Ryanair and…Ethics: How Cheap Is Too C[heap]... ign (Ch. 5)

Morgan Stanley and…Ethics: Was Morgan Stanley Too Cozy? (Ch. 8)

Tenet Healthcare and . . . Ethics: When Doctors Lead the Group (Ch. 9)

J.P. Morgan and…Ethics: Bank-Community Partnerships (Ch. 10)

Wal-Mart and…Ethics: Is Wal-Mart Invading Customer Privacy? (Ch. 14)

DaimlerChrysler and…Ethics: A Marriage…Or an Abduction? (Ch. 17)

The Organizational Behavior Discussion assists students in the transition from textbook learning to real-world application.

Employees to the 100th Power (Ch. 1)

Diversity, Aussie Style (Ch. 2)

The Best Bagelers in Boston (Ch. 3)

CollabNet Overcomes the Silo Effect (Ch. 4)

Alternative Work Arrangements at Hewlett Packard (Ch. 5)

Performance Management at Merrill Lynch (Ch. 6)

Stress and the Professional Musician (Ch. 7)

Decisions and Consequences at Morgan Stanley (Ch. 8)

Effective Group Decisions at the Denver Broncos (Ch. 9)

The Rainmakers (Ch. 10)

Communicating in a Family-Run Business (Ch. 11)

The "Reality-Distortion Field" of Steve Jobs (Ch. 12)

Teaching Leaders at Accenture (Ch. 13)

Justice for Wal-Mart's Workers (Ch. 14)

Xerox's Unique Approach to Labor-Management Relations (Ch. 15)

Nissan's New Organization Structure (Ch. 16)

The Right Structure for Build-A-Bear Workshop (Ch. 17)

The Fast-Breaking Culture of Whole Foods Market (Ch. 18)

Toyota Reinvented (Ch. 19)

Experiencing Organizational Behavior

Relating OB and Popular Culture (Ch. 1)

Understanding Your Own Stereotypes About Others (Ch. 2)

Matching Personalities and Jobs (Ch. 3)

Understanding the Dynamics of Expectancy Theory (Ch. 4)

Using Compensation to Motivate Workers (Ch. 6)

Learning How Stress Affects You (Ch. 7)

Programmed and Nonprogrammed Decisions (Ch. 8)

Learning the Benefits of a Group (Ch. 9)

Using Teams (Ch. 10)

The Importance of Feedback in Oral Communication (Ch. 11)

Understanding Successful and Unsuccessful Leadership (Ch. 12)

Understanding Leadership Substitutes (Ch. 13)

Learning About Ethics and Power (Ch. 14)

Learning Negotiation Skills (Ch. 15)

Understanding Organization Structure (Ch. 16)

Studying a Real Organization (Ch. 17)

Culture of the Classroom (Ch. 18)

Planning a Change at the University (Ch. 19)

Self Assessment Exercises

Assessing Your Own Management Skills (Ch. 1)

Cross-Cultural Awareness (Ch. 2)

Assessing Your Locus of Control (Ch. 3)

Assessing Your Equity Sensitivity (Ch. 4)

The Job Characteristics Inventory (Ch. 5)

Diagnosing Poor Performance and Enhancing Motivation (Ch. 6)

Are You Type A or Type B? (Ch. 7)

Rational Versus Practical Approaches to Decision Making (Ch. 8)

Group Cohesiveness (Ch. 9)

Understanding the Benefits of Teams (Ch. 10)

Diagnosing Your Listening Skills (Ch.11)

Applying Vroom's Decision Tree Approach (Ch. 12)

Are You a Charismatic Leader? (Ch. 13)

Assessing Organizational Justice Where You Work (Ch. 14)

Comfort with Conflict (Ch. 15)

Making Delegation Work (Ch. 16)

Diagnosing Organization Structure (Ch. 17)

An Empowering Culture: What It Is and What It Is Not (Ch. 18)

Support for Change (Ch. 19)

Integrative Running Case

Organizational Behavior

MANAGING PEOPLE AND ORGANIZATIONS

Eighth Edition

Ricky W. Griffin
Texas A&M University

Gregory Moorhead
Arizona State University

Houghton Mifflin Company   *Boston   New York*

For my daughter Ashley—A wife and successful business professional, but still her daddy's sweet and shining star. —R.W.G.
For my family: Linda, Alex, and Lindsay. —G.M.

V.P., Publisher: *George Hoffman*
Senior Sponsoring Editor: *Lisé Johnson*
Associate Editor: *Julia Perez*
Senior Project Editor: *Fred Burns*
Editorial Assistant: *Brett Pasinella*
Senior Manufacturing Buyer: *Renee Ostrowski*
Senior Art and Design Coordinator: *Jill Haber*
Composition Buyer: *Chuck Dutton*
Executive Marketing Manager: *Steven W. Mikels*
Marketing Specialist: *Lisa E. Boden*

Cover image credit: © Benjamin Shearn/TAXI/Getty Images

Printed in the U.S.A.

Library of Congress Control Number: 2005936317

Instructor's exam copy:
ISBN 13: 978-0-618-73212-8
ISBN 10: 0-618-73212-8

For orders, use student text ISBNs:
ISBN 13: 978-0-618-61158-4
ISBN 10: 0-618-61158-4

2 3 4 5 6 7 8 9—VH—10 09 08 07 06

Brief Contents

Contents

Part 2   Individual Processes in Organizations

Preface

Change continues to be the watchword for managers everywhere. Now more than ever before managers need a complete and sophisticated understanding of the assets, tools, and resources they can draw upon to compete most effectively. And understanding the people who comprise organizations—operating employees, managers, engineers, support people, sales representatives, decision makers, professionals, maintenance workers, and administrative employees—is critical for any manager who aspires to understanding change and how his or her organization needs to respond to that change.

As we prepared this edition of *Organizational Behavior: Managing People and Organizations*, we once again relied on a fundamental assumption that has helped the book remain a market leader since the publication of its first edition two decades ago: We must equip today's students (and tomorrow's managers) with a perspective on managing people that allows them to create, interpret, judge, imagine, and build behaviors and relationships. This perspective requires students to gain a firm grasp of the fundamentals of human behavior in organizations—the basic foundations of behavior—so that they can develop new answers to the new problems they encounter. As new challenges are thrust upon us from around the world by global competition, new technologies, newer and faster information processes, new worldwide uncertainties, and customers who demand the best in quality and service, the next generation of managers will need to go back to basics—the fundamentals—and then combine those basics with valid new experiences in a complex world, and ultimately develop creative new solutions, processes, products, or services to gain competitive advantage.

The Text That Meets the Challenge

This edition of *Organizational Behavior: Managing People and Organizations* takes on that charge by providing the basics in each area, bolstered by the latest research in the field, and infused with examples of what companies are doing in each area. To help meet our goals, we have made several structural changes in the book, which are detailed below. In terms of the chapters themselves, we open each one with a textual introduction that weaves in a new opening incident and provides an immediate example of how the topic of the chapter is relevant in organizations. Chapter outlines and learning objectives are also presented at the beginning of each chapter. We continue to build and reinforce learning techniques at the end of each chapter in order to provide more opportunities to work with the chapter content. In addition to the end-of-chapter case, experiential exercise, and self-assessment exercise, we have added an opportunity for students to build their own managerial skills with the building managerial skills exercise. We have also kept the in-depth running case that is presented at the end of each part of the book. The running case for this edition follows the stunning success of Starbucks.

Organizational Behavior: Managing People and Organizations, Eighth Edition, prepares and energizes managers of the future for the complex and challenging tasks of the new century while it preserves the past contributions of the classics. It is comprehensive in its presentation of practical perspectives, backed up by the research and learning of the experts. We expect each reader to be inspired by the most exciting task of the new century: managing people in organizations.

Content and Organization

The eighth edition of *Organizational Behavior: Managing People and Organizations* retains the same basic overall organization that has worked so well for over twenty years. But within that framework, we are also introducing several exciting and innovative changes that will further enhance the book's usefulness.

Part 1 discusses the managerial context of organizational behavior. In Chapter 1 we introduce the basic concepts of the field, discuss the importance of the study of organizational behavior, and relate organizational behavior to the broader field of management. Our new Chapter 2 focuses on the changing environment of organizations. The key topics addressed in this chapter are globalization, diversity, technology, ethics and corporate governance, and new employment relationships.

Part 2 includes six chapters that focus on the fundamental individual processes in organizations: individual behavior, motivation, employee performance, work stress, and decision making. Chapter 3 presents the foundations for understanding individual behavior in organizations by discussing the psychological nature of people, elements of personality, individual attitudes, perceptual processes, and workplace behavior. New coverage of emotional intelligence has also been added to this chapter. Chapter 4 focuses on the two primary categories of motivation theories: need-based approaches and process-based approaches. In our previous editions, these theories were spread across two chapters; we believe the more economical treatment provided in this new approach will be well-received. Chapters 5 and 6, meanwhile, move away from theory per se and describe some of the more important methods and techniques used by organizations to actually implement the theories of motivation, with Chapter 5 discussing work-related methods for motivating employees and Chapter 6 addressing reward-based approaches to motivation. Work stress, another important element of individual behavior in organizations, is covered in Chapter 7. Finally, Chapter 8, decision making and problem solving has been moved from Part 3 into Part 2 and refocused more on individual decision making. (The material on creativity, previously discussed in Chapter 3, has been moved to this chapter; meanwhile, the material on group decision making has been moved to the chapter on group dynamics.)

In Part 3 we move from the individual aspects of organizational behavior to the more interpersonal aspects of the field, including communication, groups and teams, leadership and influence processes, power and politics, and conflict and negotiations. Chapters 9 and 10 are a two-chapter sequence on groups and teams in organizations. We believe there is too much important material to just have one chapter on these topics. Therefore, we present the basics of understanding the dynamics of small group behavior in Chapter 9 and discuss the more applied material on teams in Chapter 10. In this manner readers get to understand the more basic processes first before attacking the more complex issues in developing teams in organizations. Chapter 11 describes the behavioral aspects of communication in organizations. We present leadership in a two-chapter sequence, examining models and concepts in Chapter 12 and contemporary views in Chapter 13. We believe users will especially enjoy Chapter 13, with its new coverage of strategic, ethical, and virtual leadership, as well as gender and cross-cultural impacts on leadership. Closely related to leadership are the concepts of power, politics, and workplace justice. This material was covered in the last edition as well, but has been repositioned and refocused as a completely new Chapter 14 for more thorough coverage. Part 3 closes with Chapter 15, also new, that is devoted to conflict and negotiations in organizations.

In Part 4 we address more macro and system-wide aspects of organizational behavior. Chapter 16, the first of a two-chapter sequence on organization structure and design, describes the basic building blocks of organizations—division of labor, specialization, centralization, formalization, responsibility, and authority—and then presents the classical view of organizations. Chapter 17 describes more about the factors and the process through which the structure of an organization is matched to fit the demands of change, new technology, and expanding competition, including global issues. Chapter 18 moves on to the more elusive concept of organizational culture. The final chapter, Chapter 19, could really be the cornerstone of every chapter, because it presents the classical and contemporary views of organizational change. Due to the demands on organizations today, as stated earlier and by every management writer alive, change is the order of the day, the year, the decade, and the new century. Finally, two appendixes provide additional coverage of research in organizational behavior and the historical foundations of the field.

Features of the Book

This edition of *Organizational Behavior: Managing People and Organizations* is guided by our continuing devotion to the preparation of the next generation of managers. This is reflected in four key elements of the book which we believe stem from this guiding principle: a strong student orientation; contemporary content; a real world, applied approach; and effective pedagogy.

Student Orientation

We believe that students, instructors, and other readers will agree with our students' reactions to the book as being easy and even enjoyable to read with its direct and active style. We have tried to retain the comprehensive nature of the book while writing in a style that is active and lively and geared to the student reader. We want your students to enjoy reading the book while they learn from it. The cartoons and their content-rich captions tie the humorous intent of the cartoons to the concepts in the text. All of the figures include meaningful captions, again to tie the figure directly to the concepts. The end-of-chapter features retain the popular experiential exercises and the diagnostic questionnaire, or self-assessments, and the real-world cases that show how the chapter material relates to actual practice.

Contemporary Content Coverage

This edition continues our tradition of presenting the most modern management approaches as expressed in the popular press and in academic research. The basic structure of the book remains the same, but you will find new coverage that represents the most recent research in many areas of the book.

Real World, Applied Approach

The organizations cited in the opening incidents, examples, cases, and boxed features throughout this edition represent a blend of large, well-known and smaller, less well-known organizations so that students will see the applicability of the material in a variety of organizational settings. Each chapter opens and closes with concrete examples of relevant topics from the chapter. The running end-of-part case on Starbucks provides a more in-depth case for class discussion. Each chapter also contains two boxes, selected from the five types of boxed features included in this edition. Each box has a unique, identifying icon that distinguishes it and makes it easier for students to identify.

But unlike previous editions and completely unlike other books, we have achieved a very exciting new form of integration with the boxed inserts in this edition. One box in the chapter continues the story from the opening case and then ties it to one of the thematic concepts described below. The second box in each chapter introduces a different thematic concept, one which is then carried forward to the end-of-chapter case.

 Each "… and Technology" box describes how a company uses advances in computer and information technology to improve its business.

 Each "… and Change" box shows an organization rethinking its methods of operation to respond to changes in the business climate.

 Each "… and Globalization" box describes an organization meeting the needs of its increasingly complex global environment.

 Each "… and Diversity" box shows an organization dealing with its increasingly diverse work force.

 Each "… and Ethics" box shows an organization's ethical perspective when making decisions or dealing with complicated situations.

Effective Pedagogy

Our guiding intent continues to be to put together a package that enhances student learning. The package includes several features of the book, many of which have already been mentioned.

- Each chapter begins with a chapter outline and objectives and ends with a synopsis.
- Discussion questions at the end of each chapter stimulate interaction among students and provide a guide to complete studying of the chapter concepts.
- An "Experiencing Organizational Behavior" exercise at the end of each chapter helps students make the transition from textbook learning to real-world applications. The end-of-chapter case, "Organizational Behavior Case for Discussion," also assists in this transition.
- A "Self Assessment" activity at the end of each chapter gives students the opportunity to apply a concept from the chapter to a brief self-assessment or diagnostic activity.
- The "Building Managerial Skills" activity provides an opportunity for students to "get their hands dirty" and really use something discussed in the chapter.
- The opening and closing cases, and accompanying boxed inserts, illustrate chapter concepts with real-life applications.
- The Integrative Running Case on Starbucks at the end of each part provides an opportunity for students to discuss an actual ongoing management situation with significant organizational behavior facets.
- The Test Prepper, a self-test found at the end of each chapter, serves as a handy review and study tool. Each self-test offers questions with answers appearing at the end of the text so students can evaluate their own progress.

- Figures, tables, photographs, and cartoons offer visual and humorous support for the text content. Explanatory captions to figures, photographs, and cartoons enhance their pedagogical value.
- A running marginal glossary and a complete glossary on the textbook website provide additional support for identifying and learning key concepts.

A new design reflects this edition's content, style, and pedagogical program. The colors remain bold to reflect the dynamic nature of the behavioral and managerial challenges facing managers today, and all interior photographs are new to this edition and have been specially selected to highlight the dynamic world of organizational behavior.

We would like to hear from you about your experiences in using the book. We want to know what you like and what you do not like about it. Please write to us via-e-mail to tell us about your learning experiences. You may contact us at:

Greg Moorhead
greg.moorhead@asu.edu

Ricky Griffin
rgriffin@tamu.edu

A Complete Teaching and Learning Package

A complete package of teaching and learning support materials accompanies the eighth edition.

For Students

The **Student Web Site** provides chapter synopses and objectives, ACE practice tests, links to companies highlighted in the text, Flashcards, a visual glossary, career snapshots, OB Online, Experiencing Organizational Behavior and Self-Assessment exercises from the end-of-chapter sections, a resource center with links to OB-related sites, and additional cases and experiential exercises.

OB in Action, *Eighth Edition,* written by Steven B. Wolff provides additional cases and hands-on experiential exercises to help students bridge the gap between theory and practice. Working individually or with teams, students tackle problems and find solutions, using organizational theories as their foundation.

For Instructors

***Online OB in Action* Instructor's Resource Manual** correlates with *OB in Action* exercises. It includes a topic area grid, a section with icebreaker materials, and teaching notes for all cases and exercises in the *OB in Action* text.

Online Instructor's Resource Manual, written by Paul Keaton of the University of Wisconsin- La Crosse, includes a chapter overview, chapter learning objectives, lecture outline, text discussion questions with suggested answers, notes on the experiential exercises (Building Managerial Skills, Experiencing Organizational Behavior, Self-Assessment), Organizational Behavior case questions with suggested answers, a mini-lecture, and additional experiential exercise ideas. Also included are a table of contents, a transition guide, sample syllabi, suggested course outlines, and a section on learning and teaching ideologies. Printed copies are available upon request to the Faculty Service Group.

Online Test Bank, written by David Glew of the University of North Carolina, Wilmington, contains completely updated true/false, multiple-choice, matching, completion, and essay questions for each chapter. A text page reference and a learning-level indicator accompany each question. Printed copies are available upon request to the Faculty Service Group.

Instructor Web Site includes downloadable files for the IRM, PowerPoint slides, Video Guide, and Transparencies, as well as a resource center that includes sample syllabi, a table of contents, learning and teaching ideologies, a visual glossary, chapter overviews, mini-lectures, notes on the experiential exercises (Building Managerial Skills, Experiencing Organizational Behavior, OB Online, Self-Assessments), text discussion questions with suggested answers, *OB in Action* Instructor Notes and notes on additional cases, Organizational Behavior case questions with suggested answers, and additional cases and notes.

PowerPoint Slides are available in both basic and premium versions. Basic PowerPoint Slides follow the text's structure, including headings and figures. The Premium Slides offer all of the content found in the Basic Slides, along with video and photos.

Online Transparencies contain all of the figures from the main text. Printed copies are available upon request to the Faculty Service Group.

HMClassPrep™ CD-ROM with HM Testing includes the complete Instructor's Resource Manual in electronic format (Word and PDF formats), PowerPoint Slides for classroom presentation, the Online Transparencies, sample syllabi, transition guide, chapter overviews, mini-lectures, lecture outlines, a visual glossary, video guide and select video case segments, learning and teaching ideologies, notes on the experiential exercises (Building Managerial Skills, Experiencing Organizational Behavior, OB Online, Self-Assessments), text discussion questions with suggested answers, Organizational Behavior case questions with suggested answers, additional experiential exercises and cases with notes, and end-of-chapter exercises. The computerized version of the *Test Bank* allows instructors to select, edit, and add questions, or to generate randomly selected questions to produce a test master for easy duplication.

Video features video case segments highlighting management and organizational behavior scenarios. A correlated Video Guide is available.

Blackboard® /WebCT® CD-ROM includes ACE practice tests plus additional self-test questions, additional cases and experiential exercises, text discussion questions with suggested answers, end-of-chapter experiential exercises with instructor notes (Building Managerial Skills, Experiencing Organizational Behavior, OB Online, Self-Assessments), *OB in Action* Instructor Notes and notes on additional cases, PowerPoint slides, HMTesting, Online Transparencies, sample syllabi, transition guide, learning and teaching ideologies, Career Snapshot and Visual Glossary video segments, a video guide, chapter overviews and objectives, mini-lectures, lecture outlines, Flashcards, Organizational Behavior cases with questions and suggested answers, and links to the instructor and student websites, and to companies highlighted in the text.

Acknowledgments

Although this book bears our two names, numerous people have contributed to it. Through the years we have had the good fortune to work with many fine professionals who helped us to sharpen our thinking about this complex field and to develop new and more effective ways of discussing it. Their contributions were essential to the development of this edition. Any and all errors of omission, interpretation, and emphasis remain the responsibility of the authors.

Several reviewers made essential contributions to the development of this and previous editions. We would like to express a special thanks to them for taking the time to provide us with their valuable assistance:

Abdul Aziz, *College of Charleston*
Steve Ball, *Cleary College*
Brendan Bannister, *Northeastern University*
Greg Baxter, *Southeastern Oklahoma State University*
Jon W. Beard, *Purdue University*
Mary-Beth Beres, *Mercer University Atlanta*
Ronald A. Bigoness, *Stephen F. Austin State University*
Allen Bluedorn, *University of Missouri Columbia*
Bryan Bonner, *University of Utah*
Wayne Boss, *University of Colorado—Boulder*
Murray Brunton, *Central Ohio Technical College*
John Bunch, *Kansas State University*
Mark Butler, *San Diego State University*
Richaurd R. Camp, *Eastern Michigan University*
Anthony Chelte, *Western New England College*
Anne Cooper, *St. Petersburg Community College*
Dan R. Dalton, *Indiana University Bloomington*
Carla L. Dando, *Idaho State University*
T. K. Das, *Baruch College*
George deLodzia, *University of Rhode Island*
Ronald A. DiBattista, *Bryant College*
Thomas W. Dougherty, *University of Missouri Columbia*
Cathy Dubois, *Kent State University*
Earlinda Elder-Albritton, *Detroit College of Business*
Stanley W. Elsea, *Kansas State University*
Jan Feldbauer, *Austin Community College*
Maureen J. Fleming, *The University of Montana—Missoula*
Joseph Forest, *Georgia State University*
Eliezer Geisler, *Northeastern Illinois University*
Robert Giacalone, *University of Richmond*
Bob Goddard, *Appalachian State University*
Lynn Harland, *University of Nebraska at Omaha*
Stan Harris, *Lawrence Tech University*

Nell Hartley, *Robert Morris College*
Peter Heine, *Stetson University*
William Hendrix, *Clemson University*
John Jermier, *University of South Florida*
Avis L. Johnson, *University of Akron*
Bruce Johnson, *Gustavus Adolphus College*
Gwen Jones, *Bowling Green State University*
Robert T. Keller, *University of Houston*
Michael Klausner, *University of Pittsburgh at Bradford*
Stephen Kleisath, *University of Wisconsin*
Barbara E. Kovatch, *Rutgers University*
David R. Lee, *University of Dayton*
Richard Leifer, *Rensselaer Polytechnic Institute*
Robert Leonard, *Lebanon Valley College*
Fengru Li, *University of Montana*
Peter Lorenzi, *University of Central Arkansas*
Joseph B. Lovell, *California State University, San Bernardino*
Patricia Manninen, *North Shore Community College*
Edward K. Marlow, *Eastern Illinois University*
Edward Miles, *Georgia State University*
C. W. Millard, *University of Puget Sound*
Alan N. Miller, *University of Nevada Las Vegas*
Herff L. Moore, *University of Central Arkansas*
Robert Moorman, *West Virginia University*
Stephan J. Motowidlo, *Pennsylvania State University*
Richard T. Mowday, *University of Oregon*
Margaret A. Neale, *Northwestern University*
Christopher P. Neck, *Virginia Tech*
Linda L. Neider, *University of Miami*
Mary Lippitt Nichols, *University of Minnesota Minneapolis*
Ranjna Patel, *Bethune-Cookman College*
Robert J. Paul, *Kansas State University*
John Perry, *Pennsylvania State University*
Pamela Pommerenke, *Michigan State University*
James C. Quick, *University of Texas at Arlington*
Richard Raspen, *Wilkes University*
Elizabeth Rawlin, *University of South Carolina*
Gary Reinke, *University of Maryland*
Joan B. Rivera, *West Texas A&M University*
Bill Robinson, *Indiana University of Pennsylvania*
Hannah Rothstein, *CUNY—Baruch College*
Carol S. Saunders, *University of Oklahoma*
Daniel Sauers, *Winona State University*
Constance Savage, *Ashland University*
Mary Jane Saxton, *University of Colorado at Denver*
Ralph L. Schmitt, *Macomb Community College*
Randall S. Schuler, *Rutgers University*
Amit Shah, *Frostburg State University*
Gary Shields, *Wayne State University*
Randall G. Sleeth, *Virginia Commonwealth University*
Dayle Smith, *University of San Francisco*

William R. Stevens, *Missouri Southern State College*
Steve Taylor, *Boston College*
Donald Tompkins, *Slippery Rock University*
Ahmad Tootoonchi, *Frostburg State University*
Matthew Valle, *Troy State University at Dothan*
Linn Van Dyne, *Michigan State University*
David D. Van Fleet, *Arizona State University West*
Bobby C. Vaught, *Southwest Missouri State University*
Sean Valentine, *University of Wyoming*
Jack W. Waldrip, *American Graduate School of International Management*
John P. Wanous, *The Ohio State University*
Judith Y. Weisinger, *Northeastern University*
Albert D. Widman, *Berkeley College*

The eighth edition could never have been completed without the support of Arizona State University and Texas A&M University. Robert Mittelstaedt, Dean of the W. P. Carey School of Business; and Jerry Strawser, Dean of Mays Business School at Texas A&M University facilitated our work by providing the environment that encourages scholarly activities and contributions to the field. Several secretaries and graduate and undergraduate assistants were also involved in the development of the eighth edition. We extend our appreciation to Linda Perry and Emily Emmer.

We would also like to acknowledge the outstanding team of professionals at Houghton Mifflin Company who helped us prepare this book. Julia Perez has been steadfast in her commitment to quality and her charge to us to raise quality throughout the book. Fred Burns has again been a master of professionalism. George Hoffman, Lisé Johnson, and Steve Mikels were also key players in planning the book and supplements package from start to finish. Others who made significant contributions to this edition's team are Lisa Boden, Jill Haber, and Brett Pasinella.

Finally, we would like to acknowledge the role of change in our own lives. One of us has successfully fought cancer, and the other has had a complete lower leg reconstruction. The techniques that led us to where we are today did not exist when we wrote the first edition of this book. Hence, change has touched the two of us in profound ways. We also continue to be mindful of the daily reminders that we get from our families about the things that really matter in life. Without the love and support of our families our lives would be far less enriched and meaningful. It is with all of our love that we dedicate this book to them.

G.M.

R.W.G.

An Overview of Organizational Behavior

CHAPTER 1

After studying this chapter, you should be able to:

Chapter Outline

What Is Organizational Behavior?

Organizational Behavior and the Management Process

Organizational Behavior and Managerial Work

Contemporary Organizational Behavior

Contextual Perspectives on Organizational Behavior

▸ **Define organizational behavior.**

▸ **Identify the functions that comprise the management process and relate them to organizational behavior.**

▸ **Relate organizational behavior to basic managerial roles and skills.**

▸ **Describe contemporary organizational behavior.**

Managing the World's Mightiest Army

The U.S. Army is the largest employer in the United States, with 500,000 full-time soldiers, 700,000 reservists, and 250,000 civilian workers. Currently, 150,000 soldiers, sailors, and marines are stationed in or near Iraq, the largest U.S. military deployment since the Vietnam War ended in 1972. Management of this large-scale operation presents serious challenges to the Army's leaders on a daily basis.

Consider the problems of logistics and supply. The Army spends millions of dollars each month to acquire housing, food, gasoline, repair parts, and many other necessities. These resources must then be transported to remote, hazardous locations, in some cases without roads or airports. The Army must set up and maintain hospitals, dining halls, computer and communication networks, and other facilities. Thousands of vehicles, planes, helicopters, and weapon systems are required too. Everything must be measured, budgeted, and accounted for. And all of this must happen with the maximum attention to security. Yet these problems are minor compared to thornier issues.

Planning is a challenge in this complex environment. The movement of materials and personnel is one area that requires a great deal of planning. Battle strategy and tactics must also be carefully planned. The war is also prompting senior Army managers to question the size and structure of the U.S. military forces, as questions are

> **❝A true leader is that remarkable person [who] moves from memorizing a creed to actually living that creed.❞**
> GENERAL ERIC SHINSEKI, CHIEF OF STAFF, U.S. ARMY

asked about the Army's heavy reliance on reservists, its old-fashioned emphasis on large unwieldy vehicles, the limited training in urban warfare, and more. This type of long-range planning may seem to have little impact on current events in Iraq, but it has the potential to start a major transformation in American foreign policies and actions.

Leadership and motivation are critical issues for the Army. Officers and non-commissioned officers receive special training in leadership techniques, to ensure that their soldiers are motivated to perform correctly, even in stressful conditions. The U.S. Army Leadership Manual is a training device that specifies what leaders must be, know, and do. "Be" includes values and attributes such as physical fitness, respect, loyalty, and personal courage. "Know" refers to technical, interpersonal, and other skills. Learning, communicating, planning, and other actions make up the "Do" component.

However, classroom exercises are tame in comparison to the reality of leading soldiers in battle. General Eric Shinseki, Chief of Staff, U.S. Army, writes, "Leadership starts at the top, with the character of the leader . . . A true leader is that remarkable person [who] moves from memorizing a creed to actually living that creed." In a situation in which leadership calls for asking others to risk or sacrifice their lives, the ability to motivate subordinates takes on heightened importance. Addressing this point, Shinseki comments, "Trained soldiers know what they're supposed to do, but under stress, their instincts might tell them to do something different . . . This is when the leader must step in—when things are falling apart, when there seems to be no hope—and get the job done."

For Army leaders, the stakes are high, in terms of soldiers' lives, Iraq's future, and the spread of democracy in the region. In addition, complexity is increased further because the operation is being carried out in conjunction with so many other nations. See this chapter's boxed insert *The U.S. Army and . . . Globalization* on page 9 for more about the challenges posed by international coordination in Iraq.

References: Army Leadership, "Be, Know, Do," *Leader to Leader*, Fall 2002, www.pfdf.org on February 24, 2005; "Multinational Defence Co-Operation," U.K. Ministry of Defence, www.mod.uk on February 25, 2005 (quotation); "Non-US Forces in Iraq—15 January 2005," Global Security report, www.globalsecurity.org on February 24, 2005; The U.S. Army Leadership Field Manual, Department of the Army, 1999 (quotation).

Regardless of their size, scope, or location, all organizations have at least one thing in common—they are comprised of people. It is those people who make decisions about the strategic direction of a firm. They buy resources the firm uses to create new products and then sell those products; they manage a firm's corporate headquarters, its warehouses, and its information technology; and they clean up at the end of the day. No matter how effective a manager might be, all organizational successes—and failures—are the result of the behaviors of many people. Indeed, no manager can succeed without the assistance of others.

Thus, any manager—whether responsible for an industrial giant like General Electric, Honda, Wal-Mart, or British Airways, for a not-for-profit organization such as the U.S. Army or the American Red Cross, for a niche business like the Boston Celtics basketball team or the Mayo Clinic, or for a local Pizza Hut restaurant or dry cleaning establishment—must strive to understand the people who work in the organization. This book is about those people. It is also about the organization itself and the managers who operate it. The study of organizations and of the people who work in them constitutes the field of organizational behavior. Our starting point in exploring this field begins with a more detailed discussion of its meaning and its importance to managers.

What Is Organizational Behavior?

What exactly is meant by the term "organizational behavior"? And why should it be studied? Answers to these two fundamental questions will help establish both our foundation for discussion and analysis and help you better appreciate the rationale as to how and why understanding the field can be of value to you in the future.

The Meaning of Organizational Behavior

Organizational behavior (OB) is the study of human behavior in organizational settings, of the interface between human behavior and the organization, and of the organization itself.[1] Although we can focus on any one of these three areas, we must remember that all three are ultimately necessary for a comprehensive understanding of organizational behavior. For example, we can study individual behavior without explicitly considering the organization. But because the organization influences and is influenced by the individual, we cannot fully understand the individual's behavior without learning something about the organization. Similarly, we can study organizations without focusing explicitly on the people within them. But again, we are looking at only a portion of the puzzle. Eventually we must consider the other pieces, as well as the whole.

Figure 1.1 illustrates this view of organizational behavior. It shows the linkages among human behavior in organizational settings, the individual-organization interface, the organization, and the environment surrounding the organization. Each individual brings to an organization a unique set of personal background and characteristics, as well as experiences from other organizations. In considering the people who work in organizations, therefore, a manager must look at the unique perspective each individual brings to the work setting. For example, suppose The Home Depot hires a consultant to investigate employee turnover. As a starting point, the consultant might analyze the types of people the company usually hires. The goal would be to learn as much as possible about the nature of the company's workforce as individuals—their expectations, their personal goals, and so forth.

But individuals do not work in isolation. They come in contact with other people and with the organization in a variety of ways. Points of contact include managers, coworkers, the formal policies and procedures of the organization, and various changes implemented by the organization. Over time, the individual changes, too, as a function both of personal experiences and maturity and of work experiences and the organization. The organization, in turn, is affected by the presence and eventual absence of the individual. Clearly, then, managers must also consider how the individual and the organization interact. Thus, the consultant studying turnover at The Home Depot might next look at the orientation procedures for newcomers to the organization. The goal of this phase of

> Organizational behavior is the study of human behavior in organizational settings, the interface between human behavior and the organization, and the organization itself.

FIGURE 1.1

The Nature of Organizational Behavior

The field of organizational behavior attempts to understand human behavior in organizational settings, the organization itself, and the individual—organization interface. As illustrated here, these areas are highly interrelated. Thus, although it is possible to focus on only one of these areas at a time, a complete understanding of organizational behavior requires knowledge of all three areas.

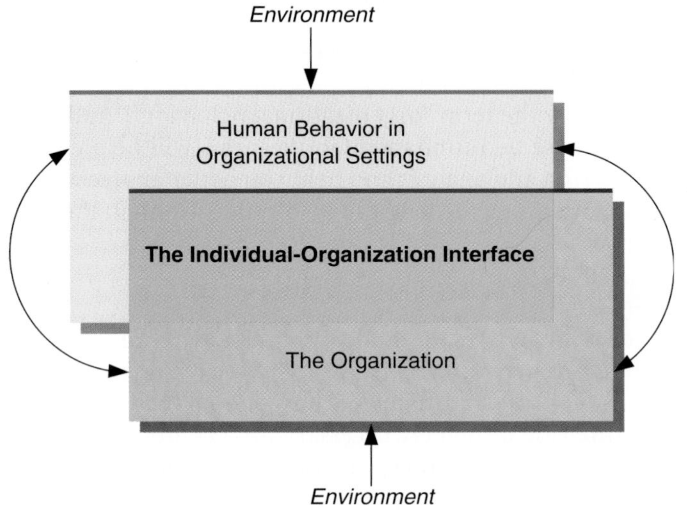

Environment

Human Behavior in
Organizational Settings

The Individual-Organization Interface

The Organization

Environment

the study would be to understand some of the dynamics of how incoming individuals are introduced to and interact with the broader organizational context.

An organization, of course, exists before a particular person joins it and continues to exist after he or she leaves. Thus, the organization itself represents a crucial third perspective from which to view organizational behavior. For instance, the consultant studying turnover would also need to study the structure and culture of The Home Depot. An understanding of factors such as the firm's performance evaluation and reward systems, its decision-making and communication patterns, and the structure of the firm itself can provide added insight into why some people choose to leave a company and others elect to stay.

Clearly, then, the field of organizational behavior is both exciting and complex. Myriad variables and concepts accompany the interactions just described, and together these factors greatly complicate the manager's ability to understand, appreciate, and manage others in the organization. They also provide unique and important opportunities to enhance personal and organizational effectiveness.

The Importance of Organizational Behavior

The importance of organizational behavior may now be clear, but we should nonetheless take a few moments to make it even more explicit. Most people are born and educated in organizations, acquire most of their material possessions from organizations, and die as members of organizations. Many of our activities are regulated by the various organizations that make up our governments. And most adults spend the better part of their lives working in organizations. Because organizations influence our lives so powerfully, we have every reason to be concerned about how and why those organizations function.

In our relationships with organizations, we may adopt any one of several roles or identities. For example, we can be consumers, employees, suppliers, competitors, owners, or investors. Since most readers of this book are either present or future managers, we will adopt a managerial perspective throughout our discussion. The study of organizational behavior can greatly clarify the factors that affect how managers manage. Hence, the field attempts to describe the complex human context of organizations and to define the opportunities, problems, challenges, and issues associated with that realm. The value of organizational behavior is that it isolates important aspects of the manager's job and offers specific perspectives on the human side of management: people as organizations, people as resources, and people as people. Clearly, then, an understanding of organizational behavior can play a vital role in managerial work. To most effectively use the knowledge provided by this field, managers must thoroughly understand its various concepts, assumptions, and premises. To provide this foundation, we next tie organizational behavior even more explicitly to management and then turn to a more detailed examination of management itself.

People represent the essence of an organization, regardless of the size of the organization or the technology it uses. Honda, for instance, relies on automated robotic assembly systems to create automobiles. But people design, install, operate, and repair those systems. These Honda employees are celebrating the launch of a new product line coming off the assembly line at Honda's factory in Marysville, Ohio.

Organizational Behavior and Management

Virtually all organizations have managers with titles such as chief financial officer, marketing manager, director of public relations, vice president for human resources, and plant manager. But probably no organization has a position called "organizational behavior manager." The reason is simple: Organizational behavior is not a defined business function or area in the same way as finance or marketing. Rather, an understanding of organizational behavior is a perspective that provides a set of insights and tools that all managers can use to carry out their jobs more effectively.[2]

An appreciation and understanding of organizational behavior helps managers better understand why others in the organization behave as they do.[3] For example, most managers in an organization are directly responsible for the work-related behaviors of a set of other people—their immediate subordinates. Typical managerial activities in this realm include motivating employees to work harder, ensuring that employees' jobs are properly designed, resolving conflicts, evaluating performance, and helping workers set goals to achieve rewards. The field of organizational behavior abounds with models and research relevant to each of these functions.[4]

Unless they happen to be chief executive officers (CEOs), managers also report to others in the organization (and even the CEO reports to the board of directors). In dealing with these individuals, an understanding of basic issues associated with leadership, power and political behavior, decision making, organization structure and design, and organization culture can be extremely beneficial. Again, the field of organizational behavior provides numerous valuable insights into these processes.

Managers can also use their knowledge of organizational behavior to better understand their own needs, motives, behaviors, and feelings, which will help them improve decision-making capabilities, control stress, communicate better, and comprehend how career dynamics unfold. The study of organizational behavior provides insights into all of these concepts and processes.

Managers interact with a variety of colleagues, peers, and coworkers inside the organization. An understanding of attitudinal processes, individual differences, group dynamics, intergroup dynamics, organization culture, and power and political behavior can help managers handle such interactions more effectively. Organizational behavior provides a variety of practical insights into these processes. Virtually all of the behavioral processes already mentioned are also valuable in interactions with people outside the organization—suppliers, customers, competitors, government officials, representatives of citizens' groups, union officials, and potential joint-venture partners. In addition, a special understanding of the environment, technology, and global issues is valuable. Again, organizational behavior offers managers many different insights into how and why things happen as they do.

Finally, these patterns of interactions hold true regardless of the type of organization. Whether a business is large or small, domestic or international, growing or stagnating, its managers perform their work within a social context. And the same can be said of managers in healthcare, education, government, and student organizations such as fraternities, sororities, and professional clubs. We see, then, that it is essentially impossible to understand and practice management without considering the numerous areas of organizational behavior. Further, as more and more organizations hire managers from other countries, the processes of understanding human behavior in organizations will almost certainly grow increasingly complicated. We now address the nature of the manager's job in more detail before returning to our primary focus on organizational behavior.

Organizational Behavior and the Management Process

Managerial work is fraught with complexity and unpredictability and enriched with opportunity and excitement. However, in characterizing managerial work, most educators and other experts find it useful to conceptualize the activities performed by managers as reflecting one or more of four basic functions. These functions are generally referred to as *planning, organizing, leading,* and *controlling.* While these functions are often described in a sequential manner, in reality, of course, most managerial work involves all four functions simultaneously.

Similarly, organizations use many different resources in the pursuit of their goals and objectives. As with management functions, though, these resources can also generally be classified into four groups: *human, financial, physical,* and/or *information* resources. As illustrated in Figure 1.2, managers combine these resources through the four basic functions, with the ultimate purpose of efficiently and effectively attaining the goals of the organization. That is, the figure shows how managers apply the basic functions across resources to advance the organization toward its goals.

Planning, the first managerial function, is the process of determining the organization's desired future position and deciding how best to get there. The planning process at Sears, for example, includes studying and analyzing the environment, deciding on appropriate goals, outlining strategies for achieving those goals, and developing tactics to help execute the strategies. Behavioral processes and characteristics pervade each of these activities. Perception, for instance, plays a major role in environmental scanning, and creativity and motivation influence how managers set goals, strategies, and tactics for their organization. Larger corporations such as General Electric and IBM usually rely on their top management teams to handle most planning activities. In smaller firms, the owner usually takes care of planning.

The second managerial function is **organizing**—the process of designing jobs, grouping jobs into manageable units, and establishing patterns of authority among jobs and groups of jobs. This process produces the basic structure, or framework, of the organization. For large organizations such as Sears, that structure can be extensive and complicated. The structure includes several hierarchical layers and spans myriad activities and areas of responsibility. Smaller firms can often function with a relatively simple and straightforward form of organization. As noted earlier, the processes and characteristics of the organization itself are a major theme of organizational behavior.

Leading, the third major managerial function, is the process of motivating members of the organization to work together toward the organization's goals. A Sears manager, for example, must hire people, train them, and motivate them. Major components of leading include motivating employees, managing group dynamics, and the actual process leadership itself. These are all closely related to major areas of organizational behavior. All managers, whether they work in a huge multinational corporation spanning dozens of countries or a small neighborhood business serving a few square city blocks, must understand the importance of leading.

The fourth managerial function, **controlling**, is the process of monitoring and correcting the actions of the organization and its people to keep them headed toward their goals. A Sears manager has to control costs, inventory, and so on. Again, behavioral processes and characteristics are a key part of this function. Performance evaluation, reward systems, and motivation, for example, all apply to control. Control is of vital importance to all businesses, but it may be especially critical to smaller ones. General Motors, for example, can withstand with relative ease a loss of several thousand dollars due to poor control, but an equivalent loss may be devastating to a small firm.

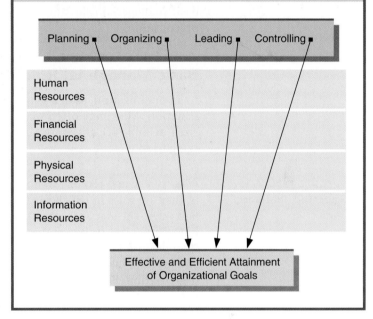

FIGURE 1.2

Basic Managerial Functions

Managers engage in the four basic functions of planning, organizing, leading, and controlling. These functions are applied to human, financial, physical, and information resources, with the ultimate purpose of attaining organizational goals efficiently and effectively.

Planning is the process of determining an organization's desired future position and the best means of getting there.

Organizing is the process of designing jobs, grouping jobs into units, and establishing patterns of authority between jobs and units.

Leading is the process of getting the organization's members to work together toward the organization's goals.

Controlling is the process of monitoring and correcting the actions of the organization and its members to keep them directed toward their goals.

Organizational Behavior and Managerial Work

As they engage in the basic management functions described above, managers often find themselves playing a variety of different roles. Moreover, in order to perform the functions most effectively and to be successful in their various roles, managers must also draw upon a set of critical skills. *The U.S. Army and . . . Globalization* previews a variety of managerial functions, roles, and skills. This section first introduces the basic managerial roles and then describes the core skills necessary for success in an organization.

Basic Managerial Roles

In an organization, as in a play or a movie, a role is the part a person plays in a given situation. Managers often play a number of different roles. In general, as summarized in Table 1.1, there are ten basic managerial roles that cluster into three general categories.[5]

Key **interpersonal roles** are the figurehead, the leader, and the liaison.

Interpersonal Roles The **interpersonal roles** are primarily social in nature; that is, they are roles in which the manager's main task is to relate to other people in certain ways. The manager sometimes may serve as a *figurehead* for the organization. Taking visitors to dinner and attending ribbon-cutting ceremonies are part of the figurehead role. In the role of *leader*, the manager works to hire, train, and motivate employees. Finally, the *liaison* role consists of relating to others outside the group or organization. For example, a manager at Intel might be responsible for handling all price negotiations with a key supplier of electronic circuit boards. Obviously, each of these interpersonal roles involves behavioral processes.

Key **informational roles** are the monitor, the disseminator, and the spokesperson.

Informational Roles The three **informational roles** involve some aspect of information processing. The *monitor* actively seeks information that might be of value to the organization in general or to specific managers. The manager who transmits this information to others is carrying out the role of *disseminator*. The *spokesperson* speaks for the organization to outsiders. A manager chosen by Dell Computer to appear at a

	Category	Role	Example
TABLE 1.1 Important Managerial Roles	**Interpersonal**	Figurehead	Attend employee retirement ceremony
		Leader	Encourage workers to increase productivity
		Liaison	Coordinate activities of two committees
	Informational	Monitor	Scan *Business Week* for information about competition
		Disseminator	Send out memos outlining new policies
		Spokesperson	Hold press conference to announce new plant
	Decision-Making	Entrepreneur	Develop idea for new product and convince others of its merits
		Disturbance handler	Resolve dispute
		Resource allocator	Allocate budget requests
		Negotiator	Settle new labor contract

The U.S. Army and . . . GLOBALIZATION

Managing a Multinational Military Force

"War represents a failure of diplomacy," says British politician Tony Benn. War involves conflict but it can also unite. In spite of ongoing conflict, the war in the Middle East has brought together soldiers from dozens of countries. In January 2005, there were 30,000 international troops in Iraq from nations as diverse as the U.K., Japan, Ukraine, and El Salvador. Japanese Prime Minister Junichiro Koizumi said, "We want to contribute our

> ### "When the international community acts together . . . the political effect . . . is much greater than when individual countries act alone."
>
> *THE U.K. MINISTRY OF DEFENCE WEBSITE*

share . . . in achieving a stable and democratic reconstruction," demonstrating that troops serve in both combatant and non-combatant peacekeeping roles. Coordination and management of the largest international force since World War II is testing and strengthening the capabilities of leaders.

At times, international troops work fairly independently, reducing the need for coordination and cooperation. However, in some cases, troops from several nations must work together. For example, Operation Telic in southern Iraq includes troops from nine countries and is commanded by the British. Coordination needs are clearly important to Operation Telic in every area, from communication in a common language to agreement on procedures to interchangeable weapon systems. For decades, the British military has conducted joint training operations with other European Union nations, providing a solid foundation for today's cooperation.

One area of special risk in the use of multinational troops is decision making. The U.K. Ministry of Defence writes, "We need to guard against [decision-making] arrangements which lead to inefficiency and delay in decision making." Soldiers in a multinational force must be trained to rely on coalition leaders, rather than officers of their own nationality.

Advantages of multinational coalitions include greater efficiency, more mutual trust, and expanded capabilities. As the U.K. Ministry of Defence claims, "When the international community acts together . . . the political effect of military action is much greater than when individual countries act alone."

References: "Multinational Defence Co-Operation," U.K. Ministry of Defence, www.mod.uk on February 25, 2005 (quotation); "Non-US Forces in Iraq—15 January 2005," Global Security report, www.globalsecurity.org on February 24, 2005; Spencer E. Ante, "The Pentagon's 'Major Modernizer,'" *BusinessWeek*, December 22, 2004, www.businessweek.com on February 24, 2005.

---

press conference announcing a new product launch or other major deal, such as a recent decision to undertake a joint venture with Microsoft, would be serving in this role. Again, behavioral processes are part of each of these roles, because information is almost always exchanged between people.

Decision-Making Roles   Finally, there are also four **decision-making roles**. The *entrepreneur* voluntarily initiates change, such as innovations or new strategies, in the organization. The *disturbance handler* helps settle disputes between various parties, such as other managers and their subordinates. The *resource allocator* decides who will get what—how resources in the organization will be distributed among various individuals and groups. The *negotiator* represents the organization in reaching agreements with other organizations, such as contracts between management and labor unions. Again, behavioral processes clearly are crucial in each of these decisional roles.

Important **decision-making roles** are the entrepreneur, the disturbance handler, the resource allocator, and the negotiator.

Critical Managerial Skills

Another important element of managerial work is the skills necessary to carry out basic functions and fill fundamental roles. In general, most successful managers have a strong combination of technical, interpersonal, conceptual, and diagnostic skills.[6]

Technical skills are the skills necessary to accomplish specific tasks within the organization.

Technical Skills   **Technical skills** are skills necessary to accomplish specific tasks within the organization. Designing a new computer for Dell Computer, developing a new formula for a frozen food additive for Conagra, and writing a press release for Halliburton require technical skills. Hence, these skills are generally associated with the operations employed by the organization in its production processes. For example, David Packard and Bill Hewlett, founders of Hewlett-Packard, started out their careers as engineers. Other examples of managers with strong technical skills include H. Lee Scott (president and CEO of Wal-Mart, who started his career as a store manager) and Gordon Bethune (former CEO of Continental, who began his career as a pilot).

The manager uses **interpersonal skills** to communicate with, understand, and motivate individuals and groups.

Interpersonal Skills   The manager uses **interpersonal skills** to communicate with, understand, and motivate individuals and groups. As we have noted, managers spend a large portion of their time interacting with others, so it is clearly important that they get along with other people. For instance, Andrall Pearson is CEO of YUM! Brands, the firm that owns KFC, Pizza Hut, and Taco Bell. Pearson is able to relate to employees throughout the firm. He is also known to his employees as a caring, compassionate, and honest person. These qualities inspire others throughout the firm and help motivate them to work hard to help Pearson meet the firm's goals.

The manager uses **conceptual skills** to think in the abstract.

Conceptual Skills   **Conceptual skills** are the manager's ability to think in the abstract. A manager with strong conceptual skills is able to see the "big picture." That is, she or he can see opportunity where others see roadblocks or problems. For example, after Steve Wozniak and Steve Jobs built a small computer of their own design in a garage, Wozniak saw just a new toy that could be tinkered with. Jobs, however, saw far more and convinced his partner that they should start a company to make and sell the computers. The result? Apple Computer. More recently Jobs has also used his conceptual skills to identify the potential in digital media technologies, leading to the introduction of such products as the iPod and iTunes and overseeing the creation of the firm's Pixar animation studio.

Diagnostic Skills   Most successful managers also bring diagnostic skills to the organization. **Diagnostic skills** allow managers to better understand cause-and-effect relationships and to recognize the optimal solutions to problems. For instance, Ed Whitacre, chairman and CEO of SBC Communications (formerly Southwestern Bell),

Managers play a number of essential organizational roles, including the role of negotiator. These managers represent General Motors and the United Auto Workers, GM's largest union. The two groups are about to begin negotiating a new labor agreement. While they are all smiling as the negotiations begin, their moods will no doubt change as they argue and deliberate over what each side is willing to accept.

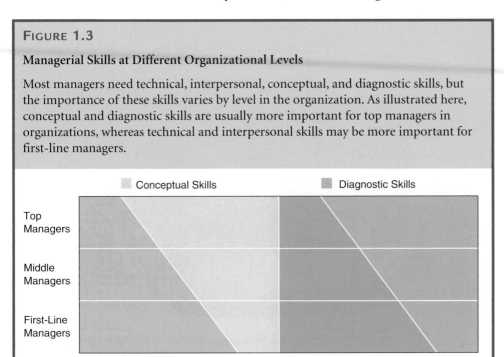

FIGURE 1.3

Managerial Skills at Different Organizational Levels

Most managers need technical, interpersonal, conceptual, and diagnostic skills, but the importance of these skills varies by level in the organization. As illustrated here, conceptual and diagnostic skills are usually more important for top managers in organizations, whereas technical and interpersonal skills may be more important for first-line managers.

recognized that while his firm was performing well in the consumer market, it lacked strong brand identification in the business environment. He then carefully identified and next implemented an action to remedy the firm's shortcoming—SBC would buy AT&T (for $16 billion), acquiring in the process the very name recognition that his company needed. And it was his diagnostic skills that pulled it all together.[7]

Of course, not every manager has an equal measure of these four basic types of skills. Nor are equal measures critical. As shown in Figure 1.3, for example, the optimal skills mix tends to vary with the manager's level in the organization. First-line managers generally need to depend more on their technical and interpersonal skills and less on their conceptual and diagnostic skills. Top managers tend to exhibit the reverse combination—more emphasis on conceptual and diagnostic skills and less dependence on technical and interpersonal skills. Middle managers require a more even distribution of skills. Similarly, the mix of skills needed can vary depending on economic prosperity. One recent survey suggested that during very tough economic times, the most important skills for a CEO are that he or she be an effective communicator and motivator, be decisive, and be a visionary.[8]

The manager uses **diagnostic skills** to understand cause-and-effect relationships and to recognize the optimal solutions to problems.

Contemporary Organizational Behavior

Now, with this additional understanding of managerial work, we can return to our discussion of organizational behavior. We first introduce two fundamental characteristics of contemporary organizational behavior that warrant special discussion; we then identify the particular set of concepts that are generally accepted as defining the field's domain.

Stress has emerged as an important individual-level outcome in many organizations. Organizational factors can both cause and be affected by stress among the firm's workers. While few employees may actually exhibit the stress levels shown here, many firms do actively seek ways to help people better cope with stress.

Characteristics of the Field

Managers and researchers who use concepts and ideas from organizational behavior must recognize that it has an interdisciplinary focus and a descriptive nature; that is, it draws from a variety of other fields and it attempts to describe behavior (rather than to predict how behavior can be changed in consistent and predictable ways).

An Interdisciplinary Focus   In many ways, organizational behavior synthesizes several other fields of study. Perhaps the greatest contribution is from psychology, especially organizational psychology. Psychologists study human behavior, whereas organizational psychologists deal specifically with the behavior of people in organizational settings. Many of the concepts that interest psychologists, such as individual differences and motivation, are also central to students of organizational behavior. These concepts are covered in Chapters 3–8.

Sociology, too, has had a major impact on the field of organizational behavior. Sociologists study social systems such as families, occupational classes, and organizations. Because a major concern of organizational behavior is the study of organization structures, the field clearly overlaps with areas of sociology that focus on the organization as a social system. Chapters 16–19 reflect the influence of sociology on the field of organizational behavior.

Anthropology is concerned with the interactions between people and their environments, especially their cultural environment. Culture is a major influence on the structure of organizations and on the behavior of people in organizations. Culture is discussed in Chapters 2 and 18.

Political science also interests organizational behaviorists. We usually think of political science as the study of political systems such as governments. But themes of interest to political scientists include how and why people acquire power and such topics as political behavior, decision making, conflict, the behavior of interest groups, and coalition formation. These are also major areas of interest in organizational behavior, as is shown in Chapters 9–15.

Economists study the production, distribution, and consumption of goods and services. Students of organizational behavior share the economist's interest in areas such as labor market dynamics, productivity, human resource planning and forecasting, and cost-benefit analysis. Chapters 2, 5, and 6 most strongly illustrate these issues.

Engineering has also influenced the field of organizational behavior. Industrial engineering in particular has long been concerned with work measurement, productivity measurement, work flow analysis and design, job design, and labor relations. Obviously these areas are also relevant to organizational behavior and are discussed in Chapters 2, 5, and 10.

Most recently, medicine has come into play in connection with the study of human behavior at work, specifically in the area of stress. Increasingly, research is showing that controlling the causes and consequences of stress in and out of organizational settings is important for the well-being of both the individual and the organization. Chapter 7 is devoted to stress.

A Descriptive Nature   A primary goal of studying organizational behavior is to describe relationships between two or more behavioral variables. The theories and concepts of the field, for example, cannot predict with certainty that changing a specific set of workplace variables will improve an individual employee's performance by a certain amount.[9] At best, the field can suggest that certain general concepts or variables tend to be related to one another in particular settings. For instance, research might indicate that in one organization, employee satisfaction and individual perceptions of working conditions are positively related. However, we may not know if better working conditions lead to more satisfaction, if satisfied people see their jobs differently than dissatisfied people, or if both satisfaction and perceptions of working conditions are actually related through other variables. Also, the relationship between satisfaction and perceptions of working conditions observed in one setting may be considerably stronger, weaker, or nonexistent in other settings.

Organizational behavior is descriptive for several reasons: the immaturity of the field, the complexities inherent in studying human behavior, and the lack of valid,

Contemporary organizational behavior reinforces the need for a strong interdisciplinary focus. For example, consider these Vietnamese employees working in a Nike contract factory in their homeland. Managers cannot simply take their understanding of U.S. workers and blindly apply it in a setting such as this. Instead, managers need to have an understanding of how psychological, sociological, anthropological, political, and economic forces vary across cultures in general and how they apply to Vietnam in particular if they are to work effectively in that country.

reliable, and accepted definitions and measures. Whether the field will ever be able to make definitive predictions and prescriptions is still an open question. But even if they never succeed in their endeavors, the value of studying organizational behavior is firmly established. Because behavioral processes pervade most managerial functions and roles, and because the work of organizations is done primarily by people, the knowledge and understanding gained from the field can help managers significantly in many ways.[10]

Basic Concepts of the Field

The central concepts of organizational behavior can be grouped into three basic categories: (1) individual processes, (2) interpersonal processes, and (3) organizational processes and characteristics. As Figure 1.4 shows, these categories provide the basic framework for this book.

This chapter and the next develop a managerial perspective on organizational behavior and link the core concepts of organizational behavior with actual management for organizational effectiveness. Chapter 2 describes the changing environment of organizations, especially relating to diversity, globalization, and similar trends and issues. Together, the two chapters in Part I provide a fundamental introduction to organizational behavior.

The six chapters of Part 2 cover individual processes in organizations. Chapter 3 explores key individual differences in such characteristics as personality and attitudes. Chapter 4 provides an introduction to and discussion of basic models useful for understanding employee work motivation. Chapters 5 and 6 are devoted to various methods and strategies that managers can use to enhance employee motivation and performance. Chapter 7 covers the causes and consequences of stress in the workplace. Finally, Chapter 8 explores decision making, problem solving, and creativity.

Part 3 is devoted to interpersonal processes in organizations. Chapter 9 introduces the foundations of interpersonal behavior through its coverage of group dynamics. Chapter 10 describes how managers are using teams in organizations today, while Chapter 11 explores communications process in organizations. Chapter 12 discusses leadership models and concepts, while Chapter 13 describes contemporary views of leadership in organizations. Power, politics, and workplace justice are covered in Chapter 14. Chapter 15 covers conflict and negotiation processes in organizations. *Google and . . . Diversity* clearly illustrates the importance of interpersonal processes as they relate to diverse people in modern organizations.

Part 4 is devoted to organizational processes and characteristics. Chapter 16 sets the stage with its coverage of the foundations of organization structure; Chapter 17 is an in-depth treatment of organization design. Organization culture is discussed in Chapter 18. Organization change and development are covered in Chapter 19. Finally, research methods in organizational behavior and the field's historical development are covered in Appendices 1 and 2.

Contextual Perspectives on Organizational Behavior

Several contextual perspectives—most notably the systems and contingency perspectives and the interactional view—also influence organizational behavior. Many of the concepts and theories discussed in the chapters that follow reflect these perspectives;

FIGURE 1.4

The Framework for Understanding Organizational Behavior

Organizational behavior is an exciting and complex field of study. The specific concepts and topics that constitute the field can be grouped into three categories: individual, interpersonal, and organizational processes and characteristics. Here these concepts and classifications are used to provide an overall framework for the organization of this book.

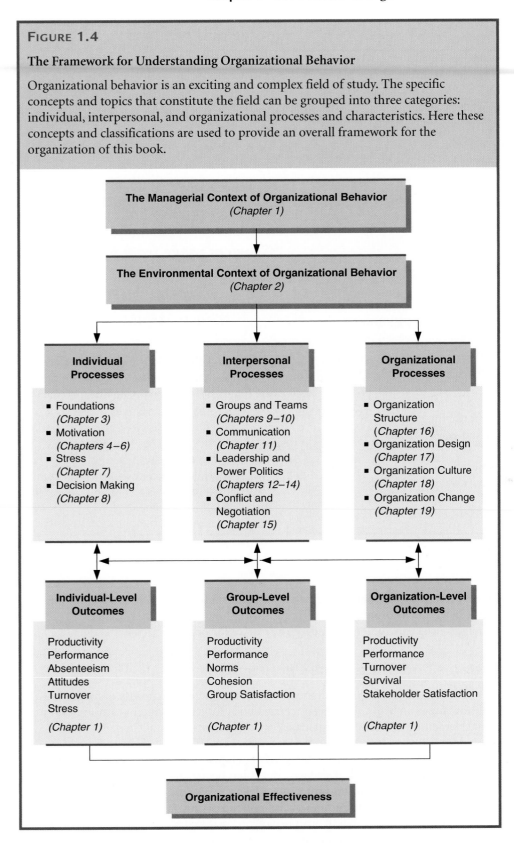

Google and . . . **DIVERSITY**

The Diversity of Googlers

Sergey Brin and Larry Page founded Google as computer science graduate students at Stanford University. From the beginning, the firm sought diversity as a way to increase innovation. Google employees are a diverse group, with a diverse mix of prior work experiences. According to the Google website, Googlers (as employees are called) "range from former neurosurgeons, CEOs, and U.S. puzzle champions to alligator wrestlers and Marines." The result is a variety of perspectives, skills, and values that lead to enhanced creativity.

Google employees speak dozens of languages and represent many nationalities, which supports the company's international users and customers. The majority of Googlers are young and male, like many high-tech firms, but there are a number of older workers and women in key roles throughout the company.

When employees are diverse, multiple viewpoints help the firm to identify many opportunities for improvement. For example, Google search depends on properly spelled search words. One engineer responded to the problem of typing errors by creating a clever spell checker.

Diversity is imbedded in Google in an even more fundamental way—through its users. The search technique used by Google relies on feedback from users. In effect, users are "voting" on the best search results. Those 82 million users per month come from hundreds of countries, access Google through one of ninety-seven different languages, and represent a tremendous pool of diverse needs and ideas.

Arthur Schopenhauer, a nineteenth-century philosopher, famously said, "Talent hits a target no one else can hit. Genius hits a target no one else can see." Diversity is

> *"Googlers range from former neurosurgeons and CEOs to alligator wrestlers."*
>
> **GOOGLE WEBSITE**

an important factor in helping Google repeatedly find those targets that no other competitor can see. The chapter closing case highlights more factors that contribute to Google's success.

References: "Corporate Information," Google website, www.google.com on January 12, 2005 (quotation); Ben Elgin, "Google: Whiz Kids or Naughty Boys?" *BusinessWeek*, August 19, 2004, www.businessweek.com on February 12, 2005; Paul S. Piper, "Google Spawn: The Culture Surrounding Google," *Information Today*, June 2004, www.infotoday.com on February 7, 2005.

they represent basic points of view that influence much of our contemporary thinking about behavior in organizations. In addition, they allow us to more clearly see how managers use behavioral processes as they strive for organizational effectiveness.

Systems and Situational Perspectives

The systems and situational perspectives share related viewpoints on organizations and how they function. Each is concerned with interrelationships among organizational elements and between organizational and environmental elements.

The Systems Perspective   The systems perspective, or the theory of systems, was first developed in the physical sciences, but it has been extended to other areas, such as management.[11] A **system** is an interrelated set of elements that function as a whole. Figure 1.5 shows a general framework for viewing organizations as systems.

According to this perspective, an organizational system receives four kinds of inputs from its environment: material, human, financial, and informational (note that

A **system** is a set of interrelated elements functioning as a whole.

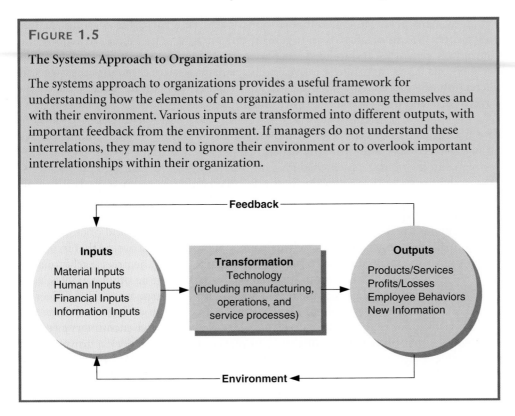

FIGURE 1.5

The Systems Approach to Organizations

The systems approach to organizations provides a useful framework for understanding how the elements of an organization interact among themselves and with their environment. Various inputs are transformed into different outputs, with important feedback from the environment. If managers do not understand these interrelations, they may tend to ignore their environment or to overlook important interrelationships within their organization.

this is consistent with our earlier description of management functions). The organization's managers then combine and transform these inputs and return them to the environment in the form of products or services, employee behaviors, profits or losses, and additional information. Then the system receives feedback from the environment regarding these outputs.

As an example, we can apply systems theory to Shell Oil Company. Material inputs include pipelines, crude oil, and the machinery used to refine petroleum. Human inputs are oil field workers, refinery workers, office staff, and other people employed by the company. Financial inputs take the form of money received from oil and gas sales, stockholder investment, and so forth. Finally, the company receives information inputs from forecasts about future oil supplies, geological surveys on potential drilling sites, sales projections, and similar analyses.

Through complex refining and other processes, these inputs are combined and transformed to create products such as gasoline and motor oil. As outputs, Shell sells these products to the consuming public. Profits from operations are fed back into the environment through taxes, investments, and dividends; losses, when they occur, hit the environment by reducing stockholders' incomes. In addition to having on-the-job contacts with customers and suppliers, employees live in the community and participate in a variety of activities away from the workplace, and their behavior is influenced in part by their experiences as Shell workers. Finally, information about the company and its operations is also released into the environment. The environment, in turn, responds to these outputs and influences future inputs. For example, consumers may buy more or less gasoline depending on the quality and price of Shell's product, and banks may be more or less willing to lend Shell money based on financial information released about the company.

The systems perspective is valuable to managers for a variety of reasons. First, it underscores the importance of an organization's environment. Failing to acquire the appropriate resources and to heed feedback from the environment, for instance, can be disastrous. The systems perspective also helps managers conceptualize the flow and interaction of various elements of the organization as they enter the system, are transformed by it, and then re-enter the environment.

The Situational Perspective   Another useful viewpoint for understanding behavior in organizations comes from the **situational perspective**. In the earlier days of management studies, managers searched for universal answers to organizational questions. They sought prescriptions, the "one best way" that could be used in any organization under any conditions, searching, for example, for forms of leadership behavior that would always lead employees to be more satisfied and to work harder. Eventually, however, researchers realized that the complexities of human behavior and organizational settings make universal conclusions virtually impossible. They discovered that in organizations most situations and outcomes are contingent; that is, the precise relationship between any two variables is likely to be situational—dependent on other variables.[12]

Figure 1.6 distinguishes the universal and situational perspectives. The universal model, shown at the top of the figure, presumes a direct cause-and-effect linkage between variables. For example, it suggests that whenever a manager encounters a certain problem or situation (such as motivating employees to work harder), a universal approach exists (such as raising pay or increasing autonomy) that will lead to the desired outcome. The situational perspective, on the other hand, acknowledges that several other variables alter the direct relationship. In other words, the appropriate managerial action or behavior in any given situation depends on elements of that situation.

> The **situational perspective** suggests that in most organizations situations and outcomes are influenced by other variables.

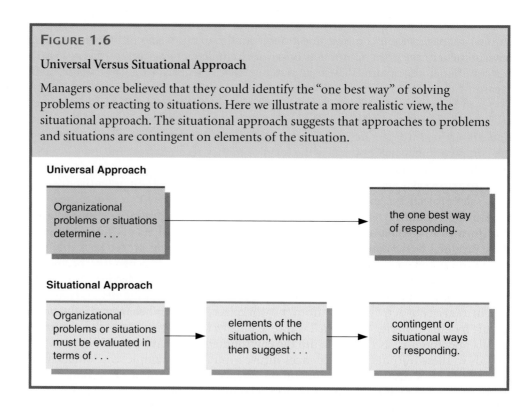

FIGURE 1.6

Universal Versus Situational Approach

Managers once believed that they could identify the "one best way" of solving problems or reacting to situations. Here we illustrate a more realistic view, the situational approach. The situational approach suggests that approaches to problems and situations are contingent on elements of the situation.

Universal Approach

Organizational problems or situations determine . . . → the one best way of responding.

Situational Approach

Organizational problems or situations must be evaluated in terms of . . . → elements of the situation, which then suggest . . . → contingent or situational ways of responding.

The field of organizational behavior gradually has shifted from a universal approach in the 1950s and early 1960s to a situational perspective. The situational perspective is especially strong in the areas of motivation (Chapters 4), job design (Chapter 5), leadership (Chapters 12 and 13), and organization design (Chapter 17), but it is becoming increasingly important throughout the field.

Interactionalism: People and Situations

Interactionalism is another useful perspective to help better understand behavior in organizational settings. First presented in terms of interactional psychology, this view assumes that individual behavior results from a continuous and multidirectional interaction between characteristics of the person and characteristics of the situation. More specifically, **interactionalism** attempts to explain how people select, interpret, and change various situations.[13] Figure 1.7 illustrates this perspective. Note that the individual and the situation are presumed to interact continuously. This interaction is what determines the individual's behavior.

The interactional view implies that simple cause-and-effect descriptions of organizational phenomena are not enough. For example, one set of research studies may suggest that job changes lead to improved employee attitudes. Another set of studies may propose that attitudes influence how people perceive their jobs in the first place. Both positions probably are incomplete: Employee attitudes may influence job perceptions, but these perceptions may in turn influence future attitudes. Because interactionalism is a fairly recent contribution to the field, it is less prominent in the chapters that follow than the systems and contingency theories. Nonetheless, the interactional view appears to offer many promising ideas for future development.

Managing for Effectiveness

Earlier in this chapter we noted that managers work toward various goals. We are now in a position to elaborate on the nature of these goals in detail. In particular, as shown in Figure 1.8, goals—or outcomes—exist at three specific levels in an organization: individual-level outcomes, group-level outcomes, and organizational-level outcomes. Of course, it may sometimes be necessary to make tradeoffs among these different kinds of outcomes, but, in general, each is seen as a critical component of organizational effectiveness. The sections that follow elaborate on these different levels in more detail.

Individual-Level Outcomes

Several different outcomes at the individual level are important to managers. Given the focus of the field of organizational behavior, it should not be surprising that most

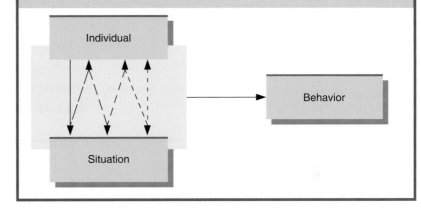

FIGURE 1.7

The Interactionist Perspective on Behavior in Organizations

When people enter an organization, their own behaviors and actions shape that organization in various ways. Similarly, the organization itself shapes the behaviors and actions of each individual who becomes a part of it. This interactionist perspective can be useful in explaining organizational behavior.

Interactionalism suggests that individuals and situations interact continuously to determine individuals' behavior.

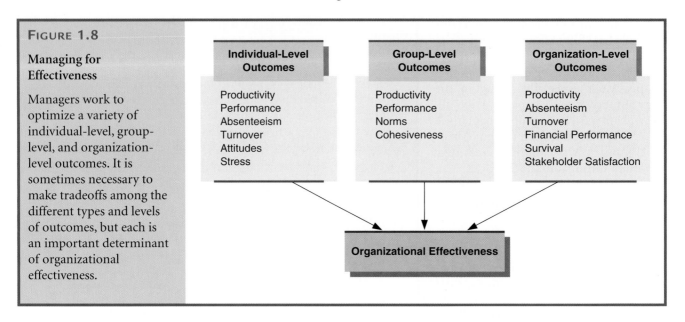

FIGURE 1.8

Managing for Effectiveness

Managers work to optimize a variety of individual-level, group-level, and organization-level outcomes. It is sometimes necessary to make tradeoffs among the different types and levels of outcomes, but each is an important determinant of organizational effectiveness.

Individual-Level Outcomes	Group-Level Outcomes	Organization-Level Outcomes
Productivity	Productivity	Productivity
Performance	Performance	Absenteeism
Absenteeism	Norms	Turnover
Turnover	Cohesiveness	Financial Performance
Attitudes		Survival
Stress		Stakeholder Satisfaction

Organizational Effectiveness

of these outcomes are directly or indirectly addressed by various theories and models. (We provide a richer and more detailed analysis of individual-level outcomes in Chapter 3.)

Individual Behaviors   First, several individual behaviors result from a person's participation in an organization. One important behavior is productivity. A person's productivity is an indicator of his or her efficiency and is measured in terms of the products or services created per unit of input. For example, if Bill makes 100 units of a product in a day and Sara makes only 90 units in a day, then assuming that the units are of the same quality and that Bill and Sara make the same wages, Bill is more productive than Sara.

Performance, another important individual-level outcome variable, is a somewhat broader concept. It is made up of all work-related behaviors. For example, even though Bill is highly productive, it may also be that he refuses to work overtime, expresses negative opinions about the organization at every opportunity, and will do nothing unless it falls precisely within the boundaries of his job. Sara, on the other hand, may always be willing to work overtime, is a positive representative of the organization, and goes out of her way to make as many contributions to the organization as possible. Based on the full array of behaviors, then, we might conclude that Sara actually is the better performer.

Two other important individual-level behaviors are absenteeism and turnover. Absenteeism is a measure of attendance. Although virtually everyone misses work occasionally, some people miss far more than others. Some look for excuses to miss work and call in sick regularly just for some time off; others miss work only when absolutely necessary. Turnover occurs when a person leaves the organization. If the individual who leaves is a good performer or if the organization has invested heavily in training the person, turnover can be costly.

Individual Attitudes and Stress   Another set of individual-level outcomes influenced by managers consists of individual attitudes. (We discuss attitudes more fully in Chapter 3.) Levels of job satisfaction or dissatisfaction, organizational commitment, and organizational involvement all play an important role in organizational behavior. Stress, discussed more fully in Chapter 7, is another important individual-level outcome variable. Given its costs, both personal and organizational, it should not be surprising that stress is becoming an increasingly important topic for both researchers in organizational behavior and practicing managers.

Group- and Team-Level Outcomes

Another set of outcomes exists at the group and team levels. Some of these outcomes parallel the individual-level outcomes just discussed. For example, if an organization makes extensive use of work teams, team productivity and performance are important outcome variables. On the other hand, even if all the people in a group or team have the same or similar attitudes toward their jobs, the attitudes themselves are individual-level phenomena. Individuals, not groups, have attitudes.

Work teams are being increasingly used in a wide variety of organizations. This team, for example, works in a New Balance shoe assembly plant in Maine. Its six members have crossed-trained each other so that each team member has a primary job but also knows how to perform other jobs as well. This allows them to help each other out when somebody gets behind or needs to miss work.

But groups or teams can also have unique outcomes that individuals do not share. For example, as we will discuss in Chapter 9, groups develop norms that govern the behavior of individual group members. Groups also develop different levels of cohesiveness. Thus, managers need to assess both common and unique outcomes when considering the individual and group levels.

Organization-Level Outcomes

Finally, a set of outcome variables exists at the organization level. As before, some of these outcomes parallel those at the individual and group levels, but others are unique. For example, we can measure and compare organizational productivity. We can also develop organization-level indicators of absenteeism and turnover. But profitability is generally assessed only at the organizational level.

Organizations are also commonly assessed in terms of financial performance: stock price, return on investment, growth rates, and so on. They are also evaluated in terms of their ability to survive and of the extent to which they satisfy important stakeholders such as investors, government regulators, employees, and unions.

Clearly, then, the manager must balance different outcomes across all three levels of analysis. In many cases, these outcomes appear to contradict one another. For example, paying workers high salaries can enhance satisfaction and reduce turnover, but it also may detract from bottom-line performance. Similarly, exerting strong pressure to increase individual performance may boost short-term profitability but increase turnover and job stress. Thus, the manager must look at the full array of outcomes and attempt to balance them in an optimal fashion. The manager's ability to do this is a major determinant of the organization's success.

Chapter Review

Synopsis

Organizational behavior is the study of human behavior in organizational settings, the interface between human behavior and the organization, and the organization itself. The study of organizational behavior is important because organizations have a powerful influence over our lives. It also directly relates to management in organizations. Indeed, by its very nature, management requires an understanding of human behavior, to help managers better comprehend those at different levels in the organization, those at the same level, those in other organizations, and themselves.

The manager's job can be characterized in terms of four functions. These basic managerial functions are planning, organizing, leading, and controlling. Planning is the process of determining the organization's desired future position and deciding how best to get there. Organizing is the process of designing jobs, grouping jobs into manageable units, and establishing patterns of authority among jobs and groups of jobs. Leading is the process of motivating members of the organization to work together toward the organization's goals. Controlling is the process of monitoring and correcting the actions of the organization and its people to keep them headed toward their goals.

Managerial work involves ten basic roles and requires the use of four skills. The roles consist of three interpersonal roles (figurehead, leader, and liaison), three informational roles (monitor, disseminator, and spokesperson), and four decision-making roles (entrepreneur, disturbance handler, resource allocator, and negotiator). The four basic skills necessary for effective management are technical, interpersonal, conceptual, and diagnostic skills.

Contemporary organizational behavior attempts to describe, rather than prescribe, behavioral forces in organizations. Ties to psychology, sociology, anthropology, political science, economics, engineering, and medicine make organizational behavior an interdisciplinary field. The basic concepts of the field are divided into three categories: individual processes, interpersonal processes, and organizational processes and characteristics. Those categories form the framework for the organization of this book.

Important contextual perspectives on the field of organizational behavior are the systems and situational perspectives and interactionalism. There are also a number of very important individual-, group-, and organizational-level outcomes related to effectiveness.

Discussion Questions

1. Some people have suggested that understanding human behavior at work is the single most important requirement for managerial success. Do you agree or disagree with this statement? Why?

2. In what ways is organizational behavior comparable to functional areas such as finance, marketing, and production? In what ways is it different from these areas? Is it similar to statistics in any way?

3. Identify some managerial jobs that are highly affected by human behavior and others that are less so. Which would you prefer? Why?

4. The text identifies four basic managerial functions. Based on your own experiences or observations, provide examples of each function.

5. Which managerial skills do you think are among your strengths? Which are among your weaknesses? How might you improve the latter?

6. Suppose you have to hire a new manager. One candidate has outstanding technical skills but poor interpersonal skills. The other has exactly the opposite mix of skills. Which would you hire? Why?

7. Some people believe that individuals working in an organization have a basic human right to satisfaction with their work and to the opportunity to grow and develop. How would you defend this position? How would you argue against it?

8. Many universities offer a course in industrial or organizational psychology. The content of those courses is quite similar to the content of this one. Do you think that behavioral material is best taught in a business or psychology program, or is it best to teach it in both?

9. Do you believe the field of organizational behavior has the potential to become prescriptive as opposed to descriptive? Why or why not?

10. Are the notions of systems, situationalism, and interactionalism mutually exclusive? If not, describe ways in which they are related.

11. Get a recent issue of a popular business magazine such as *BusinessWeek* or *Fortune* and scan its major articles. Do any of them reflect concepts from organizational behavior? Describe.

12. Do you read Dilbert? Do you think it accurately describes organization life? Are there other comic strips that reflect life and work in contemporary organizations?

Relating OB and Popular Culture

Purpose: This exercise will help you appreciate the importance and pervasiveness of organizational behavior concepts and processes in both contemporary organizational settings and popular culture.

Format: Your instructor will divide the class into groups of three to five members. Each group will be assigned a specific television program to watch before the next class meeting.

Procedure: Arrange to watch the program as a group. Each person should have a pad of paper and a pencil handy. As you watch the show, jot down examples of individual behavior, interpersonal dynamics, organizational characteristics, and other concepts and processes relevant to organizational behavior. After the show, spend a few minutes comparing notes. Compile one list for the entire group. (It is advisable to turn off the television set during this discussion!)

During the next class meeting, have someone in the group summarize the plot of the show and list the concepts it illustrated. The following television shows are especially good for illustrating behavioral concepts in organizational settings:

Network Shows	Syndicated Shows
Survivor	*Seinfeld*
The West Wing	*Cheers*
Lost	*Star Trek*
Scrubs	*Home Improvement*
24	*L.A. Law*
C.S.I.	*Gilligan's Island*

Follow-up Questions

1. What does this exercise illustrate about the pervasiveness of organizations in our contemporary society?

2. What recent or classic movies might provide similar kinds of examples?

3. Do you think television programs from countries other than the United States would provide more or fewer examples of shows set in organizations?

Assessing Your Own Management Skills

The questions below are intended to provide insights into your confidence about your capabilities regarding the management skills discussed in this chapter. Answer each question by circling the scale value that best reflects your feelings.

1. I generally do well in quantitative courses like math, statistics, accounting, and finance.

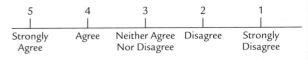

5	4	3	2	1
Strongly Agree	Agree	Neither Agree Nor Disagree	Disagree	Strongly Disagree

2. I get along well with most people.

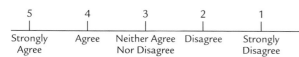

3. It is usually easy for me to see how material in one of my classes relates to material in other classes.

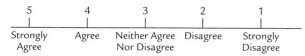

4. I can usually figure out why a problem occurred.

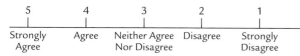

5. When I am asked to perform a task or to do some work, I usually know how to do it or else can figure it out pretty quickly.

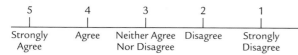

6. I can usually understand why people behave as they do.

7. I enjoy classes that deal with theories and concepts.

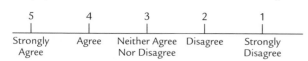

8. I usually understand why things happen as they do.

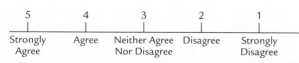

9. I like classes that require me to "do things"—write papers, solve problems, research new areas, and so forth.

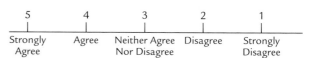

10. Whenever I work in a group, I can usually get others to accept my opinions and ideas.

11. I am much more interested in understanding the "big picture" than in dealing with narrow, focused issues.

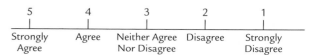

12. When I know what I am supposed to do, I can usually figure out how to do it.

Instructions: Add up your point values for questions 1, 5, and 9; this total reflects your assessment of your technical skills. The point total for questions 2, 6, and 10 reflects interpersonal skills; the point total for questions 3, 7, and 11 reflects conceptual skills; the point total for questions 4, 8, and 12 reflects diagnostic skills. Higher scores indicate stronger confidence in that realm of management. [*Note:* This brief instrument has not been scientifically validated and is to be used for classroom discussion only.]

Building Managerial Skills

Exercise Overview: Conceptual skills refer to a manager's ability to think in the abstract, while diagnostic skills focus on responses to situations. These skills must frequently be used together to better understand the behavior of others in the organization, as illustrated by this exercise.

Exercise Background: Human behavior is a complex phenomenon in any setting, but especially so in organizations. Understanding how and why people choose particular behaviors can be difficult, frustrating, but quite important. Consider, for example, the following scenario.

Sandra Buckley has worked in your department for several years. Until recently, she has been a "model" employee. She was always on time, or early, for work, and stayed late whenever necessary to get her work done. She was upbeat, cheerful, and worked very hard. She frequently said that the company was the best place she had ever worked, and that you were the

began to see
to occasion-
mber the last
so complains
her, because
suspect that

Exercise Task: Using the scenario described above as background, do the following:

1. Assume that you have done some background work to find out what has happened. Write a brief case with more information that explains why Sandra's behavior has changed (i.e., your case might include the fact that you recently promoted someone else when Sandra might have expected to get the job). Make the case as descriptive as possible.

2. Relate elements of your case to the various behavioral concepts discussed in this chapter.

3. Decide whether or not you might be about to resolve things with Sandra in order to overcome whatever issues have arisen.

4. Which behavioral process or concept discussed in this chapter is easiest to change? Which is the most difficult to change?

Organizational Behavior Case for Discussion

capability, was
ed to the 100th
eros), to reflect
the company's ability to organize... mense amount of information available on the World Wide Web.

Every month, 82 million individuals, half of them from outside the United States, access the Google website, one of the five most popular Internet sites in the world. There they find more than eight billion web pages presented in an easy-to-use format. The company charges firms to sponsor links to corporate websites so the service is free to customers and avoids irritating pop-up ads.

How does Google continue to develop innovative technology and techniques, staying ahead of such tough competitors as Yahoo! and Microsoft? The key ingredient in Google's success is people.

Google began as a project of two Stanford graduate students, Larry Page and Sergey Brin, and an informal, collegial spirit still guides the firm. Googlers are encour-

aged to work on projects of their own choosing for one day each week. The time to freely experiment has led to innovations such as the ability to translate pages into various languages. Innovation is so important to the firm that its website states, "We don't talk much about what lies ahead, because . . . one of our chief competitive advantages is surprise. Surprise and innovation."

Collaboration is another key value for Google workers. Google facilities contain on-site sports fields and shared office spaces. Employees from new hires to the CEO eat lunch together, play on the same hockey team, and mingle in the office lounges. Google's website claims, "Google . . . favors ability over experience." Position within the corporate hierarchy plays a relatively minor role.

In an environment where pressure can be intense, Googlers must know how to relax. Employees play billiards or ping pong and bring their dogs to work. Even recruiting is fun. When Google sought new programmers, they didn't use traditional techniques. Instead, the company conducted an on-line programming skills contest, giving cash prizes and job offers to top-performing competitors.

In spite of their emphasis on fun, Googlers are serious about productivity, quality, and cost cutting. To stay focused on customer needs, a large world map is prominently displayed at headquarters. Points of light represent current searches while color coding shows the language used by the searcher. Current searches are displayed around the office too, so staff remain constantly aware of their far-flung customers.

Google's commitment to excellence is characterized on the company's website: "[We] continue to look for those who share an obsessive commitment to creating search perfection." Although Google uses diversity to drive innovation, the firm concentrates on just one aspect of Internet service: search. One of the company's key values, stated on the website, is "It's best to do one thing really, really well." "Never settle for the best," the Google corporate philosophy, sums up the company's relentless drive to perfection.

Of course, Google isn't perfect. While top leaders are technology wizards, their business expertise is not as strong. Managers made serious missteps during the company's initial public offering of stock in 2004. The mistakes were serious enough to spark an SEC inquiry, which found errors but no intent to defraud. Observers credit those mistakes to arrogance. One investment banker characterizes Brin and Page as "challenging and difficult" and speculates that the stock market will "crush" that arrogance.

Looking to the future, stock analysts and investors have expressed concerns about the ability of Google managers to handle an organization that is rapidly growing. A more complex corporate structure, with facilities located on three continents, also adds to the management challenges.

Google's greatest challenge at this time, however, seems to be increased competition. While Internet search

> ## "*Never settle for the best.*"
> GOOGLE CORPORATE PHILOSOPHY

has thus far escaped the attention of larger competitors, that is about to change. Microsoft, for example, has recently introduced a test version of a new search engine. Google's search procedures yield better-quality results, yet it's only a matter of time before a well-funded and smart competitor will duplicate their methods. To ensure continued success, Google must keep its expert workforce loyal, motivated, and productive. Only then will Google innovate and stay ahead of its competition.

Case Questions

1. In your opinion, what types of management skills are most important at Google? Explain your answer.

2. How do individual processes at Google reflect the company's focus on customer needs, innovation, and teamwork? How do team processes and organizational processes reflect the company's priorities? Use Figure 1.4, "The Framework for Understanding Organizational Behavior," to help you answer these questions.

3. Consider Google as a system. Give an example of each type of input available to Google. Give examples of transformation processes and outputs at Google. What impact does the environment have on Google and what impact does Google have on the environment?

References: "Corporate Information," "Google Job Opportunities," Google website, www.google.com on February 12, 2005 (quotation); Sergey Brin and Lawrence Page, "The Anatomy of a Large-Scale Hypertextual Web Search Engine," *Computer Networks and ISDN Systems*, 1998, www-db.stanford.edu on February 7, 2005; Fernando Ribeiro Correa, "Interview with Google's Sergey Brin," *Linux Gazette*, November 2000, www.linuxgazette.com on February 7, 2005; Ben Elgin, "Google: Whiz Kid or Naughty Boys?" *BusinessWeek*, August 19, 2004, www.businessweek.com on February 12, 2005; Stephanie Olsen, "Google Seeking a Few Good Code Jockeys," C/Net News.com, September 17, 2003, news.com.com on February 7, 2005; Paul S. Piper, "Google Spawn: The Culture Surrounding Google," *Information Today*, June 2004, www.infotoday.com on February 7, 2005.

You have read the chapter and studied the key terms. Think you're ready to ace the exam? Take this sample test to gauge your comprehension of chapter material and check your answers at the back of the book. Want more test questions? Take the ACE quizzes found on the student website: http://college.hmco.com/business/students/ (select Griffin/Moorhead, *Organizational Behavior*, 8e, from the Management menu).

T   F   1. Organizational behavior (OB) is the study of how companies expand their market shares, deal with competitors, and successfully satisfy customer expectations.

T   F   2. Many students who take an organizational behavior course go on to become Organizational Behavior Managers in their future careers.

T   F   3. Motivating employees is a fundamental part of the leading function of management.

T   F   4. First-line managers generally require higher levels of conceptual and diagnostic skills than they do technical and interpersonal skills.

T   F   5. An understanding of organizational behavior allows managers to make specific, accurate predictions about their employees.

T   F   6. The systems perspective says organizations receive inputs from the environment, combine and transform them, and then return them to the environment.

T   F   7. A person's behavior is likely influenced by his or her personal characteristics as well as characteristics of the situation the person is in.

8. This is probably your first course in organizational behavior. You will learn about all of the following by reading this text, except
   a. human behavior in organizational settings.
   b. the unique perspectives employees bring to work settings.
   c. the interface between human behavior and the organization.
   d. competition and how it affects the stock prices of publicly held firms.
   e. organizations themselves.

9. A manager who designs jobs, groups jobs into manageable units, and establishes patterns of authority among jobs is performing which basic management function?
   a. Leading
   b. Organizing
   c. Planning
   d. Synthesizing
   e. Controlling

10. A manager acting in the role of monitor would do which of the following?
    a. Carefully supervise employees
    b. Check to see that time cards are properly completed
    c. Actively seek information that might be of value to the organization
    d. Upgrade computer systems whenever necessary
    e. Develop central goals and strategies for achieving those goals

11. Martha is a top manager at a large manufacturing firm. Which of the following skills are most likely to help Martha do her job?
    a. Conceptual and technical skills
    b. Technical and interpersonal skills
    c. Interpersonal and financial skills
    d. Financial and diagnostic skills
    e. Diagnostic and conceptual skills

12. The field of organizational behavior is best described as
    a. scientific and individual in nature.
    b. behavioral and organizational in nature.
    c. innovative and traditional in nature.
    d. interdisciplinary and descriptive in nature.
    e. cross-functional and predictive in nature.

13. According to the systems perspective,
    a. a company will be most successful if it can seal its borders.
    b. inputs such as raw materials and money are created inside the organization.
    c. organizations are interrelated sets of elements that function as a whole.
    d. orderly, logical management practices are the most effective.
    e. inputs are combined and transformed in the environment outside the organization.

14. Organizational behavior examines outcomes at which three levels?
    a. Organization, industry, division
    b. Organization, division, department
    c. Department, individual, group
    d. Individual, group, organization
    e. Group, organization, industry

CHAPTER 2

The Changing Environment of Organizations

Chapter Outline

Nearshoring Is the New Offshoring at SAP

During the 1990s, offshoring, hiring a foreign firm to perform some business functions, became popular. In its early uses, a company typically implemented offshoring by moving production facilities overseas to take advantage of low-cost labor. In the last few years, however, offshoring has taken on a different character. Today, companies are increasingly using offshoring for the performance of technology functions that require a high degree of education, training, and skill. Some of the business functions that can be effectively performed through offshoring are computer programming, customer service centers, and new product design.

American firms with offshoring needs frequently turn to India, with its abundance of expert engineers, designers, and computer scientists. Indian workers are fluent in English and willing to work for low wages, often half or less of the pay demanded by skilled American and European employees. For non-English-speaking countries, such as Germany and France, India may not be the most desirable offshoring partners. "India seems an awfully long way away," says analyst Ian Marriott. Firms in these countries are turning to Eastern Europe, in a process that has been named "nearshoring."

> ❝ *People want to be able to pick up the phone and resolve problems.* ❞
> *ERRAN CARMEL, PROFESSOR, AMERICAN UNIVERSITY*

German-based SAP, the third largest software firm in the world, is investing in Bulgaria. The firm has hired 180 Bulgarian computer scientists to write innovative Web-services software. For SAP, Eastern Europe offers many German speakers and closer interpersonal ties. "Cultural, linguistic, and even ethnic connections are very important in nearshoring," says Erran Carmel, a professor at American University. "People want to be able to pick up the phone and resolve problems."

Through its use of nearshoring, SAP has reduced costs, an essential tactic in the competitive software industry. While SAP's revenues grew only 7 percent last year, profits increased by 20 percent. Most of the savings came in the form of labor costs; a Bulgarian engineer earns just $6,500 annually, about one-tenth of a German engineer's wages.

Developing countries in Eastern Europe welcome the influx of capital and jobs. Today, India accounts for about half of the $25 billion global offshore market, but Eastern Europe's share is growing rapidly. As Eastern European countries join the European Union over the next few years, nearshoring may become even easier.

Some experts believe that increased use of nearshoring will increase the standard of living in poorer countries while reducing it in more developed regions. Backing up this claim, Bernhard Schreier, CEO of a German manufacturer, says, "When we find a certain product can be made with a 50 percent decrease in salary costs in another country, we cannot avoid that if we want to stay competitive." Marc Andreessen, co-founder of Netscape, disagrees. "Lower-value jobs vanish over time . . . New jobs are getting created that are better jobs . . . Growth leads to growth." SAP's experience is more in line with Andreessen's prediction, as the company has increased hiring in Germany while increasing nearshoring.

Right now, however, German workers are fearful about losing their jobs to foreigners. Perhaps they will find that offshoring creates more opportunities for them at home, as is happening at SAP. *SAP and . . . Change,* found on page 31, describes further changes occurring at SAP.

References: "The Best & Worst Managers of 2004: Henning Kagermann of SAP," *Business Week,* January 10, 2005, www .businessweek.com on February 14, 2005; Robert D. Hof, "Outsourcing Isn't a 'Zero-Sum' Game," *Business Week,* March 1, 2004, www.businessweek.com on February 14, 2005; Carol Matlack, "European Workers' Losing Battle," *Business Week,* August 9, 2004, p. 41; Andy Reinhardt, "Forget India, Let's Go To Bulgaria," *Business Week,* March 1, 2004, www.businessweek.com on February 14, 2005 (quotation).

The environment of business is changing at an unprecedented rate. Indeed, in some industries, such as consumer electronics, popular entertainment, and information technology, the speed and magnitude of change are truly breathtaking. Industries that have more staid and predictable environments, such as retailing and heavy manufacturing, also face sweeping environmental changes today. Understanding and addressing the environment of a business has traditionally been the purview of top managers. But the effects of today's changing environment permeate the entire organization. Hence, to truly understand the behavior of people in organizational settings, it is also necessary to understand the changing environment of business. This chapter is intended to provide the framework for such understanding. Specifically, we introduce and examine five of the central environmental forces for change faced by today's organizations: globalization, diversity, technology, ethics and corporate governance, and new employment relationships. An understanding of these forces will then set the stage for our in-depth discussion of contemporary organizational behavior.

Globalization and Business

> **Globalization** is the internationalization of business activities and the shift toward an integrated global economy.

Perhaps the most significant source of change impacting many organizations today is the increasing **globalization** of organizations and management. Of course, in many ways, international management is nothing new. Centuries ago, the Roman army was forced to develop a management system to deal with its widespread empire.[1] Moreover, many notable early explorers like Christopher Columbus were actually seeking new trade routes to boost international trade. Likewise, the Olympic Games, the Red Cross, and other organizations have international roots. From a business standpoint in the United States, however, the widespread concerns for and effects of international management are relatively new.

The Growth of International Business

In 2005, the volume of international trade in current dollars was almost fifty times greater than the amount in 1960. What has led to this dramatic increase? As Figure 2.1 shows, four major factors account for much of the momentum.

First, communication and transportation have advanced dramatically over the past several decades. Telephone service has improved, communication networks span the globe and can interact via satellite, and once-remote areas have become routinely accessible. Fax machines and electronic mail allow managers to send documents around the world in seconds as opposed to the days it took just a few years ago. In short, it is simply easier to conduct international business today.

Second, businesses have expanded internationally to increase their markets. Companies in smaller countries, such as Nestlé in Switzerland and Heineken in The Netherlands, recognized long ago that their domestic markets were too small to sustain much growth and moved into international arenas. Many U.S. firms, on the other hand, found it advantageous to enter foreign markets only in the last half century. Now, though, most mid-size and even many small firms routinely buy and/or sell their products and services in other countries.

Third, more and more firms are moving into international markets to reduce labor costs. This does not always work out as planned, but many firms are successfully using inexpensive labor in Asia and Mexico.[2] In searching for lower labor costs, some companies have discovered

FIGURE 2.1

Forces That Have Increased International Business

Movement along the continuum from domestic to international business is due to four forces. Businesses subject to these forces are becoming more international.

Domestic Business

International Business

Improved Communication and Transportation Facilities
Larger Potential Market
Lower Costs of Production and Distribution
Response to International Activity of Competitors

SAP and . . .

SAP Is No Longer Stodgy

As we previewed in our chapter opener, SAP is a large German-based software company. Its products allow 25,000 of the world's largest corporations to manage marketing, manufacturing, logistics, and other basic business functions. In the past, though, the company has often been accused of being slow to innovate and has been called "stodgy" and "plodding."

Give credit to CEO Henning Kagermann, who took over the top spot in 1993, with encouraging a culture of change. Kagermann describes SAP's innovative response to an anticipated upturn in demand for new technology applications, saying, "The waves of change are coming faster."

SAP is not only participating in globalization; through its products, it is also contributing to globalization. SAP's new Web-services software will allow businesses to link their many different sales, accounting, inventory, and human resources applications into one connected system using the Internet. This system makes it easier for companies to use domestic and foreign outsourcing, by simplifying the integration of data from complex and far-flung operations.

SAP is facing a number of changes in other areas. Some of the changes are guided by updates to German business law. SAP is increasing its focus on ethics, corporate governance, and investor transparency. German companies, including SAP, are also changing the employment contract, to implement pay for performance compensation, increase the workweek, and reduce worker dependence on lifelong employment and unions.

Kagermann says, "Success is the ongoing realization of new ideas—and their validation by the market." There are many new ideas at SAP today, and one of the most significant areas of change is the company's attitude toward change.

> *"The waves of change are coming faster."*
>
> HENNING KAGERMANN, CEO, SAP

References: Andy Reinhardt, "Forget India, Let's Go To Bulgaria," *Business Week,* March 1, 2004, www.businessweek .com on February 14, 2005; "SAP Annual Report 2004," SAP website, www.sap.com on June 7, 2005; "The Best Managers of 2004: Henning Kagermann of SAP," *Business Week,* January 10, 2005, www.businessweek.com on February 14, 2005 (quotation).

well-trained workers and built more efficient plants that are closer to international markets.[3] India, for instance, has emerged as a major force in the high-tech sector. And many foreign automakers have built plants in the United States.

Finally, many organizations have become international in response to competition. If an organization starts gaining strength in international markets, its competitors often must follow suit to avoid falling too far behind in sales and profitability. Exxon Mobil Corporation and Chevron realized they had to increase their international market share to keep pace with foreign competitors such as BP and Royal Dutch/Shell. The *SAP and . . . Change* box further highlights the role of change as a firm becomes more global in its orientation.

Cross-Cultural Differences and Similarities

The globalization of business has brought into focus the differences and similarities in behavior across cultures. While there is relatively little research in this area, interesting findings are beginning to emerge.

General Observations   At one level, it is possible to make several general observations about similarities and differences across cultures. For one thing, cultural and

These four workers in Alcatel's switch-making plant in Shanghai, China, exemplify the rapid changes in manufacturing in that country. Once known for cheap and low-skilled labor that made cheap trinkets, toys, textiles, and knock-offs of higher-quality goods, China has become a haven for high-tech manufacturing. Sophisticated electronic equipment, photonics, ceramic casings, liquid crystal display screens, digital switching systems, and much more are now among the goods being produced there. China's emergence is creating rapid shifts in investment around the world, as manufacturers move to take advantage of the cheaper labor, high-quality workmanship, sophisticated engineering expertise, and proximity to the huge Chinese marketplace. Investment that used to go to Japan and other countries in Southeast Asia is now going to China. In fact, Japanese, European, and U.S. producers of high-tech equipment, such as OMRON, Nokia, and Alcatel, are now investing billions in new manufacturing plants in China.

Culture is the set of shared values, often taken for granted, that help people in a group, organization, or society understand which actions are considered acceptable and which are deemed unacceptable.

national boundaries do not necessarily coincide. Some areas of Switzerland are very much like Italy, other parts like France, and still other parts like Germany. Similarly, within the United States there are large cultural differences across, say, Southern California, Texas, and the East Coast.[4]

Given this basic assumption, one major review of the literature on international management reached five basic conclusions.[5] First, behavior in organizational settings does indeed vary across cultures. Thus, employees in companies based in Japan, the United States, and Germany are likely to have different attitudes and patterns of behavior. The behavior patterns are also likely to be widespread and pervasive within an organization.

Second, culture itself is one major cause of this variation. **Culture** is the set of shared values, often taken for granted, that help people in a group, organization, or society understand which actions are considered acceptable and which are deemed unacceptable (we use this same definition to frame our discussion of organizational culture in Chapter 18). Thus, although the behavioral differences just noted may be caused in part by different standards of living, different geographical conditions, and so forth, culture itself is a major factor apart from other considerations.

Third, although the causes and consequences of behavior within organizational settings remain quite diverse across cultures, organizations and the way they are structured appear to be growing increasingly similar. Hence, managerial practices at a general level may be becoming more and more alike, but the people who work within organizations still differ markedly.

Fourth, the same individual behaves differently in different cultural settings. A manager may adopt one set of behaviors when working in one culture but change those behaviors when moved to a different culture. For example, Japanese executives who come to work in the United States slowly begin to act more like U.S. managers and less like Japanese managers. This is often a source of concern for them when they are transferred back to Japan.[6]

Finally, cultural diversity can be an important source of synergy in enhancing organizational effectiveness. More and more organizations are coming to appreciate the virtues of diversity, but they still know surprisingly little about how to manage it.[7] Organizations that adopt a multinational strategy can—with effort—become more than a sum of their parts. Operations in each culture can benefit from operations in other cultures through an enhanced understanding of how the world works.[8]

Specific Cultural Issues   Geert Hofstede, a Dutch researcher, studied workers and managers in sixty countries and found that specific attitudes and behaviors differed significantly because of the values and beliefs that characterized those countries.[9] Table 2.1 shows how Hofstede's categories can help us summarize differences for several countries.

The two primary dimensions that Hofstede found are the individualism/collectivism continuum and power distance. **Individualism** exists to the extent that people in a culture define themselves primarily as individuals rather than as part of one or more groups or organizations. At work, people from more individualistic cultures tend to be more concerned about themselves as individuals than about their work group, individual tasks are more important than relationships, and hiring and promotion are usually based on skills and rules. **Collectivism**, on the other hand, is characterized by tight social frameworks in which people tend to base their identities on the group or organization to which they belong. At work, this means that employee-employer links are more like family relationships, relationships are more important than individuals or tasks, and hiring and promotion are based on group membership. In the United States, a very individualistic culture, it is important to perform better than others and to stand out from the crowd. In Japan, a more collectivist culture, an individual tries to fit in with the group, strives for harmony, and prefers stability.

Power distance, which can also be called **orientation to authority**, is the extent to which people accept as normal an unequal distribution of power. In countries such as Mexico and Venezuela, for example, people prefer to be in a situation in which

> **Individualism** exists to the extent that people in a culture define themselves primarily as individuals rather than as part of one or more groups or organizations. **Collectivism** is characterized by tight social frameworks in which people tend to base their identities on the group or organization to which they belong.

> **Power distance,** which can also be called **orientation to authority,** is the extent to which people accept as normal an unequal distribution of power.

Country	Individualism/ Collectivism	Power Distance	Uncertainty Avoidance	Masculinity	Long-Term Orientation
Canada	H	M	M	M	L
Germany	M	M	M	M	M
Israel	M	L	M	M	(no data)
Italy	H	M	M	H	(no data)
Japan	M	M	H	H	H
Mexico	H	H	H	M	(no data)
Pakistan	L	M	M	M	L
Sweden	H	M	L	L	M
United States	H	M	M	M	L
Venezuela	L	H	M	H	(no data)

TABLE 2.1

Work-Related Differences in Ten Countries

Note: H = high; M = moderate; L = low. These are only ten of the more than sixty countries that Hofstede and others have studied.

References: Adapted from Geert Hofstede and Michael Harris Bond, "The Confucius Connection: From Cultural Roots to Economic Growth," *Organizational Dynamics*, Spring 1988, pp. 5–21; Geert Hofstede, "Motivation, Leadership, and Organization: Do American Theories Apply Abroad?" *Organizational Dynamics*, Summer 1980, pp. 42–63.

authority is clearly understood and lines of authority are never bypassed. On the other hand, in countries such as Israel and Denmark, authority is not as highly respected and employees are quite comfortable circumventing lines of authority to accomplish something. People in the United States tend to be mixed, accepting authority in some situations but not in others.

Hofstede also identified other dimensions of culture. **Uncertainty avoidance**, which can also be called **preference for stability**, is the extent to which people feel threatened by unknown situations and prefer to be in clear and unambiguous situations. People in Japan and Mexico prefer stability to uncertainty, whereas uncertainty is normal and accepted in Sweden, Hong Kong, and the United Kingdom. **Masculinity**, which might more accurately be called **assertiveness** or **materialism**, is the extent to which the dominant values in a society emphasize aggressiveness and the acquisition of money and other possessions as opposed to concern for people, relationships among people, and overall quality of life. People in the United States tend to be moderate on both the uncertainty avoidance and masculinity scales. Japan and Italy score high on the masculinity scale while Sweden scores low.

Hofstede's framework has recently been expanded to include long-term versus short-term values. **Long-term values** include focusing on the future, working on projects that have a distant payoff, persistence, and thrift. **Short-term values** are more oriented toward the past and the present and include respect for traditions and social obligations. Japan, Hong Kong, and China are highly long-term oriented. The Netherlands and Germany are moderately long-term oriented. The United States, Indonesia, West Africa, and Russia are more short-term oriented.

Hofstede's research presents only one of several ways of categorizing differences across many different countries and cultures. His findings, however, are now widely accepted and have been used by many companies. They have also prompted ongoing research by others. The important issue to remember is that people from diverse cultures value things differently from each other and that people need to take these differences into account as they work.

Managerial Behavior Across Cultures

Some individual variations in people from different cultures shape the behavior of both managers and employees. Other differences are much more likely to influence managerial behavior per se.[10] In general, these differences relate to managerial beliefs about the role of authority and power in the organization. For example, managers in Indonesia, Italy, and Japan tend to believe that the purpose of an organization structure is to let everyone know who his or her boss is (medium to high power distance). Managers in the United States, Germany, and Great Britain, in contrast, believe that organization structure is intended to coordinate group behavior and effort (low power distance). On another dimension, Italian and German managers believe it is acceptable to bypass one's boss to get things done, but among Swedish and British managers, bypassing one's superior is strongly prohibited.

Figure 2.2 illustrates findings on another interesting point. Managers in Japan strongly believe that a manager should be able to answer any question he or she is asked. Thus, they place a premium on expertise and experience. At the other extreme are Swedish managers, who have the least concern about knowing all the answers. They view themselves as problem solvers and facilitators who make no claim to omnipotence. Some evidence suggests that managerial behavior is rapidly changing, at least among European managers. In general, these managers are becoming more career oriented, better educated, more willing to work cooperatively with labor, more willing to delegate, and more cosmopolitan.[11]

Uncertainty avoidance, which can also be called **preference for stability,** is the extent to which people feel threatened by unknown situations and prefer to be in clear and unambiguous situations.

Masculinity, which might more accurately be called **assertiveness or materialism,** is the extent to which the dominant values in a society emphasize aggressiveness and the acquisition of money and other possessions as opposed to concern for people, relationships among people, and overall quality of life.

Long-term values include focusing on the future, working on projects that have a distant payoff, persistence, and thrift.

Short-term values are more oriented toward the past and the present and include respect for traditions and social obligations.

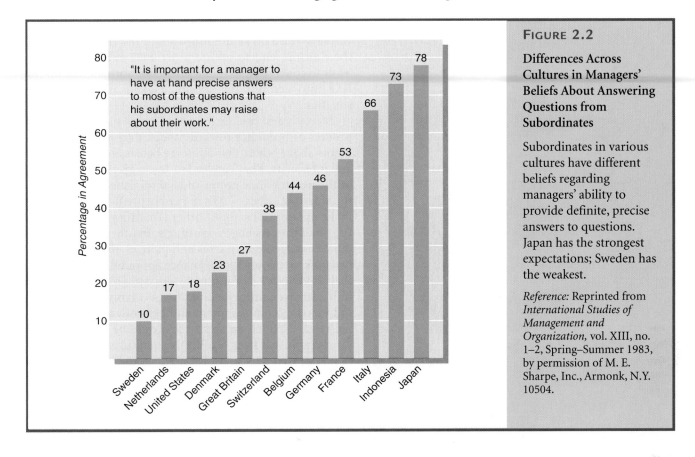

FIGURE 2.2

Differences Across Cultures in Managers' Beliefs About Answering Questions from Subordinates

Subordinates in various cultures have different beliefs regarding managers' ability to provide definite, precise answers to questions. Japan has the strongest expectations; Sweden has the weakest.

Reference: Reprinted from *International Studies of Management and Organization*, vol. XIII, no. 1–2, Spring–Summer 1983, by permission of M. E. Sharpe, Inc., Armonk, N.Y. 10504.

Diversity and Business

A second major environmental shift in recent years has been the increased attention devoted to the concept of diversity. **Workforce diversity** refers to the important similarities and differences among the employees of organizations. 3M defines its goals regarding workforce diversity as "valuing uniqueness, while respecting differences, maximizing individual potentials, and synergizing collective talents and experiences for the growth and success of 3M."[12] In a diverse workforce, managers are compelled to recognize and handle the similarities and differences that exist among the people in the organization.[13]

Employees' conceptions of work, expectations of rewards from the organization, and practices in relating to others are all influenced by diversity.[14] Managers of diverse work groups need to understand how the social environment affects employees' beliefs about work, and they must have the communication skills to develop confidence and self-esteem in members of diverse work groups.

Unfortunately, many people tend to stereotype others in organizations. A **stereotype** is a generalization about a person or a group of persons based on certain characteristics or traits. Many managers fall into the trap of stereotyping workers as being like themselves and sharing a manager's orientation toward work, rewards, and relating to coworkers. However, if workers do not share those views, values, and beliefs, problems can arise. A second situation involving stereotyping occurs when managers classify workers into some particular group based on something like age or gender. It is often easier for managers to group people based on easily identifiable characteristics and to

Workforce diversity refers to the important similarities and differences among the employees of organizations.

Stereotypes are generalizations about a person or a group of persons based on certain characteristics or traits.

Diversity training is a common method used in businesses today to better enable their employees to accept and value differences. These Pilgrim Health Care workers, for instance, are participating in a role-playing exercise as part of a diversity training program. Various individuals wear labels branding themselves as "complainer," "rookie-new hire," "opposed to change," "overweight," and so forth. As they interact with one another, they begin to see how labels affect their interactions with others at work.

Prejudices are judgments about others that reinforce beliefs about superiority and inferiority.

treat these groups as "different." Managers who stereotype workers based on assumptions about the characteristics of their group tend to ignore individual differences, which leads to making rigid judgments about others that do not take into account the specific person and the current situation.[15]

Stereotypes can lead to the even more dangerous process of prejudice toward others. **Prejudices** are judgments about others that reinforce beliefs about superiority and inferiority. They can lead to an exaggerated assessment of the worth of one group and a diminished assessment of the worth of others.[16] When people prejudge others, they make assumptions about others that may or may not be true, and they manage accordingly. In other words, people build management systems and policies, job descriptions, reward systems, and performance appraisal systems that fit their stereotypes. For instance, suppose a manager from an individualist culture assumes that everyone will strive for individual accomplishment and be motivated by individual rewards. Such an approach would be prejudicial toward employees from a collectivist culture who may focus more on group accomplishment and be motivated by group rewards.

Management systems built on stereotypes and prejudices do not meet the needs of a diverse workforce. An incentive system may offer rewards that people do not value, job descriptions that do not fit the jobs and the people who do them, and performance evaluation systems that measure the wrong things. In addition, those who engage in prejudice and stereotyping fail to recognize employees' distinctive individual talents, a situation that often leads these employees to lose self-esteem and possibly have lower levels of job satisfaction and performance. Stereotypes can also become self-fulfilling prophecies.[17] If we assume an employee is incompetent and treat the person as though he or she is, over time the employee may begin to share the same belief. This can lead to reduced productivity, lower creativity, and lower morale.

Of course, managers caught in this counterproductive cycle can change. Only when managers recognize that diversity exists in organizations can they begin to manage it appropriately. Managers who do not recognize diversity may face an unhappy, disillusioned, and underutilized workforce.

Dimensions of Diversity

In the United States, race and gender have been the primary dimensions of diversity for the past two or three decades. The earliest civil rights laws were aimed at correcting racial segregation. Other laws have dealt with discrimination on the basis of gender, age, and disability. However, diversity entails broader issues than these. In the largest sense, the diversity of the workforce refers to all of the ways that employees are similar and different. The importance of renewed interest in diversity is that it helps organizations reap the benefits of all the similarities and differences among workers.

The **primary dimensions of diversity** are those factors that are either inborn or exert extraordinary influence on early socialization. These include age, race and ethnicity, gender, physical and mental abilities, and sexual orientation.[18] These factors make up the essence of who we are as human beings. They define us to others, and because of how others react to them, these factors also define us to ourselves. These characteristics are enduring aspects of our human personality, and they can present extremely complex problems to managers.

> **Primary dimensions of diversity** are those factors that are either inborn or exert extraordinary influence on early socialization.

Secondary dimensions of diversity include factors that matter to us as individuals and that to some extent define us to others; however, they may be less permanent than primary dimensions and can be adapted or changed. These include educational background, geographical location, income, marital status, military experience, parental status, religious beliefs, and work experience. These factors may influence any given individual as much as the primary dimensions. Many veterans of the Persian Gulf War and the wars in Afghanistan and Iraq, for example, have been profoundly affected by their experience of serving in the military.

> **Secondary dimensions of diversity** include factors that matter to us as individuals and that to some extent define us to others; however, they may be less permanent than primary dimensions and can be adapted or changed.

Who Will Be the Workforce of the Future?

Employment statistics can help us understand just how different the workforce of the future will be. Figure 2.3 compares the workforce composition of 1990 to projections

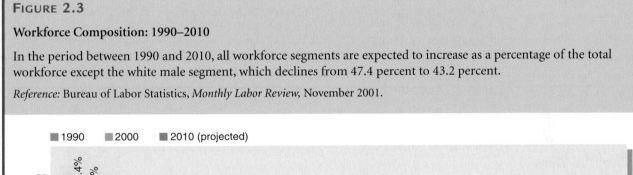

FIGURE 2.3

Workforce Composition: 1990–2010

In the period between 1990 and 2010, all workforce segments are expected to increase as a percentage of the total workforce except the white male segment, which declines from 47.4 percent to 43.2 percent.

Reference: Bureau of Labor Statistics, *Monthly Labor Review,* November 2001.

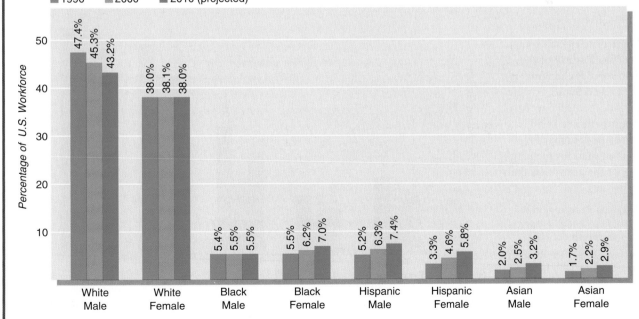

for 2010. All workforce segments will increase as a percentage of the total workforce except the white male segment, which declines from 47.4 percent to 43.2 percent. This may not seem too dramatic, but it follows decades in which the white males have dominated the workforce, making up well over 50 percent of it. When one considers that the total U.S. workforce is expected to be over 150 million people in 2010, a 4 percent drop represents a significant decline.[19]

We can also examine the nature of the growth in the workforce over the ten-year period from 2000 to 2010. Figure 2.4 shows the percentage of the growth attributable to each segment. Although the overall workforce growth is expected to be 12 percent, the growth rate for white males is expected to be only 6.7 percent. Females are expected to increase their percentage in the workforce by 15.1 percent, so that more than 62 percent of the women in the United States are expected to be working in 2010.

Examining the age ranges of the workforce gives us another view of the changes. In contrast to its standing in earlier decades, the sixteen-to-twenty-four age group will grow more rapidly than the overall population—an increase of 3.4 million (14.8 percent) between 2000 and 2010. The number of workers in the twenty-five-to-fifty-four age group is expected to increase by 5 million (5.0 percent), and the number of workers in the fifty-five-and-older group is expected to increase by 8.5 million (46.6 percent).[20]

Global Workforce Diversity

Similar statistics on workforce diversity are found in other countries. In Canada, for instance, minorities are the fastest-growing segment of the population and the workforce. In addition, women make up two-thirds of the growth in the Canadian workforce, increasing from 35 percent in the 1970s to 45 percent in 1991.[21] These

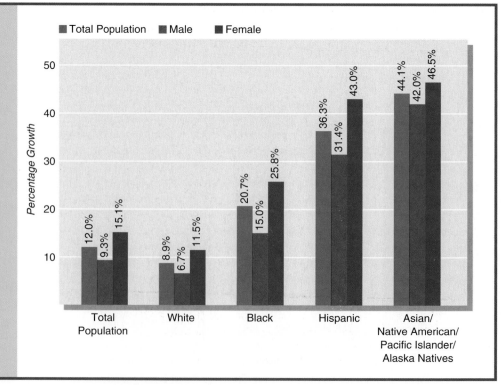

FIGURE 2.4

Expected Percentage of Growth in Workforce: 2000–2010

There is no question that the composition of the workforce is changing in the United States. For the period from 2000 to 2010, the growth rate in all segments is higher for women than for men and higher for nonwhites than for whites.

Reference: Bureau of Labor Statistics, *Monthly Labor Review,* November 2001.

changes have initiated a workforce revolution in offices and factories throughout Canada. Managers and employees are learning to adapt to changing demographics. One study found that 81 percent of the organizations surveyed by the Conference Board of Canada include diversity management programs for their employees.[22]

Increasing diversity in the workplace is even more dramatic in Europe, where employees have been crossing borders for many years. In fact, in 1991 more than 2 million Europeans were working in another European country. When the European Union opened borders in 1992, this number increased significantly. It was expected that opening borders among the European community members primarily would mean relaxing trade restrictions so that goods and services could move among the member countries. In addition, however, workers were also free to move, and they have taken advantage of the opportunity. It is clear that diversity in the workforce is more than a U.S. phenomenon. Many German factories now have a very diverse workforce that includes many workers from Turkey. Several of the newly emerging economies in Central Europe are encountering increasing diversity in their workforce. Poland, Hungary, and the Czech Republic are experiencing a steady influx of workers from Ukraine, Afghanistan, Sri Lanka, China and Somalia.[23]

Companies throughout Europe are learning to adjust to the changing workforce. Amadeus Global Travel Distribution serves the travel industry, primarily in Europe, but its staff of 650 is composed of individuals from thirty-two different countries. Amadeus developed a series of workshops to teach managers how to lead multicultural teams. Such seminars also teach them how to interact better with peers, subordinates, and superiors who come from a variety of countries.[24] Other companies experiencing much the same phenomenon in Europe and doing something about it include Mars, Hewlett-Packard Spain, Fujitsu Spain, and BP. Companies in Asia are also encountering increasing diversity. In Thailand, where there is a shortage of skilled and unskilled workers because of rapid industrialization and slow population growth, there is a growing demand for foreign workers to fill the gap, which creates problems integrating local and foreign workers.[25] Thus, the issues of workforce diversity are not prevalent only in the United States. The *Diversity Works! . . . and Globalization* box provides additional insights into the role of global diversity for Australian businesses.

The Value of Diversity

The United States has historically been seen as a "melting pot" of people from many different countries, cultures, and backgrounds. For centuries, it was assumed that people who came from other countries should assimilate themselves into the existing cultural context they were entering. Although equal employment opportunity and accompanying affirmative action legislation have had significant effects on diversifying workplaces, they sometimes focused on bringing people from culturally different groups into the workplace and assimilating them into the organization. In organizations, however, integration proved to be difficult. People were slow to change and usually resistant to the change. Substantive career advancement opportunities rarely materialized for those who were "different."

The issue of workforce diversity has become increasingly more important in the last few years as employees, managers, consultants, and the government finally realized that the composition of the workforce affects organizational productivity. Today, instead of a melting pot, the workplace in the United States is regarded as more of a "tossed salad" made up of different flavors, colors, and textures. Rather than trying to assimilate those who are different into a single organizational culture, the current view holds that organizations need to celebrate the differences and utilize the variety of talents, perspectives, and backgrounds of all employees.

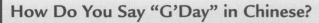

Diversity Works! . . . and GLOBALIZATION

How Do You Say "G'Day" in Chinese?

Australia is a diverse country, including indigenous people, Europeans, and others, with Asians as the largest minority group. The Australian government uses a program called Diversity Works! to educate and encourage companies about the beneficial aspects of diversity. Several of the projects recently undertaken at Diversity Works! focus on China, because Chinese-Australians make up the largest group of non-English speakers in the country. Almost half a million Australians speak Mandarin or Cantonese as their primary language and know little or no English.

Sovereign Hill, a historical park, teaches visitors about Australia's gold rush, which included 9,000 Chinese immigrant miners. Multilingual tour guides aid foreign guests and Chinese-Australian staff from Diversity Works! train all of Sovereign Hill's staff in cultural awareness. A Chinese-speaking marketer visits China to establish relationships with tour operators. "What has been most powerful is the increased understanding of the context for language and behavior," says Tim Sullivan, Deputy CEO. "This includes knowing something about the places the visitors come from, what their lives are like, and how they like to work and play."

Cisco, an American hardware manufacturer, has established a technical support center in Australia to support its Asian clients. Half of the workforce speaks a language other than English, ranging from Indian to Thai to Mandarin. Diversity Works! sponsors multicultural and language education. "It is not just language

skills that are important. Cultural skills are also very important, even when English is being spoken," claims senior director Karen McFadzen. Cisco and Diversity Works! support non-English-speaking personnel with cross-cultural training and events.

China is clearly important to Australian businesses. Seventeen percent of exports go to Chinese-speaking countries, including the People's Republic of China, Singapore, Hong Kong, and Taiwan. With help from Diversity Works! Australian organizations can increase their understanding of this important international market. (How *do* you say "G'day" in Chinese? "Wu an.")

For more about Australia's approach to encouraging diversity initiatives in business, see the chapter's closing case, "Diversity, Aussie Style."

> *"What has been most powerful is the increased understanding of the context for language and behavior."*
>
> TIM SULLIVAN, DEPUTY CEO, SOVEREIGN HILL

References: "Diversity and Inclusion: Our Commitment," Cisco website, www.cisco.com on June 11, 2005; "Case Studies," "Diversity of the Australian People," "Diversity Works!" Diversity Works! website, www.diversityaustralia.gov.au on June 7, 2005 (quotation); "The Sovereign Hill Charter," Sovereign Hill website, www.sovereignhill.com.au on June 11, 2005.

Assimilation is the process through which members of a minority group are forced to learn the ways of the majority group.

Assimilation   **Assimilation** is the process through which members of a minority group are forced to learn the ways of the majority group. In organizations this entails hiring people from diverse backgrounds and attempting to mold them to fit into the existing organizational culture. One way that companies attempt to make people fit in is by requiring that employees speak only one language. In Chicago, Carlos Solero was fired three days after he refused to sign a work agreement that included a policy of English-only at a suburban manufacturing plant. Management said the intent of the English-only policy was to improve communication among workers at the plant. In response, Solero and seven other Spanish speakers filed lawsuits against the plant.[26] Attempts to assimilate diverse workers by imposing English-only rules can lead to a variety of organizational problems. Most organizations develop systems such as performance evaluation and incentive programs that reinforce the values of the dominant group. (Chapter 18 discusses organizational culture as a means of reinforcing the organizational values and affecting the behavior of workers.) By universally applying the values of the majority group throughout the organization, as-similation tends to perpetuate false stereotypes and prejudices. Workers who are different are expected to meet the standards for dominant group members.[27]

Dominant groups tend to be self-perpetuating. Majority group members may avoid people who are "different" simply because they find communication difficult. Moreover, informal discussions over coffee and lunch and during after-hours socializing tend to be lim-ited to people in the dominant group. As a result, those who are not in the dominant group miss out on the informal communication opportunities in which office politics, company policy, and other issues are often discussed in rich detail. Subsequently, employees not in the dominant group often do not understand the more for-mal communication and may not be included in necessary action taken in response. The dominant group likewise remains unaware of opinions from the "outside."

Similarly, since the dominant group makes decisions based on their values and beliefs, the minority group has little say in deci-sions regarding compensation, facility location, benefit plans, per-formance standards, and other work issues that pertain directly to all workers. Workers who differ from the majority very quickly get the idea that to succeed in such a system, one must be like the dominant group in terms of values and beliefs, dress, and most other characteristics. Since success depends on assimilation, dif-ferences are driven underground.

Most organizations have a fairly predictable dominant group. Table 2.2 shows the results of interviews with members of several organizations who were asked to list the attributes reinforced by their organization's culture. Typically, white men in organizations view themselves as quite diverse. Others in the organizations view them as quite homogeneous, however, having attributes similar to those listed. Also typically, those who work in these dominant groups tend to be less aware of the problems that homogeneity can cause. Generally, those not in the dominant group feel the ef-fects more keenly.

Not paying attention to diversity can be very costly to the organization. In addition to blocking minority involvement in communication and decision making, it can

Fast Company, February–March 1999, p. 66. Richard Cline.

"Wilkens, the next time we catch you coming to work in suit and tie, I'm afraid we're going to have to let you go."

Fitting into the corporate model is not exactly what it used to be with all of the Internet start-ups these days. In this situation, the "boss" expects the older gentleman in the suit and tie to conform to the more informal "dress code." But fitting in is not necessarily the best in every situation. Doing the right job in the right way is more important than wearing the right clothes and fitting in. The lessons of valuing diversity should have shown us that by now.

Rational, linear thinker	Ages 35–49
Impersonal management style	Competitive
Married with children	Protestant or Jewish
Quantitative	College graduate
Adversarial	Tall
Careerist	Heterosexual
Individualistic	Predictable
Experience in competitive team sports	Excellent physical condition
In control	Willing to relocate
Military veteran	

TABLE 2.2

Attributes Reinforced by the Culture in Typical Organizations

Reference: Marilyn Loden and Judy B. Rosener, *Workforce America! Managing Employee Diversity as a Vital Resource* (Homewood, IL: Business One Irwin, 1991), p. 43. Copyright © 1991 by Business One Irwin. Used with permission.

result in tensions among workers, lower productivity, increased costs due to increasing absenteeism, increased employee turnover, increased equal employment opportunity and harassment suits, and lower morale among the workers.[28]

Valuing diversity means putting an end to the assumption that everyone who is not a member of the dominant group must assimilate.

Benefits of Valuing Diversity   **Valuing diversity** means putting an end to the assumption that everyone who is not a member of the dominant group must assimilate. This is not easily accomplished in most organizations. Truly valuing diversity is not merely giving lip service to an ideal, putting up with a necessary evil, promoting a level of tolerance for those who are different, or tapping into the latest fad. It is an opportunity to develop and utilize all of the human resources available to the organization for the benefit of the workers as well as the organization.

Valuing diversity is not just the right thing to do for workers; it is the right thing to do for the organization, both financially and economically. One of the most important benefits of diversity is the richness of ideas and perspectives that it makes available to the organization. Rather than relying on one homogeneous dominant group for new ideas and alternative solutions to increasingly complex problems, companies that value diversity have access to more perspectives of a problem. These fresh perspectives may lead to development of new products, opening of new markets, or improving service to existing customers.

Overall, the organization wins when it truly values diversity. Workers who recognize that the organization truly values them are likely to be more creative, motivated, and productive. Valued workers in diverse organizations experience less interpersonal conflict because the employees understand each other. When employees of different cultural groups, backgrounds, and values understand each other, they have a greater sense of teamwork, stronger identification with the team, and deeper commitment to the organization and its goals.

Technology and Business

Technology refers to the methods used to create products, including both physical goods and intangible services.

Technology refers to the methods used to create products, including both physical goods and intangible services. Technological change has become a major driver for other forms of organization change. Moreover, it also has widespread effects on the behaviors of people inside an organization. Three specific areas of technology worth noting here are the shift toward a service-based economy, the growing use of technology for competitive advantage, and mushrooming change in information technology.

Manufacturing and Service Technologies

Manufacturing is a form of business that combines and transforms resources into tangible outcomes that are then sold to others.

Manufacturing is a form of business that combines and transforms resources into tangible outcomes that are then sold to others. The Goodyear Tire and Rubber Company is a manufacturer because it combines rubber and chemical compounds and uses blending equipment and molding machines to create tires. Broyhill is a manufacturer because it buys wood and metal components, pads, and fabric and then combines them into furniture.

During the 1970s, manufacturing entered a long period of decline in the United States, primarily because of foreign competition. U.S. firms had grown lax and sluggish, and new foreign competitors came onto the scene with better equipment and much higher levels of efficiency. For example, steel companies in the Far East were able to produce high-quality steel for much lower prices than were U.S. companies like Bethlehem Steel and U.S. Steel (now USX Corporation). Faced with a battle for survival, many companies underwent a long and difficult period of change by eliminating waste and transforming themselves into leaner and more efficient and responsive entities. They reduced their workforces dramatically, closed antiquated or unnecessary plants, and modernized their remaining plants. In the last decade their efforts have started to pay dividends as U.S. business has regained its competitive position in many different industries. Although manufacturers from other parts of the world are still formidable competitors and U.S. firms may never again be competitive in some markets, the overall picture is much better than it was just a few years ago. And prospects continue to look bright.[29]

During the decline of the manufacturing sector, a tremendous growth in the service sector kept the U.S. economy from declining at the same rate. A **service organization** is one that transforms resources into an intangible output and creates time or place utility for its customers. For example, Merrill Lynch makes stock transactions for its customers, Avis leases cars to its customers, and your local hairdresser cuts your hair. In 1947, the service sector was responsible for less than half of the U.S. gross national product (GNP). By 1975, however, this reached 65 percent, and by 2005 it was over 75 percent. The service sector has been responsible for almost 90 percent of all new jobs created in the United States during the 1990s.

Managers have come to see that many of the tools, techniques, and methods that are used in a factory are also useful to a service firm. For example, managers of automobile plants and hair salons each have to decide how to design their facility, identify the best location for it, determine optimal capacity, make decisions about inventory storage, set procedures for purchasing raw materials, and set standards for productivity and quality. At the same time, though, service-based firms must hire and train employees based on a different skill set than is the case of most manufacturers. For instance, consumers seldom come into contact with the Toyota employee who installs the seats in their car, so that person can be hired based on technical skills. But Avis must hire people who not only know how to do a job but can also effectively interface with a variety of consumers.

> A **service organization** is one that transforms resources into an intangible output and creates time or place utility for its customers.

Technology and Competition

Technology is the basis of competition for some firms, especially those whose goals include being the technology leaders in their industries. A company, for example, might focus its efforts on being the low-cost producer or always having the most technologically advanced products on the market. But because of the rapid pace of new developments, keeping a leadership position based on technology is increasingly challenging. Another challenge is meeting constant demands to decrease cycle time—the time from beginning to end that it takes a firm to accomplish some recurring activity or function.

Businesses have increasingly found that they can be more competitive if they can systematically decrease cycle times. Many companies, therefore, now focus on decreasing cycle times in areas ranging from developing products to making deliveries and collecting credit payments. Twenty years ago, it took a car maker about five years from the decision to launch a new product until it was available in dealer showrooms. Now most companies can complete the cycle in less than two years. The speedier process allows them to respond more quickly to changing economic conditions, consumer preferences, and new competitive products while recouping their product-development costs more quickly. Some firms compete directly on how quickly they can get things done for consumers. In the early days of personal computers, for instance, getting a made-to-order system took six to eight weeks. Today, firms like Dell can usually ship exactly what the customer wants in a matter of days.

Information Technology

Most people are very familiar with advances in information technology. Cellular telephones, PDAs, the iPod, and digital cameras are just a few of the many recent technological innovations that have changed how people live and work. Breakthroughs in information technology have resulted in leaner organizations, more flexible operations, increased collaboration among employees, more flexible work sites, and improved management processes and systems. On the other hand, they have also resulted in less personal communication, less "down time" for managers and employees, and an increased sense of urgency vis-à-vis decision making and communication—changes that have not necessarily always been beneficial. We discuss information technology and its relationship to organizational behavior in more detail in Chapter 11.

Ethics and Corporate Governance

While ethics have long been of relevance to businesses, what seems like an epidemic of ethical breaches in recent years has placed ethics in the mainstream of managerial thought today. One special aspect of business ethics, corporate governance, has also taken on increased importance. Ethics also increasingly relate to information technology.

Contemporary Ethical Issues

A central issue today revolves around the fact that rapid changes in business relationships, organizational structures, and financial systems pose unsurpassed difficulties in keeping accurate track of a company's financial position. The public—current and potential investors—often get blurred pictures of a firm's competitive health. Stakeholders, however—employees, stockholders, consumers, unions, creditors, and government—are entitled to a fair accounting so they can make enlightened personal and business decisions. Even the American Institute for Certified Public Accountants (AICPA) admits that keeping up with today's increasingly fast-paced business activities is putting a strain on the accounting profession's traditional methods for auditing, financial reporting, and time-honored standards for professional ethics.

The Enron scandal, for example, involved extended enterprises using fast-moving financial transactions among layers of subsidiary firms, some domestic and many offshore, with large-scale borrowing from some of the world's largest financial institutions. Electronic transactions flooded through a vast network of quickly formed and rapidly dissolved partnerships among energy brokers and buyers. This network was so complex that Enron's accounting reports failed completely to reflect the firm's disastrous financial and managerial condition. In a blatant display of unethical conduct, Enron's public reports concealed many of its partnerships (and obligations) with other companies, thus hiding its true operating condition.

Furthermore, why did Arthur Andersen, the accounting firm that audited Enron's finances, not catch its client's distorted reports? Auditors are supposed to provide an objective and independent assessment of the accuracy of financial information reported by corporations to key stakeholders, such as investors and governmental agencies. Indeed, publicly traded corporations are legally required to use an external auditor for just this purpose.

The answer to this question reveals a further illustration of the hazards faced by today's extended firm. Andersen, like other major accounting firms, had expanded from auditing into more lucrative non-accounting areas such as management consulting. Reports suggest that Andersen's desire for future high-revenue consulting services with Enron may have motivated the CPA's auditors to turn a blind eye on questionable practices that eventually turned up during audits of Enron's finances.

Beyond these large-scale issues, other contemporary ethical concerns involve such areas as executive compensation, environmental protection, working conditions in foreign factories, pricing policies, and the pressures to balance profits against costs as businesses continue to globalize. We discuss ethical issues in several places later in this book, including Chapter 8 (decision making) and Chapter 13 (contemporary views of leadership).

Ethical Issues in Corporate Governance

A related area of emerging concern relates to ethical issues in **corporate governance**—the oversight of a public corporation by its board of directors. The board of a public corporation is expected to ensure that the business is being properly managed and that the decisions made by its senior management are in the best interests of shareholders and other stakeholders. But in far too many cases the recent ethical scandals alluded to above have actually started with a breakdown in the corporate governance structure. For instance, WorldCom's board approved a $366 million personal loan to the firm's CEO, Bernard Ebbers, when there was little evidence that he could repay it. Likewise, Tyco's board approved a $20 million bonus for one of its own members for helping with the acquisition of a firm owned by that individual (this bonus was in addition to the purchase price!).

But boards of directors are also being increasingly criticized even when they are not directly implicated in wrongdoing. The biggest complaint here often relates to board independence. Disney, for instance, has faced this problem. Several key members of the firm's board of directors are from companies that do business with Disney, and others are longtime friends with former Disney CEO Michael Eisner. The concern, then, is that Eisner may have been given more autonomy than might otherwise be warranted because of his various relationships with board members. While board

> **Corporate governance** refers to the oversight of a public corporation by its board of directors.

Corporate governance has become a major issue in corporate America. One of the more visible examples has been the long-running feud between two former Walt Disney Company directors, Roy Disney and Stanley Gold, and the current board. Disney and Gold claim that the current board lacks independence, has been too slow in forcing longtime CEO Michael Eisner to leave the company's top spot, and too slow in developing an executive succession plan. Recent events have placated Disney and Gold, but they nevertheless are keeping a careful eye on the Disney board's activities.

members need to have some familiarity with both the firm and its industry in order to function effectively, they also need to have sufficient independence as might be necessary to carry out their oversight function.[30]

Ethical Issues in Information Technology

Another set of issues that have emerged in recent times involves information technology. Among the specific questions in this area are individual rights to privacy and the potential abuse of information technology by individuals. Indeed, online privacy has become a hot issue as companies sort out the ethical and management issues. DoubleClick, an online advertising network, is one of the firms at the center of the privacy debate. The company has collected data on the habits of millions of Web surfers, recording which sites they visit and on which ads they click. DoubleClick insists the profiles are anonymous and are used to better match surfers with appropriate ads. However, after the company announced a plan to add names and addresses to its database, it was forced to back down because of public concerns over invasion of online privacy.

DoubleClick isn't the only firm gathering personal data about people's Internet activities. People who register at Yahoo! are asked to list date of birth, among other details. Amazon.com, eBay, and other sites also ask for personal information. As Internet usage increases, however, surveys show that people are troubled by the amount of information being collected and who gets to see it.

One way many companies have addressed these concerns is by posting a privacy policy on their websites. The policy usually explains what data the company collects and who gets to see it, gives people a choice about having their information shared with others, and provides an option to bypass data collection altogether. Disney, IBM, and other companies support this position by refusing to advertise on websites that have no posted privacy policies.

In addition, companies can offer Web surfers the opportunity to review and correct information that has been collected, especially medical and financial data. In the offline world, consumers are legally allowed to inspect credit and medical records. In the online world, this kind of access can be costly and cumbersome, because data are often spread across several computer systems. Despite the technical difficulties, government agencies are already working on Internet privacy guidelines, which means that companies will need internal guidelines, training, and leadership to ensure compliance.

New Employment Relationships

A final significant area of environmental change that is particularly relevant for businesses today involves what we call new employment relationships. While we discuss employment relationships from numerous perspectives in Part 2 of this book, two particularly important areas today involve the management of knowledge workers and the outsourcing of jobs to other businesses, especially when those businesses are in other countries.

The Management of Knowledge Workers

Knowledge workers are those employees who add value in an organization simply because of what they know.

Traditionally, employees added value to organizations because of what they did or because of their experience. However, as we enter the "information age" in the workplace, many employees add value simply because of what they know.[31] These employees are usually referred to as **knowledge workers**. How well these employees are managed is seen as a major factor in determining which firms will be successful in the future.[32] Knowledge workers include computer scientists, physical scientists, engineers, product designers, and video game developers. They tend to work in high-technology firms, and are usually experts in some abstract knowledge base. They often believe they have the right to work in an autonomous fashion, and identify more strongly with their profession than any organization—even to the extent of defining performance in terms recognized by other members of their profession.[33]

As the importance of information-driven jobs grows, the need for knowledge workers will grow as well. But these employees require extensive and highly specialized training, and not everyone is willing to make the human capital investments necessary to move into these jobs. In fact, even after knowledge workers are on the job, retraining and training updates are critical so that their skills do not become obsolete. It has been suggested, for example, that the "half-life" for a technical education in engineering is about three years. Further, the failure to update the required skills will not only result in the organization losing competitive advantage but will also increase the likelihood that the knowledge worker will go to another firm that is more committed to updating these skills.[34]

Compensation and related policies for knowledge workers must also be specially tailored. For example, in many high-tech organizations, engineers and scientists have the option of entering a technical career path that parallels a management career path. This allows the knowledge worker to continue to carry out specialized work without taking on large management responsibilities, while at the same time offering worker compensation that is equivalent to that available to management. But in other high-tech firms, the emphasis is on pay for performance, with profit sharing based on projects or products developed by the knowledge workers. In addition, in most firms employing these workers there has been a tendency to reduce the number of levels of the organization to allow the knowledge workers to react more quickly to the external environment and to reduce the need for bureaucratic approval.[35]

Outsourcing

Outsourcing is the practice of hiring other firms to do work previously performed by the organization itself. It is an increasingly popular strategy because it helps firms focus on their core activities and avoid getting sidetracked onto secondary activities.

> **Outsourcing** is the practice of hiring other firms to do work previously performed by the organization itself.

The cafeteria at a large bank may be important to employees and some customers, but running it is not the bank's main line of business and expertise. Bankers need to focus on money management and financial services, not food-service operations. That's why most banks outsource cafeteria operations to food-service management companies whose main line of business includes cafeterias. The result, ideally, is more attention to banking by bankers, better food service for cafeteria customers, and formation of a new supplier-client relationship (food-service company/bank). Firms today often outsource numerous activities, including payroll, employee training, facility maintenance, and research and development.

Up to a point, at least, outsourcing makes good business sense in areas that are highly unrelated to a firm's core business activities. However, it has attracted considerable more attention in recent years because of the growing trend toward outsourcing abroad in order to lower labor costs. Many software firms, for example, have found that there is an abundance of talented programmers in India who are willing to work for much lower salaries than their American counterparts. Likewise, many firms that operate large call centers find that they can handle those operations at much lower costs from other parts of the world. As a result, domestic jobs may be lost. And some firms attract additional criticism when they require their domestic workers—soon to be out of jobs—to train their newly hired foreign replacements! Clearly, there are numerous behavioral and motivational issues involved in practices such as these.

Chapter Review

Synopsis

Globalization is playing a major role in the environment of many firms today. The volume of international trade has grown significantly, and continues to grow at a very rapid pace. There are four basic reasons for this growth: (1) communication and transportation have advanced dramatically over the past several decades, (2) businesses have expanded internationally to increase their markets, (3) firms are moving into international markets to control costs, especially to reduce labor costs, and (4) many organizations have become international in response to competition. There are numerous cross-cultural differences and similarities that affect behavior within organizations.

A second major environmental shift in recent years has been the increased attention devoted to the concept of diversity. Workforce diversity refers to the important similarities and differences among the employees of organizations. Unfortunately, many people tend to stereotype others in organizations. Stereotypes can lead to the even more dangerous process of prejudice toward others. Managers should be cognizant of both primary and secondary dimensions of diversity, as well as the wide array of benefits to be derived from having a diverse workforce.

Technology refers to the methods used to create products, including both physical goods and intangible services. Technological change has become the driving force for other forms of organization change. Moreover, it also has widespread effects on the behaviors of people inside an organization. Three specific areas of technology relevant to the study of organizational behavior are the shift toward a service-based economy, the growing use of technology for competitive advantage, and mushrooming change in information technology.

While ethics have long been of relevance to businesses, what seems like an epidemic of ethical breaches in recent years has placed ethics in the mainstream of managerial thought today. One special aspect of business ethics, corporate governance, has also taken on increased importance. Ethics also increasingly relate to information technology. A central issue today revolves around the fact that rapid changes in business relationships, organizational structures, and financial systems pose unsurpassed difficulties in keeping accurate track of a company's financial position.

Another significant area of environmental change that is particularly relevant for businesses today involves new employment relationships. Knowledge workers are those who add value to an organization because of what they know. How well these employees are managed is seen as a major factor in determining which firms will be successful in the future. Outsourcing is the practice of hiring other firms to do work previously performed by the organization itself. It is an increasingly popular strategy because it helps firms focus on their core activities and avoid getting sidetracked onto secondary activities. However, it grows controversial when the jobs being outsourced are really being exported to foreign countries in ways that reduce domestic job opportunities.

Discussion Questions

1. Identify ways in which the internationalization of business affects businesses in your community.

2. What would you imagine to be the major differences between working for a domestic firm in the United States, working for a foreign company in the United States, and working for an American firm abroad?

3. Why do organizations need to be interested in managing diversity? Is it a legal or moral obligation, or does it have some other purpose?

4. Summarize in your own words what the statistics tell us about the workforce of the future.

5. All things considered, do you think people from diverse cultures are more alike or more different? Explain the reasons for your answer.

6. What roles does changing technology play in your daily activities?

7. How concerned are you regarding Internet security? Are your concerns increasing? Why or why not?

8. Do you think concerns regarding ethics will remain central in managerial thinking, or will these concerns eventually become less important? Why?

9. Do you anticipate becoming a "knowledge worker"? How do you think this will shape your own thinking regarding an employer, compensation, and so forth?

10. What are your personal opinions about the use of international outsourcing?

11. How does multiculturalism contribute to competitive advantage for an organization?

Understanding Your Own Stereotypes About Others

Purpose: This exercise will help you better understand your own stereotypes and attitudes toward others.

Format: You will be asked to evaluate a situation and the assumptions you make in doing so. Then you will compare your results with those of the rest of the class.

Procedure: First, read the following description of the situation to yourself, and decide who it is that is standing at your door and why you believe it to be that person. Make some notes that explain your rationale for eliminating the other possibilities and selecting the one that you did. Then answer the follow-up questions.

Next, working in small groups or with the class as a whole, discuss who might be standing at your door and why you believe it to be that person. Record the responses of class members by using the grid at the end of this exercise.

Finally, in a class discussion, reflect on the stereotypes used to reach a decision and consider the following:

1. How hard was it to let go of your original belief once you had formed it?

2. What implications do first impressions of people have concerning how you treat them, what you expect of them, and your assessment of whether the acquaintance is likely to go beyond the initial stage?

3. What are the implications of your responses to these questions concerning how you, as a manager, might treat a new employee? What will the impact be on that employee?

4. What are the implications of your answers for yourself in terms of job hunting?

Situation: You have just checked into a hospital room for some minor surgery the next day. When you get to your room, you are told that the following people will be coming to speak with you within the next several hours.

1. The surgeon who will do the operation

2. A nurse

3. The secretary for the department of surgery

4. A representative of the company that supplies televisions to the hospital rooms

5. A technician who does laboratory tests

6. A hospital business manager

7. The dietitian

(Note: You have never met any of these people before and do not know what to expect.)

About half an hour after your arrival, a woman who seems to be of Asian ancestry appears at your door dressed in a straight red wool skirt, a pink-and-white-striped polyester blouse with a bow at the neck, and red medium-high-heeled shoes that match the skirt. She is wearing gold earrings, a gold chain necklace, a gold wedding band, and a white hospital laboratory coat. She is carrying a clipboard.

Follow-up Questions

1. Of the seven people listed, which of them is standing at your door? How did you reach this conclusion?

2. If the woman had not been wearing a white hospital laboratory coat, how might your perceptions of her have differed? Why?

3. If you find out that she is the surgeon who will be operating on you in the morning, and you thought initially that she was someone else, how confident do you now feel in her ability as a surgeon? Why?

4. What implications can you draw from this exercise regarding the management of knowledge workers?

Self-Assessment Exercise

Cross-Cultural Awareness

The following questions are intended to provide insights into your awareness of other cultures. Please indicate the best answers to the questions listed below. There is no passing or failing answer. Use the following scale, recording it in the space before each question.

1 = definitely no

2 = not likely

3 = not sure

4 = likely

5 = definitely yes

1. I can effectively conduct business in a language other than my native language.

2. I can read and write in a language other than my native language with great ease.

3. I understand the proper protocol for conducting a business card exchange in at least two countries other than my own.

4. I understand the role of the *keiretsu* in Japan or the *chaebol* in Korea.

5. I understand the differences in manager–subordinate relationships in two countries other than my own.

6. I understand the differences in negotiation styles in at least two countries other than my own.

7. I understand the proper protocols for gift giving in at least three countries.

8. I understand how a country's characteristic preference for individualism versus collectivism can influence business practices.

9. I understand the nature and importance of demographic diversity in at least three countries.

10. I understand my own country's laws regarding giving gifts or favors while on international assignments.

11. I understand how cultural factors influence the sales, marketing, and distribution systems of different countries.

12. I understand how differences in male-female relationships influence business practices in at least three countries.

13. I have studied and understand the history of a country other than my native country.

14. I can identify the countries of the European Union without looking them up.

15. I know which gestures to avoid using overseas because of their obscene meanings.

16. I understand how the communication style practiced in specific countries can influence business practices.

17. I know in which countries I can use my first name with recent business acquaintances.

18. I understand the culture and business trends in major countries in which my organization conducts business.

19. I regularly receive and review news and information from and about overseas locations.

20. I have access to and utilize a cultural informant before conducting business at an overseas location.

_____ = Total Score

When you have finished, add up your score and compare it with those of others in your group. Discuss the areas of strengths and weaknesses of the group members. (Note: This brief instrument has not been scientifically validated and is to be used for classroom discussion purposes only.)

Reference: Neal R. Goodman, "Cross-Cultural Training for the Global Executive," in *Improving Intercultural Interactions: Modules for Cross-Cultural Training Programs,* eds. Richard W. Brislin and Tomoko Yoshida, pp. 35–36. Copyright © 1994 by Sage Publications, Inc. Reprinted by permission of Sage Publications, Inc.

Building Managerial Skills

Exercise Overview: Conceptual skills refer to a manager's ability to think in the abstract while diagnostic skills focus on responses to situations. These skills must frequently be used together to better understand the behavior of others in an organization, as illustrated by the following exercise.

Exercise Background: We can read about creating an organization in which diverse workers are welcomed and included in everyday work activities. However, working with a diverse workforce every day can be more difficult. Consider, for example, the following situation.

> You are the office manager for a large call center in an urban area. You interview applicants, explain the type of work, and give them a short, job-oriented test. At the call center employees sit at a desk in front of a computer screen and answer calls and inquiries about the products of several different companies. Employees must answer each call, determine the product, access the appropriate screen that contains all of the information about the product, and, if possible, complete the sale of the product and hopefully extend the purchase to related products. Employees must be able to use a computer and speak well. One day you interview and hire a new employee, Sarah Jane. She completes the simple test that involves sitting at the desk, using the computer, and answering mock calls. Consequently, you hire Sarah Jane, who reports to work the next Monday.
>
> About two weeks after her first day, Sarah Jane shows up with her seeing-eye dog. As it turns out, while modestly sighted, Sarah Jane is legally blind and

has decided to start walking to work rather than taking a bus. Because the call stations are built to fit a normal-size person in a desk chair in front of a computer, there is no room for her rather large seeing-eye dog. Sarah Jane requests a special accommodation for her dog. Other employees are concerned about having a large dog sitting underneath the workstations and complain to you about the situation.

Exercise Task: Using the scenario previously described as background, do the following:

1. You have to decide what to do and have to write a report to your boss as well as to Sarah Jane and the other employees. What do you decide? Do you fire Sarah Jane because she is legally blind but did not inform you of this? Do you fire Sarah Jane because her dog is bothering the other employees by sitting underneath the workstations? Do you keep her and find her a separate workstation that is larger and would allow her dog to sit under it without bothering the other employees?

2. What role might outsourcing have played in this incident? How might it affect your response?

3. Are there any technologically based solutions you might be able to identify?

Organizational Behavior
Case for Discussion

Diversity, Aussie Style

Diversity has, at times, been a troubling topic for Australians. Relations between white Europeans and Australia's indigenous people, the Aborigines, have been difficult since 1770, when Captain James Cook explored Australia and was nearly killed. Aborigines were afflicted by diseases introduced by whites, had their lands taken by force, and were banished to Australia's most inhospitable regions. Add to that the arrival of explorers from European nations, the English convict ships that brought 162,000 felons, and the gold rush in the 1850s that attracted adventurers of every race. Chinese immigrants and African slaves provided cheap labor, adding to the ethnic mix.

While Australia's past has included race relations challenges, today the nation prides itself on its ethnic and racial diversity. Over 40 percent of the population of

19 million consists of immigrants or children of immigrants. Sixteen percent of Australia's workforce does not speak English at home. Diversity has a strong impact on Australian businesses. Twenty-nine percent of Australian small businesses are owned by immigrants. The volume of exports has doubled over the last 20 years and export companies create one in every five jobs.

To help employers address diversity issues effectively, the Australian government's Department of Immigration and Multicultural and Indigenous Affairs has established a program called "Diversity Works!" The program has been extremely successful in helping businesses to address their diversity concerns.

The program stresses the benefits of diversity, including use of multicultural staff to train other personnel, utilization of business networks of recent immigrants to penetrate markets abroad, increase of targeted and effective advertising, and development of insight into foreign business practices. Diversity Works! provides training, advice, diversity statistics, and information about legal requirements. It encourages businesses to use their employees' skills to:

> **❝We are helping pull up these industries, but we are not pushing them up.❞**
> CHRIS MARA, GOVERNMENT RELATIONS ADVISOR, COLES SUPERMARKETS

- expand markets and form new markets. Australian supermarket chain Coles produces a line of "bush" foods, grown and processed by Aboriginal people. The program increases employment, teaches entrepreneurial skills, and develops local infrastructure. Coles manager Chris Mara says, "We are helping pull up these industries, but we are not pushing them up. There are clear benefits for us . . . The Coles Taste Australia range is commercially successful." Diversity Works! uses Coles as a case study to demonstrate the significant financial benefits of diversity.

- tap into international markets. Australia's beef industry is one of the largest exporters in the world, and about 30 percent of exports go to Muslim countries such as Indonesia and Malaysia. Australian beef producers, with support from Diversity Works! have worked with Islamic organizations in Australia to certify some beef as *halal*, or appropriate for consumption by Muslims.

- hit the target with market research. Vicky Mar Fashions, an Australian maker of women's wear, uses Diversity Works! information and help from immigrant employees to produce special occasion outfits for special ethnic and religious holidays. Multilingual advertising supports sales.

- focus product development. To provide better service for customers living in remote areas, Australia's leading telecommunications company, Telstra, invented pay telephones that would withstand cyclone-force winds, dusty dry conditions, and heat. The remote phones link via satellite, enabling many indigenous people to have access to reliable service for the first time. Telstra helps to promote diversity at other organizations by providing facilities and advertising for Diversity Works!

- enhance customer service. With advice and the loan of Diversity Works! personnel, Centrelink, the Australian government's social services agency, presents information in sixty-four languages— from Assyrian to Urdu— through their website, documents, call center, and multilingual seminars. Centrelink's *Guide to Naming Conventions* "gives advice about the order in which names appear such as whether the family name comes first or last," says Terry Cahill, Centrelink employee. "It also advises about how children and women are named and . . . about pronunciation of names."

- become an employer of choice. Diversity Works! helped engine maker Cummins South Pacific hire mechanics from Peru and Mexico when the company faced a labor shortage in Australia. Diversity is valued worldwide at Cummins, as shown by these excerpts from a speech by founder Irwin Miller. "Character, ability and intelligence are not concentrated in one sex over the other, nor in persons with certain accents or in certain races . . . When we indulge ourselves in such irrational prejudices we damage ourselves most of all, and ultimately assure ourselves of failure in competition with those more open and less biased."

Case Questions

1. Which dimensions of diversity are the focus of the Diversity Works! program? Are these characteristics primary or secondary dimensions of diversity?

2. The companies highlighted in the case are not trying to assimilate employees from different cultures. What are some advantages these companies may gain from this policy? What are some of the limitations or potential problems these companies may face as they implement this policy?

3. In your opinion, is a voluntary program such as Diversity Works! likely to be more or less effective in increasing diversity than a legally mandated program? Explain.

References: "Coles Cares About the Community," Coles website, www.coles.com.au on June 11, 2005; "Case Studies," "Diversity Is an Economic Advantage," "Diversity of the Australian People," "Diversity Works!" "Valuing and Celebrating Diversity," Diversity Works! website, www.diversityaustralia.gov.au on June 7, 2005 (quotation); "Welcome to Centrelink," Centrelink website, www.centrelink.gov.au on June 11, 2005.

TEST PREPPER

You have read the chapter and studied the key terms. Think you're ready to ace the exam? Take this sample test to gauge your comprehension of chapter material and check your answers at the back of the book. Want more test questions? Take the ACE quizzes found on the student website: http://college.hmco.com/business/students/ (select Griffin/Moorhead, Organizational Behavior, 8e from the Management menu).

T   F   1. The most significant source of change impacting organizations today is a reduction in the globalization of business.

T   F   2. The same manager will behave the same way regardless of what cultural settings he or she is in.

T   F   3. Stereotypes can lead to the even more dangerous process of prejudice toward others.

T   F   4. Assimilation is the process through which members of a minority group are forced to learn the ways of the majority group.

T   F   5. In the last decades many U.S. businesses have regained their competitive positions in manufacturing industries.

T   F   6. One of the primary ethical issues related to advances in information technologies is individual rights to privacy.

T   F   7. Outsourcing an area that is highly unrelated to a firm's core business activity makes good business sense.

8. The major factors that account for much of the growth in international business include all of the following except
   a. expansion due to communication and transportation advances.
   b. expansion to increase market size.
   c. expansion to reduce labor costs.
   d. expansion to meet trade agreement requirements.
   e. expansion in response to competition.

9. One of Hofstede's cultural dimensions is named power distance. Another name for power distance is
   a. assertiveness.
   b. orientation to authority.
   c. uncertainty avoidance.
   d. materialism.
   e. masculinity.

10. Truly valuing diversity means
   a. getting the most out of members of the minority group.
   b. paying members of the minority group more than the members of the majority group receive.
   c. making sure members of the minority group are promoted quickly and frequently.

   d. publishing a statement that the company appreciates employees and customers from all ethnic backgrounds and is committed to ending discrimination.
   e. putting an end to the assumption that everyone who is not a member of the dominant group must assimilate.

11. Which of the following factors is a central issue in contemporary business ethics?
   a. The speed of change in business relationships, organizational structures, and financial systems
   b. The number of minorities that are leaving the workforce to find employment in other countries
   c. The degree to which companies in other countries are outsourcing their work to the United States
   d. The public's increasing trust in corporate governance
   e. The fact that cultural assimilation is now prohibited by law in most countries

12. As we enter the "information age," many employees add value to organizations simply due to what they know. These workers are known as
   a. minority group members.
   b. majority group members.
   c. knowledge workers.
   d. assimilated workers.
   e. outsourced employees.

13. A large accounting firm in Chicago offers on-site day-care services for its employees with children. Which of the following makes the best business sense for this firm?
   a. Alter the company strategy to support a combined pursuit of accounting/day care.
   b. Outsource the day-care operation.
   c. Train senior accountants to run the day-care operation.
   d. Train new employees to run the day-care operation.
   e. Require employees to supervise their own children in the day-care facility.

The Success of Starbucks

The first time that Howard Schultz walked into a Starbucks Coffee Company store, he fell in love. In 1981, Schultz was in the Seattle store to sell drip coffeemakers. Starbucks was a local three-store chain that sold coffee beans and accessories, but the owners put great care into choosing and roasting the beans and they taught their customers that same appreciation.

Schultz said to himself, "What a great company, what a great city. I'd love to be part of that." He spent a year convincing the owners to hire him as director of marketing. "I was this East Coast person and I had so much drive and energy, I think I might have scared them at first," Schultz admits. He acknowledges that perseverance is one of the most important traits of a successful entrepreneur, adding, "I have a history of people closing doors and me saying, 'No, it's still open.'"

One year later, Schultz was struck by another lightning bolt. After a visit to Italy, he realized that coffee bars there provided a location for socializing and relaxing. Schultz believed that the social aspect would appeal to Americans, fulfilling a need that restaurants and shopping malls failed to address. Back home, Starbucks's owners refused to enter the highly competitive restaurant business. Schultz quit. He founded a successful coffee bar business and, eighteen months later, used the profits to buy Starbucks for $3.8 million.

From that uncertain beginning, Starbucks grew into a retailing powerhouse, with more than 8,000 locations, 97,000 employees, and annual sales of $5.3 billion. Starbucks appears on the *Fortune 500* list and dominates the specialty eateries industry. Dunkin' Donuts, its closest competitor, is part of the gigantic conglomerate Pernod Ricard, but has less than one-tenth the sales of Starbucks. Other popular specialty food shops, such as Cold Stone Creamery and Jamba Juice, are much smaller, boasting annual sales from $150 to $300 million.

Starbucks has grown rapidly without franchising, although it offers licenses in a few locations. Schultz avoids franchising because he believes that quality and image control are vital to success. Starbucks funds growth with current earnings and has locations in thirty-four countries. Sales revenues increase by double digits in many years. Constant innovation is another indicator of the company's effectiveness.

Starbucks has satisfied many stakeholders, including investors, customers, and employees. Stock price has risen from around $25 in mid-2003 to over $50 in mid-2005, signaling that investors are confident. The total market capitalization was $200 million in 1992, when the firm had its initial public offering. Today it's worth $19 billion. The company never advertises nationally. Starbucks's phenomenal sales growth springs from word-of-mouth from satisfied customers. And there are lots of customers—about 30 million weekly. In 2004, Starbucks was named, for the sixth time, to the *Fortune* Best Companies to Work For list. The company was ranked 34th, up from 47th in 2003.

What created this success? One of the most important factors is the management skill and ability of Howard Schultz and the subsequent CEOs, Orin Smith and Jim Donald. Schultz was raised in a Brooklyn housing project, the son of a working-class family. Schultz says about that time, "I saw the fracturing of the American dream . . . My parents didn't have much—and they didn't have much hope." After attending college on a scholarship, Schultz held positions in sales and operations for various firms, ending up as manager of U.S.

operations for Hammarplast. By 1985, he owned Starbucks, which went public in 1992. In 2000, Schultz stepped down from the CEO position, although he remains a member of the board of directors. Although he no longer has daily management responsibility, it is his vision that guides Starbucks today.

Orin C. Smith headed the firm from 2000 to 2005, after joining Starbucks in 1990. Smith's background was quite different from Schultz's. Smith has an MBA from Harvard, worked for years at management consulting firm Deloitte & Touche, and served as a top manager in several large firms before joining Starbucks. Smith was an effective manager who turned Schultz's visions into reality. He oversaw a time of rapid growth, innovation, and operational improvements.

In 2005, Starbucks gained its third CEO, Jim Donald. Donald worked as a bag boy in a supermarket during high school; by nineteen he was an assistant manager, making more money than his schoolteacher father. Donald is down-to-earth and folksy, knows everyone's name, and is willing to lend a hand. When Donald was giving a store tour, a customer spilled coffee. Donald grabbed a mop and cleaned the floor himself. "Being a grocery guy means you always know where the cleaning supplies are," he says. Before Starbucks, Donald helped Wal-Mart introduce groceries into their stores in the early 1990s, then aided Pathmark, an ailing grocery chain, in its recovery from bankruptcy.

However, no matter how skilled the managers, a company's success also relies on a number of factors from the business environment. Starbucks appeals to a demographic market segment whose needs have been ignored by the food-service industry. The typical Starbucks customer is affluent, well-educated, and thirty to fifty years old. Traditional fast-food outlets do not appeal to this segment. Above all else, these customers want customization—products that are personalized to their tastes and needs. Anne Saunders, senior vice president of marketing, worked in a Starbucks store when she was first hired, as does every executive. "I waited on hundreds of customers while working the cash registers and was struck by how every single one of them ordered something different," Saunders says. "Every single person coming in here has a different experience, designed the way they want it."

The preference for personalization is so well known that the popular movie *You've Got Mail* gently makes fun of the phenomenon. In the film, Joe (played by Tom Hanks) writes in an email, "The whole purpose of places like Starbucks is for people with no decision-making ability whatsoever to make six decisions just to buy one cup of coffee. People can get . . . an absolutely defining sense of self."

Another opportunity presented by Starbucks's environment is the potential for global expansion. Starbucks has entered thirty-three European, Asian, and Middle Eastern countries, but there are still markets the company could enter. In addition, the number of outlets in each country could be expanded. Starbucks plans to build 15,000 more overseas locations over five years, about half of the expected new stores.

Expansion plans are not stopped by the fear that selling American-style coffee and fast service to European customers, who are used to a more relaxed environment, might be tough. Plans continue in spite of anti-American sentiment that has been fueled by the war in Iraq. Some brands that are highly identified with the United States (Barbie dolls and AOL, for example) have seen their foreign sales fall in recent months.

Starbucks's operations become profitable only when there are a sufficient number of locations in a region or a country to gain economies of scale. It takes time for customers to become familiar with the company's products. Also, expenses are higher in Europe. Minimum wage in France, for instance, is $9.92 hourly, almost double the U.S. rate of $5.15. For these reasons, international operations produced adequate revenues but did not become profitable for Starbucks until 2004. Schultz explains the slow start, saying, "We're simply maturing. Not that we're getting close to maturity, because we're just scratching the surface internationally, but the markets are getting larger now."

The environment also presents some threats to Starbucks. Rising costs are a problem. The cost for employee healthcare benefits in the United States is sharply increasing. Schultz remains absolutely committed to providing health insurance for every employee who works twenty hours or more. This is a rarity in the restaurant industry, but Schultz believes that it's vital for his company to provide a living wage. Although hourly wages for overseas employees are higher, national health insurance in many countries allows Starbucks to save money on benefits.

Starbucks has been targeted by some advocate groups that are critical of the company's policies. While some of the coffee Starbucks sells is organic and shade grown, environmentalists want them to sell more. They also want Starbucks to sell more Fair Trade certified coffee, which guarantees a living wage and safe working conditions for coffee farm workers. Consumer food safety advocates want Starbucks to stop selling milk that contains hormones and other ingredients that are genetically modified.

The company claims that it is as environmentally friendly as is possible. For example, the company buys 200 million pounds of coffee each year, far more than the current worldwide supply of Fair Trade or organic coffee. Starbucks has developed Coffee and Farmer Equity (CAFE), a set of guidelines that includes some of the Fair Trade coffee requirements. The CAFE standards have been adopted by other firms and Starbucks has won awards for its environmentally friendly supplier guidelines.

Even Starbuck's very apparent success opens the company up to criticism. Writer Ruth Rosselson suggests "consumers choose non-chain shops that offer fair-trade coffee. Starbucks . . . puts local companies out of business and with this policy can never be 100 percent ethical." Many agree. On the other hand, studies have shown that when Starbucks enters a city for the first time, coffee consumption increases and local coffee houses experience increased sales. Some local coffee bar chains take advantage of this trend by opening a new store on the same block whenever Starbucks opens one.

For now, Starbucks's continued success seems assured, although skeptics claim there is a limit to the number of $4 cups of coffee people will buy. Among them is venture capitalist and author Geoffrey Moore. "Of course, no chief executive wants to say, 'Yes, our market is saturated.' The notion that 7% market share means he still has a big field to go after is silly," Moore asserts. "His market is not all coffee drinkers. His market is people who buy into an upscale 21st-century café society experience, which is much smaller."

Yet Moore and other doubters have consistently been proven wrong. Analyst Sandy Sanders believes that customers will continue to indulge. "It's a simple way of rewarding yourself without spending a ton of money," Sanders claims. Schultz is optimistic about the future of Starbucks. "We are in the infant stages of the growth of the business in America," he says. "And now seeing what we've done internationally . . . we are going to shock people in terms of what Starbucks is going to be."

> **❝ Every single person coming in here has a different experience, designed the way they want it. ❞**
> *ANNE SAUNDERS, SENIOR VICE PRESIDENT OF MARKETING, STARBUCKS*

Sources: "Corporate Social Responsibility Report 2004," "International Development," "Starbucks Corporation Board of Directors," Starbucks website, www.starbucks.com on June 25, 2005; "Biography: Howard Schultz, Starbucks," Great Entrepreneurs website, 2000, www.myprimetime.com on June 30, 2005; "Orin Smith," *Business Week,* January 12, 2004, www.businessweek.com on February 2, 2005; "Specialty Eateries," "Starbucks Corporation," *Hoover's,* www.hoovers.com on February 2, 2005; "Starbucks Coffee Company to Receive 2005 World Environment Center Gold Medal," World Environment Center website, January 2005, www.wec.org on February 2, 2005; Donna Borak, "Europeans Costing American Companies," *The Washington Times,* December 27, 2004, www.washtimes.com on June 30, 2005; Stanley Holmes, "Starbucks: An American in Paris," *Business Week,* December 8, 2003, www.businessweek.com on February 2, 2005; Peter Kafka, "Bean Counter," *Forbes,* February 28, 2005, www.forbes.com on June 30, 2005; Patricia O'Connell, "A Full-Bodied Talk with Mr. Starbucks," *Business Week,* November 22, 2004, www.businessweek.com on January 31, 2005; Alison Overholt, "Listening to Starbucks," *Fast Company,* July 2004, pp. 50–56 (quotation); Sarah Robertson, "Starbucks Under Fire in Europe for Greenwashing," Organic Consumers Association website, January 21, 2004, www.organicconsumers.org on February 2, 2005; Dan Skeen, "Howard Schultz for Hire," My Prime Time website, www.myprimetime.com on June 30, 2005; Amy Tsao, "Starbucks: A Bit Overheated?" *Business Week,* April 5, 2004, www.businessweek.com on January 31, 2005; Amy Tsao, "Starbucks' Plan to Brew Growth," *Business Week,* April 5, 2004, www.businessweek.com on January 31, 2005; Eric Wahlgren, "Will Europe Warm to Starbucks?" *Business Week,* January 24, 2004, www.businessweek.com on June 30, 2005.

Integrative Case Questions

1. Which managerial skills do Howard Schultz, Orin Smith, and Jim Donald have that allow Starbucks to prosper? How did they develop those skills?

2. What are the organizational-level outcomes experienced by Starbucks Corporation? Based on these outcomes, do you think Starbucks is an effective organization? Why or why not?

3. What forces from the environment are affecting Starbucks? Does the environment present more opportunities or more threats for Starbucks? Explain.

Foundations of Individual Behavior

CHAPTER 3

After studying this chapter, you should be able to:

Chapter Outline

People in Organizations

Personality and Organizations

Attitudes in Organizations

Perception in Organizations

Types of Workplace Behavior

- ▶ **Explain the nature of the individual-organization relationship.**

- ▶ **Define personality and describe personality attributes that affect behavior in organizations.**

- ▶ **Discuss individual attitudes in organizations and how they affect behavior.**

- ▶ **Describe basic perceptual processes and the role of attributions in organizations.**

- ▶ **Explain how workplace behaviors can directly or indirectly influence organizational effectiveness.**

The Manager of Your Sunday Afternoons

N ational Football League (NFL) commissioner Paul Tagliabue has led the football industry since 1989, years characterized by change and improved performance. Under his guidance, league profits increased from $970 million annually to $5 billion. Ratings are up, labor contracts are more equitable, scandals are fewer, there is a new NFL television channel and four new teams, improved scheduling, and more community service. What is it about Tagliabue that contributes to his amazing success?

On the one hand, Tagliabue is an unlikely candidate to lead the nation's largest sports organization. He is sometimes described as "bland" or "cerebral," qualities not usually associated with professional football. He is known as a strategic thinker and planner with a very long-term focus. Tagliabue is viewed as someone who is well-rounded, not obsessed with football.

Yet Tagliabue proves time and again that he is a leader in this very physical sport. *Business Week* and many other groups named him as one of the best managers; *Sporting News* called him "the most powerful person in U.S. sports today." Tagliabue has an excellent memory, an intimidating intellect, and great energy. He gets involved in every aspect of the sport. Broncos' owner Pat Bowlen says, "He's the guy who runs the process," and Steven Bornstein, Tagliabue's top assistant, adds, "He's the quarterback, and he's calling all the signals." Experience is also a factor in Tagliabue's success. Before assuming the top spot at the NFL, he was a lawyer who spent twenty years as the NFL's top legal advisor.

Tagliabue is widely regarded as someone who can create good working relationships even with those who disagree with him. Roger Goodell, an NFL deputy commissioner, says, "[Tagliabue] has developed political skills he didn't come to the job with. He's learned how to use his position . . . to drive change." Successful negotiations in recent years have included labor agreements with officials and players as well as lucrative new contracts with owners.

Tagliabue is a good mentor too, developing talent within NFL leadership. Under Tagliabue's supervision Bornstein recently perfected a strategy to maximize broadcasting revenues. And Tagliabue keeps the long-term needs of the industry in mind. He was the mastermind behind providing NFL executives and players with executive business training in sports management and marketing at Stanford University.

Many in the industry say that Tagliabue's confidence has grown over the years. Yet he still maintains a willingness to listen and flexibility in his decisions. He can change when change is needed. The commissioner's innovative decisions are preceded by some careful and practical consideration. Patriots owner Robert Kraft says, "[Tagliabue's] very good at gathering the facts and information he needs, and he is deliberate." Kraft goes on to say, "[Tagliabue's flexibility helps him to] understand the value of many different things and therefore to see the big picture." See the boxed insert *The NFL and . . . Change* on page 62 to find out more about how Tagliabue responds to change at the NFL.

References: "Loyola and the New Orleans Saints Present a Breakfast with Paul Tagliabue," Loyola University press release, November 14, 2003, www.loyno.edu on February 14, 2005; "Paul Tagliabue: National Football League," *Business Week*, January 12, 2004, www.businessweek.com on February 14, 2005; Susannah Chen, "Stanford Scores with the NFL," *Business Week*, July 29, 2003, www.businessweek.com on February 14, 2005; Ronald Grover, "The NFL's Big Score," *Business Week*, November 17, 2004, www.businessweek.com on February 14, 2005; Stuart Miller, "Tagliabue Tops Sporting News' Power 100," *The Sporting News*, January 4, 2005, msn.foxsports.com on February 25, 2005 (quotation).

Think about human behavior as a jigsaw puzzle. Puzzles consist of various pieces that fit together in precise ways. And of course, no two puzzles are exactly alike. They have different numbers of pieces, the pieces are of different sizes and shapes, and they fit together in different ways. The same can be said of human behavior and its determinants. Each of us is a whole picture, like a fully assembled jigsaw puzzle, but the puzzle pieces that define us and the way those pieces fit together are unique. Thus, every person in an organization is fundamentally different from everyone else. To be successful, managers must recognize that these differences exist and attempt to understand them.

In this chapter we explore some of the key characteristics that differentiate people from one another in organizations. We first investigate the psychological nature of individuals in organizations. We then look at elements of people's personalities that can influence behavior and consider individual attitudes and their role in organizations. Next, we examine the role of perception in organizations. We close this chapter with an examination of various kinds of workplace behaviors that affect organizational performance.

People in Organizations

As a starting point for understanding the behavior of people in organizations we examine the basic nature of the individual-organization relationship. Understanding this relationship helps us appreciate the nature of individual differences. That is, these differences play a critical role in determining various important workplace behaviors of special relevance to managers.

Psychological Contracts

Whenever we buy a car or sell a house, both buyer and seller sign a contract that specifies the terms of the agreement—who pays what to whom, when it's paid, and so forth. A psychological contract resembles a standard legal contract in some ways, but is less formal and well-defined. Specifically, a **psychological contract** is a person's overall set of expectations regarding what he or she will contribute to the organization and what the organization will provide in return.[1] Thus, unlike a business contract, a psychological contract is not written on paper, nor are all of its terms explicitly negotiated.

Figure 3.1 illustrates the essential nature of a psychological contract. The individual makes a variety of **contributions** to the organization—such things as effort, skills, ability, time, and loyalty. Jill Henderson, a branch manager for Merrill Lynch, uses her knowledge of financial markets and investment opportunities to help her clients make profitable investments. Her MBA in finance, coupled with hard work and motivation, have led her to become one of the firm's most promising young managers. The firm believed she had these attributes when it hired her, of course, and expected that she would do well.

A **psychological contract** is a person's set of expectations regarding what he or she will contribute to the organization and what the organization, in return, will provide to the individual.

An individual's **contributions** to an organization include such things as effort, skills, ability, time, and loyalty.

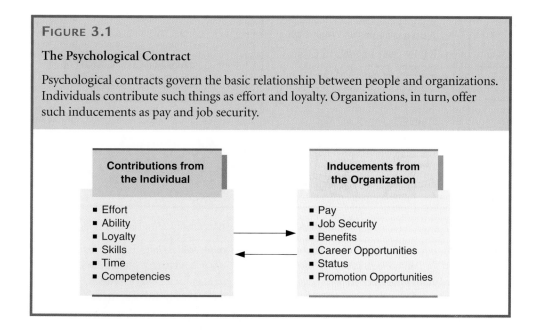

FIGURE 3.1

The Psychological Contract

Psychological contracts govern the basic relationship between people and organizations. Individuals contribute such things as effort and loyalty. Organizations, in turn, offer such inducements as pay and job security.

Contributions from the Individual	Inducements from the Organization
■ Effort	■ Pay
■ Ability	■ Job Security
■ Loyalty	■ Benefits
■ Skills	■ Career Opportunities
■ Time	■ Status
■ Competencies	■ Promotion Opportunities

Organizations provide **inducements** to individuals in the form of tangible and intangible rewards.

In return for these contributions, the organization provides **inducements** to the individual. Some inducements, such as pay and career opportunities, are tangible rewards. Others, such as job security and status, are more intangible. Jill Henderson started at Merrill Lynch at a very competitive salary and has received an attractive salary increase each of the six years she has been with the firm. She has also been promoted twice, and expects another promotion—perhaps to a larger office—in the near future.

In this instance, both Jill Henderson and Merrill Lynch apparently perceive that the psychological contract is fair and equitable. Both will be satisfied with the relationship and will do what they can to continue it. Henderson is likely to continue to work hard and effectively, and Merrill Lynch is likely to continue to increase her salary and give her promotions. In other situations, however, things might not work out as well. If either party sees an inequity in the contract, that party may initiate a change. The employee might ask for a pay raise or promotion, put forth less effort, or look for a better job elsewhere. The organization can also initiate change by training the worker to improve his skills, transferring him to another job, or by firing him.

All organizations face the basic challenge of managing psychological contracts. They want value from their employees, and they need to give employees the right inducements. For instance, underpaid employees may perform poorly or leave for better jobs elsewhere. Similarly, an employee may even occasionally start to steal organizational resources as a way to balance the psychological contract. Overpaying employees who contribute little to the organization, though, incurs unnecessary costs.

Recent trends in downsizing and cutbacks have complicated the process of managing psychological contracts. Many organizations used to offer at least reasonable assurances of job permanence as a fundamental inducement to employees. Now, however, job permanence is less likely, so alternative inducements may be needed.[2] Among the new forms of inducements some companies are providing are such things as additional training opportunities and increased flexibility in working schedules.

Increased globalization of business also complicates the management of psychological contracts. For example, the array of inducements that employees deem to be of value varies across cultures. U.S. workers tend to value individual rewards and recognition,

DILBERT reprinted by permission of United Feature Syndicate, Inc.

Psychological contracts play an important role in the relationship between an organization and its employees. As long as both parties agree that the contributions provided by an employee and the inducements provided by the organization are balanced, both parties are satisfied and will likely maintain their relationship. But if a serious imbalance occurs, one or both parties may attempt to change the relationship. As illustrated here, for example, an employee who feels sufficiently dissatisfied may even resort to using company assets for his or her own personal gain.

but Japanese workers are more likely to value group-based rewards and recognition. Workers in Mexico and Germany value leisure time and may thus prefer more time off from work, whereas workers in China place a lower premium on time off. Several years ago the Lionel Train Company, maker of toy electric trains, moved its operations to Mexico to capitalize on cheaper labor. The firm encountered problems, however, when it could not hire enough motivated employees to maintain quality standards and ended up making a costly move back to the United States.

A related problem faced by international businesses is the management of psychological contracts for expatriate managers. In some ways, this process is more like a formal contract than are other employment relationships. Managers selected for a foreign assignment, for instance, are usually given some estimate of the duration of the assignment and receive various adjustments in their compensation package, such as cost-of-living adjustments, education subsidies for children, and personal travel expenses. When the assignment is over, the manager must then be integrated back into the domestic organization, which itself may have changed in many ways—new managers, new coworkers, new procedures, new business practices, and so forth. Thus, returning managers may very well come back to an organization that is quite different from the one they left and to a job quite different from what they expected.[3]

The Person-Job Fit

One specific aspect of managing psychological contracts is managing the person-job fit. A good **person-job fit** is one in which the employee's contributions match the inducements the organization offers. In theory, each employee has a specific set of needs that she wants fulfilled and a set of job-related behaviors and abilities to contribute. If the organization can take perfect advantage of those behaviors and abilities and exactly fulfill her needs, it will have achieved a perfect person-job fit.

Person-job fit is the extent to which the contributions made by the individual match the inducements offered by the organization.

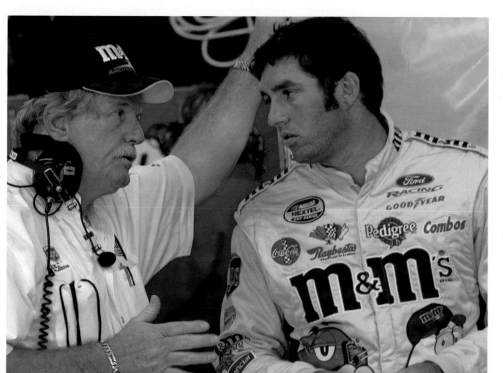

Person-job fit plays an important role in the success of any enterprise. Take NASCAR racing, for instance. Only a handful of people, such as Elliott Sadler, have the skills, nerves, and motivation to drive a race car around a narrow track at speeds in excess of 100 miles per hour sometimes only a matter of inches (or less!) from other cars. While many people find their work to be enjoyable to watch, few spectators would actually want to take their place.

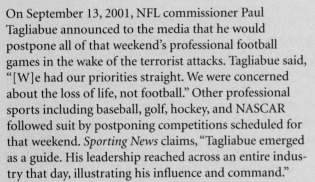

The NFL and . . . **CHANGE**

Person-Job Fit for the NFL Commissioner

On September 13, 2001, NFL commissioner Paul Tagliabue announced to the media that he would postpone all of that weekend's professional football games in the wake of the terrorist attacks. Tagliabue said, "[W]e had our priorities straight. We were concerned about the loss of life, not football." Other professional sports including baseball, golf, hockey, and NASCAR followed suit by postponing competitions scheduled for that weekend. *Sporting News* claims, "Tagliabue emerged as a guide. His leadership reached across an entire industry that day, illustrating his influence and command."

Although September 11 required a unique response, Tagliabue was already adept at managing change. A long-term strategic planner, he is known for his thoughtful analysis of trends that shape the sports industry. As the league negotiates contracts with broadcasters, Tagliabue is looking ahead ten, twenty, or even fifty years, evaluating the opportunities in traditional and emerging media such as wireless technology, interactive systems, and video-on-demand.

Another area of considerable change for the league is ethics, where safety, performance-enhancing drugs, and player behavior off the field are top concerns. One of Tagliabue's responses is an increased emphasis on community service. For example, Will Shields of the Kansas City Chiefs won the Walter Payton Man of the Year Award for community service. Shield's "Will to

Succeed" foundation helped 88,000 individuals meet needs ranging from after-school tutoring to sheltering abused women.

The NFL is facing pressure to change from inside and outside. Owners want more revenue, players want more pay, fans want more access. Tagliabue has been effective by building trust and listening. He plans ahead, so that the league is "proactive, not reactive," according to deputy commissioner Roger Goodell. Goodell is happy to see his boss use his power to influence others, saying, "[Tagliabue has] learned how to use his position . . . to drive change."

> *"[Tagliabue has] learned how to use his position . . . to drive change."*
>
> ROGER GOODELL, **NFL** DEPUTY COMMISSIONER

References: "Tagliabue, Paul," *Current Biography* (New York: The H. W. Wilson Co., 1996); "Will Shields Named Walter Payton Man of the Year," Join the Team, NFL website, www.jointheteam.com on February 27, 2005; Dennis Dillon, "Guiding Might, 2001," *The Sporting News*, www.sportingnews.com on February 14, 2005; Stuart Miller, "Tagliabue Tops Sporting News' Power 100," *The Sporting News*, January 4, 2005, msn.foxsports.com on February 25, 2005 (quotation).

Of course, such a precise person-job fit is seldom achieved. For one thing, hiring procedures are imperfect. Managers can estimate employee skill levels when making hiring decisions and can improve them through training, but even simple performance dimensions are hard to measure objectively and validly. Another factor is that both people and organizations change. An employee who finds a new job stimulating and exciting to begin with may find the same job boring and monotonous a few years later. An organization that adopts new technology needs new skills from its employees. Finally, each person is unique. Measuring skills and performance is difficult enough. Assessing attitudes and personality is far more complex. Each of these individual differences makes matching individuals with jobs a difficult and complex process.[4] *The NFL and . . . Change* box illustrates the role of person-job fit in the success of Paul Tagliabue and the NFL under his leadership.

Individual differences are personal attributes that vary from one person to another.

Individual Differences

As already noted, every individual is unique. **Individual differences** are personal attributes that vary from one person to another. Individual differences may be physical, psychological, and emotional. The individual differences that characterize a specific person make that person unique. As we see in the sections that follow, basic categories of individual differences include personality, attitudes, perception, and creativity. First, however, we need to note the importance of the situation in assessing the individual's behavior.

Are the specific differences that characterize a given person good or bad? Do they contribute to or detract from performance? The answer, of course, is that it depends on the circumstances. One person may be dissatisfied, withdrawn, and negative in one job setting but satisfied, outgoing, and positive in another. Working conditions, coworkers, and leadership are just a few of the factors that affect how a person performs and feels about a job. Thus, whenever a manager attempts to assess or account for individual differences among her employees, she must also be sure to consider the situation in which behavior occurs.

Since managers need to establish effective psychological contracts with their employees and achieve optimal fits between people and jobs, they face a major challenge in attempting to understand both individual differences and contributions in relation to inducements and contexts. A good starting point in developing this understanding is to appreciate the role of personality in organizations.

Personality and Organizations

Personality is the relatively stable set of psychological attributes that distinguish one person from another. A long-standing debate among psychologists—often expressed as "nature versus nurture"—is the extent to which personality attributes are inherited from our parents (the "nature" argument) or shaped by our environment (the "nurture" argument). In reality, both biological and environmental factors play important roles in determining our personalities. Although the details of this debate are beyond the scope of our discussion here, managers should strive to understand basic personality attributes and how they can affect people's behavior in organizational situations, not to mention their perceptions of and attitudes toward the organization.

> **Personality** is the relatively stable set of psychological attributes that distinguish one person from another.

The "Big Five" Personality Traits

Psychologists have identified literally thousands of personality traits and dimensions that differentiate one person from another. But in recent years, researchers have identified five fundamental traits that are especially relevant to organizations. Because these five traits are so important and because they are currently receiving so much attention, they are now commonly called the **"big five" personality traits**. Figure 3.2 illustrates these traits.

Agreeableness refers to a person's ability to get along with others. Agreeableness causes some people to be gentle, cooperative, forgiving, understanding, and good-natured in their dealings with others. But it results in others being irritable, short-tempered, uncooperative, and generally antagonistic toward other people. Researchers have not yet fully investigated the effects of agreeableness, but it seems likely that highly agreeable people are better at developing good working relationships with coworkers, subordinates, and higher-level managers, whereas less agreeable people are not likely to have particularly good working relationships. The same pattern might extend to relationships with customers, suppliers, and other key organizational constituents.

Conscientiousness refers to the number of goals on which a person focuses. People who focus on relatively few goals at one time are likely to be organized, systematic,

> The **"big five" personality traits** are a set of fundamental traits that are especially relevant to organizations.
> **Agreeableness** is the ability to get along with others.

> **Conscientiousness** refers to the number of goals on which a person focuses.

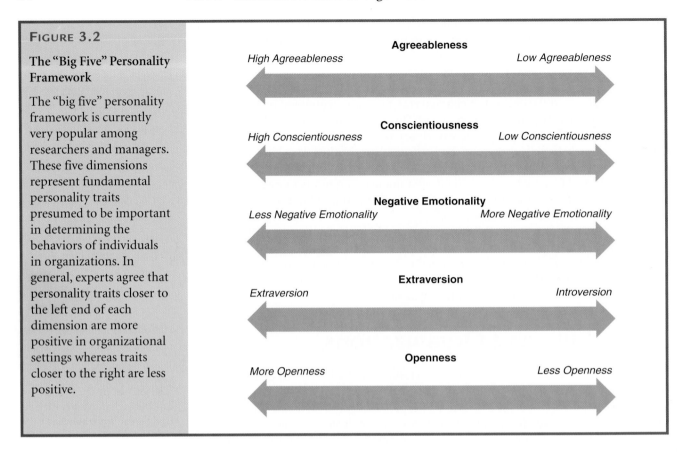

FIGURE 3.2

The "Big Five" Personality Framework

The "big five" personality framework is currently very popular among researchers and managers. These five dimensions represent fundamental personality traits presumed to be important in determining the behaviors of individuals in organizations. In general, experts agree that personality traits closer to the left end of each dimension are more positive in organizational settings whereas traits closer to the right are less positive.

careful, thorough, responsible, and self-disciplined; they tend to focus on a small number of goals at one time. Others, however, tend to pursue a wider array of goals and, as a result, to be more disorganized, careless, and irresponsible, as well as less thorough and self-disciplined. Research has found that more conscientious people tend to be higher performers than less conscientious people in a variety of different jobs. This pattern seems logical, of course, since conscientious people take their jobs seriously and approach their jobs in a highly responsible fashion.

The third of the "big five" personality dimensions is **negative emotionality**. People with less negative emotionality are relatively poised, calm, resilient, and secure; people with more negative emotionality are more excitable, insecure, reactive, and subject to extreme mood swings. People with less negative emotionality might be expected to better handle job stress, pressure, and tension. Their stability might also lead them to be seen as being more reliable than their less stable counterparts.

Extraversion reflects a person's comfort level with relationships. Extroverts are sociable, talkative, assertive, and open to establishing new relationships. Introverts are much less sociable, talkative, and assertive, and more reluctant to begin new relationships. Research suggests that extroverts tend to be higher overall job performers than introverts, and that they are more likely to be attracted to jobs based on personal relationships, such as sales and marketing positions.

Finally, **openness** reflects a person's rigidity of beliefs and range of interests. People with high levels of openness are willing to listen to new ideas and to change their own ideas, beliefs, and attitudes in response to new information. They also tend to have broad interests and to be curious, imaginative, and creative. On the other hand, people

Negative emotionality is characterized by moodiness and insecurity; those who have little negative emotionality are better able to withstand stress.

Extraversion is the quality of being comfortable with relationships; the opposite extreme, introversion, is characterized by more social discomfort.

Openness is the capacity to entertain new ideas and to change as a result of new information.

with low levels of openness tend to be less receptive to new ideas and less willing to change their minds. Further, they tend to have fewer and narrower interests and to be less curious and creative. People with more openness might be expected to be better performers due to their flexibility and the likelihood that they will be better accepted by others in the organization. Openness may also encompass a person's willingness to accept change; people with high levels of openness may be more receptive to change, whereas people with little openness may resist change.

The "big five" framework continues to attract the attention of both researchers and managers. The potential value of this framework is that it encompasses an integrated set of traits that appear to be valid predictors of certain behaviors in certain situations. Thus, managers who can both understand the framework and assess these traits in their employees are in a good position to understand how and why they behave as they do. On the other hand, managers must be careful to not overestimate their ability to assess the "big five" traits in others. Even assessment using the most rigorous and valid measures is likely to be somewhat imprecise. Another limitation of the "big five" framework is that it is primarily based on research conducted in the United States. Thus, its generalizability to other cultures presents unanswered questions. Even within the United States a variety of other factors and traits are also likely to affect behavior in organizations.

The Myers-Briggs Framework

Another interesting approach to understanding personalities in organizations is the Myers-Briggs framework. This framework, based on the classical work of Carl Jung, differentiates people in terms of four general dimensions: sensing, intuiting, judging, and perceiving. Higher and lower positions in each of the dimensions are used to classify people into one of sixteen different personality categories.

The Myers-Briggs Type Indicator (MBTI) is a popular questionnaire some organizations use to assess personality types. Indeed, it is among the most popular selection instruments used today, with as many as 2 million people taking it each year. Research suggests that the MBTI is a useful method for determining communication styles and interaction preferences. In terms of personality attributes, however, questions exist about both the validity and the stability of the MBTI.

Emotional Intelligence

The concept of emotional intelligence has been identified in recent years and provides some interesting insights into personality. **Emotional intelligence**, or **EQ**, refers to the extent to which people are self-aware, can manage their emotions, can motivate themselves, express empathy for others, and possess social skills.[5] These various dimensions can be described as follows:

> *Self-Awareness* This is the basis for the other components. It refers to a person's capacity for being aware of how they are feeling. In general, more self-awareness allows a person to more effectively guide their own lives and behaviors.
> *Managing Emotions* This refers to a person's capacity to balance anxiety, fear, and anger so that they do not overly interfere with getting things accomplished.
> *Motivating Oneself* This dimension refers to a person's ability to remain optimistic and to continue striving in the face of setbacks, barriers, and failure.
> *Empathy* Empathy refers to a person's ability to understand how others are feeling even without being explicitly told.
> *Social Skill* This refers to a person's ability to get along with others and to establish positive relationships.

Emotional intelligence (EQ) is the extent to which people are self-aware, can manage their emotions, can motivate themselves, express empathy for others, and possess social skills.

Preliminary research suggests that people with high EQs may perform better than others, especially in jobs that require a high degree of interpersonal interaction and that involve influencing or directing the work of others. Moreover, EQ appears to be something that isn't biologically based but which can be developed.[6]

Other Personality Traits at Work

Besides these complex models of personality, several other specific personality traits are also likely to influence behavior in organizations. Among the most important are locus of control, self-efficacy, authoritarianism, Machiavellianism, self-esteem, and risk propensity.

Locus of control is the extent to which people believe that their behavior has a real effect on what happens to them.[7] Some people, for example, believe that if they work hard they will succeed. They may also believe that people who fail do so because they lack ability or motivation. People who believe that individuals are in control of their lives are said to have an internal locus of control. Other people think that fate, chance, luck, or other people's behavior determines what happens to them. For example, an employee who fails to get a promotion may attribute that failure to a politically motivated boss or just bad luck, rather than to her or his own lack of skills or poor performance record. People who think that forces beyond their control dictate what happens to them are said to have an external locus of control.

Self-efficacy is a related but subtly different personality characteristic. A person's self-efficacy is that person's belief about his or her capabilities to perform a task. People with high self-efficacy believe that they can perform well on a specific task, but people with low self-efficacy tend to doubt their ability to perform a specific task. Self-assessments of ability contribute to self-efficacy, but so does the individual's personality. Some people simply have more self-confidence than others. This belief in their

A person's **locus of control** is the extent to which he believes his circumstances are a function of either his own actions or of external factors beyond his control.

A person's **self-efficacy** is that person's beliefs about his or her capabilities to perform a task.

Risk propensity is the degree to which a person is willing to take chances and make risky decisions. Top managers at Lockheed Martin demonstrated strong risk propensity in their recent quest to earn a $200 billion contract to build the new Joint Strike Fighter shown here. No fewer than three times did they essentially risk the future of the company in order to remain the leader in the bidding. Had they ultimately failed, Lockheed Martin would have suffered serious consequences for years.

ability to perform a task effectively results in their being more self-assured and better able to focus their attention on performance.

Another important personality characteristic is **authoritarianism**, the extent to which a person believes that power and status differences are appropriate within hierarchical social systems such as organizations.[8] For example, a person who is highly authoritarian may accept directives or orders from someone with more authority purely because the other person is "the boss." On the other hand, a person who is not highly authoritarian, although she may still carry out reasonable directives from the boss, is more likely to question things, express disagreement with the boss, and even refuse to carry out orders if they are for some reason objectionable.

> **Authoritarianism** is the belief that power and status differences are appropriate within hierarchical social systems such as organizations.

A highly authoritarian manager may be relatively autocratic and demanding, and highly authoritarian subordinates are more likely to accept this behavior from their leader. On the other hand, a less authoritarian manager may allow subordinates a bigger role in making decisions, and less authoritarian subordinates respond positively to this behavior. By all accounts, Dennis Kozlowski, the indicted former CEO of Tyco International, had a high degree of Machiavellianism. He apparently came to believe that his position of power in the company gave him the right to do just about anything he wanted with company resources.[9]

Machiavellianism is another important personality trait. This concept is named after Niccolo Machiavelli, a sixteenth-century author. In his book *The Prince*, Machiavelli explained how the nobility could more easily gain and use power. The term "Machiavellianism" is now used to describe behavior directed at gaining power and controlling the behavior of others. Research suggests that degree of Machiavellianism varies from person to person. More Machiavellian individuals tend to be rational and nonemotional, may be willing to lie to attain their personal goals, put little emphasis on loyalty and friendship, and enjoy manipulating others' behavior. Less Machiavellian individuals are more emotional, less willing to lie to succeed, value loyalty and friendship highly, and get little personal pleasure from manipulating others.

> People who possess the personality trait of **Machiavellianism** behave to gain power and control the behavior of others.

Self-esteem is the extent to which a person believes that he or she is a worthwhile and deserving individual. A person with high self-esteem is more likely to seek higher-status jobs, be more confident in her ability to achieve higher levels of performance, and derive greater intrinsic satisfaction from her accomplishments. In contrast, a person with less self-esteem may be more content to remain in a lower-level job, be less confident of his ability, and focus more on extrinsic rewards. Among the major personality dimensions, self-esteem is the one that has been most widely studied in other countries. Although more research is clearly needed, the published evidence suggests that self-esteem as a personality trait does indeed exist in a variety of countries and that its role in organizations is reasonably important across different cultures.

> A person's **self-esteem** is the extent to which that person believes he or she is a worthwhile and deserving individual.

Risk propensity is the degree to which a person is willing to take chances and make risky decisions. A manager with a high risk propensity, for example, might experiment with new ideas and gamble on new products. He might also lead the organization in new and different directions. This manager might be a catalyst for innovation, or on the other hand, might jeopardize the continued well-being of the organization if the risky decisions prove to be bad ones. A manager with low risk propensity might lead an organization to stagnation and excessive conservatism, or he might help the organization successfully weather turbulent and unpredictable times by maintaining stability and calm. Thus, the potential consequences of a manager's risk propensity depend heavily on the organization's environment.

> A person's **risk propensity** is the degree to which he or she is willing to take chances and make risky decisions.

High-Tech Customer Service at Finagle a Bagel

Boston restaurant chain Finagle a Bagel, owned by Laura Trust and Alan Litchman, competes for customers against coffeehouses, doughnut stores, groceries, full-service diners, fast-food eateries, and more. In order to beat that competition, their stores must offer something unique. "We provide an outstanding product at a good price point in a clean environment with a high level of customer service," states Trust. She says of other food providers, "Customer service is almost nonexistent. If you're lucky, it's horrendous."

Finagle a Bagel uses traditional methods to increase customer service, including staff training, incentives for performance, and so on. "A customer . . . just wants to know that you're going to take care of them. That you appreciate their business. That you're happy they're there. That you can talk to them in a polite manner. That you can understand their questions and concerns," says Trust. In the never-ending search for better service, the firm has also turned to a less obvious solution: automated technology.

Marketing manager Heather Robertson has always answered the phone in person to handle customer questions or feedback. She handwrites apology letters when a customer is dissatisfied. Yet when management wanted to know how many customers had complained about one server, for example, Robertson couldn't answer. So she established a customer comment database to track messages. As a result, Finagle a Bagel has retrained personnel, offered new products, and changed management policies, resulting in more loyal customers.

Another automated system manages the Frequent Finaglers cards, which can be used as gift or prepaid cards and can also track frequent buyer rewards. Customers can conveniently check their point balances or load dollars onto their card online. At the same time, the cards provide valuable information to the company about customer spending patterns. "The program . . . helps us to drive sales. It also gives us a way to manage our promotions, understand our guests, and provide our vendors information," says co-president Trust.

Automated systems, paradoxically, make it easier for Finagle a Bagel to provide high-quality customer interactions. Find out about more success factors at Finagle a Bagel in this chapter's closing case, "The Best Bagelers in Boston."

> *"A customer . . . just wants to know that you're going to take care of them."*
>
> LAURA TRUST, OWNER AND CO-PRESIDENT,
> FINAGLE A BAGEL

References: "Frequent Finaglers Get More!" Finagle a Bagel website, www.finagleabagel.com on February 28, 2005; "Customer Testimonials," Paytronix Systems Inc. website, www.paytronix.com on February 28, 2005; "Positive Attitudes at Finagle a Bagel," video case (quotation); "Zero Stage Capital Commits $3 Million to Fund Rapid Gazelle Growth," Zero Stage website, www.zerostage.com on February 27, 2005; Jennifer deJong, "Turbocharging Customer Service," *Inc.,* June 1995, pf.inc.com on February 27, 2005.

Attitudes in Organizations

Attitudes are a person's complexes of beliefs and feelings about specific ideas, situations, or other people.

People's attitudes also affect their behavior in organizations. **Attitudes** are complexes of beliefs and feelings that people have about specific ideas, situations, or other people. Attitudes are important because they are the mechanism through which most people express their feelings. An employee's statement that he feels underpaid by the organization reflects his feelings about his pay. Similarly, when a manager says that she likes the new advertising campaign, she is expressing her feelings about the organization's marketing efforts. The *Finagle a Bagel and . . . Technology* feature highlights the importance of attitudes—in concert with technology—in a real organization.

How Attitudes Are Formed

Attitudes are formed by a variety of forces, including our personal values, our experiences, and our personalities. For example, if we value honesty and integrity, we may form especially favorable attitudes toward a manager who we believe to be very honest and moral. Similarly, if we have had negative and unpleasant experiences with a particular coworker, we may form an unfavorable attitude toward her. Any of the "big five" or individual personality traits may also influence our attitudes. Understanding the basic structure of an attitude helps us see how attitudes are formed and can be changed.

Attitude Structure   Attitudes are usually viewed as stable dispositions to behave toward objects in a certain way. For any number of reasons, a person might decide that he or she does not like a particular political figure or a certain restaurant (a disposition). We would expect that person to express consistently negative opinions of the candidate or restaurant and to maintain the consistent, predictable intention of not voting for the political candidate or eating at the restaurant. In this view, attitudes contain three components: affect, cognition, and intention.

A person's **affect** is his or her feelings toward something. In many ways, affect is similar to emotion—it is something over which we have little or no conscious control. For example, most people react to words such as "love," "hate," "sex," and "war" in a manner that reflects their feelings about what those words convey. Similarly, you may like one of your classes, dislike another, and be indifferent toward a third. If the class you dislike is an elective, you may not be particularly concerned. But if it is the first course in your chosen major, your affective reaction may cause you considerable anxiety.

> A person's **affect** is his or her feelings toward something.

Cognition is the knowledge a person presumes to have about something. You may believe you like a class because the textbook is excellent, the class meets at your favorite time, the instructor is outstanding, and the workload is light. This "knowledge" may be true, partially true, or totally false. For example, you may intend to vote for a particular candidate because you think you know where the candidate stands on several issues. In reality, depending on the candidate's honesty and your understanding of his or her statements, the candidate's thinking on the issues may be exactly the same as yours, partly the same, or totally different. Cognitions are based on perceptions of truth and reality, and, as we note later, perceptions agree with reality to varying degrees.

> A person's **cognitions** constitute the knowledge a person presumes to have about something.

Intention guides a person's behavior. If you like your instructor, you may intend to take another class from him or her next semester. Intentions are not always translated into actual behavior, however. If the instructor's course next semester is scheduled for 8:00 A.M., you may decide that another instructor is just as good. Some attitudes, and their corresponding intentions, are much more central and significant to an individual than others. You may intend to do one thing (take a particular class) but later alter your intentions because of a more significant and central attitude (fondness for sleeping late).

> An **intention** is a component of an attitude that guides a person's behavior.

Cognitive Dissonance   When two sets of cognitions or perceptions are contradictory or incongruent, a person experiences a level of conflict and anxiety called **cognitive dissonance**. Cognitive dissonance also occurs when people behave in a fashion that is inconsistent with their attitudes.[10] For example, a person may realize that smoking and overeating are dangerous yet continue to do both. Because the attitudes and behaviors are inconsistent with each other, the person probably will experience a certain amount of tension and discomfort and may try to reduce these feelings by changing the attitude, altering the behavior, or perceptually distorting the circumstances. For example, the dissonance associated with overeating might be resolved by continually deciding to go on a diet "next week."

> **Cognitive dissonance** is the anxiety a person experiences when he or she simultaneously possesses two sets of knowledge or perceptions that are contradictory or incongruent.

Cognitive dissonance affects people in a variety of ways. We frequently encounter situations in which our attitudes conflict with each other or with our behaviors. Dissonance reduction is the way we deal with these feelings of discomfort and tension. In organizational settings, people contemplating leaving the organization may wonder why they continue to stay and work hard. As a result of this dissonance, they may conclude that the company is not so bad after all, that they have no immediate options elsewhere, or that they will leave "soon."

Attitude Change   Attitudes are not as stable as personality attributes. For example, new information may change attitudes. A manager may have a negative attitude about a new colleague because of his lack of job-related experience. After working with the new person for a while, however, the manager may come to realize that he is actually very talented and subsequently develop a more positive attitude. Likewise, if the object of an attitude changes, a person's attitude toward that object may also change. Suppose, for example, that employees feel underpaid and, as a result, have negative attitudes toward the company's reward system. A big salary increase may cause these attitudes to become more positive.

Attitudes can also change when the object of the attitude becomes less important or less relevant to the person. For example, suppose an employee has a negative attitude about his company's health insurance. When his spouse gets a new job with an organization that has outstanding insurance benefits, his attitude toward his own insurance may become more moderate simply because he no longer has to worry about it. Finally, as noted earlier, individuals may change their attitudes as a way to reduce cognitive dissonance.

Deeply rooted attitudes that have a long history are, of course, resistant to change. For example, over a period of years a former airline executive named Frank Lorenzo developed a reputation in the industry of being antiunion and for cutting wages and benefits. As a result, employees throughout the industry came to dislike and distrust him. When he took over Eastern Airlines, its employees had such a strong attitude of distrust toward him that they could never agree to cooperate with any of his programs or ideas. Some of them actually cheered months later when Eastern went bankrupt, even though it was costing them their own jobs!

Key Work-Related Attitudes

People in an organization form attitudes about many different things. Employees are likely to have attitudes about their salary, their promotion possibilities, their boss, employee benefits, the food in the company cafeteria, and the color of the company softball team uniforms. Of course, some of these attitudes are more important than others. Especially important attitudes are job satisfaction and organizational commitment.

Job satisfaction is the extent to which a person is gratified or fulfilled by his or her work.

Job Satisfaction   **Job satisfaction** reflects the extent to which people find gratification or fulfillment in their work. Extensive research on job satisfaction shows that personal factors such as an individual's needs and aspirations determine this attitude, along with group and organizational factors such as relationships with coworkers and supervisors and working conditions, work policies, and compensation.[11]

A satisfied employee tends to be absent less often, to make positive contributions, and to stay with the organization.[12] In contrast, a dissatisfied employee may be absent more often, may experience stress that disrupts coworkers, and may be continually looking for another job. Contrary to what a lot of managers believe, however, high levels of job satisfaction do not necessarily lead to higher levels of productivity.[13] One survey indicated that, also contrary to popular opinion, Japanese workers are less satisfied with their jobs than their counterparts in the United States.[14]

Organizational Commitment **Organizational commitment**, sometimes called job commitment, reflects an individual's identification with and attachment to the organization. A highly committed person will probably see herself as a true member of the firm (for example, referring to the organization in personal terms such as "we make high-quality products"), overlook minor sources of dissatisfaction, and see herself remaining a member of the organization. In contrast, a less committed person is more likely to see himself as an outsider (for example, referring to the organization in less personal terms like "they don't pay their employees very well"), to express more dissatisfaction about things, and to not see himself as a long-term member of the organization.[15]

Organizations can do few definitive things to promote satisfaction and commitment, but some specific guidelines are available. For one thing, if the organization treats its employees fairly and provides reasonable rewards and job security, its employees are more likely to be satisfied and committed. Allowing employees to have a say in how things are done can also promote these attitudes. Designing jobs so that they are stimulating can enhance both satisfaction and commitment. Research suggests that Japanese workers may be more committed to their organizations than are U.S. workers.[16] Other research suggests that some of the factors that may lead to commitment, including extrinsic rewards, role clarity, and participative management, are the same across different cultures.[17]

Employee attitudes such as job satisfaction and organizational commitment contribute to organizational effectiveness in a variety of works. Consequently, firms often seek ways to make their employees enjoy coming to work and to make them reluctant to consider leaving for a different job. The Oriental Trading Company warehouse in Nebraska, for instance, has set up this "cash machine." When someone makes an especially noteworthy contribution to the firm, that employee gets to spend some time in the machine catching bills as they are blown about.

Organizational commitment is a person's identification with and attachment to an organization.

Affect and Mood in Organizations

Researchers have recently started to renew their interest in the affective component of attitudes. Recall from our discussion above that the affect component of an attitude reflects our emotions. Managers once believed that emotion and feelings varied among people from day to day, but research now suggests that although some short-term fluctuation does indeed occur, there are also underlying stable predispositions toward fairly constant and predictable moods and emotional states.[18]

Some people, for example, tend to have a higher degree of **positive affectivity**. This means that they are relatively upbeat and optimistic, that they have an overall sense of well-being, and that they usually see things in a positive light. Thus, they always seem to be in a good mood. People with more **negative affectivity** are just the opposite. They are generally downbeat and pessimistic and they usually see things in a negative way. They seem to be in a bad mood most of the time.

People who possess **positive affectivity** are upbeat and optimistic, have an overall sense of well-being, and see things in a positive light.

People characterized by **negative affectivity** are generally downbeat and pessimistic, see things in a negative way, and seem to be in a bad mood.

Of course, as noted above, short-term variations can occur among even the most extreme types. People with a lot of positive affectivity, for example, may still be in a bad mood if they have just been passed over for a promotion, gotten extremely negative performance feedback, or been laid off or fired, for instance. Similarly, those with negative affectivity may be in a good mood—at least for a short time—if they have just been promoted, received very positive performance feedback, or had other good things befall them. After the initial impact of these events wears off, however, those with positive affectivity generally return to their normal positive mood, whereas those with negative affectivity gravitate back to their normal bad mood.

Perception in Organizations

Perception is the set of processes by which an individual becomes aware of and interprets information about the environment.

Perception—the set of processes by which an individual becomes aware of and interprets information about the environment—is another important element of workplace behavior. If everyone perceived everything the same way, things would be a lot simpler (and a lot less exciting!). Of course, just the opposite is true: People perceive the same things in very different ways.[19] Moreover, people often assume that reality is objective, that we all perceive the same things in the same way. To test this idea, we could ask students at the University of Florida and Florida State University to describe the most recent football game between their schools. We probably would hear two conflicting stories. These differences would arise primarily because of perception. The fans "saw" the same game but interpreted it in sharply contrasting ways.

Since perception plays a role in a variety of workplace behaviors, managers should understand basic perceptual processes. As implied in our definition, perception actually consists of several distinct processes. Moreover, in perceiving we receive information in many guises, from spoken words to visual images of movements and forms. Through perceptual processes, the receiver assimilates the varied types of incoming information for the purpose of interpreting it.[20]

Selective perception is the process of screening out information that we are uncomfortable with or that contradicts our beliefs.

Basic Perceptual Processes

Figure 3.3 shows two basic perceptual processes that are particularly relevant to managers—selective perception and stereotyping.

Selective Perception **Selective perception** is the process of screening out information that we are uncomfortable with or that contradicts our beliefs. For example, suppose a manager is exceptionally fond of a particular worker. The manager has a very positive attitude about the worker and thinks he is a top performer. One day the manager notices that the worker seems to be goofing off. Selective perception may cause the manager to quickly forget what he observed. Similarly, suppose a manager has formed a very

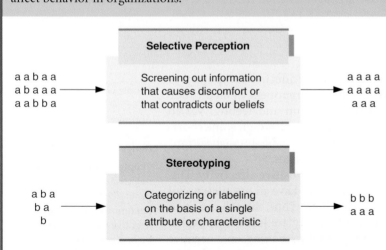

FIGURE 3.3

Basic Perceptual Processes

Perception determines how we become aware of information from our environment and how we interpret it. Selective perception and stereotyping are particularly important perceptual processes that affect behavior in organizations.

negative image of a particular worker. She thinks this worker is a poor performer who never does a good job. When she happens to observe an example of high performance from the worker, she may quickly forget it. In one sense, selective perception is beneficial because it allows us to disregard minor bits of information. Of course, the benefit occurs only if our basic perception is accurate. If selective perception causes us to ignore important information, however, it can become quite detrimental.

Stereotyping   **Stereotyping** is categorizing or labeling people on the basis of a single attribute. Certain forms of stereotyping can be useful and efficient. Suppose, for example, that a manager believes that communication skills are important for a particular job and that speech communication majors tend to have exceptionally good communication skills. As a result, whenever he interviews candidates for jobs he pays especially close attention to speech communication majors. To the extent that communication skills truly predict job performance and that majoring in speech communication does indeed provide those skills, this form of stereotyping can be beneficial. Common attributes from which people often stereotype are race and sex. Of course, stereotypes along these lines are inaccurate and can be harmful. For example, suppose a human resource manager forms the stereotype that women can perform only certain tasks and that men are best suited for other tasks. To the extent that this affects the manager's hiring practices, he or she is (1) costing the organization valuable talent for both sets of jobs, (2) violating federal law, and (3) behaving unethically.

> **Stereotyping** is the process of categorizing or labeling people on the basis of a single attribute.

Perception and Attribution

Attribution theory has extended our understanding of how perception affects behavior in organizations.[21] **Attribution theory** suggests that we observe behavior and then attribute causes to it. That is, we attempt to explain why people behave as they do. The process of attribution is based on perceptions of reality, and these perceptions may vary widely among individuals.

> **Attribution theory** suggests that we attribute causes to behavior based on our observations of certain characteristics of that behavior.

Figure 3.4 illustrates the basic attribution theory framework. To start the process, we observe behavior, either our own or someone else's. We then evaluate that behavior in terms of its degrees of consensus, consistency, and distinctiveness. Consensus is the extent to which other people in the same situation behave in the same way. Consistency is the degree to which the same person behaves in the same way at different times. Distinctiveness is the extent to which the same person behaves in the same way in different situations. We form impressions or attributions as to the causes of behavior based on various combinations of consensus, consistency, and distinctiveness. We may believe the behavior is caused internally (by forces within the person) or externally (by forces in the person's environment).

For example, suppose you observe one of your subordinates being rowdy, disrupting others' work, and generally making a nuisance of himself. If you can understand the causes of this behavior, you may be able to change it. If the employee is the only one engaging in the disruptive behavior (low consensus), if he behaves like this several times each week (high consistency), and if you have seen him behave like this in other settings (low distinctiveness), a logical conclusion would be that internal factors are causing his behavior.

Suppose, however, that you observe a different pattern: Everyone in the person's work group is rowdy (high consensus), and although the particular employee often is rowdy at work (high consistency), you have never seen him behave this way in other settings (high distinctiveness). This pattern indicates that something in the situation is causing the behavior—that is, that the causes of the behavior are external.

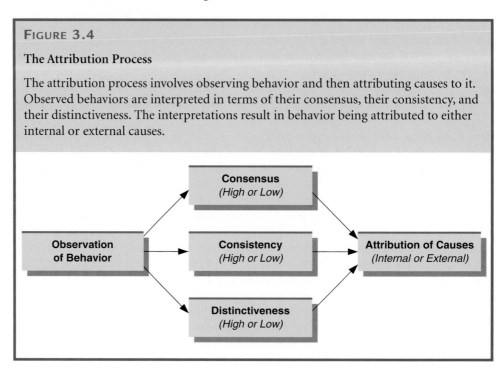

FIGURE 3.4

The Attribution Process

The attribution process involves observing behavior and then attributing causes to it. Observed behaviors are interpreted in terms of their consensus, their consistency, and their distinctiveness. The interpretations result in behavior being attributed to either internal or external causes.

Types of Workplace Behavior

Now that we have looked closely at how individual differences can influence behavior in organizations, let's turn our attention to what we mean by workplace behavior. **Workplace behavior** is a pattern of action by the members of an organization that directly or indirectly influences the organization's effectiveness. One way to talk about workplace behavior is to describe its impact on performance and productivity, absenteeism and turnover, and organizational citizenship. Unfortunately, employees can exhibit dysfunctional behaviors as well.

Performance Behaviors

Performance behaviors are the total set of work-related behaviors that the organization expects the individual to display. You might think of these as the "terms" of the psychological contract. For some jobs, performance behaviors can be narrowly defined and easily measured. For example, an assembly-line worker who sits by a moving conveyor and attaches parts to a product as it passes by has relatively few performance behaviors. He or she is expected to remain at the workstation and correctly attach the parts. Performance can often be assessed quantitatively by counting the percentage of parts correctly attached.

For many other jobs, however, performance behaviors are more diverse and much more difficult to assess. For example, consider the case of a research-and-development scientist at Merck. The scientist works in a lab trying to find new scientific breakthroughs that have commercial potential. The scientist must apply knowledge learned in graduate school and experience gained from previous research. Intuition and creativity are also important. And the desired breakthrough may take months or even years to accomplish. Organizations rely on a number of different methods to evaluate

Workplace behavior is a pattern of action by the members of an organization that directly or indirectly influences organizational effectiveness.

Performance behaviors are the total set of work-related behaviors that the organization expects the individual to display.

performance. The key, of course, is to match the evaluation mechanism with the job being performed.

Dysfunctional Behaviors

Some work-related behaviors are dysfunctional in nature. That is, **dysfunctional behaviors** are those that detract from, rather than contribute to, organizational performance. Two of the more common ones are absenteeism and turnover. **Absenteeism** occurs when an employee does not show up for work. Some absenteeism has a legitimate cause, such as illness, jury duty, or death or illness in the family. At other times, the employee may report a feigned legitimate cause that's actually just an excuse to stay home. When an employee is absent, legitimately or not, her or his work does not get done at all or a substitute must be hired to do it. In either case, the quantity or quality of actual output is likely to suffer. Obviously, some absenteeism is expected, but organizations strive to minimize feigned absenteeism and reduce legitimate absences as much as possible.

Turnover occurs when people quit their jobs. An organization usually incurs costs in replacing workers who have quit, and if turnover involves especially productive people, it is even more costly. Turnover seems to result from a number of factors, including aspects of the job, the organization, the individual, the labor market, and family influences. In general, a poor person-job fit is also a likely cause of turnover. People may also be prone to leave an organization if its inflexibility makes it difficult to manage family and other personal matters and may be more likely to stay if an organization provides sufficient flexibility to make it easier to balance work and nonwork considerations. One Chick-fil-A operator in Texas has cut the turnover rate in his stores by offering flexible work schedules, college scholarships, and such perks as free bowling trips.[22]

> **Dysfunctional behaviors** are those that detract from organizational performance. **Absenteeism** occurs when an individual does not show up for work.

> **Turnover** occurs when people quit their jobs.

Turnover in the fast-food industry is often exceedingly high. As a result, this Popeye's Fried Chicken manager has to spend a lot of his time recruiting new employees and then training them in both how to perform their jobs and how to meet safety and health standards. If firms can find ways to lower turnover, managers can devote more of their time to other important activities.

Other forms of dysfunctional behavior may be even more costly for an organization. Theft and sabotage, for example, result in direct financial costs for an organization. Sexual and racial harassment also cost an organization, both indirectly (by lowering morale, producing fear, and driving off valuable employees) and directly (through financial liability if the organization responds inappropriately). Workplace violence is also a growing concern in many organizations. Violence by disgruntled workers or former workers results in dozens of deaths and injuries each year.[23]

Organizational Citizenship

A person's degree of **organizational citizenship** is the extent to which his or her behavior makes a positive overall contribution to the organization.

Managers strive to minimize dysfunctional behaviors while trying to promote organizational citizenship. **Organizational citizenship** refers to the behavior of individuals who make a positive overall contribution to the organization.[24] Consider, for example, an employee who does work that is acceptable in terms of both quantity and quality. However, she refuses to work overtime, won't help newcomers learn the ropes, and is generally unwilling to make any contribution beyond the strict performance of her job. This person may be seen as a good performer, but she is not likely to be seen as a good organizational citizen.

Another employee may exhibit a comparable level of performance. In addition, however, he always works late when the boss asks him to, he takes time to help newcomers learn their way around, and he is perceived as being helpful and committed to the organization's success. He is likely to be seen as a better organizational citizen.

A complex mosaic of individual, social, and organizational variables determines organizational citizenship behaviors. For example, the personality, attitudes, and needs of the individual (discussed in Chapter 4) must be consistent with citizenship behaviors. Similarly, the social context, or work group, in which the individual works must facilitate and promote such behaviors (we discuss group dynamics in Chapter 9). And the organization itself, especially its culture, must be capable of promoting, recognizing, and rewarding these types of behaviors if they are to be maintained. The study of organizational citizenship is still in its infancy, but preliminary research suggests that it may play a powerful role in organizational effectiveness.

Synopsis

Understanding individuals in organizations is important for all managers. A basic framework for facilitating this understanding is the psychological contract—people's expectations regarding what they will contribute to the organization and what they will get in return. Organizations strive to achieve an optimal person-job fit, but this process is complicated by the existence of individual differences.

Personalities are the relatively stable sets of psychological and behavioral attributes that distinguish one person from another. The "big five" personality traits are agreeableness, conscientiousness, negative emotionality, extraversion, and openness. Myers-Briggs dimensions and emotional intelligence also offer insights into personalities in organizations. Other important personality traits include locus of control, self-efficacy, authoritarianism, Machiavellianism, self-esteem, and risk propensity.

Attitudes are based on emotion, knowledge, and intended behavior. Cognitive dissonance results from contradictory or incongruent attitudes, behaviors, or both. Job satisfaction or dissatisfaction and organizational commitment are important work-related attitudes. Employees' moods, assessed in terms of positive or negative affectivity, also affect attitudes in organizations.

Perception is the set of processes by which a person becomes aware of and interprets information about the environment. Basic perceptual processes include selective perception and stereotyping. Perception and attribution are also closely related.

Workplace behavior is a pattern of action by the members of an organization that directly or indirectly influences organizational effectiveness. Performance behaviors are the set of work-related behaviors the organization expects the individual to display to fulfill the psychological contract. Dysfunctional behaviors include absenteeism and turnover, as well as theft, sabotage, and violence. Organizational citizenship entails behaviors that make a positive overall contribution to the organization.

Discussion Questions

1. What is a psychological contract? Why is it important? What psychological contracts do you currently have?

2. Sometimes people describe an individual as having "no personality." What is wrong with this statement? What does this statement actually mean?

3. Describe how the "big five" personality attributes might affect a manager's own behavior in dealing with subordinates.

4. What are the components of an individual's attitude?

5. Think of a person whom you know who seems to have positive affectivity. Think of another who has more negative affectivity. How constant are they in their expressions of mood and attitude?

6. How does perception affect behavior?

7. What stereotypes have you formed about people? Are they good or bad?

8. Recall a situation in which you made attributions and describe using the framework in Figure 3.4.

9. Identify and describe several important workplace behaviors.

10. As a manager, how would you go about trying to make someone a better organizational citizen?

Matching Personalities and Jobs

Purpose: This exercise will give you insights into the importance of personality in the workplace and into some of the difficulties associated with assessing personality traits.

Format: You will first try to determine which personality traits are most relevant to different jobs. You will then write a series of questions to help assess or measure those traits in prospective employees.

Procedure: First, read each of the job descriptions below.

Sales Representative

This position involves calling on existing customers to ensure that they continue to be happy with your firm's products. The sales representative also works to get customers to buy more of your products and to attract new customers. A sales representative must be aggressive but not pushy.

Office Manager

The office manager oversees the work of a staff of twenty secretaries, receptionists, and clerks. The manager hires them, trains them, evaluates their performance, and sets their pay. The manager also schedules working hours and, when necessary, disciplines or fires workers.

Warehouse Worker

Warehouse workers unload trucks and carry shipments to shelves for storage. They also pull orders for customers from shelves and take products for packing. The job requires that workers follow orders precisely; there is little room for autonomy or interaction with others during work.

Exercise Task: Working alone, think of a single personality trait that you think is especially important for a person to be able to perform each of these three jobs effectively. Next, write five questions that will help you assess how an applicant scores on that particular trait. These questions should be of the type that can be answered on a five-point scale (i.e., strongly agree, agree, neither agree nor disagree, disagree, strongly disagree).

After completing your questions, exchange them with one of your classmates. Pretend you are a job applicant. Provide honest and truthful answers to your partner's questions. After you have both finished, discuss the traits each of you identified for each position and how well you think your classmate's questions actually measure those traits.

Follow-up Questions

1. How easy is it to measure personality?

2. How important do you believe it is for organizations to consider personality in hiring decisions?

3. Do perceptions and attitudes affect how people answer personality questions?

Self-Assessment Exercise

Assessing Your Locus of Control

Read each pair of statements below and indicate whether you agree more with statement A or with statement B. There are no right or wrong answers. In some cases, you may agree somewhat with both statements; choose the one with which you agree more.

_____ 1. **A.** Making a lot of money is largely a matter of getting the right breaks.
   B. Promotions are earned through hard work and persistence.

_____ 2. **A.** There is usually a direct correlation between how hard I study and the grades I get.
   B. Many times the reactions of teachers seem haphazard to me.

_____ 3. **A.** The number of divorces suggests that more and more people are not trying to make their marriages work.
   B. Marriage is primarily a gamble.

_____ 4. **A.** It is silly to think you can really change another person's basic attitudes.
   B. When I am right, I can generally convince others.

_____ 5. **A.** Getting promoted is really a matter of being a little luckier than the next person.
   B. In our society, a person's future earning power is dependent upon her or his ability.

—— 6. **A.** If one knows how to deal with people, they are really quite easily led.
   B. I have little influence over the way other people behave.

—— 7. **A.** The grades I make are the result of my own efforts; luck has little or nothing to do with it.
   B. Sometimes I feel that I have little to do with the grades I get.

—— 8. **A.** People like me can change the course of world affairs if we make ourselves heard.
   B. It is only wishful thinking to believe that one can readily influence what happens in our society at large.

—— 9. **A.** A great deal that happens to me probably is a matter of chance.
   B. I am the master of my life.

——10. **A.** Getting along with people is a skill that must be practiced.

B. It is almost impossible to figure out how to please some people.

Give yourself 1 point each if you chose the following answers: 1B, 2A, 3A, 4B, 5B, 6A, 7A, 8A, 9B, 10A.

Sum your scores and interpret them as follows:

8–10 = high internal locus of control
6–7 = moderate internal locus of control
5 = mixed internal/external locus of control
3–4 = moderate external locus of control
1–2 = high external locus of control

(Note: This is an abbreviated version of a longer instrument. The scores obtained here are only an approximation of what your score might be on the complete instrument.)

Reference: Adapted from J. B. Rotter, "External Control and Internal Control," *Psychology Today*, June 1971, p. 42. Reprinted with permission from *Psychology Today Magazine*. Copyright © 2002 Sussex Publishers, Inc.

Building Managerial Skills

Exercise Overview: Conceptual skills are the manager's ability to think in the abstract. This exercise will help you apply conceptual skills in a way designed to better understand the concepts of attitude formation and cognitive dissonance.

Exercise Task: Begin by considering the following situation. Assume that a new restaurant has just opened near your house, apartment, or dorm. You decide to give it a try and have one of the worst nights of your life. You wait thirty minutes to get seated, and then another thirty minutes before your waitperson stops by. The menu you are handed is dirty, and your water glass has a dead fly floating in it. Your food is served cold (unintentionally), the waitperson spills food on you when clearing the table, the food is way overpriced, and when you return to your car you find that it has been towed! All in all, not a pleasant experience. As a result, you vow to never set foot back in that restaurant again.

Now suppose that there is someone that you have been trying for months to date. While he or she seems to have an interest in dating you as well, circumstances have always kept the two of you apart. This person has just called you, however, and indicated a strong interest in going out with you next week, but only if the two of you can have dinner at the restaurant you hate.

Using the situation above as background, answer the following questions:

1. Explain how your attitude about the restaurant was formed.

2. Explain how your attitude toward the other person was formed.

3. Explain what you would do when confronted with this choice.

4. Explain the role of cognitive dissonance in this situation.

The Best Bagelers in Boston

Finagle a Bagel was founded in 1982 by Larry Smith, who was selling cheesecakes based on his father's recipe in Boston's Faneuil Hall marketplace. As the store concept evolved, Smith switched to bagels and added locations. He encountered problems finding enough financing to continue expansion. Smith began to consider selling the business in order to pursue other opportunities and have more time for his family.

> **❝ The fun part of the business is you get to use all aspects of your education. ❞**
> LAURA TRUST, OWNER AND CO-PRESIDENT,
> FINAGLE A BAGEL

At the same time, husband-and-wife team Laura Trust and Alan Litchman, both recent graduates of MIT's Sloan School of Business, were living in Hong Kong. She was working in the clothing manufacturing business and he was looking for a job in real estate. Together they were considering opening a bagel shop in Hong Kong, reasoning that the cosmopolitan residents would appreciate authentic American food. While in the United States doing research on the bagel business, they met Smith. Trust and Litchman decided they preferred to buy Smith's company rather than invest in a Hong Kong start-up.

Positive attitudes are essential for an entrepreneur and play a big part in the success of Finagle a Bagel. Trust says, "The fun part of the business is you get to use all aspects of your education . . . You don't have a sixty-man Marketing Department, you don't have a Finance Department. *You're* the Finance Department . . . Every day there is a different challenge to be met, there's a different need in the business." She goes on, "Every experience you have teaches you something. Even if it's *not* what you love. It shows you perhaps what you don't like about a particular career choice or a career path. In my case in the garment manufacturing business that I was in, we sold to a retailer who then went on to sell to a consumer. What I learned was that I liked being in contact with the consumer directly."

While Trust and Litchman clearly love their jobs, there are challenges, including the lack of personal time. The two co-presidents are together all day at work and then spend their non-work hours together too. Litchman tells the story of a "typical" workday, which begins with being awakened by his young son at 6 A.M. Business is conducted from home over the phone, while in the shower, and during his son's mealtimes. "The day never ends," states Trust. "Alan and I don't have the opportunity to go on vacations or just not answer the phone or have an evening out without the phone on. Something is always going to happen and it's always ultimately [our] responsibility."

Yet overall, the positives outweigh the negatives for the couple. It shows in the way that Litchman and Trust work to make Finagle a Bagel fit into the Boston neighborhoods where the stores are located. Bulletin boards of local happenings, family-friendly policies in suburban locations, and sponsorship of local artists and charities are designed to make the stores a part of each local community. Store employees are a diverse group to reflect the diversity of customers in each neighborhood. Other indicators of the co-presidents' positive attitudes include their hard work, commitment to the organization, and friendly relationship with subordinates.

Evidently, person-job fit is high for both Litchman and Trust. "There is a difference between people who want to run their own business," says Trust, "and people who want to be a part of a business. [Owners must] like almost all aspects of the business . . . or at least be willing to do all of them." With evident happiness, Trust adds, "Owning your own business allows you to have your hand in each pie."

Finagle a Bagel is thriving in many ways. The company was recently named one of the most popular restaurants and one of the most successful small businesses in Boston. The firm expects to achieve record profits this year, to open a new store, and to move up to a bigger and more modern headquarters and production facility. With the positive leadership and hard work of Litchman and Trust, it's easy to see why this small firm is rapidly becoming a regional leader.

Case Questions

1. Consider what Litchman and Trust say about their jobs. How would you describe the affective component of their work-related attitudes? How would you describe the cognitive and intentional components?

2. Although Litchman and Trust clearly enjoy their work, are there opportunities for them to experience cognitive dissonance in their work-related attitudes? Explain why or why not.

3. What workplace behaviors do Litchman and Trust display? Are these behaviors a result of their attitudes? Explain.

References: "About Our Company," "Fabulous Finagle Flavors," "Family Fun," "The Buzz," Finagle a Bagel website, www.finagleabagel.com on February 28, 2005; "Finagle a Bagel to Move HQ to Newton," *Boston Business Journal*, January 13, 2005, boston.bizjournals.com on February 27, 2005; "Positive Attitudes at Finagle a Bagel," video case (quotation); Jennifer deJong, "Turbocharging Customer Service," *Inc.*, June 1995, pf.inc.com on February 27, 2005; Jay Fitzgerald, "Finagling His Way," *Boston Business Journal*, December 8, 1997, boston.bizjournals.com on February 27, 2005.

TEST PREPPER

You have read the chapter and studied the key terms. Think you're ready to ace the exam? Take this sample test to gauge your comprehension of chapter material and check your answers at the back of the book. Want more test questions? Take the ACE quizzes found on the student website: http://college.hmco.com/business/students/ (select Griffin/Moorhead, Organizational Behavior, 8e from the Management menu).

T   F   1. Managers should make sure their psychological contract is written down.

T   F   2. One reason precise person-job fit is seldom achieved is hiring procedures are imperfect.

T   F   3. Negative emotionality is a personality dimension that reflects how much an employee complains.

T   F   4. Managers with high emotional intelligence can motivate themselves and express empathy for other people.

T   F   5. A high Machiavellian manager would be interested in gaining power and controlling the behavior of other people.

T   F   6. A worker who hates the work he does, but loves the salary he receives is likely to experience cognitive dissonance.

T   F   7. If one of your employees who is always on time shows up late for work one day, you are likely to make an internal attribution.

8. Which of the following is not a contribution an individual makes in a psychological contract?
   a. Effort
   b. Skills
   c. Salary
   d. Ability
   e. Loyalty

9. Achieving a good person-job fit is difficult for all of the following reasons, except
   a. people change.
   b. organizations change.
   c. hiring procedures are imperfect.
   d. each person is unique.
   e. achieving a good person-job fit is difficult for all of the above reasons.

10. Which of the following "big five" personality dimensions has been linked to higher job performance?
    a. Sensing
    b. Conscientiousness
    c. Intuition
    d. Judging
    e. Perception

11. Janice believes she can do well on the exam if she studies enough. William believes it won't really matter how much or little he studies – his performance all depends on how hard the professor makes the test. Janice and William differ in their
    a. authoritarianism.
    b. Machiavellianism.
    c. self-esteem.
    d. locus of control.
    e. risk propensity.

12. Adam is an ambitious employee who loves his job and intends to keep it, but he knows it offers little, if any, advancement potential. Adam is likely to experience
    a. negative affectivity.
    b. self-efficacy.
    c. openness to experience.
    d. cognitive dissonance.
    e. negative emotionality.

13. Managers ought to expect all of the following from satisfied employees, except
    a. lower absenteeism.
    b. higher levels of productivity.
    c. lower turnover.
    d. positive contributions.
    e. Managers ought to expect all of the above from satisfied employees.

14. Jennifer believes her manager is incompetent. Even when her manager makes a good decision, Jennifer is likely to screen out that information through a process called
    a. selective perception.
    b. stereotyping.
    c. attribution.
    d. distinctiveness.
    e. organizational citizenship.

15. In general, poor person-job fit will likely cause higher
    a. negative affectivity.
    b. self-efficacy.
    c. turnover.
    d. performance.
    e. stereotyping.

Motivation in Organizations

After studying this chapter, you should be able to:

Corporate Volunteering Motivates Workers

▶ **Characterize the nature of motivation, including its importance and basic historical perspectives.**

▶ **Identify and describe the need-based perspectives on motivation.**

▶ **Identify and describe the major process-based perspectives on motivation.**

▶ **Describe learning-based perspectives on motivation.**

The U.S. government and citizens give generously, donating billions of dollars to troubled regions desperate for aid and assistance. Yet one of the biggest contributions from Americans isn't money, it's time. Each year 64.5 million Americans volunteer, collectively investing 3.4 billion hours. Volunteers derive satisfaction from their efforts. In addition, corporations that support volunteers are very effective in recruiting and retaining workers, making profitable business connections, and promoting excellent corporate public relations.

Corporate-sponsored volunteers work within the United States and abroad. For example, at drugmaker Pfizer, workers volunteered to provide services to low-income communities from the Philippines to the Bronx. Cisco Systems, a networking provider, sent an executive to Southeast Asia for a year. He set up wireless networks to coordinate aid workers throughout the region. Microsoft employee Frank Schott visited a refugee camp in Kosovo and came away convinced that his company needed to help. Schott says, "It's very hard to go on a mission to a refugee camp and go out of there without thinking, 'Gosh, we've got to do something.'" Microsoft built a software system to register refugees, making it easier for families to reunite, and then sent 400 employees to Kosovo to implement it.

Robert Nardelli, the CEO of Home Depot, participated personally in building schools and playgrounds and sponsored a program in which Home Depot employees volunteered 250,000 hours in 2004. He notes that IBM, Target, UPS, and Avon, among other firms, have strong corporate volunteering programs. "Each corporation should play to its strength. The specific tactics should be tied to the specific skills of the corporation," says Nardelli. "For us . . . it's about building things."

Beth Miller runs a consulting firm that formerly provided information consulting services. When the company couldn't recruit enough skilled programmers in a tight job market, it began a corporate-sponsored volunteering program. The program was so successful that it became a full-time concern for Miller, whose company now helps corporations form philanthropy partnerships with nonprofits. Miller found that the volunteering program made recruiting easier, reduced turnover, and enabled employees to develop in skills and leadership, leading her to believe that volunteering increases worker satisfaction. "Satisfied employees are worth their weight in gold," according to Miller. "[A volunteering] program would be especially appealing to Generation Y—those socially conscious workers now in their twenties who grew up doing community service."

Volunteering can motivate workers by increasing their sense of self esteem, fulfilling their need for achievement, and satisfying other higher-level needs. Workers whose companies support volunteering feel pride in their employer too. And corporations clearly benefit, as do communities in need. When asked about whether companies that support corporate volunteering are promoting a cause or their own self-interest, Nardelli says, "They're inseparably linked. Not only does a corporation have to provide financial value, it also has to build itself on values." For more about corporate values, see the boxed insert *Corporate Volunteering and . . . Ethics* on page 88.

References: "Caring for Community," Pfizer website, www.pfizer.com on February 28, 2005; "Volunteers by Annual Hours," Bureau of Labor Statistics website, September 2004, www.bls.gov on February 28, 2005; Jessi Hempel, "A Corporate Peace Corps Catches On," *Business Week,* January 31, 2005, www.businessweek.com on February 28, 2005; William J. Holstein, "The Snowball Effect of Volunteer Work," *The New York Times,* November 21, 2004, p. BU12 (quotation); Simon Kuper, "Office Angels," *Financial Times Weekend,* January 2, 2005, pp. W1–2; Jerry Norton, "Tsunami Relief Aid at $6.28 Billion— U.N." *Washington Post,* February 25, 2005, www.washingtonpost .com on February 28, 2005.

G iven the complex array of individual differences discussed in Chapter 3, it should be obvious that people work for a wide variety of different reasons. Some people want money, some want challenge, some want power, and some want the intrinsic pleasure that comes from helping others. What people in an organization want from work and how they think they can achieve it play an instrumental role in determining their motivation to work. As we see in this chapter, motivation is vital to all organizations. Indeed, the difference between highly effective organizations and less effective ones often lies in the motivations of their members. Thus, managers need to understand the nature of individual motivation, especially as it applies to work situations. In this chapter we first explore various need-based perspectives on motivation. We then turn our attention to the more sophisticated process-based perspectives. We conclude with a discussion of learning-based perspectives on motivation.[1]

The Nature of Motivation

Motivation is the set of forces that causes people to engage in one behavior rather than some alternative behavior.[2] Students who stay up all night to ensure that their term papers are the best they can be, salespeople who work on Saturdays to get ahead, and doctors who make follow-up phone calls to patients to check on their conditions are all motivated people. Of course, students who avoid the term paper by spending the day at the beach, salespeople who go home early to escape a tedious sales call, and doctors who skip follow-up calls to have more time for golf are also motivated, but their goals are different. From the manager's viewpoint, the objective is to motivate people to behave in ways that are in the organization's best interest.[3]

> **Motivation** is the set of forces that leads people to behave in particular ways.

The Importance of Motivation

Managers strive to motivate people in the organization to perform at high levels. This means getting them to work hard, to come to work regularly, and to make positive contributions to the organization's mission. But job performance depends on ability and environment as well as motivation. This relationship can be stated as follows:

$$P = M + A + E$$

with P = performance, M = motivation, A = ability, and E = environment. To reach high levels of performance, an employee must want to do the job well (motivation), must be able to do the job effectively (ability), and must have the materials, resources, equipment, and information to do the job (environment). A deficiency in any one of these areas hurts performance. A manager should thus strive to ensure that all three conditions are met.[4] In most settings motivation is the most difficult of these factors to manage. If an employee lacks the ability to perform, she or he can be sent to training programs to learn new job skills. If the person cannot learn those skills, she or he can be transferred to a simpler job and replaced with a more skilled worker. If an employee lacks materials, resources, equipment, and/or information, the manager can take steps to provide them. For example, if a worker cannot complete a project without sales forecast data from marketing, the manager can contact marketing and request that information. But if motivation is deficient, the manager faces the more complex situation of determining what will motivate the employee to work harder.

Motivating performance is an important role for any manager, regardless of the circumstance. Take Lance Armstrong, for instance. During his unprecedented string of victories in the Tour de France, he had to inspire and motivate his team members to do their best each and every day as they pushed forward to victory. And they had to excel under arduous conditions and with no hope of winning—since their job was to help Armstrong!

The Motivational Framework

We can start to understand motivation by looking at need deficiencies and goal-directed behaviors. Figure 4.1 shows the basic motivational framework we use to organize our discussion.

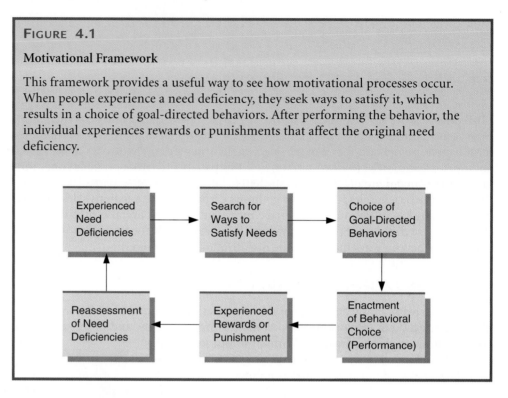

FIGURE 4.1

Motivational Framework

This framework provides a useful way to see how motivational processes occur. When people experience a need deficiency, they seek ways to satisfy it, which results in a choice of goal-directed behaviors. After performing the behavior, the individual experiences rewards or punishments that affect the original need deficiency.

A **need** is anything an individual requires or wants.

A **need**—something an individual requires or wants—is the starting point.[5] Motivated behavior usually begins when a person has one or more important needs. Although a need that is already satisfied may also motivate behavior (for example, the need to maintain a standard of living one has already achieved), unmet needs usually result in more intense feelings and behavioral changes. For example, if a person has yet to attain the standard of living she desires, this unmet need may stimulate her to action.

A need deficiency usually triggers a search for ways to satisfy it. Consider a person who feels her salary and position are deficient because she wants more income and because they do not reflect the importance to the organization of the work she does. She may feel she has three options: to simply ask for a raise and a promotion, to work harder in the hope of earning a raise and a promotion, or to look for a new job with a higher salary and a more prestigious title.

Next comes a choice of goal-directed behaviors. Although a person might pursue more than one option at a time (such as working harder while also looking for another job), most effort is likely to be directed at one option. In the next phase, the person actually carries out the behavior chosen to satisfy the need. She will probably begin putting in longer hours, working harder, and so forth. She will next experience either rewards or punishment as a result of this choice. She may perceive her situation to be punishing if she ends up earning no additional recognition and not getting a promotion or pay raise. Alternatively, she may actually be rewarded by getting the raise and promotion because of her higher performance.

Finally, the person assesses the extent to which the outcome achieved fully addresses the original need deficiency. Suppose the person wanted a 10 percent raise and a promotion to vice president. If she got both, she should be satisfied. On the other hand, if she got only a 7 percent raise and a promotion to associate vice president, she will have to decide whether to keep trying, to accept what she got, or to choose one of the other options considered earlier. (Sometimes, of course, a need may go unsatisfied altogether despite the person's best efforts.)

Historical Perspectives on Motivation

Historical views on motivation, although not always accurate, are of interest for several reasons. For one thing, they provide a foundation for contemporary thinking about motivation. For another, because they generally were based on common sense and intuition, an appreciation of their strengths and weaknesses can help managers gain useful insights into employee motivation in the workplace (we discuss these historical perspectives more fully in Appendix B).

The Traditional Approach   One of the first writers to address work motivation—over a century ago—was Frederick Taylor. Taylor developed a method for structuring jobs that he called **scientific management**. As one basic premise of this approach, Taylor assumed that employees are economically motivated and work to earn as much money as they can.[6] Hence, he advocated incentive pay systems. He believed that managers knew more about the jobs being performed than did workers, and he assumed that economic gain was the primary thing that motivated everyone. Other assumptions of the traditional approach were that work is inherently unpleasant for most people and that the money they earn is more important to employees than the nature of the job they are performing. Hence, people could be expected to perform any kind of job if they were paid enough. Although the role of money as a motivating factor cannot be dismissed, proponents of the traditional approach took too narrow a view of the role of monetary compensation and also failed to consider other motivational factors.

> The **scientific management approach** assumes that employees are motivated by money.

The Human Relations Approach   The human relations approach supplanted scientific management in the 1930s.[7] The **human relations approach** assumed that employees want to feel useful and important, that employees have strong social needs, and that these needs are more important than money in motivating employees. Advocates of the human relations approach advised managers to make workers feel important and allow them a modicum of self-direction and self-control in carrying out routine activities. The illusion of involvement and importance were expected to satisfy workers' basic social needs and result in higher motivation to perform. For example, a manager might allow a work group to participate in making a decision, even though he or she had already determined what the decision would be. The symbolic gesture of seeming to allow participation was expected to enhance motivation, even though no real participation took place.

> The **human relations approach** to motivation suggests that favorable employee attitudes result in motivation to work hard.

The Human Resource Approach   The **human resource approach** to motivation carries the concepts of needs and motivation one step farther. Whereas the human relationists believed that the illusion of contribution and participation would enhance motivation, the human resource view, which began to emerge in the 1950s, assumes that the contributions themselves are valuable to both individuals and organizations. It assumes that people want to contribute and are able to make genuine contributions. Management's task, then, is to encourage participation and to create a work environment that makes full use of the human resources available. This philosophy guides most contemporary thinking about employee motivation. At Ford, Westinghouse, Texas Instruments, and Hewlett-Packard, for example, work teams are being called upon to solve a variety of problems and to make substantive contributions to the organization.

> The **human resource approach** to motivation assumes that people want to contribute and are able to make genuine contributions.

Need-Based Perspectives on Motivation

Need-based theories of motivation assume that need deficiencies cause behavior.

Need-based perspectives represent the starting point for most contemporary thought on motivation, although these theories also attract critics.[8] The basic premise of **need-based theories** and models, consistent with our motivation framework introduced earlier, is that humans are motivated primarily by deficiencies in one or more important needs or need categories. The *Corporate Volunteering and . . . Ethics* box highlights the role of needs when people choose to volunteer their time to help others. Need theorists have attempted to identify and categorize the needs that are most important to people. (Some observers call these "content theories" because they deal with the content, or substance, of what motivates behavior.) The best-known need theories are the hierarchy of needs and the ERG theory.

Corporate Volunteering and . . .  ETHICS

Volunteering as a Motivator

Companies with corporate volunteering programs are operating at a highly ethical level. They satisfy the needs of workers and local communities despite the costs. Other organizations are also promoting volunteers, including firms that support philanthropic corporations and media organizations that recognize ethical firms.

Firms such as Atlanta-based MA&A Group help corporations with "corporate social investing," building long-term relationships with community organizations. MA&A uses author Curt Weeden's definition: "Corporate social investing is a strategic plan that sets specific goals for contributions, targets its giving toward causes that provide return to the company, and gives shareholders a means to hold the company accountable for its nonprofit investments."

Numerous nonprofit firms also support philanthropy. Social Venture Partners (SVP) works like a venture capital firm, distributing corporate donations to promising nonprofits and coordinating corporate volunteers in areas from marketing to technology. Building Blocks International (BBI) recruits corporate managers to volunteer overseas on long-term projects, in a program they named Global Social Entrepreneur. Rick Van der Kamp, a manager from Accenture consulting firm, reports that his BBI experience was "great preparation for a continued career . . . I have the confidence and capability to take on challenges I would have shied away from before."

Media is important too, because it provides the positive public relations companies desire. The Committee to Encourage Corporate Philanthropy annually selects corporations, including Target, Hasbro, and Whole Foods, with excellent records for philanthropy. *Fast Company,* a magazine devoted to emerging business issues, developed an innovative award for nonprofits that highlights outstanding achievement. In 2005, award winners included College Summit, which educated thousands of low-income high school students about the college application process.

Volunteering is a benefit to workers, corporations, and communities. Corporations that actively assist volunteers deserve applause. So, too, do those organizations that help and support corporations in this worthwhile endeavor.

> *"I have the confidence and capability to take on challenges I would have shied away from before."*
>
> RICK VAN DER KAMP, ACCENTURE

References: "About SVP," "SVP Investments and Outcomes," Social Venture Partners website, www.svpseattle.org on February 28, 2005; "MA&A Group, Inc.," MA&A Group website, www.maagroup.com on February 28, 2005; "Participant's Profiles," Building Blocks International website, www.bblocks.org on February 28, 2005 (quotation); "Programs on Philanthropy/Excellence Awards," Committee to Encourage Corporate Philanthropy website, www.corpphilanthropy.org on February 28, 2005; "Social Capitalists," *Fast Company,* January 2005, www.fastcompany.com on February 28, 2005.

The Hierarchy of Needs

The hierarchy of needs, developed by psychologist Abraham Maslow in the 1940s, is the best-known needs theory.[9] Influenced by the human relations school, Maslow argued that human beings are "wanting" animals: They have innate desires to satisfy a given set of needs. Furthermore, Maslow believed that these needs are arranged in a hierarchy of importance, with the most basic needs at the foundation of the hierarchy.

Figure 4.2 shows **Maslow's hierarchy of needs**. The three sets of needs at the bottom of the hierarchy are called deficiency needs, because they must be satisfied for the individual to be fundamentally comfortable. The top two sets of needs are termed growth needs because they focus on personal growth and development.

The most basic needs in the hierarchy are *physiological needs*. They include the needs for food, sex, and air. Next in the hierarchy are *security needs:* things that offer safety and security, such as adequate housing and clothing and freedom from worry and anxiety. *Belongingness needs*, the third level in the hierarchy, are primarily social. Examples include the need for love and affection and the need to be accepted by peers. The fourth level, *esteem needs*, actually encompasses two slightly different kinds of needs: the need for a positive self-image and self-respect and the need to be respected by others. At the top of the hierarchy are *self-actualization needs*. These involve a person's realizing her full potential and becoming all that she can be.

Maslow believed that each need level must be satisfied before the level above it can become important. Thus, once physiological needs have been satisfied, their importance diminishes, and security needs emerge as the primary sources of motivation. This escalation up the hierarchy continues until the self-actualization needs become the primary motivators. Suppose, for example, that Jennifer Wallace earns all the money she needs and is very satisfied with her standard of living. Additional income may have little or no motivational impact on her behavior. Instead, Jennifer will strive to satisfy other needs, such as a desire for higher self-esteem.

However, if a previously satisfied lower-level set of needs becomes deficient again, the individual returns to that level. For example, suppose that Jennifer unexpectedly loses her job. At first, she may not be too worried because she has savings and confidence that she can find another good job. As her savings dwindle, however, she will become increasingly

> **Maslow's hierarchy of needs theory** assumes that human needs are arranged in a hierarchy of importance.

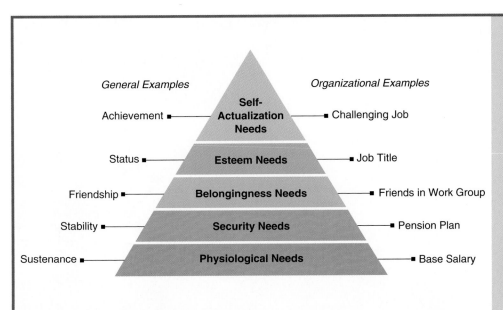

FIGURE 4.2

The Hierarchy of Needs

Maslow's hierarchy of needs consists of five basic categories of needs. This figure illustrates both general and organizational examples of each type of need. Of course, each individual has a wide variety of specific needs within each category.

Reference: Adapted from Abraham H. Maslow, "A Theory of Human Motivation," *Psychological Review,* 1943, vol. 50, pp. 374–396.

General Examples — *Organizational Examples*

Achievement ■—— **Self-Actualization Needs** ——■ Challenging Job

Status ■—— **Esteem Needs** ——■ Job Title

Friendship ■—— **Belongingness Needs** ——■ Friends in Work Group

Stability ■—— **Security Needs** ——■ Pension Plan

Sustenance ■—— **Physiological Needs** ——■ Base Salary

motivated to seek new income. Initially, she may seek a job that both pays well and that satisfies her esteem needs. But as her financial situation grows increasingly worse, she may lower her expectations regarding esteem and instead focus almost exclusively on simply finding a job with a reliable paycheck.

In most businesses, physiological needs are probably the easiest to evaluate and to meet. Adequate wages, toilet facilities, ventilation, and comfortable temperatures and working conditions are measures taken to satisfy this most basic level of needs. Security needs in organizations can be satisfied by such things as job continuity (no layoffs), a grievance system (to protect against arbitrary supervisory actions), and an adequate insurance and retirement system (to guard against financial loss from illness and to ensure retirement income).

Most employees' belongingness needs are satisfied by family ties and group relationships both inside and outside the organization. In the workplace, people usually develop friendships that provide a basis for social interaction and can play a major role in satisfying social needs. Managers can help satisfy these needs by fostering a sense of group identity and interaction among employees. At the same time, managers can be sensitive to the probable effects on employees (such as low performance and absenteeism) of family problems or lack of acceptance by coworkers. Esteem needs in the workplace are met at least partially by job titles, choice offices, merit pay increases, awards, and other forms of recognition. Of course, to be sources of long-term motivation, tangible rewards such as these must be distributed equitably and be based on performance.

Self-actualization needs are perhaps the hardest to understand and the most difficult to satisfy. For example, it is difficult to assess how many people completely meet their full potential. In most cases, people who are doing well on Maslow's hierarchy will have satisfied their esteem needs and will be moving toward self-actualization. Working toward self-actualization, rather than actually achieving it, may be the ultimate motivation for most people. In recent years there has been a pronounced trend toward people leaving well-paying but less fulfilling jobs to take lower-paying but more fulfilling jobs such as nursing and teaching. This might indicate that they are actively working toward self-actualization.[10]

People can be motivated by a wide variety of factors. Jay Schwartz provides a vivid example. After a distinguished and lucrative career as Director of Institutional Financial Strategies for a major insurance company, he decided to seek greater fulfillment as a high school math teacher in the Bronx. Mr. Schwartz is shown here with 9,000 of his new colleagues filling out orientation forms before their school year opens.

Research shows that the need hierarchy does not generalize very well to other countries. In Greece and Japan, for example, security needs may motivate employees more than self-actualization needs. Likewise, belongingness needs are especially important in Sweden, Norway, and Denmark. Research has also found differences in the relative importance of different needs in Mexico, India, Peru, Canada, Thailand, Turkey, and Puerto Rico.[11]

Maslow's need hierarchy makes a certain amount of intuitive sense. And because it was the first motivation theory to become popular, it is also one of the best known among practicing managers. However, research has revealed a number of deficiencies in the theory. For example, five levels of needs are not always present, the actual hierarchy of needs does not always conform to Maslow's model, and need structures are more unstable and variable than the theory would lead us to believe.[12] And sometimes managers are overly clumsy or superficial in their attempts to use a theory such as this one. Thus, the theory's primary contribution seems to lie in providing a general framework for categorizing needs.

ERG Theory

The **ERG theory**, developed by Yale psychologist Clayton Alderfer, is another historically important need theory of motivation.[13] In many respects, ERG theory extends and refines Maslow's needs hierarchy concept, although there are also several important differences between the two. The *E, R,* and *G* stand for three basic need categories: existence, relatedness, and growth. *Existence needs*—those necessary for basic human survival—roughly correspond to the physiological and security needs of Maslow's hierarchy. *Relatedness needs*, those involving the need to relate to others, are similar to Maslow's belongingness and esteem needs. Finally, *growth needs* are analogous to Maslow's needs for self-esteem and self-actualization.

The **ERG theory** describes existence, relatedness, and growth needs.

In contrast to Maslow's approach, ERG theory suggests that more than one kind of need, for example, relatedness and growth needs, may motivate a person at the same time. A more important difference from Maslow's hierarchy is that ERG theory includes a satisfaction-progression component and a frustration-regression component. The satisfaction-progression concept suggests that after satisfying one category of needs, a person progresses to the next level. On this point, the need hierarchy and ERG theory agree. The need hierarchy, however, assumes the individual remains at the next level until the needs at that level are satisfied. In contrast, the frustration-regression component of ERG theory suggests that a person who is frustrated by trying to satisfy a higher level of needs eventually will regress to the preceding level.[14]

Suppose, for instance, that Nick Hernandez has satisfied his basic needs at the relatedness level and now is trying to satisfy his growth needs. That is, he has many friends and social relationships and is now trying to learn new skills and advance in his career. For a variety of reasons, such as organizational constraints (i.e., few challenging jobs, a glass ceiling, etc.) and the lack of opportunities to advance, he is unable to satisfy those needs. No matter how hard he tries, he seems stuck in his current position. According to ERG theory, frustration of his growth needs will cause Nick's relatedness needs to once again become dominant as motivators. As a result, he will put renewed interest into making friends and developing social relationships.

The Dual-Structure Theory

Another important need-based theory of motivation is the **dual-structure theory**, which in many ways is similar to the need theories just discussed. This theory was originally called the "two-factor theory," but the more contemporary name used here

The **dual-structure theory** identifies motivation factors, which affect satisfaction, and hygiene factors, which determine dissatisfaction.

is more descriptive. This theory has played a major role in managerial thinking about motivation, and even though few researchers today accept the theory, it is nevertheless widely known and accepted among practicing managers.

Development of the Theory   Frederick Herzberg and his associates developed the dual-structure theory in the late 1950s and early 1960s.[15] Herzberg began by interviewing approximately two hundred accountants and engineers in Pittsburgh. He asked them to recall times when they felt especially satisfied and motivated by their jobs and times when they felt particularly dissatisfied and unmotivated. He then asked them to describe what caused the good and bad feelings. The responses to the questions were recorded by the interviewers and later subjected to content analysis. (In a content analysis, the words, phrases, and sentences used by respondents are analyzed and categorized according to their meanings.)

To his surprise, Herzberg found that entirely different sets of factors were associated with the two kinds of feelings about work. For example, a person who indicated "low pay" as a source of dissatisfaction would not necessarily identify "high pay" as a source of satisfaction and motivation. Instead, people associated entirely different causes, such as recognition or achievement, with satisfaction and motivation. The findings led Herzberg to conclude that prevailing thinking about satisfaction and motivation was incorrect. As Figure 4.3 shows, at the time job satisfaction was being viewed as a single construct ranging from satisfaction to dissatisfaction. If this were the case, Herzberg reasoned, one set of factors should therefore influence movement back and forth along the continuum. But because his research had identified differential influences from two different sets of factors, Herzberg argued that two different dimensions must be involved. Thus, he saw motivation as a dual-structured phenomenon.

FIGURE 4.3	
The Dual-Structure Theory of Motivation The traditional view of satisfaction suggested that satisfaction and dissatisfaction were opposite ends of a single dimension. Herzberg's dual-structure theory found evidence of a more complex view. In this theory, motivation factors affect one dimension, ranging from satisfaction to no satisfaction. Other workplace characteristics, called "hygiene factors," are assumed to affect another dimension, ranging from dissatisfaction to no dissatisfaction.	**The Traditional View** Satisfaction ⟷ Dissatisfaction **Herzberg's View** Satisfaction ⟷ No Satisfaction *Motivation Factors* ■ Achievement ■ Recognition ■ The Work Itself ■ Responsibility ■ Advancement and Growth Dissatisfaction ⟷ No Dissatisfaction *Hygiene Factors* ■ Supervision ■ Working Conditions ■ Interpersonal Relationships ■ Pay and Job Security ■ Company Policies

Figure 4.3 also illustrates the dual-structure concept that there is one dimension ranging from satisfaction to no satisfaction and another ranging from dissatisfaction to no dissatisfaction. The two dimensions must presumably be associated with the two sets of factors identified in the initial interviews. Thus, this theory proposed, employees might be either satisfied or not satisfied and, at the same time, dissatisfied or not dissatisfied.[16]

In addition, Figure 4.3 lists the primary factors identified in Herzberg's interviews. **Motivation factors** such as achievement and recognition were often cited by people as primary causes of satisfaction and motivation. When present in a job, these factors apparently could cause satisfaction and motivation; when they were absent, the result was feelings of no satisfaction rather than dissatisfaction. The other set of factors, **hygiene factors**, came out in response to the question about dissatisfaction and lack of motivation. The respondents suggested that pay, job security, supervisors, and working conditions, if seen as inadequate, could lead to feelings of dissatisfaction. When these factors were considered acceptable, however, the person still was not necessarily satisfied; rather, he or she was simply not dissatisfied.[17]

To use the dual-structure theory in the workplace, Herzberg recommended a two-stage process. First, the manager should try to eliminate situations that cause dissatisfaction, which Herzberg assumed to be the more basic of the two dimensions. For example, suppose that Susan Kowalski wants to use the dual-structure theory to enhance motivation in the group of seven technicians she supervises. Her first goal would be to achieve a state of no dissatisfaction by addressing hygiene factors. Imagine, for example, that she discovers that their pay is a bit below market rates and that a few of them are worried about job security. Her response would be to secure a pay raise for them and to allay their concerns about job security.

According to the theory, once a state of no dissatisfaction exists, trying to further improve motivation through hygiene factors is a waste of time.[18] At that point, the motivation factors enter the picture. Thus, when Susan Kowalski is sure that she has adequately dealt with hygiene issues, she should try to increase opportunities for achievement, recognition, responsibility, advancement, and growth. As a result, she would be helping her subordinates feel satisfied and motivated.

Unlike many other theorists, Herzberg described explicitly how managers could apply his theory. In particular, he developed and described a technique called "job enrichment" for structuring employee tasks.[19] (We discuss job enrichment in Chapter 5.) Herzberg tailored this technique to his key motivation factors. This unusual attention to application may explain the widespread popularity of the dual-structure theory among practicing managers.

Motivation factors are intrinsic to the work itself and include factors such as achievement and recognition.

Hygiene factors are extrinsic to the work itself and include factors such as pay and job security.

Evaluation of the Theory Because it gained popularity so quickly, the dual-structure theory has been scientifically scrutinized more than almost any other organizational behavior theory.[20] The results have been contradictory, to say the least. The initial study by Herzberg and his associates supported the basic premises of the theory, as did a few follow-up studies.[21] In general, studies that use the same methodology as Herzberg did (content analysis of recalled incidents) tend to support the theory. However, this methodology has itself been criticized, and studies that use other methods to measure satisfaction and dissatisfaction frequently obtain results quite different from Herzberg's.[22] If the theory is "method bound," as it appears to be, its validity is therefore questionable.

Several other criticisms have been directed against the dual-structure theory. Critics say the original sample of accountants and engineers may not represent the general working population. Furthermore, they maintain that the theory fails to account for individual differences. Also, subsequent research has found that a factor such as pay may affect satisfaction in one sample and dissatisfaction in another and that the effect of a given factor depends on the individual's age and organizational level. In addition, the theory does not define the relationship between satisfaction and motivation.

Research has also suggested that the dual-structure framework varies across cultures. Only limited studies have been conducted, but findings suggest that employees in New Zealand and Panama assess the impact of motivation and hygiene factors differently than U.S. workers.[23] It is not surprising, then, that the dual-structure theory is no longer held in high esteem by organizational behavior researchers. Indeed, the field has since adopted far more complex and valid conceptualizations of motivation, most of which we discuss in Chapter 6. But because of its initial popularity and its specific guidance for application, the dual-structure theory merits a special place in the history of motivation research.

Other Important Needs

Each theory discussed so far describes interrelated sets of important individual needs within specific frameworks. Several other key needs have been identified; these needs are not allied with any single integrated theoretical perspective. The three most frequently mentioned are the needs for achievement, affiliation, and power.

The **need for achievement** is the desire to accomplish a task or goal more effectively than was done in the past.

The Need for Achievement   The **need for achievement** is most frequently associated with the work of David McClelland.[24] This need arises from an individual's desire to accomplish a goal or task more effectively than in the past. Individuals who have a high need for achievement tend to set moderately difficult goals and to make moderately risky decisions. Suppose, for example, that Mark Cohen, a regional manager for a national retailer, sets a sales increase goal for his stores of either 1 percent or 50 percent. The first goal is probably too easy and the second is probably impossible to reach; either would suggest a low need for achievement. But a mid-range goal of, say, 15 percent might present a reasonable challenge and also be within reach. Setting this goal might more accurately reflect a high need for achievement.

High-need achievers also want immediate, specific feedback on their performance. They want to know how well they did something as quickly after finishing it as possible. For this reason, high-need achievers frequently take jobs in sales, where they get almost immediate feedback from customers, and avoid jobs in areas such as research and development, where tangible progress is slower and feedback comes at longer intervals. If Mark Cohen asks his managers for their sales performance only on a periodic basis, he might not have a high need for achievement. But if he is constantly calling each store manager in his territory to ask about their sales increases, this activity indicates a high need for achievement on his part.

Preoccupation with work is another characteristic of high-need achievers. They think about it on their way to the workplace, during lunch, and at home. They find it difficult to put their work aside, and they become frustrated when they must stop working on a partly completed project. If Cohen seldom thinks about his business in the evening, he may not be a high-need achiever. However, if work is always on his mind, he might indeed be a high-need achiever.

Finally, high-need achievers tend to assume personal responsibility for getting things done. They often volunteer for extra duties and find it difficult to delegate part of a job to someone else. Accordingly, they derive a feeling of accomplishment when they have done more work than their peers without the assistance of others. Suppose Mark Cohen visits a store one day and finds that the merchandise is poorly displayed, that the floor is dirty, and that sales clerks don't seem motivated to help customers. If he has a low need for achievement, he might point out the problems to the store manager and then leave.

But if his need for achievement is high, he may very well stay in the store for a while, personally supervising the changes that need to be made.

Although high-need achievers tend to be successful, they often do not achieve top management posts. The most common explanation is that although a high need for achievement helps these people advance quickly through the ranks, the traits associated with the need often conflict with the requirements of high-level management positions. Because of the amount of work they are expected to do, top executives must be able to delegate tasks to others. In addition, they seldom receive immediate feedback, and they often must make decisions that are either more or less risky than those with which a high-need achiever would be comfortable.[25] High-need achievers tend to do well as individual entrepreneurs with little or no group reinforcement. Steve Jobs, the co-founder of Apple Computer, and Bill Gates, the co-founder of Microsoft, are both recognized as being high-need achievers.

The Need for Affiliation Individuals also experience the **need for affiliation**—the need for human companionship.[26] Researchers recognize several ways that people with a high need for affiliation differ from those with a lower need. Individuals with a high need tend to want reassurance and approval from others and usually are genuinely concerned about others' feelings. They are likely to act and think as they believe others want them to, especially those with whom they strongly identify and desire friendship. As we might expect, people with a strong need for affiliation most often work in jobs with a lot of interpersonal contact, such as sales and teaching positions.

> The **need for affiliation** is the need for human companionship.

For example, suppose that Watanka Jackson is seeking a job as a geologist or petroleum field engineer, a job that will take her into remote areas for long periods of time with little interaction with coworkers. Aside from her academic training, one reason for the nature of her job search might be that she has a low need for affiliation. In contrast, a classmate of hers, William Pfeffer, may be seeking a job in the corporate headquarters of a petroleum company. His preferences might be dictated, at least in part, by a desire to be around other people in the workplace; he thus has a higher need for affiliation. A recent Gallup survey suggests that people who have at least one good friend at work are much more likely to be highly engaged with their work and to indicate higher levels of job satisfaction.[27]

The Need for Power A third major individual need is the **need for power**—the desire to control one's environment, including financial, material, informational, and human resources.[28] People vary greatly along this dimension. Some individuals spend much time and energy seeking power; others avoid power if at all possible. People with a high need for power can be successful managers if three conditions are met. First, they must seek power for the betterment of the organization rather than for their own interests. Second, they must have a fairly low need for affiliation because fulfilling a personal need for power may well alienate others in the workplace. Third, they need plenty of self-control to curb their desire for power when it threatens to interfere with effective organizational or interpersonal relationships.[29]

> The **need for power** is the desire to control the resources in one's environment.

Process-Based Perspectives on Motivation

Process-based perspectives are concerned with how motivation occurs. Rather than attempting to identify motivational stimuli, process-based perspectives focus on why people choose certain behavioral options to satisfy their needs and how they evaluate their satisfaction after they have attained these goals. Three useful process-based perspectives on motivation are the equity, expectancy, and goal-setting theories.

> The **process-based perspectives on motivation** focus on how people behave in their efforts to satisfy their needs.

The equity theory of motivation suggests that people compare themselves with others in terms of their inputs to their organization relative to their outcomes. But in these days of high-stress jobs and overworked employees, equity perceptions may be about as stable as a house of cards. Take Sherri Stoddard, for example. Stoddard is a registered nurse. Efforts to lower healthcare costs have caused nurses to take on ever-growing patient loads. In addition, they often have mandatory overtime requirements and mountains of paperwork. While their compensation has grown slightly, many nurses like Stoddard are feeling that they are being asked to do too much for what they are paid.

The Equity Theory of Motivation

The **equity theory** of motivation is based on the relatively simple premise that people in organizations want to be treated fairly.[30] The theory defines **equity** as the belief that we are being treated fairly in relation to others and **inequity** as the belief that we are being treated unfairly compared with others. Equity theory is just one of several theoretical formulations derived from social comparison processes. Social comparisons involve evaluating our own situation in terms of others' situations. The equity theory is the most highly developed of the social comparison approaches and the one that applies most directly to the work motivation of people in organizations.

Forming Equity Perceptions   People in organizations form perceptions of the equity of their treatment through a four-step process. First, they evaluate how they are being treated by the firm. Second, they form a perception of how a "comparison-other" is being treated. The comparison-other might be a person in the same work group, someone in another part of the organization, or even a composite of several people scattered throughout the organization.[31] Third, they compare their own circumstances with those of the comparison-other and then use this comparison as the basis for forming an impression of either equity or inequity. Fourth, depending on the strength of this feeling, the person may choose to pursue one or more of the alternatives discussed in the next section.

Equity theory focuses on people's desire to be treated with what they perceive as equity and to avoid perceived inequity.

Equity is the belief that we are being treated fairly in relation to others; **inequity** is the belief that we are being treated unfairly in relation to others.

Equity theory describes the equity comparison process in terms of an input-to-outcome ratio. Inputs are an individual's contributions to the organization—such factors as education, experience, effort, and loyalty. Outcomes are what the person receives in return—pay, recognition, social relationships, intrinsic rewards, and similar things. In effect, then, this part of the equity process is essentially a personal assessment of one's psychological contract. A person's assessments of inputs and outcomes for both self and others are based partly on objective data (for example, the person's own salary) and partly on perceptions (such as the comparison-other's level of recognition). The equity comparison thus takes the following form:

$$\frac{\text{Outcome (self)}}{\text{Inputs (self)}} \quad \text{compared with} \quad \frac{\text{Outcomes (other)}}{\text{Inputs (other)}}$$

If the two sides of this psychological equation are comparable, the person experiences a feeling of equity; if the two sides do not balance, a feeling of inequity results. We

should stress, however, that a perception of equity does not require that the perceived outcomes and inputs be equal, but only that their ratios be the same. A person may believe that his comparison-other deserves to make more money because she works harder, thus making her higher ratio of outcome-to-input acceptable. Only if the other person's outcomes seem disproportionate to her inputs does the comparison provoke a perception of inequity.

Responses to Equity and Inequity   Figure 4.4 summarizes the results of an equity comparison. If a person feels equitably treated, she is generally motivated to maintain the status quo. For example, she will continue to provide the same level of input to the organization as long as her outcomes do not change and the inputs and outcomes of the comparison-other do not change. But a person who is experiencing inequity—real or imagined—is motivated to reduce it. Moreover, the greater the inequity, the stronger the level of motivation.

People may use one of six common methods to reduce inequity.[32] First, we may change our own inputs. Thus, we may put more or less effort into the job, depending on which way the inequity lies, as a way to alter our ratio. If we believe we are being underpaid, for example, we may decide not to work as hard.

Second, we may change our own outcomes. We might, for example, demand a pay raise, seek additional avenues for growth and development, or even resort to stealing as a way to "get more" from the organization. Or we might alter our perceptions of the value of our current outcomes, perhaps by deciding that our present level of job security is greater and more valuable than we originally thought.

A third, more complex response is to alter our perceptions of ourselves and our behavior. After perceiving an inequity, for example, we may change our original self-assessment and decide that we are really contributing less but receiving more than we originally believed. For example, we might decide that we are not really working as many hours as we first thought—for example, that some of our time spent in the office is really just socializing and not really contributing to the organization.

Fourth, we may alter our perception of the other's inputs or outcomes. After all, much of our assessment of other people is based on perceptions, and perceptions can be changed. For example, if we feel under-rewarded, we may decide that

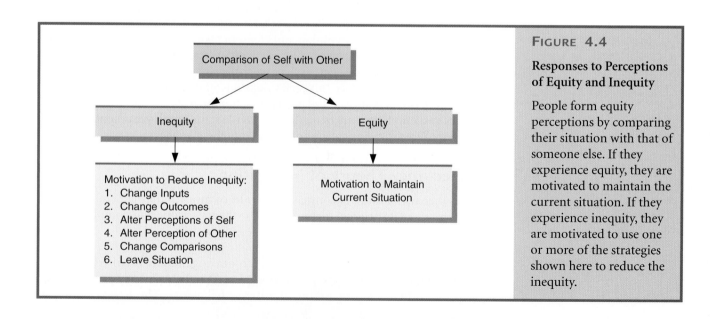

FIGURE 4.4

Responses to Perceptions of Equity and Inequity

People form equity perceptions by comparing their situation with that of someone else. If they experience equity, they are motivated to maintain the current situation. If they experience inequity, they are motivated to use one or more of the strategies shown here to reduce the inequity.

our comparison-other is working more hours than we originally believed—say by coming in on weekends and taking work home at night.

Fifth, we may change the object of comparison. We may conclude, for instance, that the current comparison-other is the boss's personal favorite, is unusually lucky, or has special skills and abilities. A different person would thus provide a more valid basis for comparison. Indeed, we might change comparison-others fairly often.

Finally, as a last resort, we may simply leave the situation. That is, we might decide that the only way to feel better about things is to be in a different situation altogether. Transferring to another department or seeking a new job may be the only way to reduce the inequity.

Evaluation and Implications   Most research on equity theory has been narrowly focused, dealing with only one ratio—between pay (hourly and piece-rate) and the quality or quantity of worker output given overpayment and underpayment.[33] Findings support the predictions of equity theory quite consistently, especially when the worker feels underpaid. When people being paid on a piece-rate basis experience inequity, they tend to reduce their inputs by decreasing quality and to increase their outcomes by producing more units of work. When a person paid by the hour experiences inequity, the theory predicts an increase in quality and quantity if the person feels overpaid and a decrease in quality and quantity if the person feels underpaid. Research provides stronger support for responses to underpayment than for responses to overpayment, but overall, most studies appear to uphold the basic premises of the theory. One interesting new twist on equity theory suggests that some people are more sensitive than others to perceptions of inequity. That is, some people pay a good deal of attention to their relative standing within the organization. Others focus more on their own situation without considering the situations of others.[34]

Social comparisons clearly are a powerful factor in the workplace. For managers, the most important implication of equity theory concerns organizational rewards and reward systems. Because "formal" organizational rewards (pay, task assignments, and so forth) are more easily observable than "informal" rewards (intrinsic satisfaction, feelings of accomplishment, and so forth), they are often central to a person's perceptions of equity.

Equity theory offers managers three messages. First, everyone in the organization needs to understand the basis for rewards. If people are to be rewarded more for high-quality work rather than for quantity of work, for instance, that fact needs to be clearly communicated to everyone. Second, people tend to take a multifaceted view of their rewards; they perceive and experience a variety of rewards, some tangible and others intangible. Finally, people base their actions on their perceptions of reality. If two people make exactly the same salary, but each thinks the other makes more, each will base his or her experience of equity on the perception, not the reality. Hence, even if a manager believes two employees are being fairly rewarded, the employees themselves may not necessarily agree if their perceptions differ from the manager's.

The Expectancy Theory of Motivation

Expectancy theory is a more encompassing model of motivation than equity theory. Over the years since its original formulation, the theory's scope and complexity have continued to grow.

The Basic Expectancy Model   Victor Vroom is generally credited with first applying the theory to motivation in the workplace.[35] The theory attempts to determine how individuals choose among alternative behaviors. The basic premise of

expectancy theory is that motivation depends on how much we want something and how likely we think we are to get it.

A simple example further illustrates this premise. Suppose a recent college graduate is looking for her first managerial job. While scanning the want ads, she sees that Shell Oil is seeking a new executive vice president to oversee its foreign operations. The starting salary is $800,000. The student would love the job, but she does not bother to apply because she recognizes that she has no chance of getting it. Reading on, she sees a position that involves scraping bubble gum from underneath desks in college classrooms. The starting pay is $5.85 an hour, and no experience is necessary. Again, she is unlikely to apply—even though she assumes she could get the job, she does not want it.

Then she comes across an advertisement for a management training position with a large company known for being an excellent place to work. No experience is necessary, the primary requirement is a college degree, and the starting salary is $37,000. She will probably apply for this position because (1) she wants it, and (2) she thinks she has a reasonable chance of getting it. (Of course, this simple example understates the true complexity of most choices. Job-seeking students may have strong geographic preferences, have other job opportunities, and also be considering graduate school. Most decisions of this type, in fact, are quite complex.)

Figure 4.5 summarizes the basic expectancy model. The model's general components are effort (the result of motivated behavior), performance, and outcomes. Expectancy theory emphasizes the linkages among these elements, which are described in terms of expectancies and valences.

Effort-to-Performance Expectancy **Effort-to-performance expectancy** is a person's perception of the probability that effort will lead to successful performance. If we believe our effort will lead to higher performance, this expectancy is very strong, perhaps approaching a probability of 1.0, where 1.0 equals absolute certainty that the outcome will occur. If we believe our performance will be the same no matter how much effort

> **Expectancy theory** suggests that people are motivated by how much they want something and the likelihood they perceive of getting it.

> **Effort-to-performance expectancy** is a person's perception of the probability that effort will lead to performance.

FIGURE 4.5

The Expectancy Theory of Motivation

The expectancy theory is the most complex model of employee motivation in organizations. As shown here, the key components of expectancy theory are effort-to-performance expectancy, performance-to-outcome expectancy, and outcomes, each of which has an associated valence. These components interact with effort, the environment, and the ability to determine an individual's performance.

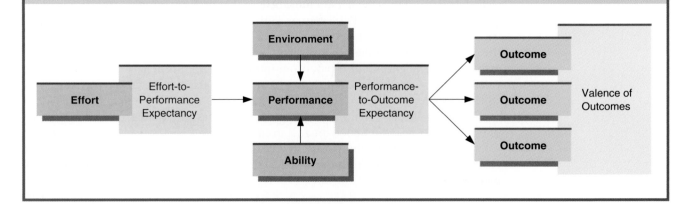

we make, our expectancy is very low—perhaps as low as 0, meaning that there is no probability that the outcome will occur. A person who thinks there is a moderate relationship between effort and subsequent performance—the normal circumstance—has an expectancy somewhere between 1.0 and 0. Mia Hamm, a star soccer player who believes that she has a great chance of scoring higher than any opponent when she puts forth maximum effort, clearly sees a link between her effort and performance.

Performance-to-outcome expectancy is the individual's perception of the probability that performance will lead to certain outcomes.

Performance-to-Outcome Expectancy   **Performance-to-outcome expectancy** is a person's perception of the probability that performance will lead to certain other outcomes. If a person thinks a high performer is certain to get a pay raise, this expectancy is close to 1.0. At the other extreme, a person who believes raises are entirely independent of performance has an expectancy close to 0. Finally, if a person thinks performance has some bearing on the prospects for a pay raise, his or her expectancy is somewhere between 1.0 and 0. In a work setting, several performance-to-outcome expectancies are relevant because, as Figure 4.5 shows, several outcomes might logically result from performance. Each outcome, then, has its own expectancy. Philadelphia's quarterback Donovan McNabb may believe that if he plays aggressively all the time (performance), he has a great chance of leading his team to the playoffs. Playing aggressively may win him individual honors like the Most Valuable Player award, but he may also experience more physical trauma and throw more interceptions. (All three anticipated results are outcomes.)

An **outcome** is anything that results from performing a particular behavior.

Valence is the degree of attractiveness or unattractiveness a particular outcome has for a person.

Outcomes and Valences   An **outcome** is anything that might potentially result from performance. High-level performance conceivably might produce such outcomes as a pay raise, a promotion, recognition from the boss, fatigue, stress, or less time to rest, among others. The **valence** of an outcome is the relative attractiveness or unattractiveness—the value—of that outcome to the person. Pay raises, promotions, and recognition might all have positive valences whereas fatigue, stress, and less time to rest might all have negative valences.

The strength of outcome valences varies from person to person. Work-related stress may be a significant negative factor for one person but only a slight annoyance to another. Similarly, a pay increase may have a strong positive valence for someone desperately in need of money, a slight positive valence for someone interested mostly in getting a promotion—or, for someone in an unfavorable tax position, even a negative valence!

The basic expectancy framework suggests that three conditions must be met before motivated behavior occurs. First, the effort-to-performance expectancy must be well above zero. That is, the worker must reasonably expect that exerting effort will produce high levels of performance. Second, the performance-to-outcome expectancies must be well above zero. Thus, the person must believe that performance will realistically result in valued outcomes. Third, the sum of all the valences for the potential outcomes relevant to the person must be positive. One or more valences may be negative as long as the positives outweigh the negatives. For example, stress and fatigue may have moderately negative valences, but if pay, promotion, and recognition have very high positive valences, the overall valence of the set of outcomes associated with performance will still be positive.

Conceptually, the valences of all relevant outcomes and the corresponding pattern of expectancies are assumed to interact in an almost mathematical fashion to determine a person's level of motivation. Most people do assess likelihoods of and preferences for various consequences of behavior, but they seldom approach them in such a calculating manner.

The Porter-Lawler Model The original presentation of expectancy theory placed it squarely in the mainstream of contemporary motivation theory. Since then, the model has been refined and extended many times. Most modifications have focused on identifying and measuring outcomes and expectancies. An exception is the variation of expectancy theory developed by Porter and Lawler. These researchers used expectancy theory to develop a novel view of the relationship between employee satisfaction and performance.[36] Although the conventional wisdom was that satisfaction leads to performance, Porter and Lawler argued the reverse: If rewards are adequate, high levels of performance may lead to satisfaction.

The Porter-Lawler model appears in Figure 4.6. Some of its features are quite different from the original version of expectancy theory. For example, the extended model includes abilities, traits, and role perceptions. At the beginning of the motivational cycle, effort is a function of the value of the potential reward for the employee (its valence) and the perceived effort-reward probability (an expectancy). Effort then combines with abilities, traits, and role perceptions to determine actual performance.

Performance results in two kinds of rewards. Intrinsic rewards are intangible—a feeling of accomplishment, a sense of achievement, and so forth. Extrinsic rewards are tangible outcomes such as pay and promotion. The individual judges the value of his or her performance to the organization and uses social comparison processes

---

FIGURE 4.6

The Porter-Lawler Model

The Porter and Lawler expectancy model provides interesting insights into the relationships between satisfaction and performance. As illustrated here, this model predicts that satisfaction is determined by the perceived equity of intrinsic and extrinsic rewards for performance. That is, rather than satisfaction causing performance, which many people might predict, this model argues that it is actually performance that eventually leads to satisfaction.

Reference: Figure from Lyman W. Porter and Edward E. Lawler, *Managerial Attitudes and Performance.* Copyright © 1968. Reproduced by permission of the publisher, McGraw-Hill, Inc.

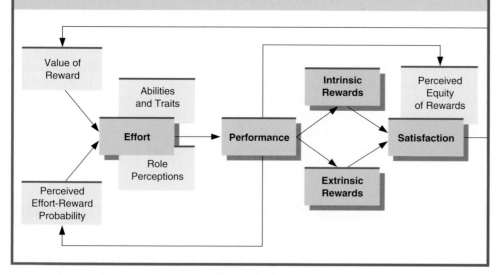

(as in equity theory) to form an impression of the equity of the rewards received. If the rewards are regarded as equitable, the employee feels satisfied. In subsequent cycles, satisfaction with rewards influences the value of the rewards anticipated, and actual performance following effort influences future perceived effort-reward probabilities.

Evaluation and Implications   Expectancy theory has been tested by many different researchers in a variety of settings and using a variety of methods.[37] As noted earlier, the complexity of the theory has been both a blessing and a curse.[38] Nowhere is this double-edged quality more apparent than in the research undertaken to evaluate the theory. Several studies have supported various parts of the theory. For example, both kinds of expectancy and valence have been found to be associated with effort and performance in the workplace.[39] Research has also confirmed expectancy theory's claims that people will not engage in motivated behavior unless they (1) value the expected rewards, (2) believe their efforts will lead to performance, and (3) believe their performance will result in the desired rewards.[40]

However, expectancy theory is so complicated that researchers have found it quite difficult to test. In particular, the measures of various parts of the model may lack validity, and the procedures for investigating relationships among the variables have often been less scientific than researchers would like. Moreover, people are seldom as rational and objective in choosing behaviors as expectancy theory implies. Still, the logic of the model, combined with the consistent, albeit modest, research support for it, suggests that the theory has much to offer.

Research has also suggested that expectancy theory is more likely to explain motivation in the United States than in other countries. People from the United States tend to be very goal oriented and to think that they can influence their own success. Thus, under the right combinations of expectancies, valences, and outcomes, they will be highly motivated. But different patterns may exist in other countries. For example, many people from Moslem countries think that God determines the outcome of every behavior, so the concept of expectancy is not applicable.[41]

Because expectancy theory is so complex, it is difficult to apply directly in the workplace. A manager would need to figure out what rewards each employee wants and how valuable those rewards are to each person, measure the various expectancies, and finally adjust the relationships to create motivation. Nevertheless, expectancy theory offers several important guidelines for the practicing manager. The following are some of the more fundamental guidelines:

1. Determine the primary outcomes each employee wants.
2. Decide what levels and kinds of performance are needed to meet organizational goals.
3. Make sure the desired levels of performance are possible.
4. Link desired outcomes and desired performance.
5. Analyze the situation for conflicting expectancies.
6. Make sure the rewards are large enough.
7. Make sure the overall system is equitable for everyone.[42]

Learning-Based Perspectives on Motivation

Learning is a relatively permanent change in behavior or behavioral potential resulting from direct or indirect experience.

Learning is another key component in employee motivation. In any organization, employees quickly learn which behaviors are rewarded and which are ignored or punished. Thus, learning plays a critical role in maintaining motivated behavior. **Learning**

is a relatively permanent change in behavior or behavioral potential that results from direct or indirect experience. For example, we can learn to use a new software application program by practicing and experimenting with its various functions and options.

How Learning Occurs

The Traditional View: Classical Conditioning   The most influential historical approach to learning is classical conditioning, developed by Ivan Pavlov in his famous experiments with dogs.[43] **Classical conditioning** is a simple form of learning in which a conditioned response is linked with an unconditioned stimulus. In organizations, however, only simple behaviors and responses can be learned in this manner. For example, suppose an employee receives very bad news one day from his boss. It's possible that the employee could come to associate, say, the color of the boss's suit that day with bad news. Thus, the next time the boss wears that same suit to the office, the employee may experience dread and foreboding.

But this form of learning is obviously simplistic and not directly relevant to motivation. Learning theorists soon recognized that although classical conditioning offered some interesting insights into the learning process, it was inadequate as an explanation of human learning. For one thing, classical conditioning relies on simple cause-and-effect relationships between one stimulus and one response; it cannot deal with the more complex forms of learned behavior that typify human beings. For another, classical conditioning ignores the concept of choice; it assumes that behavior is reflexive, or involuntary. Therefore, this perspective cannot explain situations in which people consciously and rationally choose one course of action from among many. Because of these shortcomings of classical conditioning, theorists eventually moved on to other approaches that seemed more useful in explaining the processes associated with complex learning.

Classical conditioning is a simple form of learning that links a conditioned response with an unconditioned stimulus.

The Contemporary View: Learning as a Cognitive Process   Although it is not tied to a single theory or model, contemporary learning theory generally views learning as a cognitive process; that is, it assumes that people are conscious, active participants in how they learn.[44]

First, the cognitive view suggests that people draw on their experiences and use past learning as a basis for their present behavior. These experiences represent knowledge, or cognitions. For example, an employee faced with a choice of job assignments will use previous experiences in deciding which one to accept. Second, people make choices about their behavior. The employee recognizes that she has two alternatives and chooses one. Third, people recognize the consequences of their choices. Thus, when the employee finds the job assignment rewarding and fulfilling, she will recognize that the choice was a good one and will understand why. Finally, people evaluate those consequences and add them to prior learning, which affects future choices. Faced with the same job choices next year, the employee will probably be motivated to choose the same one. As implied earlier, several perspectives on learning take a cognitive view. Perhaps foremost among them is reinforcement theory. Although reinforcement theory per se is not really new, it has been applied to organizational settings only in the last few years.

Reinforcement Theory and Learning

Reinforcement theory (also called "operant conditioning") is generally associated with the work of B. F. Skinner.[45] In its simplest form, **reinforcement theory** suggests that behavior is a function of its consequences.[46] Behavior that results in pleasant consequences is more likely to be repeated (the employee will be motivated to repeat the current

Reinforcement theory is based on the idea that behavior is a function of its consequences.

behavior), and behavior that results in unpleasant consequences is less likely to be repeated (the employee will be motivated to engage in different behaviors). Reinforcement theory also suggests that in any given situation, people explore a variety of possible behaviors. Future behavioral choices are affected by the consequences of earlier behaviors. Cognitions, as already noted, also play an important role. Therefore, rather than assuming the mechanical stimulus-response linkage suggested by the traditional classical view of learning, contemporary theorists believe that people consciously explore different behaviors and systematically choose those that result in the most desirable outcomes.

Suppose a new employee at Monsanto in St. Louis wants to learn the best way to get along with his boss. At first, the employee is very friendly and informal, but the boss responds by acting aloof and, at times, annoyed. Because the boss does not react positively, the employee is unlikely to continue this behavior. In fact, the employee next starts acting more formal and professional and finds the boss much more receptive to this posture. The employee will probably continue this new set of behaviors because they have resulted in positive consequences.

Types of Reinforcement in Organizations

The consequences of behavior are called **reinforcement**. Managers can use various kinds of reinforcement to affect employee behavior. There are four basic forms of reinforcement—positive reinforcement, avoidance, extinction, and punishment.

Positive reinforcement is a reward or other desirable consequence that follows behavior. Providing positive reinforcement after a particular behavior motivates employees to maintain or increase the frequency of that behavior. A compliment from the boss after an employee has completed a difficult job and a salary increase following a worker's period of high performance are examples of positive reinforcement. This type of reinforcement has been used at Corning's ceramics factory in Virginia, where workers receive bonuses for pulling blemished materials from assembly lines before they go into more expensive stages of production.[47]

Reinforcement is the consequences of behavior.

Positive reinforcement is a reward or other desirable consequence that a person receives after exhibiting behavior.

Positive reinforcement, of course, can be a powerful force in organizations and can help sustain motivated behaviors. But in order to really work, reinforcement should be of value to the individual and conform to one of the five schedules, as discussed in the text. However, if someone is truly desperate for a pat on the back, a simple device such as the one shown here might have some hidden market potential!
Reference: © Harley Schwadron

Avoidance, also known as **negative reinforcement**, is another means of increasing the frequency of desirable behavior. Rather than receiving a reward following a desirable behavior, the person is given the opportunity to avoid an unpleasant consequence. For example, suppose that a boss habitually criticizes employees who dress casually. To avoid criticism, an employee may routinely dress to suit the supervisor's tastes. The employee is thus motivated to engage in desirable behavior (at least from the supervisor's viewpoint) to avoid an unpleasant, or aversive, consequence.

Extinction decreases the frequency of behavior, especially behavior that was previously rewarded. If rewards are withdrawn for behaviors that were previously reinforced, the behaviors will probably become less frequent and eventually die out. For example, a manager with a small staff may encourage frequent visits from subordinates as a way of keeping in touch with what is going on. Positive reinforcement might include cordial conversation, attention to subordinates' concerns, and encouragement to come in again soon. As the staff grows, however, the manager may find that such unstructured conversations make it difficult to get her own job done. She then might begin to brush off casual conversation and reward only to-the-point "business" conversations. Withdrawing the rewards for casual chatting will probably extinguish that behavior. We should also note that if managers, inadvertently or otherwise, stop rewarding valuable behaviors such as good performance, those behaviors also may become extinct.

Punishment, like extinction, also tends to decrease the frequency of undesirable behaviors. Punishment is an unpleasant, or aversive, consequence of a behavior.[48] Examples of punishment are verbal or written reprimands, pay cuts, loss of privileges, layoffs, and termination. Many experts question the value of punishment and believe that managers use it too often and use it inappropriately. In some situations, however, punishment may be an appropriate tool for altering behavior. Many instances of life's unpleasantness teach us what to do by means of punishment. Falling off a bike, drinking too much, or going out in the rain without an umbrella all lead to punishing consequences (getting bruised, suffering a hangover, and getting wet), and we often learn to change our behavior as a result. Furthermore, certain types of undesirable behavior may have far-reaching negative effects if they go unpunished. For instance, an employee who sexually harasses a coworker, a clerk who steals money from the petty cash account, and an executive who engages in illegal stock transactions all deserve punishment.

Schedules of Reinforcement in Organizations Should the manager try to reward every instance of desirable behavior and punish every instance of undesirable behavior? Or is it better to apply reinforcement according to some plan or schedule? As you might expect, it depends on the situation. Table 4.1 summarizes five basic **schedules of reinforcement** that managers can use.

Continuous reinforcement rewards behavior every time it occurs. Continuous reinforcement is very effective in motivating desirable behaviors, especially in the early stages of learning. When reinforcement is withdrawn, however, extinction sets in very quickly. But continuous reinforcement poses serious difficulties because the manager must monitor every behavior of an employee and provide effective reinforcement. This approach, then, is of little practical value to managers. Offering partial reinforcement according to one of the other four schedules is much more typical.

Fixed-interval reinforcement is reinforcement provided on a predetermined, constant schedule. The Friday-afternoon paycheck is a good example of a fixed-interval reinforcement. Unfortunately, in many situations the fixed-interval schedule does not necessarily maintain high performance levels. If employees know the boss will drop by to check on them every day at 1:00 P.M., they may be motivated to work hard at that

---

Avoidance, or **negative reinforcement**, is the opportunity to avoid or escape from an unpleasant circumstance after exhibiting behavior.

Extinction decreases the frequency of behavior by eliminating a reward or desirable consequence that follows that behavior.

Punishment is an unpleasant, or aversive, consequence that results from behavior.

Schedules of reinforcement indicate when or how often managers should reinforce certain behaviors.

With **continuous reinforcement**, behavior is rewarded every time it occurs.

Fixed-interval reinforcement provides reinforcement on a fixed time schedule.

TABLE 4.1

Schedules of
Reinforcement

Schedule of Reinforcement	Nature of Reinforcement
Continuous	Behavior is reinforced every time it occurs.
Fixed-Interval	Behavior is reinforced according to some predetermined, constant schedule based on time.
Variable-Interval	Behavior is reinforced after periods of time, but the time span varies from one time to the next.
Fixed-Ratio	Behavior is reinforced according to the number of behaviors exhibited, with the number of behaviors needed to gain reinforcement held constant.
Variable-Ratio	Behavior is reinforced according to the number of behaviors exhibited, but the number of behaviors needed to gain reinforcement varies from one time to the next.

time, hoping to gain praise and recognition or to avoid the boss's wrath. At other times of the day, the employees probably will not work as hard because they have learned that reinforcement is unlikely except during the daily visit.

Variable-interval reinforcement also uses time as the basis for applying reinforcement, but it varies the interval between reinforcements. This schedule is inappropriate for paying wages, but it can work well for other types of positive reinforcement, such as praise and recognition, and for avoidance. Consider again the group of employees just described. Suppose that instead of coming by at exactly 1:00 P.M. every day, the boss visits at a different time each day: 9:30 A.M. on Monday, 2:00 P.M. on Tuesday, 11:00 A.M. on Wednesday, and so on. The following week, the times change. Because the employees do not know exactly when to expect the boss, they may be motivated to work hard for a longer period—until her visit. Afterward, though, they may drop back to lower levels because they have learned that she will not be back until the next day.

The fixed- and variable-ratio schedules gear reinforcement to the number of desirable or undesirable behaviors rather than to blocks of time. With **fixed-ratio reinforcement**, the number of behaviors needed to obtain reinforcement is constant. Assume, for instance, that a work group enters its cumulative performance totals into the firm's computer network every hour. The manager of the group uses the network to monitor its activities. He might adopt a practice of dropping by to praise the group every time it reaches a performance level of five hundred units. Thus, if the group does this three times on Monday, he stops by each time; if it reaches the mark only once on Tuesday, he stops by only once. The fixed-ratio schedule can be fairly effective in maintaining desirable behavior. Employees may acquire a sense of what it takes to be reinforced and may be motivated to maintain their performance.

With **variable-ratio reinforcement**, the number of behaviors required for reinforcement varies over time. An employee performing under a variable-ratio schedule is motivated to work hard because each successful behavior increases the probability that the next one will result in reinforcement. With this schedule, the exact number of behaviors needed to obtain reinforcement is not crucial; what is important is that the intervals between reinforcement not be so long that the worker gets discouraged and stops trying. The supervisor in the fixed-ratio example could reinforce his work group after it reaches performance levels of 325, 525, 450, 600, and so on. A variable-ratio schedule can be quite effective, but it is difficult and cumbersome to use when formal organizational rewards, such as pay increases and promotions, are the reinforcers. A fixed-interval system is the best way to administer these rewards.

Variable-interval reinforcement varies the amount of time between reinforcements.

Fixed-ratio reinforcement provides reinforcement after a fixed number of behaviors.

Variable-ratio reinforcement varies the number of behaviors between reinforcements.

CollabNet and . . .

Software Development Is a Team Effort

CollabNet, a software company founded by Brian Behlendorf, is changing the way that corporations create software. As an undergraduate, Behlendorf produced Apache, a software that powers 70 percent of Internet websites. If Apache cost what Microsoft charges, revenues would be $500 million, yet Behlendorf made the product free.

CollabNet is based on the same idea—that the best software is created through openness. CollabNet provides a common development environment for "over 400,000 people, in hundreds of cities, in dozens of countries, in multiple languages." Programmers around the world create code, then share the results. Companies avoid paying thousands or millions of dollars to software giants.

Avalanche, one of CollabNet's new products, is a database of open source code that is freely shared among member corporations in a cooperative arrangement. Josten's chief information officer, Andrew Black, found a program developed by Best Buy that met its needs. "That's something north of $170,000 I won't be spending on a vendor product," Black claims. "My return on investment is just fabulous."

Behlendorf wants to benefit programmers too. "Corporations have been killing the risk-taking and exploration that makes software great," Behlendorf says. "They have tried to rip the soul out of development." CollabNet's business model allows programmers to feel a greater sense of achievement, as they tackle more complex tasks. It also brings needed social and intellectual interaction to a group of workers than can often feel isolated.

Behlendorf encourages corporations to make the relationship between effort and performance clear for programmers and to reward those who contribute the most, but is modest about his impact. "I'm not enforcing a structure for social change," he claims. "I'm giving these companies the tools to do that if they wish." See this chapter's closing case, "CollabNet Overcomes the Silo Effect," to learn more about the motivating nature of the company's culture and practices.

> *"Corporations have been killing the risk-taking and exploration that makes software great."*
>
> BRIAN BEHLENDORF, FOUNDER, COLLABNET

References: "About," "How Does CollabNet Work," "Services," CollabNet website, www.collab.net on March 1, 2005; Charles Babcock, "Co-Op Puts a New Twist on Open Source," *Information Week,* September 6, 2004, www.informationweek .com on March 1, 2005; Tim Cloonan and Matt Otepka, "CollabNet Environment Enables Distributed Development Among Avalanche Cooperative Partner Organizations," CollabNet news release, www.avalanchecorporatetechnology. net on March 1, 2005; Victoria Murphy, "The Collaborator," *Forbes,* March 14, 2005, www.forbes.com on March 1, 2005 (quotation).

Social Learning in Organizations

In recent years, managers have begun to recognize the power of social learning. The subtle power of social learning is previewed in the *CollabNet and . . . Change* box. **Social learning** occurs when people observe the behaviors of others, recognize their consequences, and alter their own behavior as a result. A person can learn to do a new job by observing others or by watching videotapes. Or an employee may learn to avoid being late by seeing the boss chew out fellow workers. Social learning theory, then, suggests that individual behavior is determined by a person's cognitions and social environment. More specifically, people are presumed to learn behaviors and attitudes at least partly in response to what others expect of them.

Several conditions must be met to produce an appropriate environment for social learning. First, the behavior being observed and imitated must be relatively simple. Although we can learn by watching someone else how to push three or four buttons to

Social learning occurs when people observe the behaviors of others, recognize their consequences, and alter their own behavior as a result.

set specifications on a machine or to turn on a computer, we probably cannot learn a complicated sequence of operations for the machine or how to run a complex software package without also practicing the various steps ourselves. Second, social learning usually involves observed and imitated behavior that is concrete, not intellectual. We can learn by watching others how to respond to the different behaviors of a particular manager or how to assemble a few component parts into a final assembled product. But we probably cannot learn through simple observation how to write computer software, how to write complicated text, how to conceptualize, or how to think abstractly. Finally, for social learning to occur, we must possess the physical ability to imitate the behavior observed. Most of us, even if we watch televised baseball games or tennis matches every weekend, cannot hit a fastball like Alex Rodriguez or execute a backhand like Venus Williams.

Social learning influences motivation in a variety of ways. Many of the behaviors we exhibit in our daily work lives are learned from others. Suppose a new employee joins an existing work group. She already has some basis for knowing how to behave from her education and previous experience. However, the group provides a set of very specific cues she can use to tailor her behavior to fit her new situation. The group may indicate how the organization expects its members to dress, how people are "supposed" to feel about the boss, and so forth. Hence, the employee learns how to behave in the new situation partly in response to what she already knows and partly in response to what others suggest and demonstrate.

Organizational Behavior Modification

Learning theory alone has important implications for managers, but organizational behavior modification has even more practical applications. Organizational behavior modification is an important application of reinforcement theory some managers use to enhance motivation and performance.

Social learning plays a major role in organizations. These volunteers from Thrivent Financial are constructing a Habitat for Humanity house in a low-income neighborhood in Miami, Florida. No doubt some of the participants signed on for the program after seeing the satisfaction from such work that some of their colleagues were achieving.

Behavior Modification in Organizations   **Organizational Behavior modification**, or **OB mod**, is the application of reinforcement theory to people in organizational settings.[49] Reinforcement theory says that we can increase the frequency of desirable behaviors by linking those behaviors with positive consequences and decrease undesirable behaviors by linking them with negative consequences. OB mod characteristically uses positive reinforcement to encourage desirable behaviors in employees. Figure 4.7 illustrates the basic steps in OB mod.

The first step is to identify performance-related behavioral events—that is, desirable and undesirable behaviors. A manager of an electronics store might decide that the most important behavior for salespeople working on commission is to greet customers warmly and show them the exact merchandise they came in to see. Note in Figure 4.7 that three kinds of organizational activity are associated with this behavior: the behavioral event itself, the performance that results, and the organizational consequences that befall the individual.

Next, the manager measures baseline performance—the existing level of performance for each individual. This usually is stated in terms of a percentage frequency across different time intervals. For example, the electronics store manager may observe that a particular salesperson presently is greeting around 40 percent of the customers each day as desired. Performance management techniques, described in Chapter 6, are used for this purpose.

The third step is to identify the existing behavioral contingencies, or consequences, of performance; that is, what happens now to employees who perform at various levels? If an employee works hard, does he or she get a reward or just get tired? The electronics store manager may observe that when customers are greeted warmly and assisted competently, they buy something 40 percent of the time, whereas customers who are not properly greeted and assisted make a purchase only 20 percent of the time.

At this point, the manager develops and applies an appropriate intervention strategy. In other words, some element of the performance-reward linkage—structure, process, technology, groups, or task—is changed to make high-level performance more rewarding. Various kinds of positive reinforcement are used to guide employee behavior in desired directions. The electronics store manager might offer a sales commission plan whereby salespeople earn a percentage of the dollar amount taken in by each sale. The manager might also compliment salespeople who give appropriate greetings and ignore those who do not. This reinforcement helps shape the behavior of salespeople. In addition, an individual salesperson who does not get reinforced may imitate the behavior of more successful salespersons. In general, this step relies on the reward system in the organization, as discussed previously.

After the intervention step, the manager again measures performance to determine whether the desired effect has been achieved. If not, the manager must redesign the intervention strategy or repeat the entire process. For instance, if the salespeople in the electronics store are still not greeting customers properly, the manager may need to look for other forms of positive reinforcement—perhaps a higher commission.

If performance has increased, the manager must try to maintain the desirable behavior through some schedule of positive reinforcement. For example, higher commissions might be granted for every other sale, for sales over a certain dollar amount, and so forth. (As we saw earlier, a reinforcement schedule defines the interval at which reinforcement is given.)

Finally, the manager looks for improvements in individual employees' behavior. Here the emphasis is on offering significant longer-term rewards, such as promotions and salary adjustments, to sustain ongoing efforts to improve performance.

Organizational Behavior modification, or OB mod, is the application of reinforcement theory to people in organizational settings.

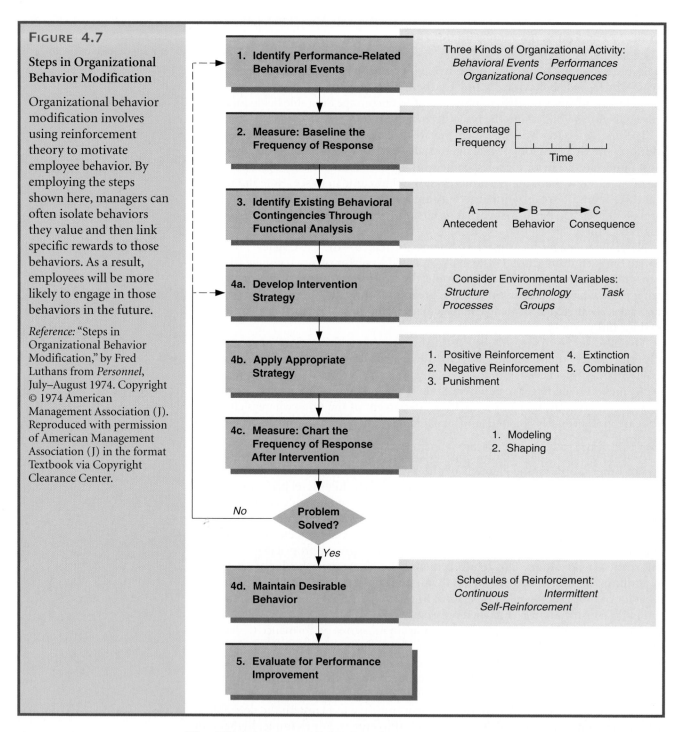

FIGURE 4.7

Steps in Organizational Behavior Modification

Organizational behavior modification involves using reinforcement theory to motivate employee behavior. By employing the steps shown here, managers can often isolate behaviors they value and then link specific rewards to those behaviors. As a result, employees will be more likely to engage in those behaviors in the future.

Reference: "Steps in Organizational Behavior Modification," by Fred Luthans from *Personnel,* July–August 1974. Copyright © 1974 American Management Association (J). Reproduced with permission of American Management Association (J) in the format Textbook via Copyright Clearance Center.

The Effectiveness of OB Mod   Since the OB mod approach is relatively simple, it has been used by many types of organizations, with varying levels of success.[50] A program at Emery Air Freight prompted much of the initial enthusiasm for OB mod, and other success stories have caught the attention of practicing managers.[51] B. F. Goodrich increased productivity over 300 percent and Weyerhaeuser increased productivity by at least 8 percent in three different work groups.[52] These results suggest that OB mod is a valuable method for improving employee motivation in many situations.

OB mod also has certain drawbacks. For one thing, not all applications have worked. A program at Standard Oil of Ohio was discontinued because it failed to meet its objectives; another program at Michigan Bell was only modestly successful. In addition, managers frequently have only limited means for providing meaningful reinforcement for their employees. Furthermore, much of the research testing OB mod has gone on in laboratories and thus is hard to generalize to the real world. And even if OB mod works for a while, the impact of the positive reinforcement may wane once the novelty has worn off, and employees may come to view it as a routine part of the compensation system.[53]

The Ethics of OB Mod   Although OB mod has considerable potential for enhancing motivated behavior in organizations, its critics raise ethical issues about its use. The primary ethical argument is that use of OB mod compromises individual freedom of choice. Managers may tend to select reinforcement contingencies that produce advantages for the organization with little or no regard for what is best for the individual employee. Thus, workers may be rewarded for working hard, producing high-quality products, and so forth. Behaviors that promote their own personal growth and development or that reduce their level of personal stress may go unrewarded.

An element of manipulation is also involved in OB mod. Indeed, its very purpose is to shape the behaviors of others. Thus, rather than giving employees an array of behaviors from which to choose, managers may continually funnel employee efforts through an increasingly narrow array of behavioral options so that they eventually have little choice but to select the limited set of behaviors approved of by managers.

These ethical issues are, of course, real concerns that should not be ignored. At the same time, many other methods and approaches used by managers have the same goal of shaping behavior. Thus, OB mod is not really unique in its potential for misuse or misrepresentation. The keys are for managers to recognize and not abuse their ability to alter subordinate behavior and for employees to maintain control of their own work environment to the point that they are fully cognizant of the behavioral choices they are making.

Chapter Review

Synopsis

Motivation is the set of forces that cause people to behave as they do. Motivation starts with a need. People search for ways to satisfy their needs and then behave accordingly. Their behavior results in rewards or punishment. To varying degrees, an outcome may satisfy the original need. Scientific management asserted that money is the primary human motivator in the workplace. The human relations view suggested that social factors are primary motivators.

According to Abraham Maslow, human needs are arranged in a hierarchy of importance, from physiological to security to belongingness to esteem and, finally, to self-actualization. The ERG theory is a refinement of Maslow's original hierarchy that includes a frustration-regression component. In Herzberg's dual-structure theory, satisfaction and dissatisfaction are two distinct dimensions instead of opposite ends of the same dimension. Motivation factors are presumed to affect satisfaction and hygiene factors to affect dissatisfaction. Herzberg's theory is well known among managers but has several deficiencies. Other important individual needs include the needs for achievement, affiliation, and power.

The equity theory of motivation assumes that people want to be treated fairly. It hypothesizes that people compare their own input-to-outcome ratio in the organization with the ratio of a comparison-other. If they feel their treatment has been inequitable, they take steps to reduce the inequity. Expectancy theory, a somewhat more complicated model, follows from the assumption that people are motivated to work toward a goal if they want it and think that they have a reasonable chance of achieving it.

Effort-to-performance expectancy is the belief that effort will lead to performance. Performance-to-outcome expectancy is the belief that performance will lead to certain outcomes. Valence is the desirability to the individual of the various possible outcomes of performance. The Porter-Lawler version of expectancy theory provides useful insights into the relationship between satisfaction and performance. This model suggests that performance may lead to a variety of intrinsic and extrinsic rewards. When perceived as equitable, these rewards lead to satisfaction.

Learning also plays a role in employee motivation. Various kinds of reinforcement provided according to different schedules can increase or decrease motivated behavior. People are affected by social learning processes. Organizational behavior modification is a strategy for using learning and reinforcement principles to enhance employee motivation and performance. This strategy relies heavily on the effective measurement of performance and the provision of rewards to employees after they perform at a high level.

Discussion Questions

1. Is it possible for someone to be unmotivated, or is all behavior motivated?

2. When has your level of performance been directly affected by your motivation? By your ability? By the environment?

3. Identify examples from your own experience that support, and others that refute, Maslow's hierarchy of needs theory.

4. Do you agree or disagree with the basic assumptions of Herzberg's dual-structure theory? Why?

5. How do you evaluate yourself in terms of your needs for achievement, affiliation, and power?

6. Have you ever experienced inequity in a job or a class? How did it affect you?

7. Which is likely to be a more serious problem—perceptions of being under-rewarded or perceptions of being over-rewarded?

8. What are some managerial implications of equity theory beyond those discussed in the chapter?

9. Do you think expectancy theory is too complex for direct use in organizational settings? Why or why not?

10. Do the relationships between performance and satisfaction suggested by Porter and Lawler seem valid? Cite examples that both support and refute the model.

11. Think of occasions on which you experienced each of the four types of reinforcement.

12. Identify the five types of reinforcement that you receive most often. On what schedule do you receive each of them?

13. What is your opinion about the ethics of OB mod?

Experiencing Organizational Behavior

Understanding the Dynamics of Expectancy Theory

Purpose: This exercise will help you recognize both the potential value and the complexity of expectancy theory.

Format: Working alone, you will be asked to identify the various aspects of expectancy theory that are pertinent to your class. You will then share your thoughts and results with some of your classmates.

Procedure: Considering your class as a workplace and your effort in the class as a surrogate for a job, do the following:

1. Identify six or seven things that might happen as a result of good performance in your class (for example,

getting a good grade or a recommendation from your instructor). Your list must include at least one undesirable outcome (for example, a loss of free time).

2. Using a value of 10 for "extremely desirable," −10 for "extremely undesirable," and 0 for "complete neutrality," assign a valence to each outcome. In other words, the valence you assign to each outcome should be somewhere between 10 and −10, inclusive.

3. Assume you are a high performer. On that basis, estimate the probability of each potential outcome. Express this probability as a percentage.

4. Multiply each valence by its associated probability and add the results. This total is your overall valence for high performance.

5. Assess the probability that if you exert effort, you will be a high performer. Express that probability as a percentage.

6. Multiply this probability by the overall valence for high performance calculated in step 4. This score reflects your motivational force—that is, your motivation to exert strong effort.

Now form groups of three or four. Compare your scores on motivational force. Discuss why some scores differ widely. Also, note whether any group members had similar force scores but different combinations of factors leading to those scores.

Follow-up Questions

1. What does this exercise tell you about the strengths and limitations of expectancy theory?

2. Would this exercise be useful for a manager to run with a group of subordinates? Why or why not?

Assessing Your Equity Sensitivity

The questions that follow are intended to help you better understand your equity sensitivity. Answer each question on the scales by circling the number that best reflects your personal feelings.

1. I think it is important for everyone to be treated fairly.

2. I pay a lot of attention to how I am treated in comparison to how others are treated.

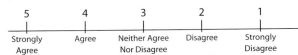

3. I get really angry if I think I'm being treated unfairly.

4. It makes me uncomfortable if I think someone else is not being treated fairly.

5. If I thought I were being treated unfairly, I would be very motivated to change things.

6. It doesn't really bother me if someone else gets a better deal than I do.

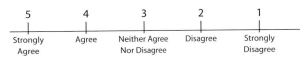

7. It is impossible for everyone to be treated fairly all the time.

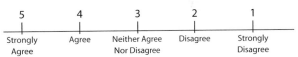

8. When I'm a manager, I'll make sure that all of my employees are treated fairly.

9. I would quit my job if I thought I was being treated unfairly.

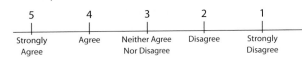

10. Short-term inequities are okay because things all even out in the long run.

Instructions: Add up your total points (note that some items have a "reversed" numbering arrangement). If you scored 35 or higher, you are highly sensitive to equity and fairness; 15 or lower, you have very little sensitivity to equity and fairness; between 35 and 15, you have moderate equity sensitivity.

Building Managerial Skills

Exercise Overview: Interpersonal skills—the ability to understand and motivate individuals and groups—are especially critical when managers attempt to deal with issues associated with equity and justice in the workplace. This exercise will provide you with insights into how these skills may be used.

Exercise Background: You are the manager of a group of professional employees in the electronics industry. One of your employees, David Brown, has asked to meet with you. You think you know what David wants to discuss, and you are unsure about how to proceed.

You hired David about ten years ago. During his time in your group, he has been a solid, but not an outstanding, employee. His performance, for example, has been satisfactory in every respect, but seldom outstanding. As a result, he has consistently received average performance evaluations, pay increases, and so forth. Indeed, he actually makes a somewhat lower salary today than do a few people in the group with less tenure but with stronger performance records.

The company has just announced an opening for a team leader position in your group, and you know that David wants the job. He feels that he has earned the opportunity to have the job on the basis of his consistent efforts. Unfortunately, you see things a bit differently. You really want to appoint another individual, Becky Thomas, to the job. Becky has worked for the firm for only six years, but she is your top performer. You want to reward her performance and think that she will do an excellent job. On the other hand, you do not want to lose David because he is a solid member of the group.

Exercise Task: Using the previous information, answer the following questions:

1. Using equity theory as a framework, how do you think David and Becky are likely to see the situation?

2. Outline a conversation with David in which you will convey your decision to him. What will you say?

3. What advice might you offer Becky in her new job? About interacting with David?

4. What other rewards might you offer David to keep him motivated?

Organizational Behavior Case for Discussion

CollabNet Overcomes the Silo Effect

Experienced managers refer to "the silo effect," in which various departments within an organization or across organizations act as if each were a stand-alone unit, ignoring important shared resources and interactions. One "silo effect" area that is a constant concern for many corporations is the tense, even hostile relationship that often exists between workers in the sales and marketing departments.

To an outsider, sales and marketing may appear to be compatible and harmonious complements—both, after all, are a bridge between the organization and its customers. Yet in many, if not most, organizations, sales-

people claim that marketers are too abstract, too academic, too focused on creativity and not focused enough on outcomes. But most of all, they claim that marketing staff doesn't understand sales, because they never have to interact directly with a customer. On the other side, marketers claim that salespeople are too egotistical, too focused on making the sale at any cost, and don't understand the organization's strategy.

According to Christopher Kenton, president of marketing firm Cymbic, neither the marketers nor the salespeople understand the relationship that should exist between them. Kenton explains the ideal relationship as similar to that between professional sports coaches and their players. "Every year [coaches] get fired while flashy players get fame and million-dollar contracts. Marketers are coaches and salespeople are players. Whatever role you choose, you need to understand that it's meaningless without your partner. If you fail to recognize you're joined at the hip, your team will lose."

How then can organizations inspire marketers and salespeople so that employees in each department are motivated, satisfied, and productive? CollabNet, a unique software company, provides a great answer. Marketing and sales departments cooperate. This requires marketing to start viewing the sales department, not the buyer, as their customer. "[Sales] is our customer. They're the ones who will be in front of the client," says CollabNet's marketing vice president Bernie Mills. "And treating sales as a customer means understanding their requirements." Rather than resenting the other department, each unit is encouraged to see the different yet equitable treatment they both receive.

Managers in both units realize that their probability of success and rewards is greater when both take on tasks that will benefit the other department. Marketing staff, for example, go on sales calls with salespeople. They meet customers, they watch negotiations, they begin to understand how to build a relationship with a customer. When CollabNet's marketing department created a sales kit for a new product launch, salespeople were involved in every aspect of the process. Mills says, "We showed up at the launch with a sales kit already [approved] by sales." These techniques ensure that the resources marketing provides are helpful and needed by the salespeople.

Sales is also doing more to support marketing. As part of a sales call, salespeople now ask questions about competing products and customer expenditures to gain useful market research for the marketing department. With constant customer contact, salespeople hear bits of market intelligence that might be useful to marketing staff, and now the relationship between the two units ensures that the intelligence is passed on.

The sales and marketing personnel seem very satisfied with the new way of conducting business. "I love our

> **❝ [Sales] is our customer. They're the ones who will be in front of the client. ❞**
> *Bernie Mills, marketing vice president, CollabNet*

marketing department," says CollabNet salesperson Bart Tilly. "They're great." Tilly lists more participation and collaboration in sales calls, meetings, and strategy formulation as some of the ways that marketing provides support to sales. Marketing vice president Mills describes himself as "thrilled" by the developments and gives the credit for the initial collaborative efforts to his counterpart in sales.

According to Mills, both departments have a lot to gain through collaboration and shared goal setting. "Sales is selling one-to-one. Marketing is selling one-to-many. For sales, that means selling deal-to-deal, quarter-to-quarter, while marketing needs to focus on the longer-term picture," Mills asserts. "We need to understand and respect that difference." Mills still sees marketing as responsible for the big picture, but adds, "Marketing needs to lead with a listening ear. Marketing doesn't need to have all the good ideas, they just need to recognize them." Sounds like CollabNet has already recognized the best idea of all—collaboration.

Case Questions

1. Describe the jobs of salesperson and marketer at a typical firm in terms of the employee needs that are being met. Then describe the jobs of salesperson and marketer at CollabNet in terms of met needs. What are the differences?

2. Use equity theory to compare inputs and outcomes for a salesperson and a marketer at CollabNet. In your opinion, does equity exist? Why or why not?

3. Based on what you read in the case, does worker satisfaction seem to lead to higher performance at CollabNet? Or does higher performance lead to satisfaction? Explain.

References: "Services," CollabNet website, www.collab.net on March 1, 2005; Christopher Kenton, "Reps and Marketers: Across the Great Divide," *Business Week,* May 26, 2004, www .businessweek.com on March 1, 2005 (quotation); Christopher Kenton, "When Sales Meets Marketing: Part I, II, and III," *Business Week,* February 19, 2005, www.businessweek.com on March 1, 2005; Victoria Murphy, "The Collaborator," *Forbes,* March 14, 2005, www.forbes.com on March 1, 2005.

TEST PREPPER

You have read the chapter and studied the key terms. Think you're ready to ace the exam? Take this sample test to gauge your comprehension of chapter material and check your answers at the back of the book. Want more test questions? Take the ACE quizzes found on the student website: http://college.hmco.com/business/students/ (select Griffin/Moorhead, Organizational Behavior, 8e from the Management menu).

T F 1. Motivation is the only factor that influences employee performance.

T F 2. The human resource approach to motivation assumed that the illusion of employee contribution and participation would enhance motivation.

T F 3. According to Alderfer's ERG theory, a person who is frustrated by trying to satisfy a higher-level need will eventually regress to the preceding level.

T F 4. High-need achievers are preoccupied with work and want immediate, specific feedback on their performance.

T F 5. According to equity theory, if you feel you are being underpaid, you will work harder.

T F 6. Reinforcement theory suggests behavior is a function of its consequences.

T F 7. The best way to administer rewards such as pay is a fixed-interval system.

8. Performance is a function of all of the following except
   a. motivation.
   b. ability.
   c. environment.
   d. organizational behavior.
   e. All of the above influence performance.

9. The easiest needs for managers to evaluate and meet are
   a. physiological needs.
   b. safety needs.
   c. belongingness needs.
   d. self-actualization needs.
   e. social needs.

10. To use Herzberg's dual-structure theory
    a. first eliminate situations that cause dissatisfaction, then focus on elements that increase satisfaction.
    b. first focus on situations that cause satisfaction, then eliminate elements that increase dissatisfaction.
    c. first focus on lower-level needs, then satisfy higher-level needs.
    d. first satisfy higher-level needs, then focus on lower-level needs.
    e. make the workplace as fair as possible.

11. The basis of equity theory is
    a. people in organizations want to be treated equally.
    b. different factors influence dissatisfaction and satisfaction.

    c. the psychological contract is irrelevant once employment begins.
    d. people in organizations want to be treated fairly.
    e. managers must focus on motivation, ability, and environment to enhance performance.

12. Samantha needs to motivate her employees to perform a difficult task. According to Vroom's expectancy theory, Samantha needs to make sure her employees believe which of the following?
    a. Outcomes will be distributed fairly.
    b. Performing the task will result in valued outcomes.
    c. High levels of performance will reduce dissatisfaction.
    d. The task satisfies self-actualization needs.
    e. Rewards for performance will increase satisfaction.

13. During the regular staff briefing each morning, Mike makes jokes at the back of the room. If Mike's manager were to use extinction to decrease the frequency of this behavior, he might
    a. send Mike out of the room the next time he made a joke.
    b. ask the other employees not to laugh at Mike's jokes.
    c. give Mike a bonus for not making jokes.
    d. glare at Mike until he stopped making jokes.
    e. ask the other employees to sit closer to Mike.

14. Organizational Behavior modification, or OB mod, uses _____ to encourage desirable behaviors in employees.
    a. punishment
    b. extinction
    c. avoidance
    d. social learning
    e. positive reinforcement

15. The primary ethical dilemma regarding Organizational Behavior modification, or OB mod, is
    a. outcomes typically exceed inputs when managers use OB mod.
    b. behaviors that promote personal growth and development are over-rewarded.
    c. use of OB mod compromises individual freedom of choice.
    d. OB mod fails to link valued outcomes with desired levels of performance.
    e. lower-level needs are left unsatisfied.

Motivating Employee Performance Through Work

CHAPTER 5

After studying this chapter,
you should be able to:

Chapter Outline

Motivation and Employee Performance

Work Design in Organizations

Employee Involvement and Motivation

Alternative Work Arrangements

- ▶ **Relate motivation and employee performance.**

- ▶ **Discuss work design, including its evolution and alternative approaches.**

- ▶ **Relate employment involvement in work and motivation.**

- ▶ **Identify and describe key alternative work arrangements.**

Happiness on the Job

Thousands of articles, books, and television shows address the unhappiness many Americans feel at work. Increased competition, longer hours, an uncertain economy, technology that allows workers to work continuously—all of these have been blamed for the trend. Employees of video game maker Electronic Arts, for example, claim they routinely work between sixty-five and eighty-five hours a week, without overtime pay, which has led to some unhappy workers and at least one lawsuit. The consequences for businesses, in terms of increased turnover, lost efficiency, low morale, and so on, is high, and the consequences for workers are even worse. Although statistics are inconclusive, observers report that white-collar injuries, illnesses, and even suicides related to work have risen recently. One study in 2000 found that 23 percent of male stockbrokers were clinically depressed, three times the national average for U.S. men.

Yet there are individuals who have found happiness. One study describes 40 percent of American workers as excited about their jobs, eager to begin work on Monday mornings, and loving what they do. In many cases, happy workers have jobs that are easy to love. Sandor Zombori was working as an engineer but always longed to cook. He walked away from his job, invested his savings in a restaurant, and twenty years later is the owner and chef at an award-winning restaurant. "All the time, I am soaking it up, like a sponge, trying to learn as much as I can," Zombori explains. Artists, game inventors, knitters, and architects have a passion to express themselves and learn, which leads to career happiness.

For others, more traditional careers hold rewards. Robert Sunday, associate marketing manager of Cheerios brand at General Mills, says about his job, "I truly love it! As the parent of a toddler, it's exciting to have the coolest job at preschool." For college professors, nurses, bank loan officers, and executive assistants, job happiness comes from satisfying intellectual curiosity, helping others, giving back to the community, and feeling needed. Sometimes the job can be defined to increase satisfaction. Richard Karlgaard is the publisher of *Forbes* magazine. He enjoys acting as an editor at large and writing about technology, while leaving most of the financial reporting to others.

Some individuals don't find their jobs rewarding and can't change the job itself. In these cases, looking elsewhere may be the best option. Mary Lou Quinlan was the CEO of a New York advertising agency, the pinnacle of her profession, but chose to quit and start a small consulting business. The pay is less but she is happier. "Finally, I'm doing something I can picture doing for a long, long time," Quinlan says. Harvard University lecturer Laura Nash agrees that individuals can be happier in their personal and professional lives if they separate notions of success and money. If you can't be a star ballerina, Nash recommends, "you can start a ballet company or design a new ballet shoe, or even supply shoes to the dancers." For another viewpoint on job happiness and unhappiness, see the boxed insert titled *Happiness and . . . Diversity* on page 121.

References: Daniel Akst, "White-Collar Stress? Stop the Whining," *New York Times,* September 19, 2004, p. BU6; Lisa Belkin, "Take This Job and Hug It," *New York Times,* February 13, 2005, p. W1 (quotation); Claudia H. Deutsch, "Grab the Brass Ring, or Just Enjoy the Ride?" *New York Times,* June 27, 2004, p. BU7; Claudia H. Deutsch, "She Didn't Stop the World, but She Slowed It Down," *New York Times,* February 13, 2005, p. BU6; Claudia H. Deutsch, "Yes, You Can Follow Your Bliss to Anytown, U.S.A." *New York Times,* October 31, 2004, p. BU7; Keith Dunnavant, "Cooking Up a New Life," *Business Week Small Biz,* Fall 2004, pp. 53–55; Randall Stross, "When Long Hours at a Video Game Stop Being Fun," *New York Times,* November 21, 2004, p. BU3; Landon Thomas Jr., "Depression, A Frequent Visitor to Wall St.," *New York Times,* September 12, 2004, pp. BU1, 9.

Managers determine what jobs will be performed in their organizations and how those jobs will be performed. But managers must also determine how to motivate people and how to optimize their performance. The long-term key to success in business is to create jobs that optimize the organization's requirements for productivity and efficiency while simultaneously motivating and satisfying the employees who perform those jobs. As people and organizations change, and as we continue to learn more about management, it is important to look back occasionally at those jobs and make whatever changes are necessary to improve them.

This chapter is the first of two that address the strategies managers use to optimize the performance of their employees. We begin with a discussion of work design, starting with a look at historical approaches. Then we discuss an important contemporary perspective on jobs, the job characteristics theory. Next, we review the importance of employee involvement through participation in their work. Finally, we discuss alternative work arrangements that can be used to enhance motivation and performance. To begin, we will introduce a general framework that can guide managers as they attempt to put into practice various theories and models of motivation.

Motivation and Employee Performance

Chapter 4 described a variety of perspectives on motivation. But no single theory or model completely explains motivation—each covers only some of the factors that actually result in motivated behavior. Moreover, even if one theory were applicable in a particular situation, a manager might still need to translate that theory into operational terms. Thus, while using the actual theories as tools, managers need to understand various operational procedures, systems, and methods for enhancing motivation and performance.

Figure 5.1 illustrates a basic framework for relating various theories of motivation to potential and actual motivation and to operational methods for translating this potential and actual motivation into performance. The left side of the figure illustrates

FIGURE 5.1

Enhancing Performance in Organizations

Managers can use a variety of methods to enhance performance in organizations. The need- and process-based perspectives on motivation explain some of the factors involved in increasing the potential for motivated behavior directed at enhanced performance. Managers can then use such means as goal setting, job design, alternative work arrangements, performance management, rewards, and organizational behavior modification to help translate this potential into actual enhanced performance.

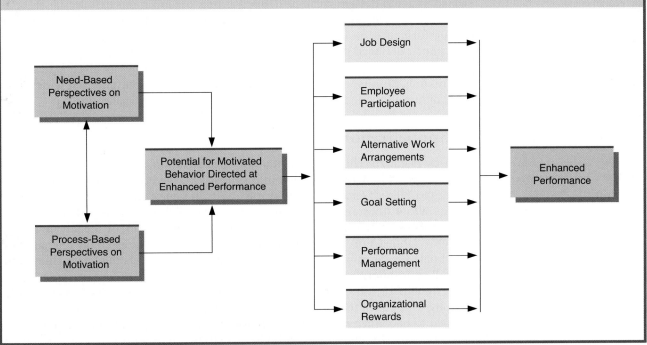

that motivated behavior can be induced by need-based or process-based circumstances. That is, people may be motivated to satisfy various specific needs or through various processes such as perceptions of inequity, expectancy relationships, and reinforcement contingencies.

These need-, process-, and learning-based concepts result in the situation illustrated in the center of the figure—a certain potential exists for motivated behavior directed at enhanced performance. For example, suppose that an employee wants more social relationships—that is, he wants to satisfy belongingness, relatedness, or affiliation needs. This means that there is potential for the employee to want to perform at a higher level if he thinks that higher performance will satisfy those social needs. Likewise, if an employee's high performance in the past was followed by strong positive reinforcement, there is again a potential for motivation directed at enhanced performance.

But managers may need to take certain steps to translate the potential for motivation directed at enhanced performance into real motivation and real enhanced performance. In some cases, these steps may be tied to the specific need or process that has created the existing potential. For example, providing more opportunities for social interaction contingent on improved performance might capitalize on an employee's social needs. More typically, however, a manager needs to go further to help translate potential into real performance.

The right side of Figure 5.1 names some of the more common methods used to enhance performance. This chapter covers the first three—job design, employee participation and empowerment, and alternative work arrangements. The other three—goal setting, performance management, and organizational rewards—are discussed in Chapter 6.

Work Design in Organizations

Work design is an important method managers can use to enhance employee performance.[1] When work design is addressed at the individual level, it is most commonly referred to as **job design**; it can be defined as how organizations define and structure jobs. As we will see, properly designed jobs can have a positive impact on the motivation, performance, and job satisfaction of those who perform them. On the other hand, poorly designed jobs can impair motivation, performance, and job satisfaction. The *Happiness and . . . Diversity* box discusses some of the issues involved in designing certain kinds of jobs to enhance motivation and satisfaction. The first widespread model of how individual work should be designed was job specialization.

Job design is how organizations define and structure jobs.

Job Specialization

Frederick Taylor, the chief proponent of **job specialization**, argued that jobs should be scientifically studied, broken down into small component tasks, and then standardized across all workers doing those jobs.[2] Taylor's view grew from the historical writings about division of labor advocated by Scottish economist Adam Smith. In practice, job specialization generally brought most, if not all, of the advantages its advocates claimed. Specialization paved the way for large-scale assembly lines and was at least partly responsible for the dramatic gains in output U.S. industry achieved for several decades after the turn of the twentieth century.

On the surface, job specialization appears to be a rational and efficient way to structure jobs. The jobs in many factories, for instance, are highly specialized and are often designed to maximize productivity. In practice, however, performing those jobs can cause problems, foremost among them the extreme monotony of highly specialized

Job specialization, as advocated by scientific management, can help improve efficiency, but it can also promote monotony and boredom.

Happiness and . . . **DIVERSITY**

White-Collar Whiners

To increase happiness, white-collar workers have options, but what about low-skill workers? In the *New York Times,* journalist Daniel Akst wrote an article titled, "White-Collar Stress? Stop the Whining." Akst points out that workplace unhappiness "is not a new phenomenon. Work is not a picnic. It's always tough for people." Akst admonishes his readers, "If you find the modern, air-conditioned workplace stressful—all that email!—just think back to the work most Americans used to do." Contrast today's modern office work with farming, the most common occupation a century ago. Farmers at that time performed hard outdoor labor seven days per week, for uncertain pay, in social isolation, and with no benefits or retirement plans.

Just as a focus on the past shows us how fortunate middle-class workers truly are, so too does a comparison of middle- and working-class employees. The Bureau of Labor Statistics reports that in 2003, 6.4 million U.S. managers earned an average salary of $83,400, while 10.3 million food-service workers earned only $17,400. The disparity is even greater when benefits and other rewards are considered.

Organizations face a stiff challenge in designing jobs for low-skill workers that are richer and more rewarding. Even if pay were greater, motivation theory theorizes that repetitive, routine jobs with little autonomy will not create worker happiness or motivation. Innovative job design for barbers, grounds workers, fishing crews, and nursing aides seems very difficult, yet could affect tens of millions of individuals nationwide.

The U.S. Census reports that 6.6 million individuals in households headed by full-time year-round workers were below the federal poverty threshold. If money and an appealing job create happiness, low-skill workers must be pretty unhappy.

> *"White-collar stress? Stop the whining."*
> DANIEL AKST, JOURNALIST, NEW YORK TIMES

References: "National Cross-Industry Estimates of Employment and Mean Annual Wage for Major Occupational Groups," Bureau of Labor Statistics, November 2003, www.bls.gov on March 4, 2005; Daniel Akst, "White-Collar Stress? Stop the Whining," *New York Times,* September 19, 2004, p. BU6 (quotation); Lisa Belkin, "Take This Job and Hug It," *New York Times,* February 13, 2005, p. W1.

tasks. Consider the job of assembling toasters. A person who does the entire assembly may find the job complex and challenging, albeit inefficient. If the job is specialized so that the worker simply inserts a heating coil into the toaster as it passes along on an assembly line, the process may be efficient, but it is unlikely to interest or challenge the worker. A worker numbed by boredom and monotony may be less motivated to work hard and more inclined to do poor-quality work or to complain about the job. For these reasons, managers began to search for job design alternatives to specialization.

One of the primary catalysts for this search was a famous study of jobs in the automobile industry. The purpose of this study was to assess how satisfied automobile workers were with various aspects of their jobs.[3] The workers indicated that they were reasonably satisfied with their pay, working conditions, and the quality of their supervision. However, they expressed extreme dissatisfaction with the actual work they did. The plants were very noisy, and the moving assembly line dictated a rigid, grueling pace. Jobs were highly specialized and standardized.

The workers complained about six facets of their jobs: mechanical pacing by an assembly line, repetitiveness, low skill requirements, involvement with only a portion of the total production cycle, limited social interaction with others in the workplace, and lack of control over the tools and techniques used in the job. These sources of dissatisfaction were a consequence of the job design prescriptions of scientific management. Thus, managers began to recognize that although job specialization might lead to efficiency, if carried too far, it would have a number of negative consequences.[4]

Job specialization has been a common method for structuring jobs for over a hundred years. Take this young woman, for instance. She works in a Samsung electronics assembly plant in northern Mexico. The plant manufactures, among many other things, video tuning devices. Her job involves inserting tiny electronic components into the tuners as they pass along an assembly line. While specialization allows her to work quickly and efficiently, her job is also very monotonous.

Early Alternatives to Job Specialization

In response to the automobile plant study, other reported problems with job specialization, and a general desire to explore ways to create less monotonous jobs, managers began to seek alternative ways to design jobs. Managers initially formulated two alternative approaches: job rotation and job enlargement.

Job Rotation   **Job rotation** involves systematically shifting workers from one job to another to sustain their motivation and interest. Under specialization, each task is broken down into small parts. For example, assembling fine writing pens such as those made by Mont Blanc or Cross might involve four discrete steps: testing the ink cartridge, inserting the cartridge into the barrel of the pen, screwing the cap onto the barrel, and inserting the assembled pen into a box. One worker might perform step one, another step two, and so forth.

When job rotation is introduced, the tasks themselves stay the same. However, the workers who perform them are systematically rotated across the various tasks. Jones, for example, starts out with task 1 (testing ink cartridges). On a regular basis—perhaps weekly or monthly—she is systematically rotated to task 2, to task 3, to task 4, and back to task 1. Gonzalez, who starts out on task 2 (inserting cartridges into barrels), rotates ahead of Jones to tasks 3, 4, 1, and back to 2.

Numerous firms have used job rotation, including American Cyanamid, Baker Hughes, Ford, and Prudential Insurance. Job rotation did not entirely live up to its expectations, however.[5] The problem was again narrowly defined, routine jobs. That is, if a rotation cycle takes workers through the same old jobs, the workers simply experience several routine and boring jobs instead of just one. Although a worker may begin each job shift with a bit of renewed interest, the effect usually is short-lived.

Job rotation is systematically moving workers from one job to another in an attempt to minimize monotony and boredom.

Rotation may also decrease efficiency. For example, it clearly sacrifices the proficiency and expertise that grow from specialization. At the same time, job rotation is an effective training technique because a worker rotated through a variety of related jobs acquires a larger set of job skills. Thus, there is increased flexibility in transferring workers to new jobs. Many U.S. firms now use job rotation for training or other purposes, but few rely on it to motivate workers. Pilgrim's Pride, one of the largest chicken-processing firms in the United States, uses job rotation, for instance, but not for motivation. Because workers in a chicken-processing plant are subject to cumulative trauma injuries such as carpel tunnel syndrome, managers at Pilgrim's believe that rotating workers across different jobs can reduce these injuries.[6]

Job enlargement involves giving workers more tasks to perform.

Job Enlargement   **Job enlargement**, or horizontal job loading, is expanding a worker's job to include tasks previously performed by other workers. For instance, if job enlargement were introduced at a Cross pen plant, the four tasks noted above might be combined into two "larger" ones. Hence, one set of workers might each test cartridges and then insert them into barrels (old steps one and two); another set of workers might then attach caps to the barrels and put the pens into boxes (old steps three and four). The logic behind this change is that the increased number of tasks in each job reduces monotony and boredom.

Maytag was one of the first companies to use job enlargement.[7] In the assembly of washing machine water pumps, for example, jobs done sequentially by six workers at a conveyor belt were modified so that each worker completed an entire pump alone. Other organizations that implemented job enlargement included AT&T, the U.S. Civil Service, and Colonial Life Insurance Company.

Unfortunately, job enlargement also failed to have the desired effects. Generally, if the entire production sequence consisted of simple, easy-to-master tasks, merely doing more of them did not significantly change the worker's job. If the task of putting two bolts on a piece of machinery was "enlarged" to putting on three bolts and connecting two wires, for example, the monotony of the original job essentially remained.

Job Enrichment

Job rotation and job enlargement seemed promising but eventually disappointed managers seeking to counter the ill effects of extreme specialization. They failed partly because they were intuitive, narrow approaches rather than fully developed, theory-driven methods. Consequently, a new, more complex approach to task design—job enrichment—was developed. **Job enrichment** is based on the dual-structure theory of motivation, which is discussed in Chapter 4. That theory contends that employees can be motivated by positive job-related experiences such as feelings of achievement, responsibility, and recognition. To achieve these, job enrichment relies on vertical job loading—not only adding more tasks to a job, as in horizontal loading, but also giving the employee more control over those tasks.[8]

AT&T, Texas Instruments, IBM, and General Foods have all used job enrichment. For example, AT&T utilized job enrichment in a group of eight typists who were responsible for preparing service orders. Managers believed turnover in the group was too high and performance too low. Analysis revealed several deficiencies in the work. The typists worked in relative isolation, and any service representative could ask them to type work orders. As a result, they had little client contact or responsibility, and they received scant feedback on their job performance. The job enrichment program focused on creating a typing team. Each member of the team was paired with a service representative, and the tasks were restructured: Ten discrete steps were replaced with three more complex ones. In addition, the typists began to get specific feedback on performance, and their job titles were changed to reflect their greater responsibility and status. As a result of these changes, the number of orders delivered on time increased from 27 to 90 percent, accuracy improved, and turnover decreased significantly.[9]

One of the first published reports on job enrichment told how Texas Instruments had used this technique to improve janitorial jobs. The company had given janitors more control over their schedules and let them sequence their own cleaning jobs and purchase their own supplies. As a direct result, turnover dropped, cleanliness improved, and the company reported estimated cost savings of approximately $103,000.[10]

At the same time, we should note that many job enrichment programs have failed. Some companies have found job enrichment to be cost-ineffective, and others believe that it simply did not produce the expected results.[11] Several programs at Prudential Insurance, for example, were abandoned because managers believed they were benefiting neither employees nor the firm. Some of the criticism is associated with the dual-structure theory of motivation, on which job enrichment is based: The theory

Job enrichment entails giving workers more tasks to perform and more control over how to perform them.

confuses employee satisfaction with motivation, is fraught with methodological flaws, ignores situational factors, and is not convincingly supported by research.

Because of these and other problems, job enrichment recently has fallen into disfavor among managers. Yet some valuable aspects of the concept can be salvaged. The efforts of managers and academic theorists ultimately have led to more complex and sophisticated viewpoints. Many of these advances are evident in the job characteristics theory, which we consider next.

The Job Characteristics Theory

> The **job characteristics theory** identifies five motivational properties of tasks and three critical psychological states of people.

The **job characteristics theory** focuses on the specific motivational properties of jobs. The theory, diagrammed in Figure 5.2, was developed by Hackman and Oldham.[12] At the core of the theory is the idea of critical psychological states. These states are presumed to determine the extent to which characteristics of the job enhance employee responses to the task. The three critical psychological states are:

1. *Experienced meaningfulness of the work*—the degree to which the individual experiences the job as generally meaningful, valuable, and worthwhile
2. *Experienced responsibility for work outcomes*—the degree to which individuals feel personally accountable and responsible for the results of their work
3. *Knowledge of results*—the degree to which individuals continuously understand how effectively they are performing the job

If employees experience these states at a sufficiently high level, they are likely to feel good about themselves and to respond favorably to their jobs. Hackman and Oldham suggest that the three critical psychological states are triggered by the following five characteristics of the job, or core job dimensions:

1. *Skill variety*—the degree to which the job requires a variety of activities that involve different skills and talents
2. *Task identity*—the degree to which the job requires completion of a "whole" and an identifiable piece of work; that is, the extent to which a job has a beginning and an end with a tangible outcome

Job sharing is an employment option some firms use. Job sharing involves two part-time employees sharing a single full-time job. A primary benefit to employees is a shorter workweek, allowing them more time for other pursuits such as education, leisure, childcare, and so forth. But also, as shown here, individuals sharing jobs also earn only about half as much money as they would if they were working full-time.

www.cartoonwork.com

Why job sharing never really took off

"Okay, she got the right side of the paycheck, so you get the left."

FIGURE 5.2

The Job Characteristics Theory

The job characteristics theory is an important contemporary model of how to design jobs. By using five core job characteristics, managers can enhance three critical psychological states. These states, in turn, can improve a variety of personal and work outcomes. Individual differences also affect how the job characteristics affect people.

Reference: Reprinted from J. R. Hackman and G. R. Oldham, "Motivation Through the Design of Work: Test of a Theory," *Organizational Behavior and Human Performance,* vol. 16, pp. 250–279. Copyright 1976, with permission of Elsevier.

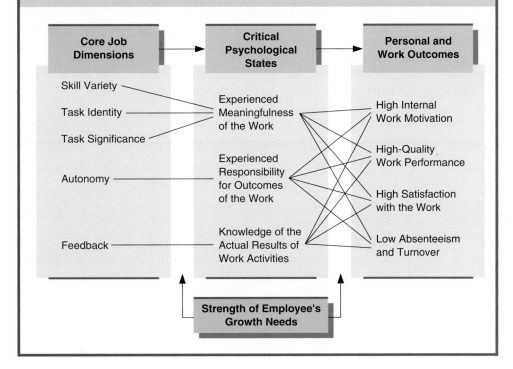

3. *Task significance*—the degree to which the job affects the lives or work of other people, both in the immediate organization and in the external environment
4. *Autonomy*—the degree to which the job allows the individual substantial freedom, independence, and discretion to schedule the work and determine the procedures for carrying it out
5. *Feedback*—the degree to which the job activities give the individual direct and clear information about the effectiveness of his or her performance

Figure 5.2 shows that these five job characteristics, operating through the critical psychological states, affect a variety of personal and work outcomes: high internal work motivation (that is, intrinsic motivation), high-quality work performance, high satisfaction with the work, and low absenteeism and turnover. The figure also suggests that individual differences play a role in job design. People with strong needs for personal growth and development will be especially motivated by the five core job characteristics. On the other hand, people with weaker needs for personal growth and development are less likely to be motivated by the core job characteristics.

Figure 5.3 expands the basic job characteristics theory by incorporating general guidelines to help managers implement it.[13] Managers can use such means as forming natural work units (that is, grouping similar tasks together), combining existing tasks into more complex ones, establishing direct relationships between workers and clients, increasing worker autonomy through vertical job loading, and opening feedback channels. Theoretically, such actions should enhance the motivational properties of each task. Using these guidelines, sometimes in adapted form, several firms, including 3M, Volvo, AT&T, Xerox, Texas Instruments, and Motorola, have successfully implemented job design changes.[14]

Much research has been devoted to this approach to job design.[15] This research has generally supported the theory, although performance has seldom been found to correlate with job characteristics.[16] Several apparent weaknesses in the theory have also come to light. First, the measures used to test the theory are not always as valid and reliable as they should be. Further, the role of individual differences frequently has not been supported by research. Finally, guidelines for implementation are not specific, so managers usually tailor them to their own particular circumstances. Still, the theory remains a popular perspective on studying and changing jobs.[17]

FIGURE 5.3

Implementing the Job Characteristics Theory

Managers should use a set of implementation guidelines if they want to apply the job characteristics theory in their organization. This figure shows some of these guidelines. For example, managers can combine tasks, form natural work units, establish client relationships, vertically load jobs, and open feedback channels.

Reference: J. R. Hackman, G. R. Oldham, R. Janson, and K. Purdy, "A New Stage for Job Enrichment." Copyright © 1975 by the Regents of the University of California. Reprinted from *California Management Review,* vol. 17, no. 4. By permission of The Regents.

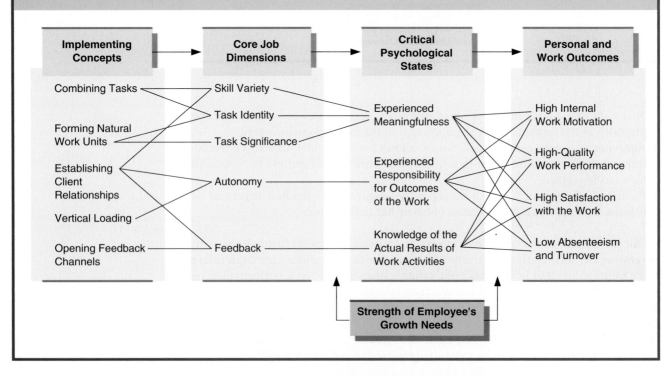

Employee Involvement and Motivation

Employee involvement in their work can also play an important role in motivation. Involvement is most often enhanced through participative management and empowerment. In most cases, managers who use these techniques are attempting to enhance employee motivation. In a sense, participation and empowerment are extensions of job design because each fundamentally alters how employees in an organization perform their jobs. **Participation** occurs when employees have a voice in decisions about their own work. (One important model that helps managers determine the optimal level of employee participation, the Vroom-Yetton-Jago model, is discussed in Chapter 13.) **Empowerment** is the process of enabling workers to set their own work goals, make decisions, and solve problems within their spheres of responsibility and authority. Thus, empowerment is a somewhat broader concept that promotes participation in a wide variety of areas, including but not limited to work itself, work context, and work environment.[18]

Participation entails giving employees a voice in making decisions about their own work.

Empowerment is the process of enabling workers to set their own work goals, make decisions, and solve problems within their sphere of responsibility and authority.

Early Perspectives on Employee Involvement

The human relations movement, in vogue from the 1930s through the 1950s, assumed that employees who are happy and satisfied will work harder. This view stimulated management interest in having workers participate in a variety of organizational activities. Managers hoped that if employees had a chance to participate in decision making concerning their work environment, they would be satisfied, and this satisfaction would supposedly result in improved performance. However, managers tended to see employee participation merely as a way to increase satisfaction, not as a source of potentially valuable input. Eventually, managers began to recognize that employee input was useful in itself, apart from its presumed effect on satisfaction. In other words, they came to see employees as valued human resources who can contribute to organizational effectiveness.[19]

Autonomous work teams have become an increasingly popular form of work design in organizations. This team works at the NASA Jet Propulsion Laboratory in Pasadena. The team is working on a rover device used to explore Mars. The team is accountable for meeting NASA performance goals and expectations, but also has considerable autonomy over how it does its work.

The role of participation and empowerment in motivation can be expressed in terms of both the need-based perspectives and the expectancy theory discussed in Chapter 4. Employees who participate in decision making may be more committed to executing decisions properly. Furthermore, successfully making a decision, executing it, and then seeing the positive consequences can help satisfy one's need for achievement, provide recognition and responsibility, and enhance self-esteem. Simply being asked to participate in organizational decision making may also enhance an employee's self-esteem. In addition, participation should help clarify expectancies; that is, by participating in decision making, employees may better understand the linkage between their performance and the rewards they want most.

Areas of Employee Involvement

At one level, employees can participate in addressing questions and making decisions about their own jobs. Instead of just telling them how to do their jobs, for example, managers can ask employees to make their own decisions about how to do them. Based on their own expertise and experience with their tasks, workers might be able to improve their own productivity. In many situations, they might also be well qualified to make decisions about what materials to use, what tools to use, and so forth.

Chaparral Steel, a small steel producer near Dallas, allows its workers considerable autonomy in how they perform their jobs. For example, when the firm recently needed a new rolling mill lathe, it budgeted $1 million for its purchase, then put the purchase decision in the hands of an operating machinist. This machinist, in turn, investigated various options, visited other mills in Japan and Europe, and then recommended an alternative piece of machinery costing less than half of the budgeted amount. The firm also helped pioneer an innovative concept called "open-book management"—any employee at Chaparral can see any company document, record, or other piece of information at any time and for any reason.

It might also help to let workers make decisions about administrative matters, such as work schedules. If jobs are relatively independent of one another, employees might decide when to change shifts, take breaks, go to lunch, and so forth. A work group or team might also be able to schedule vacations and days off for all of its members. Furthermore, employees are getting increasing opportunities to participate in broader issues of product quality. Involvement of this type has become a hallmark of successful Japanese and other international firms, and many U.S. companies have followed suit.

Techniques and Issues in Employee Involvement

In recent years many organizations have actively sought ways to extend employee involvement beyond the traditional areas. Simple techniques such as suggestion boxes and question-and-answer meetings allow a certain degree of participation, for example. The basic motive has been to better capitalize on the assets and capabilities inherent in all employees. Thus, many managers today prefer the term "empowerment" to "participation" because it implies a more comprehensive level of involvement.

One method some firms use to empower their workers is the use of work teams. This method grew out of early attempts to use what Japanese firms call "quality circles." A *quality circle* is a group of employees who voluntarily meet regularly to identify and propose solutions to problems related to quality. This use of quality circles quickly grew to encompass a wider array of work groups, now generally called "work teams." These teams are collections of employees empowered to plan, organize, direct, and control their own work. Their supervisor, rather than being a traditional "boss," plays more the role of a coach. We discuss work teams more fully in Chapter 10.

The other method some organizations use to facilitate employee involvement is to change their overall method of organizing. The basic pattern is for an organization to eliminate layers from its hierarchy, thereby becoming much more decentralized. Power, responsibility, and authority are delegated as far down the organization as possible, so control of work is squarely in the hands of those who actually do it.

Regardless of the specific technique used, however, empowerment only enhances organizational effectiveness if certain conditions exist. First, the organization must be sincere in its efforts to spread power and autonomy to lower levels of the organization. Token efforts to promote participation in just a few areas are unlikely to succeed. Second, the organization must be committed to maintaining participation and empowerment. Workers will be resentful if they are given more control only to later have it reduced or taken away altogether. Third, the organization must be systematic and patient in its efforts to empower workers. Turning over too much control too quickly can spell disaster. Finally, the organization must be prepared to increase its commitment to training. Employees being given more freedom concerning how they work are likely to need additional training to help them exercise that freedom most effectively.

Alternative Work Arrangements

Beyond the actual redesigning of jobs and the use of employee involvement, many organizations today are experimenting with a variety of alternative work arrangements. These arrangements are generally intended to enhance employee motivation and performance by giving workers more flexibility about how and when they work. The *Hewlett-Packard . . . and Change* box illustrates the importance of worker flexibility at Hewlett-Packard. Among the more popular alternative work arrangements are variable work schedules, flexible work schedules, job sharing, and telecommuting.[20]

Variable Work Schedules

There are many exceptions, of course, but the traditional work schedule in the United States has long been days that start at 8:00 or 9:00 in the morning and end at 5:00 in the evening, five days a week (and, of course, managers and other professionals often work many additional hours outside of these times). Although the exact starting and ending times vary, most companies in other countries have also used a well-defined work schedule. But such a schedule makes it difficult for workers to attend to routine personal business—going to the bank, seeing a doctor or dentist for a checkup, having a parent-teacher conference, getting an automobile serviced, and so forth. Employees locked into this work schedule may find it necessary to take a sick or vacation day to handle these activities. On a more psychological level, some people may feel so powerless and constrained by their job schedules that they grow resentful and frustrated.

To help counter these problems, one alternative some businesses use is a compressed work schedule.[21] An employee following a **compressed workweek** schedule works a full forty-hour week in fewer than the traditional five days. Most typically, this schedule involves working ten hours a day for four days, leaving an extra day off. Another alternative is for employees to work slightly less than ten hours a day but to complete the forty hours by lunchtime on Friday. And a few firms have tried having employees work twelve hours a day for three days, followed by four days off. Firms that have used these forms of compressed workweeks include John Hancock, ARCO, and R. J. Reynolds. One problem with this schedule is that if everyone in the organization is off at the same time, the firm may have no one on duty to handle problems or deal with outsiders on the off day. On the other hand, if a company staggers days off across

In a **compressed workweek**, employees work a full forty-hour week in fewer than the traditional five days.

Hewlett-Packard and . . .   **CHANGE**

Making a Living *and* Having a Life at HP

Competition heats up and companies change their work habits. To avoid downtime some firms ask their computer supplier to resolve equipment problems at night or on weekends. Smart? Sure. But that creates problems for high-tech manufacturer Hewlett-Packard (HP). Overtime for HP engineering staff doubled. "Overtime just gets you old [and] tired," says engineering manager Ron Kegle, adding that the engineers were "zombies." Kegle notes that turnover grew from 4 percent to 10 percent and transfers to other divisions further reduced personnel.

Kegle was frustrated by the limitations of traditional work/life programs, which accommodate workers' needs but not the business's needs. He started a change process that resulted in new work arrangements. "We threw a lot of our work rules out the window. We wanted to completely rethink the way the job gets done," states Kegle.

The revised schedule called for some engineers to work twelve-hour days Friday through Sunday and one-half day on Monday. Engineers were allowed to choose between the traditional and the alternative schedule. The schedule satisfied the goals of employees and the firm. The results? Overtime was reduced, engineers were happier, and customers received faster and better service. The program was so successful that it is now used at many other divisions at HP.

HP has long been at the forefront of redesigning work to improve employee motivation. Telecommuting, which can increase employee satisfaction and productivity, is used extensively at HP. Telecommuting is also beneficial to the environment. HP estimates that its telecommuting program in North America saved 50 million miles of road travel in 2004, helping to reduce pollution. Other work/life programs at HP include job sharing and flextime.

As competition, cost cutting, downsizing, and stress escalate, companies that are flexible and adaptive, like HP, will find it easier to attract and retain capable, motivated workers.

For more about Hewlett-Packard's flexible work arrangements, see the closing case titled "Alternative Work Arrangements at Hewlett-Packard."

> *"We threw a lot of our work rules out the window."*
>
> RON KEGLE, MANAGER, HEWLETT-PACKARD

References: "Employee Travel and Commuting," "Work/Life Navigation," Hewlett-Packard website, www.hp.com on June 24, 2005; Christine Canabou, "How HP Solved the Work-Life Conundrum," *Fast Company*, September 2001, www.fastcompany.com on June 24, 2005 (quotation); Burt Helm, "Paving the Road for Telecommuters," *Business Week*, September 29, 2004, www.businessweek.com on June 24, 2005.

the workforce, people who don't get the more desirable days off (Monday and Friday, for most people) may be jealous or resentful. Another problem is that when employees put in too much time in a single day, they tend to get tired and perform at a lower level later in the day.

A popular schedule some organizations are beginning to use is called a "nine-eighty" schedule. Under this arrangement, an employee works a traditional schedule one week and a compressed schedule the next, getting every other Friday off. That is, they work eighty hours (the equivalent of two weeks of full-time work) in nine days. By alternating the regular and compressed schedules across half of its workforce, the organization is staffed at all times but still gives employees two additional full days off each month. Shell Oil and Amoco Chemicals are two businesses that currently use this schedule.

Flexible work schedules, or flextime, give employees more personal control over the hours they work each day.

Flexible Work Schedules

Another promising alternative work arrangement is **flexible work schedules**, sometimes called **flextime**. The compressed work schedules previously discussed give employees time off during "normal" working hours, but they must still follow a regular

> **FIGURE 5.4**
>
> **Flexible Work Schedules**
>
> Flexible work schedules are an important new work arrangement used in some organizations today. All employees must be at work during "core time." In the hypothetical example shown here, core time is from 9 to 11 A.M. and 1 to 3 P.M. The other time, then, is flexible—employees can come and go as they please during this time, as long as the total time spent at work meets organizational expectations.

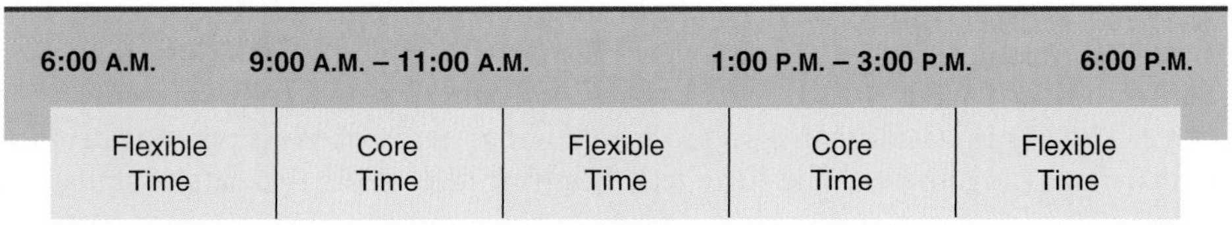

6:00 A.M.	9:00 A.M. – 11:00 A.M.		1:00 P.M. – 3:00 P.M.	6:00 P.M.
Flexible Time	Core Time	Flexible Time	Core Time	Flexible Time

and defined schedule on the days when they do work. Flextime, however, usually gives employees less say about what days they work but more personal control over the times when they work on those days.[22]

Figure 5.4 illustrates how flextime works. The workday is broken down into two categories: flexible time and core time. All employees must be at their workstations during core time, but they can choose their own schedules during flexible time. Thus, one employee may choose to start work early in the morning and leave in mid-afternoon, another to start in the late morning and work until late afternoon, and a third to start early in the morning, take a long lunch break, and work until late afternoon.

The major advantage of this approach, as already noted, is that workers get to tailor their workday to fit their personal needs. A person who needs to visit the dentist in the late afternoon can just start work early. A person who stays out late one night can start work late the next day. And the person who needs to run some errands during lunch can take a longer midday break. On the other hand, flextime is more difficult to manage because others in the organization may not be sure when a person will be available for meetings other than during the core time. Expenses such as utilities will also be higher since the organization must remain open for a longer period each day.

Some organizations have experimented with a plan in which workers set their own hours but then must follow that schedule each day. Others allow workers to modify their own schedule each day. Organizations that have used the flexible work schedule method for arranging work include Control Data Corporation, DuPont, Metropolitan Life, Chevron Texaco, and some offices in the U.S. government. One recent survey found that as many as 43 percent of U.S. workers have the option to modify their work schedules; most of those who choose to do so start earlier than normal so as to get off work earlier in the day.[23]

Job Sharing

Yet another potentially useful alternative work arrangement is job sharing. In **job sharing**, two part-time employees share one full-time job. Job sharing may be desirable for people who want to work only part-time or when job markets are tight. For its part,

In **job sharing**, two or more part-time employees share one full-time job.

the organization can accommodate the preferences of a broader range of employees and may benefit from the talents of more people. Perhaps the simplest job-sharing arrangement to visualize is that of a receptionist. To share this job, one worker would staff the receptionist's desk from, say, 8:00 A.M. to noon each day, the office might close from noon to 1:00 P.M., and a second worker would staff the desk from 1:00 in the afternoon until 5:00. To the casual observer or visitor to the office, the fact that two people serve in one job is essentially irrelevant. The responsibilities of the job in the morning and the afternoon are not likely to be interdependent. Thus, the position can easily be broken down into two or perhaps even more components.

Organizations sometimes offer job sharing as a way to entice more workers to the organization. If a particular kind of job is difficult to fill, a job-sharing arrangement might make it more attractive to more people. There are also cost benefits for the organization. Since the employees may be working only part-time, the organization does not have to give them the same benefits that full-time employees receive. The organization can also tap into a wider array of skills when it provides job-sharing arrangements. The firm gets the advantage of the two sets of skills from one job.

Some workers like job sharing because it gives them flexibility and freedom. Certain workers, for example, may want only part-time work. Stepping into a shared job may also give them a chance to work in an organization that otherwise wants to hire only full-time employees. When the job sharer isn't working, she or he may attend school, take care of the family, or simply enjoy leisure time.

Job sharing does not work for every organization, and it isn't attractive to all workers, but it has produced enough success stories to suggest that it will be around for a long time. Among the organizations that are particularly committed to job-sharing programs are the Bank of Montreal, United Airlines, and the National School Board Association. Each of these organizations, and dozens more like them, reports that job sharing has become a critically important part of its human resource system. Although job sharing has not been scientifically evaluated, it appears to be a useful alternative to traditional work scheduling.

Job sharing is an alternative work arrangement in which two part-time employees share one full-time job. For example, Amy Frank (left) and Denise Brown share the job of vice president of fixed-income sales at Bank of America. Frank works 9:00 to 5:00 Monday and Tuesday, and 9:00 to noon on Wednesday, while Brown works Wednesday afternoon, and all day on Thursday and Friday. This arrangement allows each of them to pursue a career, earn a reasonable income, and spend time at home with their children.

Telecommuting

A relatively new approach to alternative work arrangements is telecommuting—allowing employees to spend part of their time working off-site, usually at home. By using email, computer networks, and other technology, many employees can maintain close contact with their organization and do as much work at home as they could in their offices. The increased power and sophistication of modern communication technology is making telecommuting easier and easier.[24]

On the plus side, many employees like telecommuting because it gives them added flexibility. By spending one or two days a week at home, for instance, they have the same kind of flexibility to manage personal activities as is afforded by flextime or compressed schedules. Some employees also feel that they get more work done by staying at home because they are less likely to be interrupted. Organizations may benefit for several reasons as well: (1) They can reduce absenteeism and turnover since employees will need to take less "formal" time off, and (2) they can save on facilities such as parking spaces, because fewer people will be at work on any given day.

On the other hand, although many employees thrive under this arrangement, others do not. Some feel isolated and miss the social interaction of the workplace. Others simply lack the self-control and discipline to walk from the breakfast table to their desk and start working. Managers may also encounter coordination difficulties in scheduling meetings and other activities that require face-to-face contact.

Another issue with telecommuting involves workplace safety. In 2000, the Department of Labor, operating under the Occupational Safety and Health Act, began to require employers to take a proactive stance on home safety. Among other things, employers had to inspect workers' homes to ensure that all safety requirements were being met. For example, the employer had to verify that there were two external exits, that no lead paint had been used on the walls, that the employee's chairs were ergonomically sound, and that the indoor air quality met OSHA standards. This stipulation led to somewhat absurd decisions, such as corporations allowing their employees to use home telephones but not home computers if the employees' monitors did not meet low-radiation requirements. The employer could also be held accountable for employees' unsafe behaviors, such as plugging too many electrical devices into one power outlet or standing on a chair rather than on a ladder to change a light bulb. Employers complained that the requirements were too burdensome, especially as more workers began telecommuting. Employees, too, objected to the requirements as being too intrusive, invading the privacy of their homes.

So, in 2001, the ruling was lifted. However, there are still lingering legal issues and some firms still find it best to take at least some role in assessing home safety for their telecommuting employees. And there is now a new area of growing concern—cybercrime. Is a company liable if a client's confidential information is stolen because an employee's home computer didn't have hacker protection? What if the employee uses a home computer for business and also peddles online pornography? Given the trends and pressures toward telecommuting and the associated legal issues, there will no doubt continue to be significant changes in this area in the future.

Telecommuting is a work arrangement in which employees spend part of their time working off-site.

Chapter Review

Synopsis

Managers seek to enhance employee performance by capitalizing on the potential for motivated behavior intended to improve performance. Methods often used to translate motivation into performance involve work design, participation and empowerment, alternative work arrangements, performance management, goal setting, and rewards.

The essence of work design is job design—how organizations define and structure jobs. Historically, there was a general trend toward increasingly specialized jobs, but more recently the movement has consistently been away from extreme specialization. Two early alternatives to specialization were job rotation and job enlargement. Job enrichment approaches stimulated considerable interest in job design.

The job characteristics theory grew from early work on job enrichment. One basic premise of this theory is that jobs can be described in terms of a specific set of motivational characteristics. Another is that managers should work to enhance the presence of those motivational characteristics in jobs but should also take individual differences into account.

Employee involvement using participative management and empowerment can help improve employee motivation in many business settings. New management practices such as the use of various kinds of work teams and of flatter, more decentralized methods of organizing are intended to empower employees throughout the organization. Organizations that want to empower their employees need to understand a variety of issues as they go about promoting participation.

Alternative work arrangements are commonly used today to enhance motivated job performance. Among the more popular alternative arrangements are compressed workweeks, flexible work schedules, job sharing, and telecommuting.

Discussion Questions

1. What are the primary advantages and disadvantages of job specialization? Were they the same in the early days of mass production?

2. Under what circumstances might job enlargement be especially effective? Especially ineffective? How about job rotation?

3. Do any trends today suggest a return to job specialization?

4. What are the strengths and weaknesses of job enrichment? When might it be useful?

5. Do you agree or disagree that individual differences affect how people respond to their jobs? Explain.

6. What are the primary similarities and differences between job enrichment and the approach proposed by job characteristics theory?

7. What are the motivational consequences of increased employee involvement from the frame of reference of expectancy and equity theories?

8. What motivational problems might result from an organization's attempt to set up work teams?

9. Which form of alternative work schedule might you prefer?

10. How do you think you would like telecommuting?

Experiencing Organizational Behavior

Learning About Job Design

Purpose: This exercise will help you assess the processes involved in designing jobs to make them more motivating.

Format: Working in small groups, you will diagnose the motivating potential of an existing job, compare its motivating potential to that of other jobs, suggest ways to redesign the job, and then assess the effects of your redesign suggestions on other aspects of the workplace.

Procedure: Your instructor will divide the class into groups of three or four people each. In assessing the characteristics of jobs, use a scale value of 1 ("very little") to 7 ("very high").

1. Using the scale values, assign scores on each core job dimension used in the job characteristics theory (see page 124) to the following jobs: secretary, professor, food server, auto mechanic, lawyer, short-order cook, department store clerk, construction worker, and newspaper reporter.

2. Researchers often assess the motivational properties of jobs by calculating their motivating potential score (MPS). The usual formula for MPS is

$$\text{(Variety + Identity + Significance)}/3 \times \text{Autonomy} \times \text{Feedback}$$

Use this formula to calculate the MPS for each job in step 1.

3. Your instructor will now assign your group one of the jobs from the list. Discuss how you might reasonably go about enriching the job.

4. Calculate the new MPS score for the redesigned job, and check its new position in the rank ordering.

5. Discuss the feasibility of your redesign suggestions. In particular, look at how your recommended changes might necessitate changes in other jobs, in the reward system, and in the selection criteria used to hire people for the job.

6. Briefly discuss your observations with the rest of the class.

Follow-up Questions

1. How might your own pre-existing attitudes explain some of your own perceptions in this exercise?

2. Are some jobs simply impossible to redesign?

The Job Characteristics Inventory

The questionnaire below was developed to measure the central concepts of the job characteristics theory. Answer the questions in relation to the job you currently hold or the job you most recently held.

Skill Variety

1. How much *variety* is there in your job? That is, to what extent does the job require you to do many different things at work, using a variety of your skills and talents?

1	2	3	4	5	6	7
Very little; the job requires me to do the same routine things over and over again.			Moderate variety			Very much; the job requires me to do many different things, using a number of different skills and talents.

2. The job requires me to use a number of complex or high-level skills.

How accurate is the statement in describing your job?

1	2	3	4	5	6	7
Very inaccurate	Mostly inaccurate	Slightly inaccurate	Uncertain	Slightly accurate	Mostly accurate	Very accurate

3. The job is quite simple and repetitive.*

How accurate is the statement in describing your job?

1	2	3	4	5	6	7
Very inaccurate	Mostly inaccurate	Slightly inaccurate	Uncertain	Slightly accurate	Mostly accurate	Very accurate

Task Identity

1. To what extent does your job involve doing a *"whole" and identifiable piece of work*? That is, is the job a complete piece of work that has an obvious beginning and end? Or is it only a small *part* of the overall piece of work, which is finished by other people or by automatic machines?

1	2	3	4	5	6	7

My job is only a tiny part of the overall piece of work; the results of my activities cannot be seen in the final product or service.

My job is a moderate-sized "chunk" of the overall piece of work; my own contribution can be seen in the final outcome.

My job involves doing the whole piece of work, from start to finish; the results of my activities are easily seen in the final product or service.

2. The job provides me a chance to completely finish the pieces of work I begin.

How accurate is the statement in describing your job?

1	2	3	4	5	6	7
Very inaccurate	Mostly inaccurate	Slightly inaccurate	Uncertain	Slightly accurate	Mostly accurate	Very accurate

3. The job is arranged so that I do *not* have the chance to do an entire piece of work from beginning to end.*

How accurate is the statement in describing your job?

1	2	3	4	5	6	7
Very inaccurate	Mostly inaccurate	Slightly inaccurate	Uncertain	Slightly accurate	Mostly accurate	Very accurate

Task Significance

1. In general, how significant or important is your job? That is, are the results of your work likely to significantly affect the lives or well-being of other people?

1	2	3	4	5	6	7

Not very significant; the outcomes of my work are *not* likely to have important effects on other people.

Moderately significant

Highly significant; the outcomes of my work can affect other people in very important ways.

2. This job is one in which a lot of people can be affected by how well the work gets done.

How accurate is the statement in describing your job?

1	2	3	4	5	6	7
Very inaccurate	Mostly inaccurate	Slightly inaccurate	Uncertain	Slightly accurate	Mostly accurate	Very accurate

3. The job itself is *not* very significant or important in the broader scheme of things.*

How accurate is the statement in describing your job?

1	2	3	4	5	6	7
Very inaccurate	Mostly inaccurate	Slightly inaccurate	Uncertain	Slightly accurate	Mostly accurate	Very accurate

Autonomy

1. How much *autonomy* is there in your job? That is, to what extent does your job permit you to decide *on your own* how to go about doing your work?

1	2	3	4	5	6	7

Very little; the job gives me almost no personal "say" about how and when the work is done.

Moderate autonomy; many things are standardized and not under my control, but I can make some decisions about the work.

Very much; the job gives me almost complete responsibility for deciding how and when the work is done.

2. The job gives me considerable opportunity for independence and freedom in how I do the work.

How accurate is the statement in describing your job?

1	2	3	4	5	6	7
Very inaccurate	Mostly inaccurate	Slightly inaccurate	Uncertain	Slightly accurate	Mostly accurate	Very accurate

3. The job denies me any chance to use my personal initiative or judgment in carrying out the work.*

How accurate is the statement in describing your job?

1	2	3	4	5	6	7
Very inaccurate	Mostly inaccurate	Slightly inaccurate	Uncertain	Slightly accurate	Mostly accurate	Very accurate

Feedback

1. To what extent does *doing the job itself* provide you with information about your work performance? That is, does the actual *work itself* provide clues about how well you are doing—aside from any "feedback" coworkers or supervisors may provide?

1	2	3	4	5	6	7
Very little; the job itself is set up so I could work forever without finding out how well I am doing.			Moderately; sometimes doing the job provides "feedback" to me; sometimes it does not.			Very much; the job is set up so that I get almost constant "feedback" as I work about how well I am doing.

2. Just doing the work required by the job provides many chances for me to figure out how well I am doing.

How accurate is the statement in describing your job?

1	2	3	4	5	6	7
Very inaccurate	Mostly inaccurate	Slightly inaccurate	Uncertain	Slightly accurate	Mostly accurate	Very accurate

3. The job itself provides very few clues about whether or not I am performing well.*

How accurate is the statement in describing your job?

1	2	3	4	5	6	7
Very inaccurate	Mostly inaccurate	Slightly inaccurate	Uncertain	Slightly accurate	Mostly accurate	Very accurate

Scoring: Responses to the three items for each core characteristic are averaged to yield an overall score for that characteristic. Items marked with an asterisk (*) should be scored as follows: 1 = 7; 2 = 6; 3 = 5; 6 = 2; 7 = 1

Building Managerial Skills

Exercise Overview: Conceptual skills refer to a person's abilities to think in the abstract. This exercise will help you develop your conceptual skills as they relate to designing jobs.

Exercise Background: Begin by thinking of three different jobs, one that appears to have virtually no enrichment, one that seems to have moderate enrichment, and one that appears to have a great deal of enrichment. These jobs might be ones that you have personally held or ones that you have observed and about which you can make some educated or informed judgments.

Evaluate each job along the five dimensions described in the job characteristics theory. Next, see if you can identify ways to improve each of the five dimensions for each job. That is, see if you can determine how to enrich the jobs by using the job characteristics theory as a framework.

Finally, meet with a classmate and share results. See if you can improve your job enrichment strategy based on the critique offered by your classmate.

Exercise Task: Using the background information about the three jobs you examined as context, answer the following questions.

1. What job qualities make some jobs easier to enrich than others?

2. Can all jobs be enriched?

3. Even if a particular job can be enriched, does that always mean that it should be enriched?

4. Under what circumstances might an individual prefer to have a routine and unenriched job?

Organizational Behavior Case for Discussion

Alternative Work Arrangements at Hewlett-Packard

Imagine an organization that must attract and retain a skilled workforce to stay at the forefront of technological innovation. Imagine further that highly qualified workers are scarce, expensive, and switch employers readily. What can this organization do to motivate its employees?

Hewlett-Packard (HP), a provider of computer products and services, knows. "Being known as a great place to work makes it easier to attract top talent," reads HP's website. "For us, being a great place to work is good business." The challenge is great. HP employs more than 140,000 workers worldwide in every function. Alternative work arrangements are one effective way to motivate such a diverse group of employees.

HP provides a "flexible, supportive environment to manage work and personal life demands, including flexible time, telecommuting, and job-sharing," according to its website. Vice president of diversity and work/life Sid Reed acknowledges that motivation can result from alternative work arrangements. "We very definitely see that employees feel empowered when they are able to work in a schedule and a location that suits their needs. They have some flexibility to really integrate in a positive way their personal life and their work life," Reed asserts.

One motivated employee is Kristy Ward, a marketing manager. With more than two decades at HP, she has experienced several types of alternative work arrangements and is currently job sharing. "Much of what I've been able to do seems uncommon in the rest of the industry," Ward relates. "I talk to my friends that work at other companies. They don't have the same alternatives . . . That has really added to my loyalty to the company."

Ward explains that HP determines each individual's optimal work environment based on the employee's and the company's needs: "Some have the two-minute commute, downstairs in the house. Others still drive to be able to be in a work environment with other employees. There's a lot of personal preference." HP engineer Cheryl Marks says, "One of the reasons I stay with HP is because they allow me to telework. I get burned out if I can't be as productive as I want to be." Nikki Cheatham telecommutes and estimates it takes her roughly half as much time to absorb complex information at home than in her office cubicle. For just $3,500, HP set up a telework arrangement for a systems engineer with a physical handicap to work at home. The company helped this valuable worker keep his job and saved the cost of finding a replacement.

Among the significant benefits to employees are shorter or nonexistent commuting times, the ability to control their level of interaction with others, and support for family or personal needs. Yet the benefits to the organization are just as great or greater. In addition to support for recruiting and retention, alternative work arrangements can help to increase diversity by encouraging employees with various needs. Reed says, "It's a part of the overall inclusion and diversity strategy . . . We support employees so that they can contribute to their full potential." Other advantages are the lowered costs for office and parking space, the ability to hire the best talent regardless of location, the ease in forming virtual teams, and the capacity to better manage emergencies such as storms or power failures.

Yet surely the greatest benefit to the organization is the increased motivation experienced by workers when they feel supported by their employer. *ComputerWorld* magazine recently surveyed 17,000 high-tech professionals and found that access to leading technology, training, and flexible workplaces were the top three issues of concern. HP employees show that flexibility is becoming more popular at the firm—telecommuting has grown from 10 percent in 1999 to virtually 100 percent today. Many are also trying other alternatives such as job sharing and part-time work.

Tom Johnson, an HP human resources manager, says, "We have enough hard data and anecdotal evidence to suggest telework can increase productivity, [but] most important is fit." Another human resource manager, Darryl Roberts, characterizes telework as an "employee-driven business decision," a win-win agreement between HP and employees. Ward would certainly agree, as she states with evident satisfaction, "The nice thing about HP is you can do what suits your work style."

Case Questions

1. What types of employees are likely to be motivated by alternative work arrangements? Why?

2. Consider HP's use of flextime, job sharing, and telecommuting. What are some of the potential drawbacks or limitations of these approaches? What can HP do to prepare for, reduce, or eliminate these negative outcomes?

3. In your "job" as a student, do you think you would be more or less effective if you had the opportunity to telecommute (or do more telecommuting, if you already use distance learning)? Explain your answer.

> **"[E]mployees feel empowered when they are able to work in a schedule and a location that suits their needs."**
> *SID REED, VICE PRESIDENT OF DIVERSITY AND WORK/LIFE, HEWLETT PACKARD*

"Work/Life Navigation," Hewlett-Packard Company website, www.hp.com on March 5, 2005; "Alternative Work Arrangements at Hewlett-Packard," video case (quotation); "Case Study: Hewlett-Packard Company," Commuter Challenge website, 1999, www.commuter.challenge.org on March 5, 2005; Mary Brandel, "Overview: 100 Best Places to Work in IT," *ComputerWorld,* June 14, 2004, www.computerworld.com on March 6, 2005.

References: "About Us," "Awards and Recognitions," "Jobs at HP,"

TEST PREPPER

You have read the chapter and studied the key terms. Think you're ready to ace the exam? Take this sample test to gauge your comprehension of chapter material and check your answers at the back of the book. Want more test questions? Take the ACE quizzes found on the student website: http://college.hmco.com/business/students/ (select Griffin/Moorhead, Organizational Behavior, 8e from the Management menu).

T   F   1. Job specialization is a technique in which managers assign certain high-performing employees to the best jobs in the company.

T   F   2. Many organizations today rely on job rotation to motivate employees.

T   F   3. Job enrichment adds more tasks to a job and gives employees more control over those tasks.

T   F   4. According to job characteristics theory, all individuals are equally motivated by core job characteristics.

T   F   5. A quality circle is a technique to continually raise employees' perceptions of product quality by alternating between economy and premium versions.

T   F   6. In job sharing, two part-time employees share one full-time job.

T   F   7. Employers currently must ensure telecommuters' homes comply with the specific requirements of the Occupational Safety and Health Act.

8. Which of the following is not true about job specialization?
   a. Jobs are broken down into small component tasks.
   b. Specialization paved the way for large-scale assembly lines.
   c. Specialization typically raises employees' job motivation.
   d. Specialization increases efficiency.
   e. Problems with specialization led to the study of alternative job designs.

9. Job enrichment combines job enlargement with
   a. a piece-rate incentive system.
   b. commission-based wages.
   c. hygiene factors from dual-structure theory.
   d. greater employee control over their tasks.
   e. job characteristics theory.

10. Which of the following is not a core job dimension in job characteristics theory?
    a. Feedback
    b. Specialization
    c. Skill variety
    d. Task identity
    e. Autonomy

11. Larry has a strong need for personal growth and development. According to job characteristics theory
    a. Larry will be especially motivated by the five core job dimensions.
    b. Larry will thrive in an environment of high specialization.
    c. Larry will seek knowledge of results but avoid responsibility for work outcomes.
    d. high levels of task identity and task significance will potentially lower Larry's motivation.
    e. the core job dimensions will be only minimally motivating to Larry.

12. Allison's manager solicits her participation when making decisions in the department. Allison's participation is likely to lead to her
    a. eventual turnover.
    b. increased commitment to executing the decisions properly.
    c. frustration in trying to satisfy her need for achievement and recognition.
    d. belief that job specialization is a superior job design.
    e. ability to separate her work life from her private life.

13. Matthew drives a delivery truck and works a full forty-hour week in four ten-hour days. Matthew's schedule is called
    a. telecommuting.
    b. job sharing.
    c. flextime.
    d. core time.
    e. a compressed work week.

14. For empowerment to enhance organizational effectiveness, all of the following conditions must exist except
    a. the organization must arrange to pay workers more than in the past.
    b. the organization must be sincere in its efforts to spread power and autonomy to lower levels of the organization.
    c. the organization must be committed to maintaining participation and empowerment.
    d. the organization must be systematic and patient in its efforts to empower workers.
    e. the organization must increase its commitment to training.

Motivating Employee Performance Through Rewards

CHAPTER 6

After studying this chapter, you should be able to:

- ▶ Describe goal setting and relate it to motivation.
- ▶ Discuss performance management in organizations.
- ▶ Identify the key elements in understanding individual rewards in organizations.
- ▶ Describe the issues and processes involved in managing reward systems.

Chapter Outline

Goal Setting and Motivation

Performance Management in Organizations

Individual Rewards in Organizations

Managing Reward Systems

One Goal at Ryanair: Low Costs Support Low Prices

Ryanair CEO Michael O'Leary designed his U.K. firm to mimic Southwest's winning formula of low costs and low prices. Ryanair fares often cost one-half or less of rival airlines, with fares priced as low as 99 pence. On the Ryanair website, potential employees see this statement of the firm's overall goals: "Low fares and friendly, efficient service—that's our way. And how do we do it? Superb cost management."

O'Leary has a single-minded focus on costs and he communicates that vision to employees and outsiders alike. Ryanair chairman David Bonderman states, "O'Leary and his management team are absolutely the best at adopting a winning strategy and sticking to it relentlessly."

However, perhaps the most significant contributors to the low cost structure at Ryanair are its employees. Contrary to expectations for a low-cost carrier, compensation at Ryanair is at or above the industry average in most cases. In 2004, a difficult year for airlines, Ryanair increased employee pay by 3 percent, higher than competitors.

Instead of squeezing salaries, the airline aims for higher productivity. One measure of productivity is the number of dollars of revenue earned for every dollar of labor expense—a higher ratio is more productive. While major European airlines have a ratio of 3.9 and major U.S. airlines have a ratio of 2.3, Ryanair is at an astonishing 9.5, a higher level of productivity than any commercial airline in the world.

Employee expenses are the single largest cost of an airline, so "the productivity-cost relationship is key," according to Rigas Doganis, former CEO of Olympic Airlines. One of the keys to Ryanair's high productivity is the question "WTGBRFDT?" claims business writer Jason Jennings. The question, "What's the good business reason for doing this?" allows the airline to identify the essential pieces of any task, simplifying and standardizing work to increase efficiency and productivity.

Another factor in Ryanair's productivity is the ability to "incentivize" the work of most of its personnel. The firm offers rewards, including pay raises, bonuses, stock options, and rapid promotion, to high-performing teams. Almost half of Ryanair employees qualified for stock options in the first offering, creating employees that are more committed to reaching the organization's goals.

Teamwork also enhances productivity. Jennings says, "The traits these [highly productive] companies have in common are that they put people on teams and they pay teams real money." Internal communication is extensive, especially about the organization's goals and progress.

Ryanair is reducing costs, but it is not skimping on safety items. The company's strategy statement includes the following: "Management does not seek to extend Ryanair's low cost operating strategy to the areas of safety, maintenance, training or quality assurance."

Ryanair's low-cost, low-price strategy has paid off handsomely. The firm is first in Europe in lowest fares, most on-time flights, least cancellations, and fewest lost bags. As the Ryanair website claims, "We compete with some of Europe's biggest and strongest airlines, and in all cases we beat the socks off them."

For a different view on Ryanair's cost-cutting strategy, see the boxed insert on page 147 titled, *Ryanair and . . . Ethics.*

References: "2004 Annual Report," "Strategy," "Working for Ryanair," Ryanair website, www.ryanair.com on April 5, 2005; "Cost In Focus," BradyNet Forum website, March 21, 2003, www.bradynet.com on April 5, 2005; Kerry Capell, "Ryanair Rising," *Business Week*, June 2, 2003, www.businessweek.com on April 5, 2005; Joanna L. Krotz, "Reward Your Employees for Teamwork in 2003," Business Training Media website, www.business-marketing.com on April 5, 2005.

For decades management experts have advocated the importance of providing meaningful rewards for employees. Most managers initially focused on pay as the basic reward offered to employees. But now many people understand that employees actually seek and respond to a variety of rewards from their work. As we established at the beginning of Chapter 5, managers can use a number of things to capitalize on the potential for motivated behavior directed at enhanced performance in order to transform that potential into actual enhanced performance. Subsequent discussions in that chapter identified various work-related elements that can help with that transformation.

In this chapter we examine several other organizational methods and elements that can promote enhanced performance. We begin with a discussion of goals and how they relate to both motivation and performance. Next, we describe performance management per se, as well as how performance relates to total quality management. Individual rewards are then introduced and related to motivated performance. Finally, we conclude with a discussion of a variety of issues that affect the management of reward systems.

Goal Setting and Motivation

Goal setting is a very useful method of enhancing employee performance.[1] From a motivational perspective, a **goal** is a meaningful objective. Goals are used for two purposes in most organizations. First, they provide a useful framework for managing motivation. Managers and employees can set goals for themselves and then work toward them. Thus, if the organization's overall goal is to increase sales by 10 percent, a manager can use individual goals to help attain that organizational goal. Second, goals are an effective control device (control is the monitoring by management of how well the organization is performing). Comparing people's short-term performances with their goals can be an effective way to monitor the organization's long-run performance.

A **goal** is a desirable objective.

Social learning theory perhaps best describes the role and importance of goal setting in organizations.[2] This perspective suggests that feelings of pride or shame about performance are a function of the extent to which people achieve their goals. A person who achieves a goal will be proud of having done so whereas a person who fails to achieve a goal will feel personal disappointment, and perhaps even shame. People's degree of pride or disappointment is affected by their **self-efficacy**, the extent to which they feel that they can still meet their goals even if they failed to do so in the past.

Our **self-efficacy** is the extent to which we believe we can accomplish our goals even if we failed to do so in the past.

Goal-Setting Theory

Social learning theory provides insights into why and how goals can motivate behavior. It also helps us understand how different people cope with failure to reach their goals. The research of Edwin Locke and his associates most clearly established the utility of goal-setting theory in a motivational context.[3]

Locke's goal-setting theory of motivation assumes that behavior is a result of conscious goals and intentions. Therefore, by setting goals for people in the organization, a manager should be able to influence their behavior. Given this premise, the challenge is to develop a thorough understanding of the processes by which people set goals and then work to reach them. In the original version of goal-setting theory, two specific goal characteristics—goal difficulty and goal specificity—were expected to shape performance.

Goal Difficulty   **Goal difficulty** is the extent to which a goal is challenging and requires effort. If people work to achieve goals, it is reasonable to assume that they will work harder to achieve more difficult goals. But a goal must not be so difficult that it is unattainable. If a new manager asks her sales force to increase sales by 300 percent, the group may ridicule her charge as laughable because they regard it as impossible to reach. A more realistic but still difficult goal—perhaps a 20 percent increase in sales— would probably be a better incentive.

Goal difficulty is the extent to which a goal is challenging and requires effort.

A substantial body of research supports the importance of goal difficulty.[4] In one study, managers at Weyerhauser set difficult goals for truck drivers hauling loads of timber from cutting sites to wood yards. Over a nine-month period, the drivers increased the quantity of wood they delivered by an amount that would have required $250,000 worth of new trucks at the previous per-truck average load.[5] Reinforcement also fosters motivation toward difficult goals. A person who is rewarded for achieving a difficult goal will be more inclined to strive toward the next difficult goal than will someone who received no reward for reaching the first goal.

Goals, or desirable objectives, play two important roles in organizations: They provide a framework for managing motivation and they are effective control devices. For example, Dr. Taryn Rose started her career as an orthopedic surgeon. But since one of her earliest interests was fashion, she was motivated to create fashionable women's footwear that was comfortable and less damaging to feet than traditional designer shoes. Motivated by her sense of style and her understanding of bone structures, she launched a line of designer shoes in 1997. Today the pricey shoes are sold in her two boutiques (in Beverly Hills and New York City) as well as in over 200 other retail outlets such as Neiman Marcus and Nordstrom. She still practices medicine, but spends most of her time running her growing shoe empire.

Goal specificity is the clarity and precision of a goal.

Goal Specificity   **Goal specificity** is the clarity and precision of the goal. A goal of "increasing productivity" is not very specific, whereas a goal of "increasing productivity by 3 percent in the next six months" is quite specific. Some goals, such as those involving costs, output, profitability, and growth, can easily be stated in clear and precise terms. Other goals, such as improving employee job satisfaction and morale, company image and reputation, ethical behavior, and social responsibility, are much harder to state in specific terms.

Like difficulty, specificity has been shown to be consistently related to performance. The study of timber truck drivers previously mentioned also examined goal specificity. The initial loads the truck drivers were carrying were found to be 60 percent of the maximum weight each truck could haul. The managers set a new goal for drivers of 94 percent, which the drivers were soon able to reach. Thus, the goal was quite specific as well as difficult.

Locke's theory attracted widespread interest and research support from both researchers and managers, so Locke, together with Gary Latham, eventually proposed an expanded model of the goal-setting process. The expanded model, shown in Figure 6.1, attempts to capture more fully the complexities of goal setting in organizations.

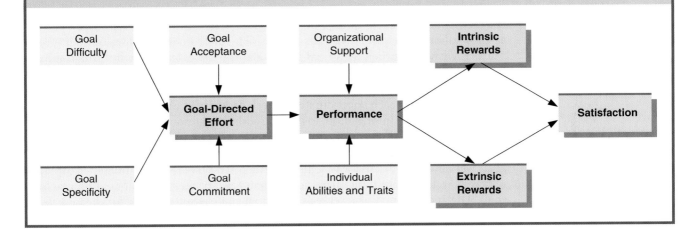

FIGURE 6.1

The Goal-Setting Theory of Motivation

The goal-setting theory of motivation provides an important means of enhancing the motivation of employees. As illustrated here, appropriate goal difficulty, specificity, acceptance, and commitment contribute to goal-directed effort. This effort, in turn, has a direct impact on performance.

Reference: Reprinted from *Organizational Dynamics,* Autumn 1979, Gary P. Latham et al., "The Goal-Setting Theory of Motivation." Copyright 1979, with permission of Elsevier.

The expanded theory argues that goal-directed effort is a function of four goal attributes: difficulty and specificity, which we already discussed, and acceptance and commitment. **Goal acceptance** is the extent to which a person accepts a goal as his or her own. **Goal commitment** is the extent to which he or she is personally interested in reaching the goal. The manager who vows to take whatever steps are necessary to cut costs by 10 percent has made a commitment to achieving the goal. Factors that can foster goal acceptance and commitment include participating in the goal-setting process, making goals challenging but realistic, and believing that goal achievement will lead to valued rewards.[6]

The interaction of goal-directed effort, organizational support, and individual abilities and traits determines actual performance. Organizational support is whatever the organization does to help or hinder performance. Positive support might mean providing whatever resources are needed to meet the goal; negative support might mean failing to provide such resources, perhaps due to cost considerations or staff reductions. Individual abilities and traits are the skills and other personal characteristics necessary to do a job. As a result of performance, a person receives various intrinsic and extrinsic rewards that, in turn, influence satisfaction. Note that the latter stages of this model are quite similar to those of the Porter and Lawler expectancy model discussed in Chapter 4.

Broader Perspectives on Goal Setting

Some organizations undertake goal setting from the somewhat broader perspective of **management by objectives**, or **MBO**. MBO is essentially a collaborative goal-setting process through which organizational goals systematically cascade down through the

Goal acceptance is the extent to which a person accepts a goal as his or her own.

Goal commitment is the extent to which a person is personally interested in reaching a goal.

Management by objectives (MBO) is a collaborative goal-setting process through which organizational goals cascade down throughout the organization.

organization. Our discussion describes a generic approach, but many organizations adapt MBO to suit their own purposes.

A successful MBO program starts with top managers establishing overall goals for the organization. After these goals have been set, managers and employees throughout the organization collaborate to set subsidiary goals. First, the overall goals are communicated to everyone. Then each manager meets with each subordinate. During these meetings, the manager explains the unit goals to the subordinate, and the two together determine how the subordinate can contribute to the goals most effectively. The manager acts as a counselor and helps ensure that the subordinate develops goals that are verifiable. For example, a goal of "cutting costs by 5 percent" is verifiable whereas a goal of "doing my best" is not. Finally, manager and subordinate ensure that the subordinate has the resources needed to reach his or her goals. The entire process spirals downward as each subordinate meets with his or her own subordinates to develop their goals. Thus, as we noted earlier, the initial goals set at the top cascade down through the entire organization.

During the time frame set for goal attainment (usually one year), the manager periodically meets with each subordinate to check progress. It may be necessary to modify goals in light of new information, to provide additional resources, or to take some other action. At the end of the specified time period, managers hold a final evaluation meeting with each subordinate. At this meeting, manager and subordinate assess how well goals were met and discuss why. This meeting often serves as the annual performance review as well, determining salary adjustments and other rewards based on reaching goals. This meeting may also serve as the initial goal-setting meeting for the next year's cycle.

Evaluation and Implications

Goal-setting theory has been widely tested in a variety of settings. Research has demonstrated fairly consistently that goal difficulty and specificity are closely associated with performance. Other elements of the theory, such as acceptance and commitment, have been studied less frequently. A few studies have shown the importance of acceptance and commitment, but little is currently known about how people accept and become committed to goals. Goal-setting theory may also focus too much attention on the short run at the expense of long-term considerations. The *Ryanair and . . . Ethics* box also raises some ethical implications that can result from too much emphasis on goals. Despite these questions, however, goal setting is clearly an important way for managers to convert motivation into actual improved performance.

From the broader perspective, MBO remains a very popular technique. Alcoa, Tenneco, Black & Decker, General Foods, and Du Pont, for example, have used versions of MBO with widespread success. The technique's popularity stems in part from its many strengths. For one thing, MBO clearly has the potential to motivate employees because it helps implement goal-setting theory on a systematic basis throughout the organization. It also clarifies the basis for rewards, and it can stimulate communication. Performance appraisals are easier and more clear-cut under MBO. Further, managers can use the system for control purposes.

However, using MBO also presents pitfalls, especially if a firm takes too many shortcuts or inadvertently undermines how the process is supposed to work. Sometimes, for instance, top managers do not really participate; that is, the goals really are established in the middle of the organization and may not reflect the real goals of top management. If employees believe this situation to be true, they may become cynical, interpreting the lack of participation by top management as a sign that the goals are not important and that their own involvement is therefore a waste of time. MBO also has a tendency to overem-

Ryanair and . . . **ETHICS**

How Cheap Is Too Cheap?

Ryanair, a U.K.-based airline, is a dedicated cost-cutter. The company has triggered a price war and vowed to reduce fares by 5 percent every year. To win that war, Ryanair must wring further cost savings out of a business that is already very lean.

Cost-cutting goals, implemented to the exclusion of other goals, can be inappropriate, unsafe, or just plain weird. The airline charges staff and customers for drinks and snacks. Miss your flight? Sorry, buy another ticket. Using a credit card? Costs $7.50. Checking luggage? Extra.

Ryanair recently acquired rival Buzz and dismissed many of the staff with three weeks' wages. "Ryanair's unnecessary sackings paint an accurate picture of a callous and malevolent employer who doesn't give a %&@# for anyone or anything apart from making a profit," claims union leader Ed Blissett.

Ryanair lost a lawsuit brought by a passenger with cerebral palsy, who was charged 36 pounds ($68) for use of a wheelchair. Now Ryanair adds 36 pence to each ticket to cover wheelchair charges, generating 9.5 million pounds (almost $18 million) in revenue annually.

Ryanair is the loser in another legal action, a suit to keep government-owned, regional airports from offering discounts to airlines. The European Commission ruled that this practice violates E.U. rules against state sponsorship of private enterprise. Just at Charleroi airport in Belgium, Ryanair will give up $6 million in annual discounts.

Pilots are involved in another lawsuit, following Ryanair's attempt to disrupt a union-run website that offers anonymous criticisms and concerns about excessive cost cutting. Andrew Clark, writing for *The Guardian*, says, "Pilots use online forums to report safety concerns. If anonymity is jeopardized, concerns may never be aired."

Positive outcomes of cost cutting—higher profits, lower fares—are matched by concerns—safety, inappropriate actions, disgruntled staff and consumers. Customer to Ryanair: "Thanks for the low fares, but don't go too far."

> *"Ryanair's unnecessary sackings paint an accurate picture of a callous and malevolent employer."*
>
> ED BLISSETT, SENIOR ORGANIZER, GMB, BRITAIN'S GENERAL UNION

References: Mike Berry, "Airlines and Airports Both Responsible for Assisting Disabled Passengers," *Personnel Today*, December 21, 2004, www.personneltoday.co.uk on May 7, 2005; Kerry Capell, "Airing Ryanair's Beef with the E.C.," *Business Week*, February 16, 2004, www.businessweek.com on April 5, 2005; Kerry Capell, "Ryanair Rising," *Business Week*, June 2, 2003, www.businessweek.com on April 5, 2005; Andrew Clark, "Ryanair Draws First Blood in Battle over Pilots' Web Attack," *The Guardian*, March 30, 2005, www.guardian.co.uk on April 5, 2005; Andrew Clark, "Buzz Workers Win Compensation after Ryanair Takeover," *The Guardian*, August 4, 2004, www.guardian.co.uk on April 5, 2005.

phasize quantitative goals to enhance verifiability. Another potential liability is that an MBO system requires a great deal of paperwork and record keeping since every goal must be documented. Finally, some managers do not really let subordinates participate in goal setting but, instead, merely assign goals and order subordinates to accept them.

On balance, MBO is often an effective and useful system for managing goal setting and enhancing performance in organizations. Research suggests that it can actually do many of the things its advocates claim but that it must also be handled carefully. In particular, most organizations need to tailor it to their own unique circumstances. Properly used, MBO can also be an effective approach to managing an organization's reward system. It requires, however, individual, one-on-one interactions between each supervisor and each employee, and these one-on-one interactions can often be difficult because of the time they take and the likelihood that at least some of them will involve critical assessments of unacceptable performance.

Performance Management in Organizations

As described earlier, most goals are oriented toward some element of performance. Managers can do a variety of things to enhance employee motivation and performance, including redesigning jobs, allowing greater participation, creating alternative work arrangements, and setting goals. They may also fail to do things that might have improved motivation and performance, and they may inadvertently even do things that reduce motivation and performance. Thus, it is clearly important that performance be approached as something that can and should be managed.[7]

The Nature of Performance Management

The core of performance management is the actual measurement of the performance of an individual or group. **Performance measurement**, or **performance appraisal**, is the process by which someone (1) evaluates an employee's work behaviors by measurement and comparison with previously established standards, (2) documents the results, and (3) communicates the results to the employee.[8] A **performance management system** **(PMS)** comprises the processes and activities involved in performance appraisals, as shown in Figure 6.2.

Performance measurement, or **performance appraisal,** is the process by which someone (1) evaluates an employee's work behaviors by measurement and comparison with previously established standards, (2) documents the results, and (3) communicates the results to the employee.

A **performance management system** comprises the processes and activities involved in performance appraisals.

FIGURE 6.2

The Performance Management System

An organization's performance management system plays an important role in determining its overall level of effectiveness. This is especially true when the organization is attempting to employ total quality management. Key elements of a performance management system, as shown here, include the timing and frequency of evaluations, the choice of who does the evaluation, the choice of measurement procedures, the storage and distribution of performance information, and the recording methods. These elements are used by managers and employees in most organizations.

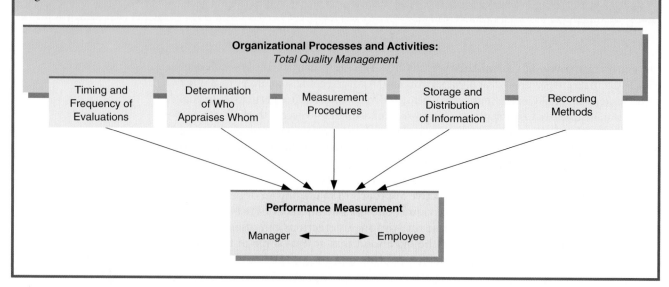

Simple performance appraisal involves a manager and an employee; the PMS incorporates the total quality management context along with the organizational policies, procedures, and resources that support the activity being approved. The timing and frequency of evaluations, choice of who appraises whom, measurement procedures, methods of recording the evaluations, and storage and distribution of information are all aspects of the PMS.

Purposes of Performance Measurement

Performance measurement may serve many purposes. The ability to provide valuable feedback is one critical purpose. Feedback, in turn, tells the employee where she or he stands in the eyes of the organization. Appraisal results, of course, are also used to decide and justify reward allocations. Performance evaluations may be used as a starting point for discussions of training, development, and improvement. Finally, the data produced by the performance appraisal system can be used to forecast future human resource needs, to plan management succession, and to guide other human resource activities such as recruiting, training, and development programs.

Providing job performance feedback is the primary use of appraisal information. Performance appraisal information can indicate that an employee is ready for promotion or that he or she needs additional training to gain experience in another area of company operations. It may also show that a person does not have the skills for a certain job and that another person should be recruited to fill that particular role. Other purposes of performance appraisal can be grouped into two broad categories, judgment and development, as shown in Figure 6.3.

Performance appraisals with a judgmental orientation focus on past performance and are concerned mainly with measuring and comparing performance and with the uses of the information generated. Appraisals with a developmental orientation focus on the future and use information from evaluations to improve performance. If improved

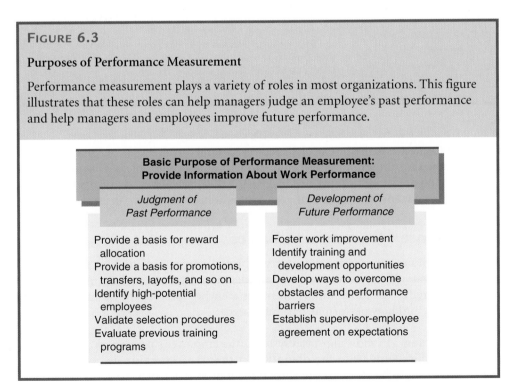

<figure>FIGURE **6.3**

Purposes of Performance Measurement

Performance measurement plays a variety of roles in most organizations. This figure illustrates that these roles can help managers judge an employee's past performance and help managers and employees improve future performance.

**Basic Purpose of Performance Measurement:
Provide Information About Work Performance**

Judgment of Past Performance	*Development of Future Performance*
Provide a basis for reward allocation	Foster work improvement
Provide a basis for promotions, transfers, layoffs, and so on	Identify training and development opportunities
Identify high-potential employees	Develop ways to overcome obstacles and performance barriers
Validate selection procedures	Establish supervisor-employee agreement on expectations
Evaluate previous training programs	|</figure>

Merrill Lynch and . . . **DIVERSITY**

"Not a Level Playing Field" at Merrill Lynch

Merrill Lynch is updating its performance evaluation system to help recruit and retain excellent personnel. At the same time, however, the company is facing over 900 lawsuits alleging that the giant brokerage discriminates against women and racial minorities. Morgan Stanley, J.P. Morgan Chase, Smith Barney, and others are accused of the same problems.

Charges of discrimination are not new. Valery Craane, a Spanish-speaking Merrill Lynch broker from Venezuela, worked for the company in the 1970s but quit because she felt the firm didn't give her the support it gave to her male coworkers. She eventually returned to Merrill and her daughter Janine joined the firm in the 1990s. In 2004, however, Valery and Janine filed a lawsuit against the company, claiming that the firm gives preferential treatment to whites and males, while allowing racial slurs, sexually suggestive behavior, and other forms of harassment.

For example, the women allege that when the brokerage distributed choice accounts, over half went to just seven male brokers, while the Craanes received 2 percent. Meanwhile, the Craanes were among Merrill's top performers, managing accounts worth $900 million and generating $4.5 million in annual revenues for Merrill. Today, Valery says that in spite of her team's contribution to Merrill, "It's just not a level playing field for us women. This is all about a profound lack of respect for who we are and what we do."

The Craanes are not poorly compensated, netting over $1 million for their work. Their lawsuit shows that racial and sexual discrimination can strike at any level.

In the early 1990s, as Merrill stalled in addressing one class-action lawsuit, female brokers chartered a plane to circle a Merrill-sponsored golf tournament in Pebble Beach. The plane towed a banner reading: "Merrill Lynch Discriminates Against Women." Maybe it's time for the Craanes to consider hiring a plane.

"Performance Management at Merrill Lynch," this chapter's closing case, describes the new performance management system at Merrill Lynch in more detail.

> **"This is all about a profound lack of respect for who we are and what we do."**
>
> VALERY CRAANE, BROKER, MERRILL LYNCH

References: Mara Der Hovanesian, "J.P. Morgan Loses a Veteran," *Business Week*, September 22, 2004, www.businessweek.com on April 16, 2005; Patrick McGeehan, "What Merrill's Women Want," *New York Times*, August 22, 2004, pp. BU1, 4 (quotation); Susan E. Reed, "When a Workplace Dispute Goes Very Public," *New York Times*, November 25, 2001, www.nytimes.com on March 29, 2005; Emily Thornton, "Fed Up and Fighting Back," *Business Week*, September 20, 2004, www.businessweek.com on March 30, 2005; Emily Thornton, "A Firefight in the Street's Gender Wars," *Business Week*, September 17, 2004, www.businessweek.com on March 30, 2005.

future performance is the intent of the appraisal process, the manager may focus on goals or targets for the employee, on eliminating obstacles or problems that hinder performance, and on future training needs. The *Merrill Lynch and . . . Diversity* box shows what can happen, however, if performance appraisal in an organization is mismanaged.

Performance Measurement Basics

Employee appraisals are common in every type of organization, but how they are performed may vary. Many issues must be considered in determining how to conduct an appraisal. Three of the most important issues are who does the appraisals, how often they are done, and how performance is measured.

The Appraiser   In most appraisal systems, the employee's primary evaluator is the supervisor. This stems from the obvious fact that the supervisor is presumably in the best position to be aware of the employee's day-to-day performance. Further, it is

Measuring job performance is an important part of performance management. For example, Jeffrey Lauden, an elementary school principal in Los Angeles, is assessing the classroom performance of Yoland Morales, a fifth-grade teacher. By carefully observing her performance, he can glean insights into her strengths and weaknesses as a teacher. He can then convey this information to her in ways that should make her an even better teacher.

the supervisor who has traditionally provided performance feedback to employees and determined performance-based rewards and sanctions. Problems often arise, however, if the supervisor has incomplete or distorted information about the employee's performance. For example, the supervisor may have little firsthand knowledge of the performance of an employee who works alone outside the company premises, such as a salesperson making solo calls on clients or a maintenance person handling equipment problems in the field. Similar problems may arise when the supervisor has a limited understanding of the technical knowledge involved in an employee's job.

One solution to these problems is a multiple-rater system that incorporates the ratings of several people familiar with the employee's performance. Another alternative is to use the employee as an evaluator. Although they may not actually do so, most employees are actually very capable of evaluating themselves in an unbiased manner.

One of the more interesting approaches being used in many companies today is something called **360-degree feedback**—a performance management system in which people receive performance feedback from those on all "sides" of them in the organization—their boss, their colleagues and peers, and their own subordinates. Thus, the feedback comes from all around them, or from 360 degrees. This form of performance evaluation can be very beneficial to managers because it typically gives them a much wider range of performance-related feedback than a traditional evaluation provides. That is, rather than focusing narrowly on objective performance, such as sales increases or productivity gains, 360 feedback often focuses on such things as interpersonal relations and style. For example, one person may learn that she stands too close to other people when she talks, another that he has a bad temper. These are the kinds of things a supervisor might not even be aware of, much less report as part of a performance appraisal. Subordinates or peers are much more willing to provide this sort of feedback.

Of course, to benefit from 360-degree feedback, a manager must have a thick skin. The manager is likely to hear some personal comments on sensitive topics, which may be threatening. Thus, a 360-feedback system must be carefully managed so that its

360-degree feedback is a performance management system in which people receive performance feedback from those on all sides of them in the organization—their boss, their colleagues and peers, and their own subordinates.

focus remains on constructive rather than destructive criticism.[9] Because of its potential advantages and in spite of its potential shortcomings, many companies today are using this approach to performance feedback. AT&T, Nestlé, Pitney Bowes, and Chase Manhattan Bank are just a few of the major companies today using 360-degree feedback to help managers improve a wide variety of performance-related behaviors.[10]

Frequency of the Appraisal   Another important issue is the frequency of appraisals. Regardless of the employee's level of performance, the type of tasks being performed, or the employee's need for information on performance, the organization usually conducts performance appraisals on a regular basis, typically once a year. Annual performance appraisals are convenient for administrative purposes such as record keeping and predictability. Some organizations also conduct appraisals semiannually.[11] Several systems for monitoring employee performance on an "as-needed" basis have been proposed as an alternative to the traditional annual system.

Managers in international settings must ensure that they incorporate cultural phenomena in their performance appraisal strategies. For example, in highly individualistic cultures such as that of the United States, appraising performance at the individual level is both common and accepted. But in collectivistic cultures such as Japan, performance appraisals almost always need to be focused more on group performance and feedback. And in countries where people put a lot of faith in destiny, fate, or some form of divine control, employees may not be receptive to performance feedback at all, believing that their actions are irrelevant to the results that follow them.

Measuring Performance   The cornerstone of a good PMS is the method for measuring performance. Detailed descriptions of the many different methods for measuring performance are beyond the scope of this book; they are more appropriately covered in a course in human resource management or a specialized course in performance appraisal. However, we can present a few general comments about how to measure performance.

The measurement method provides the information managers use to make decisions about salary adjustment, promotion, transfer, training, and discipline. The courts and Equal Employment Opportunity guidelines have mandated that performance measurements be based on job-related criteria rather than on some other factor such as friendship, age, sex, religion, or national origin. In addition, to provide useful information for the decision maker, performance appraisals must be valid, reliable, and free of bias. They must not produce ratings that are consistently too lenient or too severe or that all cluster in the middle. They must also be free of perceptual and timing errors.

Some of the most popular methods for evaluating individual performance are graphic rating scales, checklists, essays or diaries, behaviorally anchored rating scales, and forced-choice systems. These systems are easy to use and familiar to most managers. However, two major problems are common to all individual methods. The first is a tendency to rate most individuals at about the same level, and the second is the inability to discriminate among variable levels of performance.

Comparative methods evaluate two or more employees by comparing them with each other on various performance dimensions. The most popular comparative methods are ranking, forced distribution, paired comparisons, and the use of multiple raters in making comparisons. Comparative methods, however, are more difficult to use than the individual methods, are unfamiliar to many managers, and may require sophisticated development procedures and a computerized analytical system to extract usable information.

Individual Rewards in Organizations

As noted earlier, one of the primary purposes of performance management is to provide a basis for rewarding employees. We now turn our attention to rewards and their impact on employee motivation and performance. The **reward system** consists of all organizational components—including people, processes, rules and procedures, and decision-making activities—involved in allocating compensation and benefits to employees in exchange for their contributions to the organization.[12] As we examine organizational reward systems, it is important to keep in mind their role in psychological contracts (as discussed in Chapter 3) and employee motivation (as discussed in Chapter 4). Rewards constitute many of the inducements that organizations provide to employees as their part of the psychological contract. Rewards also satisfy some of the needs employees attempt to meet through their choice of work-related behaviors.

> The **reward system** consists of all organizational components, including people, processes, rules and procedures, and decision-making activities, involved in allocating compensation and benefits to employees in exchange for their contributions to the organization.

Roles, Purposes, and Meanings of Rewards

The purpose of the reward system in most organizations is to attract, retain, and motivate qualified employees. The organization's compensation structure must be equitable and consistent to ensure equality of treatment and compliance with the law. Compensation should also be a fair reward for the individual's contributions to the organization, although in most cases these contributions are difficult, if not impossible, to measure objectively. Given this limitation, managers should be as fair and as equitable as possible. Finally, the system must be competitive in the external labor market for the organization to attract and retain competent workers in appropriate fields.[13]

Beyond these broad considerations, an organization must develop its philosophy of compensation based on its own conditions and needs, and this philosophy must be defined and built into the actual reward system. For example, Wal-Mart has a policy that none of its employees will be paid the minimum wage. Even though it may pay some people only slightly more than this minimum, the firm nevertheless wants to communicate to all workers that it places a higher value on their contributions than just having to pay them the lowest wage possible.

The organization needs to decide what types of behaviors or performance it wants to encourage with a reward system because what is rewarded tends to recur. Possible behaviors include performance, longevity, attendance, loyalty, contributions to the "bottom line," responsibility, and conformity. Performance measurement, as described earlier, assesses these behaviors, but the choice of which behaviors to reward is a function of the compensation system. A reward system must also take into account volatile economic issues such as inflation, market conditions, technology, labor union activities, and so forth.

It is also important for the organization to recognize that organizational rewards have many meanings for employees. Intrinsic and extrinsic rewards carry both surface and symbolic value. The **surface value** of a reward to an employee is its objective meaning or worth. A salary increase of 5 percent, for example, means that an individual has 5 percent more spending power than before whereas a promotion, on the surface, means new duties and responsibilities. But managers must recognize that rewards also carry **symbolic value**. If a person gets a 3 percent salary increase when everyone else gets 5 percent, one plausible meaning is that the organization values other employees more. But if the same person gets 3 percent and all others get only 1 percent, the meaning may be just the opposite—the individual is seen as the most valuable employee. Thus, rewards convey to people not only how much they are valued by the organization but also their importance relative to others. Managers need to tune in to

> The **surface value** of a reward to an employee is its objective meaning or worth.
> The **symbolic value** of a reward to an employee is its subjective and personal meaning or worth.

the many meanings rewards can convey—not only to the surface messages but to the symbolic messages as well.

Types of Rewards

Most organizations use several different types of rewards. The most common are base pay (wages or salary), incentive systems, benefits, perquisites, and awards. These rewards are combined to create an individual's **compensation package**.

> An individual's **compensation package** is the total array of money (wages, salary, commission), incentives, benefits, perquisites, and awards provided by the organization.

Base Pay   For most people, the most important reward for work is the pay they receive. Obviously, money is important because of the things it can buy, but as we just noted, it can also symbolize an employee's worth. Pay is very important to an organization for a variety of reasons. For one thing, an effectively planned and managed pay system can improve motivation and performance. For another, employee compensation is a major cost of doing business—as much as 50 to 60 percent in many organizations—so a poorly designed system can be an expensive proposition. Finally, since pay is considered a major source of employee dissatisfaction, a poorly designed system can result in problems in other areas such as turnover and low morale.

> **Incentive systems** are plans in which employees can earn additional compensation in return for certain types of performance.

Incentive Systems   **Incentive systems** are plans in which employees can earn additional compensation in return for certain types of performance. Examples of incentive programs include the following:

1. *Piecework programs*, which tie a worker's earnings to the number of units produced
2. *Gain-sharing programs*, which grant additional earnings to employees or work groups for cost-reduction ideas
3. *Bonus systems*, which provide managers with lump-sum payments from a special fund based on the financial performance of the organization or a unit
4. *Long-term compensation*, which gives managers additional income based on stock price performance, earnings per share, or return on equity
5. *Merit pay plans*, which base pay raises on the employee's performance
6. *Profit-sharing plans*, which distribute a portion of the firm's profits to all employees at a predetermined rate
7. *Employee stock-option plans*, which set aside stock in the company for employees to purchase at a reduced rate

Plans oriented mainly toward individual employees may cause increased competition for the rewards and some possibly disruptive behaviors, such as sabotaging a coworker's performance, sacrificing quality for quantity, or fighting over customers. A group incentive plan, on the other hand, requires that employees trust one another and work together. Of course, incentive systems have advantages and disadvantages.

Long-term compensation for executives is particularly controversial because of the large sums of money involved and the basis for the payments. Indeed, executive compensation is one of the more controversial subjects that U.S. businesses have had to face in recent years. News reports and the popular press seem to take great joy in telling stories about how this or that executive has just received a huge windfall from his or her organization. Clearly, successful top managers deserve significant rewards. The job of a senior executive, especially a CEO, is grueling and stressful and takes talent and decades of hard work to reach. Only a small handful of managers ever attain a top position in a major corporation. The question is whether some companies are over-rewarding such managers for their contributions to the organization.[14]

© Mike Baldwin / Cornered

www.cartoonstock.com

"Worked all weekend to finish the report
and all I get is a stupid Pat on the back."

Incentive compensation systems can serve as powerful motivators. Of course, in order for incentives to have a meaningful impact on performance, the incentives that high performers earn must actually be rewards that they want. A pat on the back, for instance, only reinforces performance if the employee actually wants this form of encouragement and recognition (but as shown here, even a "pat" can be carried too far!).

When a firm is growing rapidly, and its profits are also growing rapidly, relatively few objections can be raised to paying the CEO well. However, objections arise when an organization is laying off workers, its financial performance is perhaps less than might be expected, and the CEO is still earning a huge amount of money. It is these situations that dictate that a company's board of directors take a close look at the appropriateness of its actions.[15]

Indirect Compensation   Another major component of the compensation package is **indirect compensation**, also commonly referred to as the employee benefits plan. Typical **benefits** provided by businesses include the following:

Indirect compensation, commonly known as benefits, is an important element in most compensation plans.

1. *Payment for time not worked*, both on and off the job. On-the-job free time includes lunch, rest, coffee breaks, and wash-up or get-ready time. Off-the-job time not worked includes vacation, sick leave, holidays, and personal days.
2. *Social Security contributions.* The employer contributes half the money paid into the system established under the Federal Insurance Contributions Act (FICA). The employee pays the other half.
3. *Unemployment compensation.* People who have lost their jobs or are temporarily laid off get a percentage of their wages from an insurance-like program.
4. *Disability and workers' compensation benefits.* Employers contribute funds to help workers who cannot work due to occupational injury or ailment.
5. *Life and health insurance programs.* Most organizations offer insurance at a cost far below what individuals would pay to buy insurance on their own.
6. *Pension or retirement plans.* Most organizations offer plans to provide supplementary income to employees after they retire.

A company's Social Security, unemployment, and workers' compensation contributions are set by law. But how much to contribute for other kinds of benefits is up to each

The relationship between pay and performance is an important part of the motivational process in organizations. Bill Ford, chairman and CEO of Ford Motor Company, has asked the firm's board of directors to tie his pay more directly to the company's performance. He has also agreed to forego all compensation until Ford has achieved sustainable profitability.

Perquisites are special privileges awarded to selected members of an organization, usually top managers.

company. Some organizations contribute more to the cost of these benefits than others. Some companies pay the entire cost; others pay a percentage of the cost of certain benefits, such as health insurance, and bear the entire cost of other benefits. Offering benefits beyond wages became a standard component of compensation during World War II as a way to increase employee compensation when wage controls were in effect. Since then, competition for employees and employee demands (expressed, for instance, in union bargaining) have caused companies to increase these benefits. In many organizations today, benefits now account for 30 to 40 percent of the payroll.

The burden of providing employee benefits is growing heavier for firms in the United States than it is for organizations in other countries, especially among unionized firms. For example, consider the problem that General Motors faces. Workers at GM's brake factory in Dayton, Ohio, earn an average of $27 an hour in wages. They also earn another $16 an hour in benefits, including full healthcare coverage with no deductibles, full pension benefits after thirty years of service, life and disability insurance, and legal services. Thus, GM's total labor costs per worker at the factory average $43 an hour. A German rival, Robert Bosch GmbH, meanwhile, has a nonunionized brake plant in South Carolina. It pays its workers an average of $18 an hour in wages, and its hourly benefit cost is around $5. Bosch's benefits include medical coverage with a $2,000 deductible, 401-K retirement plans with employee participation, and life and disability coverage. Bosch's total hourly labor costs per worker, therefore, are only $23. Toyota, Nissan, and Honda buy most of their brakes for their U.S. factories from Bosch whereas General Motors must use its own factory to supply brakes. Thus, foreign competitors realize considerable cost advantages over GM in the brakes they use, and this pattern runs across a variety of other component parts as well.[16]

Perquisites   **Perquisites** are special privileges awarded to selected members of an organization, usually top managers. For years, the top executives of many businesses were allowed privileges such as unlimited use of the company jet, motor home, vacation home, and executive dining room. In Japan, a popular perquisite is a paid membership in an exclusive golf club; a common perquisite in England is first-class travel. In the United States, the Internal Revenue Service has recently ruled that some "perks" constitute a form of income and thus can be taxed. This decision has substantially changed the nature of these benefits, but they have not entirely disappeared, nor are they likely to. Today, however, many perks tend to be more job-related. For example, popular perks currently include a car and driver (so that the executive can work while being transported to and from work) and cellular telephones (so that the executive can conduct business anywhere). More than anything else, though, perquisites seem to add to the status of their recipients and thus may increase job satisfaction and reduce turnover.[17]

Awards   At many companies, employees receive awards for everything from seniority to perfect attendance, from zero defects (quality work) to cost reduction suggestions. Award programs can be costly in the time required to run them and in money if cash awards are given. But award systems can improve performance under the right conditions. In one medium-size manufacturing company, careless work habits were pushing

up the costs of scrap and rework (the cost of scrapping defective parts or reworking them to meet standards). Management instituted a zero-defects program to recognize employees who did perfect or near-perfect work. During the first month, two workers in shipping caused only one defect in over two thousand parts handled. Division management called a meeting in the lunchroom and recognized each worker with a plaque and a ribbon. The next month, the same two workers had two defects, so there was no award. The following month, the two workers had zero defects, and once again top management called a meeting to give out plaques and ribbons. Elsewhere in the plant, defects, scrap, and rework decreased dramatically as workers evidently sought recognition for quality work. What worked in this particular plant may or may not work in others.[18]

Managing Reward Systems

Much of our discussion on reward systems has focused on general issues. As Table 6.1 shows, however, the organization must address other issues when developing organizational reward systems. The organization must consider its ability to pay employees at certain levels, economic and labor market conditions, and the impact of the pay system on organizational financial performance. In addition, the organization must consider the relationship between performance and rewards as well as the issues of reward system flexibility, employee participation in the reward system, pay secrecy, and expatriate compensation.

Linking Performance and Rewards

For managers to take full advantage of the symbolic value of pay, there must be a perception on the part of employees that their rewards are linked to their performance.

Issue	Important Examples
Pay Secrecy	• Open, closed, partial • Link with performance appraisal • Equity perceptions
Employee Participation	• By human resource department • By joint employee/management committee
Flexible System	• Cafeteria-style benefits • Annual lump sum or monthly bonus • Salary versus benefits
Ability to Pay	• Organization's financial performance • Expected future earnings
Economic and Labor Market Factors	• Inflation rate • Industry pay standards • Unemployment rate
Impact on Organizational Performance	• Increase in costs • Impact on performance
Expatriate Compensation	• Cost-of-living differentials • Managing related equity issues

TABLE 6.1

Issues to Consider in Developing Reward Systems

For example, if everyone in an organization starts working for the same hourly rate and then receives a predetermined wage increase every six months or year, there is clearly no relationship between performance and rewards. Instead, the organization is indicating that all entry-level employees are worth the same amount, and pay increases are tied solely to the length of time an employee works in the organization. This holds true whether the employee is a top, average, or mediocre employee. The only requirement is that the employee work well enough to avoid being fired.

At the other extreme, an organization might attempt to tie all compensation to actual performance. Thus, each new employee might start at a different wage, as determined by his or her experience, education, skills, and other job-related factors. After joining the organization, the individual then receives rewards based on actual performance. One employee, for example, might start at $15 an hour because she has ten years of experience and a good performance record at her previous employer. Another might start the same job at a rate of $10.50 an hour because he has only four years' experience and an adequate but not outstanding performance record. Assuming the first employee performs up to expectations, she might also get several pay increases, bonuses, and awards throughout the year whereas the second employee might get only one or two small increases and no other rewards. Of course, organizations must ensure that pay differences are based strictly on performance (including seniority), not on factors that do not relate to performance (such as gender, ethnicity, or other discriminatory factors).

In reality, most organizations attempt to develop a reward strategy somewhere between these two extremes. Because it is really quite difficult to differentiate all the employees, most firms use some basic compensation level for everyone. For example, they might start everyone performing a specific job at the same rate, regardless of experience. They might also work to provide reasonable incentives and other inducements for high performers while making sure that they don't ignore the average employees. The key fact for managers to remember is simply that if they expect rewards to motivate perfor-

When firms are allocating rewards and benefits to their employees, it is important that they do so in a fair and equitable manner. Defensible methods for making these allocations include performance and/or seniority. However, companies sometimes make the mistake of allowing discriminatory practices to influence rewards. These women represent 1.6 million current and former women workers at Wal-Mart. They allege that the firm discriminated against women regarding both pay and promotion opportunities for several years.

mance, employees must see a clear, direct link between their own job-related behaviors and the attainment of those rewards.[19]

Flexible Reward Systems

Flexible, or cafeteria-style, reward systems are a recent and increasingly popular variation on the standard compensation system. A **flexible reward system** allows employees, within specified ranges, to choose the combination of benefits that best suits their needs. For example, a younger worker just starting out might prefer to have especially strong healthcare coverage with few deductibles. A worker with a few years of experience might prefer to have more childcare benefits. A midcareer employee with more financial security might prefer more time off with pay. And older workers might prefer to have more rewards concentrated into their retirement plans.

A flexible reward system allows employees to choose the combination of benefits that best suits their needs.

Some organizations are starting to apply the flexible approach to pay. For example, employees sometimes have the option of taking an annual salary increase in one lump sum rather than in monthly increments. General Electric recently implemented such a system for some of its managers. UNUM Corporation, a large insurance firm, allows all of its employees the option of drawing a full third of their annual compensation in the month of January. This makes it easier for them to handle such major expenses as purchasing a new automobile, buying a home, or covering college education costs for children. Obviously, the administrative costs of providing this level of flexibility are greater, but many employees value this flexibility and may develop strong loyalty and attachment to an employer who offers this kind of compensation package.

Participative Pay Systems

In keeping with the current trend toward worker involvement in organizational decision making, employee participation in the pay process is also increasing. A participative pay system may involve the employee in the system's design, administration, or both. A pay system can be designed by staff members of the organization's human resources department, a committee of managers in the organization, an outside consultant, the employees, or a combination of these sources. Organizations that have used a joint management employee task force to design the compensation system have generally succeeded in designing and implementing a plan that managers could use and that employees believed in. Employee participation in administering the pay system is a natural extension of having employees participate in its design. Examples of companies that have involved employees in the administration of the pay system include Romac Industries, where employees vote on the pay of other employees; Graphic Controls, where each manager's pay is determined by a group of peers; and the Friedman-Jacobs Company, where employees set their own wages based on their perceptions of their performance.[20]

Pay Secrecy

When a company has a policy of open salary information, the exact salary amounts for employees are public knowledge. State governments, for instance, make public the salaries of everyone on their payrolls. A policy of complete secrecy means that no information is available to employees regarding other employees' salaries, average or percentage raises, or salary ranges. The National Labor Relations Board recently upheld an earlier ruling that an employer starting or enforcing a rule that forbids "employees to discuss their salaries" constitutes interference, restraint, and coercion of protected employee rights under the National Labor Relations Act. Although a few organizations

have completely public or completely secret systems, most have systems somewhere in the middle.

Expatriate Compensation

Expatriate compensation is yet another important issue in managing reward systems.[21] Consider, for example, a manager living and working in Houston currently making $250,000 a year. That income allows the manager to live in a certain kind of home, drive a certain kind of car, have access to certain levels of medical care, and live a certain kind of lifestyle. Now suppose the manager is asked to accept a transfer to Tokyo, Geneva, or London, cities where the cost of living is considerably higher than in Houston. The same salary cannot begin to support a comparable lifestyle in those cities. Consequently, the employer is almost certain to redesign the manager's compensation package so that the employee's lifestyle in the new location will be comparable to that in the old.

Now consider a different scenario. Suppose the same manager is asked to accept a transfer to an underdeveloped nation. The cost of living in this nation might be quite low by U.S. standards. But there may also be relatively few choices in housing, poorer schools and medical care, a harsh climate, greater personal danger, or similar unattractive characteristics. The firm will probably have to pay the manager some level of additional compensation to offset the decrement in quality of lifestyle. Thus, developing rewards for expatriates is a complicated process.

Figure 6.4 illustrates the approach to expatriate compensation used by one major multinational corporation. The left side of the figure shows how a U.S. employee currently uses her or his salary—part of it goes for taxes, part is saved, and the rest is consumed. When a person is asked to move abroad, a human resource manager works with the employee to develop an equitable balance sheet for the new compensation package. As shown on the right side of the figure, the individual's compensation package will potentially consist of six components. First, the individual will receive income to cover what his or her taxes and Social Security payments in the United States will be. The individual may also have to pay foreign taxes and additional U.S. taxes as a result of the move, so the company covers these as well.

Next, the firm also pays an amount adequate to the employee's current consumption levels in the United States. If the cost of living is greater in the foreign location than at home, the firm pays the excess foreign costs. The employee also receives income for saving comparable to what he or she is currently saving. Finally, if the employee faces a hardship because of the assignment, an additional foreign service premium or hardship allowance is added by the firm. Not surprisingly, then, expatriate compensation packages can be very expensive for an organization and must be carefully developed and managed.[22]

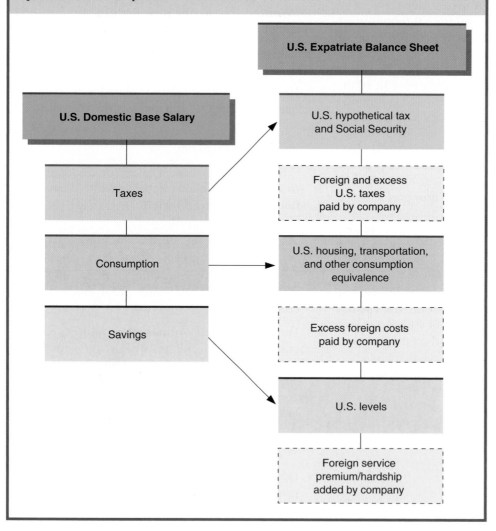

FIGURE 6.4

The Expatriate Compensation Balance Sheet

Organizations that ask employees to accept assignments in foreign locations must usually adjust their compensation levels to account for differences in cost of living and similar factors. Amoco uses the system shown here. The employee's domestic base salary is first broken down into the three categories shown on the left. Then adjustments are made by adding compensation to the categories on the right until an appropriate, equitable level of compensation is achieved.

Chapter Review

Synopsis

A goal is a desirable objective. The goal-setting theory of motivation suggests that appropriate goal difficulty, specificity, acceptance, and commitment will result in higher levels of motivated performance. Management by objectives, or MBO, extends goal setting throughout an organization by cascading goals down from the top of the firm to the bottom.

Performance measurement is the process by which work behaviors are measured and compared with established standards and the results recorded and communicated. Its purposes are to evaluate employees' work performance and to provide information for organizational uses such as compensation, personnel planning, and employee training and development. Three primary issues in performance appraisal are who does the appraisals, how often they are done, and how performance is measured.

The purpose of the reward system is to attract, retain, and motivate qualified employees and to maintain a pay structure that is internally equitable and externally competitive. Rewards have both surface and symbolic value. Rewards take the form of money, indirect compensation or benefits, perquisites, awards, and incentives. Factors such as motivational impact, cost, and fit with the organizational system must be considered when designing or analyzing a reward system.

The effective management of a reward system requires that performance be linked with rewards. Managing rewards entails dealing with issues such as flexible reward systems, employee participation in the pay system, the secrecy of pay systems, and expatriate rewards.

Discussion Questions

1. Critique the goal-setting theory of motivation.

2. Develop a framework whereby an instructor could use goal setting in running a class such as this one.

3. Why are employees not simply left alone to do their jobs instead of having their performance measured and evaluated all the time?

4. In what ways is your performance as a student evaluated?

5. How is the performance of your instructor measured? What are the limitations of this method?

6. Can performance on some jobs simply not be measured? Why or why not?

7. What conditions make it easier for an organization to achieve continuous improvement? What conditions make it more difficult?

8. As a student in this class, what "rewards" do you receive in exchange for your time and effort? What are the rewards for the professor who teaches this class? How do your contributions and rewards differ from those of some other student in the class?

9. Do you expect to obtain the rewards you discussed in question 8 on the basis of your intelligence, your hard work, the number of hours you spend in the library, your height, your good looks, your work experience, or some other personal factor?

10. What rewards are easiest for managers to control? What rewards are more difficult to control?

11. Often institutions in federal and state governments give the same percentage pay raise to all their employees. What do you think is the effect of this type of pay raise on employee motivation?

Using Compensation to Motivate Workers

Purpose: The purpose of this exercise is to illustrate how compensation can be used to motivate employees.

Format: You will be asked to review eight managers and make salary adjustments for each.

Procedure: Listed below are your notes on the performance of eight managers who work for you. You (either individually or as a group, depending on your instructor's choice) have to recommend salary increases for eight managers who have just completed their first year with the company and are now to be considered for their first annual raise. Keep in mind that you may be setting precedents and that you need to keep salary costs down. However, there are no formal company restrictions on the kind of raises you can give. Indicate the sizes of the raise that you would like to give each manager by writing a percentage next to each name.

Variations: The instructor might alter the situation in one of several ways. One way is to assume that all of the eight managers entered the company at the same salary, say $30,000, which gives a total salary expense of $240,000. If upper management has allowed a salary raise pool of 10 percent of the current salary expenses, then you as the manager have $24,000 to give out as raises. In this variation, students can deal with actual dollar amounts rather than just percentages for the raises. Another interesting variation is to assume that all of the managers entered the company at different salaries, averaging $30,000. (The instructor can create many interesting possibilities for how these salaries might vary.) Then, the students can suggest salaries for the different managers.

_____ % Abraham McGowan. Abe is not, as far as you can tell, a good performer. You have checked your view with others, and they do not feel that he is effective either. However, you happen to know he has one of the toughest work groups to manage. His subordinates have low skill levels, and the work is dirty and hard. If you lose him, you are not sure whom you could find to replace him.

_____ % Benjy Berger. Benjy is single and seems to live the life of a carefree bachelor. In general, you feel

that his job performance is not up to par, and some of his "goofs" are well known to his fellow employees.

_____ % Clyde Clod. You consider Clyde to be one of your best subordinates. However, it is obvious that other people do not consider him to be an effective manager. Clyde has married a rich wife, and as far as you know, he does not need additional money.

_____ % David Doodle. You happen to know from your personal relationship with "Doodles" that he badly needs more money because of certain personal problems he is having. As far as you are concerned, he also happens to be one of the best of your subordinates. For some reason, your enthusiasm is not shared by your other subordinates, and you have heard them make joking remarks about his performance.

_____ % Ellie Ellesberg. Ellie has been very successful so far in the tasks she has undertaken. You are particularly impressed by this since she has a hard job. She needs money more than many of the other people, and you are sure that they respect her because of her good performance.

_____ % Fred Foster. Fred has turned out to be a very pleasant surprise to you. He has done an excellent job and it is generally accepted among the others that he is one of the best people. This surprises you because he is generally frivolous and does not seem to care very much about money and promotion.

_____ % Greta Goslow. Your opinion is that Greta is just not cutting the mustard. Surprisingly enough, however, when you check to see how others feel about her, you discover that her work is very highly regarded. You also know that she badly needs a raise. She was just recently widowed and is finding it extremely difficult to support her household and her young family of four.

_____ % Harry Hummer. You know Harry personally, and he just seems to squander his money continually. He has a fairly easy job assignment, and your view is that he does not do it particularly well. You are, therefore, quite surprised to find that several of the other new managers think that he is the best of the new group.

After you have made the assignments for the eight people, you will have a chance to discuss them either in groups or in the larger class.

Follow-up Questions

1. Is there a clear difference between the highest and lowest performer? Why or why not?

2. Did you notice differences in the types of information that you had available to make the raise decisions? How did you use the different sources of information?

3. In what ways did your assignment of raises reflect different views of motivation?

Reference: Edward E. Lawler III, "Motivation Through Compensation," adapted by D. T. Hall, in *Instructor's Manual for Experiences in Management and Organizational Behavior* (New York: John Wiley & Sons, 1975). Reprinted by permission of the author.

Self-Assessment Exercise

Diagnosing Poor Performance and Enhancing Motivation

Introduction: Formal performance appraisal and feedback are part of assuring proper performance in an organization. The following assessment is designed to help you understand how to detect poor performance and overcome it.

Procedure: Please respond to the following statements by writing a number from the following rating scale in the left-hand column. Your answers should reflect your attitudes and behaviors as they are *now*.

Strongly agree   = 6
Agree   = 5
Slightly agree   = 4
Slightly disagree   = 3
Disagree   = 2
Strongly disagree = 1

When another person needs to be motivated,

_____ 1. I always approach a performance problem by first establishing whether it is caused by a lack of motivation or ability.

_____ 2. I always establish a clear standard of expected performance.

_____ 3. I always offer to provide training and information, without offering to do the task myself.

_____ 4. I am honest and straightforward in providing feedback on performance and assessing advancement opportunities.

_____ 5. I use a variety of rewards to reinforce exceptional performance.

_____ 6. When discipline is required, I identify the problem, describe its consequences, and explain how it should be corrected.

_____ 7. I design task assignments to make them interesting and challenging.

_____ 8. I determine what rewards are valued by the person and strive to make those available.

_____ 9. I make sure that the person feels fairly and equitably treated.

_____ 10. I make sure that the person gets timely feedback from those affected by task performance.

_____ 11. I carefully diagnose the causes of poor performance before taking any remedial or disciplinary actions.

_____ 12. I always help the person establish performance goals that are challenging, specific, and time-bound.

_____ 13. Only as a last resort do I attempt to reassign or release a poorly performing individual.

_____ 14. Whenever possible, I make sure that valued rewards are linked to high performance.

_____ 15. I consistently discipline when effort is below expectations and capabilities.

_____ 16. I try to combine or rotate assignments so that the person can use a variety of skills.

_____**17.** I try to arrange for the person to work with others in a team, for the mutual support of all.

_____**18.** I make sure that the person is using realistic standards for measuring fairness.

_____**19.** I provide immediate compliments and other forms of recognition for meaningful accomplishments.

_____**20.** I always determine if the person has the necessary resources and support to succeed in the task.

Reference: David A. Whetten and Kim S. Cameron, *Developing Management Skills,* 2nd ed., pp. 336–337. Copyright © 1991 by HarperCollins. Reprinted by permission of Pearson Education, Inc., Upper Saddle River, NJ.

Building Managerial Skills

Exercise Overview: All managers must be able to communicate effectively with others in the organization. Communication is especially important in terms of dealing with employment-related issues.

Exercise Background: As noted in the chapter, many companies provide various benefits to their workers. These benefits may include such things as pay for time not worked, insurance coverage, pension plans, and so forth. These benefits are often very costly to the organization. Benefits often equal one-third or more of what employees are paid in wages and salaries. In some countries, such as Germany, the figures are even higher.

However, many employees often fail to appreciate the actual value of the benefits their employers provide to them. For example, they frequently underestimate the dollar value of their benefits. In addition, when comparing their income with that of others or when comparing alternative job offers, many people focus almost entirely on direct compensation—wages and salaries directly paid to the individual.

For example, consider a college graduate who has two offers. One job offer is for $40,000 a year, and the other is for $42,000. The individual is likely to see the second offer as being more desirable, even though the first offer may have sufficiently more attractive benefits that would make the total compensation packages equivalent to each other.

Exercise Task: With this information as context, respond to the following questions:

1. Why do you think most people focus on pay when assessing their compensation?

2. If you were the human resource manager for a firm, how would you go about communicating benefit values to your employees?

3. Suppose an employee comes to you and says that he is thinking about leaving for a "better job." You then learn that he is defining "better" only in terms of higher pay. How might you go about helping him compare the total compensation (including benefits) packages of his current job and of the "better job"?

4. Some firms today are cutting their benefits. How would you go about communicating a benefit cut to your employees?

Organizational Behavior Case for Discussion

Performance Management at Merrill Lynch

In 2001, investors and government regulators accused financial services firm Merrill Lynch of dishonest practices, including involvement with the Enron scandal. The stock market was down, reducing the firm's profits. On September 11, 2001, Merrill headquarters, located next to New York's World Trade Center, were damaged and three

employees died. The events of 2001 caused Merrill managers to re-evaluate the company's direction and make sweeping changes. One area targeted for change was the firm's performance management and reward system.

> **"*The conversation really is, how do we work together to improve performance?*"**
> LINDA MURPHY, DIRECTOR OF GLOBAL PERFORMANCE MANAGEMENT, MERRILL LYNCH

Under the old process, employees were ranked against each other. Rewards were distributed to those with higher performance according to a predetermined formula. This system focused on competition between employees and forced managers to look for justifications for their ranking choices. It created tension among employees and between employees and managers.

Today, "the whole emphasis has shifted from one of justifying a rating to one of improving performance," says Linda Murphy, Merrill Lynch's director of global performance management. "We're looking at how we can help the employee improve his or her performance. And because of that, there's much more concentration on the coaching, the feedback, and the conversations that occur between the manager and the employee . . . The conversation really is, how do we work together to improve performance?" Instead of focusing on the past, the new system looks forward, to improve future performance.

The new process begins with each employee and his or her managers agreeing on a set of performance objectives. The objectives are closely tied to Merrill's business goals. Goals can be adjusted as needed at any time. Feedback is ongoing, with required reviews at mid-year and year-end, and lots of opportunities for spontaneous suggestions and mentoring. Joint goal setting strengthens the cooperative relationship between manager and worker, while performance measured against standards reduces competition among workers.

To de-emphasize the importance of ratings in this highly competitive industry, the company has moved to a simple three-point scale. Murphy states, "[The new scale] allows the manager to say to the employee, 'The middle category is an acceptable level of performance. Most of us are in that category. Now, let's talk about how, relative to your peers, we can move you up in the rankings.'"

Another important aspect of the new process is the use of 360-degree feedback, where each employee is evaluated by superiors, peers, and clients. Peer reviews are most useful in assessing an employee's performance as a team member, which accounts for about one-third of the overall evaluation at Merrill.

In the brokerage industry, most companies have many limitations on their performance evaluation system, including too much reliance on subjective criteria, reliance on a single criteria, and refusal to publicize the criteria. Merrill, on the other hand, relies on numerous, mostly objective criteria for evaluation, including profit margin, ROE, market share, growth of new businesses, and expense reduction. And its evaluation criteria are published in-house and publicly, through the Internet.

The new system has other benefits, too, including better appeal to a diverse pool of applicants and ease in recruiting and retention. "This is a critical element that will help us be more competitive in the war for talent," says Murphy.

The new performance management system is described as having a neutral effect on compensation, to calm employees' fears of lost wages. Yet CEO Stan O'Neal, who moved into that spot in 2003, is known for his strategy of radical change and cost cutting. Under O'Neal's leadership, 22,000 workers, about one-third of the payroll, have been laid off. O'Neal is looking for areas to slash and labor costs are the biggest item in Merrill's budget. Business writer Emily Thornton describes O'Neal's approach as "a Darwinian code that encourages managers to take risks and gives them six months to a year to show they can succeed—or get out."

Forecasts predict that the brokerage industry will become even more cutthroat over the next few years, increasing pressures for efficiency. If Merrill Lynch can successfully implement an innovative and supportive performance management system, it might be able to outrun this very fast and very resourceful pack.

Case Questions

1. Describe Merrill Lynch's new approach to motivation in terms of goal difficulty and goal specificity. What are the likely outcomes for goal acceptance and goal commitment?

2. Should Merrill make customers an important source of data for its 360-degree feedback program? Why or why not?

3. What are the benefits of linking pay with performance? Are there any pitfalls or limitations that Merrill managers should be aware of as they link pay with performance?

References: "New Performance Management System Replacing Annual Performance Review," Missouri Small Business Development Centers website, 2001, www.missouribusiness.net on March 29, 2005; David Bushley, "How Are Peer Reviews Used for Compensation?" *Workforce Management*, September 5, 2001, www.workforce.com on March 29, 2005; Dayton Fandray, "Managing Performance the Merrill Lynch Way," *Workforce Management*, May 2001, pp. 36–40 (quotation); Paul Hodgson, "The Wall Street Example—Bringing Excessive Executive Compensation into Line," *Ivey Business Journal*, May/June 2004, www.iveybusinessjournal.com on March 29, 2005; Jeffrey Rothfeder, "The Road Less Traveled—Merrill Lynch and Co.," *CIO Insight*, March 1, 2004, www.cioinsight.com on March 29, 2005; Emily Thornton, "The New Merrill Lynch," *Business Week*, May 5, 2003, www.businessweek.com on March 29, 2005.

TEST PREPPER

You have read the chapter and studied the key terms. Think you're ready to ace the exam? Take this sample test to gauge your comprehension of chapter material and check your answers at the back of the book. Want more test questions? Take the ACE quizzes found on the student website: http://college.hmco.com/ business/students/ (select Griffin/Moorhead, Organizational Behavior, 8e from the Management menu).

T F 1. Goals are effective control devices.

T F 2. Research shows "do your best" goals are the most effective.

T F 3. The purpose of the reward system in most organizations is to attract, retain, and motivate qualified employees.

T F 4. Social Security contributions, lunch breaks, and sick leave are all examples of indirect compensation.

T F 5. A predetermined wage increase at the end of every year employed at the organization fails to appropriately link performance and rewards.

T F 6. Expatriate compensation packages are usually more expensive for the organization than those for similar employees working locally.

7. Social learning theory suggests goals in organizations
   a. limit the ability for people to learn from one another.
   b. create feelings of pride when people achieve their goals.
   c. need to be broad "try your hardest" objectives.
   d. may lower the self-efficacy of employees.
   e. should be socially-oriented objectives aimed at increasing satisfaction.

8. Which of the following best describes management by objectives (MBO)?
   a. Market forces determine organizational goals.
   b. Top managers determine goals for each employee in the organization.
   c. Objective performance goals are set for the organization as a whole, but not for individual employees.
   d. Managers and subordinates meet and jointly determine goals for the subordinate.
   e. Subordinates are trained to set personal goals without the help of managers.

9. Performance measurement serves all of the following purposes, except
   a. feedback to the employee.
   b. decide and justify reward allocations.
   c. meet legal requirements for publicly held firms.
   d. forecast future human resource needs.
   e. starting point for discussions of training, development, and improvement.

10. Organizations typically conduct performance appraisals
    a. daily.
    b. weekly.
    c. monthly.
    d. bi-monthly.
    e. once a year.

11. An employee's compensation package might include all of the following, except
    a. base pay.
    b. performance appraisal.
    c. benefits.
    d. awards.
    e. perquisites.

12. A flexible reward system
    a. allows employees to choose the combination of benefits that best suits their needs.
    b. changes reward allocations based on the size of the organization.
    c. requires workers to accept whatever rewards are offered by the company.
    d. treats employees, managers, and staff differently.
    e. replaces the need for fixed reward costs in the organization.

13. Mike is worried some of his employees will be dissatisfied if they know each other's salaries, so he is thinking about instituting a pay secrecy policy. What advice would you give Mike?
    a. Employee dissatisfaction doesn't come from knowing salaries.
    b. Pay secrecy will lead to other forms of secrecy.
    c. He should at least tell his subordinates his own salary, since he knows theirs.
    d. Pay secrecy rules have been ruled illegal.
    e. If he adopts a pay secrecy policy, he must strictly enforce it if it is to be effective.

Managing Stress and the Work-Life Balance

After studying this chapter, you should be able to:

▶ **Define and describe the nature of stress.**

▶ **Identify basic individual differences related to stress.**

▶ **Identify and describe common causes of stress.**

▶ **Discuss the central consequences of stress.**

▶ **Describe various ways that stress can be managed.**

▶ **Discuss work-life linkages and their relation to stress.**

The Stress of "Controlled Chaos"

FedEx provides air cargo express services, moving everything from an urgent business letter to a human heart for transplant. FedEx employs thousands of aircraft, vehicles, and workers in dozens of countries. At FedEx's Memphis airport hub, the company typically processes 5 million packages—per day—and up to 7.5 million items during holidays. Looking around on a recent, typical night, Reginald Owens, Sr., vice president, admits it may look like controlled chaos, but in reality "is a well-conditioned, well-organized machine."

Yet FedEx jobs can be stressful. For example, FedEx package handlers and couriers sort, load, and deliver items. They work outside, with heavy machinery, on day and night shifts, using physical coordination, strength, speed, and attention to detail.

Call center employees face different sources of stress. In that environment, workers must answer a high volume of calls with accuracy, courtesy, and speed. Employee performance is evaluated by supervisors who listen in on calls.

Even managers at FedEx experience stress. Executive vice president T. Michael Glenn explains that performance is critical: "We've got to work our people pretty hard to guarantee that every child gets her

> **"** *Everything we do, we're managing to a time clock.* **"**
>
> JOHN G. DUNAVANT, MANAGING DIRECTOR FOR GLOBAL OPERATIONS CONTROL, FEDEX

Christmas doll on time." Nightly deadlines contribute to the urgency, and managing director for global operations control John G. Dunavant says, "Everything we do, we're managing to a time clock."

In addition, the business environment holds intense competition, a high need for security, and unpredictable weather, further adding to stress.

High stress can cause mental and physical problems and reduce motivation. These can lead to increased absenteeism and turnover, burnout, and loss of productivity. FedEx competes in a customer-oriented service industry, where these consequences could be devastating.

FedEx uses two strategies to effectively address employee stress. First, it reduces the stress inherent in jobs, to the extent that is possible. For example, the company conducts time-and-motion studies to identify less tiring ways of completing tasks. Employees are then trained in the proper techniques. Employee suggestions are used to redesign jobs to make them less stressful. Automated tools, such as bar code scanners and computerized package tracking systems, handle some of the repetitive tasks.

FedEx's second strategy helps employees more effectively cope with stress. Job duties can be modified if an employee needs a temporary break. Benefits include paid sick time and leave, and assistance with stressful life events such as birth, adoption, or death. An employee assistance program provides counseling and help for legal, financial, mental health, relationship, childcare, and eldercare problems.

While stress seems inevitable at FedEx, the company's strategies are beneficial. FedEx has been named as one of the best companies for workers by *Fortune*, *ComputerWorld*, *Wall Street Journal*, and *Business Ethics*. For more about electronic monitoring at FedEx and its effect on worker stress, see the boxed insert *FedEx and . . . Technology* on page 183.

References: "FedEx Philosophy," "Team Member Benefits," FedEx website, www.fedex.com on March 14, 2005; "HR's Push for Productivity," *Employee InfoLink*, August 23, 2002, www.doc .state.ok.us on March 14, 2005; Claudia H. Deutsch, "Planes, Trucks and 7.5 Million Packages: FedEx's Big Night," *New York Times*, December 21, 2003, p. BU 1 (quotation); Shu Shin Luh, "Asian Employers Give Workers Training, Respect and Merit Pay," *Asian Wall Street Journal*, www.shushinluh.com on March 14, 2005.

I n several of our earlier chapters we discussed motivational forces and organizational methods that might lead people to be more motivated. However, there are also dark sides to these same perspectives. Many people today work long hours, face constant deadlines, and are subject to pressure to produce more and more. Organizations and the people who run them are under constant pressure to increase income while keeping costs in check. To do things faster and better—but with fewer people—is the goal of many companies today. An unfortunate effect of this trend is to put too much pressure on people—operating employees, other managers, and oneself. The results can indeed be increased performance, higher profits, and faster growth. But stress, burnout, turnover, aggression, and other unpleasant side effects can also occur.

In this chapter, we examine how and why stress occurs in organizations and how to better understand and control it. First, we explore the nature of stress. Then we look at such important individual differences as Type A and Type B personality profiles and their role in stress. Next, we discuss a number of causes of stress and consider the potential consequences of stress. We then highlight several things people and organizations can do to manage stress at work. We conclude by discussing an important factor related to stress—linkages between work and nonwork parts of people's lives.

The Nature of Stress

Many people think of stress as a simple problem. In reality, however, stress is complex and often misunderstood.[1] To learn how job stress truly works, we must first define it and then describe the process through which it develops.

Stress Defined

Stress has been defined in many ways, but most definitions say that stress is caused by a stimulus, that the stimulus can be either physical or psychological, and that the individual responds to the stimulus in some way.[2] Therefore, we define **stress** as a person's adaptive response to a stimulus that places excessive psychological or physical demands on him or her.

> **Stress** is a person's adaptive response to a stimulus that places excessive psychological or physical demands on that person.

Given the underlying complexities of this definition, we need to examine its components carefully. First is the notion of adaptation. As we will discuss presently, people may adapt to stressful circumstances in any of several ways. Second is the role of the stimulus. This stimulus, generally called a *stressor*, is anything that induces stress. Third, stressors can be either psychological or physical. Finally, the demands the stressor places on the individual must be excessive for stress to actually result. Of course, what is excessive for one person may be perfectly tolerable for another. The point is simply that a person must perceive the demands as excessive or stress will not actually be present.

There has been a marked increase in stress reported by airline workers in the last few years. Pressure for salary and benefit reductions, threats to pensions, demotions, layoffs, and heavier workloads have all become more pronounced since September 11. And today's rising energy prices are likely to increase these pressures. As a result, more airline workers than ever before are seeking counseling services; turnover and absenteeism are also on the rise.[3]

The Stress Process

Much of what we know about stress today can be traced to the pioneering work of Dr. Hans Selye.[4] Among Selye's most important contributions were his identification of the general adaptation syndrome and the concepts of eustress and distress.

General Adaptation Syndrome   Figure 7.1 graphically shows the **general adaptation syndrome (GAS)**. According to this model, each of us has a normal level of resistance to stressful events. Some of us can tolerate a great deal of stress and others much less, but we all have a threshold at which stress starts to affect us.

> The **general adaptation syndrome (GAS)** identifies three stages of response to a stressor: alarm, resistance, and exhaustion.

The GAS begins when a person first encounters a stressor. The first stage is called "alarm." At this point, the person may feel some degree of panic and begin to wonder how to cope. The individual may also have to resolve a "fight-or-flight" question: Can I deal with this, or should I run away? For example, suppose a manager is assigned to

FIGURE 7.1

The General Adaptation Syndrome

The general adaptation syndrome, or GAS, perspective describes three stages of the stress process. The initial stage is called alarm. As illustrated here, a person's resistance often dips slightly below the normal level during this stage. Next comes actual resistance to the stressor, usually leading to an increase above the person's normal level of resistance. Finally, in stage 3, exhaustion may set in, and the person's resistance declines sharply below normal levels.

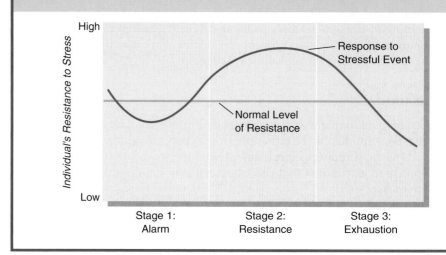

write a lengthy report overnight. Her first reaction may be "How will I ever get this done by tomorrow?"

If the stressor is too extreme, the person may simply be unable to cope with it. In most cases, however, the individual gathers his or her strength (physical or emotional) and begins to resist the negative effects of the stressor. The manager with the long report to write may calm down, call home to say she's working late, roll up her sleeves, order out for dinner, and get to work. Thus, at stage 2 of the GAS, the person is resisting the effects of the stressor.

Often, the resistance phase ends the GAS. If the manager completes the report earlier than she expected, she may drop it in her briefcase, smile to herself, and head home tired but happy. On the other hand, prolonged exposure to a stressor without resolution may bring on stage 3 of the GAS: exhaustion. At this stage, the person literally gives up and can no longer fight the stressor. For example, the manager may fall asleep at her desk at 3 A.M. and fail to finish the report.

Distress and Eustress   Selye also pointed out that the sources of stress need not be bad. For example, receiving a bonus and then having to decide what to do with the money can be stressful. So can getting a promotion, making a speech as part of winning a major award, getting married, and similar "good" things. Selye called this type of stress **eustress**. As we will see later, eustress can lead to a number of positive outcomes for the individual.

Of course, there is also negative stress. Called **distress**, this is what most people think of when they hear the word *stress*. Excessive pressure, unreasonable demands

Eustress is the pleasurable stress that accompanies positive events.

Distress is the unpleasant stress that accompanies negative events.

on our time, and bad news all fall into this category. As the term suggests, this form of stress generally results in negative consequences for the individual. For purposes of simplicity, we will continue to use the simple term *stress* throughout this chapter. But as you read and study the chapter, remember that stress can be either good or bad. It can motivate and stimulate us, or it can lead to any number of dangerous side effects.

Individual Differences and Stress

We have already alluded to the fact that stress can affect different people in different ways. Given our earlier discussion of individual differences back in Chapter 3, of course, this should come as no surprise.[5] The most fully developed individual difference relating specifically to stress is the distinction between Type A and Type B personality profiles.

Type A and Type B Personality Profiles

Type A and Type B profiles were first observed by two cardiologists, Meyer Friedman and Ray Rosenman,[6] when a worker repairing the upholstery on their waiting-room chairs commented that many of the chairs were worn only on the front. After further study, the two cardiologists realized that many of their heart patients were anxious and had a hard time sitting still—they were literally sitting on the edges of their seats!

Using this observation as a starting point, Friedman and Rosenman began to study the phenomenon more closely. They eventually concluded that their patients were exhibiting one of two very different types of behavior patterns. Their research also led them to conclude that the differences were personality-based. They labeled these two behavior patterns Type A and Type B.

The extreme **Type A** individual is extremely competitive, very devoted to work, and has a strong sense of time urgency. Moreover, this person is likely to be aggressive, impatient, and highly work oriented. He or she has a lot of drive and motivation and wants to accomplish as much as possible in as short a time as possible.

The extreme **Type B** person, in contrast, is less competitive, is less devoted to work, and has a weaker sense of time urgency. This person feels less conflict with either people or time and has a more balanced, relaxed approach to life. She or he has more confidence and is able to work at a constant pace.

A commonsense expectation might be that Type A people are more successful than Type B people. In reality, however, this is not necessarily true—the Type B person is not necessarily any more or less successful than the Type A. There are several possible explanations for this. For example, Type A people may alienate others because of their drive and may miss out on important learning opportunities in their quest to get ahead. Type Bs, on the other hand, may have better interpersonal reputations and may learn a wider array of skills.

Friedman and Rosenman pointed out that most people are not purely Type A or Type B; instead, people tend toward one or the other type. For example, an individual might exhibit marked Type A characteristics much of the time but still be able to relax once in a while and even occasionally forget about time. Likewise, even the most laid-back Type B person may occasionally spend some time obsessing about work.

Type A people are extremely competitive, highly committed to work, and have a strong sense of time urgency.

Type B people are less competitive, less committed to work, and have a weaker sense of time urgency.

Friedman and Rosenman's initial research on the Type A and Type B profile differences yielded some alarming findings. In particular, they suggested that Type As were much more likely to get coronary heart disease than were Type Bs. In recent years, however, follow-up research by other scientists has suggested that the relationship between Type A behavior and the risk of coronary heart disease is not all that straightforward.

Although the reasons are unclear, recent findings suggest that Type As are much more complex than originally believed. For example, in addition to the characteristics already noted, they are also more likely to be depressed and hostile. Any one of these characteristics or a combination of them can lead to heart problems. Moreover, different approaches to measuring Type A tendencies have yielded different results.

Finally, in one study that found Type As to actually be less susceptible to heart problems than Type Bs, the researchers offered an explanation consistent with earlier thinking: Because Type As are relatively compulsive, they may seek treatment earlier and are more likely to follow their doctors' orders![7]

Hardiness and Optimism

Two other important individual differences related to stress are hardiness and optimism. Research suggests that some people have what are termed hardier personalities than others.[8] **Hardiness** is a person's ability to cope with stress. People with hardy personalities have an internal locus of control, are strongly committed to the activities in their lives, and view change as an opportunity for advancement and growth. Such people are seen as relatively unlikely to suffer illness if they experience high levels of pressure and stress. On the other hand, people with low hardiness may have more difficulties in coping with pressure and stress.

Another potentially important individual difference is optimism. **Optimism** is the extent to which a person sees life in positive or negative terms. A popular expression used to convey this idea concerns the glass "half filled with water." An optimistic person will tend to see it as half full, whereas a person with less optimism (a pessimist) will often see the glass as half empty. Optimism is also related to positive and negative affectivity, as discussed earlier in Chapter 3. In general, optimistic people tend to handle stress better. They will be able to see the positive characteristics of the situation and recognize that things may eventually improve. In contrast, less optimistic people may focus more on the negative characteristics of the situation and expect things to get worse, not better.

Cultural differences also are important in determining how stress affects people. For example, research suggests that American executives may experience less stress than executives in many other countries, including Japan and Brazil. The major causes of stress also differ across countries. In Germany, for example, major causes of stress are time pressure and deadlines. In South Africa, long work hours more frequently lead to stress. And in Sweden, the major cause of stress is the encroachment of work on people's private lives.[9]

Other research suggests that women are perhaps more prone to experience the psychological effects of stress, whereas men may report more physical effects.[10] Finally, some studies suggest that people who see themselves as complex individuals are better able to handle stress than people who view themselves as relatively simple.[11] We should add, however, that the study of individual differences in stress is still in its infancy. It would therefore be premature to draw rigid conclusions about how different types of people handle stress.

Hardiness is a person's ability to cope with stress.

Optimism is the extent to which a person sees life in relatively positive or negative terms.

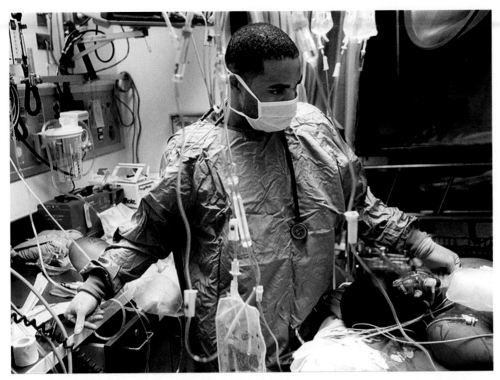

Considerable hardiness is required for many high-stress jobs. Dr. Chris Ervin is a third-year emergency medicine resident in Chicago's Cook County Hospital trauma unit. As part of his four-week rotation, he must work a 24-hour shift every three days, plus four to six hours on the other days. Fortunately, the stressful demands of the job are offset by his motivation to become a physician.

Common Causes of Stress

Many things can cause stress. Figure 7.2 shows two broad categories: organizational stressors and life stressors. It also shows three categories of stress consequences: individual consequences, organizational consequences, and burnout.

Organizational Stressors

Organizational stressors are various factors in the workplace that can cause stress. Four general sets of organizational stressors are task demands, physical demands, role demands, and interpersonal demands.

Task Demands   **Task demands** are stressors associated with the specific job a person performs. Some occupations are by nature more stressful than others. The jobs of surgeons, air-traffic controllers, and professional football coaches are generally more stressful than those of general practitioners, airline ticket agents, and football team equipment managers. Table 7.1 lists a representative sample of stressful jobs from among a total set of 250 jobs studied. As you can see, the job of U.S. president was found to be the most stressful, followed by the jobs of firefighter and senior executive. Toward the middle of the distribution are jobs such as mechanical engineer, chiropractor, technical writer, and bank officer. The jobs of

> **Organizational stressors** are factors in the workplace that can cause stress.

> **Task demands** are stressors associated with the specific job a person performs.

FIGURE 7.2

Causes and Consequences of Stress

The causes and consequences of stress are related in complex ways. As shown here, most common causes of stress can be classified as either organizational stressors or life stressors. Similarly, common consequences include individual and organizational consequences, as well as burnout.

Reference: Adapted from James C. Quick and Jonathan D. Quick, *Organizational Stress and Preventive Management* (McGraw-Hill, 1984) pp. 19, 44, and 76.

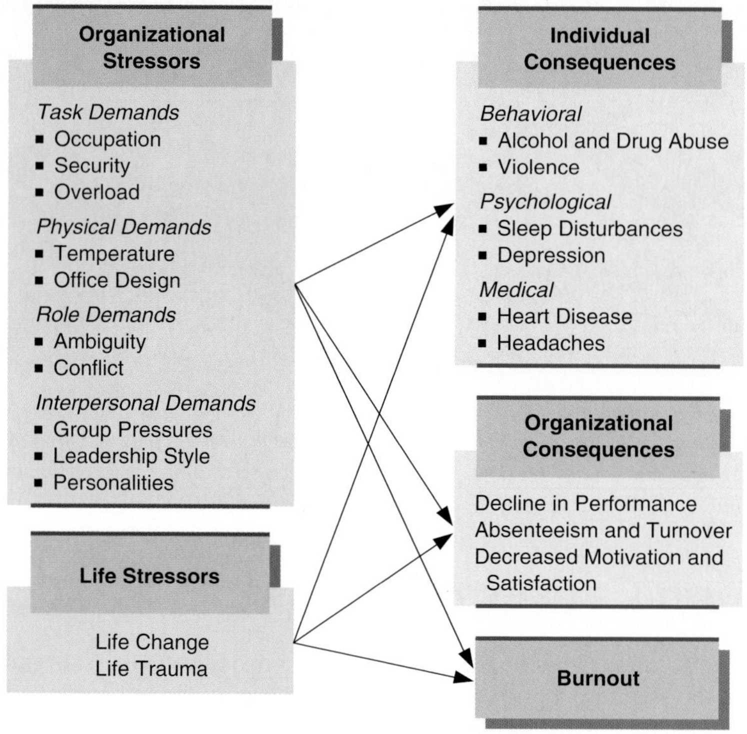

Organizational Stressors

Task Demands
- Occupation
- Security
- Overload

Physical Demands
- Temperature
- Office Design

Role Demands
- Ambiguity
- Conflict

Interpersonal Demands
- Group Pressures
- Leadership Style
- Personalities

Life Stressors

Life Change
Life Trauma

Individual Consequences

Behavioral
- Alcohol and Drug Abuse
- Violence

Psychological
- Sleep Disturbances
- Depression

Medical
- Heart Disease
- Headaches

Organizational Consequences

Decline in Performance
Absenteeism and Turnover
Decreased Motivation and
Satisfaction

Burnout

---

broadcast technician, bookkeeper, and actuary were among the least stressful jobs in this study.

Beyond specific task-related pressures, other aspects of a job may pose physical threats to a person's health. Unhealthy conditions exist in occupations such as coal mining and toxic waste handling. Security is another task demand that can cause stress. Someone in a relatively secure job is not likely to worry unduly about losing that position. Threats to job security can increase stress dramatically. For example, stress generally increases throughout an organization during a period of layoffs or immediately after a merger with another firm. This has been observed at a number of organizations, including AT&T, Safeway, and General Motors.

A final task demand stressor is overload. Overload occurs when a person simply has more work than he or she can handle. The overload can be either quantitative (the person has too many tasks to perform or too little time to perform them) or qualitative (the person may believe he or she lacks the ability to do the job). We should note that the

Rank	Occupation	Stress Score	Rank	Occupation	Stress Score
1	U.S. president	176.6	103	Market-research analyst	42.1
2	Firefighter	110.9	104	Personnel recruiter	41.8
3	Senior executive	108.6	113	Hospital administrator	39.6
6	Surgeon	99.5	119	Economist	38.7
10	Air-traffic controller	83.1	122	Mechanical engineer	38.3
12	Public-relations executive	78.5	124	Chiropractor	37.9
16	Advertising account executive	74.6	132	Technical writer	36.5
17	Real-estate agent	73.1	144	Bank officer	35.4
20	Stockbroker	71.7	149	Retail salesperson	34.9
22	Pilot	68.7	150	Tax examiner/collector	34.8
25	Architect	66.9	154	Aerospace engineer	34.6
31	Lawyer	64.3	166	Industrial designer	32.1
33	Physician (general practitioner)	64.0	173	Accountant	31.1
35	Insurance agent	63.3	193	Purchasing agent	28.9
42	Advertising salesperson	59.9	194	Insurance underwriter	28.5
47	Auto salesperson	56.3	212	Computer programmer	26.5
50	College professor	54.2	216	Financial planner	26.3
60	School principal	51.7	229	Broadcast technician	24.2
67	Psychologist	50.0	241	Bookkeeper	21.5
81	Executive-search consultant	47.3	245	Actuary	20.2

TABLE 7.1

The Most Stressful Jobs

How selected occupations ranked in an evaluation of 250 jobs*

*Among the criteria used in the rankings: overtime, quotas, deadlines, competitiveness, physical demands, environmental conditions, hazards encountered, initiative required, stamina required, win-lose situations, and working in the public eye.

Reference: The Most Stressful Jobs, February 26, 1996. Republished with permission of Dow Jones, from *Wall Street Journal*, February 26, 1996; permission conveyed through Copyright Clearance Center, Inc.

opposite of overload may also be undesirable. As Figure 7.3 shows, low task demands can result in boredom and apathy just as overload can cause tension and anxiety. Thus, a moderate degree of workload-related stress is optimal, because it leads to high levels of energy and motivation.

Physical Demands   The **physical demands** of a job are its physical requirements on the worker; these demands are a function of the physical characteristics of the setting and the physical tasks the job involves. One important element is temperature. Working outdoors in extreme temperatures can result in stress, as can working in an improperly heated or cooled office. Strenuous labor such as loading heavy cargo or lifting packages can lead to similar results. Office design also can be a problem. A poorly designed office can make it difficult for people to have privacy or promote too much or too little social interaction. Too much interaction may distract a person from his or her task, whereas too little may lead to boredom or loneliness. Likewise, poor lighting, inadequate work surfaces, and similar deficiencies can create stress. And shift work can cause disruptions for people because of the way it affects their sleep and leisure-time activities.

Physical demands are stressors associated with the job's physical setting, such as the adequacy of temperature and lighting and the physical requirements the job makes on the employee.

Role Demands   **Role demands** also can be stressful to people in organizations. A **role** is a set of expected behaviors associated with a particular position in a group or organization. As such, it has both formal (i.e., job-related and explicit) and informal (i.e., social and implicit) requirements. People in an organization or work group expect a person in a particular role to act in certain ways. They transmit these expectations both formally and informally. Individuals perceive role expectations with varying de-

Role demands are stressors associated with the role a person is expected to play. A **role** is a set of expected behaviors associated with a particular position in a group or organization.

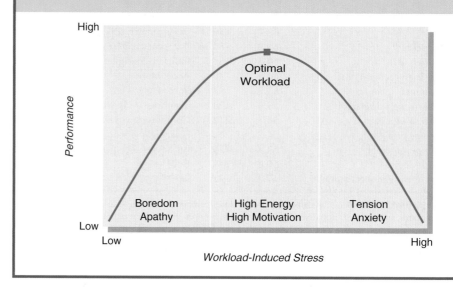

FIGURE 7.3

Workload, Stress, and Performance

Too much stress is clearly undesirable, but too little stress can also lead to unexpected problems. For example, too little stress may result in boredom and apathy and be accompanied by low performance. And although too much stress can cause tension, anxiety, and low performance, for most people there is an optimal level of stress that results in high energy, motivation, and performance.

grees of accuracy, and then attempt to enact that role. However, "errors" can creep into this process, resulting in stress-inducing problems called role ambiguity, role conflict, and role overload.

Role ambiguity arises when a role is unclear. If your instructor tells you to write a term paper but refuses to provide more information, you will probably experience ambiguity. You do not know what the topic is, how long the paper should be, what format to use, or when the paper is due. In work settings, role ambiguity can stem from poor job descriptions, vague instructions from a supervisor, or unclear cues from coworkers. The result is likely to be a subordinate who does not know what to do. Role ambiguity can thus be a significant source of stress.

Role conflict occurs when the messages and cues from others about the role are clear but contradictory or mutually exclusive.[12] One common form is *interrole conflict*—conflict between roles. For example, if a person's boss says that to get ahead one must work overtime and on weekends, and the same person's spouse says that more time is needed at home with the family, conflict may result. *Intrarole conflict* may occur when the person gets conflicting demands from different sources within the context of the same role. A manager's boss may tell her that she needs to put more pressure on subordinates to follow new work rules. At the same time, her subordinates may indicate that they expect her to get the rules changed. Thus, the cues are in conflict, and the manager may be unsure about which course to follow.

Intrasender conflict occurs when a single source sends clear but contradictory messages. This might occur if the boss says one morning that there can be no more overtime for the next month but after lunch tells someone to work late that same evening. *Person-role conflict* results from a discrepancy between the role requirements and the

> **Role ambiguity** arises when a role is unclear.

> **Role conflict** occurs when the messages and cues constituting a role are clear but contradictory or mutually exclusive.

individual's personal values, attitudes, and needs. If a person is told to do something un-ethical or illegal, or if the work is distasteful (for example, firing a close friend), person-role conflict is likely. Role conflict of all varieties is of particular concern to managers. Research has shown that conflict may occur in a variety of situations and lead to a variety of adverse consequences, including stress, poor performance, and rapid turnover.

A final consequence of a weak role structure is **role overload**, which occurs when expectations for the role exceed the individual's capabilities. When a manager gives an employee several major assignments at once while increasing the person's regular work-load, the employee will probably experience role overload. Role overload may also result when an individual takes on too many roles at one time. For example, a person trying to work extra hard at his job, run for election to the school board, serve on a committee in church, coach Little League baseball, maintain an active exercise program, and be a contributing member to his family will probably encounter role overload.

Interpersonal Demands A final set of organizational stressors consists of three **interpersonal demands**: group pressures, leadership, and interpersonal conflict. Group pressures may include pressure to restrict output, pressure to conform to the group's norms, and so forth. For instance, as we have noted before, it is quite common for a work group to arrive at an informal agreement about how much each member will produce. Individuals who produce much more or much less than this level may be pressured by the group to get back in line. An individual who feels a strong need to vary from the group's expectations (perhaps to get a pay raise or promotion) will experience a great deal of stress, especially if acceptance by the group is also important to him or her.

Leadership style also may cause stress. Suppose an employee needs a great deal of social support from his leader. The leader, however, is quite brusque and shows no concern or compassion for him. This employee will probably feel stressed. Similarly,

> **Role overload** occurs when expectations for the role exceed the individual's capabilities.

> **Interpersonal demands** are stressors associated with group pressures, leadership, and personality conflicts.

Some jobs impose considerable physical demands on workers. Soel Morales, a migrant farm worker, is shown here picking cotton on a Kentucky farm. The job involves repetitive bending motions to pick the cotton balls and then stuff them into a sack worn across the back. The more cotton that gets picked, the heavier the bag becomes. And the job has to get done regardless of the weather conditions.

assume an employee feels a strong need to participate in decision making and to be active in all aspects of management. Her boss is very autocratic and refuses to consult subordinates about anything. Once again stress is likely to result.

Finally, conflicting personalities and behaviors may cause stress. Conflict can occur when two or more people must work together even though their personalities, attitudes, and behaviors differ. For example, a person who always wants to control how things turn out might get frustrated working with a person who likes to wait and just let things happen. Likewise, a smoker and a nonsmoker who are assigned adjacent offices obviously will experience stress.[13]

Life Stressors

Stress in organizational settings also can be influenced by events that take place outside the organization. Life stressors can be categorized in terms of life change and life trauma.

A **life change** is any meaningful change in a person's personal or work situation; too many life changes can lead to health problems.

Life Change
Thomas Holmes and Richard Rahe first developed and popularized the notion of life change as a source of stress.[14] A **life change** is any meaningful change in a person's personal or work situation. Holmes and Rahe reasoned that major changes in a person's life can lead to stress and eventually to disease. Table 7.2

TABLE 7.2

Life Changes and Life Change Units

Rank	Life Event	Mean Value	Rank	Life Event	Mean Value
1	Death of spouse	100	23	Son or daughter leaving home	29
2	Divorce	73	24	Trouble with in-laws	29
3	Marital separation	65	25	Outstanding personal achievement	28
4	Jail term	63	26	Spouse beginning or ending work	26
5	Death of close family member	63	27	Beginning or ending school	26
6	Personal injury or illness	53	28	Change in living conditions	25
7	Marriage	50	29	Revision of personal habits	24
8	Fired at work	47	30	Trouble with boss	23
9	Marital reconciliation	45	31	Change in work hours or conditions	20
10	Retirement	45	32	Change in residence	20
11	Change in health of family member	44	33	Change in schools	20
12	Pregnancy	40	34	Change in recreation	19
13	Sex difficulties	39	35	Change in church activities	19
14	Gain of new family member	39	36	Change in social activities	18
15	Business readjustment	39	37	Small mortgage or loan	17
16	Change in financial state	38	38	Change in sleeping habits	16
17	Death of close family friend	37	39	Change in the number of family get-togethers	15
18	Change to different line of work	36			
19	Change in number of arguments with spouse	35	40	Change in eating habits	15
20	Large mortgage	31	41	Vacation	13
21	Foreclosure of mortgage or loan	30	42	Christmas or other major holiday	12
22	Change in responsibilities of work	29	43	Minor violations of the law	11

The amount of life stress that a person has experienced in a given period of time, say one year, is measured by the total number of life change units (LCUs). These units result from the addition of the values (shown in the right-hand column) associated with events that the person has experienced during the target time period.

Reference: Reprinted from *Journal of Psychosomatic Research*, vol. 11, Thomas H. Holmes and Richard H. Rahe, "The Social Adjustment Rating Scale," Copyright © 1967, with permission from Elsevier.

summarizes their findings on major life change events. Note that several of these events relate directly (fired from work, retirement) or indirectly (change in residence) to work.

Each event's point value supposedly reflects the event's impact on the individual. At one extreme, a spouse's death, assumed to be the most traumatic event considered, is assigned a point value of 100. At the other extreme, minor violations of the law rank only 11 points. The points themselves represent life change units, or LCUs. Note also that the list includes negative events (divorce and trouble with the boss) as well as positive ones (marriage and vacations).

Holmes and Rahe argued that a person can handle a certain threshold of LCUs, but beyond that level problems can set in. In particular, they suggest that people who encounter more than 150 LCUs in a given year will experience a decline in their health the following year. A score of between 150 and 300 LCUs supposedly carries a 50 percent chance of major illness, while the chance of major illness is said to increase to 70 percent if the number of LCUs exceeds 300. These ideas offer some interesting insights into the potential cumulative impact of various stressors and underscore our limitations in coping with stressful events. However, research on Holmes and Rahe's proposals has provided only mixed support.

Life Trauma Life trauma is similar to life change, but it has a narrower, more direct, and shorter-term focus. A **life trauma** is any upheaval in an individual's life that alters his or her attitudes, emotions, or behaviors. To illustrate, according to the life change view, a divorce adds to a person's potential for health problems in the following year. At the same time, the person will obviously also experience emotional turmoil during the actual divorce process itself. This turmoil is a form of

A **life trauma** is any upheaval in an individual's life that alters his or her attitudes, emotions, or behaviors.

Life stressors can be addressed by different people in different ways. Take Brian Benavidez, for example. After being laid off from his job as an investment banker during the 2002 recession, Benavidez spent his days watching television. One day he watched a documentary about— of all things—hot dogs. But he also noticed that everyone engaged in the process of making, selling, and eating hot dogs seemed to be happy! So rather than trying to get back into the corporate rat race, he has decided to open his own hot dog stand.

life trauma and will clearly cause stress, much of which may spill over into the workplace.[15]

Major life traumas that may cause stress include marital problems, family difficulties, and health problems initially unrelated to stress. For example, suppose a person learns she has developed arthritis that will limit her favorite activity, skiing. Her dismay over the news may translate into stress at work. Similarly, a worker coping with the traumatic aftermath of the death of a child will almost certainly go through difficult periods, some of which will affect job performance. And millions of individuals experienced traumatic stress in the wake of the September 11, 2001, terrorist attacks on New York and again following the July 7, 2005, attacks in London.

Consequences of Stress

Stress can have a number of consequences. As we already noted, if the stress is positive, the result may be more energy, enthusiasm, and motivation. Of more concern, of course, are the negative consequences of stress. Referring back to Figure 7.2, we see that stress can produce individual consequences, organizational consequences, and burnout.

We should first note that many of the factors listed are obviously interrelated. For example, alcohol abuse is shown as an individual consequence, but it also affects the organization the person works for. An employee who drinks on the job may perform poorly and create a hazard for others. If the category for a consequence seems somewhat arbitrary, be aware that each consequence is categorized according to the area of its primary influence.

Individual Consequences

The individual consequences of stress, then, are the outcomes that mainly affect the individual. The organization also may suffer, either directly or indirectly, but it is the individual who pays the real price. Stress may produce behavioral, psychological, and medical consequences. The *FedEx and . . . Technology* box illustrates how these consequences can emerge.

Behavioral Consequences   The behavioral consequences of stress may harm the person under stress or others. One such behavior is smoking. Research has clearly documented that people who smoke tend to smoke more when they experience stress. There is also evidence that alcohol and drug abuse are linked to stress, although this relationship is less well documented. Other possible behavioral consequences are accident proneness, violence, and appetite disorders.

Psychological Consequences   The psychological consequences of stress relate to a person's mental health and well-being. When people experience too much stress at work, they may become depressed or find themselves sleeping too much or not enough.[16] Stress may also lead to family problems and sexual difficulties.

Medical Consequences   The medical consequences of stress affect a person's physical well-being. Heart disease and stroke, among other illnesses, have been linked to stress. Other common medical problems resulting from too much stress include headaches, backaches, ulcers and related stomach and intestinal disorders, and skin conditions such as acne and hives.

FedEx and . . . **TECHNOLOGY**

Watching Workers at FedEx

As we saw at the beginning of this chapter, to deliver millions of time-sensitive items daily and create customer satisfaction FedEx must effectively evaluate worker performance. Electronic monitoring provides data for performance evaluation, although there are concerns about its use.

Package handlers at FedEx must correctly and quickly identify and load packages. A barcode scanner electronically identifies each package and its movements. A Global Positioning System (GPS) satellite-based locator pinpoints each worker's exact location. These technologies allow managers to calculate productivity and accuracy. Customer call center representatives must demonstrate speed, courtesy, and accuracy. Representatives' conversations are electronically recorded and then reviewed by supervisors.

The electronic monitors gather data efficiently and are legal, but can increase employee stress. FedEx couriers worry that a GPS system can monitor the length and location of their breaks and personal time. Studies of electronic monitoring show that monitored workers feel a loss of control, lower social support, and more pressure to perform. Workers also perceive reduced job security, even though their jobs are not at risk. Researchers John R. Aiello and Kathryn J. Kolb say, "Monitoring induces stress in a manner that is not completely explained [objectively]."

In the 1980s, FedEx required representatives to reduce the average time per call by one second and implemented electronic monitoring. Stress, increased absenteeism, and higher turnover resulted. Representatives cut off callers who asked lengthy questions, reducing quality. When the negative effects caused the company to stop electronic monitoring, performance then improved to a level better than the original level.

Today FedEx tries to use electronic monitoring responsibly, for example, by monitoring only a few random phone calls and by allowing employees to switch off the GPS system during personal time. The company seems to be effectively balancing the needs of management for performance data with a concern for employee privacy and stress.

> *"Monitoring induces stress."*
>
> JOHN R. AIELLO AND KATHRYN J. KOLB, RESEARCHERS

References: "Electronic Monitoring: A Poor Solution to Management Problems," National Workrights Institute, www.workrights.org on March 14, 2005; "FedEx Philosophy," "On Your Tracks: GPS Tracking in the Workplace," National Workrights Institute, www.workrights.org on March 14, 2005; "Team Member Benefits," FedEx website, www.fedex.com on March 14, 2005; Claudia H. Deutsch, "Planes, Trucks and 7.5 Million Packages: FedEx's Big Night," *New York Times*, December 21, 2003, p. BU 1.

Organizational Consequences

Clearly, any of the individual consequences just discussed can also affect the organization. Other results of stress have even more direct consequences for organizations. These include decline in performance, withdrawal, and negative changes in attitudes.

Performance   One clear organizational consequence of too much stress is a decline in performance. For workers, such a decline can translate into poor-quality work or a drop in productivity. For managers, it can mean faulty decision making or disruptions in working relationships as people become irritable and hard to get along with.[17]

Withdrawal   Withdrawal behaviors also can result from stress. For the organization, the two most significant forms of withdrawal behavior are absenteeism and quitting. People who are having a hard time coping with stress in their jobs are more likely to call in sick or consider leaving the organization for good. Stress can also

Burnout can cause even a previously motivated and committed employee to lose interest in work. This poor canine, for instance, no doubt once truly enjoyed howling at the moon. But stress has evidently taken its toll, causing the poor animal to be experiencing burnout and hence no longer motivated to care much for the moon.

produce other, more subtle forms of withdrawal. A manager may start missing deadlines or taking longer lunch breaks. An employee may withdraw psychologically by ceasing to care about the organization and the job. As noted above, employee violence is a potential individual consequence of stress. This also has obvious organizational implications as well, especially if the violence is directed at an employee or at the organization in general.[18]

Attitudes   Another direct organizational consequence of employee stress relates to attitudes. As we just noted, job satisfaction, morale, and organizational commitment can all suffer, along with motivation to perform at high levels. As a result, people may be more prone to complain about unimportant things, do only enough work to get by, and so forth.

Burnout is a general feeling of exhaustion that develops when an individual simultaneously experiences too much pressure and has too few sources of satisfaction.

Burnout   Burnout, another consequence of stress, has clear implications for both people and organizations. **Burnout** is a general feeling of exhaustion that develops when a person simultaneously experiences too much pressure and has too few sources of satisfaction.[19]

People with high aspirations and a strong motivation to get things done are often prime candidates for burnout. They are especially vulnerable when the organization suppresses or limits their initiative while constantly demanding that they serve the organization's own ends.

Burnout generally develops in such a situation, because the individual is likely to put too much of himself or herself into the job. In other words, the person may well keep trying to meet his or her own agenda while simultaneously trying to fulfill the organization's expectations. The most likely effects of this situation are prolonged stress, fatigue, frustration, and helplessness under the burden of overwhelming demands. The person literally exhausts his or her aspirations and motivation, much as a candle burns itself out. Loss of self-confidence and psychological withdrawal follow. Ultimately, burnout results. At this point, the individual may start dreading going to work in the morning, may put in longer hours but accomplish less than before, and may generally display mental and physical exhaustion.[20]

Managing Stress in the Workplace

Given that stress is widespread and so potentially disruptive in organizations, it follows that people and organizations should be concerned about how to manage it more effectively. And in fact they are. Many strategies have been developed to help manage stress in the workplace. Some are for individuals and others are geared toward organizations.[21] *The New York Philharmonic and . . . Diversity* box discusses both the potential advantages and shortcomings of some of these proactive efforts.

The New York Philharmonic and . . . **DIVERSITY**

Opportunities for Minority Musicians

A career in classical music represents a "dream job," but it may be an impossible dream for minorities, which make up only a handful of today's performers. Many orchestras conduct "blind" auditions, with applicants performing behind a screen, so the disparity isn't caused by the recruiting process. The problem occurs earlier—when public schools have limited funds for music education. "Most kids who grow up in urban environments don't have the resources [for classical music training]," says musician and Sphinx founder Aaron Dworkin. "If you don't get involved before you're a senior in high school, it's too late."

Sphinx was founded in 1996 as a national non-profit organization to seek out, nurture, educate, and encourage young African Americans and Latin Americans in classical music. Sphinx programs include Sphinx Symphony, made up of minority musicians, and a recital series that entertains families in inner-city shopping areas. Sphinx provides music training, sends professional musicians into schools, and creates educational materials for teachers.

In Massachusetts, Sphinx conducts a full-scholarship summer camp for promising string players. Sphinx donates funds to purchase instruments and to attend music festivals and training programs. For more advanced musicians, Sphinx gives college scholarships and career mentoring. Works by minority composers are commissioned and performed. New York Philharmonic

musicians support Sphinx's musicians and the orchestra offers them a chance to perform with the orchestra.

Increased diversity would be a benefit to a symphony or opera company, because creativity would flourish. Diversity could also attract a more diverse audience, an important goal of many classical music organizations. Early exposure to classical music can create lifelong fans and young people benefit from expanded career options. Thanks to Sphinx, classical music institutions and musicians can both win from increased diversity. For more about a performer's career, read "Stress and the Professional Musician" on page 193.

> *"If you don't get involved before you're a senior in high school, it's too late."*
>
> AARON DWORKIN, PROFESSIONAL MUSICIAN AND FOUNDER OF SPHINX

References: "Activities for Kids," The New York Philharmonic website, newyorkphilharmonic.org on March 14, 2005; "Sphinx Celebrates Black Composers of Classical Music," *Detroit Free Press*, February 15, 2004, www.freep.com on March 16, 2005; Kevin McKeough, "The Sphinx Stands Alone," *Strings*, January 2003, no. 107, www.stringsmagazine.com on March 16, 2005; Mark Stryker, "Programs – Sphinx Symphony," Sphinx website, www.sphinxmusic.org on March 15, 2005.

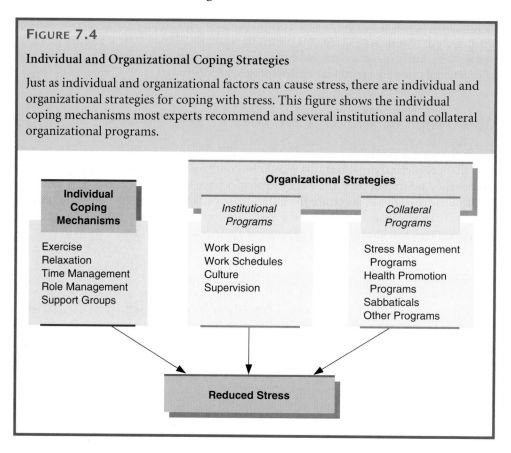

FIGURE 7.4

Individual and Organizational Coping Strategies

Just as individual and organizational factors can cause stress, there are individual and organizational strategies for coping with stress. This figure shows the individual coping mechanisms most experts recommend and several institutional and collateral organizational programs.

Individual Coping Strategies

Many strategies for helping individuals manage stress have been proposed. Figure 7.4 lists five of the more popular.

Exercise   Exercise is one method of managing stress. People who exercise regularly are less likely to have heart attacks than inactive people. More directly, research has suggested that people who exercise regularly feel less tension and stress, are more self-confident, and show greater optimism. People who do not exercise regularly feel more stress, are more likely to be depressed, and experience other negative consequences.

Relaxation   A related method of managing stress is relaxation. We noted at the beginning of the chapter that coping with stress requires adaptation. Proper relaxation is an effective way to adapt. Relaxation can take many forms. One way to relax is to take regular vacations. One study found that people's attitudes toward a variety of workplace characteristics improved significantly following a vacation.[22] People can also relax while on the job. For example, it has been recommended that people take regular rest breaks during their normal workday.[23] A popular way of resting is to sit quietly with closed eyes for ten minutes every afternoon. (Of course, it might be necessary to have an alarm clock handy!)

Time Management   Time management is often recommended for managing stress. The idea is that many daily pressures can be eased or eliminated if a person does a better job of managing time. One popular approach to time management is to make a list every morning of the things to be done that day. Next, the items on the list are grouped into three categories: critical activities that must be performed, important activities that should be performed, and optional or trivial things that can be delegated or postponed. Then, of course, the things on the list are done in their order of importance. This strategy helps people get more of the important things done every day. It also encourages delegation of less important activities to others.

Role Management   Somewhat related to time management is the idea of role management, in which the individual actively works to avoid overload, ambiguity, and conflict. For example, if you do not know what is expected of you, you should not sit and worry about it. Instead, ask for clarification from your boss. Another role management strategy is to learn to say "no." As simple as saying "no" might sound, a lot of people create problems for themselves by always saying "yes." Besides working in their regular jobs, they agree to serve on committees, volunteer for extra duties, and accept extra assignments. Sometimes, of course, we have no choice but to accept an extra obligation (if our boss tells us to complete a new project, we will probably have to do it). In many cases, however, saying "no" is an option.[24]

Support Groups   A final method for managing stress is to develop and maintain support groups. A support group is simply a group of family members or friends with whom a person can spend time. Going out after work with a couple of coworkers to a basketball game, for example, can help relieve the stress that builds up during the day. Supportive family and friends can help people deal with normal stress on an ongoing basis. Support groups can be particularly useful during times of crisis. For example, suppose an employee has just learned that she did not get the promotion she has been working toward for months. It may help her tremendously if she has good friends to lean on, be it to talk to or to yell at.

Organizational Coping Strategies

Organizations are also increasingly realizing that they should be involved in managing their employees' stress. There are two different rationales for this view. One is that because the organization is at least partly responsible for creating the stress, it should help relieve it. The other is that workers experiencing lower levels of harmful stress will function more effectively. Two basic organizational strategies for helping employees manage stress are institutional programs and collateral programs.

Institutional Programs   *Institutional programs* for managing stress are undertaken through established organizational mechanisms. For example, properly designed jobs and work schedules (both discussed in Chapter 5) can help ease stress. Shift work, in particular, can cause major problems for employees, because they are constantly adjusting their sleep and relaxation patterns. Thus, the design of work and work schedules should be a focus of organizational efforts to reduce stress.

The organization's culture (covered in Chapter 18) also can be used to help manage stress. In some organizations, for example, there is a strong norm against taking time off or going on vacation. In the long run, such norms can cause major stress. Thus, the organization should strive to foster a culture that reinforces a healthy mix of work and nonwork activities.

Finally, supervision can play an important institutional role in managing stress. A supervisor can be a major source of overload. If made aware of their potential for assigning stressful amounts of work, supervisors can do a better job of keeping work-loads reasonable.

Collateral Programs   In addition to institutional efforts aimed at reducing stress, many organizations are turning to collateral programs. A *collateral stress program* is an organizational program specifically created to help employees deal with stress. Organizations have adopted stress management programs, health promotion programs, and other kinds of programs for this purpose. More and more companies are developing their own programs or adopting existing programs of this type. For example, Lockheed Martin offers screening programs for its employees to detect signs of hypertension.

Many firms today also have employee fitness programs. These programs attack stress indirectly by encouraging employees to exercise, which is presumed to reduce stress. On the negative side, this kind of effort costs considerably more than stress management programs, because the firm must invest in physical facilities. Still, more and more companies are exploring this option.[25] L.L. Bean, for example, has state-of-the-art fitness centers for its employees.

Finally, organizations try to help employees cope with stress through other kinds of programs. For example, existing career development programs, like the one at General Electric, are used for this purpose. Other companies use programs promoting everything from humor to massage to yoga as antidotes for stress.[26] Of course, little or no research supports some of the claims made by advocates of these programs. Thus, managers must take steps to ensure that any organizational effort to help employees cope with stress is at least reasonably effective.

Work-Life Linkages

At numerous points in this chapter we have alluded to relationships between a person's work and life. In this final brief section we will make these relationships a bit more explicit.

Fundamental Work-Life Relationships

Work-life relationships can be characterized in any number of ways. Consider, for example, the basic dimensions of the part of a person's life tied specifically to work. Common dimensions would include such things as an individual's current job (including working hours, job satisfaction, and so forth), his or her career goals (the person's aspirations, career trajectory, and so forth), interpersonal relations at work (with the supervisor, subordinates, coworkers, and others), and job security.

Part of each person's life is also distinctly separate from work. These dimensions might include the person's spouse or life companion, dependents (such as children or elderly parents), personal life interests (hobbies, leisure-time interests, religious affiliations, community involvement), and friendship networks.

Work-life relationships are interrelationships between a person's work life and personal life.

Work-life relationships, then, include any relationships between dimensions of the person's work life and the person's personal life. For example, a person with numerous dependents (a nonworking spouse or domestic partner, dependent children, dependent parents, etc.) may prefer a job with a relatively high salary, fewer overtime demands, and less travel. On the other hand, a person with no dependents may be less interested in salary, more receptive to overtime, and enjoy job-related travel.

Stress will occur when there is a basic inconsistency or incompatibility between a person's work and life dimensions. For example, if a person is the sole care provider

for a dependent elderly parent but has a job that requires considerable travel and evening work, stress is likely to result.

Balancing Work-Life Linkages

Balancing work-life linkages is, of course, no easy thing to do. Demands from both sides can be extreme, and people may need to be prepared to make tradeoffs. The important thing is to recognize the potential tradeoffs in advance so that they can be carefully weighed and a comfortable decision made. Some of the strategies for doing this were discussed earlier. For example, working for a company that offers flexible work schedules may be an attractive option.[27]

Individuals must also recognize the importance of long-term versus short-term perspectives in balancing their work and personal lives. For example, people may have to respond a bit more to work than to life demands in the early years of their career. In mid-career, they may be able to achieve a more comfortable balance. In later career stages they may be able to put life dimensions first, by refusing to relocate, by working shorter hours, and so forth.

People also have to decide for themselves what they value and what tradeoffs they are willing to make. For instance, consider the dilemma faced by a dual-career couple when one partner is being transferred to another city. One option is for one of the partners to subordinate her or his career for the other partner, at least temporarily. For example, the partner being transferred can turn it down, risking a potential career setback or the loss of the job. Or the other partner may resign from his or her current position and seek another one in the new location. The couple might also decide to live apart, with one moving and the other staying. The partners might also come to realize that their respective careers are more important to them than their relationship and decide to go their separate ways.[28]

Chapter Review

Synopsis

Stress is a person's adaptive response to a stimulus that places excessive psychological or physical demands on that person. According to the general adaptation syndrome perspective, the three stages of response to stress are alarm, resistance, and exhaustion. Two important forms of stress are eustress and distress.

Type A personalities are more competitive and time-driven than Type B personalities. Initial evidence suggested that Type As are more susceptible to coronary heart disease, but recent findings provide less support for this idea. Hardiness, optimism, cultural context, and gender may also affect stress.

Stress can be caused by many factors. Major organizational stressors are task demands, physical demands, role demands, and interpersonal demands. Life stressors include life change and life trauma.

Stress has many consequences. Individual consequences can include behavioral, psychological, and medical problems. On the organizational level, stress can affect performance and attitudes or cause withdrawal. Burnout is another possibility.

Primary individual mechanisms for managing stress are exercise, relaxation, time management, role management, and support groups. Organizations use both institutional and collateral programs to control stress.

People have numerous dimensions to their work and personal lives. When these dimensions are interrelated, individuals must decide for themselves which are more important and how to balance them.

Discussion Questions

1. Describe two recent times when stress had both good and bad consequences for you.

2. Describe a time when you successfully avoided stage 3 of the GAS and another time when you got to stage 3.

3. Do you consider yourself a Type A or a Type B person? Why?

4. Can a person who is a Type A change? If so, how?

5. What are the major stressors for a student?

6. Is an organizational stressor or a life stressor likely to be more powerful?

7. What consequences are students most likely to suffer as a result of too much stress?

8. Do you agree that a certain degree of stress is necessary to induce high energy and motivation?

9. What can be done to prevent burnout? If someone you know is suffering burnout, how would you advise that person to recover from it?

10. Do you practice any of the stress reduction methods discussed in the text? Which ones? Do you use others not mentioned in the text?

11. Has the work-life balance been an issue in your life?

Experiencing Organizational Behavior

Learning How Stress Affects You

Purpose: This exercise is intended to help you develop a better understanding of how stress affects you.

Format: The following is a set of questions about your job. If you work, respond to the questions in terms of your job. If you do not work, respond to the questions in terms of your role as a student.

Procedure: This quiz will help you recognize your level of stress on the job. Take the test, figure your score, and then see if your stress level is normal, beginning to be a problem, or dangerous. Answer the following statements by putting a number in front of each:

1—seldom true
2—sometimes true
3—mostly true

_____ 1. Even over minor problems, I lose my temper and do embarrassing things, like yell or kick a garbage can.

_____ 2. I hear every piece of information or question as criticism of my work.

_____ 3. If someone criticizes my work, I take it as a personal attack.

_____ 4. My emotions seem flat whether I'm told good news or bad news about my performance.

_____ 5. Sunday nights are the worst time of the week.

_____ 6. To avoid going to work, I'd even call in sick when I'm feeling fine.

_____ 7. I feel powerless to lighten my work load or schedule, even though I've always got far too much to do.

_____ 8. I respond irritably to any request from coworkers.

_____ 9. On the job and off, I get highly emotional over minor accidents, such as typos or spilt coffee.

_____ 10. I tell people about sports or hobbies that I'd like to do but say I never have time because of the hours I spend at work.

_____ 11. I work overtime consistently yet never feel caught up.

_____ 12. My health is running down; I often have headaches, backaches, stomachaches.

_____ 13. If I even eat lunch, I do it at my desk while working.

_____ 14. I see time as my enemy.

_____ 15. I can't tell the difference between work and play; it all feels like one more thing to be done.

_____ 16. Everything I do feels like a drain on my energy.

_____ 17. I feel like I want to pull the covers over my head and hide.

_____ 18. I seem off center, distracted—I do things like walk into mirrored pillars in department stores and excuse myself.

_____ 19. I blame my family—because of them, I have to stay in this job and location.

_____ 20. I have ruined my relationship with coworkers whom I feel I compete against.

Scoring: Add up the points you wrote beside the questions. Interpret your score as follows:

20–29: You have normal amounts of stress.

30–49: Stress is becoming a problem. You should try to identify its source and manage it.

50–60: Stress is at dangerous levels. Seek help, or it could result in worse symptoms such as alcoholism or illness.

Follow-up Questions

1. How valid do you think your score is?

2. Is it possible to anticipate stress ahead of time and plan ways to help manage it?

Reference: "Stress on the job? Ask yourself," _USA Today_, June 16, 1987. Copyright 1987, _USA Today_. Reprinted with permission.

Self-Assessment Exercise

Are You Type A or Type B?

This test will help you develop insights into your own tendencies toward Type A or Type B behavior patterns. Answer the questions honestly and accurately about either your job or your school, whichever requires the most time each week. Then calculate your score according to the instructions that follow the questions. Discuss your results with a classmate. Critique each other's answers and see if you can help each other develop a strategy for reducing Type A tendencies.

Choose from the following responses to answer the questions that follow:

a. Almost always true
b. Usually true
c. Seldom true
d. Never true

_____ **1.** I do not like to wait for other people to complete their work before I can proceed with mine.

_____ **2.** I hate to wait in most lines.

_____ **3.** People tell me that I tend to get irritated too easily.

_____ **4.** Whenever possible, I try to make activities competitive.

_____ **5.** I have a tendency to rush into work that needs to be done before knowing the procedure I will use to complete the job.

_____ **6.** Even when I go on vacation, I usually take some work along.

_____ **7.** When I make a mistake, it is usually because I have rushed into the job before completely planning it through.

_____ **8.** I feel guilty about taking time off from work.

_____ **9.** People tell me I have a bad temper when it comes to competitive situations.

_____ **10.** I tend to lose my temper when I am under a lot of pressure at work.

_____ **11.** Whenever possible, I will attempt to complete two or more tasks at once.

_____ **12.** I tend to race against the clock.

_____ **13.** I have no patience with lateness.

_____ **14.** I catch myself rushing when there is no need.

Score your responses according to the following key:

■ *An intense sense of time urgency* is a tendency to race against the clock, even when there is little reason to. The person feels a need to hurry for hurry's sake alone, and this tendency has appropriately been called hurry sickness. Time urgency is measured by items 1, 2, 8, 12, 13, and 14. Every *a* or *b* answer to these six questions scores one point.

■ *Inappropriate aggression and hostility* reveal themselves in a person who is excessively competitive and who cannot do anything for fun. This inappropriately aggressive behavior easily evolves into frequent displays of hostility, usually at the slightest provocation or frustration. Competitiveness and hostility are measured by items 3, 4, 9, and 10. Every *a* or *b* answer scores one point.

■ *Polyphasic behavior* refers to the tendency to undertake two or more tasks simultaneously at inappropriate times. It usually results in wasted time because of an inability to complete the tasks. This behavior is measured by items 6 and 11. Every *a* or *b* answer scores one point.

■ *Goal directedness without proper planning* refers to the tendency of an individual to rush into work without really knowing how to accomplish the desired result. This usually results in incomplete work or work with many errors, which in turn leads to wasted time, energy, and money. Lack of planning is measured by items 5 and 7. Every *a* or *b* response scores one point.

TOTAL SCORE _____

If your score is 5 or greater, you may possess some basic components of the Type A personality.

Reference: From Daniel A. Girdano, George S. Everly Jr., and Dorothy E. Dusek, *Controlling Stress and Tension: A Holistic Approach*, 6th ed. Copyright © 2001 by Allyn & Bacon. Reprinted by permission of Pearson Education, Inc.

Building Managerial Skills

Exercise Overview: Time management skills help people prioritize work, work more efficiently, and to delegate appropriately. Poor time management, in turn, may result in stress. This exercise will help you relate time management skills to stress reduction.

Exercise Background: Make a list of several of the major things that cause stress for you. Stressors might involve school (i.e., hard classes, too many exams, etc.), work (i.e., financial pressures, demanding work schedule), and/or personal circumstances (i.e., friends, romance, family, etc.). Try to be as specific as possible. Also try to identify at least ten different stressors.

Exercise Task: Using the list you have developed, do each of the following:

1. Evaluate the extent to which poor time management on your part plays a role in how each stressor affects you. For example, do exams cause stress because you delay studying for them?

2. Develop a strategy for using time more efficiently in relation to each stressor that relates to time.

3. Note interrelationships among different kinds of stressors and time. For example, financial pressures may cause you to work, but work may interfere with school. Can any of these interrelationships be more effectively managed vis-à-vis time?

4. How do you manage the stress in your life? Is it possible to manage stress in a more time-effective manner?

Organizational Behavior Case for Discussion

Stress and the Professional Musician

The New York Philharmonic Orchestra, with 106 musicians, is the most renowned classical music group in the United States. Playing with the Philharmonic may seem an ideal career, where musicians play just nineteen hours weekly for salaries above $100,000. Yet the job poses unique challenges.

The physical demands are a source of stress for musicians due to repetitive injuries. Cellist Carter Brey says, "You can get tennis elbow. If you don't warm up before playing, you can hurt your hand." Glenn Dicterow, violinist, claims, "Your right arm can feel like it's falling off. We have this fatigue . . . [just] holding this instrument up." Sitting for hours can be painful and the noise can be deafening. "When the trumpets and trombones are behind us, it's agonizing," states bassoonist Judy LeClair. "It's so loud it physically hurts." Percussionist Joe Pereira agrees: "Hearing loss is a real problem." Even when not playing, the musicians must protect their hands, their fingertip calluses, their lips and teeth.

Conflict between personal and professional roles is another stressor. Time demands are intense. David Grossman, a bass player, says, "Music is not like a 9-to-5 job . . . Music . . . engrosses you and encompasses you." Flutist Mindy Kaufman adds, "We work on Saturday nights and almost every holiday . . . and then there's practice time." "It's a way of life—it totally envelops your life," says Dicterow. "Four nights a week you're away. And when you come home, you're exhausted."

The demanding schedule is especially hard on musicians' families. Trombonist Jim Markey states, "We have concerts at night, so we're usually working when others . . . are with their families. When people are going to the movies on a Saturday night, we're playing." On the other hand, some musicians enjoy being home during the day or after school with their children.

The strain of working closely with a small group can be stressful. "When problems come up, it's really just due to personality conflicts—and we have a lot of strong, intense personalities," says Brey. Careers are measured in decades and French horn player Philip Myers emphasizes the need to maintain good working relationships: "When you get . . . to the Philharmonic, you're with people that you're going to be living with for the rest of your life."

Additional stressors include the responsibility to purchase or care for an instrument worth thousands or millions of dollars, worries about waning ability due to aging, and even perfectionism.

The musicians try to manage their stress. Members use special chairs to alleviate the strain of sitting. Many practice relaxation and strengthening routines to reduce repetitive injuries. Most of them exercise to reduce stress and to keep fit for their demanding work. Grossman compares his job to that of an athlete, saying, "You have to listen to your body, just like in sports . . . I'm in tune with my body enough to know when something's really wrong." Others limit practice time or take days off. To rest their senses, some recommend not listening to music at home. Many of the Philharmonic musicians are married to musicians. Kaufman states, "Other musicians understand the time commitment; understand why you have to practice."

The Philharmonic helps too, buying instruments for some musicians, for example. The pay at the Philharmonic is high for a professional musician, reducing financial worries. The organization's policies about work-life relationships are generous. "I waited so long to have a child . . . I didn't think I'd have enough time," LeClair says. "Finding balance is tough . . . [but] if you need time off, the Philharmonic is wonderful."

In spite of stress, the Philharmonic musicians love their jobs, love to entertain and enlighten others, love to teach and volunteer. "It's a fantastic experience to be a musician," says Markey. "There are so many rewards." Brey agrees, "I love the overwhelming power that a symphony orchestra can generate—and I love being in the middle of that." LeClair sums up her colleagues' feelings: "[People] say, 'Oh, it must be so fabulous, to do something you love, all the time.' And I'm thinking, well, it's hard work, too, and we don't always love it. But it's still better than going to an office job."

Case Questions

1. Categorize the various types of organizational stressors experienced by Philharmonic musicians. Is the

> **"***It's hard work . . . but it's still better than going to an office job.***"**
> Judy LeClair, bassoonist, New York Philharmonic Orchestra

Philharmonic doing everything it can to reduce these stressors? If so, explain why. If not, tell what additional steps the Philharmonic could take to reduce stress.

2. The Philharmonic musicians are among the best musicians in the world. In your opinion, is stress greater for an employee who has reached the very top of his or her career than one who is about average in achievement? What is the stress level of someone with very low achievement? Explain your answers.

3. Musical careers often require nontraditional schedules. What positive and negative impacts can a nontraditional schedule have on an individual's work-life balance?

References: Jacqueline Cardinale and Laurent Lapierre, "Zarin Mehta and the New York Philharmonic," *The International Journal of Arts Management,* Fall 2003, vol. 6, no.1, www.hec.ca on March 15, 2005; Beth Nissen, "Bassist David Grossman: 'Not a 9-to-5 Job,' " "Bassoonist Judy LeClair: 'A Family Was My Answer,' " "Cellist Carter Brey: 'Renaissance Lumber,' " "Flutist Mindy Kaufman: 'Music Is a Language,' " "Glenn Dicterow, Concertmaster: 'Music as Medicine,' " "Jim Markey, Trombonist: 'A Great Career,' " "Percussionist Joe Pereira: 'Just Do Some Sounds,' " "Philip Myers, French Hornist: 'Practice Attacks,' " CNN Careers Series, February 23, 2001 to April 12, 2001, archives.cnn.com on February 20, 2005.

TEST PREPPER

You have read the chapter and studied the key terms. Think you're ready to ace the exam? Take this sample test to gauge your comprehension of chapter material and check your answers at the back of the book. Want more test questions? Take the ACE quizzes found on the student website: http://college.hmco.com/business/students/ (select Griffin/Moorhead, Organizational Behavior, 8e from the Management menu).

T   F   1. Stress is an adaptive response.

T   F   2. A Type B person is very competitive, devoted to work, and has a strong sense of time urgency.

T   F   3. Overload can occur if a person believes he or she lacks the ability to do the job.

T   F   4. Negative and positive life events may both be sources of stress.

T   F   5. Burnout is a general feeling of exhaustion when a person has too few positive sources of stress.

T   F   6. Collateral stress programs focus on repairing the damage stress does to those outside the organization.

T   F   7. Flexible work schedules may help employees balance work-life linkages.

8. For an employee to experience stress
   a. the demands on the employee must be physical.
   b. the demands on the employee must be psychological.
   c. the demands must prevent the employee from adapting.
   d. the demands on the employee must be excessive.
   e. the demands must be greater than the employee has experienced in the past.

9. Which of the following does not describe a Type A person as compared to a Type B person?
   a. Impatient
   b. Confident
   c. Strong sense of time urgency
   d. Very devoted to work
   e. Extremely competitive

10. Of 250 jobs studied, the most stressful job found was
   a. broadcast technician.
   b. mechanical engineer.
   c. actuary.
   d. bank officer.
   e. U.S. president.

11. Thomas believes in always telling the truth. His manager asks him to "bend" the truth when discussing the technical specifications of the machinery they are selling because the customers will really never know the difference. Thomas is likely to experience
   a. intrasender conflict.
   b. intersender conflict.

   c. role ambiguity.
   d. person-role conflict.
   e. role overload.

12. According to research by Holms and Rahe, excessive life changes are expected to result in
   a. a decline in the person's health.
   b. a sensation of accomplishment.
   c. a tendency to become a Type A person.
   d. a tendency to become a Type B person.
   e. increased role overload.

13. Too much stress at work can be expected to have all the following consequences for organizations except
   a. a decline in performance.
   b. withdrawal behaviors.
   c. employees spending more time at work.
   d. lower organizational commitment.
   e. burnout.

14. One of your subordinates tells you she is experiencing a lot of stress. There doesn't seem to be anything wrong with the organization, so you assume an individual coping strategy might help her the most. Which of the following would you not recommend?
   a. Exercise
   b. Role management
   c. Relaxation
   d. Time management
   e. All of the above are individual coping strategies you might recommend.

15. Balancing work-life linkages sometimes requires people to make tradeoffs. Which of the following best describes the process to make these tradeoffs?
   a. Always respond to work demands early in your career.
   b. Always respond to life demands later in your career.
   c. Always subordinate your career for your partner's career.
   d. Never subordinate your career for your partner's career.
   e. Decide for yourself what you value and what tradeoffs you are willing to make.

CHAPTER 8

Decision Making and Problem Solving

- ▶ **Describe the nature of decision making and distinguish it from problem solving.**

- ▶ **Discuss the decision-making process for a variety of perspectives.**

- ▶ **Identify and discuss related behavioral aspects of decision making.**

- ▶ **Discuss the nature of creativity and relate it to decision making and problem solving.**

Chapter Outline

The Nature of Decision Making

The Decision-Making Process

Related Behavioral Aspects of Decision Making

Creativity, Problem Solving, and Decision Making

Coptervision's Creativity

In the film *Collateral Damage*, viewers see Arnold Schwarzenegger jump down an elevator shaft. The camera's point of view moves with the actor, so that viewers feel the sensation of falling. This special effect is created through the use of a new camera that, at fifteen pounds, is so light it can be strapped onto an actor's back. "The idea of a camera head that can pan and tilt and roll is not brand new," says Mark Centkowski, president of a production equipment rental firm. "Coptervision has taken that idea and made it very lightweight and portable, and that's the uniqueness."

Coptervision is a California-based firm whose second product is a tiny camera, called Rollvision, which can be attached to a person, a horse, a bicycle, or just about anything. The company's first product, Coptervision, is a lightweight microwave-controlled camera mounted on a small unmanned helicopter. The entire system is just six feet across. Coptervision allows filming under bridges, inside buildings, or in tunnels, creating exciting action sequences.

The two products have been used for numerous films and television shows, including *The Scorpion King* and *Charmed*, as well as for music videos, commercials, and sports programs. "What we specialize in is close-range aerial images," says Coptervision vice president Daniela Meltzer. "So if you have a shot where you want to chase a car on the open road, then go through a tunnel and come out the other end to reveal a cityscape, we can do that. There's nothing else out there that can do that kind of thing." Compared to full-size helicopters, Coptervision's products lower costs by half or more and increase safety.

The Coptervision company began in 1997, but the inspiration came much earlier, from the founder's background. Carlos Hoyos, the son of a photographer, began shooting still photographs at 16, and later became a cinematographer, producer, and director. As a boy, he was interested in radio-controlled airplanes. In 1996, he moved to Los Angeles, where he joined a model helicopter club and began to experiment with cameras mounted on mini-helicopters. Hoyos took on partners Sarita Spiwak, a fellow Colombian, and his daughter Meltzer. The partners do the technical development themselves, while a team of trained pilots and technicians work on each production.

After the creation of Coptervision, filmmakers began to express interest in using the lightweight camera alone, without the helicopter. The partners improvised. "A lot of people expressed interest in the camera design itself . . . The idea for Rollvision

started with that. We took it off the helicopter and put it on different platforms," says Meltzer.

The company recently released new aerial still-photography equipment, and future goals include the completion of products for surveillance and navigation applications for the U.S. military and NASA. A new book of aerial photographs by Hoyos has been praised as "giving us a pair of wings with which to look at the world." Want to see that view yourself? You can, for Coptervision's price of about $8,000 per day.

See *Coptervision and . . . Technology*, a boxed insert, for more about innovation at Coptervision.

References: "About Us," "Coptervision," "Rollvision," Coptervision website, www.coptervision.com on May 28, 2005; "Breathtaking Aerial Photography Exhibit Comes to Beverly Hills," Press Release Newswire website, May 28, 2005, www.prweb.com on May 28, 2005; Shelly Garcia, "Wireless Camera Puts Fans in the Action," *Los Angeles Business Journal*, July 30, 2001, www.la-businessjournal.com on May 28, 2005; Stephen Porter, "Bird's Eye View," *Video Systems*, February 1, 2002, videosystems.com on May 28, 2005 (quotation); David Wiener, "Bird's Eye View," *American Cinematographer*, August 2000, www.theasc.com on May 28, 2005.

Managers routinely make both tough and easy decisions. Regardless of which decisions are made, though, it is almost certain that some observers will criticize and others will applaud. Indeed, in the rough-and-tumble world of business, there are few simple or easy decisions to make. Some managers claim to be focused on the goal of what is good for the company in the long term and make decisions accordingly. Others clearly focus on the here and now. Some decisions deal with employees, some with investors, and others with dollars and cents. But all require careful thought and consideration.

This chapter describes many different perspectives of decision making. We start by examining the nature of decision making and distinguishing it from problem solving. Next, we describe several different approaches to understanding the decision-making process. We then identify and discuss related behavioral aspects of decision making. Finally, we discuss creativity, a key ingredient in many effective decisions.

The Nature of Decision Making

Decision making is choosing one alternative from among several. Consider a game of football, for example. The quarterback can run any of perhaps a hundred plays. With the goal of scoring a touchdown always in mind, he chooses the play that seems to promise the best outcome. His choice is based on his understanding of the game situation, the likelihood of various outcomes, and his preference for each outcome.

Problem solving, on the other hand, is a special form of decision making in which the issue is unique—it requires developing and evaluating alternatives. Suppose after running a play the quarterback sees that a referee has thrown a flag to signal a rules infraction. The referee explains to the quarterback that the defensive team committed a foul and that the offense now has a choice. The offense can accept the play that was just run without a sanction against the defense or else they can impose the sanction and run the play again. If the play resulted in a 30-yard gain, whereas the penalty would mean only 5 yards, the answer is to refuse the penalty and take the play. But if the play had resulted in a big loss, the penalty would be accepted.

Note that in some situations decision making and problem solving start out alike. Suppose the issue is to identify the best location for a new plant. After evaluating each of the primary locations only one viable choice remains, so there is really no decision left to make. But if three locations each meet the firm's basic requirements and have different relative strengths, the manager will then have to make a decision from among the options. Most of our discussion in this chapter relates to decision making. However, we will identify implications for problem solving as relevant.

Figure 8.1 shows the basic elements of decision making. A decision maker's actions are guided by a goal. Each of several alternative courses of action is linked with various outcomes. Information is available on the alternatives, on the likelihood that each outcome will occur, and on the value of each outcome relative to the goal. The decision maker chooses one alternative on the basis of his or her evaluation of the information.

Decisions made in organizations can be classified according to frequency and to information conditions. In a decision-making context, frequency is how often a particular decision situation recurs, and information conditions describe how much information is available about the likelihood of various outcomes.

> **Decision making** is the process of choosing from among several alternatives.

> **Problem solving** is a special form of decision making in which the issue is unique—it requires developing and evaluating alternatives.

Types of Decisions

The frequency of recurrence determines whether a decision is programmed or nonprogrammed. A **programmed decision** recurs often enough for decision rules to be developed. A **decision rule** tells decision makers which alternative to choose once they have predetermined information about the decision situation. The appropriate decision rule is used whenever the same situation is encountered. Programmed decisions usually are highly structured; that is, the goals are clear and well known, the decision-making procedure is already established, and the sources and channels of information are clearly defined.[1] Note that in problem solving, alternatives can be developed and evaluated without the aid of a decision rule.

Airlines use established procedures when an airplane breaks down and cannot be used on a particular flight. Passengers may not view the issue as a programmed decision because they experience this situation relatively infrequently. But the airlines know that equipment problems that render a plane unfit for service arise regularly. Each airline has its own set of clear and defined procedures to use in the event of equipment problems. A given flight may be delayed, canceled, or continued on a different plane, depending on the nature of the problem and other circumstances (such

> A **programmed decision** is a decision that recurs often enough for a decision rule to be developed.
>
> A **decision rule** is a statement that tells a decision maker which alternative to choose based on the characteristics of the decision situation.

FIGURE 8.1

Elements of Decision Making

A decision maker has a goal, evaluates the outcomes of alternative courses of action in terms of the goal, and selects one alternative to be implemented.

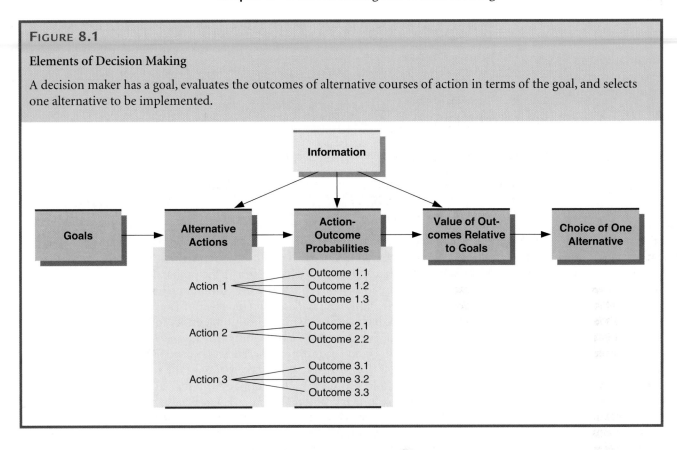

as the number of passengers booked, the next scheduled flight for the same destination, and so forth).

When a problem or decision situation has not been encountered before, however, a decision maker cannot rely on previously established decision rules. Such a decision is called a **nonprogrammed decision**, and it requires problem solving. Nonprogrammed decisions are poorly structured because information is ambiguous, there is no clear procedure for making the decision, and the goals are often vague. Many of the decisions that had to be made by government, military, and business leaders in the wake of the events of September 11, 2001, were clearly this type.

Table 8.1 summarizes the characteristics of programmed and nonprogrammed decisions. Note that programmed decisions are more common at the lower levels of the organization, whereas a primary responsibility of top management is to make the difficult, nonprogrammed decisions that determine the organization's long-term effectiveness. By definition, the strategic decisions for which top management is responsible are poorly structured and nonroutine and have far-reaching consequences.[2] Programmed decisions, then, can be made according to previously tested rules and procedures. Nonprogrammed decisions generally require that the decision maker exercise judgment and creativity. In other words, all problems require a decision, but not all decisions require problem solving.

A **nonprogrammed decision** is a decision that recurs infrequently and for which there is no previously established decision rule.

Information Required for Decision Making

Decisions are made to bring about desired outcomes, but the information available about those outcomes varies. The range of available information can be considered as a

TABLE 8.1

Characteristics of
Programmed and
Nonprogrammed
Decisions

Characteristics	Programmed Decisions	Nonprogrammed Decisions
Type of Decision	Well structured	Poorly structured
Frequency	Repetitive and routine	New and unusual
Goals	Clear, specific	Vague
Information	Readily available	Not available, unclear channels
Consequences	Minor	Major
Organizational Level	Lower levels	Upper levels
Time for Solution	Short	Relatively long
Basis for Solution	Decision rules, set procedures	Judgment and creativity

continuum whose endpoints represent complete certainty when all alternative outcomes are known and complete uncertainty when alternative outcomes are unknown. Points between the two extremes create risk—the decision maker has some information about the possible outcomes and may be able to estimate the probability of their occurrence.

Different information conditions present different challenges to the decision maker.[3] For example, suppose the marketing manager of PlayStation is trying to determine whether to launch an expensive promotional effort for a new video game (see Figure 8.2). For simplicity, assume there are only two alternatives: to promote the game or not to promote it. Under a **condition of certainty**, the manager knows the outcomes of each alternative. If the new game is promoted heavily, the company will realize a $10 million profit. Without promotion, the company will realize only a $2 million profit. Here the decision is simple: Promote the game. (Note: These figures are created for the purposes of this example and are not actual profit figures for any company.)

Under a **condition of risk**, the decision maker cannot know with certainty what the outcome of a given action will be but has enough information to estimate the probabilities of various outcomes. Thus, working from information gathered by the market research department, the marketing manager in our example can estimate the likelihood of each outcome in a risk situation. In this case, the alternatives are defined by the size of the market. The probability for a large video game market is 0.6, and the probability for a small market is 0.4. The manager can calculate the expected value of the promotional effort based on these probabilities and the expected profits associated with each. To find the expected value of an alternative, the manager multiplies each outcome's value by the probability of its occurrence. The sum of these calculations for all possible outcomes represents that alternative's expected value. In this case, the expected value of alternative 1—to promote the new game—is as follows:

$$0.6 \times \$10,000,000 = \$6,000,000 + 0.4 \times \$2,000,000 = \$800,000$$

$$\text{Expected value of alternative 1} = \$6,800,000$$

The expected value of alternative 2—not to promote the new game—is $1,400,000 (see Figure 8.2). The marketing manager should choose the first alternative, because its expected value is higher. The manager should recognize, however, that although the numbers look convincing, they are based on incomplete information and are only estimates of probability.

The decision maker who lacks enough information to estimate the probability of outcomes (or perhaps even to identify the outcomes at all) faces a **condition of uncertainty**. In the PlayStation example, this might be the case if sales of video games had recently collapsed, and it was not clear whether the precipitous drop was temporary or permanent or when information to clarify the situation would be available. Under such circumstances, the decision maker may wait for more information to reduce

Under the **condition of certainty**, the manager knows the outcomes of each alternative.

Under the **condition of risk**, the decision maker cannot know with certainty what the outcome of a given action will be but has enough information to estimate the probabilities of various outcomes.

Under the **condition of uncertainty**, the decision maker lacks enough information to estimate the probability of possible outcomes.

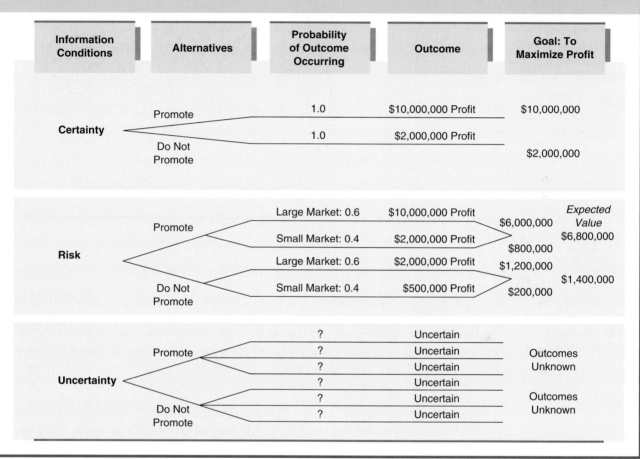

FIGURE 8.2

Alternative Outcomes Under Different Information Conditions

The three decision-making conditions of certainty, risk, and uncertainty for the decision about whether to promote a new video game to the market.

uncertainty or rely on judgment, experience, and intuition to make the decision. Of course, it is also important to remember that decision making is not always so easy to classify in terms of certainty, uncertainty, and risk.

The Decision-Making Process

Several approaches to decision making offer insights into the process by which managers arrive at their decisions. The rational approach is appealing because of its logic and economy. Yet these very qualities raise questions about this approach because actual decision making often is not a wholly rational process. The behavioral approach, meanwhile, attempts to account for the limits on rationality in decision making. The practical approach combines features of the rational and behavioral approaches. Finally, the personal approach focuses on the decision-making processes individuals use in difficult situations.

The Rational Approach

The **rational decision-making approach** is a systematic, step-by-step process for making decisions.

The **rational decision-making approach** assumes that managers follow a systematic, step-by-step process. It further assumes the organization is economically based and managed by decision makers who are entirely objective and have complete information.[4] Figure 8.3 identifies the steps of the process, starting with stating a goal and running logically through the process until the best decision is made, implemented, and controlled.

State the Situational Goal   The rational decision-making process begins with the statement of a situational goal—that is, a goal for a particular situation. The goal of a marketing department, for example, may be to obtain a certain market share by the end of the year. (Some models of decision making do not start with a goal. We include it because it is the standard used to determine whether there is a decision to be made.)

Identify the Problem   The purpose of problem identification is to gather information that bears on the goal. If there is a discrepancy between the goal and the actual state, action may be needed. In the marketing example, the group may gather information about the company's actual market share and compare it with the desired market share. A difference between the two represents a problem that necessitates a decision. Reliable information is very important in this step. Inaccurate information can lead to an unnecessary decision or no decision when one is required.

Determining Decision Type   Next, the decision makers must determine if the problem represents a programmed or a nonprogrammed decision. If a programmed decision is needed, the appropriate decision rule is invoked, and the process moves on to the choice among alternatives. A programmed marketing decision may be called for if analysis reveals that competitors are outspending the company on print advertising. Because creating print advertising and buying space for it are well-established functions of the marketing group, the problem requires only a programmed decision.

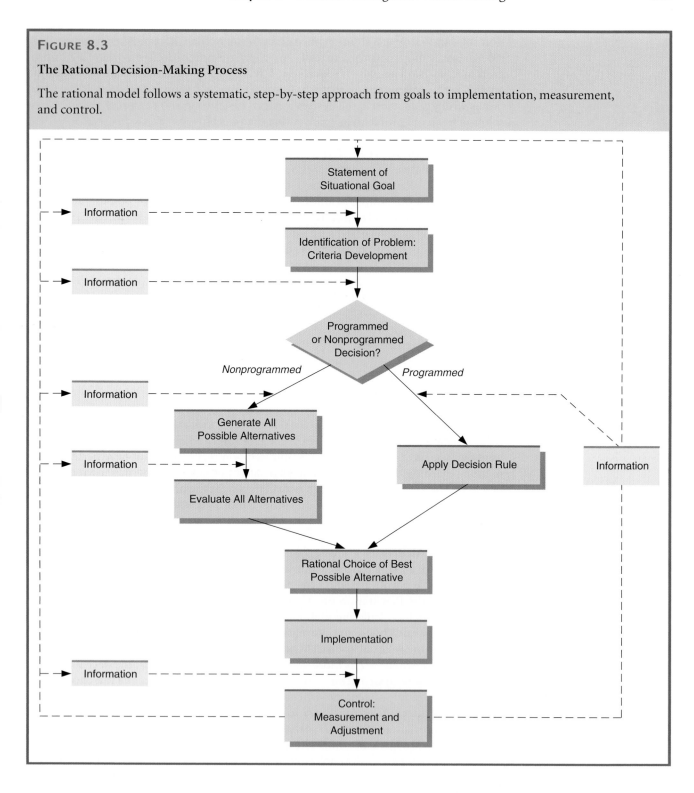

FIGURE 8.3

The Rational Decision-Making Process

The rational model follows a systematic, step-by-step approach from goals to implementation, measurement, and control.

Although it may seem simple to diagnose a situation as programmed, apply a decision rule, and arrive at a solution, mistakes can still occur. Choosing the wrong decision rule or assuming the problem calls for a programmed decision when a nonprogrammed decision actually is required can result in poor decisions. The same caution applies to the determination that a nonprogrammed decision is called for. If the situation is wrongly diagnosed, the decision maker wastes time and resources seeking a new solution to an old problem, or "reinventing the wheel."

Generate Alternatives   The next step in making a nonprogrammed decision is to generate alternatives. The rational process assumes that decision makers will generate all the possible alternative solutions to the problem. However, this assumption is unrealistic because even simple business problems can have scores of possible solutions. Decision makers may rely on education and experience as well as knowledge of the situation to generate alternatives. In addition, they may seek information from other people such as peers, subordinates, and supervisors. Decision makers may analyze the symptoms of the problem for clues or fall back on intuition or judgment to develop alternative solutions.[5] If the marketing department in our example determines that a nonprogrammed decision is required, it will need to generate alternatives for increasing market share.

Evaluate Alternatives   Evaluation involves assessing all possible alternatives in terms of predetermined decision criteria. The ultimate decision criterion is "Will this alternative bring us nearer to the goal?" In each case, the decision maker must examine each alternative for evidence that it will reduce the discrepancy between the desired state and the actual state. The evaluation process usually includes (1) describing the anticipated outcomes (benefits) of each alternative, (2) evaluating the anticipated costs of each alternative, and (3) estimating the uncertainties and risks associated with each alternative.[6] In most decision situations, the decision maker does not have perfect information regarding the outcomes of all alternatives. At one extreme, as shown earlier in Figure 8.2, outcomes may be known with certainty; at the other, the decision maker has no information whatsoever, so the outcomes are entirely uncertain. But risk is the most common situation.

Choose an Alternative   Choosing an alternative is usually the most crucial step in the decision-making process. Choosing consists of selecting the alternative with the highest possible payoff, based on the benefits, costs, risks, and uncertainties of all alternatives. In the PlayStation promotion example, the decision maker evaluated the two alternatives by calculating their expected values. Following the rational approach, the manager would choose the alternative with the largest expected value.

Even with the rational approach, however, difficulties can arise in choosing an alternative. First, when two or more alternatives have equal payoffs, the decision maker must obtain more information or use some other criterion to make the choice. Second, when no single alternative will accomplish the objective, some combination of two or three alternatives may have to be implemented. Finally, if no alternative or combination of alternatives will solve the problem, the decision maker must obtain more information, generate more alternatives, or change the goals.[7]

An important part of the choice phase is the consideration of **contingency plans**—alternative actions that can be taken if the primary course of action is unexpectedly disrupted or rendered inappropriate.[8] Planning for contingencies is part of the transition between choosing the preferred alternative and implementing it. In developing contingency plans, the decision maker usually asks such questions as "What if something unexpected happens during the implementation of this alternative?" or "If the economy

Contingency plans are alternative actions to take if the primary course of action is unexpectedly disrupted or rendered inappropriate.

goes into a recession, will the choice of this alternative ruin the company?" or "How can we alter this plan if the economy suddenly rebounds and begins to grow?"

Implement the Plan   Implementation puts the decision into action. It builds on the commitment and motivation of those who participated in the decision-making process (and may actually bolster individual commitment and motivation). To succeed, implementation requires the proper use of resources and good management skills. Following the decision to promote the new PlayStation game heavily, for example, the marketing manager must implement the decision by assigning the project to a work group or task force. The success of this team depends on the leadership, the reward structure, the communications system, and group dynamics. Sometimes the decision maker begins to doubt a choice already made. This doubt is called post-decision dissonance, or more generally, **cognitive dissonance**.[9] To reduce the tension created by the dissonance, the decision maker may seek to rationalize the decision further with new information.

> **Cognitive dissonance** is doubt about a choice that has already been made.

Control: Measure and Adjust   In the final stage of the rational decision-making process, the outcomes of the decision are measured and compared with the desired goal. If a discrepancy remains, the decision maker may restart the decision-making process by setting a new goal (or reiterating the existing one). The decision maker, unsatisfied with the previous decision, may modify the subsequent decision-making process to avoid another mistake. Changes can be made in any part of the process, as Figure 8.3 illustrates by the arrows leading from the control step to each of the other steps. Decision making therefore is a dynamic, self-correcting, and ongoing process in organizations.

Suppose a marketing department implements a new print advertising campaign. After implementation, it constantly monitors market research data and compares its new market share with the desired market share. If the advertising has the desired effect, no changes will be made in the promotion campaign. If, however, the data indicate no change in the market share, additional decisions and implementation of a contingency plan may be necessary. For example, when Nissan introduced its luxury car line Infiniti, it relied on a Zen-like series of ads that featured images of rocks, plants, and water—but no images of the car. At the same time, Toyota was featuring close-up pictures of its own luxury car line, Lexus, which quickly established itself as a market leader. When Infiniti managers realized their mistake, they quickly pulled the old ads and started running new ones centered around images of their car.[10]

Strengths and Weaknesses of the Rational Approach   The rational approach has several strengths. It forces the decision maker to consider a decision in a logical, sequential manner, and the in-depth analysis of alternatives enables the decision maker to choose on the basis of information rather than emotion or social pressure. But the rigid assumptions of this approach often are unrealistic.[11] The amount of information available to managers usually is limited by either time or cost constraints, and most decision makers have limited ability to process information about the alternatives. In addition, not all alternatives lend themselves to quantification in terms that will allow for easy comparison. Finally, because they cannot predict the future, it is unlikely that decision makers will know all possible outcomes of each alternative.

The Behavioral Approach

Whereas the rational approach assumes that managers operate logically and rationally, the behavioral approach acknowledges the role and importance of human behavior in

The decision-making process is supposed to be logical and rational but is instead often affected by behavioral, practical, and personal considerations. Consider, for example, Gabrielle Melchionda. Ms. Melchionda is a Maine entrepreneur whose skin-care product business is booming. She was recently offered a lucrative contract to begin exporting her products to Turkey. But she turned it down when she learned that the exporter also sold weapons. Had rational decision-making prevailed, she would have jumped on the idea. But her own personal values kept her focused on what was important to her as a person—and it wasn't just the money!

the decision-making process. In particular, a crucial assumption of the behavioral approach is that decision makers operate with bounded rationality rather than with the perfect rationality assumed by the rational approach. **Bounded rationality** is the idea that although individuals may seek the best solution to a problem, the demands of processing all the information bearing on the problem, generating all possible solutions, and choosing the single best solution are beyond the capabilities of most decision makers. Thus, they accept less-than-ideal solutions based on a process that is neither exhaustive nor entirely rational. For example, one recent study found that under time pressure, groups usually eliminate all but the two most favorable alternatives and then process the remaining two in great detail.[12] Thus, decision makers operating with bounded rationality limit the inputs to the decision-making process and base decisions on judgment and personal biases as well as on logic.[13]

The **behavioral approach** is characterized by (1) the use of procedures and rules of thumb, (2) suboptimizing, and (3) satisficing. Uncertainty in decision making can initially be reduced by relying on procedures and rules of thumb. If, for example, increasing print advertising has increased a company's market share in the past, that linkage may be used by company employees as a rule of thumb in decision making. When the previous month's market share drops below a certain level, the company might increase its print advertising expenditures by 25 percent during the following month.

Suboptimizing is knowingly accepting

Bounded rationality is the idea that decision makers cannot deal with information about all the aspects and alternatives pertaining to a problem and therefore choose to tackle some meaningful subset of it.

The **behavioral approach** uses rules of thumb, suboptimizing, and satisficing in making decisions.

less than the best possible outcome. Frequently it is not feasible to make the ideal decision in a real-world situation given organizational constraints. The decision maker often must suboptimize to avoid unintended negative effects on other departments, product lines, or decisions.[14] An automobile manufacturer, for example, can cut costs dramatically and increase efficiency if it schedules the production of one model at a time. Thus, the production group's optimal decision is single-model scheduling. But the marketing group, seeking to optimize its sales goals by offering a wide variety of models, may demand the opposite production schedule: short runs of entirely different models. The groups in the middle, design and scheduling, may suboptimize the benefits the production and marketing groups seek by planning long runs of slightly different models. This is the practice of the large auto manufacturers such as General Motors and Ford, which make several body styles in numerous models on the same production line.

The final feature of the behavioral approach is **satisficing**—examining alternatives only until a solution that meets minimal requirements is found and then ceasing to look

for a better one.[15] The search for alternatives usually is a sequential process guided by procedures and rules of thumb based on previous experiences with similar problems. The search often ends when the first minimally acceptable choice is encountered. The resulting choice may narrow the discrepancy between the desired and the actual states, but it is not likely to be the optimal solution. As the process is repeated, incremental improvements slowly reduce the discrepancy between the actual and desired states.

The Practical Approach

Because of the unrealistic demands of the rational approach and the limited, short-run orientation of the behavioral approach, neither is entirely satisfactory. However, the worthwhile features of each can be combined into a practical approach to decision making, shown in Figure 8.4. The steps in this process are the same as in the rational approach; however, the conditions recognized by the behavioral approach are added to provide a more realistic process. For example, the **practical approach** suggests that rather than generating all alternatives, the decision maker should try to go beyond rules of thumb and satisficing limitations and generate as many alternatives as time, money, and other practicalities of the situation allow. In this synthesis of the two other approaches, the rational approach provides an analytical framework for making decisions, whereas the behavioral approach provides a moderating influence.

In practice, decision makers use some hybrid of the rational, behavioral, and practical approaches to make the tough day-to-day decisions in running organizations. Some decision makers use a methodical process of gathering as much information as possible, developing and evaluating alternatives, and seeking advice from knowledgeable people before making a decision. Others fly from one decision to another, making seemingly hasty decisions and barking out orders to subordinates. The second group would seem not to use much information or a rational approach to making decisions. Recent research, however, has shown that managers who make decisions very quickly probably are using just as much, or more, information and generating and evaluating as many alternatives as slower, more methodical decision makers.[16]

The Personal Approach

Although the models just described have provided significant insight into decision making, they do not fully explain the processes people engage in when they are nervous, worried, and agitated over making a decision that has major implications for them, their organization, or their families. In short, they still do not reflect the conditions under which many decisions are made. One attempt to provide a more realistic view of individual decision making is the model presented by Irving Janis and Leon Mann.[17] The Janis-Mann concept, called the **conflict model**, is based on research in social psychology and individual decision processes and is a very personal approach to decision making. Although the model may appear complex, if you examine it one step at a time and follow the example in this section, you should easily understand how it works. The model has five basic characteristics:

1. It deals only with important life decisions—marriage, schooling, career, and major organizational decisions—that commit the individual or the organization to a certain course of action following the decision.
2. It recognizes that procrastination and rationalization are mechanisms by which people avoid making difficult decisions and coping with the associated stress.
3. It explicitly acknowledges that some decisions probably will be wrong and that the fear of making an unsound decision can be a deterrent to making any decision at all.

Suboptimizing is knowingly accepting less than the best possible outcome to avoid unintended negative effects on other aspects of the organization.

Satisficing is examining alternatives only until a solution that meets minimal requirements is found.

The **practical approach** to decision making combines the steps of the rational approach with the conditions in the behavioral approach to create a more realistic approach for making decisions in organizations.

The **conflict model** is a very personal approach to decision making because it deals with the personal conflicts that people experience in particularly difficult decision situations.

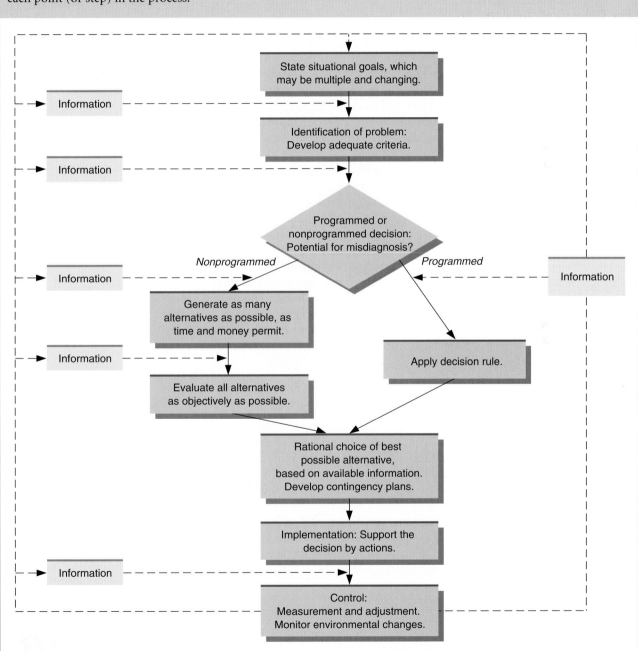

Practical Approach to Decision Making with Behavioral Guidelines

The practical model applies some of the conditions recognized by the behavioral approach to the rational approach to decision making. Although similar to the rational model, the practical approach recognizes personal limitations at each point (or step) in the process.

Information

Information

Information

Information

Information

Information

State situational goals, which may be multiple and changing.

Identification of problem: Develop adequate criteria.

Programmed or nonprogrammed decision: Potential for misdiagnosis?

Nonprogrammed   *Programmed*

Generate as many alternatives as possible, as time and money permit.

Apply decision rule.

Evaluate all alternatives as objectively as possible.

Rational choice of best possible alternative, based on available information. Develop contingency plans.

Implementation: Support the decision by actions.

Control: Measurement and adjustment. Monitor environmental changes.

4. It provides for **self-reactions**—comparisons of alternatives with internalized moral standards. Internalized moral standards guide decision making as much as economic and social outcomes do. A proposed course of action may offer many economic and social rewards, but if it violates the decision maker's moral convictions, it is unlikely to be chosen.

5. It recognizes that at times the decision maker is ambivalent about alternative courses of action; in such circumstances, it is very difficult to make a wholehearted commitment to a single choice. Major life decisions seldom allow compromise, however; usually they are either-or decisions that require commitment to one course of action.

> **Self-reactions** are comparisons of alternatives with internalized moral standards.

The Janis-Mann conflict model of decision making is shown in Figure 8.5. A concrete example will help explain each step. Suppose Richard is a thirty-year-old engineer with a working wife and two young children. Richard has been employed at a large manufacturing company for eight years. He keeps abreast of his career progress through visits with peers at work and in other companies, through feedback from his manager and others regarding his work and future with the firm, through the alumni magazine from his university, and through other sources.

At work one morning, Richard learns that he has been passed over for a promotion for the second time in a year. He investigates the information, which can be considered negative feedback, and confirms it. As a result, he seeks out other information regarding his career at the company, the prospect of changing employers, and the possibility of going back to graduate school to get an MBA. At the same time, he asks himself, "Are the risks serious if I do not make a change?" If the answer is "no," Richard will continue his present activities. In the model's terms, this option is called **unconflicted adherence**. If instead the answer is "yes" or "maybe," Richard will move to the next question in the model.

> **Unconflicted adherence** entails continuing with current activities if doing so does not entail serious risks.

The second step asks, "Are the risks serious if I do make a change?" If Richard goes on to this step, he will gather information about potential losses from making a change. He may, for example, find out whether he would lose health insurance and pension benefits if he changed jobs or went back to graduate school. If he believes that changing presents no serious risks, Richard will make the change, called an **unconflicted change**. Otherwise, Richard will move on to the next step.

> **Unconflicted change** involves making decisions in present activities if doing so presents no serious risks.

But suppose Richard has determined that the risks are serious whether or not he makes a change. He believes he must make a change because he will not be promoted further in his present company, yet serious risks are also associated with making a change—perhaps loss of benefits, uncertain promotion opportunities in another company, or lost income from going to graduate school for two years. In the third step, Richard wonders, "Is it realistic to hope to find a better solution?" He continues to look for information that can help him make the decision. If the answer to this third question is "no," Richard may give up hope of finding anything better and opt for what Janis and Mann call **defensive avoidance**; that is, he will make no change and avoid any further contact with the issue. A positive response, however, will move Richard onward to the next step.

> **Defensive avoidance** entails making no changes in present activities and avoiding further contact with associated issues because there appears to be no hope of finding a better solution.
> **Hypervigilance** is frantic, superficial pursuit of some satisficing strategy.

Here the decision maker, who now recognizes the serious risks involved yet expects to find a solution, asks, "Is there sufficient time to search and deliberate?" Richard now asks himself how quickly he needs to make a change. If he believes that he has little time to deliberate, perhaps because of his age, he will experience what Janis and Mann call **hypervigilance**. In this state, he may suffer severe psychological stress and engage in frantic, superficial pursuit of some satisficing strategy. (This might also be called "panic"!) If, on the other hand, Richard believes that he has two or three years to consider various alternatives, he will undertake vigilant information processing, in which

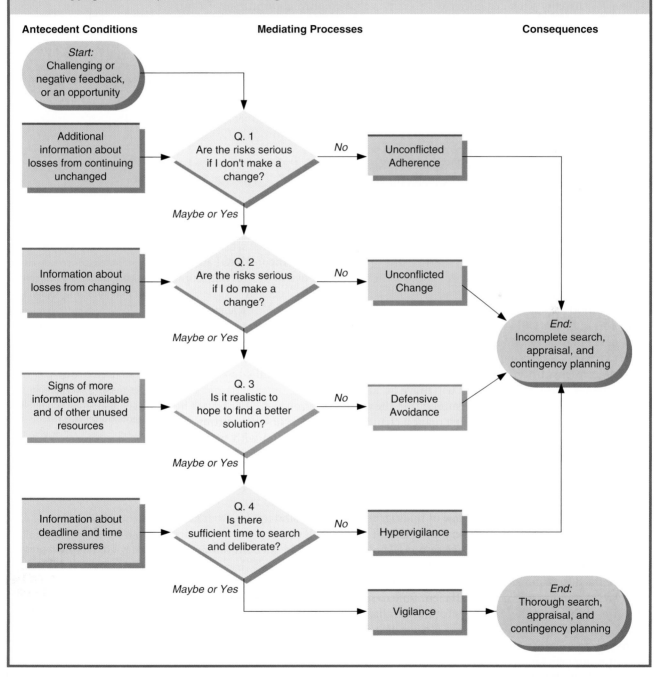

he will thoroughly investigate all possible alternatives, weigh their costs and benefits before making a choice, and develop contingency plans.

Negative answers to the questions in the conflict model lead to responses of unconflicted adherence, unconflicted change, defensive avoidance, and hypervigilance. All are coping strategies that result in incomplete search, appraisal, and contingency planning. A decision maker who gives the same answer to all the questions will always engage in the same coping strategy. However, if the answers change as the situation changes, the individual's coping strategies may change as well. The decision maker who answers "yes" to each of the four questions is led to **vigilant information processing**, a process similar to that outlined in the rational decision-making model. The decision maker objectively analyzes the problem and all alternatives, thoroughly searches for information, carefully evaluates the consequences of all alternatives, and diligently plans for implementation and contingencies.

> **Vigilant information processing** involves thoroughly investigating all possible alternatives, weighing their costs and benefits before making a decision, and developing contingency plans.

Related Behavioral Aspects of Decision Making

The behavioral, practical, and personal approaches each have behavioral components, but the manager should also be aware of other behavioral aspects of decision making as well. These include political forces, intuition, escalation of commitment, risk propensity, and ethics.

Political Forces in Decision Making

Political forces can play a major role in how decisions are made. We cover political behavior in Chapter 14, but one major element of politics, coalitions, is especially relevant to decision making. A **coalition** is an informal alliance of individuals or groups formed to achieve a common goal. This common goal is often a preferred decision alternative. For example, coalitions of stockholders frequently band together to force a board of directors to make a certain decision. Indeed, many of the recent power struggles between management and dissident shareholders at Disney Corporation have relied on coalitions as each side tried to gain the upper hand against the other.[18]

> A **coalition** is an informal alliance of individuals or groups formed to achieve a common goal.

The impact of coalitions can be either positive or negative. They can help astute managers get the organization on a path toward effectiveness and profitability, or they can strangle well-conceived strategies and decisions. Managers must recognize when to use coalitions, how to assess whether coalitions are acting in the best interests of the organization, and how to constrain their dysfunctional effects.[19]

Intuition

Intuition is an innate belief about something without conscious consideration. Managers sometimes decide to do something because it "feels right" or they have a hunch. This feeling is usually not arbitrary, however. Rather, it is based on years of experience and practice in making decisions in similar situations. An inner sense may help managers make an occasional decision without going through a full-blown rational sequence of steps. The recent best-selling book by Malcolm Gladwell entitled *Blink: The Power of Thinking Without Thinking* made strong arguments that intuition is both used more commonly and results in better decisions than had previously been believed.

A few years ago the New York Yankees called three major sneaker manufacturers, Nike, Reebok, and Adidas, and informed them that they were looking to make a

> **Intuition** is innate belief about something without conscious consideration.

sponsorship deal. While Nike and Reebok were carefully and rationally assessing the possibilities, managers at Adidas quickly realized that a partnership with the Yankees made a lot of sense for them. They responded very quickly to the idea, and ended up hammering out a contract while the competitors were still analyzing details.[20] Of course, all managers, but most especially inexperienced ones, should be careful not to rely on intuition too heavily. If rationality and logic are continually flaunted for what "feels right," the odds are that disaster will strike one day.

Escalation of Commitment

Escalation of commitment occurs when a decision maker stays with a decision even when it appears to be wrong.

Another important behavioral process that influences decision making is **escalation of commitment** to a chosen course of action. In particular, decision makers sometimes make decisions and then become so committed to the course of action suggested by that decision that they stay with it, even when it appears to have been wrong.[21] For example, when people buy stock in a company, they sometimes refuse to sell it even after repeated drops in price. They chose a course of action—buying the stock in anticipation of making a profit—and then stay with it even in the face of increasing losses.

For years Pan American World Airways ruled the skies and used its profits to diversify into real estate and other businesses. But with the advent of deregulation, Pan Am began to struggle and lose market share to other carriers, and managers began to realize how ineffective airline operations had become. Experts today point out that the "rational" decision would have been to sell off the remaining airline operations and concentrate on the firm's more profitable businesses. But because they still saw the company as being first and foremost an airline, Pan Am's managers instead began to slowly sell off the firm's profitable holdings to keep the airline flying. Eventually, the company was left with nothing but an ineffective and inefficient airline, and then had to sell off its more profitable routes before eventually being taken over by Delta. Had Pan Am's managers made the more rational decision years earlier, chances are the firm could still be a profitable enterprise today, albeit one with no involvement in the airline industry.[22]

Decision makers must walk a fine line. On the one hand, they must guard against sticking with an incorrect decision too long. To do so can bring about financial decline. On the other hand, managers should not bail out of a seemingly incorrect decision too soon, as did Adidas several years ago. Adidas once dominated the market for professional athletic shoes. It subsequently entered the market for amateur sports shoes and did well there also. But managers incorrectly interpreted a sales slowdown as a sign that the boom in athletic shoes was over. They thought that they had made the wrong decision and ordered drastic cutbacks. The market took off again with Nike at the head of the pack, and Adidas never recovered. Fortunately, a new management team has changed the way Adidas makes decisions, and, as illustrated earlier, the firm is again on its way to becoming a force in the athletic shoe and apparel markets.

Risk Propensity and Decision Making

Risk propensity is the extent to which a decision maker is willing to gamble in making a decision.

The behavioral element of **risk propensity** is the extent to which a decision maker is willing to gamble when making a decision. (Recall that we introduced risk propensity back in Chapter 3.) Some managers are cautious about every decision they make. They try to adhere to the rational model and are extremely conservative in what they do. Such managers are more likely to avoid mistakes, and they infrequently make decisions that lead to big losses. Other managers are extremely

aggressive in making decisions and are willing to take risks.[23] They rely heavily on intuition, reach decisions quickly, and often risk big investments on their decisions. As in gambling, these managers are more likely than their conservative counterparts to achieve big successes with their decisions; they are also more likely to incur greater losses.[24] The organization's culture is a prime ingredient in fostering different levels of risk propensity.

Ethics and Decision Making

Ethics are a person's beliefs about what constitutes right and wrong behavior. Ethical behavior is that which conforms to generally accepted social norms; unethical behavior does not conform to generally accepted social norms. Some decisions made by managers may have little or nothing to do with their own personal ethics, but many other decisions are influenced by the manager's ethics. For example, decisions involving such disparate issues as hiring and firing employees, dealing with customers and suppliers, setting wages and assigning tasks, and maintaining one's expense account are all subject to ethical influences.

In general, ethical dilemmas for managers may center on direct personal gain, indirect personal gain, or simple personal preferences. Consider, for example, a top executive contemplating a decision about a potential takeover. His or her stock-option package may result in enormous personal gain if the decision goes one way, even though stockholders may benefit more if the decision goes the other way. An indirect

> **Ethics** are a person's beliefs about what constitutes right and wrong behavior.

Ethics play a critical role in the kinds of decisions that people make. In light of recent ethical scandals, many organizations today are actively attempting to promote ethical decision making by their managers. These individuals are the top elected officials in the state of Hawaii. They are undergoing a mandatory ethics training program in order to help them better understand and assess the ethical issues they confront as part of their jobs.

Morgan Stanley and . . .  **ETHICS**

Was Morgan Stanley Too Cozy?

In 1997, when Dean Witter Discover merged with Morgan Stanley Dean Witter, CEO Phil Purcell became head of the combined firm. Purcell seemed a good choice because of his belief in offering diversified financial services, from consumer investment accounts to investment banking.

However, seven years later, Morgan Stanley had failed to achieve the expected synergies. The fault appeared to lie with Purcell and several of his misguided decisions. Among the disturbing choices: (1) mishandling a fraud investigation and destroying evidence, resulting in a judgment of $1.5 billion against the firm, (2) forcing out several capable leaders, resulting in the defection of dozens of top staff including twenty-four managing directors, and (3) refusing to consider divestiture of high-performing divisions, resulting in a possible hostile takeover bid from HSBC bank.

Many investors, regulators, and current and former employees blamed Purcell, but they also accused the board of directors of ineffective oversight. One website asked, "How many more talented employees must leave before the Board understands that . . . the Firm is facing a crisis of confidence in the Chairman and CEO?"

When outsiders asked the board to investigate Purcell's leadership, "they found no specific errors of judgment." Instead, the board approved sharp increases in Purcell's compensation. Why did the board refuse to stop Purcell's escalation of commitment to poor decisions? Many of the board members were his close friends. Several worked for Sears or McKinsey Consulting, where Purcell had worked

before joining Dean Witter, or lived in Chicago, Purcell's hometown. One-quarter of the board served on Dean Witter's board, so some of the directors had long-standing relationships with Purcell.

The relationship between a corporate board of directors and the CEO must be close, with trust and shared information. But when the relationship is too cozy, imperfect choices go unchallenged and the firm's shareholders are the losers.

For more about Purcell's troubled decision making, see this chapter's closing case, entitled "Decisions and Consequences at Morgan Stanley."

> ### "The Firm is facing a crisis of confidence in the Chairman and CEO."
>
> *Eight former Morgan Stanley directors*

References: "Open Letter to Morgan Stanley Shareholders," The Future of Morgan Stanley website, May 12, 2005, www.futureofms.com on May 31, 2005 (quotation); Christopher Burba, "Morgan Stanley: Too Pliant a Board," *Business Week*, April 20, 2005, www.businessweek.com on May 23, 2005; Emily Thornton, "Can Phil Purcell Change His Spots?" *Business Week*, April 18, 2005, www.businessweek.com on May 23, 2005; Emily Thornton, "Morgan Stanley's No-Win Situation," *Business Week*, May 11, 2005, www.businessweek.com on May 23, 2005; Emily Thornton, "Only Making It Worse," *Business Week*, April 11, 2005, pp. 90–91; Emily Thornton, "Up and Out at Morgan Stanley," *Business Week*, May 30, 2005, www.businessweek.com on May 23, 2005.

personal gain may result when a decision does not directly add value to a manager's personal worth but does enhance her or his career. Or the manager may face a choice about relocating a company facility in which one of the options is closest to his or her residence.

Managers should carefully and deliberately consider the ethical context of every one of their decisions. The goal, of course, is for the manager to make the decision that is in the best interest of the firm, as opposed to the best interest of the manager. Doing this requires personal honesty and integrity. Managers also find it helpful to discuss potential ethical dilemmas with colleagues. Others can often provide an objective view of a situation that may help a manager avoid unintentionally making an unethical decision.

Creativity, Problem Solving, and Decision Making

Creativity is an important individual difference variable that exists in everyone. However, rather than discuss it with other individual-level concepts in Chapter 3, we describe it here because it plays such a central role in both decision making and problem solving. **Creativity** is the ability of an individual to generate new ideas or to conceive new perspectives of existing ideas. Hence, creativity can play a role in how a problem or decision situation is defined, what alternatives are identified, and how each is evaluated. Creativity can also enable a manager to identify a new way of looking at things.

Creativity is a person's ability to generate new ideas or to conceive of new perspectives on existing ideas.

What makes a person creative? How does the creative process work? Although psychologists have not yet discovered complete answers to these questions, examining a few general patterns can help us understand the sources of individual creativity within organizations and the processes through which creativity emerges.[25]

The Creative Individual

Numerous researchers have focused their efforts on attempting to describe the common attributes of creative individuals. These attributes generally fall into three categories: background experiences, personal traits, and cognitive abilities.

Background Experiences and Creativity   Researchers have observed that many creative individuals were raised in an environment in which creativity was nurtured. Mozart was raised in a family of musicians and began composing and performing music at age 6. Pierre and Marie Curie, great scientists in their own right, also raised a daughter, Irene, who won the Nobel Prize in Chemistry. Thomas Edison's creativity was nurtured by his mother. However, people with background experiences very different from theirs have also been creative. The African American abolitionist and writer Frederick Douglass was born into slavery in Tuckahoe, Maryland, and had very limited opportunities for education. Nonetheless, his powerful oratory and creative thinking helped lead to the Emancipation Proclamation, which outlawed slavery in the United States.

Personal Traits and Creativity   Certain personal traits have also been linked to creativity in individuals. The traits shared by most creative people are openness; an attraction to complexity; high levels of energy, independence, and autonomy; strong self-confidence; and a strong belief that one is, in fact, creative. Individuals who possess these traits are more likely to be creative than are those who do not have them.

Cognitive Abilities and Creativity   Cognitive abilities are an individual's power to think intelligently and to analyze situations and data effectively. Intelligence may be a precondition for individual creativity—although most creative people are highly intelligent, not all intelligent people necessarily are creative. Creativity is also linked with the ability to think divergently and convergently. Divergent thinking is a skill that allows people to see differences between situations, phenomena, or events. Convergent thinking is a skill that allows people to see similarities between situations, phenomena, or events. Creative people are generally very skilled at both divergent and convergent thinking.

Coptervision and . . . TECHNOLOGY

Behind the Magic of Coptervision

Coptervision's unique products make for easy filming of impossible shots. Film crews and photographers use the company's remote-controlled mini-helicopters to create never-before-seen live action sequences and still shots.

Coptervision's helicopters were designed by company founder Carlos Hoyos, who began his career as a film director. Hoyos's creativity springs from his convergent thinking—he combined his passion for film production with his passion for flying model aircraft. Hoyos prepared by spending years mastering photography, film direction and production, and radio-controlled model helicopters.

Behind Hoyos's inventive creativity, however, lay a host of other technological developments. These innovations made it possible for Hoyos to create his breakthrough products. The Global Positioning Systems (GPS), consisting of 24 satellites that communicate with ground devices to identify locations precisely, is essential. The U.S. military first created this system and began its use in the 1990s. Coptervision uses GPS to pinpoint the helicopters' real-time locations. The proliferation of commercial communication satellites make it easy for ground-based pilots to maneuver Coptervision helicopters remotely. Satellite communications replace less reliable radio-based communications and allow the helicopters to roam further.

Other supporting innovations include strong and light carbon fiber materials that replace aluminum and steel. Solar-powered battery technology reduces weight

and allows for longer flights. "For every two paper clips in weight we lose, we get another kilometer in range," says a mini-helicopter maker.

More features, longer flights, and other improvements increase the range of uses for unmanned aerial vehicles (UAVs). Proposals range from spy drones for military applications to airborne cell phone towers. Coptervision is exploring opportunities with NASA and the U.S. Army. "The UAV industry is crawling," says James Massey, editor of *Unmanned Vehicles*. "But we're going to go from a crawl to a walk to a run in a tenth the time manned aviation did."

> *"The UAV industry is crawling, but we're going to go from a crawl to a walk to a run in a tenth the time manned aviation did."*
>
> JAMES MASSEY, EDITOR, UNMANNED VEHICLES

References: "About Us," "Coptervision," "Rollvision," Coptervision website, www.coptervision.com on May 28, 2005; "Breathtaking Aerial Photography Exhibit Comes to Beverly Hills," Press Release Newswire website, May 28, 2005, www.prweb.com on May 28, 2005; Stephen Porter, "Bird's Eye View," *Video Systems*, February 1, 2002, video-systems.com on May 28, 2005; Noah Shachtman, "Flying Solo, in the Extreme," *New York Times*, November 14, 2002, www.nytimes.com on July 20, 2005 (quotation).

The Creative Process

Although creative people often report that ideas seem to come to them "in a flash," individual creative activity actually tends to progress through a series of four stages: preparation, incubation, insight, and verification. While Figure 8.6 summarizes the major stages of the creative process, we use the story of Bruce Roth to illustrate how the creative process can work in an individual. Keep in mind that not all creative activity has to follow these four stages, but much of it does.

Preparation, usually the first stage in the creative process, includes education and formal training.

Preparation   The creative process normally begins with a period of **preparation**. Formal education and training are usually the most efficient ways of becoming familiar with this vast amount of research and knowledge. To make a creative contribution to business management or business services, individuals must usually receive formal training and education in business. This is one reason for the strong demand for undergraduate

and master's-level business education. Formal business education can be an effective way for an individual to get "up to speed" and begin making creative contributions quickly. Experiences that managers have on the job after their formal training has finished can also contribute to the creative process. Bruce Roth earned a Ph.D. in chemistry and then spent years working in the pharmaceutical industry learning more and more about chemical compounds and how they work in human beings. In an important sense, the education and training of creative people never really ends. It continues as long as they remain interested in the world and curious about the way things work.

Incubation   The second phase of the creative process is **incubation**—a period of less intense conscious concentration during which the knowledge and ideas acquired during preparation mature and develop. A curious aspect of incubation is that it is often helped along by pauses in concentrated rational thought. Some creative people rely on physical activity such as jogging or swimming to provide a "break" from thinking. Others may read or listen to music. Sometimes sleep may even supply the needed pause. Bruce Roth eventually joined Warner-Lambert, an up-and-coming drug company, to help develop medication to lower cholesterol. In his spare time, Roth read mystery novels and hiked in the mountains. He later acknowledged that this was when he did his best thinking.

Insight   Usually occurring after preparation and incubation, insight is a spontaneous breakthrough in which the creative person achieves a new understanding of some problem or situation. **Insight** represents a coming together of all the scattered thoughts and ideas that were maturing during incubation. It may occur suddenly or develop slowly over time. Insight can be triggered by some external event, such as a new experience or an encounter with new data that forces the individual to think about old issues and problems in new ways, or it can be a completely internal event in which patterns of thought finally coalesce in ways that generate new understanding. One day Bruce Roth was reviewing some data from some earlier studies that had found the new drug under development to be no more effective than other drugs already available. But this time he saw some statistical relationships that had not been identified previously. He knew then that he had a major breakthrough on his hands.

Verification   Once an insight has occurred, **verification** determines the validity or truthfulness of the insight. For many creative ideas, verification includes scientific experiments to determine whether or not the insight actually leads to the results expected. Verification may also include the development of a product or service prototype. A prototype is one or a very small number of products built just to see if the ideas behind the

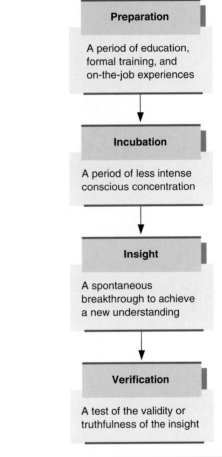

FIGURE 8.6

The Creative Process

The creative process generally follows the four steps illustrated here. Of course, there are exceptions, and the process is occasionally different. In most cases, however, these steps capture the essence of the creative process.

Preparation

A period of education, formal training, and on-the-job experiences

Incubation

A period of less intense conscious concentration

Insight

A spontaneous breakthrough to achieve a new understanding

Verification

A test of the validity or truthfulness of the insight

Incubation is the stage of less intense conscious concentration during which a creative person lets the knowledge and ideas acquired during preparation mature and develop.

Insight is the stage in the creative process when all the scattered thoughts and ideas that were maturing during incubation come together to produce a breakthrough.

Creativity often makes the difference between business success and failure. Take Betsey Johnson, for instance. Her company owns 40 retail shops and the Betsey Johnson label is represented in more than 1,000 stores worldwide. Ms. Johnson is the creative force behind the trendy and cutting-edge clothing company, and her daily business attire is a clear reflection of her own personal creative energy.

In **verification**, the final stage of the creative process, the validity or truthfulness of the insight is determined.

new product actually work. Product prototypes are rarely sold to the public but are very valuable in verifying the insights developed in the creative process. Once the new product or service is developed, verification in the marketplace is the ultimate test of the creative idea behind it. Bruce Roth and his colleagues set to work testing the new drug compound and eventually won FDA approval. The drug, named Lipitor, is already the largest-selling pharmaceutical in history. And Pfizer, the firm that bought Warner-Lambert in a hostile takeover, is expected to soon earn more than $10 billion a year on the drug.[26]

Enhancing Creativity in Organizations

Managers who wish to enhance and promote creativity in their organizations can do so in a variety of ways.[27] One important method for enhancing creativity is to make it a part of the organization's culture, often through explicit goals. Firms that truly want to stress creativity, like 3M and Rubbermaid, for example, state goals that some percent of future revenues are to be gained from new products. This clearly communicates that creativity and innovation are valued and that they should strive to help achieve the kinds of creative breakthroughs necessary to meet relevant goals.

Another important part of enhancing creativity is to reward creative successes, while being careful to not punish creative failures. Many ideas that seem worthwhile on paper fail to pan out in reality. If the first person to come up with an idea that fails is fired or otherwise punished, others in the organization will become more cautious in their own work. And as a result, fewer creative ideas will emerge.

Synopsis

Decision making is the process of choosing one alternative from among several. Problem solving is finding the answer to a question. The basic elements of decision making include choosing a goal; considering alternative courses of action; assessing potential outcomes of the alternatives, each with its own value relative to the goal; and choosing one alternative based on an evaluation of the outcomes. Information is available regarding the alternatives, outcomes, and values.

Programmed decisions are well-structured, recurring decisions made according to set decision rules. Nonprogrammed decisions involve nonroutine, poorly structured situations with unclear sources of information; these decisions cannot be made according to existing decision rules. Decision making may also be classified according to the information available. The classifications—certainty, risk, and uncertainty—reflect the amount of information available regarding the outcomes of alternatives.

The rational approach views decision making as a completely rational process in which goals are established, a problem is identified, alternatives are generated and evaluated, a choice is made and implemented, and control is exercised. The use of procedures and rules of thumb, suboptimizing, and satisficing characterize the behavioral model. The rational and behavioral views can be combined into a practical model. The Janis-Mann conflict model recognizes the personal anxiety individuals face when they must make important decisions.

A variety of other behavioral processes also influence decision making in organizations. Political activities by coalitions, managerial intuition, and the tendency to become increasingly committed to a chosen course of action are all important. Risk propensity is also an important behavioral perspective on decision making. Finally, ethics also affect how managers make decisions.

Creativity is the capacity to generate new ideas. Numerous individual and background factors are likely to influence any given individual's level of creativity. The creative process itself generally involves four phases: preparation, incubation, insight, and verification.

Managers can enhance or reduce creativity in their organizations through various means.

Discussion Questions

1. Some have argued that people, not organizations, make decisions and that the study of "organizational" decision making is therefore pointless. Do you agree with this argument? Why or why not?

2. What information did you use in deciding to enter the school you now attend?

3. When your alarm goes off each morning, you have a decision to make: whether to get up and go to school or work, or to stay in bed and sleep longer. Is this a programmed or nonprogrammed decision? Why?

4. Describe at least three points in the decision-making process at which information plays an important role.

5. How does the role of information in the rational model of decision making differ from the role of information in the behavioral model?

6. Why does it make sense to discuss several different models of decision making?

7. Can you think of a time when you satisficed when making a decision? Have you ever suboptimized?

8. Describe a situation in which you experienced escalation of commitment to an ineffective course of action. What did you do about it? Do you wish you had handled it differently? Why or why not?

9. How comfortable or uncomfortable are you in making risky decisions?

10. Do you consider yourself to be relatively more or less creative? Recall an instance in which you made a discovery using the four phases of the creative process.

Experiencing Organizational Behavior

Decisions

Purpose: This exercise will allow you to take part in making a hypothetical decision and help you understand the difference between programmed and nonprogrammed decisions.

Format: You will be asked to perform a task both individually and as a member of a group.

Procedure: The following is a list of typical organizational decisions. Read it, and then determine whether they are programmed or nonprogrammed decisions. Number your paper, and write *P* for programmed or *N* for nonprogrammed next to each number.

Your instructor will divide the class into groups of four to seven. All groups should have approximately the same number of members. The group's task is to make the determinations just outlined using the same list. The group should discuss the difference between programmed and nonprogrammed decisions and each decision situation until all members at least partly agree with the decision. While deliberating, do not use techniques such as voting or negotiating ("Okay, I'll give in on this one if you'll give in on that one").

Decision List

1. Hiring a specialist for the research staff in a highly technical field

2. Assigning workers to daily tasks

3. Determining the size of dividend to be paid to shareholders in the ninth consecutive year of strong earnings growth

4. Deciding whether to officially excuse an employee's absence for medical reasons

5. Selecting the location for another branch of a 150-branch bank in a large city

6. Approving the appointment of a new law school graduate to the corporate legal staff

7. Making annual assignments of graduate assistants to faculty

8. Approving an employee's request to attend a local seminar in his or her special area of expertise

9. Selecting the appropriate outlets for print advertisements for a new college textbook

10. Determining the location for a new fast-food restaurant in a small but growing town on the major interstate highway between two very large metropolitan areas

Follow-up Questions

1. To what extent did group members disagree about which decisions were programmed and which were nonprogrammed?

2. What primary factors did the group discuss in making each decision?

3. Were there any differences between the members' individual lists and the group lists? If so, discuss the reasons for the differences.

Self-Assessment Exercise

Rational Versus Practical Approaches to Decision Making

Managers need to recognize and understand the different models that they use to make decisions. They also need to understand the extent to which they are predisposed to be relatively autocratic or relatively participative in making decisions. To develop your skills in these areas, perform the following activity.

First, assume you are the manager of a firm that is rapidly growing. Recent sales figures strongly suggest the need for a new plant to produce more of your firm's products. Key issues include where the plant might be built and how large it might be (for example, a small, less expensive plant to meet current needs that could be expanded in the future versus a large and more expensive plant that might have excess capacity today but could better meet long-term needs).

Using the rational approach diagrammed in Figure 8.3, trace the process the manager might use to make the decision. Note the kinds of information that might be required and the extent to which other people might need to be involved in making a decision at each point.

Next, go back and look at various steps in the process where behavioral processes might intervene and affect the overall process. Will bounded rationality come into play? How about satisficing?

Finally, use the practical approach shown in Figure 8.4 and trace through the process again. Again note where other input may be needed. Try to identify places in the process where the rational and practical approaches are likely to result in the same outcome and places where differences are most likely to occur.

Building Managerial Skills

Exercise Overview: Interpersonal skills refer to the manager's ability to understand and motivate individuals and groups. This exercise will allow you to practice your interpersonal skills in a role-playing exercise.

Exercise Background: You supervise a group of six employees who work in an indoor facility in a relatively isolated location. The company you work for has recently adopted an ambiguous policy regarding smoking. Essentially, the policy states that all company work sites are to be smoke free unless the employees at a specific site choose differently and at the discretion of the site supervisor.

Four members of the work group you supervise are smokers. They have come to you with the argument that since they constitute the majority, they should be allowed to smoke at work. The other two members of the group, both nonsmokers, have heard about this request and have also discussed the situation with you. They argue that the health-related consequences of secondary smoke should outweigh the preferences of the majority.

To compound the problem further, your boss wrote the new policy and is quite defensive about it—numerous individuals have already criticized the policy. You know that your boss will get very angry with you if you also raise concerns about the policy. Finally, you are personally indifferent to the issue. You do not smoke yourself, but your spouse does smoke. Secondary smoke does not bother you, and you do not have strong opinions about it. Still, you have to make a decision about what to do. You see that your choices are to (1) mandate a smoke-free environment, (2) allow smoking in the facility, or (3) ask your boss to clarify the policy.

Exercise Task: Based on the background previously presented, assume that you are the supervisor and do the following:

1. Assume that you have chosen option 1. Write down an outline that you will use to announce your decision to the four smokers.

2. Assume that you have chosen option 2. Write down an outline that you will use to announce your decision to the two nonsmokers.

3. Assume that you have chosen option 3. Write down an outline that you will use when you meet with your boss.

4. Are there other alternatives?

5. What would you do if you were actually the group supervisor?

Decisions and Consequences at Morgan Stanley

Top managers make risky and non-routine decisions on a daily basis. Yet in today's rapidly changing economic and legal environment, chief executives in the financial services industry face especially daunting challenges. Phil Purcell, former leader of Morgan Stanley, one of the biggest and most prominent Wall Street investment banks, faced many criticisms for decisions he made about his top management team. The trouble began when Purcell headed Dean Witter Discover, which combined a brokerage firm for small individual investors with the Discover card business. In 1997, Morgan Stanley acquired Dean Witter. At that time, Morgan Stanley was a prestigious New York investment firm, known for its highly profitable mergers and acquisitions and IPO (initial public offering) markets. Morgan Stanley wanted to diversify into other financial services and Dean Witter's focus on small investors and credit card services seemed ideal. Purcell was named CEO of the merged firm.

From the beginning, Purcell's business model for Morgan Stanley included retail banking, credit cards, and investment banking. However, the Discover division performed poorly, never claiming more than 6 percent of the credit card market, and Dean Witter lagged behind both traditional and online retail investments companies. Many outside observers believed that the company would be better off if it sold the Dean Witter and Discover businesses. Analyst Lauren Smith estimated profits from the sale at $20 billion, and Morgan Stanley could keep the investment bank.

In response, Purcell points to the success of the investment banking divisions, saying, "Number one in global underwriting. That's some failure . . . Number one in global IPOs. Is that a failure too?" While accurate, these comments ignored the problems in other divisions. The synergies investors expected to see from the merged firm never materialized, and the CEO seemed unable or unwilling to see that his vision was flawed.

To add to his troubles, Purcell forced two managers who had been vocal about the problems at Morgan Stanley to resign. When eight former senior executives complained about Purcell's removal of the managers,

> **❝** *The company is a jewel. But nobody is willing to give this guy a chance anymore.* **❞**
> RICHARD BOVE, ANALYST, PUNK ZIEGEL & CO.

Purcell accused the group of attempting a "coup." The former executives wrote a letter to the board of directors stating that "unless immediate action is taken to reverse the loss of talent, the Firm's ability to restore its reputation and its competitive edge will be put at risk. We believe that the immediate removal of Mr. Purcell will stem the tide and possibly convince those who have left to return as leaders."

Some Morgan Stanley employees were critical of Purcell, calling him aloof, stubborn, and arrogant. Some feared a repeat of earlier situations, when Purcell fought with President John Mack in 2001 and President Robert Scott in 2003, resulting in their departures from the firm. Those who were most bitter were in the investment banking divisions, where Purcell was still seen as an outsider to Wall Street.

Purcell's refusal to change his original decisions, even when presented with evidence that those decisions might be faulty, seems to point to escalation of commitment. Purcell believed that the situation could turn around, while many others believed that it was time to make new strategic decisions. The CEO placed the blame on outside forces, including the managers who resigned, the former executives, the economy, and others. "The media frenzy over recent events has been disruptive," said Purcell.

Profits had dropped 30 percent at Morgan Stanley and the bank's share price had been volatile, declining 27 percent over four years, revealing a lack of investor confidence. Continued complaints against Purcell hurt the firm too. "The company is a jewel," said analyst Richard Bove. "But nobody is willing to give this guy a chance anymore." Meanwhile, Purcell kept repeating his message: "Morgan Stanley is winning. The business model works." Ultimately, however, the business model did not work. Pressure for Purcell to step down continued to intensify, and he resigned in June of 2005. Former president and CEO John Mack was named as his replacement. For more on Morgan Stanley, see the boxed insert entitled *Morgan Stanley and . . . Ethics.*

tendency or lack of a tendency toward escalation of commitment in the current situation.

References: Monica Gagnier, "They've Had Their Phil," *Business Week*, May 23, 2005, www.businessweek.com on May 23, 2005; Michael J. Martinez, "Purcell Says Morgan Stanley Will Thrive," Associated Press, May 10, 2005, biz.yahoo.com on May 23, 2005; David Rynecki, "Morgan Stanley's Man on the Spot," *Fortune*, November 15, 2004, pp. 120–127; Emily Thornton, "Can Phil Purcell Change His Spots?" *Business Week*, April 18, 2005, www.businessweek.com on May 23, 2005; Emily Thornton, "Morgan Stanley's No-Win Situation," *Business Week*, May 11, 2005, www.businessweek.com on May 23, 2005 (quotation); Emily Thornton, "Only Making It Worse," *Business Week*, April 11, 2005, pp. 90–91.

PORTLAND STATE RESERVES FINES

Reserve late charges start at

1. 1hr, 2hr, 4hr & 24hr checkout - $1.00 for the first hour then $.25 for each additional hour to 96hrs, then **BILLED AS LOST.**

2. 2 day, 3 day & 7 day checkout - $1.00 per day to $5.00, then **BILLED AS LOST.**

3. Reserves items may not be renewed, but if there are multiple copies available, you may checkout a different copy.

4. Charges for reserves items that have been declared lost are non-refundable. These charges will include the cost of the item, processing & shipping, and any late charges (Minimum $75).

5. Patrons are responsible for all checked out material until items are checked in by library staff.

TEST PREPPER

You have read the chapter and studied the key terms. Think you're ready to ace the exam? Take this sample test to gauge your comprehension of chapter material and check your answers at the back of the book. Want more test questions? Take the ACE quizzes found on the student website: http://college.hmco.com/ business/students/ (select Griffin/Moorhead, Organizational Behavior, 8e from the Management menu).

T F 1. Decision making is finding the correct answer to a question.

T F 2. Predicting the roll of the dice occurs under a decision condition of risk.

T F 3. A contingency plan is the action managers expect their competitors to take.

T F 4. In practice, managers use some hybrid of the rational, behavioral, and practical decision-making approaches.

T F 5. Coalitions can help astute managers get the organization on a path toward effectiveness and profitability.

T F 6. A common ethical dilemma for managers is deciding whether to pursue personal or organizational interests.

T F 7. It is important to reward creative successes and punish creative failures.

8. When managers make programmed decisions, they apply
   a. a condition of risk.
   b. a decision rule.
   c. their intuition.
   d. their creativity.
   e. the choice of a coalition.

9. Kevin owns a small business and is considering opening a second store in a different location. He has consulted with several small business experts regarding his decision and now is able to predict the probabilities that the new store will reach certain profit levels. Kevin is operating under which decision condition?
   a. Programmed
   b. Certainty
   c. Risk
   d. Uncertainty
   e. Expertise

10. Decision makers ask the question "What if something happens during the implementation of this alternative?" in order to develop
    a. group consensus.
    b. ethical guidelines.
    c. post-decision dissonance.
    d. contingency plans.
    e. nonprogrammed decisions.

11. The practical decision-making approach suggests managers should
    a. use rules of thumb to make decisions.
    b. generate as many alternatives as time and money allow.
    c. satisfice whenever possible.
    d. never satisfice.
    e. train others to make their own decisions.

12. Which of the following questions is not one decision makers ask themselves in the conflict model of decision making proposed by Janis and Mann?
    a. Are the risks serious if I do not make a change?
    b. Are the risks serious if I do make a change?
    c. Is it realistic to hope to find a better solution?
    d. Has this decision been made before in the past?
    e. Is there sufficient time to search and deliberate?

13. Which of the following managers would be best suited to rely on his or her intuition?
    a. An experienced manager with practice in making similar decisions
    b. An inexperienced manager with a degree in advanced decision sciences
    c. A manager who is part of a strong coalition
    d. A manager who is extremely creative
    e. A manager who is extremely ethical

14. Tammy chose to expand her retail clothing line by offering specialty uniforms for healthcare workers. Despite a large initial investment in design and advertising, the uniforms did not sell well the first year. In the second year, Tammy increased the advertising budget and offered the uniforms in two different fabrics, but they continued to sell poorly. Now at the beginning of the third year, Tammy is considering expanding the advertising budget once again. Tammy is experiencing
    a. an ethical dilemma.
    b. a programmed decision.
    c. prolonged creative incubation.
    d. a condition of risk.
    e. escalation of commitment.

The Success of Individuals at Starbucks

Starbucks sells food and drinks, but the most important component of a customer's purchase is the service. Customers demand high-quality service that is personal, friendly, fast, and accurate. They want a relaxing and social store atmosphere. Customer satisfaction is crucial to generating profitable repeat buyers, as the most loyal customers visit Starbucks eighteen times a month or more. "When . . . the person behind the counter says hello and maybe greets you by name, you feel a connection you don't find with most retailers anymore. It makes you feel welcome and it makes you want to come back," says Dave Pace, executive vice president. To offer that level of service and atmosphere, Starbucks depends on its 97,000 worldwide employees.

Success starts with choosing workers, called "baristas" (from the Italian word for barkeeper), for front-line positions. A good person-job fit is created by selecting individuals with the right skills and personality. Baristas must be knowledgeable about the various items that Starbucks sells. They are constantly on their feet, must lift heavy items frequently, use dangerously hot machinery, and communicate and cooperate with their coworkers. Most importantly, they must provide a satisfying, personal interaction to hundreds of customers each day. "Our baristas are the foundation of our business," claims the company. "Baristas deliver legendary customer service to all customers by acting with a 'customer comes first' attitude and connecting with the customer. They discover and respond to customer needs." To meet high customer expectations, Starbucks "looks for people who are adaptable, self-motivated, passionate, creative team players."

It's not hard to find individuals with the minimal skills needed for entry-level jobs. However, it's more difficult to identify who can contribute the most and who is most likely to stay. Applicants undergo interviews with two managers, to assess complex abilities such as social and communication skills. Each applicant completes a behavioral assessment designed to measure cooperativeness, extroversion, honesty, and conscientiousness.

"It's not hard to recruit at this company," claims vice president Sheri Southern. "People want to work here. We're very fortunate that way." The company has a reputation for being a great employer. A 2004 survey found that 82 percent of employees were satisfied or very satisfied. In January 2005, Starbucks was named #2 on *Fortune* magazine's list of best large employers. One tangible measure of the good person-job fit at Starbucks is the low annual turnover rate among baristas—80 percent—compared to 200 percent for the quick-serve food industry. Starbucks CEO Jim Donald is intensely interested in generating enough applicants to keep up with growth while maintaining the quality of personnel. The company must hire 200 new workers each day, for vacancies at existing stores and for new locations. "My biggest fear isn't the competition, although I respect it," Donald says. "It's having a robust pipeline of people to open and manage the stores who will also be able to take their next steps with the company."

Although Starbucks's baristas are generally satisfied, their jobs can be stressful. There are the physical demands of constant standing and walking. At the same time, baristas must properly prepare orders and work in a constrained physical space with others. Interpersonal stress can also be high. It is difficult to establish a personal and positive relationship with a stranger in just a few seconds, and baristas must do this over and over again for hours. As in any job with heavy customer contact, there is the potential for unpleasant interactions and encounters with difficult customers. For example, some of Starbucks's customers are irritated by the language the company uses. Although customers may order Starbucks's products by using the words "small, medium, large," the baristas are required by the company to respond with the official terms of "tall, grande, venti." "Customers will mock the drink sizes and get snippy with the barista over how they think it's stupid to not just use small, medium, and large. And that's when I find myself tempted to be rude. To simply say, 'Oh, thank you, mister! I'm so glad you're taking on the corporate dominance of Starbucks by irritating an hourly employee!'" says one barista.

Another factor in creating success through the efforts of individuals is to properly design the work. The job of barista combines physical production, personal interaction, and planning and time management. Therefore, workers use a variety of skills and switch tasks frequently, reducing boredom and fatigue. The barista participates in the entire process, from the time the customer enters the store through payment. Baristas receive constant feedback from customers about their performance. Based on Hackman and Oldham's job characteristics theory, these qualities of the barista job should result in higher satisfaction and motivation. On the other hand, baristas do not have a lot of autonomy. The products must be prepared consistently, reducing creative opportunities. Also, although providing good customer service is a priority, baristas may feel that their job does not have a significant impact on others. These factors would tend to reduce satisfaction and motivation.

Another important aspect of job design at Starbucks is work scheduling. About two-thirds of Starbucks's 75,000 U.S. workers have part-time work schedules. Of those, about one-half work twenty hours or more each week. Operating hours for each Starbucks location is determined by local demand; however, many stores open as early as 6:00 A.M. and remain open until 11:00 P.M. The busiest hours at most stores are between 8:00 A.M. and 10:00 A.M. Clearly then, work scheduling is a complex task. Stores use a flexible scheduling approach. Many baristas appreciate the part-time and flexible nature of their work hours, so they may attend school or meet other needs. Some workers, however, would prefer a more predictable schedule. In addition, the total number of hours worked per week has a significant impact on income and benefits eligibility, so some workers are displeased when their hours vary.

From 2000 to 2005, then CEO Orin Smith concentrated on improving operational effectiveness. Automated espresso machines were introduced to speed up coffee production, which now takes about one minute per cup, down from three minutes. The taste of the machine-made drinks is as good as those made by hand, an important point for quality-conscious Starbucks. Another factor in the decision to adopt espresso machines was worker safety. Overall, Starbucks is a very safe employer. Workers sustain injuries at about half the rate of other companies in the industry. However, burns are the most frequent injuries sustained by baristas and are a concern. Automated machines reduce baristas' burn rate by 50 percent. Workers must learn new skills in order to operate the new machinery.

Finally, success based on individual employees comes from motivating workers to perform at high levels, coupled with meaningful and appropriate rewards. CEO Donald role-models motivation skills. Every morning, he calls five store managers for a personal chat. Then he calls three hourly workers. Donald says, "We've got to be able to reach into this organization and say, 'How's it going?' and 'Good job!' If any company doesn't have the time to talk to people on the front lines, then you might as well close it up, because it's not going anywhere."

Motivation at Starbucks is accomplished through the use of rewards to meet the needs of employees. An important motivator is base pay, which at Starbucks is about average for the fast-food industry. The average annual pay for full-time hourly employees, including baristas and shift supervisors, is $35,294. However, Starbucks also offers above-average benefits to most workers. Bonuses are a rare benefit in the fast-food industry. In 2004, Starbucks paid each hourly worker a $250 annual cash bonus.

Starbucks also offers a level of healthcare benefits that is unusual, especially for part-time workers. All employees who work half-time or more can receive healthcare benefits, including medical, drug, vision, dental, and even alternative medicine. In its list of the Best Companies to Work For published in January of 2005, *Fortune* magazine said about Starbucks: "The coffee behemoth is justly famous for its generous benefits. One example: Part-timers and their same-sex or opposite-sex partners receive comprehensive health coverage. Hypnotherapy? Covered. Naturopathy? Ditto." The company pays between 50 percent and 80 percent of the cost of the care for workers and family members.

A stock purchase plan allows employees to buy shares of Starbucks at a 15 percent discount. Another program, called "Bean Stock," grants stock options to almost every employee, allowing them to purchase stock at even deeper discounts. The stock options are awarded based on an individual's pay, length of employment, and even more importantly, Starbucks's overall corporate performance. Stock ownership is seen as a way to increase wealth for hourly workers, while also helping to align their interests with those of the company. "Share success with the people who make it happen," says vice president

Emily Ericsen. "It makes everybody think like an owner, which helps them build long-term relationships with customers and influences them to do things in an efficient way."

Starbucks also offers a variety of miscellaneous benefits, including reimbursement for college tuition and adoption expenses. All employees get free beverages and one pound of free coffee beans. Time-off benefits include paid vacation for full-time employees, and personal days and time-and-a-half pay for holiday work. Extensive training improves employees' skills and prepares them for positions of greater responsibility. Finally, the benefits package is flexible. Under the Starbucks's program, called "Your Special Blend," employees can shift benefits dollars between the various components of the total pay package, customizing their compensation. Each worker can use their benefit dollars in the way that provides the best value.

With its emphasis on appropriate recruiting, job design, and motivation, Starbucks is fulfilling its mission statement, which states, "[We will] provide a great work environment and treat each other with respect and dignity." Many employees realize that Starbucks, while not perfect, is clearly one of the best employers. When a barista posted negative comments on the Internet, one employee replied with: "Starbucks work isn't much different from that of any other foodservice job. Yet employees show more loyalty and support for Starbucks than they do for any other similar employer." Another also defended the firm, writing, "Starbucks does more for its employees than any other food service or retail business. Perhaps not as good as a company where everyone has

> **❝*If any company doesn't have the time to talk to people on the front lines, then you might as well close it up, because it's not going anywhere.*❞**
> *JIM DONALD, CEO, STARBUCKS*

their Masters degrees, but it's a lot better than the McDonald's and Wal-Mart's of the world."

Sources: "Application for Employment," "Barista," "Career Paths," "Corporate Social Responsibility Report 2004," "Retail Careers," "Starbucks Mission Statement," Starbucks website, www.starbucks.com on June 30, 2005; "Man Orders a 'Medium' Starbucks Coffee," Starbucks Gossip website, starbucksgossip.typepad.com on June 30, 2005; "100 Best Companies to Work For 2005," *Fortune*, January 2005, www.fortune.com on June 30, 2005; "Ideas and Inspirations," November 25, 2003, The Employee Involvement Association website, www.eianet.org on June 30, 2005; "Industry Solutions: Taleo for Foodservice," Taleo website, www.taleo.com on June 30, 2005; Gretchen Weber, "Preserving the Starbucks' Counter Culture," *Workforce Management*, February 2005, pp. 28–34 (quotation).

Integrative Case Questions

1. Describe the psychological contract for baristas working at Starbucks. What are the inducements? What are the contributions? In your opinion, is this a reasonable and fair exchange? If so, explain why. If not, tell how it could be improved.

2. How do alternative work arrangements contribute to the motivation of baristas at Starbucks? Are there any potential limitations or drawbacks of the alternative work arrangements?

3. Consider all of the significant stakeholders of Starbucks: investors, employees, customers, and local communities. Do the generous rewards offered to baristas help or hinder each of these groups in reaching their goals? Explain.

CHAPTER 9

Foundations of Interpersonal and Group Behavior

Chapter Outline

Every Group Counts at Tenet Healthcare

The quality of a patient's hospital stay depends on good interactions between doctors, nurses, pharmacists, technicians, and patients. High-performing groups are essential to good patient outcomes. Yet Tenet, owner and operator of dozens of hospitals, was accused of dealing dishonestly and unfairly with stakeholders and the company faced lawsuits from low-income patients, investigations of Medicare billings, and nurses' strikes.

Tenet is now making changes to address these concerns. Tenet is going further than most healthcare organizations in its efforts to improve group interactions about patient care. Tenet implemented Target 100, a program seeking 100 percent staff and patient satisfaction. "The Target 100 program engages our employees—from hospital CEOs to floor nurses to admissions clerks—in a process aimed at improving customer service," reads the Tenet website. Under the Target 100 program, each Tenet hospital asks groups in various functional areas to address concerns such as patient satisfaction or employee recognition. The groups identify areas for improvement, suggest changes, and then implement the best solutions.

❝ The Target 100 program engages our employees—from hospital CEOs to floor nurses to admissions clerks. ❞

TENET HEALTHCARE WEBSITE

The Target 100 process brings together hospital staff, including administrators, nurses, and technicians, with physicians, who are not usually employed by the hospital. By bringing an outsider perspective, doctors are valuable group members who have different types of information and skills and can be more innovative. Tenet prides itself on the high participation of doctors on its hospitals' governing boards. Physicians make up over one-half of the board at most Tenet hospitals, compared to a national average of 17 percent.

Under other initiatives, Tenet is encouraging even more outside participation. Several of the company's hospitals are affiliated with medical schools. Medical school faculty and students practice at these teaching hospitals, introducing the latest and most creative techniques and ideas. Also, the firm hired outside expert consultants to study ways to improve quality. Tenet's new general counsel, formerly counsel for the U.S. Department of Health and Human Services, is improving Medicare billing and Tenet's relationship with regulators. A new Physician Advisory Board brings together Tenet's top doctors from around the country to resolve company-wide issues, establish best practices, and educate personnel. Each of these affiliations has strengthened the company by making it more innovative and responsive.

Tenet's Chief Information Officer, Stephen F. Brown, embodies the company's new approach to group dynamics. During one tense meeting, Brown asked for a "cooling-off" break. "As a leader . . . when discussions go awry, you have to stop and remind everyone that this isn't a personality contest," Brown says. "You remind them that we have to allow all ideas to exist." Alan Cranford, who works with Brown, notes, "[He is] encouraging and supportive of his staff but also gives them autonomy."

Hospitals throughout the Tenet system have made dramatic improvements in patient care, billing practices, and other areas. With the help of individuals with various skills, information, and backgrounds, Tenet will begin a new era of success, in profits and in patient outcomes. The boxed insert *Tenet Healthcare and . . . Ethics* on page 232 tells more about physician involvement in hospital management.

References: "Frequently Asked Questions: Physician Issues," Great Boards website, www.greatboards.org on March 21, 2005; "Target 100," Tenet Healthcare website, www.tenethealth.com on March 20, 2005 (quotation); "Tenet Healthcare Corporation," Hoover's, www.hoovers.com on February 20, 2005; Trevor Fetter, "Remarks at Tenet's 2004 Annual Shareholders' Meeting," May 6, 2004, www.tenethealth.com on March 20, 2005; Leslie Jaye Goff, "Tenet Healthcare Corp. Stephen F. Brown: Coach," *ComputerWorld*, January 1, 2002, www.computerworld.com on March 20, 2005.

In Chapter 1 we noted the pervasiveness of human behavior in organizations and the importance of interactions among people as critical to achieving important outcomes for organizations. Indeed, a great deal of all managerial work involves interacting with other people, both directly and indirectly and both inside and outside the organization. This chapter is the first of seven that deal primarily with interpersonal processes in organizations. We begin by reinforcing the interpersonal nature of organizations. We then introduce and describe numerous elements of group dynamics, one of the important aspects of interpersonal relations. In subsequent chapters we discuss such other forms of interpersonal activity in organizations as work teams (Chapter 10), interpersonal communication (Chapter 11), leadership (Chapters 12 and 13), power, politics, and workplace justice (Chapter 14), and conflict and negotiation in organizations (Chapter 15).

The Interpersonal Nature of Organizations

The schedule that follows is a typical day for the president of a Houston-based company, part of a larger firm headquartered in California. He kept a log of his activities for several different days so you could better appreciate the nature of managerial work.

- 7:45–8:15 A.M. Arrive at work; review hard copy mail sorted by assistant; review and respond to email; discuss day's schedule with assistant.
- 8:15–8:30 A.M. Scan *The Wall Street Journal* and online financial news sources.
- 8:30–9:00 A.M. Meet with labor officials and plant manager to resolve minor labor disputes.
- 9:00–9:30 A.M. Review internal report; read and respond to new email.
- 9:30–10:00 A.M. Meet with two marketing executives to review advertising campaign; instruct them to fax approvals to advertising agency.
- 10:00–11:30 A.M. Meet with company executive committee to discuss strategy, budgetary issues, and competition (this committee meets weekly).
- 11:30 A.M.–12:00 P.M. Send several emails; read and respond to new email.
- 12:00–1:15 P.M. Lunch with the financial vice president and two executives from another subsidiary of the parent corporation. Primary topic of discussion is the Houston Rockets basketball team. Place three business calls from cellular phone en-route to lunch, and receive one business call en-route back to office.
- 1:15–1:45 P.M. Meet with human resource director and assistant about a recent OSHA inspection; establish a task force to investigate the problems identified and to suggest solutions.
- 1:45–2:00 P.M. Read and respond to new email.
- 2:00–2:30 P.M. Conference call with four other company presidents.
- 2:30–3:00 P.M. Meet with financial vice president about a confidential issue that came up at lunch (unscheduled).
- 3:00–3:30 P.M. Work alone in office; read and respond to new email; send several emails.
- 3:30–4:15 P.M. Meet with a group of sales representatives and the company purchasing agent.
- 4:15–5:30 P.M. Make telephone call to company CEO in California to discuss various organizational issues; work alone in office.
- 5:30–7:00 P.M. Play racquetball at nearby athletic club with marketing vice president.
- 9:00–9:30 P.M. Read and respond to email from home; send email to assistant about an emergency meeting to be scheduled for the next day.

How did this manager spend his time? He spent most of it interacting with other people. This set of other people included people who report to him, his own boss, and various other groups. And this compressed daily schedule does not include several other short telephone calls, quick conversations with his assistant, and brief meetings with other managers. Moreover, myriad other meetings, conversations, and other interpersonal exchanges were taking place throughout the organization simultaneously during that same day. Clearly, interpersonal relations and group processes are a pervasive part of all organizations and a vital part of all managerial activities.[1]

Interpersonal Dynamics

The nature of interpersonal relations in an organization is as varied as the individual members themselves. At one extreme, interpersonal relations can be personal and positive. This occurs when the two parties know each other, have mutual respect and affection, and enjoy interacting with one another. Two managers who have known each other for years, play golf together on weekends, and are close personal friends will likely interact at work in a positive fashion. At the other extreme, interpersonal dynamics can be personal but negative. This is most likely when the parties dislike one another, do not have mutual respect, and do not enjoy interacting with one another. Suppose a manager has fought openly for years to block the promotion of another manager within the organization. Over the objections of the first manager, however, the other manager eventually gets promoted to the same rank. When the two of them must interact, it will most likely be in a negative manner.

Most interactions fall between these extremes, as members of the organization interact in a professional way focused primarily on goal accomplishment. The interaction deals with the job at hand, is relatively formal and structured, and is task-directed. Two managers may respect each other's work and recognize the professional competence that each brings to the job. However, they may also have few common interests and little to talk about besides the job they are doing. These different types of interaction may occur between individuals, between groups, or between individuals and groups, and they can change over time. The two managers in the second scenario, for example, might decide to bury the hatchet and adopt a detached, professional manner. The two managers in the third example could find more common ground than they anticipated and evolve to a personal and positive interaction.

Outcomes of Interpersonal Behaviors

A variety of things can happen as a result of interpersonal behaviors. Recall from Chapter 4, for example, that numerous perspectives on motivation suggest that people have social needs. Interpersonal relations in organizations can be a primary source of need satisfaction for many people. For people with a strong need for affiliation, high-quality interpersonal relations can be an important positive element in the workplace. However, when this same person is confronted with poor-quality working relationships, the effect can be just as great in the other direction.

Interpersonal relations also serve as a solid basis for social support. Suppose that an employee receives a poor performance evaluation or is denied a promotion. Others in the organization can lend support because they share a common frame of reference—an understanding of the causes and consequences of what happened. Good interpersonal relations throughout an organization can also be a source of synergy. People who support one another and who work well together can accomplish much more than people who do not support one another and who do not work well together. Another outcome, implied earlier, is conflict—people may leave an interpersonal exchange feeling angry or hostile. Understanding how and why people interact with one another is a complex process—whether the interaction occurs in a sports team, a work group, or a school committee. This is especially true when those individuals are members of the same group. The *Tenet Healthcare and . . . Ethics* box provides another perspective on these issues in the healthcare sector, as previewed in our opening case for this chapter.

Tenet Healthcare and . . .  ETHICS

When Doctors Lead the Group

As noted in the opening case, patient-care quality depends on positive group interactions. Participation by physicians, who are not hospital employees, is important because they work with hospital staff and board members. However, there are a growing number of hospitals owned by physicians, making doctors into administrators and hospital leaders.

Physician ownership can be beneficial. Many hospital owners, including Tenet Healthcare, are divesting facilities, especially in small communities or low-income areas. Yet some doctors are willing to invest their own money to keep hospitals open. Dr. John J. Regan says, "Physicians are feeling that . . . they've lost control over patient care." Physician ownership can eliminate layers of bureaucracy and insurance middlemen, making the hospital more cost-effective as well as more focused on quality.

Some regulators and patient advocates are concerned about physician ownership of medical facilities. Medicare law prohibits doctors from referring patients to a pharmacy, rehabilitation center, or other business in which the physician has an ownership interest. But the law does not prohibit referrals to physician-owned hospitals, so an unscrupulous doctor could reap financial benefits by recommending unnecessary hospital stays, for example.

Others are concerned that doctor-owners may discriminate by sending sicker or underinsured patients to public hospitals. "They will turn these hospitals into specialty clinics where they can be assured very lucrative treatments," says Jerry Flanagan, a patient advocate. Many experts don't believe that doctors can run a hospital more profitably than a large, professional corporation can.

Dr. Jack Lewin, CEO of the California Medical Association, believes that more cooperation is risky but should be tried. He says, "The economic forces don't align very well when hospitals, physicians, health plans, pharmacies, and laboratories are all competing." Experimentation may be the only way to determine whether physician ownership will lead to better interactions, more cooperation, and ultimately, better patient outcomes.

> *"The economic forces don't align very well when hospitals, physicians, health plans, pharmacies, and laboratories are all competing."*
>
> DR. JACK LEWIN, CEO,
> CALIFORNIA MEDICAL ASSOCIATION

References: "Doctor-Owned Businesses Create Conflict, Threaten Health Care System," Texas Hospital Association, news.findlaw.com on March 20, 2005; "Frequently Asked Questions: Physician Issues," Great Boards website, www.greatboards.org on March 21, 2005; Jerry Cobb, "Sick of Red Tape, Physicians are Buying Hospitals," MSNBC.com, March 5, 2005, msnbc.msn.com on March 20, 2005; Lisa Girion, "Doctors' Hospital Bids Raise Ethical Worries," *Los Angeles Times*, April 5, 2004, www.calhealthconsensus.org on March 20, 2005 (quotation).

Figure 9.1 presents a three-phase model of group dynamics. In the first phase, the reasons for forming the group determine what type of group it will be. A four-step process of group development occurs during the second stage; the precise nature of these steps depends on four primary group performance factors. In the final phase, a mature, productive, adaptive group has evolved. As the model shows, mature groups interact with other groups, meet goals, and sometimes have conflicts with other groups. This model serves as the framework for our discussion of groups in this chapter.

A **group** is two or more people who interact with one another such that each person influences and is influenced by each other person.

The Nature of Groups

Definitions of "group" are as abundant as studies of groups. Groups can be defined in terms of perceptions, motivation, organization, interdependencies, and interactions. We will define a **group** as two or more persons who interact with one another such

FIGURE 9.1

A General Model of Group Dynamics

This model serves as the framework for this chapter. In phase one, the reasons for group formation determine what type of group it will be. In the second phase, groups evolve through four stages under the influence of four performance factors. Finally, a mature group emerges that interacts with other groups and can pursue organizational goals; conflicts with other groups sometimes occur.

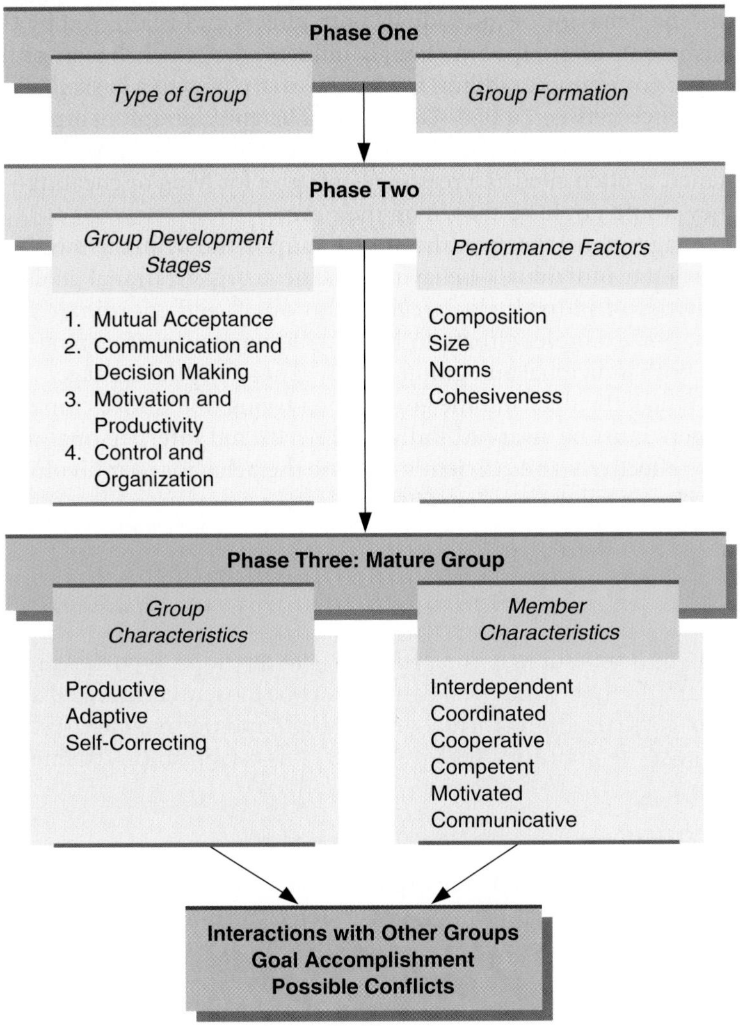

Phase One

| Type of Group | Group Formation |

Phase Two

Group Development Stages

1. Mutual Acceptance
2. Communication and Decision Making
3. Motivation and Productivity
4. Control and Organization

Performance Factors

Composition
Size
Norms
Cohesiveness

Phase Three: Mature Group

Group Characteristics

Productive
Adaptive
Self-Correcting

Member Characteristics

Interdependent
Coordinated
Cooperative
Competent
Motivated
Communicative

**Interactions with Other Groups
Goal Accomplishment
Possible Conflicts**

that each person influences and is influenced by each other person.[2] Two people who are physically near each other are not a group unless they interact and have some influence on each other. Coworkers may work side by side on related tasks, but if they do not interact, they are not a group.

Although groups often have goals, our definition does not state that group members must share a goal or motivation. This omission implies that members of a group may identify little or not at all with the group's goal. People can be a part of a group and enjoy the benefits of group membership without wanting to pursue any group goal. Members may satisfy needs just by being members, without pursuing anything. Of course, the quality of the interactions and the group's performance may be affected by members' lack of interest in the group goal. Our definition also suggests a limit on group size. A collection of people so large that its members cannot interact with and influence one another does not meet this definition. And in reality, the dynamics of large assemblies of people usually differ significantly from those of small groups. Our focus in this chapter is on small groups in which the members interact with and influence one another. Understanding the behavior of people in organizations requires that we understand the forces that affect individuals as well as how individuals affect the organization. The behavior of individuals both affects and is affected by the group. The accomplishments of groups are strongly influenced by the behavior of their individual members. For example, adding one key all-star player to a basketball team may make the difference between a bad season and a league championship. At the same time, groups have profound effects on the behaviors of their members. Group pressure, for instance, is often cited as a reason people give for lying or cheating—activities they claim they would not have chosen on their own.

From a managerial perspective, the work group is the primary means by which managers coordinate individuals' behavior to achieve organizational goals. Managers direct the activities of individuals, but they also direct and coordinate interactions within groups. For example, efforts to boost salespersons' performance have been shown to have both individual and group effects.[3] Therefore, the manager must pay attention to both the individual and the group when trying to improve employee performance. Managers must be aware of individual needs and interpersonal dynamics to manage groups effectively and efficiently because the behavior of individuals is key to the group's success or failure.[4]

Types of Groups

Our first task in understanding group processes is to develop a typology of groups that provides insight into their dynamics. Groups may be loosely categorized according to their degrees of formalization (formal or informal) and permanence (relatively permanent or relatively temporary). Table 9.1 shows this classification scheme.

Formal Groups

A **formal group** is formed by an organization to do its work.

A **command group** is a relatively permanent, formal group with functional reporting relationships and is usually included in the organization chart.

A **task group** is a relatively temporary, formal group established to do a specific task.

Affinity groups are collections of employees from the same level in the organization who meet on a regular basis to share information, capture emerging opportunities, and solve problems.

Formal groups are established by the organization to do its work. Formal groups include command (or functional) groups, task groups, and affinity groups. A **command group** is relatively permanent and is characterized by functional reporting relationships such as having a group manager and those who report to the manager. Command groups are usually included in the organization chart. A **task group** is created to perform a specific task, such as solving a particular quality problem, and is relatively temporary. **Affinity groups** are relatively permanent collections of employees from the same level in the organization who meet on a regular basis to share information, capture emerging opportunities, and solve problems.[5]

In business organizations, most employees work in command groups, as typically specified on an official organization chart. The size, shape, and organization of a company's command groups can vary considerably. Typical command groups in organizations include the quality-assurance department, the industrial engineering department, the cost-accounting department, and the personnel department. Other types of

	Relatively Permanent	Relatively Temporary	
Formal	**Command Groups**	**Task Groups**	**Affinity Groups**
	Quality-assurance department Cost-accounting group	Search Committee for a new school superintendent Task force on new-product quality	New product development group
Informal	**Friendship Groups**	**Interest Groups**	
	Friends who do many activities together (attend the theater, play games, travel)	Bowling group Women's network	

TABLE 9.1

Classification Scheme for Types of Groups

command groups include work teams organized as in the Japanese style of management, in which subsections of manufacturing and assembly processes are each assigned to a team of workers. The team members decide among themselves who will perform each task.

Teams are becoming widespread in automobile manufacturing. For instance, General Motors has organized most of its highly automated assembly lines into work teams of between five and twenty workers. Although participative teams are becoming more popular, command groups, whether entire departments or sophisticated work teams, are the dominant type of work group in organizations. Federal Express organized its clerical workers into teams that manage themselves.

Task, or special-project, groups are usually temporary and are often established to solve a particular problem. The group usually dissolves once it solves the problem or makes recommendations. People typically remain members of their command groups, or functional departments, while simultaneously serving in a task group and continuing to carry out the normal duties of their jobs. The members' command group duties may be temporarily reduced if the task group requires a great deal of time and effort. Task groups exist in all types of organizations around the world. For example, Pope John Paul II used a special task force of cardinals to study the financial condition of the Vatican and develop new ways to raise money.[6]

Affinity groups are a special type of formal group: They are set up by the organization, yet they are not really part of the formal organization structure. They are not really command groups because they are not part of the organizational hierarchy, yet they are not task groups because they stay in existence longer than any one task. Affinity groups are groups of employees who share roles, responsibilities, duties, and interests; they represent horizontal slices of the normal organizational hierarchy. Because the members share important characteristics such as roles, duties, and levels, they are said to have an affinity for one another. The members of affinity groups usually have very similar job titles and similar duties but are in different divisions or departments within the organization.

Affinity groups meet regularly, and members have assigned roles such as recorder, reporter, facilitator, and meeting organizer. Members follow simple rules such as communicating openly and honestly, listening actively, respecting confidentiality, honoring

Friendship and interest groups can be a powerful force in an organization. These women comprise the medical staff on the third floor of Capital Region Medical Center in Jefferson City, Missouri. When they discovered that a coworker had cancer, the women became an even closer-knit group and worked even harder to both support their friend and to help other cancer patients.

time agreements, being prepared, staying focused, being individually accountable, and being supportive of each other and the group. The greatest benefits of affinity groups are that they cross existing boundaries of the organization and facilitate better communication among diverse departments and divisions across the organization.

Informal Groups

Whereas formal groups are established by an organization, **informal groups** are formed by their members and consist of friendship groups, which are relatively permanent, and interest groups, which may be shorter lived. **Friendship groups** arise out of the cordial relationships among members and the enjoyment they get from being together. **Interest groups** are organized around a common activity or interest, although friendships may develop among members.

Good examples of interest groups are the networks that working women have developed. Many of these groups began as informal social gatherings of women who wanted to meet with other women working in male-dominated organizations, but they soon developed into interest groups whose benefits went far beyond their initial social purposes. The networks became information systems for counseling, job placement, and management training. Some networks were eventually established as formal, permanent associations; some remained informal groups based more on social relationships than on any specific interest; others were dissolved. These groups may be partly responsible for the dramatic increase in the percentage of women in managerial and administrative jobs.

An **informal group** is established by its members.

A **friendship group** is relatively permanent and informal and draws its benefits from the social relationships among its members.

An **interest group** is relatively temporary and informal and is organized around a common activity or interest of its members.

Stages of Group Development

Groups are not static—they typically develop through a four-stage process: (1) mutual acceptance, (2) communication and decision making, (3) motivation and productivity, and (4) control and organization.[7] The stages and the activities that typify them are shown in Figure 9.2. We treat the stages as separate and distinct. It is difficult to pinpoint exactly when a group moves from one stage to another, however, because the activities in the phases tend to overlap.

The **mutual acceptance stage** of group development is characterized by members sharing information about themselves and getting to know each other.

Mutual Acceptance

In the **mutual acceptance** stage of group development, the group forms, and members get to know one another by sharing information about themselves. They often test one another's opinions by discussing subjects that have little to do with the group, such as the weather, sports, or recent events within the organization. Some aspects of the

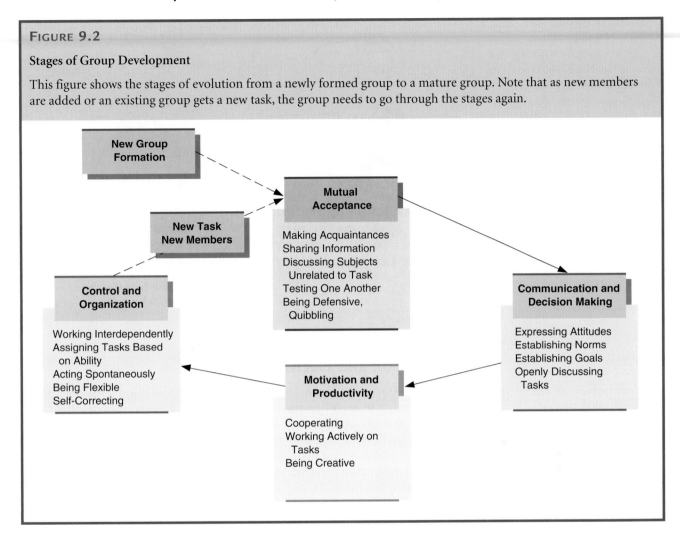

FIGURE 9.2

Stages of Group Development

This figure shows the stages of evolution from a newly formed group to a mature group. Note that as new members are added or an existing group gets a new task, the group needs to go through the stages again.

New Group Formation

New Task New Members

Mutual Acceptance

Making Acquaintances
Sharing Information
Discussing Subjects
 Unrelated to Task
Testing One Another
Being Defensive,
 Quibbling

Communication and Decision Making

Expressing Attitudes
Establishing Norms
Establishing Goals
Openly Discussing
 Tasks

Control and Organization

Working Interdependently
Assigning Tasks Based
 on Ability
Acting Spontaneously
Being Flexible
Self-Correcting

Motivation and Productivity

Cooperating
Working Actively on
 Tasks
Being Creative

group's task, such as its formal objectives, may also be discussed at this stage. However, such discussion probably will not be very productive because the members are unfamiliar with one another and do not know how to evaluate one another's comments. If the members do happen to know one another already, this stage may be brief, but it is unlikely to be skipped altogether because this is a new group with a new purpose. Besides, there are likely to be a few members whom the others do not know well or at all.

As the members get to know one another, discussion may turn to more sensitive issues, such as the organization's politics or recent controversial decisions. At this stage, members may have little arguments and feud a bit as they explore one another's views on various issues and learn about each other's reactions, knowledge, and expertise. From the discussion, members come to understand how similar their beliefs and values are and the extent to which they can trust one another. Members may discuss their expectations about the group's activities in terms of their previous group and organizational experience.[8] Eventually, the conversation turns to the business of the group. When this discussion becomes serious, the group is moving to the next stage of development, communication and decision making.

Communication and decision making are key stages of group development, but it looks like this team may have skipped an early stage like mutual acceptance. Groups need to openly discuss and agree on their goals, motivations, and individual roles before they can successfully accomplish tasks. It is essential that groups go through all four stages of development in order to become a mature, productive group.

"My team is having trouble thinking outside the box. We can't agree on the size of the box, what materials the box should be constructed from, a reasonable budget for the box, or our first choice of box vendors."

© 2001 Randy Glasbergen.
www.glasbergen.com

Communication and Decision Making

In the **communication and decision-making stage** of group development, members discuss their feelings more openly and agree on group goals and individual roles in the group.

The group progresses to the **communication and decision-making** stage once group members have begun to accept one another. In this stage, members discuss their feelings and opinions more openly; they may show more tolerance for opposing viewpoints and explore different ideas to bring about a reasonable solution or decision. The membership usually begins to develop norms of behavior during this stage. Members discuss and eventually agree on the group's goals. Then they are assigned roles and tasks to accomplish the goals.

Motivation and Productivity

In the **motivation and productivity stage** of group development, members cooperate, help each other, and work toward accomplishing tasks.

In the next stage, **motivation and productivity**, the emphasis shifts away from personal concerns and viewpoints to activities that will benefit the group. Members perform their assigned tasks, cooperate with each other, and help others accomplish their goals. The members are highly motivated and may carry out their tasks creatively. In this stage, the group is accomplishing its work and moving toward the final stage of development.

Control and Organization

In the **control and organization stage** of group development, the group is mature; members work together and are flexible, adaptive, and self-correcting.

In the final stage, **control and organization**, the group works effectively toward accomplishing its goals. Tasks are assigned by mutual agreement and according to ability. In a mature group, the members' activities are relatively spontaneous and flexible rather than subject to rigid structural restraints. Mature groups evaluate their activities and potential outcomes and take corrective actions if necessary. The characteristics of flexibility, spontaneity, and self-correction are very important if the group is to remain productive over an extended period.

Not all groups, however, go through all four stages. Some groups disband before reaching the final stage. Others fail to complete a stage before moving on to the next one. Rather than spend the time necessary to get to know one another and build trust, for example, a group may cut short the first stage of development because of pressure from its leader, from deadlines, or from an outside threat (such as the boss).[9] If members are forced into activities typical of a later stage while the work of an earlier stage remains incomplete, they are likely to become frustrated: The group may not develop completely and may be less productive than it could be.[10] Group productivity depends on successful development at each stage. A group that evolves fully through the four stages of development usually becomes a mature, effective group.[11] Its members are interdependent, coordinated, cooperative, competent at their jobs, motivated to do them, self-correcting, and in active communication with one another.[12] The process does not take a long time if the group makes a good, solid effort and pays attention to the processes.

Finally, as working conditions and relationships change, either through a change in membership or when a task is completed and a new task is begun, groups may need to re-experience one or more of the stages of development to maintain the cohesiveness and productivity characteristic of a well-developed group. The San Francisco Forty-Niners, for example, once returned from an NFL strike to an uncomfortable and apprehension-filled period. Their coach conducted rigorous practices but also allowed time for players to get together to air their feelings. Slowly, team unity returned, and players began joking and socializing again as they prepared for the rest of the season.[13] Their redevelopment as a mature group resulted in two subsequent Super Bowl victories.

Although these stages are not separate and distinct in all groups, many groups make fairly predictable transitions in activities at about the midpoint of the period available to complete a task.[14] A group may begin with its own distinctive approach to the problem and maintain it until about halfway through the allotted time. The midpoint transition is often accompanied by a burst of concentrated activity, reexamination of assumptions, dropping old patterns of activity, adopting new perspectives on the work, and making dramatic progress. Following these midpoint activities, the new patterns of

While groups naturally progress through a series of identifiable stages, events sometimes speed up the evolution of a group. In the wake of devastating hurricanes that swept across Florida in 2004, this emergency response planning team moved very quickly from the mutual acceptance and communication and decision-making stages (stages one and two) to the motivation and productivity and control and organization stages (stages three and four).

The Denver Broncos and . . . **TECHNOLOGY**

Online Recruiting for Sports Marketers

"Front office" staff, including marketing and other business functions, is just as essential to the success of professional sports teams as are athletes. Front office staff manages profitability, which determines the team's ability to recruit and support players. Recruiting excellent front office staff is challenging, due to geographic and time constraints.

The Denver Broncos and many other sports teams use technology to find qualified sports marketers. SportsPersonnel.com and TeamworkOnline.com are two of the many firms that aid teams and sports marketers in recruiting. Both of these companies offer online job posting. The jobs available at these companies' websites include positions such as Senior Account Manager of Season Ticket Sales for the Miami Dolphins, among many others. The companies allow job seekers to post résumés. Other services include online job applications, screening of applications, career counseling, message boards, career mentoring, and professional networking.

The online technology helps teams create marketing groups that are diverse in gender, race, location, and training. The technology provides access to a very large pool of job seekers at a very low cost to the organization. "Selecting candidates for job openings is still largely based on responses from a small circle of current employees who recommend someone they know," says Kent Briggs, former defensive coordinator for football at North Carolina State University and president of SportsPersonnel.com. "It's

hard to consider potential employees if there isn't enough information about who is available."

Clearly, there are many intangible factors important to a recruiting decision that cannot be captured in an online system. So websites will not replace face-to-face interviews. Yet online systems can bring together job seekers and employers quickly, conveniently, and cheaply, while increasing applicant diversity and quality. That is a winning concept. The winning ingredients for the Denver Broncos professional football team are further illustrated in this chapter's closing case.

> **"It's hard to consider potential employees if there isn't enough information about who is available."**
>
> KENT BRIGGS, PRESIDENT OF SPORTSPERSONNEL.COM

References: "AFC Teams: The Denver Broncos," NFL Join the Team website, www.jointheteam.com on March 28, 2005; "Denver Broncos," Invesco Field website, www.invescofieldatmilehigh.com on March 23, 2005; "Inside the Arena," "Jobs/Career Services," National Sports Marketing Network website, www.sportsmarketingnetwork.com on March 23, 2005; "Our Coach Speaks," SportsPersonnel.com website, www.sportspersonnel .com on April 12, 2005 (quotation); "Introduction," "How It Works," "How We Save You Money," "Testimonials," TeamWork Online website, www.teamworkonline.com on April 12, 2005.

activity may be maintained until close to the end of the period allotted for the activity. Another transition may occur just before the deadline. At this transition, groups often go into the completion stage, launching a final burst of activity to finish the job. Finally, we should also note that our current understanding about group development is based on the study of traditional face-to-face groups. As firms create more and more virtual and/or online work groups, researchers may have to develop new frameworks to explain how such groups develop. *The Denver Broncos and . . . Technology* discusses an example of one area where such groups are being developed.

Group Performance Factors

The performance of any group is affected by several factors other than its reasons for forming and the stages of its development. In a high-performing group, a group synergy often develops in which the group's performance is more than the sum of the individual contributions of its members. Several additional factors may account for this accelerated performance.[15] The four basic **group performance factors** are composition, size, norms, and cohesiveness.

Group Composition

The composition of a group plays an important role in determining group productivity.[16] **Group composition** is most often described in terms of the homogeneity or heterogeneity of the members. A group is *homogeneous* if the members are similar in one or several ways that are critical to the work of the group, such as in age, work experience, education, technical specialty, or cultural background. In *heterogeneous* groups, the members differ in one or more ways that are critical to the work of the group. Homogeneous groups often are created in organizations when people are assigned to command groups based on a similar technical specialty. Although the people who work in such command groups may differ in some ways, such as in age or work experience, they are homogeneous in terms of a critical work performance variable: technical specialty.

Much research has explored the relationship between a group's composition and its productivity. The group's heterogeneity in terms of age and tenure with the group has been shown to be related to turnover: Groups with members of different ages and experiences with the group tend to experience frequent changes in membership.[17] A homogeneous group is likely to be more productive when the group task is simple, cooperation is necessary, the group tasks are sequential, or quick action is required. A heterogeneous group is more likely to be productive when the task is complex, requires a collective effort (that is, each member does a different task, and the sum of these efforts constitutes the group output), and demands creativity, and when speed is less important than thorough deliberations. For example, a group asked to generate ideas for marketing a new product probably needs to be heterogeneous to develop as many different ideas as possible.

The link between group composition and type of task is explained by the interactions typical of homogeneous and heterogeneous groups. A homogeneous group tends to have less conflict, fewer differences of opinion, smoother communication, and more interactions. When a task requires cooperation and speed, a homogeneous group is therefore more desirable. If, however, the task requires complex analysis of information and creativity to arrive at the best possible solution, a heterogeneous group may be more appropriate because it generates a wide range of viewpoints. More discussion and more conflict are likely, both of which can enhance the group's decision making.

Group composition becomes especially important as organizations become increasingly more diverse.[18] Cultures differ in the importance they place on group membership and in how they view authority, uncertainty, and other important factors. Increasing attention is being focused on how to deal with groups made up of people from different cultures.[19] In general, a manager in charge of a culturally diverse group can expect several things. First, members will probably distrust each other. Stereotyping also will present a problem, and communication problems will almost certainly arise. Thus, the manager needs to recognize that such groups will seldom function smoothly, at least at first. Managers may need to spend more time helping a culturally diverse group through the rough spots as it matures, and they should allow a longer-than-normal time before expecting it to carry out its assigned task.

Many organizations are creating joint ventures and other types of alliances with organizations from other countries. Joint ventures have become common in the automobile and electronics industries, for example. However, managers from the United States

Group performance factors—composition, size, norms, and cohesiveness—affect the success of the group in fulfilling its goals.

Group composition is the degree of similarity or difference among group members on factors important to the group's work.

Group composition is an important factor in understanding group dynamics. These women recently attended a Women in Business seminar for women holding key executive positions in major corporations. The fact that they are all female gave them a shared frame of reference and common perspectives from which to identify key issues and to help shape the future of their respective businesses.

tend to exhibit individualistic behaviors in a group setting, whereas managers from more collectivistic countries, such as the People's Republic of China, tend to exhibit more group-oriented behaviors. Thus, when these two different types of managers work together in a joint venture, the managers must be trained to be cautious and understanding in their interactions and in the types of behaviors they exhibit.

Group Size

Group size is the number of members of the group; group size affects the number of resources available to perform the task.

A group can have as few as two members or as many members as can interact and influence one another. **Group size** can have an important effect on performance. A group with many members has more resources available and may be able to complete a large number of relatively independent tasks. In groups established to generate ideas, those with more members tend to produce more ideas, although the rate of increase in the number of ideas diminishes rapidly as the group grows.[20] Beyond a certain point, the greater complexity of interactions and communication may make it more difficult for a large group to achieve agreement.

Interactions and communication are much more likely to be formalized in larger groups. Large groups tend to set agendas for meetings and to follow a protocol or parliamentary procedure to control discussion. As a result, some time that otherwise might be available to work on tasks is taken up in administrative duties such as organizing and structuring the interactions and communications within the group. Also, the large size may inhibit participation of some people and increase absenteeism; some people may stop trying to make a meaningful contribution and may even stop coming to group meetings if their repeated attempts to contribute or participate are thwarted by the sheer number of similar efforts by other members. Furthermore, large groups present more opportunities for interpersonal attraction, leading to more social interactions and fewer task interactions. **Social loafing** is the tendency of some members of groups not to put forth as much effort in a group situation as they would working alone. Social loafing often results from the assumption by some members that if they do not work hard, other members will pick up the slack. How much of a problem this becomes

Social loafing is the tendency of some members of groups to put forth less effort in a group than they would when working alone.

depends on the nature of the task, the characteristics of the people involved, and the ability of the group leadership to be aware of the potential problem and do something about it.

The most effective size of a group, therefore, is determined by the group members' ability to interact and influence each other effectively. The need for interaction is affected by the maturity of the group, the tasks of the group, the maturity of individual members, and the ability of the group leader or manager to deal with the communication, potential conflicts, and task activities. In some situations, the most effective group size is three or four; other groups can function effectively with fifteen or more members.

Group Norms

A **norm** is a standard against which the appropriateness of a behavior is judged. Thus, norms determine the behavior expected in a certain situation. Group norms usually are established during the second stage of group development (communication and decision making) and carried forward into the maturity stage. By providing a basis for predicting others' behaviors, norms enable people to behave in a manner consistent with and acceptable to the group. Without norms, the activities in a group would be chaotic.

Norms result from the combination of members' personality characteristics, the situation, the task, and the historical traditions of the group.[21] Lack of conformity to group norms may result in verbal abuse, physical threats, ostracism, or ejection from the group. Group norms are enforced, however, only for actions that are important to group members. For example, if the office norm is for employees to wear suits to convey a professional image to clients, a staff member who wears blue jeans and a sweatshirt violates the group norm and will hear about it quickly. But if the norm is that dress is unimportant because little contact with clients occurs in the office, the fact that someone wears blue jeans may not even be noticed.

Norms serve four purposes in organizations. First, they help the group survive. Groups tend to reject deviant behavior that does not help meet group goals or contribute to the survival of the group if it is threatened. Accordingly, a successful group that is not under threat may be more tolerant of deviant behavior. Second, they simplify and make more predictable the behaviors expected of group members. Because they are familiar with norms, members do not have to analyze each behavior and decide on a response. Members can anticipate the actions of others on the basis of group norms, usually resulting in increased productivity and goal attainment. Third, norms help the group avoid embarrassing situations. Group members often want to avoid damaging other members' self-images and are likely to avoid certain subjects that might hurt a member's feelings. And finally, norms express the central values of the group and identify the group to others. Certain clothes, mannerisms, or behaviors in particular situations may be a rallying point for members and may signify to others the nature of the group.[22]

> A **norm** is a standard against which the appropriateness of a behavior is judged.

Group Cohesiveness

Group cohesiveness is the extent to which a group is committed to remaining together; it results from forces acting on the members to remain in the group. The forces that create cohesiveness are attraction to the group, resistance to leaving the group, and the motivation to remain a member of the group.[23] As shown in Figure 9.3, group cohesiveness is related to many aspects of group dynamics that we have already discussed—maturity, homogeneity, manageable size, and frequency of interactions.

> **Group cohesiveness** is the extent to which a group is committed to staying together.

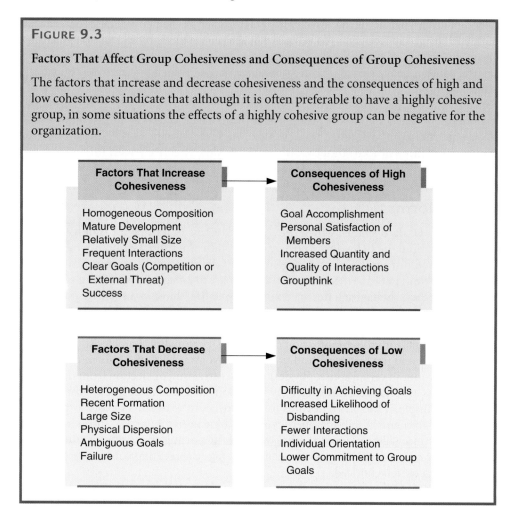

FIGURE 9.3

Factors That Affect Group Cohesiveness and Consequences of Group Cohesiveness

The factors that increase and decrease cohesiveness and the consequences of high and low cohesiveness indicate that although it is often preferable to have a highly cohesive group, in some situations the effects of a highly cohesive group can be negative for the organization.

Factors That Increase Cohesiveness

Homogeneous Composition
Mature Development
Relatively Small Size
Frequent Interactions
Clear Goals (Competition or
   External Threat)
Success

Consequences of High Cohesiveness

Goal Accomplishment
Personal Satisfaction of
   Members
Increased Quantity and
   Quality of Interactions
Groupthink

Factors That Decrease Cohesiveness

Heterogeneous Composition
Recent Formation
Large Size
Physical Dispersion
Ambiguous Goals
Failure

Consequences of Low Cohesiveness

Difficulty in Achieving Goals
Increased Likelihood of
   Disbanding
Fewer Interactions
Individual Orientation
Lower Commitment to Group
   Goals

The figure also shows that group cohesiveness can be increased by competition or by the presence of an external threat. Either factor can focus members' attention on a clearly defined goal and increase their willingness to work together. Finally, successfully reaching goals often increases the cohesiveness of a group because people are proud to be identified with a winner and to be thought of as competent and successful. This may be one reason behind the popular expression "Success breeds success." A group that is successful may become more cohesive and hence possibly even more successful. Of course, other factors can get in the way of continued success, such as personal differences, egos, and the lure of more individual success in other activities.

Research on group performance factors has focused on the relationship between cohesiveness and group productivity.[24] Highly cohesive groups appear to be more effective at achieving their goals than groups that are low in cohesiveness, especially in research and development groups in U.S. companies.[25] However, highly cohesive groups will not necessarily be more productive in an organizational sense than groups with low cohesiveness. As Figure 9.4 illustrates, when a group's goals are compatible with the organizational goals, a cohesive group probably will be more productive than one that is not cohesive. In other words, if a highly cohesive group has the goal of contributing to the good of the organization, it is very likely to be productive in organizational terms. But if such a group decides on a goal that has little to do with

FIGURE 9.4

Group Cohesiveness, Goals, and Productivity

This figure shows that the best combination is for the group to be cohesive and for the group's goals to be congruent with the organization's goals. The lowest potential group performance also occurs with highly cohesive groups when the group's goals are not consistent with the organization's goals.

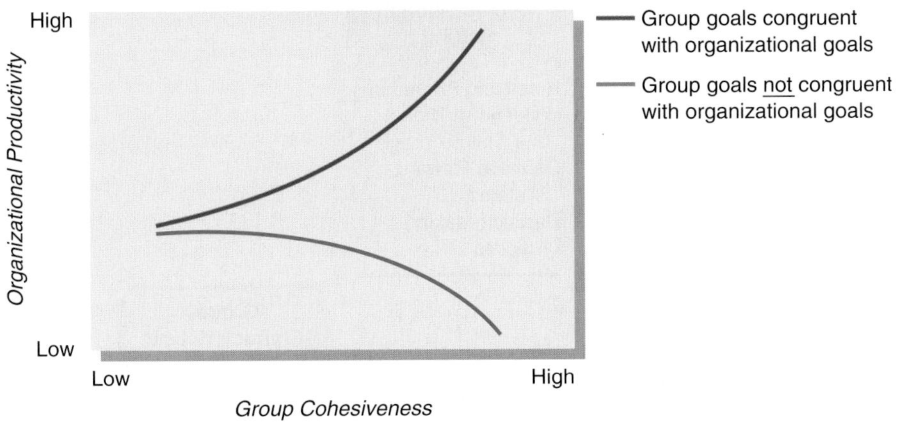

the business of the organization, it will probably achieve its own goal even at the expense of any organizational goal. In a study of group characteristics and productivity, group cohesiveness was the only factor that was consistently related to high performance for research and development engineers and technicians.

Cohesiveness may also be a primary factor in the development of certain problems for some decision-making groups. An example is **groupthink**, which occurs when a group's overriding concern is a unanimous decision rather than critical analysis of alternatives.[26] (We discuss groupthink later in this chapter.) These problems, together with the evidence regarding group cohesiveness and productivity, mean that a manager must carefully weigh the pros and cons of fostering highly cohesive groups.

Intergroup Dynamics

A group's contribution to an organization depends on its interactions with other groups as well as on its own productivity. Many organizations are expanding their use of cross-functional teams to address more complex and important organizational issues. The result has been heightened emphasis on the teams' interactions with other groups. Groups that actively interact with other groups by asking questions, initiating joint programs, and sharing their team's achievements are usually the most productive.

Interaction is the key to understanding intergroup dynamics. The orientation of the groups toward their goals takes place under a highly complex set of conditions that determine the relationships among the groups. The most important of these factors are presented in the model of intergroup dynamics in Figure 9.5. The model emphasizes three primary factors that influence intergroup interactions: group characteristics, organizational setting, and task and situational bases of interaction.

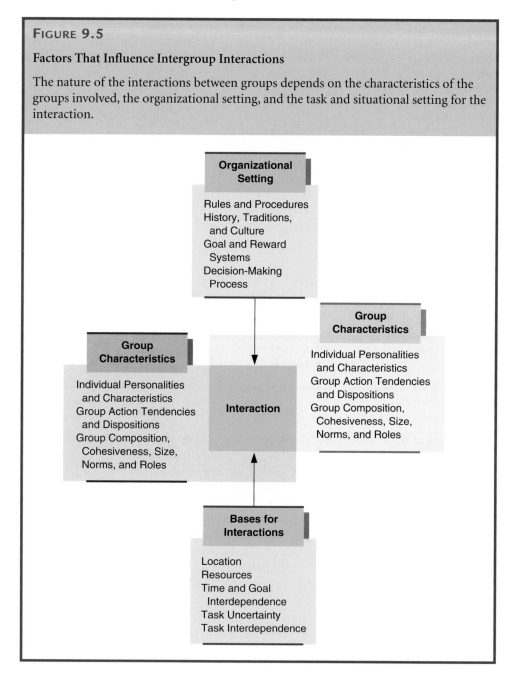

FIGURE 9.5

Factors That Influence Intergroup Interactions

The nature of the interactions between groups depends on the characteristics of the groups involved, the organizational setting, and the task and situational setting for the interaction.

First, we must understand the key characteristics of the interacting groups. Each group brings to the interaction its own unique features. As individuals become a part of a group, they tend to identify so strongly with the group that their views of other groups become biased, so harmonious relationships with other groups may be difficult to achieve.[27] Furthermore, the individuals in the group contribute to the group processes, and these contributions in turn influence the group's norms, size, composition, and cohesiveness; all of these factors affect the interactions with other groups. Thus, understanding the individuals in the group and the key characteristics of the group can help managers monitor intergroup interactions.

Second, the organizational setting in which the groups interact can have a powerful influence on intergroup interactions. The organization's structure, rules and procedures, decision-making processes, and goals and reward systems all affect interactions. For example, organizations in which frequent interactions occur and strong ties among groups exist usually are characterized as low-conflict organizations.[28] Third, the task and situational bases of interactions focus attention on the working relationships among the interacting groups and on the reasons for the interactions. As Figure 9.5 shows, five factors affect intergroup interactions: location, resources, time and goal interdependence, task uncertainty, and task interdependence. These factors both create the interactions and determine their characteristics, such as the frequency of interaction, the volume of information exchange among groups, and the type of coordination the groups need to interact and function. For example, if two groups depend heavily on each other to perform a task about which much uncertainty exists, they need a great deal of information from each other to define and perform the task.

Group Decision Making in Organizations

People in organizations work in a variety of groups—formal and informal, permanent and temporary. Most of these groups make decisions that affect the welfare of the organization and the people in it. Here we discuss several issues surrounding how groups make decisions: group polarization, groupthink, and group problem solving.

Group Polarization

Members' attitudes and opinions with respect to an issue or a solution may change during group discussion. Some studies of this tendency have showed the change to be a fairly consistent movement toward a more risky solution, called "risky shift."[29] Other studies and analyses have revealed that the group-induced shift is not always toward more risk; the group is just as likely to move toward a more conservative view.[30] Generally, **group polarization** occurs when the average of the group members' post-discussion attitudes tends to be more extreme than average pre-discussion attitudes.[31]

> **Group polarization** is the tendency for a group's average post-discussion attitudes to be more extreme than its average pre-discussion attitudes.

Several features of group discussion contribute to polarization. When individuals discover during group discussion that others share their opinions, they may become more confident about their opinions, resulting in a more extreme view. Persuasive arguments also can encourage polarization. If members who strongly support a particular position are able to express themselves cogently in the discussion, less avid supporters of the position may become convinced that it is correct. In addition, members may believe that because the group is deciding, they are not individually responsible for the decision or its outcomes. This diffusion of responsibility may enable them to accept and support a decision more radical than those they would make as individuals.

Polarization can profoundly affect group decision making. If group members are known to lean toward a particular decision before a discussion, it may be expected that their post-decision position will be even more extreme. Understanding this phenomenon may be useful for one who seeks to affect their decision.

Groupthink

As discussed earlier, highly cohesive groups and teams often are very successful at meeting their goals, although they sometimes have serious difficulties as well. One problem that can occur is groupthink. According to Irving L. Janis, **groupthink** is "a mode of thinking that people engage in when they are deeply involved in a cohesive

> **Groupthink** is a mode of thinking that occurs when members of a group are deeply involved in a cohesive in-group, and the desire for unanimity offsets their motivation to appraise alternative courses of action.

in-group, when the members' strivings for unanimity override their motivation to realistically appraise alternative courses of action."[32] When groupthink occurs, then, the group unknowingly makes unanimity rather than the best decision its goal. Individual members may perceive that raising objections is not appropriate. Groupthink can occur in many decision-making situations in organizations. The current trend toward increasing use of teams in organizations may increase instances of groupthink because of the susceptibility of self-managing teams to this type of thought.[33]

Symptoms of Groupthink   The three primary conditions that foster the development of groupthink are cohesiveness, the leader's promotion of his or her preferred solution, and insulation of the group from experts' opinions. Based on analysis of the disaster associated with the explosion of the space shuttle *Challenger* in 1986, the effects of increased time pressure and the role of the leader in not stimulating critical thinking were added to the original idea of groupthink symptoms.[34] Figure 9.6 outlines the revised groupthink process.

A group in which groupthink has taken hold exhibits eight well-defined symptoms:

1. An *illusion of invulnerability,* shared by most or all members, that creates excessive optimism and encourages extreme risk taking
2. *Collective efforts to rationalize or discount warnings* that might lead members to reconsider assumptions before recommitting themselves to past policy decisions
3. An *unquestioned belief in the group's inherent morality* that makes members inclined to ignore the ethical and moral consequences of their decisions

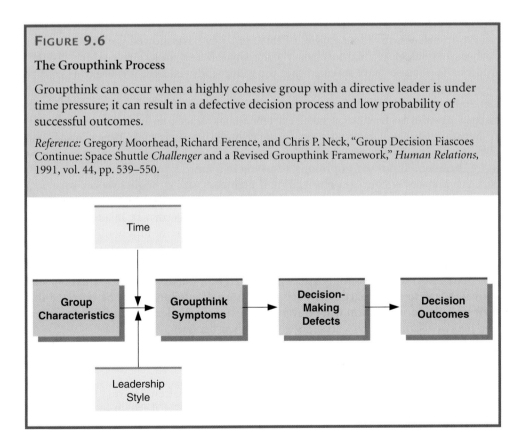

FIGURE 9.6

The Groupthink Process

Groupthink can occur when a highly cohesive group with a directive leader is under time pressure; it can result in a defective decision process and low probability of successful outcomes.

Reference: Gregory Moorhead, Richard Ference, and Chris P. Neck, "Group Decision Fiascoes Continue: Space Shuttle *Challenger* and a Revised Groupthink Framework," *Human Relations,* 1991, vol. 44, pp. 539–550.

4. *Stereotyped views of "enemy" leaders* as too evil to warrant genuine attempts to negotiate or as too weak or stupid to counter whatever risky attempts are made to defeat their purposes

5. *Direct pressure on a member* who expresses strong arguments against any of the group's stereotypes, illusions, or commitments, making clear that such dissent is contrary to what is expected of loyal members

6. *Self-censorship of deviations* from the apparent group consensus, reflecting each member's inclination to minimize the importance of his or her doubts and counter-arguments

7. A *shared illusion of unanimity,* resulting partly from self-censorship of deviations, augmented by the false assumption that silence means consent[35]

8. *The emergence of self-appointed "mindguards,"* members who protect the group from adverse information that might shatter their shared complacency about the effectiveness and morality of their decisions[36]

Janis contends that the members of the group involved in the Watergate cover-up during President Richard Nixon's administration and re-election campaign—Nixon himself, H. R. Haldeman, John Ehrlichman, and John Dean—may have been victims of groupthink. Evidence of most of the groupthink symptoms can be found in the unedited transcripts of the group's deliberations.[37]

Decision-Making Defects and Decision Quality When groupthink dominates group deliberations, the likelihood that decision-making defects will occur increases. The group is less likely to survey a full range of alternatives and may focus on only a few (often one or two). In discussing a preferred alternative, the group may fail to examine it for risks and drawbacks that are not obvious. The group may not reexamine previously rejected alternatives, even when they receive new information. The group may reject expert opinions that run counter to its own views and may choose to consider only information that supports its preferred solution. The decision to launch the space shuttle *Challenger* in January 1986 may have been a product of groupthink; because of increased time pressure to make a decision and leadership style, negative information was ignored by the group that made the decision. (Unfortunately, this same pattern may well have occurred prior to the ill-fated launch of the shuttle *Columbia* in 2003.) Finally, the group may not consider any potential setbacks or countermoves by competing groups and therefore may fail to develop contingency plans. It should be noted that Janis contends that these decision-making defects may arise from other common problems as well: fatigue, prejudice, inaccurate information, information overload, and ignorance.[38]

Defects in decision making do not always lead to bad outcomes or defeats. Even if its own decision-making processes are flawed, one side can win a battle because of the poor decisions made by the other side's leaders. Nevertheless, decisions produced by defective processes are less likely to succeed. Although the arguments for the existence of groupthink are convincing, the hypothesis has not been subjected to rigorous empirical examination. Research supports parts of the model but leaves some questions unanswered.[39]

Prevention of Groupthink Several suggestions have been offered to help managers reduce the probability of groupthink in group decision making. Summarized in Table 9.2, these prescriptions fall into four categories, depending on whether they apply to the leader, the organization, the individual, or the process. All are designed to facilitate the critical evaluation of alternatives and discourage the single-minded pursuit of unanimity.

TABLE 9.2

Prescriptions for Preventing Groupthink

A. Leader prescriptions
  1. Assign everyone the role of critical evaluator.
  2. Be impartial; do not state preferences.
  3. Assign the devil's advocate role to at least one group member.
  4. Use outside experts to challenge the group.
  5. Be open to dissenting points of view.

B. Organizational prescriptions
  1. Set up several independent groups to study the same issue.
  2. Train managers and group leaders in groupthink prevention techniques.

C. Individual prescriptions
  1. Be a critical thinker.
  2. Discuss group deliberations with a trusted outsider; report back to the group.

D. Process prescriptions
  1. Periodically break the group into subgroups to discuss the issues.
  2. Take time to study external factors.
  3. Hold second-chance meetings to rethink issues before making a commitment.

Participation

A major issue in group decision making is the degree to which employees should participate in the process. Early management theories, such as those of the scientific management school, advocated a clear separation between the duties of managers and workers: Management was to make the decisions, and employees were to implement them.[40] Other approaches have urged that employees be allowed to participate in decisions to increase their ego involvement, motivation, and satisfaction.[41] Numerous research studies have shown that whereas employees who seek responsibility and challenge on the job may find participation in the decision-making process both motivating and enriching, other employees may regard such participation as a waste of time and a management imposition.[42]

Whether employee participation in decision making is appropriate depends on the situation. In tasks that require an estimation, a prediction, or a judgment of accuracy—usually referred to as judgmental tasks—groups typically are superior to individuals simply because more people contribute to the decision-making process. However, one especially capable individual may make a better judgment than a group.

In problem-solving tasks, groups generally produce more and better solutions than do individuals. But groups take far longer than individuals to develop solutions and make decisions. An individual or very small group may be able to accomplish some things much faster than a large, unwieldy group or organization. In addition, individual decision making avoids the special problems of group decision making such as groupthink or group polarization. If the problem to be solved is fairly straightforward, it may be more appropriate to have a single capable individual concentrate on solving it. On the other hand, complex problems are more appropriate for groups. Such problems can often be divided into parts and the parts assigned to individuals or small groups who bring their results back to the group for discussion and decision making.

An additional advantage of group decision making is that it often creates greater interest in the task. Heightened interest may increase the time and effort given to the task, resulting in more ideas, a more thorough search for solutions, better evaluation of alternatives, and improved decision quality.

The Vroom decision tree approach to leadership (discussed in Chapter 12) is one popular way of determining the appropriate degree of subordinate participation.[43] The model includes decision styles that vary from "decide" (the leader alone makes the decision) to "delegate" (the group makes the decision, with each member having an equal say). The choice of style rests on seven considerations that concern the characteristics of the situation and the subordinates.

Participation in decision making is also related to organizational structure. For example, decentralization involves delegating some decision-making authority throughout the organizational hierarchy. The more decentralized the organization, the more its employees tend to participate in decision making. Whether one views participation in decision making as pertaining to leadership, organization structure, or motivation, it remains an important aspect of organizations that continues to occupy managers and organizational scholars.[44]

Group Problem Solving

A typical interacting group may have difficulty with any of several steps in the decision-making process. One common problem arises in the generation-of-alternatives phase: The search may be arbitrarily ended before all plausible alternatives have been identified. Several types of group interactions can have this effect. If members immediately express their reactions to the alternatives as they are first proposed, potential contributors may begin to censor their ideas to avoid embarrassing criticism from the group. Less confident group members, intimidated by members who have more experience, higher status, or more power, also may censor their ideas for fear of embarrassment or punishment. In addition, the group leader may limit idea generation by enforcing requirements concerning time, appropriateness, cost, feasibility, and the like. To improve the generation of alternatives, managers may employ any of three techniques to stimulate the group's problem-solving capabilities: brainstorming, the nominal group technique, or the Delphi technique.

Brainstorming   **Brainstorming** is most often used in the idea-generation phase of decision making and is intended to solve problems that are new to the organization and have major consequences. In brainstorming, the group convenes specifically to generate alternatives. The members present ideas and clarify them with brief explanations. Each idea is recorded in full view of all members, usually on a flip chart. To avoid selfcensoring, no attempts to evaluate the ideas are allowed. Group members are encouraged to offer any ideas that occur to them, even those that seem too risky or impossible to implement. (The absence of such ideas, in fact, is evidence that group members are engaging in self-censorship.) In a subsequent session, after the ideas have been recorded and distributed to members for review, the alternatives are evaluated.

The intent of brainstorming is to produce totally new ideas and solutions by stimulating the creativity of group members and encouraging them to build on the contributions of others. Brainstorming does not provide the resolution to the problem, an evaluation scheme, or the decision itself. Instead, it should produce a list of alternatives that is more innovative and comprehensive than one developed by the typical interacting group.

The Nominal Group Technique   The **nominal group technique** is another means of improving group decision making. Whereas brainstorming is used primarily to generate alternatives, this technique may be used in other phases of decision making, such as identification of the problem and of appropriate criteria for evaluating

Brainstorming is a technique used in the idea-generation phase of decision making that assists in development of numerous alternative courses of action.

With **nominal group technique** group members follow a generate-discussion-vote cycle until they reach a decision.

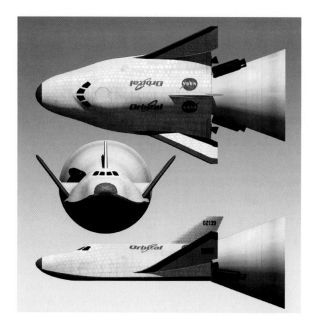

Brainstorming is a common technique for promoting the identification of new alternatives in group decision-making situations. Engineers at Northrop Grumman are helping the next generation of space vehicles to replace the aging shuttle fleet. The firm often uses groups to brainstorm new ideas. One such group, for instance, came up with this possible option—a "Space Taxi" that would take off like an airplane but still be capable of supersonic speeds.

alternatives. To use this technique, a group of individuals convenes to address an issue. The issue is described to the group, and each individual writes a list of ideas; no discussion among the members is permitted. Following the five-to-ten-minute idea-generation period, individual members take turns reporting their ideas, one at a time, to the group. The ideas are recorded on a flip chart, and members are encouraged to add to the list by building on the ideas of others. After all ideas have been presented, the members may discuss them and continue to build on them or proceed to the next phase. This part of the process can also be carried out without a face-to-face meeting or by mail, telephone, or computer. A meeting, however, helps members develop a group feeling and puts interpersonal pressure on the members to do their best in developing their lists.

After the discussion, members privately vote on or rank the ideas or report their preferences in some other agreed-upon way. Reporting is private to reduce any feelings of intimidation. After voting, the group may discuss the results and continue to generate and discuss ideas. The generation-discussion-vote cycle can continue until an appropriate decision is reached.

The nominal group technique has two principal advantages. It helps overcome the negative effects of power and status differences among group members, and it can be used to explore problems to generate alternatives, or to evaluate them. Its primary disadvantage lies in its structured nature, which may limit creativity.

The **Delphi technique** is a method of systematically gathering judgments of experts for use in developing forecasts.

The Delphi Technique   The **Delphi technique** was originally developed by RAND Corporation as a method to systematically gather the judgments of experts for use in developing forecasts. It is designed for groups that do not meet face-to-face. For instance, the product development manager of a major toy manufacturer might use the Delphi technique to probe the views of industry experts to forecast developments in the dynamic toy market.

The manager who wants the input of a group is the central figure in the process. After recruiting participants, the manager develops a questionnaire for them to complete. The questionnaire is relatively simple in that it contains straightforward questions that deal with the issue, trends in the area, new technological developments, and other factors the manager is interested in. The manager summarizes the responses and reports back to the experts with another questionnaire. This cycle may be repeated as many times as necessary to generate the information the manager needs.

The Delphi technique is useful when experts are physically dispersed, anonymity is desired, or the participants are known to have trouble communicating with one another because of extreme differences of opinion. This method also avoids the intimidation problems that may exist in decision-making groups. On the other hand, the technique eliminates the often fruitful results of direct interaction among group members.

Synopsis

Interpersonal dynamics are a pervasive element of all organizations. Interpersonal relations can vary from positive to negative and from personal to professional. Numerous outcomes can result from various forms of interpersonal relations, including different levels of need satisfaction, social support, synergy, performance, and conflict.

A group is two or more people who interact so as to influence one another. It is important to study groups because they can profoundly affect individual behavior and because the behavior of individuals in a group is key to the group's success or failure. The work group is the primary means by which managers coordinate individual behavior to achieve organizational goals. Individuals form or join groups because they expect to satisfy personal needs.

Groups may be differentiated on the bases of relative permanence and degree of formality. The three types of formal groups are command, task, and affinity groups. Friendship and interest groups are the two types of informal groups. Command groups are relatively permanent work groups established by the organization and usually are specified on an organization chart. Task groups, although also established by the organization, are relatively temporary and exist only until the specific task is accomplished. Affinity groups are formed by the organization, are composed of employees at the same level and doing similar jobs, and come together regularly to share information and discuss organizational issues. In friendship groups, the affiliation among members arises from close social relationships and the enjoyment that comes from being together. The common bond in interest groups is the activity in which the members engage.

Groups develop in four stages: mutual acceptance, communication and decision making, motivation and productivity, and control and organization. Although the stages are sequential, they may overlap. A group that does not fully develop within each stage will not fully mature as a group, resulting in lower group performance.

Four additional factors affect group performance: composition, size, norms, and cohesiveness. The homogeneity of the people in the group affects the interactions that occur and the productivity of the group. The effect of increasing the size of the group depends on the nature of the group's tasks and the people in the group. Norms help people function and relate to one another in predictable and efficient ways. Norms serve four purposes: They facilitate group survival, simplify and make more predictable the behaviors of group members, help the group avoid embarrassing situations, and express the central values of the group and identify the group to others.

To comprehend intergroup dynamics, we must understand the key characteristics of groups: that each group is unique, that the specific organizational setting influences the group, and that the group's task and setting have an effect on group behavior. The five bases of intergroup interactions determine the characteristics of the interactions among groups, including their frequency, how much information is exchanged, and what type of interaction occurs.

Interactions among work groups involve some of the most complex relationships in organizations. They are based on five factors: location, resources, time and goal interdependence, task uncertainty, and task interdependence. Being physically near one another naturally increases groups' opportunities for interactions. If groups use the same or similar resources, or if one group can affect the availability of the resources needed by another group, the potential for frequent interactions increases. The nature of the tasks groups perform, including time and goal orientation, the uncertainties of group tasks, and group interdependencies, influences how groups interact.

Group decision making involves problems as well as benefits. One possible problem is group polarization, the shift of members' attitudes and opinions to a more extreme position following group discussion. Another difficulty is groupthink, a mode of thinking in which the urge toward unanimity overrides the critical appraisal of alternatives. Yet another concern involves employee participation in decision making. The appropriate degree of participation depends on the characteristics of the situation.

Discussion Questions

1. Why is it useful for a manager to understand group behavior? Why is it useful for an employee?

2. Our definition of a group is somewhat broad. Would you classify each of the following collections of people as a group? Explain why or why not.
   a. Seventy thousand people at a football game
   b. Students taking this course
   c. People in an elevator
   d. People on an escalator
   e. Employees of IBM
   f. Employees of your local college bookstore

3. List four groups to which you belong. Identify each as formal or informal.

4. Explain why each group you listed in question 3 formed. Why did you join each group? Why might others have decided to join each group?

5. In which stage of development is each of the four groups listed in question 3? Did any group move too quickly through any of the stages? Explain.

6. Analyze the composition of two of the groups to which you belong. How are they similar in composition? How do they differ?

7. Are any of the groups to which you belong too large or too small to get their work done? If so, what can the leader or the members do to alleviate the problem?

8. List two norms each for two of the groups to which you belong. How are these norms enforced?

9. Discuss the following statement: "Group cohesiveness is the good, warm feeling we get from working in groups and is something that all group leaders should strive to develop in the groups they lead."

10. Consider one of the groups to which you belong and describe the interactions that group has with another group.

11. Recall a situation in which you may have encountered or observed groupthink (either as member of a group, as a target of a decision made by a group, or as a simple observer).

Experiencing Organizational Behavior

Learning the Benefits of a Group

Purpose: This exercise demonstrates the benefits a group can bring to a task.

Format: You will be asked to do the same task both individually and as part of a group.

Procedure: You will need a pen or pencil and a 8.5" by 11" sheet of paper. Working alone, do the following:

Part 1

1. Write the letters of the alphabet in a vertical column down the left side of the paper: A–Z.

2. Your instructor will randomly select a sentence from any written document and read out loud the first twenty-six letters in that sentence. Write these letters in a vertical column immediately to the right of the alphabet column. Everyone should have an identical set of twenty-six two-letter combinations.

3. Working alone, think of a famous person whose initials correspond to each pair of letters, and write the name next to the letters—for example, "MT Mark Twain." You will have ten minutes. Only one name

per set is allowed. One point is awarded for each legitimate name, so the maximum score is twenty-six points.

4. After time expires, exchange your paper with another member of the class and score each other's work. Disputes about the legitimacy of names will be settled by the instructor. Keep your score for use later in the exercise.

Part 2

Your instructor will divide the class into groups of five to ten people. All groups should have approximately the same number of members. Each group now follows the procedure given in part 1. Again write the letters of the alphabet down the left side of the sheet of paper, this time in reverse order: Z–A. Your instructor will dictate a new set of letters for the second column. The time limit and scoring procedure are the same. The only difference is that the groups will generate the names.

Part 3

Each team identifies the group member who came up with the most names. The instructor places these "best" students into one group. Then all groups repeat part 2, but this time the letters from the reading will be in the first column and the alphabet letters will be in the second column.

Part 4

Each team calculates the average individual score of its members on part 1 and compares it with the team score from parts 2 and 3, kept separately. Your instructor will put the average individual score and team scores from each part of each group on the board.

Follow-up Questions

1. Are there differences in the average individual scores and the team scores? What are the reasons for the differences, if any?

2. Although the team scores in this exercise usually are higher than the average individual scores, under what conditions might individual averages exceed group scores?

Reference: Adapted from *The Handbook for Group Facilitators*, pp. 19–20, by John E. Jones and J. William Pfeiffer, eds. Copyright © 1979. Reprinted with permission of John Wiley & Sons, Inc.

Self-Assessment Exercise

Group Cohesiveness

Introduction: You are probably a member of many different groups: study groups for school, work groups, friendship groups within a social club such as a fraternity or sorority, and interest groups. You probably have some feel for how tightly knit or cohesive each of those groups is. This exercise will help you diagnose the cohesiveness of one of those groups.

Instructions: First, pick one of the small groups to which you belong for analysis. Be sure that it is a small group, say between three and eight people. Next, rate on the following scale of 1 (poorly) to 5 (very well) how well you feel the group works together.

1	2	3	4	5
Poorly	Not Very Well	About Average	Pretty Well	Very Well

How well does this group work together?

Now answer the following six questions about the group. Put a check in the blank next to the answer that best describes how you feel about each question.

1. How many of the people in your group are friendly toward each other?
   _____ (5) All of them
   _____ (4) Most of them
   _____ (3) Some of them
   _____ (2) A few of them
   _____ (1) None of them

2. How much trust is there among members of your group?
   _____ (1) Distrust
   _____ (2) Little trust
   _____ (3) Average trust
   _____ (4) Considerable trust
   _____ (5) A great deal of trust

3. How much loyalty and sense of belonging is there among group members?
   _____ (1) No group loyalty of sense of belonging
   _____ (2) A little loyalty and sense of belonging
   _____ (3) An average sense of belonging
   _____ (4) An above-average sense of belonging
   _____ (5) A strong sense of belonging

4. Do you feel that you are really a valuable part of your group?
   _____ (5) I am really a part of my group.
   _____ (4) I am included in most ways.
   _____ (3) I am included in some ways but not others.
   _____ (2) I am included in a few ways but not many.
   _____ (1) I do not feel I really belong.

5. How friendly are your fellow group members toward each other?
   _____ (1) Not friendly
   _____ (2) Somewhat friendly
   _____ (3) Friendly to an average degree
   _____ (4) Friendlier than average
   _____ (5) Very friendly

6. If you had a chance to work with a different group of people doing the same task, how would you feel about moving to another group?
   _____ (1) I would want very much to move.
   _____ (2) I would rather move than stay where I am.
   _____ (3) It would make no difference to me.
   _____ (4) I would rather stay where I am than move.
   _____ (5) I would want very much to stay where I am.

Now add up the numbers you chose for all six questions and divide by 6. Total from all six questions = __ / 6 = __. This is the group cohesiveness score for your group.

Compare this number with the one you checked on the scale at the beginning of this exercise about how well you feel this group works together. Are they about the same, or are they quite different? If they are about the same, then you have a pretty good feel for the group and how it works. If they are quite different, then you probably need to analyze what aspects of the group functioning you misunderstood. (This is only part of a much longer instrument; it has not been scientifically validated in this form and is to be used for class discussion purposes only.)

Reference: The six questions were taken from the Groupthink Assessment Inventory by John R. Montanari and Gregory Moorhead, "Development of the Groupthink Assessment Inventory," *Educational and Psychological Measurement*, 1999, vol. 39, pp. 209–219. Reprinted by permission of Gregory Moorhead.

Building Managerial Skills

Exercise Overview: A manager's interpersonal skills refer to her or his ability to understand how to motivate individuals and groups. Clearly, then, interpersonal skills play a major role in determining how well a manager can interact with others in a group setting. This exercise will allow you to practice your interpersonal skills in relation to just such a setting.

Exercise Background: You have just been transferred to a new position supervising a group of seven employees. The group itself has functioned as an intact group for eight years, and the previous supervisor led them for the last five years. She was a very popular leader, and you know that you will have to work hard to succeed.

You quickly discover some underlying problems with your new assignment, however. Specifically, you realize that the group is accustomed to functioning with much more autonomy than you prefer. The previous supervisor essentially left the group alone to make its own decisions, to solve its own problems, and to develop its own work methods. You have received strong indicators from your own boss that your future promotions depend on

how much you can improve the performance of this particular work group. In order to meet these expectations, you are convinced that you will need to be much more involved in the group's work.

As soon as you begin to try to make suggestions and implement changes, the group lets you know—in no uncertain terms—that it knows how to do things better than you. In fact, as you begin to be more and more directive, you also realize that not only is the group not producing more but that its members are actually producing less. Meanwhile, you are certain that while the group does indeed know its job, you do have several ideas that could make the group more productive. But now it seems that the harder you try to help, the more sluggish the group performs.

Exercise Task: With this information as context, do the following:

1. Explain the underlying work group dimensions that exist in this situation.

2. Develop a course of action for dealing with the situation.

Effective Group Decisions at the Denver Broncos

The Denver Broncos function effectively as a team, winning the Super Bowl three times between 1987 and 1990. The team is popular with its fans too—every Broncos game since 1970 has been a sell-out. The Broncos staff is equally effective, generating revenues of $183 million in 2004. *Forbes* claims that the Broncos are among the best-run organizations in the NFL. The estimated value of the team has risen from $320 million in 1998 to $683 million today.

The Broncos' marketing group handles a vast array of decisions and tasks, from community relations, to corporate partnerships, broadcasting, advertising, merchandising, publications, websites, special events, promotions, and more. Most of the decisions are made through collaboration and participative meetings. Derek Marlin, corporate partnerships executive for the Broncos, says, "We will sit down and do different types of brainstorming . . . We will kind of bounce ideas back and forth off of each other." Collaboration and mutual support are essential when one marketing event or one game-day promotion may involve managers from several different areas within marketing. For example, Lynn Rosen, manager for Game-day Entertainment, states, "I plan events and I couldn't do that by myself."

With members who are motivated, flexible, and cooperative, it's clear that the Denver Broncos' marketing group is in the final stage of group development, called "Control and Organization." Communication in mature groups is open and honest, yet supportive. "We'll debate it back and forth and sometimes it will get pretty heated, but it's never a personal thing," says James Merilatt, marketing communications coordinator. "Ultimately, you get all sides out on the table and everybody's comfortable with the decision once that decision is made."

Mature groups tend to make effective decisions. Another factor that improves decision quality is the diversity of talents, interests, and perspectives of the members of the marketing group. Strong group performance norms are yet another factor in this group's effectiveness. Group members make comments such as, "We all take pride in

> **❝ [When] you get all sides out on the table [then] everybody's comfortable with the decision. ❞**
> *James Merilatt, marketing communications coordinator, Denver Broncos*

our work," "We are a part of a bigger picture," and "We are all heading towards the same goal." According to Marlin, "Most of the time, people have their own initiatives, but . . . you've got to say, 'What's going to be best for the team?'" Marlin's opinion is echoed by several of the marketing group members, who agree that "what's best for the team" is the most important factor in any decision. Sometimes "what's best for the team" may mean pleasing the fans, or the corporate sponsors, or the players, but it all ends up having a positive impact on revenues.

Cohesiveness is an additional factor for enhancing group performance. For the Broncos' marketing group, cohesiveness arises from a common goal as well as shared fun. "It's a good support network," says Marlin. "Everyone is in it for the same goal." Rosen agrees. "We all get along so well and that's what makes the job so fun." Coordinator of partnerships Sandy Bretzlauf mentions that work friendships extend to personal time, saying, "We all get along really well inside and outside of work and do things [together] on the weekends or after work."

Yet in spite of the strong group cohesiveness, members work hard to avoid the negative effects of groupthink. Merilatt states, "We don't have too much groupthink . . . I tend to be the counterculture kind of guy." Merilatt's willingness to challenge the group's thinking by acting as a devil's advocate can be very beneficial to the group. Amy Marolf, manager of corporate partner services, claims that group members are not hesitant to express dissenting opinions. She says, "We're very supportive of each other but if we have a point or we think one of our ideas could really improve [a coworker's] project . . . we're all pretty open to that." Merilatt has the same idea and he says, "Sometimes you just have to agree to disagree." Disagreement and a diversity of opinions, when expressed in a helpful way, are two important ways to prevent groupthink.

While Broncos marketing staff members love their ideal job and think of work as fun, it's clear that they are effective decision makers, making them effective contributors to the management of their complex and challenging organization.

Case Questions

1. Describe the decision-making process at the Denver Broncos' marketing group. Why is the group decision process beneficial for this organization?

2. What aspects of the marketing group lead to high decision quality and high effectiveness? What factors might potentially reduce decision quality or effectiveness?

3. How does the Denver Broncos' marketing group avoid groupthink? In your opinion, is there anything else the group could do to decrease the chances of groupthink? Explain your answer.

References: Bill Saporito, "The American Money Machine," *Time*, December 6, 2004, www.time.com on April 11, 2005; "Denver Broncos," Invesco Field website, www.invescofieldatmilehigh.com on March 23, 2005; "Group Decisions Support Marketing of the Denver Broncos," video case (quotation); "Marketing," Denver Broncos website, www.denverbroncos.com on April 11, 2005; Jeff Legwold, "Tagliabue Sounds the Alarm," *Rocky Mountain News*, March 22, 2005, rockymountainnews.com on April 11, 2005; Paul Munsey and Cory Suppes, "Mile High Stadium," *BallParks*, football.ballparks.com on April 11, 2005.

You have read the chapter and studied the key terms. Think you're ready to ace the exam? Take this sample test to gauge your comprehension of chapter material and check your answers at the back of the book. Want more test questions? Take the ACE quizzes found on the student website: http://college.hmco.com/business/students/ (select Griffin/Moorhead, Organizational Behavior, 8e from the Management menu).

T F 1. Interpersonal relations are a vital part of all managerial activities.

T F 2. A collection of coworkers must share a goal to qualify as a group.

T F 3. Mutual acceptance is usually the last stage of group development.

T F 4. A group must fully complete one stage of development before it can move on to the next stage.

T F 5. A homogeneous group tends to have less conflict than a heterogeneous group.

T F 6. Diffusion of responsibility for a group decision contributes to group polarization.

T F 7. In problem-solving tasks, groups generally produce more and better solutions than do individuals.

8. According to the authors of your text, a group has all of the following except
   a. two or more people.
   b. interaction among the group members.
   c. mutual influence among the group members.
   d. motivation to stay together.

9. Hannah is the manager of the large appliance department at a home improvement store. She supervises six appliance salespeople. This is an example of a
   a. task group.
   b. command group.
   c. affinity group.
   d. interest group.
   e. project group.

10. The first stage of group development is
    a. communication and decision making.
    b. planning and leading.
    c. control and organization.
    d. mutual acceptance.
    e. motivation and productivity.

11. A homogeneous group is likely to be more productive when the group task is
    a. highly challenging and long term.
    b. risky and short term.
    c. new and uncertain.
    d. simple and cooperation is necessary.
    e. complex and requires collective effort.

12. Group norms are usually established during which stage of group development?
    a. Communication and decision making
    b. Planning and leading
    c. Control and organization
    d. Mutual acceptance
    e. Motivation and productivity

13. Which of the following is an example of group polarization?
    a. Two members of a group have a clash of personalities.
    b. Individually, the members of a group try to take the group in different directions.
    c. As a whole, a group becomes more extreme in its position following a discussion than it was before.
    d. A highly cohesive group avoids seeking outside advice.
    e. A group splits in half after an emotional debate on an important issue.

14. Cameron is considering using a group to solve a problem. He knows groups generally produce better decisions than do individuals. However, which of the following disadvantages should Cameron expect?
    a. Groups usually focus on decisions that benefit themselves.
    b. Groups take far longer than individuals to develop solutions and make decisions.
    c. Groups of experts are unlikely to agree on a solution.
    d. Groups tend to reduce the interest individuals have in the task.
    e. Groups that have become polarized can never be repaired.

15. A group decision-making technique that systematically gathers the judgments of experts, even though the experts never meet face-to-face, is called
    a. the Delphi technique.
    b. the nominal group technique.
    c. synergistic decision making.
    d. the synopsis method.
    e. conservative group shift.

CHAPTER 10

Using Teams in Organizations

▶ **Differentiate teams from groups.**

▶ **Identify and discuss the benefits and costs of teams in organizations.**

▶ **Identify and describe various types of teams.**

▶ **Describe how organizations implement the use of teams.**

▶ **Discuss other essential team issues.**

Chapter Outline

Differentiating Teams from Groups

Benefits and Costs of Teams in Organizations

Types of Teams

Implementing Teams in Organizations

Essential Team Issues

Outsourcing Teamwork

Outsourcing occurs when a company hires another firm to perform internal business functions. Outsourcing is spreading to more companies and more functions today. An auto components manufacturer outsources product testing and quality control functions. A hospital outsources purchasing. The biopharmaceutical industry outsources specialty chemical production. Small businesses outsource website design, while growing companies outsource human resources.

Outsourcing can reduce costs and speed up processes, increasing company efficiency. However, outsourcing can also improve teamwork and effectiveness by allowing employees to focus more attention on functions where they can add value and by giving instant access to valuable and specific knowledge.

Teamwork can be enhanced through outsourcing when cooperation, communication, and trust are present. Dr. Harold Meckler and Kenton Shultis, vice presidents of chemical firm AMRI, state, "Successful [outsourcing] projects and customer relationships all possess the same common denominators . . . [These] allow the efficient outsourcing customer to deploy its resources on many more projects and give the customer a tremendous advantage over its competitors."

> **"An exchange of people is at the heart of outsourcing."**
>
> GORDON THOMAS, PRODUCT TEAM DIRECTOR, CSC

In some cases, company workers actually become employees of the contractor, further enriching teamwork. CSC, a provider of logistics information systems, hired 200 civilian employees formerly with the U.S. Army. "True outsourcing is not about managing services" says CSC director Gordon Thomas. "An exchange of people is at the heart of outsourcing." The workers brought years of experience in meeting the Army's needs to CSC, which in turn provided training and job security to the workers. The Army also benefited from CSC's expertise and innovation.

Yet outsourcing also provides challenges to effective teamwork. Employees from two different companies are simply not as likely to form the long-lasting and close relationships that foster teamwork. Employees may view outsourcing as a job threat or as an indicator of lack of support for workers. Merrill Lynch, for example, faced a decision in 2002 about outsourcing its human resource functions. The firm believed it could save money from outsourcing, but ultimately decided to keep the human resources functions in-house. "Especially after September 11 . . . we felt that we shouldn't do something that might help us in the short term but hurt us in the long term through employee dissatisfaction and the inability to retain future leaders," says Terry Kassel, head of Merrill Lynch's human resources.

Rick Brenner, a business consultant, asks companies considering outsourcing, "If your supplier develops an innovation or acquires an insight, will you ever become aware of it? Can that innovation or insight propagate to your competitors [who are also customers of the contractor]?" Clearly, teamwork is severely hampered by a lack of trust.

On the positive side, outsourcing can increase team diversity, maximize resource usage, enhance creativity, improve speed, and reduce costs. On the negative side, outsourcing can harm teamwork by making cooperation and communication more difficult and reducing trust. For managers, the challenge will be to choose outsourcing situations appropriately and then manage them carefully. The organization that can do this should reap tremendous benefits in teamwork. For more about the advantages and risks of global outsourcing, see the boxed insert on page 271 titled *Outsourcing and . . . Globalization.*

References: "Logistics Modernization Program," CSC website, www.csc.com on April 16, 2005 (quotation); "Outsourcing Engineering Services," Continental Design and Engineering website, www.continental-design.com on April 16, 2005; Rick Brenner, "Outsourcing Each Other's Kids," Chaco Canyon Consulting newsletter, March 10, 2004, www.chacocanyon.com on April 16, 2005; Harold Meckler and Kenton Shultis, "A Formula for Outsourcing Success," *Contract Pharma*, October 2003, www.contractpharma.com on April 16, 2005; Andrew Park, "EDS Turbocharges Its Teamwork," *Business Week*, February 28, 2005, www.businessweek.com on April 16, 2005; Jeffrey Rothfeder, "The Road Less Traveled: Merrill Lynch & Co.," *CIO Insight*, March 1, 2004, www.cioinsight.com on March 29, 2005.

Teams are an integral part of the management process in many organizations today. But the notion of using teams as a way of organizing work is not new. Neither is it an American or Japanese innovation. One of the earliest uses and analyses of teams was the work of the Tavistock Institute in the late 1940s in the United Kingdom.[1] Major companies such as Hewlett-Packard, Xerox, Procter & Gamble, General Motors, and General Mills have been using teams as a primary means of accomplishing tasks for many years. The popular business press, such as *Fortune, Business Week, Forbes*, and the *Wall Street Journal*, regularly reports on the use of teams in businesses around the world. The use of teams is not a fad of the month or some new way to manipulate workers into producing more at their own expense to enrich owners. Managers and experts agree that using teams can be among the best ways to organize and manage successfully in the twenty-first century.

This chapter presents a summary of many of the current issues involving teams in organizations. First, we define what "team" means and differentiate teams from normal work groups. We then discuss the rationale for using teams, including both the benefits and the costs. Next, we describe six types of teams in use in organizations today. Then we present the steps involved in implementing teams. Finally, we take a brief look at two essential issues that must be addressed.

Differentiating Teams from Groups

Teams have been used, written about, and studied under many names and organizational programs: self-directed teams, self-managing teams, autonomous work groups, participative management, and many other labels. Groups and teams are not the same thing, however, although the two words are often used interchangeably in popular usage. A brief look at a dictionary shows that "group" usually refers to an assemblage of people or objects gathered together, whereas "team" usually refers to people or animals organized to work together. Thus, a "team" places more emphasis on concerted action than a "group" does. In common, everyday usage, however, "committee," "group," "team," and "task force" are often used interchangeably.

In organizations, teams and groups are quite different. As we noted in Chapter 9, a group is two or more persons who interact with one another such that each person influences and is influenced by each other person. We specifically noted that individuals interacting and influencing each other need not have a common goal. The collection of people who happen to report to the same supervisor or manager in an organization can be called a "work group." Group members may be satisfying their own needs in the group and have little concern for a common objective. This is where a team and a group differ. In a team, all team members are committed to a common goal.

We could therefore simply say that a team is a group with a common goal. But teams differ from groups in other ways, too, and most experts are a bit more specific in defining teams. A more complete definition is "A **team** is a small number of people with complementary skills who are committed to a common purpose, performance goals, and approach for which they hold themselves mutually accountable."[2] Several facets of this definition need further explanation. A team typically includes few people because the interaction and influence processes needed for the team to function can only occur when the number of members is small. When many people are involved, they have difficulty interacting and influencing each other, utilizing their complementary skills, meeting goals, and holding themselves accountable. Regardless of the name, by our definition, mature, fully developed teams are self-directing, self-managing, and autonomous. If they are not, then someone from outside the group must be giving directions, so the group cannot be considered a true team.[3]

Teams include people with a mix of skills appropriate to the tasks to be done. Three types of skills are usually required in a team. First, the team needs to have members with the technical or functional skills to do the jobs. Some types of engineering, scientific, technological, legal, or business skills may be necessary. Second, some team members need to have problem-solving and decision-making skills to help the team identify problems, determine priorities, evaluate alternatives, analyze tradeoffs, and

> A **team** is a small number of people with complementary skills who are committed to a common purpose, common performance goals, and an approach for which they hold themselves mutually accountable.

make decisions about the direction of the team. Third, members need interpersonal skills to manage communication flow, resolve conflict, direct questions and discussion, provide support, and recognize the interests of all members of the team. Not all members will have all of the required skills, especially when the team first convenes; different members will have different skills. However, as the team grows, develops, and matures, team members will come to have more of the necessary skills.[4]

Having a common purpose and common performance goals sets the tone and direction of the team. A team comes together to take action to pursue a goal, unlike a work group, in which members merely report to the same supervisor or work in the same department. The purpose becomes the focus of the team, which makes all decisions and takes all actions in pursuit of the goal. Teams often spend days or weeks establishing the reason for their existence, an activity that builds strong identification and fosters commitment to the team. This process also helps team members develop trust in one another.[5] Usually, the defining purpose comes first, followed by development of specific performance goals.

For example, a team of local citizens, teachers, and parents may come together for the purpose of making the local schools the best in the state. Then the team establishes specific performance goals to serve as guides for decision making, to maintain the focus on action, to differentiate this team from other groups who may want to improve schools, and to challenge people to commit themselves to the team. One study looked at more than thirty teams and found that demanding, high-performance goals often challenge members to create a real team—as opposed to being merely a group—because when goals are truly demanding, members must pull together, find resources within themselves, develop and use the appropriate skills, and take a common approach to reach the goals.[6]

Teams have become an increasingly important mechanism for organizations to use in getting things done. For example, some large companies are beginning to suggest that small suppliers work together as partners to win major contracts. In order to facilitate such partnerships, each supplier generally provides one or more team members who work together to coordinate their effort. Woodrow Hall, owner of a plastic packaging business called Film Fabricators Inc., and Robert Johnson, owner of Johnson-Bryce Corp., a plastic bag manufacturer and printer, are working together as a team in pursuit of a major contract from Procter & Gamble.

Agreeing on a common approach is especially important for teams because it is often the approach that differentiates one team from others. The team's approach usually covers how work will be done, social norms regarding dress, attendance at meetings, tardiness, norms of fairness and ethical behavior, and what will and will not be included in the team activities.

Finally, the definition states that teams hold themselves mutually accountable for results rather than merely meeting a manager's demands for results, as in the traditional approach. If the members translate accountability to an external manager into internal, or mutual, accountability, the group moves toward acting like a team. Mutual accountability is essentially a promise that members make to each other to do everything possible to achieve their goals, and it requires the commitment and trust of all members. It is the promise of each member to hold herself or himself accountable for the team's goals that earns each individual the right to express her or his views and expect to get a fair and constructive hearing. With this promise, members maintain and strengthen the trust necessary for the team to succeed. The clearly stated high-performance goals and the common approach serve as the standards to which the team holds itself. Because teams are mutually accountable for meeting performance goals, three other differences between groups and teams become important: job categories, authority, and reward systems. The differences for traditional work groups and work teams are shown in Table 10.1.

Job Categories

The work of conventional groups is usually described in terms of highly specialized jobs that require minimal training and moderate effort. Tens or even hundreds of people may have similar job descriptions and see little relationship between their effort and the end result or finished product. In teams, on the other hand, members have many different skills that fit into one or two broad job categories. Neither workers nor management worries about who does what job as long as the team puts out the finished product or service and meets its performance goals.[7]

Authority

As shown in Table 10.1, in conventional work groups, the supervisor directly controls the daily activities of workers. In teams, the team discusses what activities need to be done and determines for itself who in the team has the necessary skills and will do each task. The team, rather than the supervisor, makes the decisions. If a "supervisor" remains on the team, the person's role usually changes from decision maker and controller to that of coach, facilitator, or one who helps the team make decisions.

TABLE 10.1

Differences Between Teams and Traditional Work Groups

Issue	Conventional Work Groups	Teams
Job Categories	Many narrow categories	One or two broad categories
Authority	Supervisor directly controls daily activities	Team controls daily activities
Reward System	Depends on the type of job, individual performance, and seniority	Based on team performance and individual breadth of skills

Reference: Adapted from Jack D. Osburn, Linda Moran, and Ed Musselwhite, with Craig Perrin, *Self-Directed Work Teams: The New American Challenge* (Homewood, IL: Business One Irwin, 1990), p. 11.

Reward Systems

How employees are rewarded is vital to the long-term success of an organization. The traditional reward and compensation systems suitable for individual motivation (discussed in Chapter 4) are simply not appropriate in a team-based organization. In conventional settings, employees are usually rewarded on the basis of their individual performance, their seniority, or their job classification. In a team-based situation, team members are rewarded for mastering a range of skills needed to meet team performance goals, and rewards are sometimes based on team performance. Such a pay system tends to promote the flexibility that teams need to be responsive to changing environmental factors. Three types of reward systems are common in a team environment: skill-based pay, gain-sharing systems, and team bonus plans.

Skill-Based Pay   Skill-based pay systems require team members to acquire a set of the core skills needed for their particular team plus additional special skills, depending on career tracks or team needs. Some programs require all members to acquire the core skills before any member receives additional pay. Usually employees can increase their base compensation by some fixed amount, say $0.30 per hour for each additional skill acquired, up to some fixed maximum. Companies using skill-based pay systems include Eastman Chemical Company, Colgate-Palmolive Company, and Pfizer.

Gain-Sharing Systems   Gain-sharing systems usually reward all team members from all teams based on the performance of the organization, division, or plant. Such a system requires a baseline performance that must be exceeded for team members to receive some share of the gain over the baseline measure. Westinghouse gives equal one-time, lump-sum bonuses to everyone in the plant based on improvements in productivity, cost, and quality. Employee reaction is usually positive because when employees work harder to help the company, they share in the profits they helped generate. On the other hand, when business conditions or other factors beyond their control make it impossible to generate improvements over the preset baseline, employees may feel disappointed and even disillusioned with the process.

Team Bonus Plans   Team bonus plans are similar to gain-sharing plans except that the unit of performance and pay is the team rather than a plant, a division, or the entire organization. Each team must have specific performance targets or baseline measures that the team considers realistic for the plan to be effective. Companies using team bonus plans include Milwaukee Insurance Company, Colgate-Palmolive, and Harris Corporation.

Changes in an organizational compensation system can be traumatic and threatening to most employees. However, matching the reward system to the way that work is organized and accomplished can have very positive benefits. The three types of team-based reward systems presented can be used in isolation for simplicity or in some combination to address different types of issues for each organization.

Benefits and Costs of Teams in Organizations

With the popularity of teams increasing so rapidly around the world, it is possible that some organizations are starting to use teams simply because everyone else is doing it, which is obviously the wrong reason. The reason for a company to create teams should

TABLE 10.2

Benefits of Teams in Organizations

Type of Benefit	Specific Benefit	Organizational Examples
Enhanced Performance	Increased productivity	Ampex: On-time customer delivery rose 98%.
	Improved quality	K Shoes: Rejects per million dropped from 5,000 to 250.
	Improved customer service	Eastman: Productivity rose 70%.
Employee Benefits	Quality of work life	Milwaukee Mutual: Employee assistance program usage dropped to 40% below industry average.
	Lower stress	
Reduced Costs	Lower turnover, absenteeism	Kodak: Reduced turnover to one-half the industry average.
	Fewer injuries	Texas Instruments: Reduced costs more than 50%.
		Westinghouse: Costs down 60%.
Organizational Enhancements	Increased innovation, flexibility	IDS Mutual Fund Operations: Improved flexibility to handle fluctuations in market activity.
		Hewlett-Packard: Innovative order-processing system.

References: Adapted from Richard S. Wellins, William C. Byham, and George R. Dixon, *Inside Teams* (San Francisco: Jossey-Bass, 1994); Charles C. Manz and Henry P. Sims Jr., *Business Without Bosses* (New York: Wiley, 1993).

be that teams make sense for that particular organization. The best reason to start teams in any organization is to recap the positive benefits that can result from a team-based environment: enhanced performance, employee benefits, reduced costs, and organizational enhancements. Four categories of benefits and some examples are shown in Table 10.2.

Enhanced Performance

Enhanced performance can come in many forms, including improved productivity, quality, and customer service. Working in teams enables workers to avoid wasted effort, reduce errors, and react better to customers, resulting in more output for each unit of employee input. Such enhancements result from pooling of individual efforts in new ways and from continuously striving to improve for the benefit of the team. For example, a General Electric plant in North Carolina experienced a 20 percent increase in productivity after team implementation.[8] K Shoes reported a 19 percent increase in productivity and significant reductions in rejects in the manufacturing process.

Employee Benefits

Employees tend to benefit as much as organizations in a team environment. Much attention has been focused on the differences between the baby-boom generation and the "postboomers" in their attitudes toward work, its importance to their lives, and what they want from it. In general, younger workers tend to be less satisfied with their work and the organization, to have lower respect for authority and supervision, and to want more than a paycheck every week. Teams can provide the sense of self-control, human dignity, identification with work, and sense of self-worth and self-fulfillment for which current workers seem to strive. Rather than relying on the traditional, hierarchical, manager-based system, teams give employees the freedom to grow and to gain respect and dignity by managing themselves, making decisions about their work, and really making a difference in the world around them.[9] As a result, employees have a better work life, face less stress at work, and make less use of employee assistance programs.

Reduced Costs

As empowered teams reduce scrap, make fewer errors, file fewer worker compensation claims, and reduce absenteeism and turnover, organizations based on teams are showing significant cost reductions. Team members feel that they have a stake in the outcomes, want to make contributions because they are valued, and are committed to their team and do not want to let it down. Wilson Sporting Goods reported saving $10 million per year for five years thanks to its teams. Colgate-Palmolive reported that technician turnover was extremely low—more than 90 percent of technicians were retained after five years—once it changed to a team-based approach.

Organizational Enhancements

Other improvements in organizations that result from moving from a hierarchically based, directive culture to a team-based culture include increased innovation, creativity, and flexibility.[10] Use of teams can eliminate redundant layers of bureaucracy and flatten the hierarchy in large organizations. Employees feel closer and more in touch with top management. Employees who think their efforts are important are more likely to make significant contributions. In addition, the team environment constantly challenges teams to innovate and solve problems creatively. If the "same old way" does not work, empowered teams are free to throw it out and develop a new way. With increasing global competition, organizations must constantly adapt to keep abreast of changes. Teams provide the flexibility to react quickly. One of Motorola's earliest teams challenged a long-standing top-management policy regarding supplier inspections in order to reduce the cycle times and improve delivery of crucial parts.[11] After several attempts, management finally allowed the team to change the system and consequently reaped the expected benefits.

Costs of Teams

The costs of teams are usually expressed in terms of the difficulty of changing to a team-based organization. Managers have expressed frustration and confusion about their new roles as coaches and facilitators, especially if they developed their managerial skills under the old traditional hierarchical management philosophy. Some managers have felt as if they were working themselves out of a job as they turned over more and more of their old directing duties to a team.[12]

Employees may also feel like losers during the change to a team culture. Some traditional staff groups, such as technical advisory staffs, may feel that their jobs are in jeopardy as teams

Teams are playing an increasingly important role in many settings. As part of the beefed-up emphasis on homeland security, many law enforcement and security agencies are using teams to help develop strategies and tactics to help thwart terrorists. A team of security experts in New Jersey, for instance, helped develop this robot. Andros, as it has been dubbed, can help disarm potential weapons of mass destruction.

do more and more of the technical work formerly done by technicians. New roles and pay scales may need to be developed for the technical staff in these situations. Often, technical people have been assigned to a team or a small group of teams and become members who fully participate in team activities.

Another cost associated with teams is the slowness of the process of full team development. As discussed elsewhere in this chapter, it takes a long time for teams to go through the full development cycle and become mature, efficient, and effective. If top management is impatient with the slow progress, teams may be disbanded, returning the organization to its original hierarchical form with significant losses for employees, managers, and the organization.

Probably the most dangerous cost is premature abandonment of the change to a team-based organization. If top management gets impatient with the team change process and cuts it short, never allowing teams to develop fully and realize benefits, all the hard work of employees, middle managers, and supervisors is lost. As a result, employee confidence in management in general and in the decision makers in particular may suffer for a long time.[13] The losses in productivity and efficiency will be very difficult to recoup. Management must therefore be fully committed before initiating a change to a team-based organization.

Types of Teams

Many different types of teams exist in organizations today. Some evolved naturally in organizations that permit various types of participative and empowering management programs. Others have been formally created at the suggestion of enlightened management. One easy way to classify teams is by what they do; for example, some teams make or do things, some teams recommend things, and some teams run things. The most common types of teams are quality circles, work teams, and problem-solving teams; management teams are also quite common.

Unfortunately, this person probably isn't going to be a very effective team member. That's too bad, because working in teams can result in enhanced performance, a reduction in errors, and an overall enhancement in performance. An organization that promotes a team environment can see positive results in terms of worker creativity, productivity, and job satisfaction.

"Before I begin, I'd just like to make it known that I didn't volunteer to do this presentation."

© 2002 Randy Glasbergen.   www.glasbergen.com

Quality Circles

Quality circles (QCs) are small groups of employees from the same work area who meet regularly (usually weekly or monthly) to discuss and recommend solutions to workplace problems.[14] QCs were the first type of team created in U.S. organizations, becoming most popular during the 1980s in response to growing Japanese competition. QCs had some success in reducing rework and cutting defects on the shop floors of many manufacturing plants. Some attempts have been made to use QCs in offices and service operations, too. They exist alongside the traditional management structure and are relatively permanent. The role of QCs is to investigate a variety of quality problems that might come up in the workplace. They do not replace the work group or make decisions about how the work is done. The usage of QCs has declined in recent years, although many companies still have them.[15] QCs are teams that make recommendations.

Quality circles are small groups of employees from the same work area who regularly meet to discuss and recommend solutions to workplace problems.

Work Teams

Work teams tend to be permanent, like QCs, but they, rather than auxiliary committees, are the teams that do the daily work.[16] The nurses, orderlies, and various technicians responsible for all patients on a floor or wing in a hospital comprise a work team. Rather than investigate a specific problem, evaluate alternatives, and recommend a solution or change, a work team does the actual daily work of the unit. The difference between a traditional work group of nurses and the patient care team is that the latter has the authority to decide how the work is done, in what order, and by whom; the entire team is responsible for all patient care. When the team decides how the work is to be organized or done, it becomes a self-managing team, to which accrue all of the benefits described in this chapter. Work teams are teams that make or do things.

Work teams include all the people working in an area, are relatively permanent, and do the daily work, making decisions regarding how the work of the team is done.

Problem-Solving Teams

Problem-solving teams are temporary teams established to attack specific problems in the workplace. Teams can use any number of methods to solve the problem, as discussed in Chapter 9. After solving the problem, the team is usually disbanded, allowing members to return to their normal work. One survey found that 91 percent of U.S. companies utilize problem-solving teams regularly.[17] High-performing problem-solving teams are often cross-functional, meaning that team members come from many different functional areas. Crisis teams are problem-solving teams created only for the duration of an organizational crisis and are usually composed of people from many different areas. Problem-solving teams are teams that make recommendations for others to implement.

Problem-solving teams are temporary teams established to attack specific problems in the workplace.

Management Teams

Management teams coordinate work teams and consist of managers from various areas. They are relatively permanent because their work does not end with the completion of a particular project or the resolution of a problem. Management teams must concentrate on the teams that have the most impact on overall corporate performance. The primary job of management teams is to coach and counsel other teams to be self-managing by making decisions within the team. The second most important task of management teams is to coordinate work between work teams that are interdependent in some manner. Digital Equipment Corporation abandoned its team matrix structure because the matrix of teams was not well organized and coordinated. Team members at all levels reported spending hours and hours in meetings trying to coordinate among teams, leaving too little time to get the real work done.[18]

Management teams consist of managers from various areas; they coordinate work teams.

Top-management teams may have special types of problems. First, the work of the top-management team may not be conducive to teamwork. Vice presidents or heads of divisions may be in charge of different sets of operations that are not related and do not need to be coordinated. Forcing that type of top-management group to be a team may be inappropriate. Second, top managers often have reached high levels in the organization because they have certain characteristics or abilities to get things done. For successful managers to alter their style, to pool resources, and to sacrifice their independence and individuality can be very difficult.[19]

Product Development Teams

Product development teams are combinations of work teams and problem-solving teams that create new designs for products or services that will satisfy customer needs. They are similar to problem-solving teams because when the product is fully developed and in production, the team may be disbanded. As global competition and electronic information storage, processing, and retrieving capabilities increase, companies in almost every industry are struggling to cut product development times. The primary organizational means of accomplishing this important task is the "blue-ribbon" cross-functional team. The team that developed Boeing's 777 commercial airplane and the platform teams of Chrysler are typical examples.

The rush to market with new designs can lead to numerous problems for product development teams. The primary problems of poor communication and coordination of typical product development processes in organizations can be rectified by creating self-managing cross-functional product development teams.[20]

Virtual Teams

Virtual teams are teams that may never actually meet together in the same room—their activities take place on the computer via teleconferencing and other electronic

Product development teams are combinations of work teams and problem-solving teams that create new designs for products or services that will satisfy customer needs.

Virtual teams work together by computer and other electronic communication utilities; members move in and out of meetings and the team itself as the situation dictates.

Boeing engineers are hard at work designing the next generation of the popular 777 long-haul aircraft. This engineer is part of a team developing new instrumentation systems for the aircraft. The team is using computer simulations to test how various instrument designs can enhance performance of the plane.

Outsourcing and . . . GLOBALIZATION

Outsourcing Our Country?

The United States led the world in engineering, science, and business for decades. Outsourcing was popular, but limited to manufacturing. Today, however, even technical and managerial occupations are at risk for overseas outsourcing.

According to author Thomas L. Friedman, the first wave of globalization occurred from 1492 to 1800, when countries globalized by empire building. From 1800 to 2000, companies sought bigger markets and cheaper labor. We are entering the third wave of globalization, in which individuals and small groups will become more empowered. People everywhere now have access through the Internet to education, resources, and contacts that enable them to effectively compete for professional jobs that can be performed in their home country. As Friedman puts it, in this phase of globalization, "You can innovate without having to emigrate."

Salaried Americans are increasingly vocal about the threat from overseas workers, making it more difficult for companies to outsource. Wipro, the Indian company that is the largest outsourcing firm in the world, has come under heavy attack. Wipro CEO Azim Premji says of his client firms, "The head wants to offshore, but the heart holds them back." Most Wipro clients now meet in secret to avoid repercussions at home.

The effects on business are difficult to determine. Outsourcing can increase creativity and reduce costs, but it can also make communication and trust more difficult. These factors, both good and bad, are even more pronounced in offshore outsourcing.

Experts focus on reversing the trend through education or hard work. But when India produces a million more college graduates per year than does the United States and China produces twice as many, education and hard work don't seem to be enough. Which is the more realistic advice: that America should produce an additional one million college graduates, or that Americans and their employers should work to improve cooperation and teamwork between workers on every continent?

> ***"You can innovate without having to emigrate."***
>
> THOMAS L. FRIEDMAN, AUTHOR

References: Thomas L. Friedman, "It's a Flat World, After All," *New York Times Magazine*, April 3, 2005, pp. 33–37 (quotation); Enrico T. Polastro, "Asia Outlook: Chinese and Indian Markets," *Contract Pharma*, October 2004, www.contractpharma.com on April 16, 2005; Saritha Rai, "An Outsourcing Giant Fights Back," *New York Times*, March 21, 2004, pp. BU1, 10; Mark A. Stein, "Outsourcing Corner Offices," *New York Times*, September 5, 2004, p. BU2;

information systems. Engineers in the United States can connect audibly and visually with counterparts all around the globe, sharing files via the Internet, electronic mail, and other communication utilities. All participants can look at the same drawing, print, or specification, so decisions are made much faster. With electronic communication systems, team members can move in or out of a team or a team discussion as the issues warrant. Moreover, as illustrated in the *Outsourcing and . . . Globalization* box, virtual teams can exist with members anywhere in the world.

Implementing Teams in Organizations

Implementing teams in organizations is not easy; it takes a lot of hard work, time, training, and patience. Changing from a traditional organizational structure to a team-based structure is much like other organizational changes (which we discuss in Chapter 19). It is really a complete cultural change for the organization. Typically, the organization is hierarchically designed in order to provide clear direction and control. However, many organizations need to be able to react quickly to a dynamic environment. Team procedures artificially imposed on existing processes are a recipe for disaster. In this section we present several essential elements peculiar to an organizational change to a team-based situation.

Planning the Change

The change to a team-based organization requires a lot of analysis and planning before it is implemented; the decision cannot be made overnight and quickly implemented. It is such a drastic departure from the traditional hierarchy and authority-and-control orientation that significant planning, preparation, and training are prerequisites. The planning actually takes place in two phases, the first leading to the decision about whether to move to a team-based approach and the second while preparing for implementation.

Making the Decision   Prior to making the decision, top management needs to establish the leadership for the change, develop a steering committee, conduct a feasibility study, and then make the go/no-go decision. Top management must be sure that the team culture is consistent with its strategy, as we discuss in Chapter 18. Quite often the leadership for the change is the chief executive officer, the chief operating officer, or another prominent person in top management. Regardless of the position, the person leading the change needs to (1) have a strong belief that employees want to be responsible for their own work, (2) be able to demonstrate the team philosophy, (3) articulate a coherent vision of the team environment, and (4) have the creativity and authority to overcome obstacles as they surface.

The leader of the change needs to put together a steering committee to help explore the organization's readiness for the team environment and lead it through the planning and preparation for the change. The steering committee can be of any workable size, from two to ten people who are influential and know the work and the organization. Members may include plant or division managers, union representatives, human resource department representatives, and operational-level employees. The work of the steering committee includes visits to sites that might be candidates for utilizing work teams, visits to currently successful work teams, data gathering and analysis, low-key discussions, and deliberating and deciding whether to use a consultant during the change process.

A feasibility study is a necessity before making the decision to use teams. The steering committee needs to know if the work processes are conducive to team use, if the employees are willing and able to work in a team environment, if the managers in the unit to be converted are willing to learn and apply the hands-off managerial style necessary to make teams work, if the organization's structure and culture are ready to accommodate a team-based organization, if the market for the unit's products or services is growing or at least stable enough to absorb the increased productive capacity that teams will be putting out, and if the community will support the transition teams. Without answers to these questions, management is merely guessing and hoping that teams will work and may be destined for many surprises that could doom the effort.

After the leadership has been established, the steering committee has been set up, and a feasibility study has been conducted, the go/no-go decision can be made. The committee and top management will need to decide jointly to go ahead if conditions are right. On the other hand, if the feasibility study indicates that questions exist as to whether the organizational unit is ready, the committee can decide to postpone implementation while changes are made in personnel, organizational structure, organizational policies, or market conditions. The committee could also decide to implement training and acculturation for employees and managers in the unit in preparation for later implementation.

Preparing for Implementation   Once the decision is made to change to a team-based organization, much needs to be done before implementation can begin. Preparation consists of the following five steps: clarifying the mission, selecting the site for the first work teams, preparing the design team, planning the transfer of authority, and drafting the preliminary plan.

The mission statement is simply an expression of purpose that summarizes the long-range benefits the company hopes to gain by moving to a team environment. It must be consistent with the organization's strategy as it establishes a common set of assumptions for executives, middle managers, support staff, and the teams. In addition, it sets the parameters or boundaries within which the change will take place. It may identify which divisions or plants will be involved or what levels will be converted to teams. The mission statement attempts to stimulate and focus the energy of those people who need to be involved in the change. The mission can focus on continuous improvement, employee involvement, increasing performance, competition, customer satisfaction, and contributions to society. The steering committee should involve many people from many different areas to foster fuller involvement in the change.

Once the mission is established, the steering committee needs to decide where teams will be implemented first. Selection of the first site is crucial because it sets the tone for the success of the total program. The best initial site would be one that includes workers from multiple job categories, one where improving performance or reaching the targets set in the mission is feasible, and one where workers accept the idea of using teams. Also valuable are a tradition or history of success and a staff that is receptive to training, especially training in interpersonal skills. One manufacturing company based its choice of sites for initial teams not on criteria such as these but on the desire to reward the managers of successful divisions or to "fix" areas performing poorly. Team implementation in that company consequently was very slow and not very successful.[21] Initial sites must also have a local "champion" of the team concept.

Once the initial sites have been identified, the steering committee needs to set up the team that will design the other teams. The design team is a select group of employees, supervisors, and managers who will work out the staffing and operational details to make the teams perform well. The design team selects the initial team members, prepares members and managers for teams, changes work processes for use with the team design, and plans the transition from the current state to the new self-managed teams. The design team usually spends the first three months learning from the steering committee, visiting sites where teams are being used successfully, and spending a significant amount of time in classroom training. Considering the composition of the teams is one of the most important decisions the design team has to make.

Planning the transfer of authority from management to teams is the most important phase of planning the implementation. It is also the most distinctive and difficult part of moving to a team-based organization. It is difficult because it is so different from the traditional, hierarchical organization management system. It is a gradual process, one that takes from two to five years in most situations. Teams must learn new skills and make new decisions related to their work, all of which take time. It is, essentially, a cultural change for the organization.

The last stage of planning the implementation is to write the tentative plan for the initial work teams. The draft plan combines the work of the steering and design committees and becomes the primary working document that guides the continuing work of the design teams and the first work teams. The draft plan (1) recommends a process

Implementing teams in organizations is a complex and multistep process, but if done well, the payoffs can be dramatic. For instance, India's Wipro Technologies moved to a team organization as a way of competing more effectively with other international software solutions firms such as EDS and IBM Global Solutions. This team helped the firm win a major contract from Home Depot. Other teams have worked effectively with clients such as General Electric and Nokia as Wipro's annual revenues approach $400 million.

for selecting the people who will be on the first teams; (2) describes roles and responsibilities for all the people who will be affected (team members, team leaders, facilitators, support teams, managers, and top management); (3) explains what training the several groups will need; (4) identifies specifically which work processes will be involved; (5) describes what other organizational systems will be affected; and (6) lays out a preliminary master schedule for the next two to three years. Once the steering committee and top management approve the preliminary plan, the organization is ready to start the implementation.

Phases of Implementation

Implementation of self-managing work teams is a long and difficult process, often taking two to five years. During this period, the teams go through a number of phases (Figure 10.1); these phases are not, however, readily apparent at the times the team is going through them.

Phase 1: Start-Up   In phase 1, team members are selected and prepared to work in teams so that the teams have the best possible chance of success. Much of the initial training is informational or "awareness" training that sends the message that top management is firmly committed to teams and that teams are not experimental. The steering committee usually starts the training at the top, and the training and information are passed down the chain to the team members. Training covers the rationale for moving to a team-based organization, how teams were selected, how they work, the roles and responsibilities of teams, compensation, and job security. In general, training covers the technical skills necessary to do the work of the team, the administrative skills necessary for the team to function within the organization, and the interpersonal skills necessary to work with people in the team and throughout the organization. Sometimes the interpersonal skills are important. Perhaps most important is establishing the idea that teams are not "unmanaged" but are "differently managed." The difference is

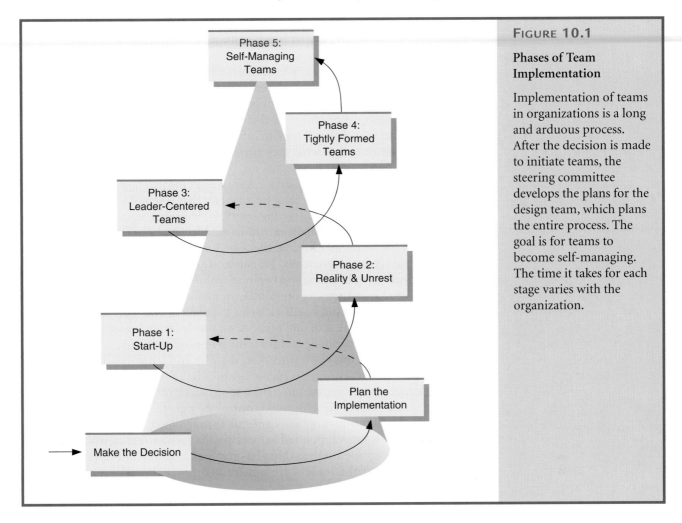

FIGURE **10.1**

Phases of Team Implementation

Implementation of teams in organizations is a long and arduous process. After the decision is made to initiate teams, the steering committee develops the plans for the design team, which plans the entire process. The goal is for teams to become self-managing. The time it takes for each stage varies with the organization.

that the new teams manage themselves. Team boundaries are also identified, and the preliminary plan is adjusted to fit the particular team situations. Employees typically feel that much is changing during the first few months, enthusiasm runs high, and the anticipation of employees is quite positive. Performance by teams increases at start-up because of this initial enthusiasm for the change.

Phase 2: Reality and Unrest After perhaps six to nine months, team members and managers report frustration and confusion about the ambiguities of the new situation. For employees, unfamiliar tasks, more responsibility, and worry about job security replace hope for the opportunities presented by the new approach. All of the training and preparation, as important as it is, is never enough to prepare for the storm and backlash. Cummins Engine Company held numerous "prediction workshops" in an effort to prepare employees and managers for the difficulties that lay ahead, all to no avail. Its employees reported the same problems that employees of other companies did. The best advice is to perform phase 1 very well and then make managers very visible, continue to work to clarify the roles and responsibilities of everyone involved, and reinforce the positive behaviors that do occur.

Some managers make the mistake of staying completely away from the newly formed teams, thinking that the whole idea is to let teams manage themselves. In reality, managers need to be very visible to provide encouragement, to monitor team performance, to act as intermediaries between teams, to help teams acquire needed resources, to foster the right type of communication, and sometimes to protect teams from those who want to see them fail. Managers, too, feel the unrest and confusion. The change they supported results in more work for them. In addition, there is the real threat, at least initially, that work will not get done, projects may not get finished, or orders will not get shipped on time and that they will be blamed for the problems.[22] Managers also report that they still have to intervene and solve problems for the teams because the teams do not know what they are doing.

Phase 3: Leader-Centered Teams   As the discomfort and frustrations of the previous phase peak, teams usually long for a system that resembles the old manager-centered organizational structure (see Figure 10.1). However, members are learning about self-direction and leadership from within the team and usually start to focus on a single leader in the team. In addition, the team begins to think of itself as a unit as members learn to manage themselves. Managers begin to get a sense of the positive possibilities of organizing in teams and begin to withdraw slowly from the daily operation of the unit to begin focusing on standards, regulations, systems, and resources for the team.[23] This phase is not a setback to team development, although it may seem like one, because development of and reliance on one internal leader is a move away from focusing on the old hierarchy and traditional lines of authority.

The design and steering committees need to be sure that two things happen during this phase. First, they need to encourage the rise of strong internal team leaders. The new leaders can either be company appointed or team appointed. Top management sometimes prefers the additional control they get from appointing the team leaders, assuming that production will continue through the team transition. On the other hand, if the company-appointed leaders are the former managers, team members have trouble believing that anything has really changed. Team-appointed leaders can be a problem if the leaders are not trained properly and oriented toward team goals.

If the team-appointed leader is ineffective, the team usually recognizes the problem and makes the adjustments necessary to get the team back on track. Another possibility for team leadership is a rotating system in which the position changes every quarter, month, week, or even day. A rotating system fosters professional growth of all members of the team and reinforces the strength of the team's self-management.

The second important issue for this phase is to help each team develop its own sense of identity. Visits to observe mature teams in action can be a good step for newly formed teams. Recognizing teams and individuals for good performance is always powerful, especially when the teams choose the recipients. Continued training in problem-solving steps, tools, and techniques is imperative. Managers need to push as many problem-solving opportunities as possible down to the team level. Finally, as team identity develops, teams develop social activities and display T-shirts, team names, logos, and other items that show off their identity. All of these are a sure sign that the team is moving into phase 4.

Phase 4: Tightly Formed Teams   The fourth phase of team implementation is when teams become tightly formed to the point that their internal focus can become detrimental to other teams and to the organization as a whole. Such teams are usually extremely confident of their ability to do everything. They are solving problems, managing their schedule and resources, and resolving internal conflicts. However, communication with external teams begins to diminish, the team covers up for

underperforming members, and interteam rivalries can turn sour, leading to unhealthy competition.

To avoid the dangers of the intense team loyalty and isolation inherent in phase 4,
managers need to make sure that teams continue to do the things that have enabled
them to prosper thus far. First, teams need to keep the communication channels with
other teams open through councils of rotating team representatives who meet
regularly to discuss what works and what does not; teams who communicate and
cooperate with other teams should be rewarded. At the Digital Equipment plant in
Connecticut, team representatives meet weekly to share successes and failures so that
all can avoid problems and improve the ways their teams operate.[24] Second, management needs to provide performance feedback through computer terminals in the work
area that give up-to-date information on performance, or via regular feedback meetings. At TRW plants, management introduced peer performance appraisal at this stage
of the team implementation process. It found that in phase 4, teams were ready to take
on this administrative task but needed significant training in how to perform and
communicate appraisals. Third, teams need to follow the previously developed plan to
transfer authority and responsibility to the teams and to be sure that all team members have followed the plan to get training in all of the skills necessary to do the work
of the team. By the end of phase 4, the team should be ready to take responsibility for
managing itself.

Phase 5: Self-Managing Teams

Phase 5 is the end result of the months or
years of planning and implementation.
Mature teams are meeting or exceeding
their performance goals. Team members
are taking responsibility for team-related
leadership functions. Managers and supervisors have withdrawn from the daily
operations and are planning and providing counseling for teams. Probably most
important, mature teams are flexible—
taking on new ideas for improvement;
making changes as needed to membership,
roles, and tasks; and doing whatever it
takes to meet the strategic objectives of the
organization. Although the teams are mature and functioning quite well, several
things need to be done to keep them on
track. First and foremost, individuals and
teams need to continue their training in
job skills and team and interpersonal
skills. Second, support systems need to be
constantly improved to facilitate team development and productivity. Third, teams
always need to improve their internal customer and supplier relationships within
the organization. Partnerships among
teams throughout the organization can
help the internal teams continue to meet
the needs of external customers. The

*Team organizations are becoming more and more popular. Toshiba and UPS both use
teams. Recently, the two firms even created a cross-business team to make it easier for
them to work together. Essentially, UPS handles all of Toshiba's logistical support for
having its computers repaired. Toshiba, meanwhile, helps supply UPS with the latest
technology for tracking packages and moving shipments as quickly as possible. And the
team-based structures each firm uses has made their partnership even more effective.*

J.P. Morgan and . . .    **ETHICS**

Bank-Community Partnerships

J.P. Morgan Chase bank has over $1.1 trillion in assets and 161,000 employees. The firm's strong resource base supports a tradition of philanthropy and community partnerships. Support comes from the top of the organization, as the bank's website states, "Central to our history is the principle of working to improve the communities we serve."

Some of J.P. Morgan Chase's charitable activities make good business sense and comply with regulations. For example, the firm generates mortgages for low-income families, minorities, immigrants, and gays, which generate profits as well as meet the requirements of the federal Community Reinvestment Act. In 2004, the bank spent $3 billion on community development lending worldwide.

Outright gifts to needy individuals and organizations accounted for another $140 million at J.P. Morgan Chase. Programs include college scholarships, funding for literacy training, and support for Big Brothers/Big Sisters, and free concerts by the Jazzmobile.

However, perhaps the most significant community impact results from J.P. Morgan Chase's community partnerships, in which bank employees team with community members. The bank offers free seminars on basic financial skills, such as creating a budget, in disadvantaged communities. Training programs teach job skills to inner-city youth and the homeless, while graduates are offered employment at the bank. J.P. Morgan Chase employees work closely with small, family-owned businesses to provide financing and help with marketing and other business functions.

Community partnerships benefit community members, the bank, and its employees. Workers enjoy giving back to communities and appreciate the paid leave that makes volunteering possible. Participation builds team spirit, increasing loyalty to the team and the bank. J.P. Morgan Chase demonstrates that charity provides a sense of common purpose and is a great team builder, within the firm and with outside groups. For more about teamwork at J.P. Morgan Chase, see "The Rainmakers" on page 283.

> *"Central to our history is the principle of working to improve the communities we serve."*
>
> *J.P. MORGAN CHASE WEBSITE*

References: "Building a Sustainable Community Development Business," "Community Partnerships," "Strengthening Our Communities," J.P. Morgan Chase website, www.jpmorganchase.com on April 16, 2005 (quotation); "Community Reinvestment Act," Federal Financial Institutions Examination Council website, www.ffiec.gov on April 17, 2005; "Community Reinvestment Act Performance Evaluation: JPMorgan Chase Bank," Federal Reserve Bank of New York website, September 8, 2003, www.federalreserve.gov on April 17, 2005; Jessi Hempel and Lauren Gard, "The Corporate Givers," *Business Week*, November 29, 2004, www.businessweek.com on April 17, 2005.

J.P. Morgan and . . . Ethics box describes how management teams have been implemented and changed at J.P. Morgan Chase through a series of mergers.

Essential Team Issues

This chapter has described the many benefits of teams and the process of changing to a team-based organization. Teams can be utilized in small and large organizations, on the shop floor and in offices, and in countries around the world. Teams must be initiated for performance-based business reasons, and proper planning and implementation strategies must be used. In this section we discuss two essential issues that cannot be overlooked as organizations move to a team-based setup: team performance and starting at the top.

Team Performance

Organizations typically expect too much too soon when they implement teams. In fact, things often get worse before they get better.[25] Figure 10.2 shows how, shortly after implementation, team performance often declines and then rebounds to rise to the original levels and above. Management at Investors Diversified Services, the financial services giant in Minneapolis, Minnesota, expected planning for team start-up to take three or four months.

The actual planning took eight and a half months.[26] It often takes a year or more before performance levels return to at least their before-team levels. If teams are implemented without proper planning, their performance may never return to prior levels. The long lead time for improving performance can be discouraging to managers who reacted to the fad for teams and expected immediate returns.

The phases of implementation discussed in the previous sections correspond to key points on the team performance curve. At the start-up, performance is at its normal levels, although sometimes the anticipation of, and enthusiasm for, teams causes a slight increase in performance. In phase 2, reality and unrest, teams are often confused and frustrated with the training and lack of direction from top management to the point that actual performance may decline. In phase 3, leader-centered teams become more comfortable with the team idea and refocus on the work of the team. They once again have established leadership, although it is with an internal leader rather than an external manager or supervisor. Thus, their performance usually returns to at least their former levels. In phase 4, teams are beginning to experience the real potential of

---

FIGURE 10.2

Performance and Implementation of Teams

The team performance curve shows that performance initially drops as reality sets in, and team members experience frustration and unrest. However, performance soon increases and rises to record levels as the teams mature and become self-managing.

Reference: Reprinted by permission of Harvard Business School Press. From *The Wisdom of Teams: Creating the High Performance Organization* by Jon R. Katzenbach and Douglas K. Smith, Boston, MA, 1993, p. 84. Copyright © 1993 by the Harvard Business School Publishing Corporation; all rights reserved.

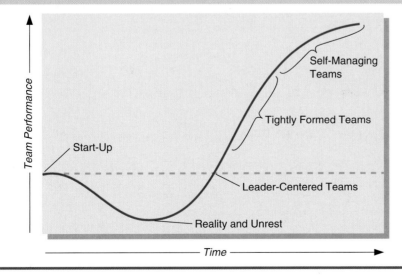

teamwork and are producing above their prior levels. Finally, in phase 5, self-managing teams are mature, flexible, and usually setting new records for performance.

Organizations changing to a team-based arrangement need to recognize the time and effort involved in making such a change. Hopes for immediate, positive results can lead to disappointment. The most rapid increases in performance occur between the leader-centered phase and the team-centered phase because teams have managed to get past the difficult, low-performance stages, have had a lot of training, and are ready to utilize their independence and freedom to make decisions about their own work. Team members are deeply committed to each other and to the success of the team. In phase 5, management needs to make sure that teams are focused on the strategic goals of the organization.

Start at the Top

The question of where to start in team implementation is really no issue at all. Change starts at the top in every successful team implementation. Top management has three important roles to play. First, top management must decide to go to a team-based organization for sound business performance–related reasons. A major cultural change cannot be made because it is the fad, because the boss went to a seminar on teams, or because a quick fix is needed. Second, top management is instrumental in communicating the reasons for the change to the rest of the organization. Third, top management has to support the change effort during the difficult periods. As discussed previously, performance usually goes down in the early phases of team implementation. Top-management support may involve verbal encouragement of team members, but organizational support systems for the teams are also needed. Examples of support systems for teams include more efficient inventory and scheduling systems, better hiring and selection systems, improved information systems, and appropriate compensation systems.

Synopsis

Groups and teams are not the same. A team is a small number of people with complementary skills who are committed to a common purpose, common performance goals, and a common approach for which they hold themselves mutually accountable. Teams differ from traditional work groups in their job categories, authority, and reward systems.

Teams are used because they make sense for a specific organization. Organizational benefits include enhanced performance, employee benefits, and reduced costs, among others.

Many different types of teams exist in organizations. Quality circles are small groups of employees from the same work area who meet regularly to discuss and recommend solutions to workplace problems. Work teams perform the daily operations of the organization and make decisions about how to do the work. Problem-solving teams are temporarily established to solve a particular problem. Management teams consist of managers from various areas; these teams are relatively permanent and coach and counsel the new teams. Product development teams are teams assigned the task of developing a new product or service for the organization. Members of virtual teams usually meet via teleconferencing, may never actually sit in the same room together, and often have a fluid membership.

Planning the change entails all the activities leading to the decision to utilize teams and then preparing the organization for the initiation of teams. Essential steps include establishing leadership for the change, creating a steering committee, conducting a feasibility study, and making the go/no-go decision. After the decision to utilize teams has been made, preparations include clarifying the mission of the change, selecting the site for the first teams, preparing the design team, planning the transfer of authority, and drafting the preliminary plan.

Implementation includes five phases: start-up, reality and unrest, leader-centered teams, tightly formed teams, and self-managing teams. Implementation of teams is really a cultural change for the organization.

For teams to succeed, the change must start with top management, who must decide why the change is needed, communicate the need for the change, and support the change. Management must not expect too much too soon because team performance tends to decrease before it returns to prior levels and then increases to record levels.

Discussion Questions

1. Why is it important to make a distinction between "group" and "team"? What kinds of behaviors might be different in these assemblages?

2. How are other organizational characteristics different for a team-based organization?

3. Some say that changing to a team-based arrangement "just makes sense" for organizations. What are the four primary reasons why this might be so?

4. If employees are happy working in the traditional boss-hierarchical organization, why should a manager even consider changing to a team-based organization?

5. How are the six types of teams related to each other?

6. Explain the circumstances under which a cross-functional team is useful in organizations.

7. Which type of team is the most common in organizations? Why?

8. Why is planning the change important in the implementation process?

9. What can happen if your organization prematurely starts building a team-based organization by clarifying the mission and then selecting the site for the first work teams?

10. What are two of the most important issues facing team-based organizations?

Experiencing Organizational Behavior

Using Teams

Introduction: The use of groups and teams is becoming more common in organizations throughout the world. The following assessment surveys your beliefs about the effective use of teams in work organizations.

Instructions: You will agree with some of the statements and disagree with others. In some cases, you may find making a decision difficult, but you should force a choice. Record your answers next to each statement according to the following scale:

4 = Agree Strongly

3 = Agree Somewhat

2 = Disagree Somewhat

1 = Disagree Strongly

_____ 1. Each individual in a work team should have a clear assignment so that individual accountability can be maintained.

_____ 2. For a team to function effectively, the team must be given complete authority over all aspects of the task.

_____ 3. One way to get teams to work is to simply assemble a group of people, tell them in general what needs to be done, and let them work out the details.

_____ 4. Once a team "gets going," management can turn its attention to other matters.

_____ 5. To ensure that a team develops into a cohesive working unit, managers should be especially careful not to intervene in any way during the initial start-up period.

_____ 6. Training is not critical to a team because the team will develop any needed skills on its own.

_____ 7. It's easy to provide teams with the support they need because they are basically self-motivating.

_____ 8. Teams need little or no structure to function effectively.

_____ 9. Teams should set their own direction, with managers determining the means to the selected end.

_____10. Teams can be used in any organization.

Reference: Adapted from J. Richard Hackman, ed., _Groups That Work (and Those That Don't)_, pp. 493–504. Copyright © 1990 by Jossey-Bass, Inc. Reprinted with permission of John Wiley & Sons, Inc.

Self-Assessment Exercise

Understanding the Benefits of Teams

Purpose: This exercise will help you understand some of the benefits of teamwork.

Format: Your instructor will divide the group into teams of four to six people. (These could be previously formed teams or new teams.) Teams should arrange their desks or chairs so that they can interact and communicate well with each other.

Procedure: Consider that your team is an engineering design team assigned to work out this difficult problem whose solution would be the key to getting a major purchase contract from a large influential buyer. The task seems simple, but working out such tasks (at different levels of complexity) can be very important to organizations.

1. It is important for your team to work together to develop your solution.

2. Look at the following figure. Your task is to create a single square by making only two straight-line cuts and then reassembling the pieces so that all material is used in the final product.

The Figure:

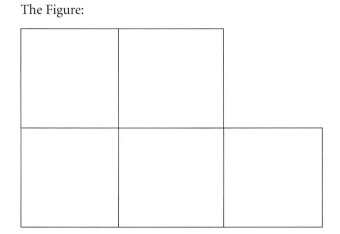

3. It might be easier to trace the design onto stiff paper or cardboard to facilitate working with the pieces.

4. Your instructor has access to the correct answer key from the *Instructor's Resource Manual*.

Follow-up Questions

1. How did the other members of your team help or hinder your ability to solve the problem?

2. Did your team have a leader throughout the exercise? If so, can you identify why that person emerged as the leader?

3. What type of training would have helped your team solve the problem better or faster?

Reference: From John W. Newstrom and Edward E. Scannell, *Games Trainers Play: Experiential Learning Exercises*, p. 259. Copyright © 1980 by McGraw-Hill Companies. Reprinted with permission of McGraw-Hill Companies, Inc.

Building Managerial Skills

Exercise Overview: Groups and teams are becoming ever more important in organizations. This exercise will allow you to practice your conceptual skills as they apply to work teams in organizations.

Exercise Background: A variety of highly effective groups exists outside the boundaries of typical business organizations. For example, each of the following represents a team:

1. A basketball team

2. An elite military squadron

3. A government policy group such as the presidential cabinet

4. A student planning committee

Exercise Task

1. Identify an example of a real team, such as the ones just listed. Choose a team (1) that is not part of a normal business and (2) that you can argue is highly effective.

2. Determine the reasons for the team's effectiveness.

3. Determine how a manager could learn from this particular team and use its success determinants in a business setting.

Organizational Behavior Case for Discussion

The Rainmakers

Modern corporate CEOs are asked to fulfill two distinct roles. On one hand, they must be decisive and bold, willing to take risks. On the other hand, they are expected to be good team players, surrounding themselves with strong subordinates and comfortable with consensus building. If a CEO is too much of a loner, capable subordinates may leave the firm, or worse. For example, former Disney CEO Michael Eisner refused to promote his long-term colleague

Jeffrey Katzenberg, who left to co-found Disney rival Dreamworks. In the same way, Sanford Weill, CEO of Citigroup, felt threatened by and fired his protégé Jamie Dimon. Dimon went on to head Bank One, taking a team of five top Citigroup managers with him.

Four years later, Bank One merged with J.P. Morgan Chase bank. At the time, J.P. Morgan Chase was still suffering from the effects of the 2000 merger between J.P. Morgan and Chase banks. In that merger, J.P. Morgan CEO Bill Harrison asked most of the Chase executives to step down, leaving J.P. Morgan personnel in charge of the new firm.

In contrast, in the merger between J.P. Morgan Chase and Bank One, Bank One personnel remained in many key roles, including the five executives Dimon lured from Citigroup. Dimon himself was named president and COO. Unlike autocratic Weill, Dimon is seen as both a risk taker and a team player. Dimon, a rainmaker himself, is expected to attract a top group of rainmakers to the merged firm. (For bankers, a rainmaker is an employee who is very successful at attracting new, wealthy clients for his or her firm.)

The merged firm is the second-largest bank in the United States, behind #1 Citigroup. "We do hope to give Citi a little bit of a run for its money," says Dimon. Dimon has proven that he can handle the delicate task of merging employees from different companies into an effective workforce and integrating functions, brands, systems, and people across all of the giant bank's businesses. He improved operations so much that a $544 million loss in 2000 became a $3.4 billion profit in 2003.

Harrison is giving Dimon his full support. In a speech introducing Dimon to J.P. Morgan Chase personnel, Harrison showed a film clip of the Detroit Pistons and said, "A team beats superstars every time." When the two leaders appear in public, they are often compared to a vaudeville team, finishing each other's sentences and playing pranks. The close cooperation on stage is an important symbol of cooperation for the merged firm's employees.

Sarah E. Nash, vice chairman of investment banking at J.P. Morgan Chase, agrees that aggressive individuals are no longer the primary determinant of success on Wall Street. "We don't want movie stars anymore," Nash says. She

> **"A team beats superstars every time."**
> BILL HARRISON, CEO, J.P. MORGAN CHASE

thinks that her firm could go further in creating a team identity, claiming that she can still recognize which bank an employee came from, based on appearance and work style. She states, "[Following a merger], the toughest thing to do is get people to . . . let go of their heritage."

The emphasis on teamwork isn't just for show either. The idea gets support all up and down the organizational hierarchy, from top managers to entry-level workers. One analyst notes, "There's very little petty office politics. It's generally very inclusive and team-oriented. There's not much backstabbing. Managing directors and vice presidents are concerned about developing junior people."

Dimon has been named as successor to Harrison and is scheduled to assume the top spot in 2006. To be sure, there are challenges ahead. Dimon has committed to finding $2.2 billion in cost savings, which can only be the result of significant change. Teamwork, however, may be just the thing to bring a little more rain to J.P. Morgan Chase. Then watch out, Weill!

Case Questions

1. Describe the steps in the process that J.P. Morgan Chase uses as it creates teams, blending its own employees and those from the banks it has acquired.

2. What benefits would J.P. Morgan Chase gain by using blended teams? What difficulties will it have to overcome as it goes through the process of team formation?

3. In your opinion, what is the likely performance of the blended teams at J.P. Morgan Chase? Describe how team performance might change over time.

References: "About J.P. Morgan Chase," "Strengthening Communities," J.P. Morgan Chase website, www.jpmorganchase.com on April 16, 2005; Bill Saporito, "Sandy's Story," *Time*, March 24, 2003, www.time.com on April 16, 2005; "Secrets to Success on Wall Street: Teamwork, Not Ego," *Knowledge@Wharton*, knowledge.wharton.upenn.edu on April 16, 2005; Landon Thomas Jr., "The Yin, the Yang, and the Deal," *New York Times*, June 27, 2004, pp. BU 1, 4 (quotation); Emily Thornton and Joseph Weber, "A Made-to-Order Banking Megamerger," *Business Week*, January 26, 2004, www.businessweek.com on April 16, 2005.

TEST PREPPER

You have read the chapter and studied the key terms. Think you're ready to ace the exam? Take this sample test to gauge your comprehension of chapter material and check your answers at the back of the book. Want more test questions? Take the ACE quizzes found on the student website: http://college.hmco.com/business/students/ (select Griffin/Moorhead, Organizational Behavior, 8e from the Management menu).

T   F   1. The use of teams is a recent innovation in the management process.

T   F   2. The members of teams hold themselves mutually accountable for results.

T   F   3. Team bonus plans are similar to gain-sharing plans, except that the unit of performance and pay is the team, not the entire organization.

T   F   4. Product development teams are combinations of work teams and problem-solving teams.

T   F   5. Once the decision is made to change to a team-based organization, managers should implement the change immediately.

T   F   6. A period of frustration and confusion is likely to occur within the first year of a change to a team-based organization.

T   F   7. An organization that has begun implementing teams should be ready for the possibility that things will get worse before they get better.

8. One basic difference between a group and a team is
   a. a group is usually larger.
   b. team members are committed to a common goal.
   c. group members have complementary skills.
   d. team members are more concerned with individual performance.
   e. a team is evaluated as a whole.

9. In traditional work groups, the supervisor directly controls the daily activities. In teams, who performs this function?
   a. Customers
   b. Senior managers
   c. The team itself
   d. Unaffiliated supervisors
   e. Management trainees

10. Which of the following is not a benefit that may result from the use of teams?
    a. Reduced frustration for managers in their new roles
    b. Enhanced performance, such as increased output
    c. Employee benefits and a sense of self-control
    d. Reduced costs
    e. Organizational enhancements and eliminated bureaucracy

11. Kim is a member of a permanent team that does the daily work of her department. Kim is a member of a
    a. management team.
    b. problem-solving team.
    c. development team.
    d. quality circle.
    e. work team.

12. The primary job of a management team is to
    a. supervise and control the work of other teams.
    b. attack specific problems in the workplace.
    c. make recommendations for others to implement.
    d. coach and counsel other teams to be self-managing.
    e. determine improvements to the work process.

13. The person leading the change to a team-based organization needs all of the following, except
    a. to believe that employees want to be responsible for their own work.
    b. to demonstrate the team philosophy.
    c. to display a strong authoritarian personality.
    d. to articulate a coherent vision of the team environment.
    e. to have the creativity and authority to overcome obstacles.

14. Performance by teams in the start-up phase is typically
    a. decreased because of confusion.
    b. increased because of initial enthusiasm.
    c. decreased because of resistance.
    d. increased because of tightly formed teams.
    e. Performance by teams in the start-up phase usually remains at about the same level.

15. Jennifer is interested in changing her company to a team-based organization. Where should Jennifer start to implement this change?
    a. At the top of the organization
    b. At the bottom of the organization
    c. At middle levels in the organization
    d. Simultaneously at all levels in the organization
    e. As long as Jennifer can create a "critical mass" of interest, it doesn't matter where she begins the implementation.

CHAPTER 11

Communication in Organizations

- Discuss the nature of communication in organizations.
- Identify and describe the primary methods of communication.
- Describe the communication process.
- Note how information technology affects communication.
- Identify and discuss the basic kinds of communication networks.
- Discuss how communication can be managed in organizations.

Chapter Outline

The Nature of Communication in Organizations

Methods of Communication

The Communication Process

Electronic Information Processing and Telecommunications

Communication Networks

Managing Communication

eBay Manages Communication Challenges

eBay, the online auction company, faces many challenges. Although providing an online space for buyers and sellers to exchange information might sound simple, the communication demands of such a business are staggering.

There are 100 million registered members of eBay worldwide. 430,000 earn their primary living as eBay sellers. If eBay sellers constituted a single organization, the firm would be the sixth-largest American employer, after the civil service, Wal-Mart, McDonald's, the military, and the post office. Communication is essential for eBay, both between individuals and between individuals and the firm.

eBay's online system allows sellers to post descriptive text and images, name prices, and set terms. The system provides a mechanism for online auctioning, including monitoring the time limit, number of bids, reserve price, and other auction details. Buyers search items by categories, view items, and submit bids.

The system also provides many additional capabilities. One of the most important features of eBay is the feedback feature. Every eBay member has an online profile that reports comments and scores from previous transactions. According to the eBay website, "Learning to trust a member of the community has a lot to do with what their past customers or sellers have to say!" eBay founder Pierre Omidyar believes that feedback provides a policing mechanism that enhances the organization's sense of community. He says, "Some people are dishonest. Or deceptive . . . But here, those people can't hide. We'll drive them away . . . Make your complaints in the open. Better yet, give your praise in the open . . . Deal with others the way you would have them deal with you." By April of 2005, eBay members had posted 3 billion feedback messages.

To further encourage communication, eBay creates online discussion boards for item categories such as dolls or motorcycles and help topics. A more sophisticated form of community discussion tool is the group—hundreds of classifications based on regions, items, or interests. The group allows for online discussion and adds capabilities for taking opinion polls, posting photos, and setting up online "meetings."

eBay doesn't neglect more traditional forms of online communication, either. The company sponsors chat rooms, frequently asked questions (FAQs) lists, and an online and email newsletter. Online town hall meetings with eBay managers are conducted through streaming audio and allow members to submit questions in advance or during the event. Workshops on various topics also rely on streaming audio.

eBay's communication systems, based on trust and the voluntary involvement of millions of people, do not always work smoothly. Feedback ratings can be maliciously manipulated or just neglected, reducing the system's effectiveness. Frequent users complain that the firm's democratic system fails to provide extra communication channels for the firm's most profitable customers. Yet some things clearly work—the hardware supporting millions of daily transactions crashes for just three seconds per month, on average.

eBay's online communication system is necessary for the firm's survival. With that in mind, the company works hard to ensure that the system performs effectively. See the boxed insert on page 290 titled *eBay and . . . Globalization* for more about eBay's international communication challenges.

References: "Community," "Founders Letter," "The Company," eBay website, www.ebay.com on April 17, 2005 (quotation); Michelle Conlin, "The eBay Way," *Business Week,* November 29, 2004, www.businessweek.com on February 14, 2005; Rob Hof, "Meet eBay's Auctioneer-in-Chief," *Business Week,* May 29, 2003, www.businessweek.com on April 17, 2005; Sarah Lacy, "Getting with the Program on eBay," *Business Week,* November 1, 2004, www.businessweek.com on February 14, 2005; Kate Murphy, "eBay Merchants Trust Their Eyes, and the Bubble Wrap," *New York Times,* October 24, 2004, p. BU 7; Amey Stone, "Well Spent," *Business Week,* February 9, 2005, www.businessweek.com on April 17, 2005.

Communication is something that most of us take for granted—we have been communicating for so long that we really pay little attention to the actual process. Even at work, we often focus primarily on doing our jobs and pay little attention to how we communicate about those jobs. However, since methods of communication play such a pervasive role in affecting behavior in organizations and represent another vital underpinning of interpersonal processes, we need to pay more attention to the processes that effectively link what we do to others in the organization.

In this chapter, we focus on interpersonal communication and information processing. First, we discuss the importance of communication in organizations and some important aspects of international communication. Next, we describe the methods of organizational communication and examine the basic communication process. Then we examine the potential effects of computerized information technology and telecommunications. Next, we explore the development of communication networks in organizations. Finally, we discuss several common problems of organizational communication and methods of managing communication.

The Nature of Communication in Organizations

Communication is the social process in which two or more parties exchange information and share meaning.

Communication is the social process in which two or more parties exchange information and share meaning. Communication has been studied from many perspectives. In this section, we provide an overview of the complex and dynamic communication process and discuss some important issues relating to international communication in organizations.

The Purposes of Communication in Organizations

Communication among individuals and groups is vital in all organizations. Some of the purposes of organizational communication are shown in Figure 11.1. The primary purpose is to achieve coordinated action.[1] Just as the human nervous system responds to stimuli and coordinates responses by sending messages to the various parts of the body, communication coordinates the actions of the parts of an organization. Without communication, an organization would be merely a collection of individual workers doing separate tasks. Organizational action would lack coordination and would be oriented toward individual rather than organizational goals.

A second purpose of communication is information sharing. The most important information relates to organizational goals, which give members a sense of purpose and direction. Another information-sharing function of communication is to give

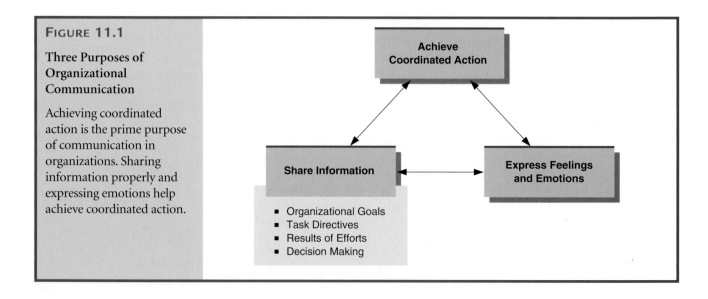

FIGURE 11.1

Three Purposes of Organizational Communication

Achieving coordinated action is the prime purpose of communication in organizations. Sharing information properly and expressing emotions help achieve coordinated action.

Achieve Coordinated Action

Share Information
- Organizational Goals
- Task Directives
- Results of Efforts
- Decision Making

Express Feelings and Emotions

specific task directions to individuals. Whereas information on organizational goals gives employees a sense of how their activities fit into the overall picture, task communication tells them what their job duties are and are not. Employees must also receive information on the results of their efforts, as in performance appraisals.

Communication is essential to the decision-making process as well, as we discuss in Chapter 8. Information and information sharing are needed to define problems, generate and evaluate alternatives, implement decisions, and control and evaluate results. Finally, communication expresses feelings and emotions. Organizational communication is far from merely a collection of facts and figures. People in organizations, like people anywhere else, often need to communicate emotions such as happiness, anger, displeasure, confidence, and fear.

Communication Across Cultures

Communication is an element of interpersonal relations that obviously is affected by the international environment, partly because of language issues and partly because of coordination issues.

Language Differences in languages are compounded by the fact that the same word can mean different things in different cultures. For example, "Coca-Cola" meant "bite the head of a dead tadpole" in the first Chinese characters that were used in its advertising. The company had to quickly find other Chinese characters to use in advertising in China. Chevrolet once tried to export a line of cars to Latin America that it called the Nova in the United States, but then found that "no va" means "doesn't go" in Spanish—not the best name for an automobile!

Elements of nonverbal communication also vary across cultures. Colors and body language can convey quite a different message in one culture than in another. For example, the American sign for "OK" (making a loop with thumb and first finger) is

Understanding communication dynamics across cultures is a challenging but important business necessity. Tyson Foods, for instance, is trying to learn more about the kinds of products and product packaging that work best in different cultures. During a recent agricultural conference in Havana, Cuba, Tyson sent a sales representative out to a local market to observe how consumers assessed and made purchase decisions about poultry products.

eBay Communicates with the World

eBay communicates globally through 26 international websites, including countries from the Americas, Asia, and Europe. About $1.4 billion, or 15 percent of the firm's total business, comes from outside of the United States.

International eBay websites all look the same. On each site, the navigation toolbar lists categories of items. Categories are similar, including items such as computers, autos, and jewelry. In 2002, eBay purchased PayPal, a company that provides a secure online payment method. PayPal enables members from around the world to trade with each other, managing the currency translation for both buyers and sellers.

In other aspects, the websites are tailored to local communication needs—Bollywood memorabilia on eBay India, for example. While sites for Italy, Korea, and Argentina are translated into their country's primary language, sites for India, the Philippines, and Sweden use English. Each site lists prices in the local currency.

eBay is aggressively expanding overseas but is not equally successful everywhere. In Japan, for example, eBay entered the online auction business after competitors had established strong market positions, charged higher fees, and failed to establish a relationship with users. "When we arrived last year, the 800-pound gorilla was already positioned," says eBay Japan president Merle Okawara. The company ceased Japanese operations in 2003.

One of the difficulties may lie in the eBay top management team. The heads of international eBay sites are often local managers. Yet the San Jose, California, headquarters team, responsible for overall company strategy and operations, has only one international member, Rajiv Dutta, the Chief Financial Officer.

As the online auction industry becomes more profitable, it will attract stronger competitors. Focusing on communication with diverse international users can lead eBay to increased success and competitive victory.

> *"When we arrived last year, the 800-pound gorilla was already positioned."*
>
> MERLE OKAWARA, PRESIDENT, EBAY JAPAN

References: "eBay Profits Miss the Mark," *CNN Money,* January 19, 2005, money.cnn.com on April 20, 2005; "Global Trade," "Welcome to eBay," eBay website, www.ebay.com on April 20, 2005; Ken Belson, "How Yahoo! Japan Beat eBay at Its Own Game," *Business Week,* June 4, 2001, www.businessweek.com on April 20, 2005 (quotation); Bambi Francisco, "All Eyes on eBay," *Market Watch,* www.marketwatch.com on April 20, 2005; Troy Wolverton, "eBay Readies Execs for Merger," *C/Net,* September 5, 2002, news.com on April 20, 2005.

considered rude in Spain and vulgar in Brazil. Managers should be forewarned that they can take nothing for granted in dealing with people from other cultures. They must take the time to become as fully acquainted as possible with the verbal and nonverbal languages of a culture. And indeed, new forms of communication technology such as email are actually changing language itself.

Coordination   International communication is closely related to issues of coordination. For example, an American manager who wants to speak with his or her counterpart in Hong Kong, Singapore, Rome, or London must contend not only with language differences but also with a time difference of many hours. When the American manager needs to talk on the telephone, the Hong Kong executive may be home asleep. Consequently, organizations are employing increasingly innovative methods for coordinating their activities in scattered parts of the globe. Merrill Lynch, for example, has its own satellite-based telephone network to monitor and participate in the worldwide money and financial markets.[2] The *eBay and . . . Globalization* box discusses some of eBay's successes—and failures—regarding communication across cultures.

Methods of Communication

The three primary methods of communicating in organizations are written, oral, and nonverbal. Often the methods are combined. Considerations that affect the choice of method include the audience (whether it is physically present), the nature of the message (its urgency or secrecy), and the costs of transmission. Figure 11.2 shows various forms each method can take.

Written Communication

Organizations typically produce a great deal of written communication of many kinds. A letter is a formal means of communicating with an individual, generally someone outside the organization. Probably the most common form of written communication in organizations is the office memorandum, or memo. Memos usually are addressed to a person or group inside the organization. They tend to deal with a single topic and are more impersonal (as they often are destined to reach more than one person) but less formal than letters. Most email is similar to the traditional memo, although it is even less formal.

Other common forms of written communication include reports, manuals, and forms. Reports generally summarize the progress or results of a project and often provide information to be used in decision making. Manuals have various functions in

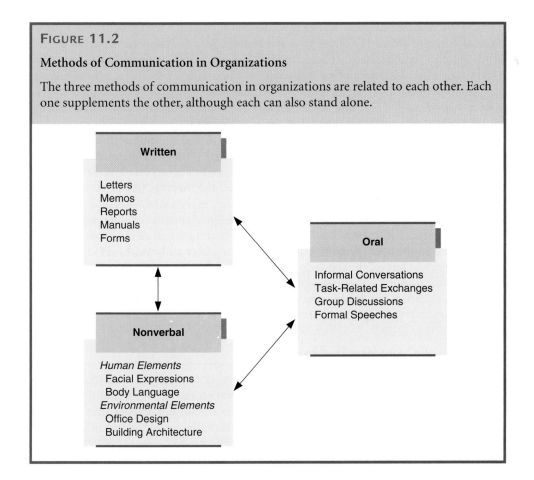

FIGURE 11.2

Methods of Communication in Organizations

The three methods of communication in organizations are related to each other. Each one supplements the other, although each can also stand alone.

Written
Letters
Memos
Reports
Manuals
Forms

Oral
Informal Conversations
Task-Related Exchanges
Group Discussions
Formal Speeches

Nonverbal
Human Elements
Facial Expressions
Body Language
Environmental Elements
Office Design
Building Architecture

organizations. Instruction manuals tell employees how to operate machines; policy and procedures manuals inform them of organizational rules; operations manuals describe how to perform tasks and respond to work-related problems. Forms are standardized documents on which to report information. As such, they represent attempts to make communication more efficient and information more accessible. A performance appraisal form is an example. We should also note that although many of these forms of written communication have historically been used in a paper-based environment, they are increasingly being put on websites and intranets in many larger companies today.

Oral Communication

The most prevalent form of organizational communication is oral. Oral communication takes place everywhere—in informal conversations, in the process of doing work, in meetings of groups and task forces, and in formal speeches and presentations. Recent studies identified oral communication skills as the number one criterion for hiring new college graduates.[3] Business school leaders have also been urged by industry to develop better communication skills in their graduates.[4] Even in Europe, employers have complained that the number one problem with current graduates is the lack of oral communication skills, citing cultural factors and changes in the educational process as primary causes.[5]

Oral forms of communication are particularly powerful because they include not only speakers' words but also their changes in tone, pitch, speed, and volume. As listeners, people use all of these cues to understand oral messages. Try this example with a friend or work colleague. Say this sentence several times, each time placing the emphasis on a different word: "The boss gave Joe a raise." See how the meaning changes depending on the emphasis! Moreover, receivers interpret oral messages in the context of previous communications and, perhaps, the reactions of other receivers. (Try saying another sentence before saying the phrase about the boss—such as "Joe is so lazy" or "Joe is such a good worker.") Quite often the top management of an organization sets the tone for oral communication throughout the organization.

Voicemail has all the characteristics of traditional verbal communication except that there is no feedback. The sender just leaves a message on the machine or network with no feedback or confirmation that the message was, or will be, received. With no confirmation, the sender does not know for sure whether the message will be received as he or she intended it. Therefore, it may be wise for the receiver of a voicemail to quickly leave a message on the sender's voicemail acknowledging that the original message was received. But then the "great voicemail phone tag" is at its worst! Also, the receiver then has an excuse in the event that something goes wrong later and can always say that a return message was left on the sender's voicemail! The receiver could also pass the blame by saying that no such voice message was received. The lack of confirmation, or two-way communication, can lead to several problems, as will be discussed in later sections of this chapter.

Nonverbal Communication

Nonverbal communication includes all the elements associated with human communication that are not expressed orally or in writing. Sometimes nonverbal communication conveys more meaning than words do. Human elements of nonverbal communication include facial expressions and physical movements, both conscious and unconscious. Facial expressions have been categorized as (1) interest-excitement, (2) enjoyment-joy, (3) surprise-startle, (4) distress-anguish, (5) fear-terror, (6) shame-humiliation,

(7) contempt-disgust, and (8) anger-rage.[6] The eyes are the most expressive component of the face.

Physical movements and "body language" are also highly expressive human elements. Body language includes both actual movement and body positions during communication. The handshake is a common form of body language. Other examples include making eye contact, which expresses a willingness to communicate; sitting on the edge of a chair, which may indicate nervousness or anxiety; and sitting back with arms folded, which may convey an unwillingness to continue the discussion.

Environmental elements such as buildings, office space, and furniture can also convey messages. A spacious office, expensive draperies, plush carpeting, and elegant furniture can combine to remind employees or visitors that they are in the office of the president and CEO of the firm. On the other hand, the small metal desk set in the middle of the shop floor accurately communicates the organizational rank of a first-line supervisor. Thus, office arrangements convey status, power, and prestige and create an atmosphere for doing business. The physical setting can also be instrumental in the development of communication networks because a centrally located person can more easily control the flow of task-related information.

The Communication Process

Communication is a social process in which two or more parties exchange information and share meaning. The process is social because it involves two or more people. It is a two-way process and takes place over time rather than instantaneously. The communication process illustrated in Figure 11.3 shows a loop between the source and the receiver.[7] Note the importance of the feedback portion of the loop; upon receiving the message, the receiver responds with a message to the source to verify the communication. Each element of the basic communication process is important. If one part is faulty, the message may not be communicated as it was intended. A simple organizational example might be when a manager attempts to give direction to an employee regarding the order in which to perform two tasks. (We refer to this example again in later discussions.) The manager wants to send a message and have the employee understand precisely the meaning she intends. Each part of the communication process is described next.

Source

The **source** is the individual, group, or organization interested in communicating something to another party. In group or organizational communication, an individual may send the message on behalf of the organization. The source is responsible for preparing the message, encoding it, and entering it into the transmission medium. In some cases, the receiver chooses the source of information, as when a decision maker seeks information from trusted and knowledgeable individuals.[8] The source in organizational communication is often the manager giving directions to employees.

The **source** is the individual, group, or organization interested in communicating something to another party.

Encoding

Encoding is the process by which the message is translated from an idea or thought into symbols that can be transmitted. The symbols may be words, numbers, pictures, sounds, or physical gestures and movements. In a simple example, the manager may use words in English as the symbols, usually spoken or written. The source must encode the message in symbols that the receiver can decode properly; that is, the source

Encoding is the process by which the message is translated from an idea or thought into transmittable symbols.

FIGURE **11.3**

The Communication Process

The communication process is a loop that connects the sender and the receiver and operates in both directions. Communication is not complete until the original sender knows that the receiver understands the message.

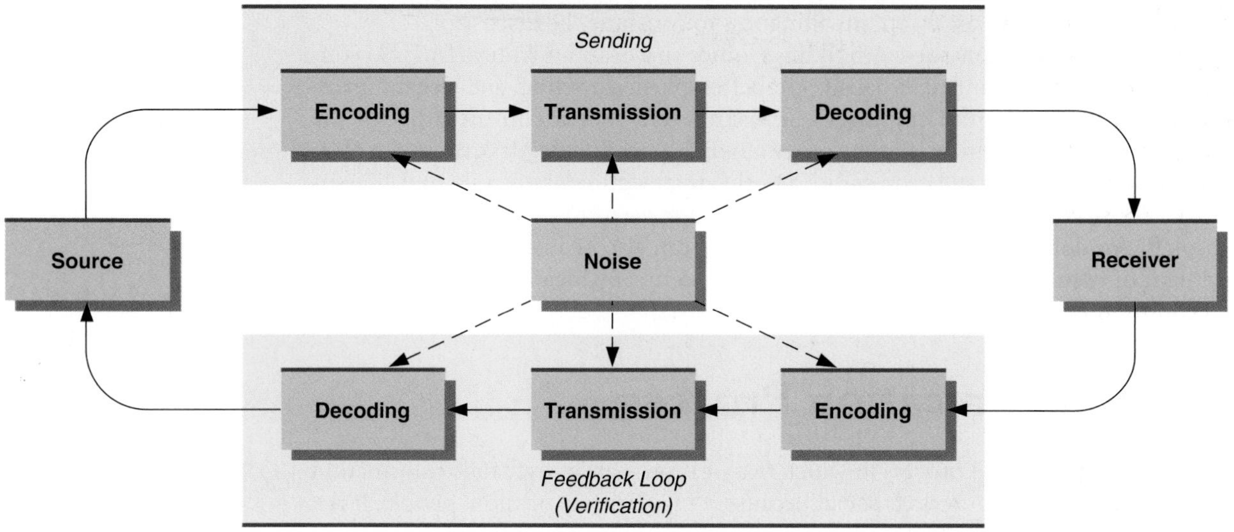

and the receiver must attach the same meaning to the symbols. When we use the symbols of a common language, we assume those symbols have the same meaning to everyone who uses them. However, the inherent ambiguity of symbol systems can lead to decoding errors. In verbal communication, for example, some words have different meanings for different people. Parents and children often use the same word, but the differences in their positions and ages may lead them to interpret words quite differently. If a manager speaks only Spanish and an employee speaks only German, the message is unlikely to be understood. The meanings of words used by the sender may differ depending on the nonverbal cues, such as facial expression, that the sender transmits along with them.

Transmission

Transmission is the process through which the symbols that represent the message are sent to the receiver.

The **medium** is the channel, or path, through which the message is transmitted.

Transmission is the process through which the symbols that carry the message are sent to the receiver. The **medium** is the channel, or path, of transmission. The medium for face-to-face conversation is sound waves. The same conversation conducted over the telephone involves not only sound waves but also electrical impulses and the lines that connect the two phones. To tell the employee in what order to perform tasks, the manager could tell the employee face-to-face or use the telephone, a memo, email, or voicemail.

Communications media range from interpersonal media, such as talking or touching, to mass media, such as newspapers, magazines, or television broadcasts. Different media have different capacities for carrying information. For example, a face-to-face conversation generally has more carrying capacity than a letter because it allows the transmission of more than just words. In addition, the medium can help determine the effect the message has on the receiver. Calling a prospective client on the telephone to make a business proposal is a more personal approach than sending a letter and is likely to elicit a different response. It is important that a sender choose the medium that is most likely to correspond to the type of message that needs to be sent and understood.

Decoding

Decoding is the process by which the receiver of the message interprets its meaning. The receiver uses knowledge and experience to interpret the symbols of the message; in some situations, he or she may consult an authority such as a dictionary or a code book. Up to this point, the receiver has been relatively inactive, but the receiver becomes more active in the decoding phase. The meaning the receiver attaches to the symbols may be the same as or different from the meaning intended by the source. If the meanings differ, of course, communication breaks down, and misunderstanding is likely. In our example, if the employee does not understand the language or a particular word, then the employee will not comprehend the same meaning as the sender (manager) and may do the tasks in the wrong order or not do them at all.

> **Decoding** is the process by which the receiver of the message interprets its meaning.

Receiver

The **receiver** of the message may be an individual, a group, an organization, or an individual acting as the representative of a group. The receiver decides whether to decode the message, whether to make an effort to understand it, and whether to respond. Moreover, the intended receiver may not get the message at all, whereas an unintended receiver may, depending on the medium and the symbols used by the source and the attention level of potential receivers. An employee may share the same language (know the symbols) used by the manager but may not want to get the sender's meaning.

> The **receiver** is the individual, group, or organization that perceives the encoded symbols; the receiver may or may not decode them to try to understand the intended message.

The key skill for proper reception of the message is good listening. The receiver may not concentrate on the sender, the message, or the medium such that the message is lost. Listening is an active process that requires as much concentration and effort from the receiver as sending the message does for the sender. The expression of emotions by the sender and receiver enters into the communication process at several points. First, the emotions may be part of the message, entering into the encoding process. For example, if the manager's directions are encoded with a sense of emotional urgency—for example, if they are given with a high-pitched or loud voice—the employee may move quickly to follow the directions. However, if the message is urgent, but the manager's tone of voice is low and does not send urgent signals, employees may not engage in quick action. Second, as the message is decoded, the receiver may let his or her emotions perceive a message different from what the sender intended. Third, emotion-filled feedback from the intended receiver can cause the sender to modify her or his subsequent message.

Feedback

Feedback is the receiver's response to the message. Feedback verifies the message by telling the source whether the receiver received and understood the message. The feedback may be as simple as a phone call from the prospective client expressing interest in the business proposal or as complex as a written brief on a complicated point of law sent from an attorney to a judge. In our example, the employee can respond to the manager's directions by a verbal or written response indicating that he or she does or does not understand the message. Feedback could also be nonverbal, as when, in our example, the employee does not do either task. With typical voicemail, the feedback loop is missing, which can lead to many communication problems.

> **Feedback** is the process in which the receiver returns a message to the sender that indicates receipt of the message.

Information overload can serve as a major source of noise in the communication process. This harried manager, for example, seems overwhelmed with the vast amount of information spread before him. His feelings of stress will no doubt affect his ability to effectively cope with the tasks he needs to accomplish. Unfortunately, advances in electronic communication seem likely to make this problem even worse in the future.

Noise

Noise is any disturbance in the communication process that interferes with or distorts communication.

Channel noise is a disturbance in communication that is primarily a function of the medium.

Noise is any disturbance in the communication process that interferes with or distorts communication. Noise can be introduced at virtually any point in the communication process. The principal type, called **channel noise**, is associated with the medium.[9] Radio static and "ghost" images on television are examples of channel noise, as is an email virus. When noise interferes in the encoding and decoding processes, poor encoding and decoding can result. Emotions that interfere with an intended communication may also be considered a type of noise. An employee may not hear the directions given by the manager owing to noisy machinery on the shop floor or competing input from other people.

Effective communication occurs when information or meaning has been shared by at least two people. Therefore, communication must include the response from the receiver back to the sender. The sender cannot know if the message has been conveyed as intended if there is no feedback from the receiver, as when we leave voicemail. Both parties are responsible for the effectiveness of the communication. The evolution of new technology in recent years presents novel problems in ensuring that communications work as sender and receiver expect them to.

Electronic Information Processing and Telecommunications

Changes in the workplace are occurring at an astonishing rate. Many innovations are based on new technologies—computerized information processing systems, new types of telecommunication systems, the Internet, organizational intranets and extranets, and various combinations of these technologies. Experts have estimated that performance of new information technology (at the same cost) doubles every eighteen months.[10] Managers can now send and receive memos and other documents to and from one person or a group scattered around the world from their computers using the Internet, and they can do so in their cars or via their notebook computers and cellular phones on the commuter train. Wireless devices such as PDAs and so-called wi-fi hotspots are making these activities even more commonplace. Indeed, many employees are now telecommuting from home rather than going to the office every day. And whole new industries are developing around information storage, transmission, and retrieval that were not even dreamed of a few years ago.

The "office of the future" is here, but it just may not be in a typical office building. Virtually every office now has a facsimile (fax) machine, a copier, and personal computers, most of them linked into a single integrated system and to numerous databases and electronic mail systems. Automobile companies advertise that their cars and trucks have equipment for your cellular telephone, computer, and fax machine. The electronic office links managers, clerical employees, professional workers, sales personnel, and often suppliers and customers as well in a worldwide communication network that uses a combination of computerized data storage, retrieval, and transmission systems.

In fact, the computer-integrated organization is becoming commonplace. Ingersol Milling Machine of Rockford, Illinois, boasts a totally computer-integrated operation in which all major functions—sales, marketing, finance, distribution, and manufacturing—exchange operating information quickly and continuously via computers. For example, product designers can send specifications directly to machines on the factory floor, and accounting personnel receive online information about sales, purchases, and prices instantaneously. The computer system parallels and greatly speeds up the entire process.

Computers are facilitating the increase in telecommuting across the United States and reducing the number of trips people make to the office to get work done. Almost ten years ago IBM provided many of its employees with notebook computers and told them not to come to the office but instead to use the computers to do the work out in the field and send it in electronically.[11] Other companies, such as Motorola and AT&T, have also encouraged such telecommuting by employees. Employees report increased productivity, less fatigue caused by commuting, reduced commuting expenses, and increased personal freedom. In addition, telecommuting may reduce air pollution and overcrowding. Some employees have reported, however, that they miss the social interaction of the office. Some managers have also expressed concerns about the quantity and quality of the work telecommuting employees do when away from the office.

Research conducted among office workers using a new electronic office system indicated that attitudes toward the system were generally favorable. On the other hand, reduction of face-to-face meetings may depersonalize the office. Some observers are also concerned that companies are installing electronic systems with little consideration for the social structures of the office. As departments adopt computerized information systems, the activities of work groups throughout the organization are likely to become more interdependent, a situation that may alter power relationships among the groups. Most employees quickly learn the system of power, politics, authority, and responsibility in the office. A radical change in work and personal relationships caused by new office technology may disrupt normal ways of accomplishing tasks, thereby reducing productivity. Other potential problems include information overload, loss of records in a "paperless" office, and the dehumanizing consequences of using electronic equipment. In effect, new information processing and transmission technologies mean new media, symbols, message transmission methods, and networks for organizational communication.

The real increases in organizational productivity due to information technology may come from the ability to communicate in new and different ways rather than from simply speeding up existing communication patterns. For example, to remain competitive in a very challenging global marketplace, companies will need to be able

While electronic communication technology may be dysfunctional in some cases, it can also help promote new methods of working, such as telecommuting. Take Carolina Amero, for instance. She works for BellSouth in Atlanta, Georgia. Rather than making the one-hour commute to and from work each day, she works from her home office two or three days a week. This arrangement helps her be more productive and to simultaneously better balance some of the demands of work and home.

to generate, disseminate, and implement new ideas more effectively. In effect, organizations will become "knowledge-based" learning organizations that are continually generating new ideas to improve themselves. This can only occur when expert knowledge is communicated and available throughout the organization.

One of these new ways of communicating is idea sharing, or knowledge sharing, by sharing information on what practices work best. A computer-based system is necessary to store, organize, and then make available to others the best practices from throughout the company.[12] For example, Eli Lilly, a large pharmaceutical company, has developed a company-wide intranet for all of its sixteen thousand employees. This system makes available internal email, corporate policies, and directories and enables information sharing throughout the organization.[13] Electronic information technology is, therefore, speeding up existing communication and developing new types of organizational communication processes with potential new benefits and problems for managers.

Communication Networks

Communication links individuals and groups in a social system. Initially, task-related communication links develop in an organization so that employees can get the information they need to do their jobs and coordinate their work with that of others in the system. Over a long period, these communication relationships become a sophisticated social system composed of both small-group communication networks and a larger organizational network. These networks structure both the flow and the content of communication and support the organizational structure.[14] The pattern and content of communication also support the culture, beliefs, and value systems that enable the organization to operate. The *Family-Run Businesses and . . . Diversity* box previews the role of communication networks in family-owned businesses.

Family-Run Businesses and . . .   **DIVERSITY**

Minority Family Businesses and Communication

Communication in family-owned businesses presents opportunities and challenges. Yet family businesses owned by African American, Asian, and Hispanic families offer unique communication patterns and complications.

According to professors Young-Ho Nam and James I. Herbert, Korean and Chinese ethnic cultures place high value on family and kinship. Therefore, Asian family businesses experience little conflict or disagreement. Communication between family members is clear, even across generations. There is a strong preference for hiring family members, which tends to reduce conflict and enhance communication. Most Korean and Chinese families do not emphasize the importance of passing the business on to their children. Rather, many hope that their children will have very different careers. This cultural value is supported by the traditional Korean saying, "Inherited wealth is difficult to transfer through three generations."

Many of the values shared by Asian families are also present in African American and Hispanic families. Family is an important value and most employees are family members. There are some differences too. For example, there is less emphasis on communications that increase family harmony and more tolerance for challenging or creative statements. Unlike many Asian families, African American and Hispanic families often intend that the family business be a source of income for many generations.

Communication about succession is therefore a high priority.

Another source of difference is language skills. While Asian and Hispanic family members may find that lack of English communication skills is a barrier to self-employment, African Americans do not.

Family communication skills are vitally important to the success of a family-owned business. Yet differences in family heritage and values can have significant impact on the way in which families communicate at home and at work. "Communicating in a Family-Run Business," the chapter closing case, describes more issues related to communication in a family firm.

> ### *"Inherited wealth is difficult to transfer through three generations."*
> TRADITIONAL KOREAN SAYING

References: "Competing With the Big Dogs," Making It! Minority Success Stories, March 6, 2005, www.makingittv.com on April 25, 2005; "LuLu's Journey," "LuLu's Philosophy," LuLu's Desserts website, www.lulusdessert.com on April 25, 2005; Young-Ho Nam and James I. Herbert, "Characteristics and Key Success Factors in Family Business: The Case of Korean Immigrant Businesses in Metro-Atlanta," Kennesaw State University website, www.kennesaw.edu on April 25, 2005 (quotation).

Small-Group Networks

To examine interpersonal communication in a small group, we can observe the patterns that emerge as the work of the group proceeds, and information flows from some people in the group to others.[15] Four such patterns are shown in Figure 11.4. The lines identify the communication links most frequently used in the groups.

A **wheel network** is a pattern in which information flows between the person at the end of each spoke and the person in the middle. Those on the ends of the spokes do not directly communicate with each other. The wheel network is a feature of the typical work group, in which the primary communication occurs between the members and the group manager. In a **chain network**, each member communicates with the person above and below, except for the individuals on each end, who communicate with only one person. The chain network is typical of communication in a vertical hierarchy, in which most communication travels up and down the chain of command. Each person in a **circle network** communicates with the people on both sides but not with anyone else. The circle network often is found in task forces and committees. Finally, in an all-channel network, all members communicate with all the other

In a **wheel network**, information flows between the person at the end of each spoke and the person in the middle.

In a **chain network**, each member communicates with the person above and below, except for the individuals on each end, who communicate with only one person.

In a **circle network**, each member communicates with the people on both sides but with no one else.

FIGURE 11.4

Small-Group Communication Networks

These four types of communication networks are the most common in organizations. The lines represent the most frequently used communication links in small groups.

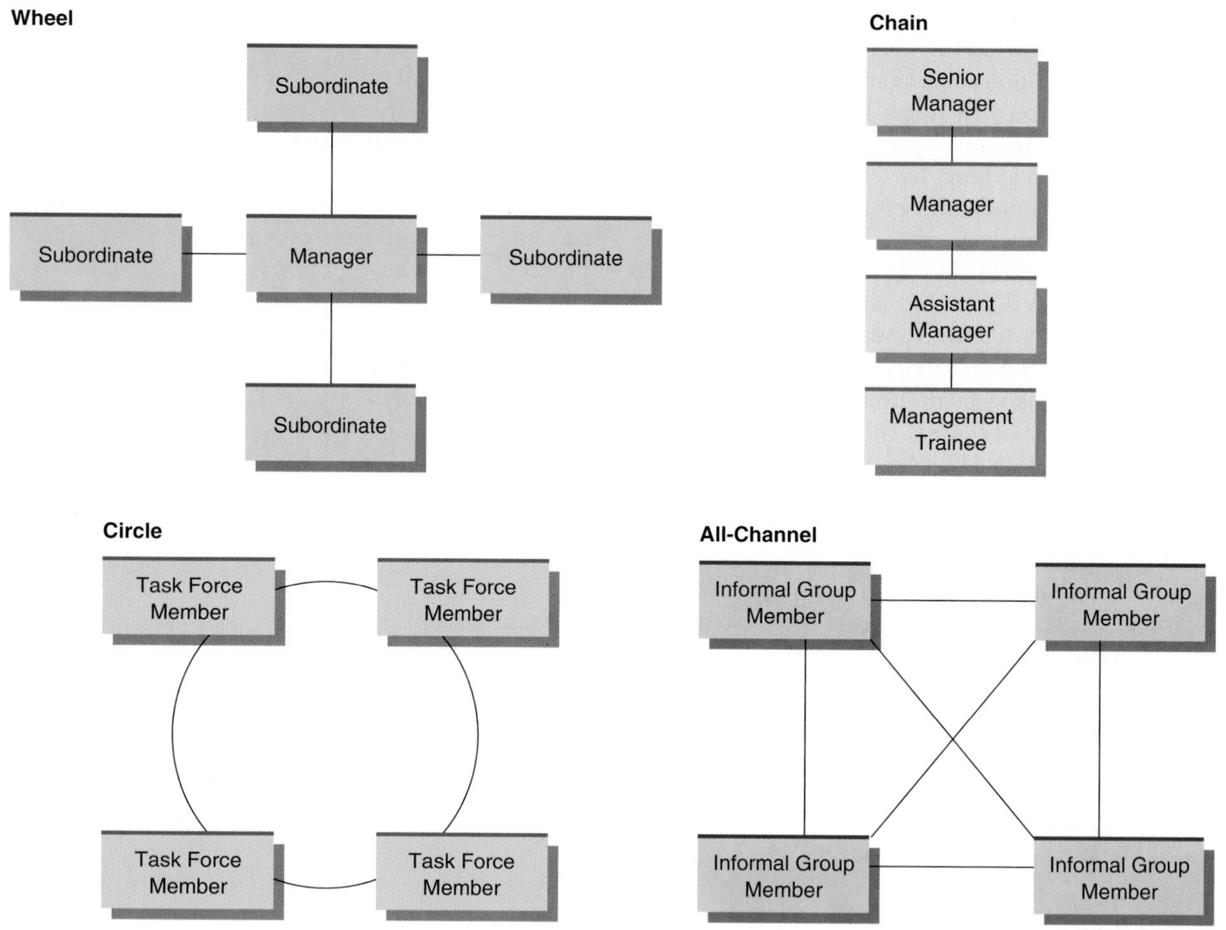

In an **all-channel network**, all members communicate with all other members.

members. The **all-channel network** often is found in informal groups that have no formal structure, leader, or task to accomplish.

Communication may be more easily distorted by noise when much is being communicated or when the communication must travel a great distance. Improvements in electronic communication technology, such as computerized mail systems and intranets, are reducing this effect. A relatively central position gives a person an opportunity to communicate with all of the other members, so a member in a relatively central position can control the information flow and may become a leader of the group. This leadership position is separate and distinct from the formal group structure, although a central person in a group may also emerge as a formal group leader over a long period.

Communication networks form spontaneously and naturally as the interactions among workers continue over time.

Communication networks form spontaneously and naturally as interactions among workers continue. They are rarely permanent since they change as the tasks, interactions, and memberships change. The task is crucial in determining the pattern of the network. If the group's primary task is decision making, an all-channel network may develop to provide the information needed to evaluate all possible alternatives. If, however, the group's task mainly involves the sequential execution of individual tasks, a chain or wheel network is more likely because communication among members may not be important to the completion of the tasks.

The environment (the type of room in which the group works or meets, the seating arrangement, the placement of chairs and tables, the geographical dispersion, and other aspects of the group's setting) can affect the frequency and types of interactions among members. For example, if most members work on the same floor of an office building, the members who work three floors down may be considered outsiders and develop weaker communication ties to the group. They may even form a separate communication network.

Personal factors also influence the development of the communication network. These include technical expertise, openness, speaking ability, and the degree to which members are acquainted with one another. For example, in a group concerned mainly with highly technical problems, the person with the most expertise may dominate the communication flow during a meeting.

The group performance factors that influence the communication network include composition, size, norms, and cohesiveness. For example, group norms in one organization may encourage open communication across different levels and functional units, whereas the norms in another organization may discourage such lateral and diagonal communication. These performance factors are discussed in Chapter 9.

Because the outcome of the group's efforts depends on the coordinated action of its members, the communication network strongly influences group effectiveness. Thus, to develop effective working relationships in the organization, managers need to

Communication networks structure both the flow and the content of communication in organizations. Take Jamie Dimon, for example. He is the CEO of Bank One and is shown here meeting with a group of branch employees in Ohio. The branch employees themselves form various small-group communication networks such as the wheel, the chain, and the circle. But when Mr. Dimon is involved, the networks become more formalized. And he plays the role of gatekeeper by controlling the flow of information in and out of the branch employee networks.

make a special effort to manage the flow of information and the development of communication networks. Managers can, for example, arrange offices and work spaces to foster communication among certain employees. Managers may also attempt to involve members who typically contribute little during discussions by asking them direct questions such as "What do you think, Tom?" or "Maria, tell us how this problem is handled in your district." Methods such as the nominal group technique, discussed in Chapter 9, can also encourage participation.

One other factor that is becoming increasingly more important in the development of communication networks is the advent of electronic groups fostered by electronic distribution lists, chat rooms, discussion boards, and other computer networking systems. This form of communication results in a network of people who may have little or no face-to-face communication but still may be considered a group communication network. For example, your professor is probably a member of an electronic group of other professors who share an interest in the topic of this course. Through the electronic group, they keep up with new ideas in the field.

Organizational Communication Networks

An organization chart shows reporting relationships from the line worker up to the CEO of the firm. The lines of an organization chart may also represent channels of communication through which information flows, yet communication may also follow paths that cross traditional reporting lines. Information moves not only from the top down—from CEO to group members—but also upward from group members to the CEO. In fact, a good flow of information to the CEO is an important determinant of the organization's success.

Several companies have realized that the key to their continuing success was improved internal communication. General Motors was known for its extremely formal, top-down communication system. In the mid-1980s, however, the formality of its system came under fire from virtually all of its stakeholders. GM's response was to embark on a massive communication improvement program that included sending employees to public-speaking workshops, improving the more than 350 publications that it sends out, providing videotapes of management meetings to employees, and using satellite links between headquarters and field operations to establish two-way conversations around the world.

Downward communication generally provides directions whereas upward communication provides feedback to top management. Communication that flows horizontally or crosses traditional reporting lines usually is related to task performance. For example, a design engineer, a manufacturing engineer, and a quality engineer may communicate about the details of a particular product design, thus making it easy to manufacture and inspect. Horizontal communication often travels faster than vertical communication because it need not follow organizational protocols and procedures.

Organizational communication networks may diverge from reporting relationships as employees seek better information with which to do their jobs. Employees often find that the easiest way to get their jobs done or to obtain the necessary information is to go directly to employees in other departments rather than through the formal channels shown on the organization chart. Figure 11.5 shows a simple organization chart and the organization's real communication network. The communication network links the individuals who most frequently communicate with one another; the firm's CEO, for example, communicates most often with employee 5. (This does not mean that individuals not linked in the communication network never communicate, but means only that their communications are relatively infrequent.) Perhaps the CEO and the employee interact frequently outside of work, in church, in service organizations such as Kiwanis, or

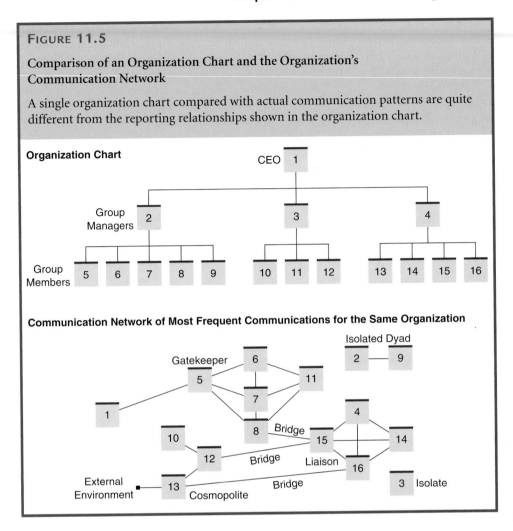

FIGURE 11.5

Comparison of an Organization Chart and the Organization's Communication Network

A single organization chart compared with actual communication patterns are quite different from the reporting relationships shown in the organization chart.

Organization Chart

CEO 1

Group Managers 2   3   4

Group Members 5 6 7 8 9   10 11 12   13 14 15 16

Communication Network of Most Frequent Communications for the Same Organization

Isolated Dyad
2 — 9

Gatekeeper 6
5   11
    7
1
        8   Bridge
10   15   14
   12   Bridge   4
External   13   Liaison 16
Environment   Cosmopolite   Bridge   3 Isolate

at sporting events. Such interactions may lead to close friendships that carry over into business relationships. The figure also shows that the group managers do not have important roles in the communication network, contrary to commonsense expectations.

The roles that people play in organizational communication networks can be analyzed in terms of their contribution to the functioning of the network.[16] The most important roles are labeled in the bottom portion of Figure 11.5. A **gatekeeper** (employee 5) has a strategic position in the network that allows him or her to control information moving in either direction through a channel. A **liaison** (employee 15) serves as a bridge between groups, tying groups together and facilitating the communication flow needed to integrate group activities. Employee 13 performs the interesting function of **cosmopolite**, who links the organization to the external environment by, for instance, attending conventions and trade shows, keeping up with outside technological innovations, and having more frequent contact with sources outside the organization. This person may also be an opinion leader in the group. Finally, the **isolate** (employee 3) and the **isolated dyad** (employees 2 and 9) tend to work alone and to interact and communicate little with others.

Each of these roles and functions plays an important part in the overall functioning of the communication network and in the organization as a whole. Understanding these roles can help both managers and group members facilitate communication. For

The **gatekeeper** has a strategic position in the network that allows him or her to control information moving in either direction through a channel.

The **liaison** serves as a bridge between groups, tying groups together and facilitating the communication flow needed to integrate group activities.

The **cosmopolite** links the organization to the external environment and may also be an opinion leader in the group.

The **isolate** and the **isolated dyad** tend to work alone and to interact and communicate little with others.

instance, the manager who wants to be sure that the CEO receives certain information is well advised to go through the gatekeeper. If the employee who has the technical knowledge necessary for a particular project is an isolate, the manager can take special steps to integrate the employee into the communication network for the duration of the project.

Recent research has indicated some possible negative impacts of communication networks. Employee turnover has been shown to occur in clusters related to employee communication networks.[17] That is, employees who communicate regularly in a network may share feelings about the organization and thus influence one another's intentions to stay or quit. Communication networks therefore may have both positive and negative consequences.

As we discuss in Chapter 16, a primary function of organizational structure is to coordinate the activities of many people doing specialized tasks. Communication networks in organizations provide this much-needed integration. In fact, in some ways, communication patterns influence organizational structure. Some companies are finding that the need for better communication forces them to create smaller divisions. The fewer managerial levels and improved team spirit of these divisions tend to enhance communication flows.

Managing Communication

As simple as the process of communication may seem, messages are not always understood. The degree of correspondence between the message intended by the source and the message understood by the receiver is called **communication fidelity**. Fidelity can be diminished anywhere in the communication process, from the source to the feedback. Moreover, organizations may have characteristics that impede the flow of information.

Improving the Communication Process

To improve organizational communication, one must understand potential problems. Using the basic communication process, we can identify several ways to overcome typical problems.

Source   The source may intentionally withhold or filter information on the assumption that the receiver does not need it to understand the communication. Withholding information, however, may render the message meaningless or cause an erroneous interpretation. For example, during a performance appraisal interview, a manager may not tell the employee all of the sources of information being used to make the evaluation, thinking that the employee does not need to know them. If the employee knew, however, he or she might be able to explain certain behaviors or otherwise alter the manager's perspective of the evaluation and thereby make it more accurate. Filtering may be more likely to occur in electronic communication such as email or voicemail since they carry an implied importance for brevity and conciseness. Selective filtering may cause a breakdown in communication that cannot be repaired, even with good follow-up communication.

To avoid filtering, the communicator needs to understand why it occurs. Filtering can result from a lack of understanding of the receiver's position, from the sender's need to protect his or her own power by limiting the receiver's access to information, or from doubts about what the receiver might do with the information. The sender's primary concern, however, should be the message. In essence, the sender must determine exactly what message he or she wants the receiver to understand, send the receiver enough information to understand the message but not enough to create an overload, and trust the receiver to use the information properly.

Communication fidelity is the degree of correspondence between the message intended by the source and the message understood by the receiver.

Encoding and Decoding   Encoding and decoding problems occur as the message is translated into or from the symbols used in transmission. Such problems can relate to the meaning of the symbols or to the transmission itself. Encoding and decoding problems include lack of common experience between source and receiver, problems related to semantics and the use of jargon, and difficulties with the medium.

Clearly, the source and the receiver must share a common experience with the symbols that express the message if they are to encode and decode them in exactly the same way. People who speak different languages or come from different cultural backgrounds may experience problems of this sort. But even people who speak the same language can misunderstand each other.

Semantics is the study of language forms, and semantic problems occur when people attribute different meanings to the same words or language forms. For example, J. Edgar Hoover, the legendary former director of the FBI, once jotted "watch the borders" on a memo he had received and sent it back to the senior agency manager who had written it. Only after dispatching several dozen agents to guard the border between the United States and Mexico did the agency manager learn what Hoover had actually meant—the margins on the memo were too narrow! Similarly, when discussing a problem employee, the division head may tell her assistant, "We need to get rid of this problem." The division head may have meant that the employee should be scheduled for more training or transferred to another division. However, the assistant may interpret the statement differently and fire the problem employee.

> **Semantics** is the study of language forms.

The specialized or technical language of a trade, field, profession, or social group is called **jargon**. Jargon may be a hybrid of standard language and the specialized language of a group. For example, experts in the computer field use terms such as "gigs," "megs," "RAM," and "bandwidth" that have little or no meaning to those unfamiliar with computers. The use of jargon makes communication within a close group of colleagues more efficient and meaningful, but outside the group it has the opposite effect. Sometimes a source person comfortable with jargon uses it unknowingly in an attempt to communicate with receivers who do not understand it, thus causing a communication breakdown. In other cases, the source may use jargon intentionally to obscure meaning or to show outsiders that he or she belongs to the group that uses the language.

> **Jargon** is the specialized or technical language of a trade, profession, or social group.

The use of jargon is acceptable if the receiver is familiar with it; otherwise, it should be avoided. Repeating a jargon-containing message in clearer terms should help the receiver understand it. In general, the source and the receiver should clarify the set of

Reprinted with special permission of King Feature Syndicate.

One of the oldest barriers to effective communication in organizations is simply poor writing. If the sender jots down some instructions or other information, but the receiver cannot accurately read the intended message, any number of problems can arise. Of course, the simplest solution is for the receiver to simply ask the sender to "translate" what she or he has written. As shown here, though, some people are reluctant to take this step, and their reluctance can sometimes spell big trouble!

symbols to be used before they communicate. Also, the receiver can ask questions frequently and, if necessary, ask the source to repeat all or part of the message. The source must send the message through a medium appropriate to the message itself and to the intended receiver. For example, a commercial run on an AM radio station will not have its intended effect if the people in the desired market segment listen only to FM radio.

Largely influenced by the Enron debacle, many investors are increasingly beginning to scrutinize the financial reporting systems of larger companies. Coca-Cola, for instance, has recently seen its own accounting practices criticized in the media. These critics contend that the firm is using increasingly complex reporting methods to make its earnings seem higher than they would have been if simpler and more straightforward accounting practices had been used.[18]

Receiver   Several communication problems originate in the receiver, including problems with selective attention, value judgments, source credibility, and overload. Selective attention exists when the receiver attends only to selected parts of a message—a frequent occurrence with oral communication. For example, in a college class, some students may hear only part of the professor's lecture as their minds wander to other topics. To focus receivers' attention on the message, senders often engage in attention-getting behaviors such as varying the volume, repeating the message, and offering rewards.

Value judgments are influenced by the degree to which a message reinforces or challenges the receiver's basic personal beliefs. If a message reinforces the receiver's beliefs, he or she may pay close attention and believe it completely, without examination. On the other hand, if the message challenges those beliefs, the receiver may entirely discount it. Thus, if a firm's sales manager predicts that the demand for new baby-care products will increase substantially over the next two years, he may ignore reports that the birthrate is declining.

The receiver may also judge the credibility of the source of the message. If the source is perceived to be an expert in the field, the listener may pay close attention to the message and believe it. Conversely, if the receiver has little respect for the source, he or she may disregard the message. The receiver considers both the message and the source in making value judgments and determining credibility. An expert in nuclear physics may be viewed as a credible source if the issue is building a nuclear power plant, yet the same person's evaluation of the birthrate may be disregarded, perhaps correctly. This is one reason that trial lawyers ask expert witnesses about their education and experience at the beginning of their testimony: to establish credibility.

A receiver experiencing communication overload is receiving more information than she or he can process. In organizations, this can happen very easily; a receiver can be bombarded with computer-generated reports and messages from superiors, peers, and sources outside the organization. It is not unusual for middle managers or telecommuters to receive one hundred email messages per day. Unable to take in all the messages, decode them, understand them, and act on them, the receiver may use selective attention and value judgments to focus on the messages that seem most important. Although this type of selective attention is necessary for survival in an information-glutted environment, it may mean that vital information is lost or overlooked.[19]

Verification is the feedback portion of communication in which the receiver sends a message to the source indicating receipt of the message and the degree to which he or she understood the message.

Feedback   The purpose of feedback is **verification**, in which the receiver sends a message to the source indicating receipt of the message and the degree to which it was understood. Lack of feedback can cause at least two problems. First, the source may need to send another message that depends on the response to the first; if the source receives no feedback, the source may not send the second message or may be forced to send the original message again. Second, the receiver may act on the unverified message; if the receiver misunderstood the message, the resulting act may be inappropriate.

Because feedback is so important, the source must actively seek it, and the receiver must supply it. Often it is appropriate for the receiver to repeat the original message as an introduction to the response, although the medium or symbols used may be different. Nonverbal cues can provide instantaneous feedback. These include body language and facial expressions such as anger and disbelief.

The source needs to be concerned with the message, the symbols, the medium, and the feedback from the receiver. Of course, the receiver is concerned with these things, too, but from a different point of view. In general, the receiver needs to be source oriented just as the source needs to be receiver oriented. Table 11.1 gives specific suggestions for improving the communication process.

Improving Organizational Factors in Communication

Organizational factors that can create communication breakdowns or barriers include noise, status differences, time pressures, and overload. As previously stated, disturbances anywhere in the organization can distort or interrupt meaningful communication. Thus, the noise created by a rumored takeover can disrupt the orderly flow of task-related information. Kmart's stock recently dropped precipitously based on rumors that it would file bankruptcy. Although the retailer did indeed eventually take this step, rumor alone caused great damage to the company in the eyes of the investment community.[20]

Status differences between source and receiver can cause some of the communication problems just discussed. For example, a firm's chief executive officer may pay little attention to communications from employees far lower on the organization chart, and employees may pay little attention to communications from the CEO. Both are instances of selective attention prompted by the organization's status system. Time pressures and communication overloads are also detrimental to communication. When the receiver is not allowed enough time to understand incoming messages, or when

| Focus | Source | | Receiver | | TABLE 11.1 |
	Question	Corrective Action	Question	Corrective Action	
Message	What idea or thought are you trying to get across?	Give more information. Give less information. Give entire message.	What idea or thought does the sender want you to understand?	Listen carefully to the entire message, not just to part of it.	**Improving the Communication Process**
Symbols	Does the receiver use the same symbols, words, jargon?	Say it another way. Employ repetition. Use receiver's language or jargon. Before sending, clarify symbols to be used.	What symbols are being used—for example, foreign language, technical jargon?	Clarify symbols before communication begins. Ask questions. Ask sender to repeat message.	
Medium	Is this a channel that the receiver monitors regularly? Sometimes? Never?	Use multiple media. Change medium. Increase volume (loudness).	What medium or media is the sender using?	Monitor several media.	
Feedback	What is the receiver's reaction to your message?	Pay attention to the feedback, especially nonverbal cues. Ask questions.	Did you correctly interpret the message?	Repeat message.	

there are too many messages, he or she may misunderstand or ignore some of them. Effective organizational communication provides the right information to the right person at the right time and in the right form.

Reduce Noise   Noise is a primary barrier to effective organizational communication. A common form of noise is the rumor **grapevine**, an informal system of communication that coexists with the formal system. The grapevine usually transmits information faster than official channels do. Because the accuracy of this information often is quite low, however, the grapevine can distort organizational communication. Management can reduce the effects of the distortion by using the grapevine as an additional channel for disseminating information and by constantly monitoring it for accuracy.

> The **grapevine** is an informal system of communication that coexists with the formal system.

Foster Informal Communication   Communication in well-run companies was once described as "a vast network of informal, open communications."[21] Informal communication fosters mutual trust, which minimizes the effects of status differences. Open communication can also contribute to better understanding between diverse groups in an organization. Monsanto Company created fifteen-member teams in its Agricultural Group, the primary objective being to increase communication and awareness among various diverse groups. Its Chemical Group set up diversity pairs of one supervisor and one worker to increase communication and awareness. In both cases, Monsanto found that increasing communication between people who were different paid handsome benefits for the organization.[22] Open communication also allows information to be communicated when it is needed rather than when the formal information system allows it to emerge. Some experts also describe communication in effective companies as chaotic and intense, supported by the reward structure and the physical arrangement of the facilities. This means that the performance appraisal and reward system, offices, meeting rooms, and work areas are designed to encourage frequent, unscheduled, and unstructured communication throughout the organization.

Develop a Balanced Information Network   Many large organizations have developed elaborate formal information networks to cope with the potential problems of information overload and time pressures. In many cases, however, the networks have created problems instead of solving them. Often they produce more information than managers and decision makers can comprehend and use in their jobs. The networks also often use only formal communication channels and ignore various informal lines of communication. Furthermore, they frequently provide whatever information the computer is set up to provide—information that may not apply to the most pressing problem at hand. The result of all these drawbacks is loss of communication effectiveness.

Organizations need to balance information load and information-processing capabilities. In other words, they must take care not to generate more information than people can handle. It is useless to produce sophisticated statistical reports that managers have no time to read. Furthermore, the new technologies that are making more information available to managers and decision makers must be unified to produce usable information. Information production, storage, and processing capabilities must be compatible with one another and, equally important, with the needs of the organization.

Some companies—for example, General Electric, Anheuser-Busch, and McDonald's—have formalized an upward communication system that uses a corporate "ombudsperson" position. A highly placed executive who is available outside the formal chain of command to hear employees' complaints usually holds this position. The system provides an opportunity for disgruntled employees to complain without fear of losing their jobs and may help some companies achieve a balanced communication system.

Chapter Review

Synopsis

Communication is the process by which two parties exchange information and share meaning. It plays a role in every organizational activity. The purposes of communication in organizations are to achieve coordinated action, to share information, and to express feelings and emotions.

People in organizations communicate through written, oral, and nonverbal means. Written communications include letters, memos, email, reports, and the like. Oral communication is the type most commonly used. Personal elements, such as facial expressions and body language, and environmental elements, such as office design, are forms of nonverbal communication.

Communication among individuals, groups, or organizations is a process in which a source sends a message and a receiver responds. The source encodes a message into symbols and transmits it through a medium to the receiver, who decodes the symbols. The receiver then responds with feedback, an attempt to verify the meaning of the original message. Noise—anything that distorts or interrupts communication—may interfere in virtually any stage of the process.

The fully integrated communication-information office system—the electronic office—links personnel in a communication network through a combination of computers and electronic transmission systems. The full range of effects of such systems has yet to be fully realized.

Communication networks are systems of information exchange within organizations. Patterns of communication emerge as information flows from person to person in a group. Typical small-group communication networks include the wheel, chain, circle, and all-channel networks.

The organizational communication network, which constitutes the real communication links in an organization, usually differs from the arrangement on an organization chart. Roles in organizational communication networks include those of gatekeeper, liaison, cosmopolite, and isolate.

Managing communication in organizations involves understanding the numerous problems that can interfere with effective communication. Problems may arise from the communication process itself and from organizational factors such as status differences.

Discussion Questions

1. How is communication in organizations an individual process as well as an organizational process?

2. Discuss the three primary purposes of organizational communication.

3. Describe a situation in which you tried to carry on a conversation when no one was listening. Were any messages sent during the "conversation"?

4. A college classroom is a forum for a typical attempt at communication as the professor tries to communicate the subject to the students. Describe classroom communication in terms of the basic communication process outlined in the chapter.

5. Is there a communication network (other than professor-to-student) in the class in which you are using this book? If so, identify the specific roles that people play in the network. If not, why has no network developed? What would be the benefits of having a communication network in this class?

6. Why might educators typically focus most communication training on the written and oral methods and pay little attention to the nonverbal methods? Do you think that more training emphasis should be placed on nonverbal communication? Why or why not?

7. Is the typical classroom means of transferring information from professor to student an effective form of communication? Where does it break down? What are the communication problems in the college classroom?

8. Whose responsibility is it to solve classroom communication problems: the student's, the professor's, or the administration's?

9. Have you ever worked in an organization in which communication was a problem? If so, what were some causes of the problem?

10. What methods were used, or should have been used, to improve communication in the situation you described in question 9?

11. Would the use of advanced computer information processing or telecommunications have helped solve the communications problem you described in question 9?

12. What types of communication problems will new telecommunications methods probably be able to solve? Why?

13. What types of communications would NOT be appropriate to send by email? Or by voicemail?

14. Which steps in the communication process are usually left out, or at least, poorly done when email and voicemail are used for communication?

Experiencing Organizational Behavior

The Importance of Feedback in Oral Communication

Purpose: This exercise demonstrates the importance of feedback in oral communication.

Format: You will be an observer or play the role of either a manager or an assistant manager trying to tell a coworker where a package of important materials is to be picked up. The observer's role is to make sure the other two participants follow the rules and to observe and record any interesting occurrences.

Procedure: The instructor will divide the class into groups of three. (Any extra members can be roving observers.) The three people in each group will take the roles of manager, assistant manager, and observer. In the second trial, the manager and the assistant manager will switch roles.

Trial 1: The manager and the assistant manager should turn their backs to each other so that neither can see the other. Here is the situation: The manager is in another city that he or she is not familiar with but that the assistant manager knows quite well. The manager needs to find the office of a supplier to pick up drawings of a critical component of the company's main product. The supplier will be closing for the day in a few minutes; the drawings must be picked up before closing time. The manager has called the assistant manager to get directions to the office. However, the connection is faulty; the manager can hear the assistant manager, but the assistant manager can hear only enough to know the manager is on the line. The manager has redialed once, but there was no improvement in the connection. Now there is no time to lose. The manager has decided

to get the directions from the assistant without asking questions.

Just before the exercise begins, the instructor will give the assistant manager a detailed map of the city that shows the locations of the supplier's office and the manager. The map will include a number of turns, stops, stoplights, intersections, and shopping centers between these locations. The assistant manager can study it for no longer than a minute or two. When the instructor gives the direction to start, the assistant manager describes to the manager how to get from his or her present location to the supplier's office. As the assistant manager gives the directions, the manager draws the map on a piece of paper.

The observer makes sure that no questions are asked, records the beginning and ending times, and notes how the assistant manager tries to communicate particularly difficult points (including points about which the manager obviously wants to ask questions) and any other noteworthy occurrences.

After all pairs have finished, each observer "grades" the quality of the manager's map by comparing it with the original and counting the number of obvious mistakes. The instructor will ask a few managers who believe they have drawn good maps to tell the rest of the class how to get to the supplier's office.

Trial 2: In trial 2, the manager and the assistant manager switch roles, and a second map is passed out to the new assistant managers. The situation is the same as in the first trial except that the telephones are working properly and the manager can ask questions of the assistant manager. The observer's role is the same as in trial 1—recording the beginning and ending times, the methods of communication, and other noteworthy occurrences.

After all pairs have finished, the observers grade the maps, just as in the first trial. The instructor then selects a few managers to tell the rest of the class how to get to the supplier's office. The subsequent class discussion should center on the experiences of the class members and the follow-up questions.

Follow-up Questions

1. Which trial resulted in more accurate maps? Why?

2. Which trial took longer? Why?

3. How did you feel when a question needed to be asked but could not be asked in trial 1? Was your confidence in the final result affected differently in the two trials?

Reference: "Diagnosing Your Listening Skills," from Ethel C. Glenn and Elliott A. Pond, "Listening Self-Inventory," *Supervisory Management,* January 1989, pp. 12–15. Copyright 1989 by American Management Association in the format textbook via Copyright Clearance Center.

Diagnosing Your Listening Skills

Introduction: Good listening skills are essential for effective communication and are often overlooked when communication is analyzed. This self-assessment questionnaire examines your ability to listen effectively.

Instructions: Go through the following statements, checking "Yes" or "No" next to each one. Mark each question as truthfully as you can in light of your behavior in the last few meetings or gatherings you attended.

Yes   No

1. I frequently attempt to listen to several conversations at the same time.

2. I like people to give me only the facts and then let me make my own interpretation.

3. I sometimes pretend to pay attention to people.

4. I consider myself a good judge of nonverbal communications.

5. I usually know what another person is going to say before he or she says it.

6. I usually end conversations that don't interest me by diverting my attention from the speaker.

7. I frequently nod, frown, or in some other way let the speaker know how I feel about what he or she is saying.

8. I usually respond immediately when someone has finished talking.

9. I evaluate what is being said while it is being said.

10. I usually formulate a response while the other person is still talking.

11. The speaker's "delivery" style frequently keeps me from listening to content.

12. I usually ask people to clarify what they have said rather than guess at the meaning.

13. I make a concerted effort to understand other people's point of view.

14. I frequently hear what I expect to hear rather than what is said.

15. Most people feel that I have understood their point of view when we disagree.

Scoring

The correct answers according to communication theory are as follows:

No for statements 1, 2, 3, 5, 6, 7, 8, 9, 10, 11, 14.

Yes for statements 4, 12, 13, 15.

If you missed only one or two responses, you strongly approve of your own listening habits, and you are on the right track to becoming an effective listener in your role as manager. If you missed three or four responses, you have uncovered some doubts about your listening effectiveness, and your knowledge of how to listen has some gaps. If you missed five or more responses, you probably are not satisfied with the way you listen, and your friends and coworkers may not feel you are a good listener, either. Work on improving your active listening skills.

Reference: "Diagnosing Your Listening Skills," from Ethel C. Glenn and Elliott A. Pond, "Listening Self-Inventory," *Supervisory Management,* January 1989, pp. 12–15. Reprinted with permission of American Management Association via Copyright Clearance Center.

Building Managerial Skills

Exercise Overview: Communication skills refer to a manager's ability both to convey ideas and information effectively to others and to receive ideas and information effectively from others. This exercise focuses on communication skills as they involve deciding how to best convey information.

Exercise Background: Assume that you are a middle manager for a large electronics firm. People in your organization generally use one of three means for communicating with one another. The most common way is oral communication, accomplished either face-to-face or by telephone. Electronic mail is also widely used. Finally, a surprisingly large amount of communication is still done on paper, such as through memos, reports, or letters.

During the course of a typical day, you receive and send a variety of messages and other communication. You generally use some combination of all of the communication methods previously noted during the course of any given day. The things that you need to communicate today include the following:

1. You need to schedule a meeting with five subordinates.

2. You need to congratulate a coworker who just had a baby.

3. You need to reprimand a staff assistant who has been coming to work late for the last several days.

4. You need to inform the warehouse staff that several customers have recently complained because their shipments were not properly packed.

5. You need to schedule a meeting with your boss.

6. You need to announce two promotions.

7. You need to fire someone who has been performing poorly for some time.

8. You need to inform several individuals about a set of new government regulations that will soon affect them.

9. You need to inform a supplier that your company will soon be cutting back on its purchases because a competing supplier has lowered its prices, and you plan to shift more of your business to that supplier.

10. You need to resolve a disagreement between two subordinates who both want to take their vacation at the same time.

Exercise Task: Using the information just presented, do the following:

1. Indicate which methods of communication would be appropriate for each situation.

2. Rank-order the methods for each communication situation from best to worst.

3. Compare your rankings with those of a classmate and discuss any differences.

Communicating in a Family-Run Business

> **❝ It is the paradox of family business that the family can be either a tremendous asset or the kiss of death. ❞**
> OTIS W. BASKIN, PROFESSOR,
> PEPPERDINE UNIVERSITY

Family-run businesses are important contributors to the U.S. economy, employing more than 70 percent of all workers, creating the majority of new jobs, and earning profits equal to 55 percent of GDP. More than one-third of the companies listed on the New York Stock Exchange and the *Fortune* 500 are family-owned.

Communication is vital to the success of family-run businesses. Internal communication between individuals and work units is just as critical as it is for other companies. In addition, "family businesses have a certain repository of knowledge and experience passed down over time that larger competitors often cannot match," claims business writer June Kim. Small firms can provide unique products and services, form a special bond with customers, and be innovative, if the family's knowledge and experiences are indeed communicated to younger members.

In some ways, communication between family members is much easier than communication between two unrelated coworkers. Communication within families can be fast, efficient, and honest. Wayne D. Messick, a business consultant, says, "By their very nature, family companies are very flexible and quicker to act since the people who make all the decisions often eat Sunday dinner together." Rick Decruz, who runs a retail business with his parents and brother, says, "As sons to their father, we take more liberty in what we say. To a regular boss . . . we would be fired."

On the other hand, communicating with family members can also be tough. Many families have unresolved conflicts that linger or are reluctant to bring up controversial issues, which makes honesty difficult. The roles individuals assume within the family may not be appropriate for their working relationships. Conflict between family and business roles can be a problem too. Jennifer Sorenson, writing about owners of family-run retail firms, says, "When both siblings and parents manage the business, they often face the difficult challenge of negotiating between two disparate value systems: the family that offers unconditional love, and the business that depends on performance and profits."

Simply spending too much time together can be a problem, as can the inability to switch from a "family" mode to a "business" mode of communicating. Decruz says, "You can't separate the family from the business. It is a twenty-four-hour-a-day job . . . It's tough." Otis W. Baskin, a professor of management at Pepperdine University, explains, "It is important for members of the family to consciously and deliberately plan how to communicate about the business in addition to whatever informal communication takes place at, say, the dinner table . . . It is important for the family's health as a family not to always be focused on the business."

Another obstacle for family businesses is the use of communication patterns based on family roles. Families tend to attach labels to individuals: the smart one, the troublemaker, and so on. As they mature, children may outgrow the behavior that led to these labels. Also, "offspring who are the peacemakers at home may find themselves mediating management conflicts between family members whether or not they have the desire or qualifications to do so," according to Nancy Bowman-Upton, director of the Institute for Family Business at Baylor University.

Communication across generations in family businesses becomes especially critical, and especially difficult, when it's time for succession planning. Older family members must decide how they will hand off responsibility and leadership to the younger generation. Professor Matthew Kaplan of Pennsylvania State University claims that family relationships are the most serious obstacle in succession planning, more serious than economic or any other considerations. Kaplan says, "When there is open communication . . . there is less conflict, greater cohesion . . . , and more agreement on basic issues . . . Family members report less stress and more satisfaction."

Communication in family-run businesses mirrors the relationships between the family members. "It is the paradox of family business that the family can be either a tremendous asset or the kiss of death. If family relationships are divisive, those negative relationships carry over into the business and are often more destructive than they would be between coworkers or managers who have no other relationship," says Baskin. When the relationship is good, however, family-run businesses can achieve a level of trust and honesty in communication that cannot be rivaled.

Case Questions

1. Are there differences in the communication methods chosen by coworkers who are part of a family-run business and those chosen by coworkers who are not related? Explain.

2. How might feedback from a member of a family-run business differ from feedback offered by a member of a corporation that is not family run? Give specific examples to support your answer.

3. Would you prefer communicating within a family-run business or a business that is not family run? Why?

References: Otis W. Baskin, "Trust as a Competitive Advantage," *The Graziado Business Report,* Pepperdine University, Spring 2001, gbr.pepperdine.edu on April 21, 2005; Nancy Bowman-Upton, "Transferring Management in the Family-Owned Business," U.S. Small Business Administration, www.sba.gov on April 21, 2005; Matthew Kaplan, "Intergenerational Communication as a Tool for Sustaining Small Family Farms," Pennsylvania State University website, intergenerational.cas.psu.edu on April 21, 2005; June Kim, "New Spins on Old-Fashioned Virtues," *Business Week,* January 27, 2005, www.businessweek.com on April 21, 2005; Jennifer Sorensen, "Family-Owned Businesses," *Baby Shop Magazine,* www.babyshopmagazine.com on April 21, 2005.

TEST PREPPER

You have read the chapter and studied the key terms. Think you're ready to ace the exam? Take this sample test to gauge your comprehension of chapter material and check your answers at the back of the book. Want more test questions? Take the ACE quizzes found on the student website: http://college.hmco.com/business/students/ (select Griffin/Moorhead, Organizational Behavior, 8e from the Management menu).

T F 1. Communication is a social process.

T F 2. A performance appraisal form is an example of communication.

T F 3. The communication sender must decode his or her message before they transmit it.

T F 4. One downside to telecommuting is the missed social interaction of the office.

T F 5. Communication networks are relatively permanent, even though tasks and organization memberships change.

T F 6. One way a manager can improve communication is to increase filtering.

T F 7. The grapevine usually transmits information faster than official channels do.

8. The primary purpose of communication in organizations is
   a. to inform customers.
   b. to achieve coordinated action.
   c. to understand different cultures.
   d. to share ideas.
   e. to make decisions.

9. The most prevalent form of organizational communication is
   a. written.
   b. visual.
   c. memos and reports.
   d. policy manuals.
   e. oral.

10. Tony wants to transmit a message to his employees, but he wants to be sure they understand how passionately he feels about the issue. He'd be best off to pick which communication media?
    a. Letter
    b. Email
    c. Memo
    d. Face-to-face
    e. All of the above have the same carrying capacity, as long as Tony makes his message clear.

11. All of the following are benefits of telecommuting, except
    a. less fatigue for employees.
    b. increased productivity.
    c. reduced commuting expenses.
    d. reduced air pollution and overcrowding.
    e. increased control over employees.

12. An organization that has a clear vertical hierarchy likely has which type of communication network?
    a. Wheel network
    b. Chain network
    c. Circle network
    d. All-channel network
    e. Virtual network

13. Nichole is a lower-level manager who wants to communicate with the company president. To accomplish this, Nichole will likely have to go through a/an
    a. gatekeeper.
    b. liaison.
    c. cosmopolite.
    d. isolate.
    e. transmitter.

14. Which is the best advice for managers with regard to the use of jargon?
    a. Use jargon to establish expertise in a particular field.
    b. Require the use of jargon by all technical employees.
    c. Use jargon during negotiations to avoid telling the other party too much.
    d. Avoid using jargon if the receiver is unfamiliar with it.
    e. Never use jargon.

15. The recommendation to managers to develop a balanced information network refers to the need to weigh
    a. the capacity of information-processing equipment with the financial cost of this equipment.
    b. the frequency of information usage with the demands on information capacity.
    c. the amount of information people can handle with the amount of information generated.
    d. the technology available to process information with the personal wants and needs of information systems employees.
    e. the information storage capabilities with the needs of the organization.

CHAPTER 12

Traditional Models for Understanding Leadership

- **Characterize the nature of leadership.**
- **Trace the early approaches to leadership.**
- **Discuss the emergence of situational theories and models of leadership.**
- **Describe the LPC theory of leadership.**
- **Discuss the path-goal theory of leadership.**
- **Describe Vroom's decision tree approach to leadership.**

Chapter Outline

Leading the Leaders at PepsiCo

PepsiCo, maker of Pepsi, Fritos, and Gatorade, is the third-largest branded food company in the world, following Nestlé and Kraft. Sixteen of PepsiCo's dozens of brands have world-wide sales revenues of over $1 billion and the firm has won many awards, for everything from diversity to advertising to recycling. PepsiCo has a history of great leaders who improved the company. Steve Reinemund, who became CEO in 2001, also seems destined to achieve great things. Reinemund is accomplishing his vision of making PepsiCo the world's leading food company by relying on six important qualities of leadership that he calls "the six Ps."

First, Reinemund believes that successful leaders must hold Principles (the first "P") and communicate them throughout the organization. "You have to have a moral compass as a leader," Reinemund says. "It starts with basic beliefs and values." Second, Reinemund suggests that Perspective, or strategic vision, is essential. Third, Passion is also important. Passion is the motivating factor that demonstrates a leader's commitment and inspires others. The fourth factor is Perseverance. Reinemund emphasizes the role of Performance, the fifth factor, saying, "Results count. If you can't get the results over the goal line, are you really a leader?" Sixth, a successful leader builds employees to

> ## "My role is to . . . develop the leaders that we have around the world."
> STEVE REINEMUND, CEO OF PEPSICO

improve the organization, a value Reinemund calls People.

Reinemund's leadership philosophy mimics the structure of the Michigan studies, which distinguished job-centered leader behavior from employee-centered leader behavior, or the Ohio State studies, which focused on consideration and initiating-structure behaviors. Principles is an example of a job-centered behavior. The leader uses principles to communicate information about what to do and what not to do. Perspective is also job-centered, as it is used to develop a long-term set of goals. Another job-centered behavior is Perseverance, with its emphasis on effort. Finally, Performance is a job-centered behavior because of its emphasis on bottom-line outcomes.

On the other hand, Passion, a motivating and inspiring commitment, is an employee-centered behavior. The final value, People, is employee-centered. Reinemund claims that he spends more time on this value than on any of the others.

The CEO places a high importance on helping to develop the leadership capabilities of others. "We all need to take a role in developing leaders," Reinemund says. "Leaders train leaders in this company." To carry through on that commitment, Reinemund personally teaches a yearly leadership course to PepsiCo middle managers. Reinemund enjoys interacting with class participants and says, "It keeps me relevant on what's going on and what our people are thinking. It gives me a chance to influence and mentor our up-and-coming leaders. Out of those classes come the CEOs of the future."

Reinemund is an effective leader, but, in the long term, his biggest contribution to PepsiCo may be the firm's future leaders, a legacy that will be valuable years from now. "My role is to be the enabler of growth," Reinemund says. "That growth is business growth, but more importantly, it's people growth and helping to develop the leaders that we have around the world." This chapter's boxed insert titled *PepsiCo and . . . Diversity* on page 321 describes more about the diverse leaders of PepsiCo.

References: "Brands and Companies," "Overview," PepsiCo website, www.pepsico.com on May 9, 2005; PepsiCo Shakes Up Leadership," *BevNet*, March 30, 2005, www.bevnet.com on May 11, 2005; "Winner of the Week: PepsiCo," *Forbes*, April 27, 2001, www.forbes .com on May 10, 2005; Diane Brady, "The Six Ps of PepsiCo's Chief," *Business Week*, January 10, 2005, www.businessweek.com on February 14, 2005 (quotation); John Deighton, "How Snapple Got Its Juice Back," *Harvard Business Review*, January 2002, hbswk.hbs.edu on May 10, 2005; "Steve S. Reinemund, "Letter to Shareholders," PepsiCo 2004 Annual Report, www.pepsico.com on May 9, 2005.

The mystique of leadership makes it one of the most widely debated, studied, and sought-after properties of organizational life. Managers talk about the characteristics that make an effective leader and the importance of leadership to organizational success, while organizational scientists have extensively studied leadership and myriad related phenomena for decades. Paradoxically, however, while leadership is among the most widely studied concepts in the entire field of management, there remain many unanswered questions. Why, then, should we continue to study leadership? First, leadership is of great practical importance to organizations. Second, in spite of many remaining mysteries, researchers have isolated and verified some key variables that influence leadership effectiveness.[1]

This chapter, the first of two devoted to leadership, introduces the fundamental traditional models that are commonly used as a basis for understanding leadership. We start with a discussion of the meaning of leadership, including its definition and the distinctions between leadership and management. Then we turn to historical views of leadership, focusing on the trait and behavioral approaches. Next, we examine three contemporary leadership theories that have formed the basis for most leadership research: the LPC theory developed by Fred Fiedler, the path-goal theory, and Victor Vroom's decision tree approach to leadership. In our next chapter we explore several contemporary views of leadership.

The Nature of Leadership

Because "leadership" is a term that is often used in everyday conversation, you might assume that it has a common and accepted meaning. In fact, just the opposite is true— like several other key organizational behavior terms such as "personality" and "motivation," "leadership" is used in a variety of ways. Thus, we first clarify its meaning as we use it in this book.

The Meaning of Leadership

Leadership is both a process and a property. As a *process*, leadership involves the use of noncoercive influence. As a *property*, leadership is the set of characteristics attributed to someone who is perceived to use influence successfully.

Influence is the ability to affect the perceptions, beliefs, attitudes, motivation, and/or behaviors of others.

We will define **leadership** in terms of both process and property.[2] As a process, leadership is the use of noncoercive influence to direct and coordinate the activities of group members to meet a goal. As a property, leadership is the set of characteristics attributed to those who are perceived to use such influence successfully.[3] **Influence**, a common element of both perspectives, is the ability to affect the perceptions, beliefs, attitudes, motivation, and/or behaviors of others. From an organizational viewpoint, leadership is vital because it has such a powerful influence on individual and group behavior.[4] Moreover, because the goal toward which the group directs its efforts is often the desired goal of the leader, it may or may not mesh with organizational goals.

Leadership involves neither force nor coercion. A manager who relies solely on force and formal authority to direct the behavior of subordinates is not exercising leadership. Thus, as discussed more fully in the next section, a manager or supervisor may or may not also be a leader. It is also important to note that a leader may possess the characteristics attributed to him or her; on the other hand, the leader may merely be perceived as possessing them.

Leadership Versus Management

From these definitions, it should be clear that leadership and management are related, but they are not the same. A person can be a manager, a leader, both, or neither.[5] Some of the basic distinctions between the two are summarized in Table 12.1. On the left side of the table are four elements that differentiate leadership from management. The two columns show how each element differs when considered from a management and a leadership point of view. For example, when executing plans, managers focus on monitoring results, comparing them with goals, and correcting deviations. In contrast, the leader focuses on energizing people to overcome bureaucratic hurdles to help reach goals.

To further underscore the differences, consider the various roles that might typify managers and leaders in a hospital setting. The chief of staff of a large hospital is clearly a manager by virtue of the position itself. At the same time, this individual may not be respected or trusted by others and may have to rely solely on the authority vested in the position to get people to do things. But an emergency-room nurse with

Activity	Management	Leadership
Creating an Agenda	**Planning and budgeting.** Establishing detailed steps and timetables for achieving needed results; allocating the resources necessary to make those needed results happen	**Establishing direction.** Developing a vision of the future, often the distant future, and strategies for producing the changes needed to achieve that vision
Developing a Human Network for Achieving the Agenda	**Organizing and staffing.** Establishing some structure for accomplishing plan requirements, staffing that structure with individuals, delegating responsibility and authority for carrying out the plan, providing policies and procedures to help guide people, and creating methods or systems to monitor implementation	**Aligning people.** Communicating the direction by words and deeds to all those whose cooperation may be needed to influence the creation of teams and coalitions that understand the vision and strategies and accept their validity
Executing Plans	**Controlling and problem solving.** Monitoring results vs. plan in some detail, identifying deviations, and then planning and organizing to solve these problems	**Motivating and inspiring.** Energizing people to overcome major political, bureaucratic, and resource barriers to change by satisfying very basic, but often unfulfilled, human needs
Outcomes	Produces a degree of predictability and order and has the potential to consistently produce major results expected by various stakeholders (e.g., for customers, always being on time; for stockholders, being on budget)	Produces change, often to a dramatic degree, and has the potential to produce extremely useful change (e.g., new products that customers want, new approaches to labor relations that help make a firm more competitive)

TABLE 12.1

Distinctions Between Management and Leadership

Reference: Reprinted with the permission of The Free Press, a Division of Simon & Schuster Adult Publishing Group, from *A Force for Change: How Leadership Differs from Management,* by John P. Kotter, 1990. Copyright © 1990 by John P. Kotter, Inc. All rights reserved.

no formal authority may be quite effective at taking charge of a chaotic situation and directing others in how to deal with specific patient problems. Others in the emergency room may respond because they trust the nurse's judgment and have confidence in the nurse's decision-making skills.

And the head of pediatrics, supervising a staff of twenty other doctors, nurses, and attendants, may also enjoy the staff's complete respect, confidence, and trust. They readily take her advice and follow directives without question, and often go far beyond what is necessary to help carry out the unit's mission. Thus, being a manager does not ensure that a person is also a leader—any given manager may or may not also be a leader. Similarly, a leadership position can also be formal, as when someone appointed to head a group has leadership qualities, or informal, as when a leader emerges from the ranks of the group according to a consensus of the members. The chief of staff described earlier is a manager but not really a leader. The emergency-room nurse is a leader but not a manager. And the head of pediatrics is likely both.

Organizations need both management and leadership if they are to be effective. For example, leadership is necessary to create and direct change and to help the organization get through tough times.[6] And management is necessary to achieve coordination and systematic results and to handle administrative activities during times of stability and predictability. Management in conjunction with leadership can help achieve planned orderly change, and leadership in conjunction with management can keep the organization properly aligned with its environment. In addition, managers and leaders

Many successful businesses are led by people who understand how to be effective leaders as well as effective managers. Meg Whitman is president and CEO of eBay, the popular online auction business. Ms. Whitman used her managerial acumen to assemble a strong top management team, shown with her here. By aligning people effectively and motivating and inspiring them to succeed, she is laying the foundation for the continued success of eBay.

also play a major role in establishing the moral climate of the organization and in determining the role of ethics in its culture.[7]

Early Approaches to Leadership

Although leaders and leadership have profoundly influenced the course of human events, careful scientific study of them began only about a century ago. Early study focused on the traits, or personal characteristics, of leaders.[8] Later research shifted to examine actual leader behaviors.

Trait Approaches to Leadership

Lincoln, Napoleon, Joan of Arc, Hitler, and Gandhi are names that most of us know quite well. Early researchers believed that notable leaders such as these had some unique set of qualities or traits that distinguished them from their peers. Moreover, these traits were presumed to be relatively stable and enduring. Following this **trait approach**, these researchers focused on identifying leadership traits, developing methods for measuring them, and using the methods to select leaders.

Hundreds of studies guided by this research agenda were conducted during the first several decades of the twentieth century. The earliest writers believed that important leadership traits included intelligence, dominance, self-confidence, energy, activity, and task-relevant knowledge. The results of subsequent studies gave rise to a long list of additional traits. Unfortunately, the list quickly became so long that it lost any semblance of practical value. In addition, the results of many studies were inconsistent.

For example, one early argument was that effective leaders such as Lincoln tended to be taller than ineffective leaders. But critics were quick to point out that Hitler and Napoleon, both effective leaders in their own way, were not tall. Some writers have even tried to relate leadership to such traits as body shape, astrological sign, or hand-

The **trait approach** to leadership attempted to identify stable and enduring character traits that differentiated effective leaders from nonleaders.

PepsiCo and . . . **DIVERSITY**

A Multitude of Leaders at PepsiCo

Diversity has always been important to Pepsi. In 1961, for instance, Pepsi's Harvey C. Russell was the first African American to be named as vice president of a major U.S. corporation.

Today, PepsiCo's top management team, board of directors, and labor force are all highly diverse. Of PepsiCo's five largest businesses, three are headed by women, one of them an Asian. A woman serves as the chief financial officer and president of PepsiCo. PepsiCo's board of directors is diverse too. The group of thirteen directors includes three women, two Latinos, two African Americans, one individual originally from India, and one originally from Switzerland. In the U.S. labor force, about 11.4 percent of workers are Hispanic. At PepsiCo, Hispanics represent 10.4 percent of all employees.

Diverse leaders, and a diverse pool of employees who represent potential leaders, provide a variety of backgrounds, experiences, and values. In a diverse environment, these leaders offer various approaches and ideas that lead to success. A diverse leadership group makes better quality decisions as well as providing role models for the labor force.

PepsiCo's website recognizes the importance of a diverse workforce when it says, "Our brands appeal to an extraordinarily diverse array of customers. And they are sold to an equally diverse group of retailers. To truly understand the needs of our customers and consumers—and succeed in the marketplace—PepsiCo must reflect

that diversity in our employees, our suppliers, and in everything we do."

PepsiCo's efforts are recognized by the business community; in 2004 the company received more than twenty significant diversity awards. But, most importantly, performance is strong. Last year, PepsiCo share value grew 12 percent, one-third more than the stock market overall. Investors have confidence in the firm's future, a confidence increased by PepsiCo's leaders and on-going commitment to diversity.

> *"To truly understand the needs of our customers and consumers . . . PepsiCo must reflect that diversity in our employees, our suppliers, and in everything we do."*
>
> PEPSICO WEBSITE

References: "Diversity@Work," "Officers and Directors," "Principal Divisions," "The Pepsi Legacy," PepsiCo website, www.pepsico.com on May 11, 2005; "PepsiCo Shakes Up Leadership," *BevNet*, March 30, 2005, www.bevnet.com on May 11, 2005; "Top 10 Companies for Executive Women," National Association of Female Executives website, January 26, 2005, www.nafe.com on May 11, 2005; Steve S. Reinemund, "Letter to Shareholders," PepsiCo 2004 Annual Report, www.pepsico.com on May 9, 2005.

writing patterns. The trait approach also had a significant theoretical problem in that it could neither specify nor prove how presumed leadership traits are connected to leadership per se. For these and other reasons, the trait approach was all but abandoned several decades ago.

In recent years, however, the trait approach has received renewed interest. For example, some researchers have sought to reintroduce a limited set of traits into the leadership literature. These traits include emotional intelligence, drive, motivation, honesty and integrity, self-confidence, cognitive ability, knowledge of the business, and charisma (which is discussed in Chapter 13).[9] Some people even believe that biological factors may play a role in leadership. Although it is too early to know whether these traits have validity from a leadership perspective, it does appear that a serious and scientific assessment of appropriate traits may further our understanding of the leadership phenomenon. As illustrated in the *PepsiCo and . . . Diversity* box, such traits as ethnicity and gender should perhaps also be studied.

Behavioral Approaches to Leadership

The **behavioral approach** to leadership tried to identify behaviors that differentiated effective leaders from nonleaders.

In the late 1940s, most researchers began to shift away from the trait approach and to look at leadership as an observable process or activity. The goal of the so-called **behavioral approach** was to determine what behaviors were associated with effective leadership.[10] The researchers assumed that the behaviors of effective leaders differed somehow from the behaviors of less effective leaders and that the behaviors of effective leaders would be the same across all situations. The behavioral approach to the study of leadership included the Michigan studies, the Ohio State studies, and the leadership grid.

The **Michigan leadership studies** defined job-centered and employee-centered leadership as opposite ends of a single leadership dimension.

The Michigan Studies

The **Michigan leadership studies** were a program of research conducted at the University of Michigan.[11] The goal of this work was to determine the pattern of leadership behaviors that results in effective group performance. From interviews with supervisors and subordinates of high- and low-productivity groups in several organizations, the researchers collected and analyzed descriptions of supervisory behavior to determine how effective supervisors differed from ineffective ones. Two basic forms of leader behavior were identified—job-centered and employee-centered—as shown in the top portion of Figure 12.1.

Job-centered leader behavior involves paying close attention to the work of subordinates, explaining work procedures, and demonstrating a strong interest in performance.

The leader who exhibits **job-centered leader behavior** pays close attention to the work of subordinates, explains work procedures, and is mainly interested in

---

FIGURE 12.1

Early Behavioral Approaches to Leadership

Two of the first behavioral approaches to leadership were the Michigan and Ohio State studies. The results of the Michigan studies suggested that there are two fundamental types of leader behavior, job-centered and employee-centered, which were presumed to be at opposite ends of a single continuum. The Ohio State studies also found two similar kinds of leadership behavior, "consideration" and "initiating-structure," but this research suggested that these two types of behavior were actually independent dimensions.

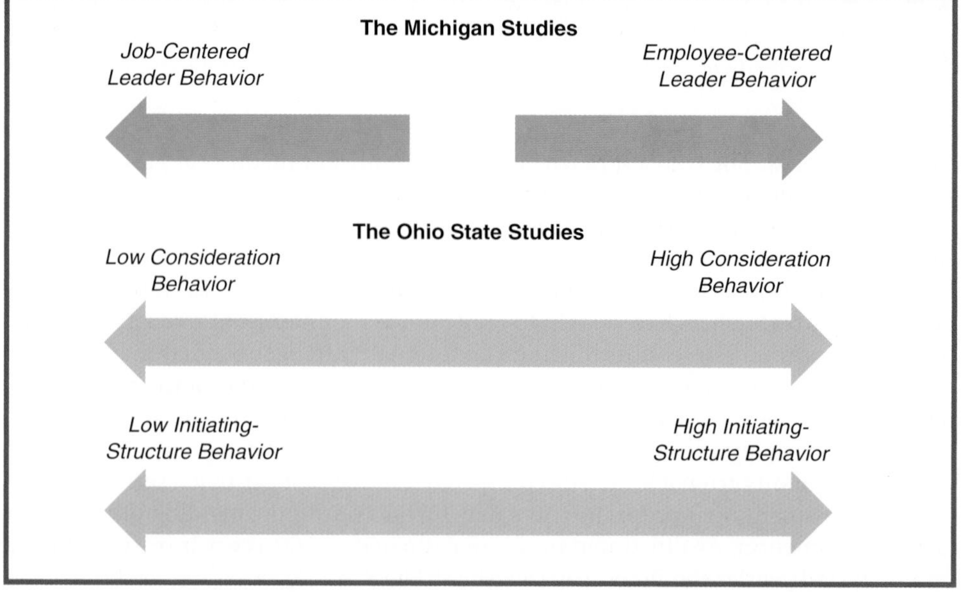

The Michigan Studies

Job-Centered Leader Behavior   *Employee-Centered Leader Behavior*

The Ohio State Studies

Low Consideration Behavior   *High Consideration Behavior*

Low Initiating-Structure Behavior   *High Initiating-Structure Behavior*

performance. The leader's primary concern is efficient completion of the task. The leader who engages in **employee-centered leader behavior** attempts to build effective work groups with high performance goals. The leader's main concern is with high performance, but that is to be achieved by paying attention to the human aspects of the group. These two styles of leader behavior were presumed to be at opposite ends of a single dimension. Thus, the Michigan researchers suggested that any given leader could exhibit either job-centered or employee-centered leader behavior, but not both at the same time. Moreover, they suggested that employee-centered leader behavior was more likely to result in effective group performance than was job-centered leader behavior.

> **Employee-centered leader behavior** involves attempting to build effective work groups with high performance goals.

The Ohio State Studies

The **Ohio State leadership studies** were conducted about the same time as the Michigan studies (in the late 1940s and early 1950s).[12] During this program of research, behavioral scientists at Ohio State University developed a questionnaire, which they administered in both military and industrial settings, to assess subordinates' perceptions of their leaders' behavior. The Ohio State studies identified several forms of leader behavior but tended to focus on the two most significant ones: consideration and initiating-structure.

> The **Ohio State leadership studies** defined leader consideration and initiating-structure behaviors as independent dimensions of leadership.

When engaging in **consideration behavior**, the leader is concerned with the subordinates' feelings and respects subordinates' ideas. The leader-subordinate relationship is characterized by mutual trust, respect, and two-way communication. When using **initiating-structure behavior**, on the other hand, the leader clearly defines the leader-subordinate roles so that subordinates know what is expected of them. The leader also establishes channels of communication and determines the methods for accomplishing the group's task.

> **Consideration behavior** involves being concerned with subordinates' feelings and respecting subordinates' ideas.
> **Initiating-structure behavior** involves clearly defining the leader-subordinate roles so that subordinates know what is expected of them.

Unlike the employee-centered and job-centered leader behaviors, consideration and initiating structure were not thought to be on the same continuum. Instead, as shown in the bottom portion of Figure 12.1, they were seen as independent dimensions of the leader's behavioral repertoire. As a result, a leader could exhibit high initiating-structure behavior and low consideration or low initiating-structure behavior and high consideration. A leader could also exhibit high or low levels of each behavior simultaneously. For example, a leader may clearly define subordinates' roles and expectations but exhibit little concern for their feelings. Alternatively, she or he may be concerned about subordinates' feelings but fail to define roles and expectations clearly. But the leader might also demonstrate concern for performance expectations and employee welfare simultaneously.

The Ohio State researchers also investigated the stability of leader behaviors over time. They found that a given individual's leadership pattern appeared to change little as long as the situation remained fairly constant.[13] Another topic they looked at was the combinations of leader behaviors that were related to effectiveness. At first, they believed that leaders who exhibit high levels of both behaviors would be most effective. An early study at International Harvester (now Navistar Corporation), however, found that employees of supervisors who ranked high on initiating-structure behavior were higher performers but also expressed lower levels of satisfaction. Conversely, employees of supervisors who ranked high on consideration had lower performance ratings but also had fewer absences from work.[14] Later research showed that these conclusions were misleading because the studies did not consider all the important variables. Nonetheless, however, the Ohio State studies represented another important milestone in leadership research.[15]

Leadership Grid

Yet another behavioral approach to leadership is the Leadership Grid (originally called the Managerial Grid).[16] The Leadership Grid provides a means

"Ok, honesty is the best policy. Let's call that option A."

Leader behavior plays an important role in setting the tone and reinforcing the culture of an organization. This executive, for instance, seems headed toward the creation of moral ambiguity in his organization!

for evaluating leadership styles and then training managers to move toward an ideal style of behavior. The most current version of the Leadership Grid is shown in Figure 12.2. The horizontal axis represents *concern for production* (similar to job-centered and initiating-structure behaviors), and the vertical axis represents *concern for people* (similar to employee-centered and consideration behavior). Note the five extremes of leadership behavior: the 1,1 manager (impoverished management) who exhibits minimal concern for both production and people; the 9,1 manager (authority-compliance) who is highly concerned about production but exhibits little concern for people; the 1,9 manager (country club management) who has the exact opposite concerns from the 9,1 manager; the 5,5 manager (middle-of-the-road management) who maintains adequate concern for both people and production; and the 9,9 manager (team management) who exhibits maximum concern for both people and production.

According to this approach, the ideal style of leadership is 9,9. The developers of this model thus created a multiphase training and development program to assist managers in achieving this style of behavior. A.G. Edwards, Westinghouse, FAA, Equicor, and other companies have used the Leadership Grid, and anecdotal evidence seems to confirm its effectiveness in some settings. However, there is little published scientific evidence regarding its true effectiveness and the extent to which it applies to all managers and/or to all settings. Indeed, as we discuss next, such evidence is not likely to actually exist.

The Emergence of Situational Leadership Models

The leader-behavior theories have played an important role in the development of more realistic, albeit more complex, approaches to leadership. In particular, they urge us not to be so preoccupied with what properties may be possessed by leaders (the trait approach) but to concentrate on what leaders actually do (their behaviors). Unfortunately, these theories also make universal generic prescriptions about what constitutes effective leadership. When we are dealing with complex social systems composed of complex individuals, however, few if any relationships are consistently predictable, and certainly no formulas for success are infallible.

Yet, behavior theorists tried to identify consistent relationships between leader behaviors and employee responses in the hope of finding a dependable prescription for effective leadership. As we might expect, they often failed. Other approaches to understanding leadership were therefore needed. The catalyst for these new approaches was the realization that although interpersonal and task-oriented dimensions might be useful to describe the behavior of leaders, they were not useful for predicting or prescribing it. The next step in the evolution of leadership theory was the creation of situational models.

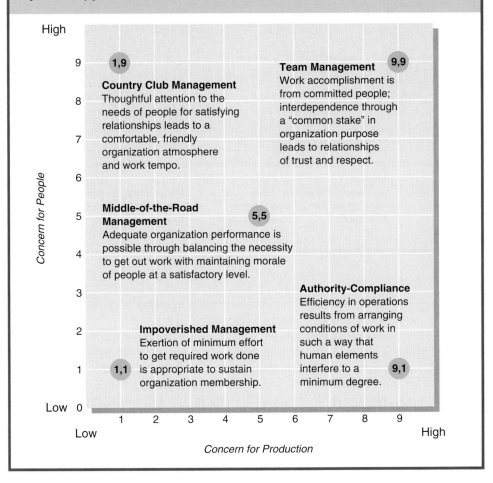

FIGURE 12.2

The Leadership Grid

The Leadership Grid® is a method of evaluating leadership styles. The overall objective of an organization using the Grid® is to train its managers using organizational development techniques so that they are simultaneously more concerned for both people and production (9,9 style on the Grid®).

Source: The Leadership Grid Figure from *Leadership Dilemmas—Grid Solutions* by Robert R. Blake and Anne Adams McCanse. (Formerly the Managerial Grid by Robert R. Blake and Jane S. Mouton.) Houston: Gulf Publishing Company, p. 29. Copyright 1997 by Grid International, Inc. Reproduced by permission of Grid International, Inc.

Situational models assume that appropriate leader behavior varies from one situation to another. The goal of a situational theory, then, is to identify key situational factors and to specify how they interact to determine appropriate leader behavior. Before discussing the major situational theories, we first discuss an important early model that in many ways laid the foundation for these theories. In a seminal article about the decision-making process, Robert Tannenbaum and Warren H. Schmidt proposed a continuum of leadership behavior. Their model is much like the original Michigan framework.[17] Besides purely job-centered behavior (or "boss-centered" behavior, as they termed it) and employee-centered ("subordinate-centered") behavior, however,

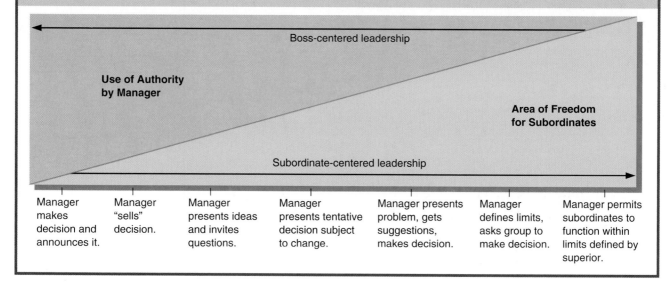

they identified several intermediate behaviors that a manager might consider. These are shown on the leadership continuum in Figure 12.3.

This continuum of behavior ranges from the one extreme of having the manager make the decision alone to the other extreme of having the employees make the decision with minimal guidance from the leader. Each point on the continuum is influenced by characteristics of the manager, subordinates, and the situation. Managerial characteristics include the manager's value system, confidence in subordinates, personal inclinations, and feelings of security. Subordinate characteristics include the subordinates' need for independence, readiness to assume responsibility, tolerance for ambiguity, interest in the problem, understanding of goals, knowledge, experience, and expectations. Situational characteristics that affect decision making include the type of organization, group effectiveness, the problem itself, and time pressures.

Hence, the leadership continuum acknowledged for the first time that leader behaviors represent a continuum rather than discrete extremes, and that various characteristics and elements of any given situation would affect the success of any given leadership style. Although this framework pointed out the importance of situational factors, it was, however, only speculative. It remained for others to develop more comprehensive and integrated theories. In the following sections, we describe three of the most important and widely accepted situational theories of leadership: the LPC theory, the path-goal theory, and Vroom's decision tree approach.

The LPC Theory of Leadership

Fred Fiedler developed the **LPC theory of leadership**. The LPC theory attempts to explain and reconcile both the leader's personality and the complexities of the situation. Originally called the "contingency theory of leadership," this phrase has come to have generic connotations and so a new label is being used to avoid confusion. "LPC" stands for "least-preferred coworker," a concept we explain later in this section. The LPC theory contends that a leader's effectiveness depends on the situation and, as a result, some leaders may be effective in one situation or organization but not in another. The theory also explains why this discrepancy may occur and identifies leader-situation matches that should result in effective performance.

> The **LPC theory of leadership** suggests that a leader's effectiveness depends on the situation.

Task Versus Relationship Motivation

Fiedler and his associates maintain that leadership effectiveness depends on the match between the leader's personality and the situation. Fiedler devised special terms to describe a leader's basic personality traits in relation to leadership: "task motivation" versus "relationship motivation." He also conceptualized the situational context in terms of its favorableness for the leader, ranging from highly favorable to highly unfavorable.

In some respects, the ideas of task and relationship motivation resemble the basic concepts identified in the behavioral approaches. Task motivation closely parallels job-centered and initiating-structure leader behavior, and relationship motivation is similar to employee-centered and consideration leader behavior. A major difference, however, is that Fiedler viewed task versus relationship motivation as being grounded in personality in a way that is basically constant for any given leader.

The LPC theory suggests that what constitutes effective leadership is determined by the situation. These Native American elders, for example, have helped gained formal recognition for the Cowlitz tribe and have recruited over 2,000 members. The leadership style they used to accomplish this task was partially dictated by what they wanted to accomplish. Now the leadership style needed to lead the tribe in its formative stages may be different. And finally, when the tribe becomes a mature and fully functional entity, yet another style may be needed.

The degree of task or relationship motivation in a given leader is measured by the **least-preferred coworker (LPC)** scale. The LPC instructions ask respondents (i.e., leaders) to think of all the persons with whom they have worked and to then select their least-preferred coworker. Respondents then describe this coworker by marking a series of sixteen scales anchored at each end by a positive or negative quality or attribute.[18] For example, three of the items Fiedler uses in the LPC are

Pleasant	8 7 6 5 4 3 2 1	Unpleasant
Inefficient	1 2 3 4 5 6 7 8	Efficient
Unfriendly	1 2 3 4 5 6 7 8	Friendly

The higher numbers on the scales are associated with a positive evaluation of the least-preferred coworker. (Note that the higher scale numbers are associated with the more favorable term and that some items reverse both the terms and the scale values. The latter feature forces the respondent to read the scales more carefully and to provide more valid answers.) Respondents who describe their least-preferred coworker in relatively positive terms receive a high LPC score whereas those who use relatively negative terms receive a low LPC score.

Fiedler assumed that these descriptions actually say more about the leader than about the least-preferred coworker. He believed, for example, that everyone's least-preferred coworker is likely to be equally "unpleasant" and that differences in descriptions actually reflect differences in personality traits among the leaders responding to the LPC scale. Fiedler contended that high-LPC leaders are basically more concerned with interpersonal relations whereas low-LPC leaders are more concerned with task-relevant problems. Not surprisingly, controversy has always surrounded the LPC scale. Researchers have offered several interpretations of the LPC score, arguing that it may be an index of behavior, personality, or some other unknown factor. Indeed, the LPC measure—and its interpretation—have long been among the most debated aspects of this theory.

Situational Favorableness

Fiedler also identified three factors that determine the favorableness of the situation. In order of importance (from most to least important), these factors are leader-member relations, task structure, and leader position power.

Leader-member relations refers to the personal relationship that exists between subordinates and their leader. It is based on the extent to which subordinates trust, respect, and have confidence in their leader, and vice versa. A high degree of mutual trust, respect, and confidence obviously indicates good leader-member relations, and a low degree indicates poor leader-member relations.

Task structure is the second most important determinant of situational favorableness. A structured task is routine, simple, easily understood, and unambiguous. The LPC theory presumes that structured tasks are more favorable because the leader need not be closely involved in defining activities and can devote time to other matters. On the other hand, an unstructured task is one that is nonroutine, ambiguous, and complex. Fiedler argues that this task is more unfavorable because the leader must play a major role in guiding and directing the activities of subordinates.

Finally, *leader position power* is the power inherent in the leader's role itself. If the leader has considerable power to assign work, reward and punish employees, and recommend them for promotion, position power is high and favorable. If, however, the leader must have job assignments approved by someone else, does not control rewards and punishment, and has no voice in promotions, position power is low and unfavorable; that is, many decisions are beyond the leader's control.

Leader-Member Relations	Good				Poor			
Task Structure	Structured		Unstructured		Structured		Unstructured	
Position Power	High	Low	High	Low	High	Low	High	Low
Situational Favorableness	Very favorable				Moderately favorable		Very unfavorable	
Recommended Leader Behavior	↓ Task-oriented behavior				↓ Person-oriented behavior		↓ Task-oriented behavior	

TABLE 12.2

The LPC Theory of Leadership

Leader Motivation and Situational Favorableness Fiedler and his associates conducted numerous studies examining the relationships among leader motivation, situational favorableness, and group performance. Table 12.2 summarizes the results of these studies.

To begin interpreting the results, let's first examine the situational favorableness dimensions shown in the table. The various combinations of these three dimensions result in eight different situations, as arrayed across the first three lines of the table. These situations in turn define a continuum ranging from very favorable to very unfavorable situations from the leader's perspective. Favorableness is noted in the fourth line of the table. For example, good relations, a structured task, and either high or low position power result in a very favorable situation for the leader. But poor relations, an unstructured task, and either high or low position power create very unfavorable conditions for the leader.

The table also identifies the leadership approach that is supposed to achieve high group performance in each of the eight situations. These linkages are shown in the bottom line of the table. A task-oriented leader is appropriate for very favorable as well as very unfavorable situations. For example, the LPC theory predicts that if leader-member relations are poor, the task is unstructured, and leader position power is low, a task-oriented leader will be effective. It also predicts that a task-oriented leader will be effective if leader-member relations are good, the task is structured, and leader position power is high. Finally, for situations of intermediate favorableness, the theory suggests that a person-oriented leader will be most likely to achieve high group performance.

Leader-Situation Match What happens if a person-oriented leader faces a very favorable or very unfavorable situation, or a task-oriented leader faces a situation of intermediate favorableness? Fiedler considers these leader-situation combinations to be "mismatches." Recall that a basic premise of his theory is that leadership behavior is a personality trait. Thus, the mismatched leader cannot readily adapt to the situation and achieve effectiveness. Fiedler contends that when a leader's style and the situation do not match, the only available course of action is to change the situation through "job engineering."[19]

For example, Fiedler suggests that if a person-oriented leader ends up in a situation that is very unfavorable, the manager should attempt to improve matters by spending more time with subordinates to improve leader-member relations and by laying down rules and procedures to provide more task structure. Fiedler and his associates have also developed a widely used training program for supervisors on how to assess situational favorableness and to change the situation, if necessary, to achieve a better match.[20] Weyerhauser and Boeing are among the firms that have experimented with Fiedler's training program.

Evaluation and Implications

The validity of Fiedler's LPC theory has been heatedly debated because of the inconsistency of the research results. Apparent shortcomings of the theory are that the LPC measure lacks validity, the theory is not always supported by research, and Fiedler's assumptions about the inflexibility of leader behavior are unrealistic.[21] The theory itself, however, does represent an important contribution because it returned the field to a study of the situation and explicitly considered the organizational context and its role in effective leadership.

The Path-Goal Theory of Leadership

The **path-goal theory of leadership** suggests that effective leaders clarify the paths (behaviors) that will lead to desired rewards (goals).

Another important contingency approach to leadership is the path-goal theory. Developed jointly by Martin Evans and Robert House, the path-goal theory focuses on the situation and leader behaviors rather than on fixed traits of the leader.[22] In contrast to the LPC theory, the path-goal theory suggests that leaders can readily adapt to different situations.

Basic Premises

The path-goal theory has its roots in the expectancy theory of motivation discussed in Chapter 4. Recall that expectancy theory says that a person's attitudes and behaviors can be predicted from the degree to which the person believes job performance will lead to various outcomes (expectancy) and the value of those outcomes (valences) to the individual. The **path-goal theory of leadership** argues that subordinates are motivated by their leader to the extent that the behaviors of that leader influence their expectancies. In other words, the leader affects subordinates' performance by clarifying the behaviors (paths) that will lead to desired rewards (goals). Ideally, of course, getting a reward in an organization depends on effective performance. Path-goal theory also suggests that a leader may behave in different ways in different situations. The *Apple Computer and . . . Technology* box discusses how Steve Jobs, CEO of Apple Computer, uses basic principles from the path-goal theory as elements of his approach to leadership.

Leader Behaviors As Figure 12.4 shows, path-goal theory identifies four kinds of leader behavior: directive, supportive, participative, and achievement-oriented. With *directive leadership*, the leader lets subordinates

The path-goal theory of leadership encompasses four kinds of leader behavior. Andrea Jung, chair and CEO of Avon, uses each of these behaviors on a regular basis. For example, she occasionally uses directive behavior to set performance expectations and provide guidance. Jung also demonstrates supportive behavior through her care and interest in those she works with. Finally, she also uses achievement-oriented leadership in that she sets challenging goals and provides constant encouragement for everyone to work toward those goals.

Apple Computer and . . . **TECHNOLOGY**

Leading for Innovation

As head of both Pixar Animation Studios and Apple Computer, Steve Jobs has overseen some astonishing developments. Jobs helped produce the first mass-market personal computer, mouse, and graphical user interface, which used icons rather than commands to send instructions to the computer. Pixar holds numerous awards, including Oscars,® for its revolutionary animation technology. Apple's Power Mac and the iPod Mini each won an Innovative Design Excellence Award (IDEA) in 2004. "Apple has changed the rules of the game for three industries—PCs, consumer electronics, and music," says writer Brent Schlender.

Jobs' leadership is more about vision than technical proficiency. "On the technical side, there are people here with skills I can't possibly match," claims Jobs. How, then, does Jobs create an environment in which engineers, computer scientists, and designers can produce cutting-edge products over and over again? According to Jobs, a leader must establish a strategic vision, hire a great group of people, provide a supportive atmosphere, and then get out of their way.

Vision: Focus on innovation. "Motives make so much difference. Our primary goal here is to make the world's best PCs—not to be the biggest or the richest," Jobs states. Jobs reminds employees, "Real artists ship." In other words, working products are the ultimate creative goal.

People: "We hire based on potential," claims Jobs. "[As a manager], you need to hire people who are better than you are."

Atmosphere: Reward teams and be fair. Jobs explains, "The artistic side and technical side are equal . . . Each has the potential to earn the same compensation . . . When one of our films does well, everybody gets a bonus."

Get out of the way: "[Steve's] talent is identifying good people and giving them free rein . . . Part of his genius is recognizing their genius and leaving them to it," says Ed Catmull, president of Pixar.

This chapter's closing case, "The 'Reality-Distortion Field' of Steve Jobs," presents more information about the leadership of Steve Jobs.

> *"[Steve Job's] talent is identifying good people and giving them free rein."*
>
> ED CATMULL, PRESIDENT, PIXAR ANIMATION STUDIOS

References: "Corporate Overview," Pixar website, www.pixar.com on May 20, 2005; Peter Burrows, "The Seed of Apple's Innovation," *Business Week*, October 12, 2004, www.businessweek.com on May 16, 2005; Justin Martin, "Inside the Pixar Dream Factory," *Fortune Small Business*, February 2003, www.fortune.com on May 20, 2005 (quotation); Brent Schlender, "How Big Can Apple Get?" *Fortune*, February 21, 2005, www.fortune.com on May 15, 2005.

know what is expected of them, gives specific guidance as to how to accomplish tasks, schedules work to be done, and maintains definitive standards of performance for subordinates. A leader exhibiting *supportive leadership* is friendly and shows concern for subordinates' status, well-being, and needs. With *participative leadership*, the leader consults with subordinates about issues and takes their suggestions into account before making a decision. Finally, *achievement-oriented leadership* involves setting challenging goals, expecting subordinates to perform at their highest level, and showing strong confidence that subordinates will put forth effort and accomplish the goals. Unlike the LPC theory, path-goal theory assumes that leaders can change their behavior and exhibit any or all of these leadership styles. The theory also predicts that the appropriate combination of leadership styles depends on situational factors.

Situational Factors The path-goal theory proposes two types of situational factors that influence how leader behavior relates to subordinate satisfaction: the

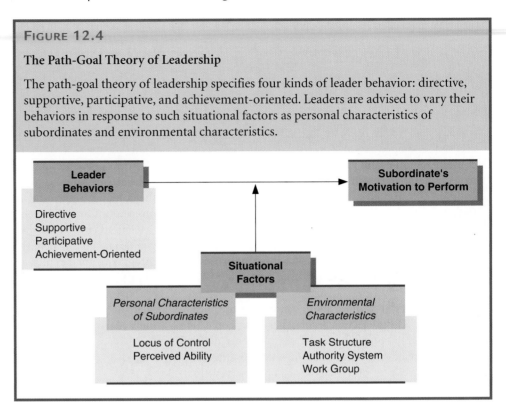

FIGURE 12.4

The Path-Goal Theory of Leadership

The path-goal theory of leadership specifies four kinds of leader behavior: directive, supportive, participative, and achievement-oriented. Leaders are advised to vary their behaviors in response to such situational factors as personal characteristics of subordinates and environmental characteristics.

personal characteristics of the subordinates and the characteristics of the environment (see Figure 12.4).

Two important personal characteristics of subordinates are locus of control and perceived ability. Locus of control, discussed in Chapter 3, refers to the extent to which individuals believe that what happens to them results from their own behavior or from external causes. Research indicates that individuals who attribute outcomes to their own behavior may be more satisfied with a participative leader (since they feel their own efforts can make a difference), whereas individuals who attribute outcomes to external causes may respond more favorably to a directive leader (since they think their own actions are of little consequence). Perceived ability pertains to how people view their own ability with respect to the task. Employees who rate their own ability relatively high are less likely to feel a need for directive leadership (since they think they know how to do the job), whereas those who perceive their own ability to be relatively low may prefer directive leadership (since they think they need someone to show them how to do the job).

Important environmental characteristics are task structure, the formal authority system, and the primary work group. The path-goal theory proposes that leader behavior will motivate subordinates if it helps them cope with environmental uncertainty created by those characteristics. In some cases, however, certain forms of leadership will be redundant, decreasing subordinate satisfaction. For example, when task structure is high, directive leadership is less necessary and therefore less effective; similarly, if the work group gives the individual plenty of social support, a supportive leader will not be especially attractive. Thus, the extent to which leader behavior matches the people and environment in the situation is presumed to influence subordinates' motivation to perform.

Evaluation and Implications

The path-goal theory was designed to provide a general framework for understanding how leader behavior and situational factors influence subordinate attitudes and behaviors. But the intention of the path-goal theorists was to stimulate research on the theory's major propositions, not to offer definitive answers. Researchers hoped that a more fully developed, formal theory of leadership would emerge from continued study. Further work actually has supported the theory's major predictions, but it has not validated the entire model. Moreover, many of the theory's predictions remain overly general and have not been fully refined and tested.

Vroom's Decision Tree Approach to Leadership

The third major contemporary approach to leadership is **Vroom's decision tree approach**. The earliest version of this model was proposed by Victor Vroom and Philip Yetton and later revised and expanded by Vroom and Arthur Jago.[23] Most recently, Vroom has developed yet another refinement of the original model.[24] Like the path-goal theory, this approach attempts to prescribe a leadership style appropriate to a given situation. It also assumes that the same leader may display different leadership styles. But Vroom's approach concerns itself with only a single aspect of leader behavior: subordinate participation in decision making.

> **Vroom's decision tree approach to leadership** attempts to prescribe how much participation subordinates should be allowed in making decisions.

Basic Premises

Vroom's decision tree approach assumes that the degree to which subordinates should be encouraged to participate in decision making depends on the characteristics of the situation. In other words, no one decision-making process is best for all situations. After evaluating a variety of problem attributes (characteristics of the problem or decision), the leader determines an appropriate decision style that specifies the amount of subordinate participation.

Vroom's current formulation suggests that managers should use one of two different decision trees.[25] To do so, the manager first assesses the situation in terms of several factors. This assessment involves determining whether the given factor is "high" or "low" for the decision that is to be made. For instance, the first factor is decision significance. If the decision is extremely important and may have a major impact on the organization (i.e., choosing a location for a new plant), its significance is high. But if the decision is routine, and its consequences not terribly important (i.e., selecting a logo for the firm's softball team uniforms), its significance is low. This assessment guides the manager through the paths of the decision tree to a recommended course of action. One decision tree is to be used when the manager is primarily interested in making the decision on the most timely basis possible; the other is to be used when time is less critical, and the manager is interested in helping subordinates to improve and develop their own decision-making skills.

The two decision trees are shown in Figures 12.5 and 12.6. The problem attributes (situational factors) are arranged along the top of the decision tree. To use the model, the decision maker starts at the left side of the diagram and assesses the first problem attribute (decision significance). The answer determines the path to the second node on the decision tree, where the next attribute (importance of commitment) is assessed.

Vroom's decision tree approach to leadership suggests that leaders should vary the degree of participation they provide to subordinates in making decisions. In the wake of financial scandal after financial scandal, some top managers have begun to systematically increase communication and participation throughout the ranks of their organization. For instance, Steve Odland (standing) is the CEO of AutoZone. He now insists that all top managers fully participate in discussions and decisions regarding the firm's finances. Indeed, he requires that each top manager certify the accuracy of his or her unit's financial performance before the results are submitted to him.

This process continues until a terminal node is reached. In this way, the manager identifies an effective decision-making style for the situation.

The various decision styles reflected at the ends of the tree branches represent different levels of subordinate participation that the manager should attempt to adopt in a given situation. The five styles are defined as follows:

- *Decide:* The manager makes the decision alone and then announces or "sells" it to the group.
- *Delegate:* The manager allows the group to define for itself the exact nature and parameters of the problem and to then develop a solution.
- *Consult (Individually):* The manager presents the program to group members individually, obtains their suggestions, and then makes the decision.
- *Consult (Group):* The manager presents the problem to group members at a meeting, gets their suggestions, and then makes the decision.
- *Facilitate:* The manager presents the problem to the group at a meeting, defines the problem and its boundaries, and then facilitates group member discussion as members make the decision.

Vroom's decision tree approach represents a very focused but quite complex perspective on leadership. To compensate for this difficulty, Vroom has developed elaborate expert system software to help managers assess a situation accurately and quickly and then make an appropriate decision regarding employee participation. Many firms, including Halliburton Company, Litton Industries, and Borland International, have provided their managers with training in how to use the various versions of this model.

FIGURE **12.5**

Vroom's Time-Driven Decision Tree

This matrix is recommended for situations in which time is of the highest importance in making a decision. The matrix operates like a funnel. You start at the left with a specific decision problem in mind. The column headings denote situational factors that may or may not be present in that problem. You progress by selecting High or Low (H or L) for each relevant situational factor. Proceed down from the funnel, judging only those situational factors for which a judgment is called for, until you reach the recommended process.

Reference: Victor H. Vroom's Time-Driven Model from *A Model of Leadership Style,* copyright 1998.

Decision Significance	Importance of Commitment	Leader Expertise	Likelihood of Commitment	Group Support	Group Expertise	Team Competence	
H	H	H	H	-	-	-	Decide
			L	H	H	H	Delegate
						L	Consult (Group)
					L	-	Consult (Group)
				L	-	-	
	H	L	H	H	H	H	Facilitate
						L	Consult (Individually)
					L	-	Consult (Individually)
				L	-	-	
		L	L	H	H	H	Facilitate
						L	Consult (Group)
					L	-	Consult (Group)
				L	-	-	
	L	H	-	-	-	-	Decide
		L	-	H	H	H	Facilitate
						L	Consult (Individually)
					L	-	Consult (Individually)
				L	-	-	
L	H	-	H	-	-	-	Decide
			L			H	Delegate
						L	Facilitate
	L	-	-	-	-	-	Decide

FIGURE 12.6

Vroom's Development-Driven Decision Tree

This matrix is to be used when the leader is more interested in developing employees than in making the decision as quickly as possible. Just as with the time-driven tree shown in Figure 12.5, the leader assesses up to seven situational factors. These factors, in turn, funnel the leader to a recommended process for making the decision.

Reference: Victor H. Vroom's Development-Driven Model from *A Model of Leadership Style,* copyright 1998.

Decision Significance	Importance of Commitment	Leader Expertise	Likelihood of Commitment	Group Support	Group Expertise	Team Competence	
P R O B L E M S T A T E M E N T							
H	H	-	H	H	H	H	Decide
						L	Facilitate
					L	-	Consult (Group)
				L	-	-	Consult (Group)
			L	H	H	H	Delegate
						L	Facilitate
					L	-	Facilitate
				L	-	-	Consult (Group)
	L	-	-	H	H	H	Delegate
						L	Facilitate
					L	-	Consult (Group)
				L	-	-	Consult (Group)
L	H	-	H	-	-	-	Decide
			L	-	-	-	Delegate
	L	-	-	-	-	-	Decide

Evaluation and Implications

Because Vroom's current approach is relatively new, it has not been fully scientifically tested. The original model and its subsequent refinement, however, attracted a great deal of attention and were generally supported by research.[26] For example, there is some support for the idea that individuals who make decisions consistent with the predictions of the model are more effective than those who make decisions inconsistent with it. The model therefore appears to be a tool that managers can apply with some confidence in deciding how much subordinates should participate in the decision-making process.

Synopsis

Leadership is both a process and a property. Leadership as a process is the use of noncoercive influence to direct and coordinate the activities of group members to meet goals. As a property, leadership is the set of characteristics attributed to those who are perceived to use such influence successfully. Leadership and management are related but distinct phenomena.

Early leadership research primarily attempted to identify important traits and behaviors of leaders. The Michigan and Ohio State studies each identified two kinds of leader behavior, one focusing on job factors, the other on people factors. The Michigan studies viewed these behaviors as points on a single continuum whereas the Ohio State studies suggested that they were separate dimensions. The Leadership Grid further refined these concepts.

Newer situational theories of leadership attempt to identify appropriate leadership styles on the basis of the situation. The leadership continuum first proposed by Tannenbaum and Schmidt was the catalyst for these theories.

Fiedler's LPC theory states that leadership effectiveness depends on a match between the leader's style (viewed as a trait of the leader) and the favorableness of the situation. Situation favorableness, in turn, is determined by task structure, leader-member relations, and leader position power. Leader behavior is presumed to reflect a constant personality trait and therefore cannot easily be changed.

The path-goal theory focuses on appropriate leader behavior for various situations. The path-goal theory suggests that directive, supportive, participative, or achievement-oriented leader behavior may be appropriate, depending on the personal characteristics of subordinates and the characteristics of the environment. Unlike the LPC theory, this view presumes that leaders can alter their behavior to best fit the situation.

Vroom's decision tree approach suggests appropriate decision-making styles based on situation characteristics. This approach focuses on deciding how much subordinates should participate in the decision-making process. Managers assess situational attributes and follow a series of paths through a decision tree that subsequently prescribes for them how they should make a particular decision.

Discussion Questions

1. How would you define "leadership"? Compare and contrast your definition with the one given in this chapter.

2. Cite examples of managers who are not leaders and leaders who are not managers. What makes them one and not the other? Also, cite examples of both formal and informal leaders.

3. What traits do you think characterize successful leaders? Do you think the trait approach has validity?

4. Recent evidence suggests that successful managers (defined by organizational rank and salary) may indeed have some of the same traits originally ascribed to effective leaders (such as an attractive appearance and relative height). How might this finding be explained?

5. What other forms of leader behavior besides those cited in the chapter can you identify?

6. Critique Fiedler's LPC theory. Are other elements of the situation important? Do you think Fiedler's assertion about the inflexibility of leader behavior makes sense? Why or why not?

7. Do you agree or disagree with Fiedler's assertion that leadership motivation is basically a personality trait? Why?

8. Compare and contrast the LPC and path-goal theories of leadership. What are the strengths and weaknesses of each?

9. Of the three major leadership theories—the LPC theory, the path-goal theory, and Vroom's decision tree approach—which is the most comprehensive? Which is the narrowest? Which has the most practical value?

10. How realistic do you think it is for managers to attempt to use Vroom's decision tree approach as prescribed? Explain.

Understanding Successful and Unsuccessful Leadership

Purpose: This exercise will help you better understand the behaviors of successful and unsuccessful leaders.

Format: You will be asked to identify contemporary examples of successful and unsuccessful leaders and then to describe how these leaders differ.

Procedure:

1. Working alone, each student should list the names of ten people he or she thinks of as leaders in public life. Note that the names should not necessarily be confined to "good" leaders but instead should also identify "strong" leaders.

2. Next, students should form small groups and compare their lists. This comparison should focus on common and unique names as well as on the kinds of individuals listed (i.e., male or female, contemporary or historical, business or nonbusiness, and so on).

3. From all the lists, choose two leaders whom most people would consider very successful and two who would be deemed unsuccessful.

4. Identify similarities and differences between the two successful leaders and between the two unsuccessful leaders.

5. Relate the successes and failures to at least one theory or perspective discussed in the chapter.

6. Select one group member to report your findings to the rest of the class.

Follow-up Questions

1. What role does luck play in leadership?

2. Are there factors about the leaders you researched that might have predicted their success or failure before they achieved leadership roles?

3. What are some criteria of successful leadership?

Applying Vroom's Decision Tree Approach

This skillbuilder will help you better understand your own leadership style regarding employee participation in decision making. Mentally play the role described in the following scenario, then make the comparisons suggested at the end of the exercise.

You are the southwestern United States branch manager of an international manufacturing and sales organization. The firm's management team is looking for ways to increase efficiency. As one part of this effort, the company recently installed an integrated computer network linking sales representatives, customer service employees, and other sales support staff. Sales were supposed to increase and sales expenses to drop as a result.

However, exactly the opposite has occurred: Sales have dropped a bit, and expenses are up. You have personally inspected the new system and believe the hardware is fine. However, you believe the software linking the various computers is less than ideal.

The subordinates you have quizzed about the system, on the other hand, think the entire system is fine. They attribute the problems to a number of factors, including inadequate training in how to use the system, a lack of incentive for using it, and generally poor morale. Whatever the reasons given, each worker queried had strong feelings about the issue.

Your boss has just called you and expressed concern about the problems. He has indicated that he has confidence in your ability to solve the problem and will leave it in your hands. However, he wants a report on how you plan to proceed within one week. First, think of how much participation you would normally be inclined to allow your subordinates in making this decision. Next, apply Vroom's decision tree approach to the problem and see what it suggests regarding the optimal level of participation. Compare your normal approach with the recommended solution.

Exercise Overview: Conceptual skills refer to the manager's ability to think in the abstract. This exercise will enable you to apply your conceptual skills to better understanding the distinction between leadership and management.

Exercise Task: First, identify someone who currently occupies a management and/or leadership position. This individual can be a manager in a large business, the owner of a small business, the president of a campus organization, or any other similar kind of position. Next, interview this individual and ask them the following questions:

1. Name three recent tasks or activities that were primarily management in nature, requiring little or no leadership.

Building Managerial Skills

2. Name three recent tasks or activities that were primarily leadership in nature, requiring little or no management.

3. Do you spend most of the time working as a manager or a leader?

4. How easy or difficult is it to differentiate activities on the basis of their being management versus leadership?

Finally, after you have completed the interview, break up into small groups with your classmates and discuss your results. What have you learned about leadership from this activity?

Organizational Behavior Case for Discussion

The "Reality-Distortion Field" of Steve Jobs

Steve Jobs, a co-founder of Apple Computer, was the visionary behind the first mass-market personal computer, while his co-founder, Steve Wozniak, was the technical wizard. The quirky, creative, and unique culture of Apple was greatly influenced by Jobs, the nonconformist CEO. Apple's unprecedented success paved the way for the PC boom of the 1980s. However, under pressure of competition from mainstream computer makers such as IBM and Compaq, Apple's performance declined. As the PC maker lost its strategic direction, Jobs reluctantly left Apple in 1985. One biography of Jobs sums up the turnover, saying, "While Jobs was a persuasive and charismatic evangelist for Apple, critics also claimed he was an erratic and tempestuous manager." In 1986, Jobs purchased Pixar from George Lucas and became CEO. The computer animation studio produced its first film, *Toy Story*, in 1995. And after a decade of mediocre results at Apple, Jobs again assumed the top spot in 1997.

As Apple's CEO, Jobs developed a reputation for brilliance, originality, and charm. At the same time, he could be arrogant and hypercritical. He expected others to meet his very high standards and was insulting when disappointed. One industry observer portrayed

Jobs as intimidating and power hungry, while others said he commanded "a cult-like following from employees and consumers."

Yet, in spite of occasional criticism, Jobs is clearly a leader who can deliver success in businesses that are evolving, highly technical, and demanding. Writer Steven Berglas says, "Jobs, the enfant terrible widely reputed to be one of the most aggressive egotists in Silicon Valley, has an unrivaled track record when it comes to pulling development teams through start-ups." Referring to the bitter battles waged in the PC industry during the period of rapid growth, Berglas believes that Jobs is an empire builder who "held up IBM as the enemy he needed to destroy." Writing about the history of the PC industry, author Robert X. Cringely states that Jobs had a "reality-distortion field" surrounding him, so that his vision became the one adopted by many in the industry. "The major advantage of having Jobs on the job during uncertain and anxious times is his capacity to dispel feelings of ambiguity," writes Berglas.

But would Jobs's charisma, confidence, and vision allow him to be a successful leader during times of prosperity and success? Berglas and some other industry observers predicted that Jobs would not be able to switch his leadership behavior to effectively manage the company during good times. However, as Apple's shares reached an all-time high of $80 and the company had the highest revenues and profits in its history in January 2005, Jobs has proved them wrong.

He is more unbeatable than ever. In a 2004 interview, Jobs discussed how his passion and focus enable the company to succeed in any type of situation or environment. "Lots of companies have tons of great engineers and smart people," said Jobs. "But ultimately, there needs to be some gravitational force that pulls it all together . . . That's what was missing at Apple for a while. There were bits and pieces of interesting things floating around, but not that gravitational pull."

Today, Pixar, Apple, and Jobs are riding high. Pixar has released a series of wildly successful movies, such as *Monsters, Inc.*, *Finding Nemo*, and *The Incredibles*. Each film has grossed more than the previous one. *The Incredibles* had sales of $143 million in its opening weekend; the DVD sold five million on the first day of release, setting a daily record of $100 million. Apple has released several versions of the hugely popular iPod, supported by the company's online music store, iTunes. The recent iMac and Mac mini have also been bestsellers.

> **❝ The major advantage of having Jobs on the job during uncertain and anxious times is his capacity to dispel feelings of ambiguity. ❞**
> — STEVEN BERGLAS, WRITER

Jobs's confidence is justified by the company's tremendous success and his confidence is growing. Jobs says, "Apple is doing the best work in its history . . . And there's a lot more coming."

Case Questions

1. Using the Michigan studies framework, describe the leader behavior of Steve Jobs. Is he likely to be an effective leader? Why or why not?

2. A manager who has very high expectations can be most effective in what types of situations? Use path-goal theory to explain your answer.

3. Based on your answer to the previous question, do you expect Steve Jobs to be an effective manager at Pixar and Apple? Explain.

References: Steven Berglas, "What You Can Learn from Steve Jobs," *Inc. Magazine*, October 1999, www.inc.com on May 5, 2005 (quotation); Peter Burrows, "Apple's Bold Swim Downstream," *Business Week*, January 24, 2005, pp. 32–35; Peter Burrows, "The Seed of Apple's Innovation," *Business Week*, October 12, 2004, www.businessweek.com on May 16, 2005; Robert X. Cringely, *Accidental Empires*, Addison-Wesley, 1992; Alan Deutschman, *The Second Coming of Steve Jobs*, Broadway Publishing, September 2001; Brent Schlender, "How Big Can Apple Get?" *Fortune*, February 21, 2005, www.fortune.com on May 15, 2005; Mike Snider, "The New Theatrical Event: DVD," *USA Today*, March 21, 2005, www.usatoday.com on May 15, 2005.

TEST PREPPER

You have read the chapter and studied the key terms. Think you're ready to ace the exam? Take this sample test to gauge your comprehension of chapter material and check your answers at the back of the book. Want more test questions? Take the ACE quizzes found on the student website: http://college.hmco.com/business/students/ (select Griffin/Moorhead, Organizational Behavior, 8e from the Management menu).

T F 1. Leadership can be a property or a process, but not both.

T F 2. The earliest study of leadership focused on leaders' behaviors.

T F 3. Leaders use initiating-structure behaviors to show respect for subordinates' feelings and ideas.

T F 4. Situation models of leadership teach a leader how to steer clear of difficult situations.

T F 5. In Fiedler's LPC theory, a leader has power when he or she can assign work and reward and punish employees.

T F 6. According to the path-goal theory of leadership, leaders motivate their subordinates by clarifying the behaviors that will be rewarded.

T F 7. Vroom's decision tree approach helps leaders determine how much subordinate participation to include in decision making.

8. Compared to managers, leaders do which of the following?
   a. Create and direct change
   b. Achieve coordination
   c. Handle administrative activities
   d. Achieve systematic results
   e. Compare results with goals

9. Although the trait approach to leadership was all but abandoned several decades ago, renewed interest in leadership traits has focused on which of the following characteristics?
   a. Emotional intelligence
   b. Motivation
   c. Honesty and integrity
   d. Cognitive ability
   e. Current interest in leadership traits has focused on all of the above characteristics.

10. The behavioral theories of leadership focused on which two basic dimensions of leadership?
    a. Profit-generating behaviors and cost-reducing behaviors
    b. Work-centered behaviors and employee-centered behaviors

   c. Personal goal-directed behaviors and organizational goal-directed behaviors
   d. Management behaviors and leadership behaviors
   e. Public behaviors and private behaviors

11. Situational models of leadership assume
    a. good leaders are made rather than born.
    b. leadership is based on personal characteristics rather than on behaviors.
    c. leaders are most effective when they focus on situations, not on people.
    d. leaders should learn as much as possible about the situation before acting.
    e. appropriate leader behavior varies from one situation to another.

12. Janice takes Fiedler's Least-Preferred Coworker (LPC) questionnaire and rates her least-preferred coworker in positive terms. According to LPC theory, Janice is which type of leader?
    a. Task motivated
    b. Decision motivated
    c. Relationship motivated
    d. Path-goal motivated
    e. Career motivated

13. According to path-goal theory, when would a directive leadership style be most appropriate?
    a. When subordinates have high motivation
    b. When subordinates have an external locus of control
    c. When subordinates have high ability
    d. When leaders have an internal locus of control
    e. When leaders have low ability

14. Thomas is interested in becoming a more effective leader. One issue he struggles with currently is how much to involve subordinates in decision making. Which of the following would likely help Thomas resolve this issue?
    a. Path-goal theory
    b. Fiedler's LPC theory
    c. The Ohio State studies
    d. Vroom's decision tree approach
    e. The Managerial Grid

CHAPTER 13

Contemporary Views of Leadership in Organizations

Chapter Outline

A New President for MIT

The Massachusetts Institute of Technology (MIT) is the nation's foremost research university, ranked first and fourth in graduate and undergraduate programs. Business, science, technology, and engineering are the school's strengths. Yet a 1999 investigation about discrimination against female faculty reported lower pay, fewer resources for research, and slower promotions. MIT's hiring of female professors hadn't increased in a decade, despite a record number of female PhDs. No women had ever headed a science department at MIT. In addition, the university has seen a decline in corporate and government spending for research in science and engineering. Also, and most alarmingly, foreign student applications for MIT have dropped sharply.

All of that is likely to change under MIT's new president, Dr. Susan Hockfield. Hockfield brings a number of important credentials to her new position. First, her specialization in neurobiology, a "life" science, complements MIT's strength in the physical sciences. Second, her experience as dean and then provost of Yale University demonstrates her skills in fund raising, collaborative research, and developing graduate students. And third, she is female and has personal knowledge and experience in issues regarding careers and gender.

> **"We all thought that women getting the jobs was all you needed to achieve equality."**
>
> NANCY HOPKINS, BIOLOGY PROFESSOR, MIT

Hockfield's qualifications clearly show that she is capable of effective transactional leadership. The question is—will she be an effective transformational leader as well? She certainly intends to try. One of her first priorities is to increase the number of women at MIT, both overall and in leadership positions. This will require adjusting MIT's male-dominated culture. In the past, "we all thought that women getting the jobs was all you needed to achieve equality," says MIT professor Nancy Hopkins. "But it turns out that the experiences of different people are not necessarily the same." Hockfield plans to address each aspect of gender inequality by implementing several changes, including pay surveys, a more flexible tenure schedule, more inclusion in decision making and leadership, and increased recruiting of female engineers.

Graduate students are also part of Hockfield's transformation plan. Post-9/11 security concerns have made it harder for international students to obtain U.S. study visas. "Nationally we've seen a 30 percent falloff in applications for graduate school from international students," Hockfield states. "If we cut off these opportunities, these people will go somewhere else. And ultimately, we could lose our position as a world leader in science and technology."

Hockfield's greatest transformational effort springs from her determination to advance science and math education in grades K–12 through research and educational symposia, publications,

speeches, and the like. "We [in the U.S.] need to raise expectations," Hockfield says. "We need to reinspire the nation to value the people who work in science and technology."

In January 2005, Harvard president Lawrence C. Summers suggested that "innate differences" between the genders might account for the lack of women in science. Hockfield joined other university presidents in writing a letter sharply rejecting Summers' idea; the letter stated that his remarks "had the untoward effect of shifting the focus of the debate to history rather than to the future." Hockfield's unwavering focus on the future will enable her to make the sweeping changes needed for organizational transformation at MIT.

A boxed insert, *MIT's Hockfield and . . . Diversity* focuses on Hockfield's leadership and gender issues at MIT.

References: "MIT Completes Ground-Breaking Studies on Status of Women" (quotation), "Susan Hockfield," MIT website, www.mit.edu on June 11, 2005; Daniel J. Hemel, "Chief Calls for 'Family Friendly' Tenure Rules," *The Harvard Crimson*, February 14, 2005, www.thecrimson.com on June 11, 2005; Lisa Scanlon, "MIT Chooses Neurobiologist Susan Hockfield as President," *Technology Review*, August 26, 2004, www.techreview.com on June 11, 2005; William C. Symonds, "A Breakthrough for MIT—and Science," *Business Week*, October 4, 2004, www.businessweek.com on June 11, 2005; William C. Symonds, "MIT's Chief on America's Slide and How to Fix It," *Business Week*, October 4, 2004, www.businessweek.com on June 11, 2005.

The three major situational theories of leadership discussed in Chapter 12 altered everyone's thinking about leadership. No longer did people feel compelled to search for the one best way to lead. Nor did they continue to seek universal leadership prescriptions or relationships. Instead, both researchers and practicing managers turned their attention to a variety of new approaches to leadership.

These new approaches, as well as other current emerging leadership issues, are the subject of this chapter. We first describe two relatively new situational theories, as well as recent refinements to the earlier theories. We then examine leadership through the eyes of followers. Recent thinking regarding potential alternatives to traditional leadership are then explored. Next we describe the changing nature of leadership. We conclude this chapter with a discussion of several emerging issues in leadership.

Contemporary Situational Theories

The LPC theory, the path-goal theory, and Vroom's decision tree approach together redirected the study of leadership. Not surprisingly, then, other situational theories have also been developed. Moreover, there continue to be changes and refinements to the original situational models.

The **leader-member exchange model (LMX)** of leadership stresses the importance of variable relationships between supervisors and each of their subordinates.

The **in-group** often receives special duties requiring more responsibility and autonomy; they may also receive special privileges, such as more discretion about work schedules.

The Leader-Member Exchange Model

The **leader-member exchange model (LMX)** of leadership, conceived by George Graen and Fred Dansereau, stresses the importance of variable relationships between supervisors and each of their subordinates.[1] Each superior-subordinate pair is referred to as a "vertical dyad." The model differs from earlier approaches in that it focuses on the differential relationship leaders often establish with different subordinates. Figure 13.1 shows the basic concepts of the leader-member exchange theory.

The model suggests that supervisors establish a special relationship with a small number of trusted subordinates referred to as the **in-group**. The in-group often receives special duties requiring more responsibility and autonomy; they may also receive special privileges, such as more discretion about work schedules. Members of the in-group are also likely to be privy to sensitive information and to know about coming

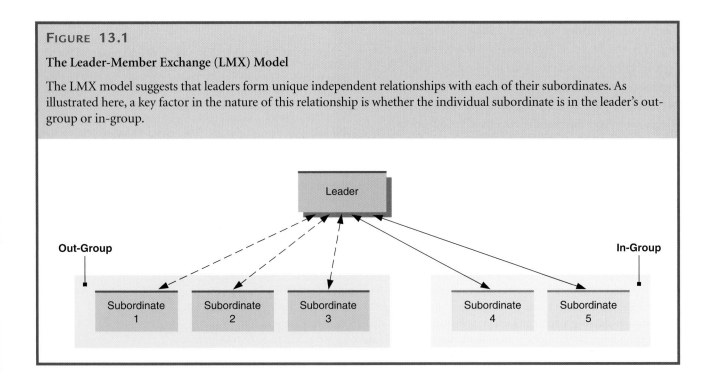

FIGURE 13.1

The Leader-Member Exchange (LMX) Model

The LMX model suggests that leaders form unique independent relationships with each of their subordinates. As illustrated here, a key factor in the nature of this relationship is whether the individual subordinate is in the leader's out-group or in-group.

events before others. They may also receive more rewards and generally stronger support from the leader.

Subordinates who are not a part of this group are called the **out-group**, and they receive less of the supervisor's time and attention. Members of the out-group are likely to be assigned the more mundane tasks the group must perform and not be "in the loop" insofar as information is being shared. They may also receive fewer rewards and overall weaker support from the leader.

Note in the figure that the leader has a dyadic, or one-to-one, relationship with each of the five subordinates. Early in his or her interaction with a given subordinate, the supervisor initiates either an in-group or an out-group relationship. It is not clear how a leader selects members of the in-group, but the decision may be based on personal compatibility and subordinates' competence. Research has confirmed the existence of in-groups and out-groups. In addition, studies generally have found that in-group members tend to have a higher level of performance and satisfaction than out-group members.[2]

> Members of the **out-group** receive less of the supervisor's time and attention, are likely to be assigned the more mundane tasks the group must perform, and are not "in the loop" insofar as information is being shared.

The Hersey and Blanchard Model

Another recent situational perspective, especially popular among practicing managers, is the Hersey and Blanchard model. Like the leadership grid discussed in the previous chapter, this model was also developed as a consulting tool. The **Hersey and Blanchard model** is based on the notion that appropriate leader behavior depends on the "readiness" of the leader's followers.[3] In this instance, readiness refers to the subordinate's degree of motivation, competence, experience, and interest in accepting responsibility. Figure 13.2 shows the basic model.

The figure suggests that as the readiness of followers improves, the leader's basic style should also change. When subordinate readiness is low, for example, the leader should rely on a "telling" style by providing direction and defining roles. When low to moderate readiness exists, the leader should use a "selling" style by offering direction and role definition accompanied by explanation and information. In a case of moderate-to-high follower readiness, the leader should use a "participating" style, allowing followers to share in decision making. Finally, when follower readiness is high, the leader is advised to use a "delegating" style by allowing followers to work independently with little or no overseeing.

> The **Hersey and Blanchard model** is based on the premise that appropriate leader behavior depends on the "readiness" of the leader's followers. In this instance, readiness refers to the subordinate's degree of motivation, competence, experience, and interest in accepting responsibility.

Refinements and Revisions of Other Theories

In addition to these somewhat newer models, the three dominant situational theories have also continued to undergo various refinements and revisions. For instance, while the version of the LPC theory presented in Chapter 12 is still the dominant model, researchers have made several attempts to improve its validity. Most recently, for example, Fiedler has added the concept of stress as a major element of situational favorableness. He also argued that the leader's intelligence and experience plays a major role in enabling her or him to cope with various levels of stress that characterize any particular situation.[4]

The path-goal theory has also undergone major refinements over the years. Its original formulation included only two forms of leader behavior. A third was later added and then, most recently, the theory evolved to include the four forms of leader behavior discussed in Chapter 12. While there has been relatively little research on this theory in recent years, its intuitive logic and general research support make it highly likely that it will again one day emerge as a popular topic for research.

Finally, Vroom's decision tree approach also continues to evolve. The version presented in Chapter 12 was the third published version. Moreover, Vroom and his

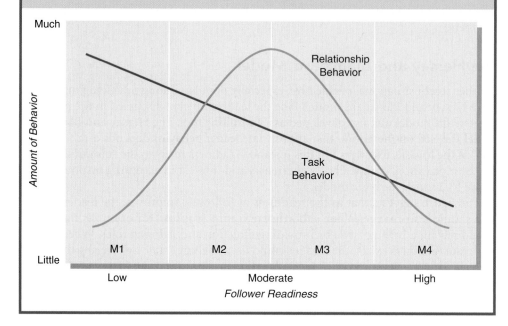

FIGURE 13.2

The Hersey and Blanchard Theory of Leadership

The Hersey and Blanchard theory suggests that leader behaviors should vary in response to the readiness of followers. This figure shows the nature of this variation. The curved line suggests that relationship leader behavior should start low, gradually increase, but then decrease again as follower readiness increases. But task behavior, shown by the straight line, should start high when followers lack readiness and then continuously diminish as they gain readiness.

Reference: The Situational Leadership Model is the registered trademark of the Center for Leadership Studies, Escondido, CA. Excerpt from P. Hersey, *Management Organizational Behavior Utilizing Human Resources,* 3rd ed., 1977, p. 165.

associates have continued to develop training and assessment materials to better enable managers to understand their own "natural" decision-making styles. In addition, there are software versions of the various models that now can quickly help managers determine the optimal level of participation in any given situation.

Leadership Through the Eyes of Followers

Another recent perspective that has been adopted by some leadership experts focuses on how leaders are seen through the eyes of followers. That is, in what ways and to what extent is it important that followers and other observers attribute leadership to others? The three primary approaches to leadership through the eyes of followers are transformational leadership, charismatic leadership, and attributions of leadership.

MIT's Hockfield and . . .   **DIVERSITY**

Does It Take a Woman to Lead a Woman?

Dr. Susan Hockfield is an accomplished university teacher, researcher, and leader. She is well qualified to be president of MIT, her job since December of 2004. The appointment of a female president also serves a symbolic role, demonstrating the university's commitment to furthering women in higher education. Beyond symbolic value, however, is Hockfield more capable of leading the female faculty members at MIT, simply because of her gender?

In one sense, yes. Hockfield is a public reminder that women can succeed in the academic world, in spite of the academic career path, which requires eight or more years of schooling followed by a six-year period of intense research. This schedule can discourage many women, but Hockfield chose to marry and have a daughter after receiving tenure, showing that this is one option that is possible. Still, prejudices remain. "If a woman decides she is going to have a family, university science departments equate that with not being serious," says Donna J. Nelson, a chemistry professor.

However, in another way, it clearly does not take a woman to lead a woman. Women are just as likely as men to possess leadership traits, including high self-confidence, strong values, good communication skills, and a desire to influence others. Barriers to effective leadership by women spring from social and organizational factors, not ability. With access to fewer resources, mentoring, and promotions, women are not well prepared for leadership positions. Societal expectations and inflexible career paths are also obstacles.

Even those who try to support women in academics betray the stereotypes in their thinking. Writing about Hockfield and the lack of female professors in the sciences, author William C. Symonds notes that "Hockfield didn't marry until the year she got tenure, wasn't distracted by a family." Is a family considered a distraction for a man? Would the author have noted the professor's delay in starting a family if Hockfield had been male? Probably not, and there lies the problem.

> *"If a woman decides she is going to have a family, university science departments equate that with not being serious."*
>
> DONNA J. NELSON, CHEMISTRY PROFESSOR, UNIVERSITY OF OKLAHOMA

References: "MIT's 16th President," "Susan Hockfield," MIT website, www.mit.edu on February 19, 2005; Lisa Scanlon, "MIT Chooses Neurobiologist Susan Hockfield as President," *Technology Review*, August 26, 2004, www.techreview.com on June 11, 2005; William C. Symonds, "A Breakthrough for MIT—and Science," *Business Week*, October 4, 2004, www.businessweek.com on June 11, 2005 (quotation).

Transformational Leadership

Recall from Chapter 12 the distinction between management and leadership. *Transactional leadership* is essentially the same as management in that it involves routine, regimented activities. Closer to the general notion of leadership, however, is **transformational leadership**, the set of abilities that allows the leader to recognize the need for change, to create a vision to guide that change, and to execute the change effectively. Only a leader with tremendous influence can hope to perform these functions successfully. Some experts believe that change is such a vital organizational function that even successful firms need to change regularly to avoid complacency and stagnation; accordingly, leadership for change is also important.[5] The *MIT's Hockfield and . . . Diversity* box further highlights the transformational leadership approach being undertaken by MIT's new president.

Transformational leadership focuses on the basic distinction between leading for change and leading for stability.[6] According to this viewpoint, much of what a leader

Transformational leadership refers to the set of abilities that allows the leader to recognize the need for change, to create a vision to guide that change, and to execute the change effectively.

Charisma is a form of inter-personal attraction that inspires support and acceptance.

Charismatic leadership is a type of influence based on the leader's personal charisma.

does occurs in the course of normal, routine work-related transactions—assigning work, evaluating performance, making decisions, and so forth. Occasionally, however, the leader has to initiate and manage major change, such as managing a merger, creating a work group, or defining the organization's culture. The first set of issues involves transactional leadership whereas the second entails transformational leadership.[7]

Moreover, some leaders can adopt either transformational or transactional perspectives, depending on their circumstances. Others are able to do one or the other, but not both. For instance, when Gordon Bethune assumed the leadership role at Continental Airlines in the early 1990s, the firm was in desperate straits, heading for its third bankruptcy in a decade. The airline's equipment was aging, it was heavily in debt, and employee morale was at an all-time low. Using dramatic transformational leadership Bethune managed to completely overhaul the firm, revitalizing it along every major dimension, and transforming the airline to become one of the most successful and admired in the world. And after the transformation was complete, Bethune was then able to transition to become a highly effective transactional role and led the firm through several more years of success before retiring in 2005.

At Walt Disney, however, the story has been different. When Michael Eisner took over the firm in 1984 it had become stagnant and was heading into decline. Relying on transformational skills, he turned things around in dramatic fashion. Among many other things, he quickly expanded the company's theme parks, built new hotels, improved Disney's movie business, created a successful Disney cruise line, launched several other major new initiatives, and changed the company into a global media powerhouse. But when the firm began to plateau and needed some time to let the changes all settle in, Eisner was unsuccessful at changing his own approach from transformational leadership to transactional leadership and was recently pressured into announcing his retirement plans.

Charismatic leadership is a type of influence based on an individual's personal charisma. Nelson Mandela is a clear example of this type of leader. During the struggles of black South Africans to end that nation's oppressive policies of apartheid, Mandela came to reflect both their triumphs and their tragedies. Not surprisingly, when the country abolished apartheid, the newly empowered black majority elected Mandela as the country's first black president. Mandela then extended the hand of reconciliation to members of the former ruling party and quickly united the divided country. And today he is seen as a national hero.

Charismatic Leadership

Perspectives based on charismatic leadership, like the trait theories discussed in Chapter 11, assume that charisma is an individual characteristic of the leader. **Charisma** is a form of interpersonal attraction that inspires support and acceptance. Accordingly, **charismatic leadership** is a type of influence based on the leader's personal charisma. All else being equal, then, someone with charisma is more likely to be able to influence others than someone without charisma. For example, a highly charismatic supervisor will be more successful in influencing subordinate behavior than a supervisor who lacks charisma. Thus, influence is again a fundamental element of this perspective.[8]

Robert House first proposed a theory of charismatic leadership based on research findings from a variety of social science disciplines.[9] His theory suggests that charismatic leaders are likely to have a lot of self-confidence, firm confidence in their beliefs and ideals, and a strong need to influence people. They also tend to communicate high expectations about follower performance and to express confidence in their followers. Gordon Bethune, described above, is an excellent example of a charismatic leader. Bethune blended a unique combination of executive skill, honesty, and playfulness. These qualities attracted a group of followers at Continental who were willing to follow his lead without question and to dedicate themselves to carrying out his decisions and policies with unceasing passion.[10] Other charismatic leaders include Herb Kelleher, Mary Kay Ash, Steve Jobs, Ted Turner, Martin Luther King, Jr., and Pope John Paul II. Unfortunately, however, charisma can also empower leaders in other directions. Adolf Hitler and Osama bin Laden, for instance, each used strong charismatic qualities for destructive purposes.

Figure 13.3 portrays the three elements of charismatic leadership in organizations that most experts acknowledge today.[11] First, charismatic leaders are able to envision likely future trends and patterns, to set high expectations for themselves and for others, and to model behaviors consistent with meeting those expectations. Next, charismatic leaders are able to energize others by demonstrating personal excitement, personal confidence, and consistent patterns of success. Finally, charismatic leaders enable others by supporting them, empathizing with them, and expressing confidence in them.[12]

The charismatic leadership perspective is quite popular among managers today and is the subject of numerous books and articles.[13] Unfortunately, few studies have specifically attempted to test the meaning and impact of charismatic leadership. Lingering ethical concerns about charismatic leadership also trouble some people. They

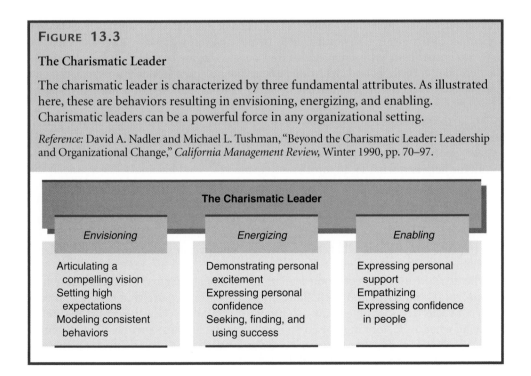

FIGURE 13.3

The Charismatic Leader

The charismatic leader is characterized by three fundamental attributes. As illustrated here, these are behaviors resulting in envisioning, energizing, and enabling. Charismatic leaders can be a powerful force in any organizational setting.

Reference: David A. Nadler and Michael L. Tushman, "Beyond the Charismatic Leader: Leadership and Organizational Change," *California Management Review,* Winter 1990, pp. 70–97.

stem from the fact that some charismatic leaders inspire such blind faith in their followers that they may engage in inappropriate, unethical, or even illegal behaviors just because the leader instructed them to do so. This tendency probably played a role in the unraveling of both Enron and Arthur Andersen as people followed orders from charismatic leaders to hide information, shred documents, and mislead investigators. Taking over a leadership role from someone with substantial personal charisma is also a challenge. For instance, the immediate successors to very successful charismatic football coaches like Vince Lombardi (Green Bay Packers), Steve Spurrier (University of Florida), and Tom Osborne (University of Nebraska) each failed to measure up to his predecessor's legacy and was subsequently fired.

Attribution and Leadership

The **attribution theory**, applied to leadership, holds that when behaviors are observed in a context associated with leadership, others may attribute varying levels of leadership ability or power to the person displaying those behaviors.

We discussed **attribution theory** back in Chapter 3 and noted then that people tend to observe behavior and then attribute causes (and hence meaning) to it. There are clear implications for attribution theory and leadership, especially when leadership is framed through the eyes of followers; when behaviors are observed in a context associated with leadership, followers may attribute varying levels of leadership ability or power to the person displaying those behaviors.

For example, suppose we observe an individual behaving confidently and decisively; we also observe that others are paying close attention to what this person says and does and that they seem to defer to and/or consult with her on various things. We might subsequently conclude that this individual is a leader because of both her behavior and the behaviors of others. However, in a different setting we observe an individual who is not especially confident or decisive; we also observe that others seem relatively indifferent to what he has to say and that he is not routinely consulted about things. In this case we are more likely to assume that this person is not really a leader.

The attributions we make subsequently affect both our own behavior and the actual capacity of an individual to behave like a leader. For instance, suppose we become a member of the group that is supervised by the first individual we observed; since we have attributed leadership qualities to that person, we are somewhat likely to mimic the behaviors of others and treat this person like our own leader. Moreover, the fact that we and others do this reinforces this person's confidence in continuing the leadership role.

To further put this into perspective, assume that a group of strangers is trapped in an elevator. One person in the group immediately steps forward and takes charge. He appears confident, has a calming effect on everyone, and assures us that he knows how to call for help and what to do until that help arrives. In all likelihood, everyone in the elevator will acknowledge his leadership, will respond positively to his behavior, and would later credit him with helping them get through the unpleasant experience. On the other hand, if in the same setting someone tries to take charge but clearly lacks confidence and/or clearly exhibits ignorance of what to do, others will quickly pick up on this, pay little attention to what the person says, and perhaps look to someone else for leadership.

The attribution perspective on leadership is especially clear during presidential campaigns. Candidates and their handlers strive to make sure that they are always shown in the best possible light—demonstrating confidence, being sympathetic, knowing what to do, looking poised and well-groomed, and so forth. George W. Bush received a lot of media attention during the early stages of the war with Iraq when he landed a jet plane on an aircraft carrier, jumped out of the cockpit, and boldly walked toward the cameras. Supporters of Bush saw this as illustration of his strong leadership, but critics no doubt saw it as a carefully orchestrated media event designed solely to make him look strong and leaderlike. Hence, each camp attributed things to Bush's leadership based on the same objective reality but heavily influenced by their own attitudes and predispositions.

Alternatives to Leadership

Another perspective on leadership that has received considerable attention in recent years has focused on alternatives to leadership. In some cases, circumstances may exist that render leadership unnecessary or irrelevant. The factors that contribute to these circumstances are called leadership substitutes. In other cases, factors may exist that neutralize or negate the influence of a leader even when that individual is attempting to exercise leadership.

Leadership Substitutes

Leadership substitutes are individual, task, and organizational characteristics that tend to outweigh the leader's ability to affect subordinates' satisfaction and performance.[14] In other words, if certain factors are present, the employee will perform his or her job

> **Leadership substitutes** are individual, task, and organizational characteristics that tend to outweigh the leader's ability to affect subordinates' satisfaction and performance.

Leadership substitutes allow people to perform effectively without the direction or supervision of a leader. The Dragon Slayers, shown here, are a volunteer group of high school girls who provide the only round-the-clock emergency care available for 3,000 people in a region of Alaska that is the size of Maryland. The girls voluntarily undergo 200 hours of medical training and respond to about 450 calls a year. And they function without supervision and without a formal leader—they simply know what to do, and then get it done in order to save lives and help people.

TABLE 13.1

Substitutes and Neutralizers for Leadership

Individual	**Group**
Individual professionalism	Group norms
Motivation	Group cohesiveness
Experience and training	**Organization**
Indifference to rewards	Rigid procedures and rules
Job	Explicit goals and objectives
Structured/automated	Rigid reward system
Highly controlled	
Intrinsically satisfying	
Embedded feedback	

capably without the direction of a leader. Unlike traditional theories, which assume that hierarchical leadership in one form or another is always important, the premise of the leadership substitutes perspective is that leader behaviors may be irrelevant in some situations. Several basic leadership substitutes are identified in Table 13.1.

Consider, for example, what happens when an ambulance with a critically injured victim screeches to the door of a hospital emergency room. Do the ER employees stand around waiting for someone to take control and instruct them on what to do? The answer is obviously no—they are highly trained and well-prepared professionals who know how to respond, who to depend on, who to communicate with, how to work together as a team, and so forth. In short, they are fully capable of carrying out their jobs without someone playing the role of leader.

Individual ability, experience, training, knowledge, motivation, and professional orientation are among the characteristics that may substitute for leadership. Similarly, a task characterized by routine, a high degree of structure, frequent feedback, and intrinsic satisfaction may also render leader behavior unnecessary. Thus, if the task gives the subordinate enough intrinsic satisfaction, she or he may not need support from a leader.

Explicit plans and goals, rules and procedures, cohesive work groups, a rigid reward structure, and physical distance between supervisor and subordinate are organizational characteristics that may substitute for leadership. For example, if job goals are explicit, and there are many rules and procedures for task performance, a leader providing directions may not be necessary. Research has provided support for the concept of leadership substitutes, but additional research is needed to identify other potential substitutes and their impact on leadership effectiveness.[15]

Leadership Neutralizers

Leadership neutralizers are factors that render ineffective a leader's attempts to engage in various leadership behaviors.

In other situations, even if a leader is present and attempts to engage in various leadership behaviors, those behaviors may be rendered ineffective—neutralized—by various factors. Suppose, for example, that a relatively new and inexperienced leader is assigned to a work group comprised of very experienced employees with long-standing performance norms and a high level of group cohesiveness. The norms and cohesiveness of the group may be so strong that there is nothing the new leader can do to change things. Of course, this pattern may also work in several different ways. The norms may dictate acceptable but not high performance, and the leader may be powerless to improve things because the group is so cohesive. Or, the norms may call for very high performance, and even a bungling and ineffective leader cannot cause any damage. In both cases, however, the process is the same—the leader's ability to alter the situation is neutralized by elements in that situation.

In addition to group factors, elements of the job itself may also limit a leader's ability to "make a difference." Consider, for example, employees working on a moving assembly line. Employees may be able to work only at the pace of the moving line, so performance quantity is constrained by the speed of the line. Moreover, if performance quality is also constrained (say, by simple tasks and/or tight quality control procedures) the leader may again be powerless to influence individual work behaviors.

Finally, organizational factors can also neutralize at least some forms of leader behavior. Suppose a new leader is accustomed to using merit pay increases as a way to motivate people. But in her or his new job, pay increases are dictated by union contracts and are based primarily on employee seniority and cost-of-living. Or suppose that an employee is already at the top of the pay grade for his or her job. In either case, the leader's previous approach to motivating people has been neutralized and new approaches will have to be identified.

The Changing Nature of Leadership

Various alternatives to leadership aside, though, many settings still call for at least some degree of leadership, although the nature of that leadership continues to evolve. Among the recent changes in leadership that managers should recognize are the increasing role of leaders as coaches and gender and cross-cultural patterns of leader behavior.

Leaders as Coaches

We noted in Chapter 10 that many organizations today are using teams. Other organizations are exploring ways to become less hierarchical—that is, to eliminate the old-fashioned command-and-control mentality often inherent in bureaucratic organizations and to motivate and empower individuals to work independently. In each case, the role of leaders is also changing. Whereas leaders were once expected to control situations, direct work, supervise people, closely monitor performance, make decisions, and structure activities, many leaders today are being asked to change how they manage people. Perhaps the best description of this new role is for the leader to become a **coach** instead of an overseer.[16]

Consider the metaphor from the standpoint of an actual coach of an athletic team. The coach plays a role in selecting the players for the team and deciding which direction to take (such as emphasizing offense versus defense). The coach also helps develop player talent, and teaches them how to execute specific plays. But at game time, the coach stays on the sideline; it's up to the players themselves to execute plays and get the job done. And while the coach may get some of the credit for the victory, he or she didn't actually score any of the points.

Likewise, then, from the standpoint of an organizational leader, a coaching perspective would call for the leader to help select team members and other new employees, to provide some general direction, to help train and develop the team and the skills of its members, and to help the team get the information and other resources it needs. The leader may also have to help resolve conflict among team members and mediate other disputes that arise. And coaches from different teams may need to play important roles in linking the activities and functions of their respective teams. But beyond these activities, the leader keeps a low profile and lets the group get its work done with little or no direct oversight from the leader.

Of course, some managers long accustomed to the traditional approach may have trouble changing to a coaching role. But others seem to make the transition with little or no difficulty. Moreover, companies such as Texas Instruments, Halliburton, and

Whereas leaders were once expected to control situations, direct work, supervise people, closely monitor performance, make decisions, and structure activities, many leaders today are being asked to change how they manage people—to become coaches.

Leaders today are increasingly being called upon to play the role of coach or mentor to others. For example, Sean Tucker and Michael Goulian play these roles in the Stars of Tomorrow program, a confederation of stunt pilots. Tucker is shown here in the Oracle plane, while Goulian is flying the plane in the lower left. They are helping the pilots of the other planes practice and hone the skills necessary to fly in close formation during intricate maneuvers.

Within the coaching role, some leaders have also excelled at taking on more responsibilities as a **mentor**—helping a less-experienced person learn the ropes and to better prepare him or her to advance within the organization.

Yum! Brands have developed very successful training programs to help their managers learn how to become better coaches. Within the coaching role, some leaders have also excelled at taking on more responsibilities as a **mentor**—helping a less-experienced person learn the ropes and to better prepare him or her to advance within the organization. Texas Instruments, again, has maintained a very successful mentoring program for years. The *Accenture and . . . Technology* box provides an example of how Accenture expects its leaders to serve as coaches.

Gender and Leadership

Another factor that is clearly changing the nature of leadership is the growing number of women advancing to higher levels in organizations. Given that most leadership theories and research studies have focused on male leaders, developing a better understanding of how females lead is clearly an important next step. For example, do women and men tend to lead differently? Some early research suggests that there are indeed fundamental differences in leadership as practiced by women and men.[17]

For instance, in contrast to original stereotypes, female leaders are not necessarily more nurturing or supportive than are male leaders. Likewise, male leaders are not systematically more harsh, controlling, or task focused than are female leaders. The one difference that does seem to arise in some cases is that women have a tendency to be slightly more democratic in making decisions, whereas men have a similar tendency to be somewhat more autocratic.[18]

There are two possible explanations for this pattern. One possibility is that women may tend to have stronger interpersonal skills than men and are able to better understand how to effectively involve others in making decisions. Men, on the other hand, may have weaker interpersonal skills and thus have a tendency to rely on their own judgment. The other possible explanation is that women may encounter more stereotypic resistance to their occupying senior roles. If this is the case, they may actively work to involve others in making decisions so as to help minimize any hostility or conflict. Clearly, however, much

Accenture and . . . **TECHNOLOGY**

Accenture's Technology Leads the World

Accenture, an international consulting, technology, and outsourcing firm, employs over 100,000 individuals in offices in forty-eight countries. The firm is shifting its leadership model to focus more on the coaching role of managers. However, it's challenging for managers to lead subordinates scattered across various physical locations.

One way that Accenture addresses this issue is by bringing teams together whenever possible. "We don't have a headquarters because we are very virtual, so our leadership team tends to work by coming together in a particular location for various meetings," says Gill Rider, Accenture chief leadership officer.

Another, less expensive solution is to bring teams together virtually. Accenture Technology Labs products support remote training, meetings, and data sharing. Accenture and Microsoft formed an independent joint venture firm called Avanade to offer these products for sale. Also, Accenture recently donated the company's online training system to an agency in Kenya for use in educating nurses. "With the current shortage of nursing instructors, training 26,000 nurses would take 100 years," says Dr. Peter Ngatia of the Kenyan Ministry of Health. "By leveraging Accenture's innovative electronic learning solutions, we are targeting to train the same number in just five years."

Technology solutions are tailored to each situation, but the information conveyed by the technology is not. "You do have to be very cognizant of people's culture and their natural style. [Accenture has] found that the fundamentals of how you develop leaders and the things that people need to focus on are the same everywhere around the world . . . Although the style in which something is executed may be different, the content is just the same around the world," claims Rider.

"Teaching Leaders at Accenture," this chapter's closing case, describes Accenture's leadership development in more detail.

> *"We don't have a headquarters because we are very virtual . . ."*
>
> GILL RIDER, CHIEF LEADERSHIP OFFICER, ACCENTURE

References: "About Avanade," Avanade website, www.avanade.com on June 11, 2005; "Accenture Gives $2.9 Million to African Medical and Research Foundation to Help Train Nurses in Kenya," Business Wire press release, June 14, 2005, biz.yahoo.com on June 14, 2005; "Developing Leaders at Accenture," video case (quotation); Cyrille Bataller, "Using Innovating Technologies to Bridge the Digital Divide," March 2003, Accenture website, www.accenture.com on June 11, 2005.

more work needs to be done in order to better understand the dynamics of gender and leadership. It is obvious, of course, that high-profile and successful female leaders such as Andrea Jung (CEO of Avon Products) and Condoleezza Rice (secretary of state) are demonstrating the effectiveness with which women can be truly exceptional leaders. We saw another example in the chapter opening case.

Cross-Cultural Leadership

Another changing perspective on leadership relates to cross-cultural issues. In this context culture is used as a broad concept to encompass both international differences and diversity-based differences within one culture. For instance, when a Japanese firm sends an executive to head up the firm's operation in the United States, that person will need to become acclimated to the cultural differences that exist between the two countries and consider changing his or her leadership style accordingly. Japan is generally characterized by collectivism, while the United States is based more on individualism. The Japanese executive, then, will find it necessary to recognize the importance of individual

Leaders today are increasingly being called upon to play the role of a coach. In this role, they don't lead and direct, but instead support and encourage. This organization has taken the bumper sticker sometimes seen on delivery vehicles ("How's My Driving?") and applied it to its managers. Employees are being asked to provide feedback on how well their "coach" is performing.

© 1998 Randy Glasbergen
www.glasbergen.com

contributions and rewards and the differences in individual and group roles that exist in Japanese and U.S. businesses.

Similarly, cross-cultural factors also play a growing role in organizations as their workforces become more and more diverse. Most leadership research, for instance, has been conducted on samples or case studies involving white male leaders (since until several years ago most business leaders were white males!). But as African Americans, Asian Americans, Hispanics, and members of other ethnic groups achieve leadership positions, it may be necessary to reassess how applicable current theories and models of leadership are when applied to an increasingly diverse pool of leaders.

Emerging Issues in Leadership

Finally, there are also three emerging issues in leadership that warrant discussion. These issues are strategic leadership, ethical leadership, and virtual leadership.

Strategic leadership is the capability to understand the complexities of both the organization and its environment and to lead change in the organization so as to achieve and maintain a superior alignment between the organization and its environment.

Strategic Leadership
Strategic leadership is a new concept that explicitly relates leadership to the role of top management. We will define **strategic leadership** as the capability to understand the complexities of both the organization and its environment and to lead change in the organization so as to achieve and maintain a superior alignment between the organization and its environment. In some ways, then, strategic leadership may be seen as an extension of the transformational leadership role discussed earlier. However, this recent focus has more explicitly acknowledged and incorporated the importance of strategy and strategic decision making. That is, while both transformational and strategic leadership include the concept of change, transformational leadership implicitly emphasizes the ability to lead change as the central focus. Strategic leadership, on the other hand, puts greater weight on the leader's ability to think and function strategically.

To be effective in this role, a manager needs to have a thorough and complete understanding of the organization—its history, its culture, its strengths, and its weaknesses. In addition, the leader needs a firm grasp of the organization's environment. This understanding must encompass current conditions and circumstances as well as significant trends and issues on the horizon. The strategic leader also needs to recognize how the firm is currently aligned with its environment—where it relates effectively, and where it relates less effectively with that environment. Finally, looking at environmental trends and issues the strategic leader works to both improve the current alignment and improve the future alignment.

Andrea Jung (CEO of Avon Products), Michael Dell (founder and CEO of Dell Computer), and A.G. Lafley (CEO of Procter & Gamble) have all been recognized as strong strategic leaders. Reflecting on his dramatic turnaround at Procter & Gamble, for instance, Lafley commented, "I have made a lot of symbolic, very physical changes so people understand we are in the business of leading change." On the other hand, Jurgen Schrempp (CEO of DaimlerChrysler), Raymond Gilmartin (CEO of Merck), and Scott Livengood (CEO of Krispy Kreme) were recently singled out by *Business Week* for their poor strategic leadership.[19]

Ethical Leadership

Most people have long assumed that top managers are ethical people. But in the wake of recent corporate scandals at firms like Enron, Boeing, and WorldCom, faith in top managers has been shaken. Hence, perhaps now more than ever high standards of ethical conduct are being held up as a prerequisite for effective leadership. More specifically, top managers are being called upon to maintain high ethical standards for their own conduct, to unfailingly exhibit ethical behavior, and to hold others in their organizations to the same standards.

The behaviors of top leaders are being scrutinized more than ever, and those responsible for hiring new leaders for a business are looking more and more closely at the backgrounds of those being considered. And the emerging pressures for stronger corporate governance models are likely to further increase commitment to select only those individuals with high ethical standards for leadership positions in business and to hold them more accountable than in the past for both their actions and the consequences of those actions.[20]

Strategic leadership has become a major force in many organizations today. When A.G. Lafley took over the reins at Procter & Gamble, he systematically revamped the firm's staid culture in order the make the company more responsive to changing consumer tastes and emerging competitive challenges. Lafley is shown here explaining one of his major strategic decisions, the acquisition of the Gillette Company, to Procter & Gamble shareholders.

Virtual Leadership

Finally, virtual leadership is also emerging as an important issue for organizations. In earlier times, leaders and their employees worked together in the same physical location and engaged in personal (i.e., face-to-face) interactions on a regular basis. But in today's world both leaders and their employees may work in locations that are far from one another. Such arrangements might include people telecommuting from a home office one or two days a week to people actually living and working far from company headquarters and seeing one another in person only very infrequently.

How, then, do managers carry out leadership when they do not have regular personal contact with their followers? And how do they help mentor and develop others? Communication between leaders and their subordinates will still occur, of course, but it may be largely by telephone and email. Hence, one implication may be that leaders in these situations simply need to work harder at creating and maintaining relationships with their employees that go beyond words on a computer screen. While nonverbal communication such as smiles and handshakes may not be possible online, managers can instead make a point of adding a few personal words in an email (whenever appropriate) to convey appreciation, reinforcement, or constructive feedback. Building on this, managers should then also take advantage of every single opportunity whenever they are in face-to-face situations to go further than they might have done under different circumstances to develop a strong relationship.

But beyond these simple prescriptions, there is no theory or research to guide managers functioning in a virtual world. Hence, as electronic communications continues to pervade the workplace, researchers and managers alike need to work together to first help frame the appropriate issues and questions regarding virtual leadership and then to help address those issues and answer those questions.

Synopsis

There are two contemporary situation theories. The leader-member exchange model (LMX) of leadership stresses the importance of variable relationships between supervisors and each of their subordinates. Each superior-subordinate pair is referred to as a "vertical dyad." The Hersey and Blanchard model argues that appropriate leader behavior depends on the subordinate's degree of motivation, competence, experience, and interest in accepting responsibility. In addition to these somewhat newer models, the three dominant situational theories have also continued to undergo various refinements and revisions.

There are three primary approaches to leadership through the eyes of followers. Transformational leadership focuses on the basic distinction between leading for change and leading for stability. Perspectives based on charismatic leadership assume that charisma is an individual characteristic of the leader. Charisma is a form of interpersonal attraction that inspires support and acceptance. The attribution perspective holds that when behaviors are observed in a context associated with leadership, others may attribute varying levels of leadership ability or power to the person displaying those behaviors.

Another perspective on leadership that has received considerable attention in recent years has focused on alternatives to leadership. In some cases, circumstances may exist that render leadership unnecessary or irrelevant. The factors that contribute to these circumstances are called leadership substitutes. In other cases, factors may exist that neutralize or negate the influence of a leader even when that individual is attempting to exercise leadership.

The nature of leadership continues to evolve. Among the recent changes in leadership that managers should recognize is the increasing role of leaders as coaches. The most frequent instance of this arrangement is when an organization uses self-managing teams. Gender differences in leader behavior are also becoming more important, especially given the increasing numbers of women advancing up the organizational ladder. Cross-cultural patterns of leadership both between and within national boundaries are also taking on growing importance.

Finally, there are three emerging issues in leadership. Strategic leadership is a new concept that explicitly relates leadership to the role of top management. In addition, leaders in all organizations are being called upon to maintain high ethical standards for their own conduct, to unfailingly exhibit ethical behavior, and to hold others in their organizations to the same standards. And the growing importance of virtual leadership needs to be further studied.

Discussion Questions

1. Compare and contrast the leader-member exchange and the Hersey and Blanchard models of leadership.

2. Are you now or have you ever been a member of an in-group? An out-group? If so, in what ways did your experiences differ?

3. Which of the three traditional situational theories discussed in Chapter 12 is most similar to the leader-member exchange model? To the Hersey and Blanchard model?

4. Identify an individual who could serve as an example of a transformational leader. How successful or unsuccessful has this person been?

5. Name the three people today whom you consider to be the most charismatic. How well do they/might they function as a leader?

6. In your opinion, is it possible for someone with little or no charisma to become charismatic? If so, how? If not, why?

7. Have you ever made direct leadership attributions about someone based on the context in which you observed them?

8. What are some of the substitutes and neutralizers to leadership that might exist in your classroom?

9. Do you believe that men and women differ in how they lead? If so, what are some of the factors that might account for the differences?

10. In what ways does strategic leadership differ from "non-strategic" leadership? In what ways do these distinctions differ?

11. Some people have held that highly successful managers and leaders all face situations in which they cannot be entirely truthful and still succeed. For instance, a politician who personally believes that a tax increase is inevitable may feel that to fully disclose this belief will result in a significant loss of votes. Do you agree or disagree with the idea that sometimes people cannot be entirely truthful and still succeed?

Experiencing Organizational Behavior

Understanding Leadership Substitutes

Purpose: This exercise will help you assess the possibilities and limitations of leadership substitutes in organizations.

Format: Working in small groups, you will identify several factors that can substitute for and/or neutralize leadership in different settings.

Procedures: Your instructor will divide the class into small groups of four to five members each. Working as a team, do the following:

1. Identify two jobs, one that is relatively simple (perhaps a custodian or a fast-food cook) and one that is much more complex (such as an airline pilot or software engineer).

2. For each job, identify as many potential leadership substitutes and neutralizers as possible.

3. Next, exchange one list with one group and the other list with a different group.

4. Review the two new lists and look for areas where you agree or disagree.

5. Exchange lists once again to get back your original lists.

6. Discuss among yourselves if there is a discernable pattern as to which type of group might be most easily substituted or neutralized.

Follow-up Questions

1. To what extent did your own experiences affect how you performed this exercise?

2. Are there some jobs for which there are no substitutes? Provide examples.

3. Should managers actively seek substitutes for leadership? Why or why not?

Self-Assessment Exercise

Are You a Charismatic Leader?

Introduction: Charismatic leaders articulate a vision, show concern for group members, communicate high expectations, and create high-performing organizations. This assessment exercise measures your charismatic potential.

Instructions: The following statements refer to the possible ways in which you might behave toward others when you are in a leadership role. Please read each statement carefully and decide to what extent it applies to you. Then put a check on the appropriate number.

To a very great extent	= 5
To a considerable extent	= 4
To a moderate extent	= 3
To a slight extent	= 2
To little or no extent	= 1

1. I pay close attention to what others say when they are talking.   1 2 3 4 5

2. I communicate clearly.   1 2 3 4 5

3. I am trustworthy.   1 2 3 4 5

4. I care about other people.   1 2 3 4 5

5. I do not put excessive energy into avoiding failure.   1 2 3 4 5

6. I make the work of others more meaningful.   1 2 3 4 5

7. I seem to focus on the key issues in a situation.   1 2 3 4 5

8. I get across my meaning effectively, often in unusual ways.   1 2 3 4 5

9. I can be relied on to follow through on commitments.   1 2 3 4 5

10. I have a great deal of self-respect.   1 2 3 4 5

11. I enjoy taking carefully calculated risks.   1 2 3 4 5

12. I help others feel more competent in what they do.   1 2 3 4 5

13. I have a clear set of priorities.   1 2 3 4 5

14. I am in touch with how others feel.   1 2 3 4 5

15. I rarely change once I have taken a clear position.   1 2 3 4 5

16. I focus on strengths, of myself and of others.   1 2 3 4 5

17. I seem most alive when deeply involved in some project.   1 2 3 4 5

18. I show others that they are all part of the same group.   1 2 3 4 5

19. I get others to focus on the issues I see as important.   1 2 3 4 5

20. I communicate feelings as well as ideas.   1 2 3 4 5

21. I let others know where I stand.   1 2 3 4 5

22. I seem to know just how I "fit" into a group.   1 2 3 4 5

23. I learn from mistakes and do not treat errors as disasters but rather as learning experiences.   1 2 3 4 5

24. I am fun to be around.   1 2 3 4 5

For interpretation, see the Interpretation Guide in the *Instructor's Resource Manual.*

The questionnaire measures six facets of charismatic leadership. Your score can range from 4 to 20 for each section. Each question is stated as a measure of the extent to which you engage in the behavior—or elicit the feelings. The higher your score, the more you demonstrate charismatic leader behaviors.

Index 1: Management of Attention (1, 7, 13, 19).
Your score: _____. You pay especially close attention to people with whom you are communicating. You are also "focused in" on the key issues under discussion and help others to see clearly these key points. You have clear ideas about the relative importance or priorities of different issues under discussion.

Index 2: Management of Meaning (2, 8, 14, 20).
Your score: _____. This set of items centers on your communication skills, specifically your ability to get the meaning of a message across, even if this means devising some quite innovative approach.

Index 3: Management of Trust (3, 9, 15, 21).
Your score: _____. The key factor is your perceived trustworthiness as shown by your willingness to follow through on promises, to avoid "flip-flop" shifts in position, and to take clear positions.

Index 4: Management of Self (4, 10, 16, 22).
Your score: _____. This index concerns your general attitudes toward yourself and others—that is, your overall concern for others and their feelings as well as for "taking care of" feelings about yourself in a positive sense (e.g., self-regard).

Index 5: Management of Risk (5, 11, 17, 23).
Your score: _____. Effective charismatic leaders are deeply involved in what they do and do not spend excessive amounts of time or energy on plans to "protect" themselves against failure. These leaders are willing to take risks, not on a hit-or-miss basis, but after careful estimation of the odds of success or failure.

Index 6: Management of Feelings (6, 12, 18, 24). Your score: _____. Charismatic leaders seem to consistently generate a set of positive feelings in others. Others feel that their work becomes more meaningful and that they are the "masters" of their own behavior—that is, they feel competent. They feel a sense of community, a "we-ness" with their colleagues and coworkers.

Reference: Marshall Sashkin, William C. Morris, and Donald Hellriegel, *Experiential Exercises in Management Book,* p. 132. Copyright © 1987, Addison-Wesley Longman. Reprinted by permission of Pearson Education, Inc., Upper Saddle River, NJ.

Building Managerial Skills

Exercise Overview: Interpersonal skills refer to a manager's ability to communicate with, understand, and motivate individuals and groups. This exercise will help you develop your interpersonal skills as they relate to leadership.

Exercise Background: As noted in the chapter, virtual leadership is an emerging phenomenon about which little is known. Begin this exercise by partnering three of your classmates (that is, create groups of four). Spend some time with your group members getting to know each other and exchanging email addresses.

Next, create a hypothetical work team. The team should identify one of you as the leader, and the other three as employees. Develop relatively detailed roles for yourselves—gender, age, work experiences, motivations and aspirations, and so forth, as well as some detail about a work project that the team has been assigned.

Between now and the next class meeting, you should all exchange numerous emails about your hypothetical work project. The leader should be especially active in the process and send a wide array of messages. Specifically, the leader should be sure to provide some encouragement, respond to questions, relay some information, provide some criticism, and so forth. The leader should also maintain a written log of the intention of each email that was sent. Employees can communicate among themselves, but should also be sure to communicate with their leader—ask questions, relay information, and so forth.

During the process of exchanging emails, it is virtually certain that you will need to "make up some things." Try to maintain realism, however, and try to be consistent with things that have already transpired. For example, an employee might "create" a problem and ask the leader's advice. However, the problem should be realistic, and it should be reasonable for the leader to be able to answer the question. For her or his part, the leader should also make a realistic effort to answer the question. Later, during subsequent exchanges, remember to account for the question and the answer if and when appropriate. End the exercise when several exchanges have taken place and you sense that the group has "run out of steam."

Exercise Task: At the next class meeting, reconvene with your team members and respond to the following questions:

1. The leader should first recount each email that was sent and then convey his or her intended meaning; the recipient(s) should then convey how the message was actually interpreted. Were there any differences between the intended message and how it was interpreted?

2. To what extent did interactions among those playing the roles of employees affect how they interpreted messages from the leader?

3. What, if anything, could the leader have done to improve communication?

Teaching Leaders at Accenture

A traditional leadership model puts the leader at the top of a hierarchy, giving him or her responsibility for making decisions, directing the activities of subordinates, and ensuring that desired outcomes are reached. Accenture, one of the largest management consulting firms in the world with over 100,000 professionals, is using a different model. Accenture's model calls for leaders to concentrate on developing the leadership potential of others.

> **"*Leaders have to have responsibility to teach other leaders.*"**
> GILL RIDER, CHIEF LEADERSHIP
> OFFICER, ACCENTURE

This model emphasizes Accenture's "leaders-teaching-leaders" approach. It explicitly acknowledges that individuals best develop their leadership skills by observing and working closely with effective leaders, who serve as mentors, role models, and coaches. This model also focuses on the long-term impact that a leader may have, rather than the short-term impact.

Gill Rider, Accenture's chief leadership officer, says, "Leaders have to have responsibility to teach other leaders . . . to think about what they've learned and what they know, then push that down the organization in a teaching way to other people who hopefully will step up to their job in the not-too-distant future." She adds, "One of the things that we really believe about people and the development of leaders is that the top leaders have to teach; they have to have a teachable point of view that allows them to teach future generations."

Accenture's new approach to leadership development began in 2002, when then CEO Joe W. Forehand noticed that he had direct contact with the chief financial officer but had no equivalent contact with the "people" side of the business. Human capital excellence is especially important in the consulting industry, where client personnel work hand in hand with consulting personnel, so Forehand knew he needed a closer relationship. He solved the problem by creating the chief leadership officer.

"My job is to think about how . . . we create a people strategy that allows us to have the right people with the right skills at the right time to be able to execute our business strategy over time. That linkage between business strategy and all our people is a very, very key aspect of my job," Rider says. While the chief leadership officer oversees traditional human resources functions such as training, the role extends further to incorporate strategic considerations. This allows Accenture to link business objectives, training requirements, performance standards, and compensation.

Accenture has always been noted for its ability to develop leaders. Some of those individuals have gone on to executive positions in the company; many more have been hired into managerial jobs at client firms. In this way, Accenture continues to influence and sustain relationships with clients after a project is completed. However, Forehand recognized that the leadership development process could be much more productive and work at every level of the firm if it was better understood. According to Rider, "We've always been this huge engine creating leaders but we've taken a step back and said, 'What is the magic source that we have about leadership?'"

A thorough study of Accenture's successes led to the creation of a leadership statement for the firm. The statement identifies three key roles for leaders: value creator, people developer, and business operator. As a value creator the leader provides something of value, either to external or internal clients. People developer is the leadership development role—that is, the leader helps others develop their own leadership skills. As a business operator the leader must promote effectiveness and efficiency throughout the organization. As the leadership statement is used at lower and lower levels of the organization, every consultant will be asked to demonstrate strategic leadership. Every professional will become responsible for making the changes necessary to more effectively align the organization with its environment.

The new emphasis on strategy seems to be working. In 2004, as corporate consulting contracts dried up, Accenture employees led a move toward more outsourcing contracts. In addition, Accenture employees bid for, and won, a $10 billion contract to provide the U.S. government with an automated system for monitoring border security. This is the largest and most ambitious contract the firm has ever entered into.

Accenture's leadership development program will create strategic leaders throughout the organization. Will their strategic decisions be effective? That remains to be seen.

Case Questions

1. Accenture relies on constantly changing teams of consultants and other professionals to staff each project. Does Accenture's organization of work support the "leaders-as-coaches" concept? Why or why not?

2. For Accenture to successfully use strategic leadership, what types of skills and information are needed by its leaders?

3. Consider Accenture's global leadership development, as described in the boxed insert titled *Accenture and . . . Technology*. In your opinion, is Rider correct? Are leadership fundamentals essentially the same everywhere, with differences existing only in style and execution? Explain.

References: "Corporate Strategy Client Successes;" Robert J. Thomas, "Basic Leadership Moves," Accenture website, www.accenture.com on June 11, 2005; "Developing Leaders at Accenture," video case (quotation); Spencer E. Ante, "Accenture Hits the Daily Double," "Accenture Rising," *Business Week*, July 12, 2004, www.businessweek.com on June 11, 2005.

TEST PREPPER

You have read the chapter and studied the key terms. Think you're ready to ace the exam? Take this sample test to gauge your comprehension of chapter material and check your answers at the back of the book. Want more test questions? Take the ACE quizzes found on the student website: http://college.hmco.com/business/students/ (select Griffin/Moorhead, Organizational Behavior, 8e from the Management menu).

T F 1. The leader-member exchange model focuses on how leaders can get the maximum level of effort from organizational members.

T F 2. According to the Hersey and Blanchard model, when subordinates are not ready to do work, leaders should adopt a "telling" style by providing direction and defining roles.

T F 3. Transactional leadership is essentially the same as management.

T F 4. Research has shown that charismatic leaders are usually less effective than non-charismatic leaders.

T F 5. Compared to the United States, Japan is a more collectivistic society.

T F 6. Existing leadership theories have quickly been adopted for use in the virtual office.

7. According to research on the leader-member exchange model, employees in the out-group are characterized by all of the following except they
   a. receive less attention from the supervisor.
   b. are assigned more mundane work.
   c. experience lower job satisfaction.
   d. receive more responsibility and autonomy.
   e. are given fewer special privileges.

8. Which of the following elements did Fiedler add as another major element of situational favorableness in his LPC theory of leadership?
   a. Stress
   b. Decision-making style
   c. Participation
   d. Charisma
   e. Rewards

9. Which of the following leadership styles would be most appropriate for a leader who needs to initiate and manage major change?
   a. Exchange
   b. Telling
   c. Selling
   d. Transformational
   e. Transactional

10. Charismatic leaders possess all of the following except the ability to
    a. set high expectations for themselves and for others.
    b. display personal excitement and confidence.
    c. envision likely future trends and patterns.
    d. build a tight-knit in-group of followers.
    e. support and empathize with followers.

11. When we attribute leadership to a person and act consistent with that attribution
    a. we engage in transactional leadership.
    b. we engage in transformational leadership.
    c. we reinforce the person's confidence in continuing the leadership role.
    d. we leave the out-group and enter the more privileged in-group.
    e. we reduce the need for leadership because of our own self-motivation.

12. John feels his attempts at leading his department are inconsequential. Which of the following is not likely to neutralize John's attempts at leadership?
    a. Experienced employees
    b. High group cohesiveness
    c. Strong performance norms
    d. Highly structured work
    e. Ambiguous role requirements

13. Which of the following differences between men and women leaders has research supported?
    a. Female leaders tend to be more democratic in making decisions.
    b. Female leaders are more nurturing of their in-groups.
    c. Male leaders are more task focused in their early careers.
    d. Male leaders are more controlling of new employees.
    e. Female leaders are more supportive of older employees.

14. Which of the following is not an element of strategic leadership?
    a. A thorough and complete understanding of the organization
    b. A firm grasp of the organization's environment
    c. A recognition of how the firm is currently aligned with its environment
    d. Leading change to improved the alignment of the organization and its environment.
    e. All of the above are elements of strategic leadership.

CHAPTER 14

Power, Politics, and Organizational Justice

- Define and discuss influence in organizations.
- Describe the types and uses of power in organizations.
- Discuss politics and political behavior in organizations.
- Describe the various forms and implications of justice in organizations.

Chapter Outline

Influence in Organizations

Power in Organizations

Politics and Political Behavior

Organizational Justice

The Face of New Labor at the SEIU

The world has changed since 1969, the peak of the U.S. labor movement, when one-third of all workers were unionized. Today's business environment is based on services, not manufacturing. Intense competition has driven prices down, forcing companies into extreme cost cutting. And companies have the option today to outsource work, even service work, overseas.

Labor is not the force that it once was. Labor unions are still run as they were fifty years ago but they are losing power. Only one-twelfth of workers are unionized today and jobs continue to move west and south, into states that limit union power. The largest labor group in the U.S., the AFL-CIO, is more of an umbrella organization that encompasses dozens of independent unions and millions of members. The Service Employees International Union (SEIU), with 1.8 million members, is the largest in the AFL-CIO, bigger than any of the unions for the manufacturing trades.

By 1984, when he came to the attention of SEIU president John Sweeney, Andy Stern had spent more than a decade working with SEIU locals. Stern looked to Sweeney as a mentor and ran Sweeney's 1995 campaign for the AFL-CIO presidency. However, as soon as Sweeney won, Stern gathered support from a coalition of locals to take Sweeney's former spot. Sweeney fired Stern, but six weeks later, Stern called upon his longtime allies in the locals and became SEIU president. Stern has been successful in building SEIU membership.

❝ What's my risk? That some people won't like me? Their risk is that they lose their jobs. ❞

ANDY STERN, PRESIDENT, SERVICE EMPLOYEES INTERNATIONAL UNION

Early in 2005 Stern and other union leaders issued a set of proposals to Sweeney and AFL-CIO leaders. These proposals recommended sweeping changes, such as consolidation into fewer unions; more focus on minority, female, and immigrant workers; and redistribution of funds from headquarters to locals. Sweeney and his team rejected the proposals, stating that gradual change is best. Some of the AFL-CIO's member union leaders had supported Stern's proposals, although they were not happy about the way in which they were delivered. To many observers, it seemed that Stern had turned on his former friend, although Stern insisted that his concern was for the workers. "If I don't have the courage to do what my members put me here to do, then how do I ask a janitor or a childcare worker to go in and see a private-sector employer and say, 'We want to have a union in this place?'" said Stern. "What's *my* risk? That some people won't like me? *Their* risk is that they lose their jobs."

Opposition to Stern seems based on the division between old labor and new—Stern looks and sounds more like management. Tom Buffenbarger, head of the International Association of Machinists, an AFL-CIO member union, says that "[Stern's] trying to corporatize the labor movement. When you listen to him talk, it's all about producers and consumers . . . I think he wants his own TV show." In fact, that's exactly what Stern wants. Among his proposals for revitalizing the labor movement is a labor television channel, a companion for SEIU's radio station, the Worker Independent News Station, or WINS.

See the boxed insert on page 369 in this chapter, *The SEIU and . . . Change* for more information about Stern's approach to unionizing today's service workforce.

References: "Five Leading Unions Form New Coalitions to Rebuild American Labor Movement," SEIU Press release, June 15, 2005, SEIU website, www.seiu.org on June 15, 2005; Matt Bai, "The New Boss," *New York Times Magazine*, January 30, 2005, pp. 38–70 (quotation); Aaron Bernstein, "The Status Quo Won't Stand," *Business Week*, September 13, 2004, www.businessweek.com on June 11, 2005; Steven Greenhouse, "Labor Tries Organizing in the Union-Wary South," *New York Times*, February 6, 2005, p. N14.

As we learned in Chapters 12 and 13, leadership is a powerful, complex, and amorphous concept. This chapter explores a variety of forces and processes in organizations that are often related to—but at the same time distinct from— leadership. These forces and processes may precede, follow from, undermine, and/or reinforce a leader's ability to function effectively. They may also occur independently of leadership and its other associated activities.

We begin by briefly revisiting the concept of influence. While we introduced influence at the beginning of Chapter 12 as a basis for defining leadership, we now examine influence a bit more completely, and also describe a specific form of influence known as impression management. We then discuss power in its myriad forms in organizations. Politics and political behavior are then introduced and described in detail. Finally, we discuss organizational justice. (Some authors treat justice in the context of motivation, but given its close association with influence, power, and politics, it seems most reasonable to cover it here.)

Influence in Organizations

Recall that in Chapter 12 we defined leadership (from a process perspective) as the use of noncoercive influence to direct and coordinate the activities of group members to meet goals. We then described a number of leadership models and theories based variously on leadership traits, behaviors, and contingencies. Unfortunately, most of these models and theories essentially ignore the influence component of leadership. That is, they tend to focus on the characteristics of the leader (traits, behaviors, or both) and the responses from followers (satisfaction, performance, or both, for instance) with little regard for how the leader actually exercises influence in an effort to bring about the desired responses from followers.

But influence should actually be seen as the cornerstone of the process of one person attempting to affect another. For instance, regardless of the leader's traits or behaviors, leadership only matters if influence actually occurs. That is, the ultimate determinant of a person's leadership is how successful that person is in affecting the behavior of others through influence. No one can truly be a leader without the ability to influence others. If someone does have the ability to influence others, he or she clearly has the potential—at least—to become a leader.

> **Influence** is the ability to affect the perceptions, attitudes, or behaviors of others.

Influence, the ability to influence the perceptions, attitudes, or behaviors of others, is a fundamental cornerstone of leadership. Childhood friends Rameck Hunt, Sampson Davis, and George Jenkins vowed to defy the limitations of their inner-city upbringings and become doctors together. Throughout the rigors of college and medical school, the friends pushed each other to do their best. And there is little doubt in any of their minds that their mutual influence was the catalyst for each of them to succeed. Now they do their best to exert that same positive influence on others who face similar challenges.

The Nature of Influence

Influence is defined as the ability to affect the perceptions, attitudes, or behaviors of others.[1] If a person can make another person recognize that her working conditions are more hazardous than she currently believes them to be (change in perceptions), influence has occurred. Likewise, if an individual can convince someone else that the organization is a much better place to work than he currently believes it to be (change in attitude), influence has occurred. And if someone can get others to work harder or to file a grievance against their boss (change in behavior), influence has occurred.[2]

Influence can be dramatic or subtle. For instance, a new leader may be able to take a group of disenchanted employees working on a flawed and poorly conceived project and energize them to work harder while simultaneously enhancing the nature and direction of their project so as to make it much more worthwhile. As a result, the group will enjoy much greater success. In a different setting, however, a specific disgruntled employee may be very unhappy and on the verge of resigning. One morning a supervisor makes an innocuous comment that the unhappy employee perceives to be a criticism. That one comment, taken alone, might objectively be seen as very trivial. But

The SEIU and . . . **CHANGE**

New Labor's New Tactics

"[The labor] movement is going out of existence," says Andy Stern, president of the 1.8-million-member Service Employees International Union (SEIU). "I don't think workers in our country have a lot of time left if we don't change." Stern is concerned about the decline in labor's power. He is using political techniques, such as coalition building, controlling decision parameters, and creating lines of communication.

To build coalitions, SEIU unionizes entire industries in one region at the same time instead of the traditional practice of unionizing from employer to employer. When SEIU wanted to unionize janitors in New Jersey, Stern promised employers that the union wouldn't take effect unless 50 percent of all the janitors in the area signed the petition. When that percentage was reached, SEIU gained 7,000 new members.

Stern positions labor as an equal partner with management, rather than an adversary. He structures deals so that employees gain wages, benefits, and security, while employers gain a better trained, loyal, and productive workforce. To gain employers' trust, Stern goes to unusual lengths. In Arkansas, Stern promised nursing homes that he would lobby the state legislature for an increase in funding if the healthcare workers organized. The union was approved and Arkansas came up with more money.

Stern creates new lines of communication through his support of international unions. When an English bus company doing business in the United States refused to allow their American workers to organize, Stern formed a relationship with British unions that pressured the firm into changing. At Stern's request, a group of European union leaders met in April 2005 for the first time, and Stern has also met with Chinese unions. Stern will need all of his political savvy to successfully answer the question: "What can unions do to improve the standard of living in developing countries, while protecting it in developed ones?"

> *"I don't think workers in our country have a lot of time left if [the unions] don't change."*
>
> ANDY STERN, PRESIDENT, SERVICE EMPLOYEES INTERNATIONAL UNION

References: "Restore the American Dream," Purple Ocean website, www.changetowin.org on June 11, 2005; Matt Bai, "The New Boss," *New York Times Magazine*, January 30, 2005, pp. 38–70 (quotation); Aaron Bernstein, "Can This Man Save Labor?" *Business Week*, September 13, 2004, www.businessweek.com on June 11, 2005; Aaron Bernstein, "The Status Quo Won't Stand," *Business Week*, September 13, 2004, www.businessweek.com on June 11, 2005.

on top of the employee's current feelings and attitudes, it's enough to prompt an immediate resignation.

We should also point out that both the source and the target of influence can be a person or group. For instance, the efforts and success of a work team might so inspire other teams as to cause them to work harder. Further, influence might be intentional or unintentional. If one employee starts coming to work dressed more casually than has been the norm, others might follow, even though the first employee did not mean to influence others in any way.

Note, too, that influence can be used in ways that are beneficial or harmful. Someone can be influenced to help clean up a city park on the weekend as part of a community service program, for example. Operating employees can be influenced to work harder, engineers can be influenced to become more creative and innovative, and teams can be influenced to increase their efficiency. Employees can also be influenced to care less about the quality of their work, engineers can be influenced to not explore or advocate new ideas, and teams can be influenced to be less efficient. Hence, influence is a major force in organizations that managers cannot afford to ignore. *The SEIU and . . . Change* box provides additional information about change at SEIU.

Impression Management

Impression management is a special—and occasionally subtle—form of influence that deserves special mention. **Impression management** is a direct, intentional effort by someone to enhance his or her image in the eyes of others. People engage in impression management for a variety of reasons. For one thing, they may do so to further their own careers. By making themselves look good, they think they are more likely to receive rewards, attractive job assignments, and promotions. They may also engage in impression management to boost their own self-esteem. When people have a positive image in an organization, others make them aware of it through their compliments, respect, and so forth. Another reason people use impression management is to acquire more power and more control.

People attempt to manage how others perceive them through a variety of mechanisms. Appearance is one of the first things people think of. Hence, a person motivated by impression management will pay close attention to choice of attire, selection of language, and the use of manners and body posture. People interested in impression management may try to be associated only with successful projects. By being assigned to high-profile projects led by highly successful managers, a person can begin to link his or her own name with such projects in the minds of others.

In its most basic sense, of course, there is nothing wrong with impression management. After all, most people want to create a positive—and honest—image of themselves in the eyes of others. Sometimes, however, a person can become obsessed by impression management and resort to dishonest or unethical means. For example, a person may start to take credit for the work of others or exaggerate or even falsify personal accomplishments in an effort to enhance his or her image. Hence, while there is clearly nothing wrong with "putting your best foot forward," people should be cognizant of the impressions they are attempting to create and make sure they are not using inappropriate methods.

Power in Organizations

Influence is also closely related to the concept of power. Power is one of the most significant forces that exist in organizations. The *Wal-Mart and . . . Ethics* box provides an interesting discussion of the potential misuse of power. Moreover, it can be an extremely important ingredient in organizational success—or organizational failure. In this section we first describe the nature of power. Then we examine the types and uses of power.

The Nature of Power

Power has been defined in dozens of different ways; no one definition is generally accepted. Drawing from the more common meanings of the term, we define **power** as the potential ability of a person or group to exercise control over another person or group.[3] Power is distinguished from influence by the element of control—the more the ability to control exists in a relationship, the more that relationship is based on power. Thus, power might be thought of as an extreme form of influence.

One obvious aspect of our definition is that it expresses power in terms of potential; that is, we may be able to control others but choose not to exercise that control. Nevertheless, simply having the potential may be enough to influence others in some settings. We should also note that power may reside in individuals (such as managers and informal leaders), in formal groups (such as departments and committees), and in informal groups

Wal-Mart and . . . **ETHICS**

Is Wal-Mart Invading Customer Privacy?

According to the Wal-Mart website, "Years ago, [Wal-Mart founder] Sam Walton challenged all Wal-Mart associates to practice what he called 'aggressive hospitality.'" Today, Wal-Mart is clearly more aggressive in offering low prices than excellent service. Those low prices are the result of dozens of strategic actions, including the use of automated data collection and analysis. Relentless data management reduces prices, but it also introduces concerns about customer privacy.

Wal-Mart, a technology pioneer, has 460 terabytes of information on its mainframe computers, twice as much as on the entire Internet. Much of that data is about stores or products, but some of it is about customers. "We know who every customer is," says Wal-Mart chief information officer Linda M. Dillman. Through credit cards, checks, and drivers' licenses, Wal-Mart can link to customers' home address and email, credit reports, buying patterns, criminal and driving history, bank account balances, marital status, medical conditions, and more.

The information is legal to gather and is used to manage inventory, determine prices, and target advertising. For its part, Wal-Mart claims that it is more interested in aggregate patterns than in the behavior of any one customer. But the potential for misuse is evident.

Wal-Mart's next wave of technology will be radio-frequency ID tags, or RFIDs. These smart-chips with tiny antennas can hold a significant amount of data and communicate with transmitters. One RFID costs about 25 cents today, but that price is expected to fall to 2 cents within two years, making it an affordable replacement for bar codes. Benetton is considering including RFIDs in its undergarments, where they will transmit information about wear patterns and even bra size! Gillette is already using RFIDs in its expensive razors to control shoplifting.

For now, observers agree that Wal-Mart is not abusing its power, but the data and the technology are available and Wal-Mart's intentions could change at any time. The power lies with the giant retailer. Who is ensuring justice for customers?

This chapter's closing case, titled "Justice for Wal-Mart's Workers," describes further consequences of Wal-Mart's continual pressure to keep prices and costs low.

> *"We know who every customer is."*
>
> LINDA M. DILLMAN, CHIEF INFORMATION OFFICER, WAL-MART

References: "Exceeding Customer Expectations," Wal-Mart website, www.walmartstores.com on June 11, 2005; Patrick Dixon, "RFIDs: Great New Logistics Business or Brave New World?" Global Change website, www.globalchange.com on June 11, 2005; Constance L. Hays, "What They Know About You," *New York Times*, November 14, 2004, pp. BU1, 9.

(such as a clique of influential people). Finally, we should note the direct link between power and influence. If a person can convince another person to change his or her opinion on some issue, to engage in or refrain from some behavior, or to view circumstances in a certain way, that person has exercised influence—and used power.

Considerable differences of opinion exist about how thoroughly power pervades organizations. Some people argue that virtually all interpersonal relations are influenced by power, whereas others believe that exercise of power is confined only to certain situations. Whatever the case, power is undoubtedly a pervasive part of organizational life. It affects decisions ranging from the choice of strategies to the color of the new office carpeting. It makes or breaks careers. And it enhances or limits organizational effectiveness.

Types of Power

Within the broad framework of our definition, there are obviously many types of power. These types usually are described in terms of bases of power and position

TABLE 14.1

Common Forms of Power in Organizations

Legitimate power	Power that is granted by virtue of one's position in the organization
Reward power	Power that exists when one person controls rewards that another person values
Coercive power	Power that exists when one person has the ability to punish or physically or psychologically harm someone else
Expert power	Power that exists when one person controls information that is valuable to someone else
Referent power	Power that exists when one person wants to be like or imitates someone else
Position power	Power that resides in a position, regardless of who is filling that position
Personal power	Power that resides in the person, regardless of the position being filled

power versus personal power. Table 14.1 identifies and summarizes the most common forms of power.

Bases of Power   The most widely used and recognized analysis of the bases of power is the classic framework developed by John R. P. French and Bertram Raven.[4] French and Raven identified five general bases of power in organizational settings: legitimate, reward, coercive, expert, and referent power.

Legitimate power, essentially the same thing as authority, is granted by virtue of one's position in an organization. Managers have legitimate power over their subordinates. The organization specifies that it is legitimate for the designated individual to direct the activities of others. The bounds of this legitimacy are defined partly by the formal nature of the position involved and partly by informal norms and traditions.

Legitimate power is power that is granted by virtue of one's position in the organization.

The lines of legitimate power are often blurred in organic high-technology companies, with patterns of influence following different paths depending on circumstances. These people, for instance, comprise a computer game team for Electronic Arts. Among other projects, they develop computer soccer games tied to the World Cup Soccer event. While Bill Harrison (in the Hawaiian shirt) is the group's "official" boss, team members know that they are free to work among themselves to keep projects moving without having to rely too heavily on Harrison's approval.

For example, it was once commonplace for managers to expect their secretaries not only to perform work-related activities such as typing and filing but to also run personal errands such as picking up laundry and buying gifts. In highly centralized, mechanistic, and bureaucratic organizations such as the military, the legitimate power inherent in each position is closely specified, widely known, and strictly followed. In more organic organizations, such as research and development labs and software firms, the lines of legitimate power often are blurry. Employees may work for more than one boss at the same time, and leaders and followers may be on a nearly equal footing.

Reward power is the extent to which a person controls rewards that are valued by another. The most obvious examples of organizational rewards are pay, promotions, and work assignments. If a manager has almost total control over the pay his subordinates receive, can make recommendations about promotions, and has considerable discretion to make job assignments, he or she has a high level of reward power. Reward power can extend beyond material rewards. As we noted in our discussions of motivation theory in Chapters 4 and 5, people work for a variety of reasons in addition to pay. For instance, some people may be motivated primarily by a desire for recognition and acceptance. To the extent that a manager's praise and acknowledgment satisfy those needs, that manager has even more reward power.

> **Reward power** is the extent to which a person controls rewards that another person values.

Coercive power exists when someone has the ability to punish or physically or psychologically harm another person. For example, some managers berate subordinates in front of their peers and colleagues, belittling their efforts and generally making their work lives miserable. Certain forms of coercion may also be more subtle than this example. In some organizations, a particular division may be notorious as a resting place for people who have no future with the company. Thus, threatening to transfer someone to a dead-end branch or some other undesirable location is a form of coercion. Clearly, the more negative the sanctions a person can bring to bear on others, the stronger is her or his coercive power. At the same time, the use of coercive power carries a considerable cost in employee resentment and hostility.

> **Coercive power** is the extent to which a person has the ability to punish or physically or psychologically harm someone else.

Control over expertise or, more precisely, over information is another source of power in an organization. For example, to the extent that an inventory manager has information that a sales representative needs, the inventory manager has **expert power** over the sales representative. The more important the information and the fewer the alternative sources for getting it, the greater the power. Expert power can reside in many niches in an organization; it transcends positions and jobs. Although legitimate, reward, and coercive power may not always correspond exactly to formal authority, they often do. Expert power, on the other hand, may be associated much less with formal authority. Upper-level managers usually decide on the organization's strategic agenda, but individuals at lower levels in the organization may have the expertise those managers need to do the tasks. A research scientist may have crucial information about a technical breakthrough of great importance to the organization and its strategic decisions. Or an assistant may take on so many of the boss's routine and mundane activities that the manager loses track of such details and comes to depend on the assistant to keep things running smoothly. In other situations, lower-level participants are given power as a way to take advantage of their expertise.

> **Expert power** is the extent to which a person controls information that is valuable to someone else.

Referent power is power through identification. If Jose is highly respected by Adam, Jose has referent power over Adam. Like expert power, referent power does not always correlate with formal organizational authority. In some ways, referent power is similar to the concept of charisma in that it often involves trust, similarity, acceptance, affection, willingness to follow, and emotional involvement. Referent power usually surfaces as imitation. For example, suppose a new department manager is the youngest person in the organization to have reached that rank. Further, it is widely believed that she is being groomed for the highest levels of the company. Other people in the department

> **Referent power** exists when one person wants to be like or imitates someone else.

may begin to imitate her, thinking that they too may be able to advance. They may begin dressing like her, working the same hours, and trying to pick up as many work-related pointers from her as possible.

Position Versus Personal Power   The French and Raven framework is only one approach to examining the origins of organizational power. Another approach categorizes power in organizations in terms of position or personal power.

> **Position power** resides in the position, regardless of who is filling that position.

Position power is power that resides in the position, regardless of who holds it. Thus, legitimate, reward, and some aspects of coercive and expert power can all contribute to position power. Position power is thus similar to authority. In creating a position, the organization simultaneously establishes a sphere of power for the person filling that position. He or she will generally have the power to direct the activities of subordinates in performing their jobs, to control some of their potential rewards, and to have a say in their punishment and discipline. There are, however, limits to a manager's position power. A manager cannot order or control activities that fall outside his or her sphere of power, such as directing a subordinate to commit crimes, to perform personal services, or to take on tasks that clearly are not part of the subordinate's job.

> **Personal power** resides in the person, regardless of the position being filled.

Personal power is power that resides with an individual, regardless of his or her position in the organization. Thus, the primary bases of personal power are referent and some traces of expert, coercive, and reward power. Charisma may also contribute to personal power. Someone usually exercises personal power through rational persuasion or by playing on followers' identification with him or her. An individual with personal power often can inspire greater loyalty and dedication in followers than someone who has only position power. The stronger influence stems from the fact that the followers are acting more from choice than from necessity (as dictated, for example, by their organizational responsibilities) and thus will respond more readily to requests and appeals. Of course, the influence of a leader who relies only on personal power is limited, because followers may freely decide not to accept his or her directives or orders.

The distinctions between formal and informal leaders are also related to position and personal power. A formal leader will have, at minimum, position power. And an informal leader will similarly have some degree of personal power. Just as a person may be both a formal and an informal leader, he or she can have both position and personal power simultaneously. Indeed, such a combination usually has the greatest potential influence on the actions of others. Figure 14.1 illustrates how personal and position power may interact to determine how much overall power a person has in a particular situation. An individual with both personal and position power will have the strongest overall power. Likewise, an individual with neither personal nor position power will have the weakest overall power. Finally, when either personal or position power is high but the other is low, the individual will have a moderate level of overall power.

FIGURE 14.1

Position Power and Personal Power

Position power resides in a job whereas personal power resides in an individual. When these two types of power are broken down into high and low levels and related to one another, the two-by-two matrix shown here is the result. For example, the upper-right cell suggests that a leader with high levels of both position and personal power will have the highest overall level of power. Other combinations result in differing levels of overall power.

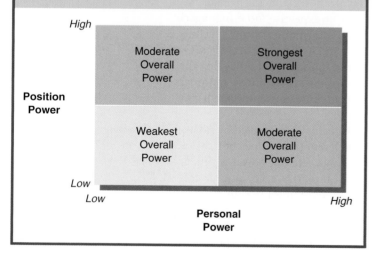

The Uses of Power in Organizations

Power can be used in many ways in an organization. Because of the potential for its misuse and the concerns that it may engender, it is important that managers fully understand the dynamics of using power. Gary Yukl has presented a useful perspective for understanding the possible consequences of using power in various ways.[5] He notes that, depending upon the circumstances, a leader using any given base of power might encounter one of three responses—commitment, compliance, or resistance. Table 14.2 indicates the outcomes that may result when a leader tries to exert power. These outcomes depend on the leader's base of power, how that base is operationalized, and the subordinate's individual characteristics (for example, personality traits or past interactions with the leader).

Commitment will probably result from an attempt to exercise power if the subordinate accepts and identifies with the leader. Such an employee will be highly motivated by requests that seem important to the leader. For example, a leader might explain that a new piece of software will greatly benefit the organization if it is developed soon. A committed subordinate will work just as hard as the leader to complete the project,

Source of Leader Influence	Type of Outcome		
	Commitment	**Compliance**	**Resistance**
Referent Power	*Likely*	*Possible*	*Possible*
	If request is believed to be important to leader	If request is perceived to be unimportant to leader	If request is for something that will bring harm to leader
Expert Power	*Likely*	*Possible*	*Possible*
	If request is persuasive and subordinates share leader's task goals	If request is persuasive but subordinates are apathetic about leader's task goals	If leader is arrogant and insulting, or subordinates oppose task goals
Legitimate Power	*Possible*	*Likely*	*Possible*
	If request is polite and very appropriate	If request or order is seen as legitimate	If arrogant demands are made or request does not appear proper
Reward Power	*Possible*	*Likely*	*Possible*
	If used in a subtle, very personal way	If used in a mechanical, impersonal way	If used in a manipulative, arrogant way
Coercive Power	*Very Unlikely*	*Possible*	*Likely*
		If used in a helpful, nonpunitive way	If used in a hostile or manipulative way

TABLE 14.2

Uses and Outcomes of Power

Reference: From Dorwin P. Cartwright ed., *Studies in Social Power*, 1959. Reprinted with permission from the Institute for Social Research, University of Michigan, Ann Arbor, Michigan.

Leaders who have high levels of commitment from their followers can accomplish astonishing things. Sam Walton, the inspirational founder of Wal-Mart, managed to achieve unusually high levels of commitment on the part of his employees. All "Mr. Sam" (as he was affectionately known) had to do was ask his employees to do something, and it wasn't a matter of if but when it might get done. This loyalty helped propel the small retailing establishment launched by Walton in 1962 to its lofty position today as the world's largest company. Even though Walton passed away in 1992, his influence still pervades the company today.

even if that means working overtime. Sam Walton once asked all Wal-Mart employees to start greeting customers with a smile and an offer to help. Because Wal-Mart employees generally were motivated by and loyal to Walton, most of them accepted his request.

Compliance means the subordinate is willing to carry out the leader's wishes as long as doing so will not require extraordinary effort. That is, the person will respond to normal, reasonable requests that are perceived to be clearly within the normal boundaries of the job. But the person will not be inclined to do anything extra or to go beyond the normal expectations for the job. Thus, the subordinate may work at a reasonable pace but refuse to work overtime, insisting that the job will still be there tomorrow. Many ordinary requests from a boss meet with compliant responses from subordinates.

Resistance occurs when the subordinate rejects or fights the leader's wishes. For example, suppose an unpopular leader asks employees to volunteer for a company-sponsored community activity project. The employees may reject this request, largely because of their feelings about the leader. A resistant subordinate may even deliberately neglect the project to ensure that it is not done as the leader wants. Continental Airlines once had a very unpopular CEO named Frank Lorenzo; some employees occasionally disobeyed his mandates as a form of protest against his leadership of the firm.

Table 14.3 suggests ways for leaders to use various kinds of power most effectively. By effective use of power, we mean using power in the way that is most likely to engender commitment or, at the least, compliance that is least likely to engender resistance. For example, to suggest a somewhat mechanistic approach, managers may enhance their referent power by choosing subordinates with backgrounds similar to their own. They might, for instance, build a referent power base by hiring several subordinates who went to the same college they did. A more subtle way to exercise referent power is through role modeling: The leader behaves as she or he wants subordinates to behave. As noted earlier, since subordinates relate to and identify with the leader with referent power, they may subsequently attempt to emulate that person's behavior.

Basis of Power	Guidelines for Use
Referent Power	Treat subordinates fairly
	Defend subordinates' interests
	Be sensitive to subordinates' needs, feelings
	Select subordinates similar to oneself
	Engage in role modeling
Expert Power	Promote image of expertise
	Maintain credibility
	Act confident and decisive
	Keep informed
	Recognize employee concerns
	Avoid threatening subordinates' self-esteem
Legitimate Power	Be cordial and polite
	Be confident
	Be clear and follow up to verify understanding
	Make sure request is appropriate
	Explain reasons for request
	Follow proper channels
	Exercise power regularly
	Enforce compliance
	Be sensitive to subordinates' concerns
Reward Power	Verify compliance
	Make feasible, reasonable requests
	Make only ethical, proper requests
	Offer rewards desired by subordinates
	Offer only credible rewards
Coercive Power	Inform subordinates of rules and penalties
	Warn before punishing
	Administer punishment consistently and uniformly
	Understand the situation before acting
	Maintain credibility
	Fit punishment to the infraction
	Punish in private

TABLE 14.3

Guidelines for
Using Power

Reference: Reprinted from Gary A. Yukl, *Leadership in Organization,* 2nd ed., © 1989, pp. 44–49, Prentice Hall, Inc., Englewood Cliffs, N.J.

In using expert power, managers may subtly make others aware of their education, experience, and accomplishments as they apply to current circumstances. But to maintain credibility, a leader should not pretend to know things that he or she really does not know. A leader whose pretensions are exposed will rapidly lose expert power. A confident and decisive leader demonstrates a firm grasp of situations and takes charge when circumstances dictate. Managers should also keep themselves informed about developments related to tasks that are valuable to the organization and relevant to their expertise.

A leader who recognizes employee concerns works to understand the underlying nature of these issues and takes appropriate steps to reassure subordinates. For example, if employees feel threatened by rumors that they will lose office space after an impending move, the leader might ask them about this concern and then find out just how much office space there will be and tell the subordinates. Finally, to avoid threatening the self-esteem of subordinates, a leader should be careful not to flaunt expertise or behave like a "know-it-all."

In general, a leader exercises legitimate power by formally requesting that subordinates do something. The leader should be especially careful to make requests diplomatically if the subordinate is sensitive about his or her relationship with the leader. This might be the case, for example, if the subordinate is older or more experienced than the leader. But although the request should be polite, it should be made confidently. The leader is in charge and needs to convey his or her command of the situation. The request should also be clear. Thus, the leader may need to follow up to ascertain that the subordinate has understood it properly. To ensure that a request is seen as appropriate and legitimate to the situation, the leader may need to explain the reasons for it. Often subordinates do not understand the rationale behind a request and consequently are unenthusiastic about it. It is important, too, to follow proper channels when dealing with subordinates.

Suppose a manager has asked a subordinate to spend his day finishing an important report. Later, while the manager is out of the office, her boss comes by and asks the subordinate to drop that project and work on something else. The subordinate will then be in the awkward position of having to choose which of two higher-ranking individuals to obey. Exercising authority regularly will reinforce its presence and legitimacy in the eyes of subordinates. Compliance with legitimate power should be the norm, because if employees resist a request, the leader's power base may diminish. Finally, the leader exerting legitimate power should attempt to be responsive to subordinates' problems and concerns in the same ways we outlined for using expert power.

Reward power is in some respects the easiest base of power to use. Verifying compliance simply means that leaders should find out whether subordinates have carried out their requests before giving rewards; otherwise, subordinates may not recognize the linkage between their performance and subsequent reward. The request that is to be rewarded must be both reasonable and feasible, of course, because even the promise of a reward will not motivate a subordinate who thinks a request should not or cannot be carried out.

The same can be said for a request that seems improper or unethical. Among other things, the follower may see a reward linked to an improper or unethical request, such as a bribe or other shady offering. Finally, if the leader promises a reward that subordinates know she or he cannot actually deliver, or if they have little use for a reward the manager can deliver, they will not be motivated to carry out the request. Further, they may grow skeptical of the leader's ability to deliver rewards that are worth something to them.

Coercion is in many ways the most difficult form of power to exercise. Because coercive power is likely to cause resentment and to erode referent power, it should be used infrequently, if at all. Compliance is about all one can expect from using coercive power, and that is only if the power is used in a helpful, non-punitive way—that is, if the sanction is mild and fits the situation and if the subordinate learns from it. In most cases, resistance is the most likely outcome, especially if coercive power is used in a hostile or manipulative way.

Violations of rules pose an unpalatable dilemma for a leader, and fully informing subordinates about rules and penalties will prevent accidental violations. Overlooking an infraction on the grounds that the perpetrator was ignorant may undermine the rule or the leader's legitimate power, but carrying out the punishment probably will create resentment. One approach is to provide reasonable warning before inflicting punishment, responding to the first violation of a rule with a warning about the consequences of another violation. Of course, a serious infraction such as a theft or violence warrants immediate and severe punishment.

The disciplinary action needs to be administered consistently and uniformly, because doing so shows that punishment is both impartial and clearly linked to the infraction.

Leaders should obtain complete information about what has happened before they punish, because punishing the wrong person or administering uncalled-for punishment can stir great resentment among subordinates. Credibility must be maintained, because a leader who continually makes threats but fails to carry them out loses both respect and power. Similarly, if the leader uses threats that subordinates know are beyond his or her ability to impose, the attempted use of coercive power will be fruitless. Obviously, too, the severity of the punishment generally should match the seriousness of the infraction. Finally, punishing someone in front of others adds humiliation to the penalty, which reflects poorly on the leader and makes those who must watch and listen uncomfortable as well.

Politics and Political Behavior

A concept closely related to power in organizational settings is politics, or political behavior. **Organizational politics** are activities people perform to acquire, enhance, and use power and other resources to obtain their preferred outcomes in a situation where there is uncertainty or disagreement. Thus, political behavior is the general means by which people attempt to obtain and use power. Put simply, the goal of such behavior is to get one's own way about things.[6]

> **Organizational politics** are activities carried out by people to acquire, enhance, and use power and other resources to obtain their desired outcomes.

The Pervasiveness of Political Behavior

One important survey provides some interesting insights into how managers perceive political behavior in their organizations.[7] Roughly one-third of the 428 managers who responded to this survey believed political behavior influenced salary decisions in their organizations, while 28 percent felt it affected hiring decisions. Moreover, three-quarters of them also believed political behavior to be more prevalent at higher levels of the organization than at lower levels. More than half believed that politics are unfair, unhealthy, and irrational but also acknowledged that successful executives must be good politicians and that it is necessary to behave politically to get ahead. The survey results suggest that managers see political behavior as an undesirable but unavoidable facet of organizational life.

Politics often are viewed as synonymous with dirty tricks or backstabbing and therefore as something distasteful and best left to others. But the results of the survey just described demonstrate that political behavior in organizations, like power, is pervasive. Thus, rather than ignoring or trying to eliminate political behavior, managers might more fruitfully consider when and how organizational politics can be used constructively.

Figure 14.2 presents an interesting model of the ethics of organizational politics.[8] In the model, a political behavior alternative (PBA) is a given course of action, largely political in character, in a particular situation. The model considers political behavior ethical and appropriate under two conditions: (1) if it respects the rights of all affected parties, and (2) if it adheres to the canons of justice (that is, to a commonsense judgment of what is fair and equitable). Even if the political behavior does not meet these tests, it may be ethical and appropriate under certain circumstances. For example, politics may provide the only possible basis for deciding which employees to let go during a recessionary period of cutbacks. In all cases where nonpolitical alternatives exist, however, the model recommends rejecting political behavior that abrogates rights or justice.

To illustrate how the model works, consider Susan Jackson and Bill Thompson, both assistant professors of English at a private university. University regulations stipulate that only one of the assistant professors may be tenured; the other must be let go (some

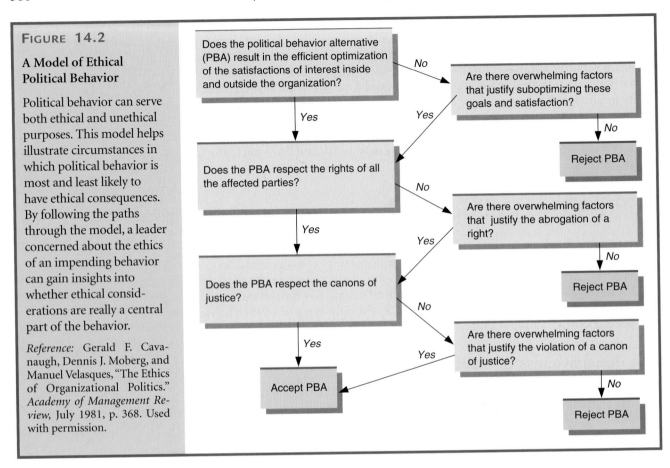

FIGURE 14.2

A Model of Ethical Political Behavior

Political behavior can serve both ethical and unethical purposes. This model helps illustrate circumstances in which political behavior is most and least likely to have ethical consequences. By following the paths through the model, a leader concerned about the ethics of an impending behavior can gain insights into whether ethical considerations are really a central part of the behavior.

Reference: Gerald F. Cavanaugh, Dennis J. Moberg, and Manuel Velasques, "The Ethics of Organizational Politics." *Academy of Management Review,* July 1981, p. 368. Used with permission.

universities actually follow this practice!). Both Susan and Bill submit their credentials for review. By most objective criteria, such as number of publications and teaching evaluations, the two faculty members' qualifications are roughly the same. Because he fears termination, Bill begins an active political campaign to support a tenure decision favoring him. For instance, he reminds the tenured faculty of his intangible contributions, such as his friendship with influential campus administrators, and points out his family ties to the university. Susan, on the other hand, decides to say nothing and let her qualifications speak for themselves. The department ultimately votes to give Bill tenure and let Susan go.

Was Bill's behavior ethical? Assuming that his comments about himself were accurate and that he said nothing to disparage Susan, his behavior did not affect her rights; that is, she had an equal opportunity to advance her own cause but chose not to do so. Bill's efforts did not directly hurt Susan but only helped himself. On the other hand, it might be argued that Bill's actions violated the canons of justice because clearly defined data on which to base the tenure decision were available. Thus, one could argue that Bill's calculated introduction of additional information into the decision was unjust.

This model has not been tested empirically. Indeed, its very nature may make it impossible to test. Further, as the preceding demonstrates, it often is difficult to give an unequivocal yes or no answer to the questions, even under the simplest circumstances. Thus, the model serves as a general framework for understanding the ethical implications of various courses of action managers might take.

How, then, should managers approach the phenomenon of political behavior? Trying to eliminate political behavior will seldom, if ever, work. In fact, such action may well increase political behavior because of the uncertainty and ambiguity it creates. At the other extreme, universal and freewheeling use of political behavior probably will lead to conflict, feuds, and turmoil. In most cases, a position somewhere in between is best: The manager does not attempt to eliminate political activity, recognizing its inevitability, and may try to use it effectively, perhaps following the ethical model just described. At the same time, the manager can take certain steps to minimize the potential dysfunctional consequences of abusive political behavior.

Managing Political Behavior

Managing organizational politics is not easy. The very nature of political behavior makes it tricky to approach in a rational and systematic way. Success will require a basic understanding of three factors: the reasons for political behavior, common techniques for using political behavior, and strategies for limiting the effects of political behavior.

Reasons for Political Behavior   Political behavior occurs in organizations for five basic reasons: ambiguous goals, scarce resources, technology and environment, nonprogrammed decisions, and organizational change (see Figure 14.3).

Most organizational goals are inherently ambiguous. Organizations frequently espouse goals such as "increasing our presence in certain new markets" or "increasing our market share." The ambiguity of such goals provides an opportunity for political behavior, because people can view a wide range of behaviors as helping to meet the goal. In reality, of course, many of these behaviors may actually be designed for the personal gain of the individuals involved. For example, a top manager might argue

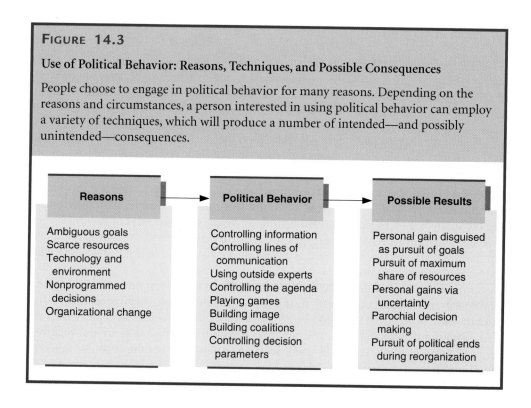

FIGURE 14.3

Use of Political Behavior: Reasons, Techniques, and Possible Consequences

People choose to engage in political behavior for many reasons. Depending on the reasons and circumstances, a person interested in using political behavior can employ a variety of techniques, which will produce a number of intended—and possibly unintended—consequences.

Reasons	Political Behavior	Possible Results
Ambiguous goals	Controlling information	Personal gain disguised as pursuit of goals
Scarce resources	Controlling lines of communication	Pursuit of maximum share of resources
Technology and environment	Using outside experts	Personal gains via uncertainty
Nonprogrammed decisions	Controlling the agenda	Parochial decision making
Organizational change	Playing games	Pursuit of political ends during reorganization
	Building image	
	Building coalitions	
	Controlling decision parameters	

that the corporation should pursue its goal of entry into a new market by buying out another firm instead of forming a new division. The manager may appear to have the good of the corporation in mind—but what if his or her spouse owns some of the target firm's stock and stands to make money on a merger or acquisition?

Whenever resources are scarce, some people will not get everything they think they deserve or need. Thus, they are likely to engage in political behavior as a means of inflating their share of the resources. In this way, a manager seeking a larger budget might present accurate but misleading or incomplete statistics to inflate the perceived importance of her department. Because no organization has unlimited resources, incentives for this kind of political behavior are often present.

Technology and environment may influence the overall design of the organization and its activities. The influence stems from the uncertainties associated with nonroutine technologies and dynamic, complex environments. These uncertainties favor the use of political behavior, because in a dynamic and complex environment, it is imperative that an organization respond to change. An organization's response generally involves a wide range of activities, from purposeful activities to uncertainty to a purely political response. In the last case, a manager might use an environmental shift as an argument for restructuring his or her department to increase his or her own power base.

Political behavior is also likely to arise whenever many nonprogrammed decisions need to be made. Nonprogrammed-decision situations involve ambiguous circumstances that allow ample opportunity for political maneuvering. The two faculty members competing for one tenured position is an example. The nature of the decision allowed political behavior, and in fact, from Bill's point of view, the nonprogrammed decision demanded political action.

As we discuss in Chapter 19, changes in organizations occur regularly and can take many forms. Each such change introduces some uncertainty and ambiguity into the organizational system, at least until it has been completely institutionalized. The period during which this is occurring usually affords much opportunity for political activity. For instance, a manager worried about the consequences of a reorganization may resort to politics to protect the scope of his or her authority.

The Techniques of Political Behavior   Several techniques are used in practicing political behavior. Unfortunately, because these techniques have not been systematically studied, our understanding of them is based primarily on informal observation and inference.[9] To further complicate this problem, the participants themselves may not even be aware that they are using particular techniques. Figure 14.3 also summarizes the most frequently used techniques.[10]

One technique of political behavior is to control as much information as possible. The more critical the information and the fewer the people who have access to it, the larger the power base and influence of those who do. For example, suppose a top manager has a report compiled as a basis for future strategic plans. Rather than distributing the complete report to peers and subordinates, he shares only parts of it with the few managers who must have the information. Because no one but the manager has the complete picture, he has power and is engaging in politics to control decisions and activities according to his own ends.

Similarly, some people create or exploit situations to control lines of communication, particularly access to others in the organization. Administrative assistants frequently control access to their bosses. An assistant may put visitors in contact with the boss, send them away, delay the contact by ensuring that phone calls are not returned promptly, and so forth. People in these positions often find that they can use this type of political behavior quite effectively.

Using outside experts, such as consultants or advisers, can be an effective political technique. The manager who hires a consultant may select one whose views match her own. Because the consultant realizes that the manager was responsible for selecting him, he feels a certain obligation to her. Although the consultant truly attempts to be objective and unbiased, he may unconsciously recommend courses of action favored by the manager. Given the consultant's presumed expertise and neutrality, others in the organization accept his recommendations without challenge. By using an outside expert, the manager has ultimately gotten what she wants.

Controlling the agenda is another common political technique. Suppose a manager wants to prevent a committee from approving a certain proposal. The manager first tries to keep the decision off the agenda entirely, claiming that it is not yet ready for consideration, or attempts to have it placed last on the agenda. As other issues are decided, he sides with the same set of managers on each deci-

Controlling agendas and information are common methods for enacting political behavior. Take White House chief of staff Andrew Card, for example. Card plays a major role in deciding what information is released to the media and what information is withheld or delayed. He also helps determine the format and scope of press releases, press conferences, and cabinet meetings. Hence, he clearly has the capacity to promote whatever political agendas he and the president want to pursue.

sion, building up a certain assumption that they are a team. When the controversial item comes up, he can defeat it through a combination of collective fatigue, the desire to get the meeting over with, and the support of his carefully cultivated allies. This technique, then, involves group polarization. A less sophisticated tactic is to prolong discussion of prior agenda items so that the group never reaches the controversial one. Or the manager may raise so many technical issues and new questions about the proposal that the committee decides to table it. In any of these cases, the manager will have used political behavior for his or her own ends.

"Game playing" is a complex technique that may take many forms. When playing games, managers simply work within the rules of the organization to increase the probability that their preferred outcomes will come about. Suppose a manager is in a position to cast the deciding vote on an upcoming issue but does not want to alienate either side by voting on it. One game she might play is to arrange to be called out of town on a crucial business trip when the vote is to take place. Assuming that no one questions the need for the trip, she will successfully maintain her position of neutrality and avoid angering either opposing camp.

Another game would involve using any of the techniques of political behavior in a purely manipulative or deceitful way. For example, a manager who will soon be making recommendations about promotions tells each subordinate, in "strictest confidence," that he or she is a leading candidate and needs only to increase his or her performance to have the inside track. Here the manager is using his control over information to play games with his subordinates. A power struggle at the W.R. Grace Company clearly illustrates manipulative practices. One senior executive fired the CEO's son and then allegedly attempted to convince the board of directors to oust the CEO and to give him the job. The CEO, in response, fired his rival and then publicly announced that the individual had been forced out because he had sexually harassed Grace employees.[11]

The technique of building coalitions has as its general goal convincing others that everyone should work together to accomplish certain things. A manager who believes she does not control enough votes to pass an upcoming agenda item may visit with other managers before the meeting to urge them to side with her. If her preferences are in the best interests of the organization, this may be a laudable strategy for her to follow. But if she herself is the principal beneficiary, the technique is not desirable from the organization's perspective.

At its extreme, coalition building, which is frequently used in political bodies, may take the form of blatant reciprocity. In return for Roberta Kline's vote on an issue that concerns him, Jose Montemayor agrees to vote for a measure that does not affect his group at all but is crucial to Kline's group. Depending on the circumstances, this practice may benefit or hurt the organization as a whole.

The technique of controlling decision parameters can be used only in certain situations and requires much subtlety. Instead of trying to control the actual decision, the manager backs up one step and tries to control the criteria and tests on which the decision is based. This allows the manager to take a less active role in the actual decision but still achieve his or her preferred outcome. For example, suppose a district manager wants a proposed new factory to be constructed on a site in his region. If he tries to influence the decision directly, his arguments will be seen as biased and self-serving. Instead, he may take a very active role in defining the criteria on which the decision will be based, such as target population, access to rail transportation, tax rates, distance from other facilities, and the like. If he is a skillful negotiator, he may be able to influence the decision parameters such that his desired location subsequently appears to be the ideal site as determined by the criteria he has helped shape. Hence, he gets just what he wants without playing a prominent role in the actual decision.

Limiting the Effects of Political Behavior

Although it is virtually impossible to eliminate political activity in organizations, managers can limit its dysfunctional consequences. The techniques for checking political activity target both the reasons it occurs in the first place and the specific techniques that people use for political gain.

Open communication is one very effective technique for restraining the impact of political behavior. For instance, if open communication is present in a situation where resources are scarce, the basis for allocating those resources will be known to everyone. This knowledge, in turn, will tend to reduce the propensity to engage in political behavior to acquire the resources, because people already know how the decisions will be made. Open communication also limits the ability of any single person to control information or lines of communication.

A related technique is to reduce uncertainty. Several of the reasons why political behavior occurs—ambiguous goals, nonroutine technology, an unstable environment, and organizational change—are associated with high levels of uncertainty. Political behavior can be limited if the manager can reduce uncertainty. Consider an organization about to transfer a major division from Florida to Michigan. Many people will resist the idea of moving north and may resort to political behavior to forestall their own transfer. However, the manager in charge of the move could announce who will stay and who will go at the same time that news of the change spreads throughout the company, thereby curtailing political behavior related to the move.

The adage "forewarned is forearmed" sums up one final technique for controlling political activity. Simply being aware of the causes and techniques of political behavior can help a manager check their effects. Suppose a manager anticipates that several impending organizational changes will increase the level of political activity. As a result of this awareness, the manager quickly infers that a particular subordinate is lobbying for the use of a certain consultant only because the subordinate thinks the consultant's recommendations will be in line with his own. Attempts to control the agenda, engage in game playing, build a certain image, and control decision parameters often are transparently obvious to the knowledgeable observer. Recognizing such behaviors for what they are, an astute manager may be able to take appropriate steps to limit their impact.

Organizational Justice

Organizational justice is an important phenomenon that has recently been introduced into the study of organizations. Justice can be discussed from a variety of perspectives, including motivation, leadership, and group dynamics. We choose to discuss it here because it is also likely to be related to power and political behavior in organizations. Basically, **organizational justice** refers to the perceptions of people in an organization regarding fairness.[12] As illustrated in Figure 14.4, there are four basic forms of organizational justice.

> **Organizational justice** refers to the perceptions of people in an organization regarding fairness.

Distributive Justice

Distributive justice refers to people's perceptions of the fairness with which rewards and other valued outcomes are distributed within the organization. Obviously related to the equity theory of motivation discussed back in Chapter 4, distributive justice takes a more holistic view of reward distribution than simply a comparison between one person and another. For instance, the compensation paid to top managers (especially the CEO), to peers and colleagues at the same level in an organization, and even entry-level hourly workers can all be assessed in terms of their relative fairness vis-à-vis anyone else in the organization.

Perceptions of distributive justice affect individual satisfaction with various work-related outcomes such as pay, work assignments, recognition, and opportunities for advancement. Specifically, the more people see rewards to be distributed as just, the more satisfied they will be with those rewards; the more they see rewards to be distributed as unjust, the less satisfied they will be. Moreover, individuals who feel that rewards are not distributed justly may be inclined to attribute such injustice to misuse of power and/or to political agendas.

"I'm making this decision on principle, just to see how it feels."

Perceptions of distributive justice play an important role in organizations. The extent to which managers make reward decisions that are seen as fair and just can impact satisfaction, motivation, and other key outcomes. Following principles of fairness and equity is therefore very important, a lesson that this executive no doubt still needs to learn!

Procedural Justice

Another important form of organizational justice is *procedural justice*—individual perceptions of the fairness used to determine various outcomes. For instance, suppose an employee's performance is evaluated by someone very familiar with the job being performed. Moreover, the evaluator clearly explains the basis for the evaluation and then discusses how that evaluation will translate in other outcomes such as promotions and pay increases. The individual will probably see this set of procedures as being fair and just. But if the evaluation is conducted by someone unfamiliar with the job and who provides no explanation as to how the evaluation is being done nor what it will mean, the individual is likely to see that process as less fair and just.

When workers perceive a high level of procedural justice, they may be motivated to participate in activities, to follow rules, and to accept relevant outcomes as being fair. But if workers perceive procedural injustice, they tend to withdraw from opportunities to participate, to pay less attention to rules and policies, and to see relevant outcomes as being unfair. In addition, perceptions of procedural injustice may be accompanied by interpretations based on the power and political behaviors of others.

Interpersonal Justice

Interpersonal justice relates to the degree of fairness people see in how they are treated by others in their organization. For instance, suppose an employee is treated by his boss with dignity and respect. The boss also provides information on a timely basis, and is always open and honest in her dealings with the subordinate. The subordinate will express high levels of interpersonal justice. But if the boss treats her subordinate with disdain and a clear lack of respect, and withholds important information and is often ambiguous or dishonest in her dealings with the subordinate, he will experience more interpersonal injustice.

Perceptions of interpersonal justice will most affect how individuals feel about those with whom they interact and communicate. If they experience interpersonal justice, they are likely to reciprocate by treating others with respect and openness. But if they experience interpersonal injustice, they may be less respectful in turn, and may be less inclined to follow the directives of their leader. Power and political behaviors are also likely to be seen as playing roles in interpersonal justice.

Informational Justice

Finally, *informational justice* refers to the perceived fairness of information used to arrive at decisions. If someone feels that a manager made a decision based on relatively complete and accurate information, and that the information was appropriately processed and considered, the person will likely experience informational justice even if they don't completely agree with the decision. But if the person feels that the decision was based on incomplete and inaccurate information and/or that important information was ignored, the individual will experience less informational justice.

Power and political behaviors are also likely to play an important role in perceptions of informational justice. Recall, for example, our earlier discussion of information control as a political tactic. To the extent that people believe that informational justice is lacking, they may very well attribute power and political behaviors as having played a major role in the decision-making process.

Synopsis

Influence can be defined as the ability to affect the perceptions, attitudes, or behaviors of others. Influence is a cornerstone of leadership. Impression management is a direct, intentional effort by someone to enhance his or her image in the eyes of others. People engage in impression management for a variety of reasons and use a variety of methods to influence how others see them.

Power is the potential ability of a person or group to exercise control over another person or group. The five bases of power are legitimate power (granted by virtue of one's position in the organization), reward power (control of rewards valued by others), coercive power (the ability to punish or harm), expert power (control over information that is valuable to the organization), and referent power (power through personal identification). Position power is tied to a position regardless of the individual who holds it. Personal power is power that resides in a person regardless of position. Attempts to use power can result in commitment, compliance, or resistance.

Organizational politics are activities people perform to acquire, enhance, and use power and other resources to obtain their preferred outcomes in a situation where uncertainty or disagreement exists. Political behavior is the general means by which people attempt to obtain and use power. Research indicates that most managers do not advocate use of political behavior but acknowledge that it is a necessity of organizational life. Because managers cannot eliminate political activity in the organization, they must learn to cope with it. Understanding how to manage political behavior requires understanding why it occurs, what techniques it employs, and strategies for limiting its effects.

Organizational justice refers to the perceptions of people in an organization regarding fairness. There are four basic forms of organizational justice: distributive, procedural, interpersonal, and informational. Power and political behaviors are likely to be attributed when any or all of these forms of justice are seen as being deficient.

Discussion Questions

1. Can a person without influence be a leader? Does having influence automatically make someone a leader?

2. Have you ever engaged in impression management? What did you hope to accomplish?

3. What might happen if two people, each with significant, equal power, attempt to influence each other?

4. Cite examples based on a professor-student relationship to illustrate each of the five bases of organizational power.

5. Is there a logical sequence in the use of power bases that a manager might follow? For instance, should the use of legitimate power usually precede the use of reward power, or vice versa?

6. Cite examples in which you have been committed, compliant, and resistant as a result of efforts to influence you. Think of times when your attempts to influence others led to commitment, compliance, and resistance.

7. Do you agree or disagree with the assertion that political behavior is inevitable in organizational settings?

8. The term "politics" is generally associated with governmental bodies. Why do you think it has also come to be associated with the behavior in organizations described in the chapter?

9. Recall examples of how you have either used or observed others using the techniques of political behavior identified in the chapter. What other techniques can you suggest?

10. Recall an instance when you have experienced each of the four forms of organizational justice in either a positive or a negative manger.

Learning About Ethics and Power

Purpose: This exercise will help you appreciate some of the ambiguities involved in assessing the ethics of power and political behavior in organizations.

Format: First, you will identify examples of more and less ethical uses of power and political behavior. Then you will discuss, compare, and contrast your examples with those generated by some of your classmates.

Procedure:

1. Identify and write down three examples of situations in which you think it would be ethical to use power and political behavior. For example, you might think it is ethical to use power and political behavior to save the job of a coworker whom you think is a very good—but misunderstood—employee.

2. Identify and write down three examples of situations in which you think it would be unethical to use power and political behavior. For instance, you might think it is unethical to use power and political behavior to gain a job for which you are really not qualified.

3. Form small groups of three or four members each. Each member of the group should read his or her examples of ethical and unethical uses of power and political behavior.

4. Discuss the extent to which the group members agree on the ethics for each situation.

5. See if your group members can think of different situations in which the ethical context changes. For example, if everyone agrees that a given situation is ethical, see if the group can think of slightly different circumstances in which, in essentially the same situation, using power and political behavior would become more unethical.

Follow-up Questions

1. How realistic was this exercise? What did you learn from it?

2. Could you assess real-life situations relating to the ethics of political activity using this same process?

Assessing Organizational Justice Where You Work

To learn about how workers respond to various types of injustices they may experience in the workplace, scientists have found it useful to use rating scales like the one shown. By completing this scale, you will gain some useful insight into your own feelings about the fairness experienced in the organization in which you work.

Directions

1. Using the following scale, respond to each of the questionnaire items by selecting a number from 1 to 5 to indicate the extent to which it applies to you.

   1 = almost never
   2 = slightly

   3 = moderately
   4 = greatly
   5 = almost always

2. In responding to each item, think about a particular organization in which you work or, if you are a student, think about a particular class.

3. Where you see the word (*outcome*), substitute a specific outcome that is relevant to you (e.g., for a worker, pay; for a student, a grade).

4. Where you see the word (*superior*), substitute a specific authority figure that is relevant to you (e.g., for a worker, one's supervisor; for a student, one's teacher).

Scale

To what extent . . .

1. _____ Is it possible for you to express your views about your (outcome)?

2. _____ Are your (outcomes) generally based on accurate information?

3. _____ Do you have an opportunity to correct decisions made about your (outcome)?

4. _____ Are you rewarded appropriately for the effort you put into your work?

5. _____ Do the (outcomes) you receive reflect the quality of your work?

6. _____ Is your (outcome) in keeping with your performance?

7. _____ Are you treated politely by your (superior)?

8. _____ Does your (superior) treat you with dignity and respect?

9. _____ Does your (superior) refrain from making inappropriate comments?

10. _____ Does your (superior) communicate openly with you?

11. _____ Does your (superior) tell you things in a timely fashion?

12. _____ Does your (superior) explain decisions to you in a thorough fashion?

Scoring

1. Add your responses to questions 1, 2, and 3. This is your *distributive justice* score.

2. Add your responses to questions 4, 5, and 6. This is your *procedural justice* score.

3. Add your responses to questions 7, 8, and 9. This is your *interpersonal justice* score.

4. Add your responses to questions 10, 11, and 12. This is your *informational justice* score.

5. For each score, higher numbers (e.g., 12–15) reflect higher perceived amounts of the type of fairness in question, whereas lower scores (e.g., 3–6 reflect lower perceived amounts of that type of fairness.

Discussion Questions

1. With respect to what particular type of fairness did you score highest? What specific experiences contributed to this assessment?

2. With respect to what particular type of fairness did you score lowest? What specific experiences contributed to this assessment?

3. What kinds of problems resulted from any violations of any type of organizational justice you may have experienced? What could have been done to avoid these violations?

Source: Jerald Greenberg, *Managing Behavior in Organizations,* 4th ed. (Upper Saddle River, NJ: Prentice Hall 2005), pp. 65–67.

Building Managerial Skills

Exercise Overview: Diagnostic skills help a manager visualize appropriate responses to a situation. One situation managers often face is whether to use power to solve a problem. This exercise will help you develop your diagnostic skills as they relate to using different types of power in different situations.

Exercise Background: Several methods have been identified for using power. These include:

1. *Legitimate request*—The manager requests that the subordinate comply because the subordinate recognizes that the organization has given the manager the right to make the request. Most day-to-day interactions between manager and subordinate are of this type.

2. *Instrumental compliance*—In this form of exchange, a subordinate complies to get the reward the manager controls. Suppose that a manager asks a subordinate

to do something outside the range of the subordinate's normal duties, such as working extra hours on the weekend, terminating a relationship with a long-standing buyer, or delivering bad news. The subordinate complies and, as a direct result, reaps praise and a bonus from the manager. The next time the subordinate is asked to perform a similar activity, that subordinate will recognize that compliance will be instrumental in her getting more rewards. Hence the basis of instrumental compliance is clarifying important performance-reward contingencies.

3. *Coercion*—This is used when the manager suggests or implies that the subordinate will be punished, fired, or reprimanded if he does not do something.

4. *Rational persuasion*—This is when the manager can convince the subordinate that compliance is in the subordinate's best interest. For example, a manager might argue that the subordinate should accept a transfer because it would be good for the subordinate's career. In some ways, rational persuasion is like reward power except that the manager does not really control the reward.

5. *Personal identification*—This is when a manager who recognizes that she has referent power over a subordinate can shape the behavior of that subordinate by

engaging in desired behaviors: the manager consciously becomes a model for the subordinate and exploits personal identification.

6. *Inspirational appeal*—This is when a manager can induce a subordinate to do something consistent with a set of higher ideals or values through inspirational appeal. For example, a plea for loyalty represents an inspirational appeal.

Exercise Task: With these ideas in mind, do the following:

1. Relate each of the uses of power listed above to the five types of power identified in the chapter. That is, indicate which type(s) of power is most closely associated with each use of power, which type may be related to each use of power, and which type(s) is unrelated to each use of power. Note: More than one type of power may be present.

2. Is a manager more likely to be using multiple forms of power at the same time or to be using a single type of power?

3. Identify other methods and approaches to using power.

4. What are some of the dangers and pitfalls associated with using power?

Organizational Behavior
Case for Discussion

Justice for Wal-Mart's Workers

With 1.7 million workers worldwide, Wal-Mart is the planet's largest employer. The company's leaders pride themselves on creating jobs, providing decent working conditions and pay, and treating individuals with respect. Wal-Mart proclaims, "Our people make the difference." However, many Wal-Mart workers tell a very different story. Wal-Mart stands accused of gender discrimination and violating worker rights to unionize.

Women employed or formerly employed by Wal-Mart accuse the giant firm of gender-based discrimination. In a document requesting that the U.S. District Court in California allow a class-action lawsuit, the plaintiffs introduce their case. "Since at least 1997, female employees of Wal-Mart Stores have been paid less than comparable male employees . . . despite having, on average, higher performance ratings and more seniority . . . Female employees at Wal-Mart Stores also receive far fewer promotions to management than do male employees, and those who are promoted must wait longer." The document goes on to note that women account for two-thirds of employees at Wal-Mart but just one-third of managers. The plaintiffs also allege that the discrimination is on-going, is worsening, and is not representative of the retail industry, where women typically hold over 50 percent of management jobs.

Wal-Mart is vigorously fighting the lawsuit and some of the actions the company has taken appear very suspect.

Delay has been Wal-Mart's first tactic. They have spent more than two years disputing the plaintiffs' rights to file as a class, instead suggesting that every woman must file a separate claim. This would increase legal costs and discourage claimants. Next, Wal-Mart has argued that pay and promotion are two separate issues that must be tried separately, again increasing costs for the female workers. Finally, Wal-Mart has claimed that the firm is composed of four different business units and thousands of stores, each of which acts autonomously. Thus, even if a pattern of discrimination is found, the company claims the blame should rest with individual store managers and not with the corporation. Wal-Mart seems unlikely to succeed in any of these tactics, but they do delay the trial and increase expenses, which can be very difficult for working families.

The right to unionize is also under attack at Wal-Mart. Wal-Mart has established a website to publicize the company's stand on issues, called Wal-Mart Facts. On that site, the company's opinion about unions is described: "Our Wal-Mart union stance is simple. There has never been a need for a Wal-Mart union due to the familiar, special relationship between Wal-Mart associates and their managers. Wal-Mart has encouraging and advantageous relationships with our loyal and happy associates on the floor of each Wal-Mart facility."

However, the company is using a variety of actions, some of them unethical or allegedly illegal, to prevent employees from unionizing. Some of those tactics include secret meetings, threats, and anti-union propaganda. These tactics are used against individuals who try to join unions, who encourage others to join unions, who are related to someone who is a union member, who just mention the word "union" at work, or who appear to be "susceptible" to unions. Wal-Mart has also denied union organizers access to employees outside of work, secretly made audio- and videotapes of employees suspected of being pro-union, and even terminated workers for showing interest in a union. Together, these actions amount to a pattern of intimidation. "The management of Wal-Mart creates the tension, they create the fear," says one associate. Chad Jordan, an associate,

> **"[F]emale employees of Wal-Mart Stores have been paid less than comparable male employees . . . despite having, on average, higher performance ratings and more seniority."**
> JOCELYN LARKIN AND CHRISTINE E. WEBER,
> ATTORNEYS FOR PLAINTIFFS

reports, "Wal-Mart says that union people are lazy, that they are poor workers, they are not intelligent, and they cannot stand up for themselves."

Wal-Mart's actions are sharply criticized by unions. According to Joe Hansen, president of United Food and Commercial Workers, Wal-Mart pays substandard wages, offers few benefits, uses child labor, discriminates against immigrants and minorities, violates safety and hiring standards, and denies workers their freedom of speech. "The average [full-time] associate makes $17,114 per year, well below the poverty level for a family of four . . . 660,000 of its employees [have no] company-provided health insurance, forcing workers to seek taxpayer-funded public assistance," says Hansen. "A U.S. congressional study found that Wal-Mart costs you, the American taxpayer, up to $2.5 billion in public assistance."

It's clear where Wal-Mart's $10 billion profit for 2004 came from, but where is the justice for Wal-Mart employees?

Case Questions

1. Describe one example of how Wal-Mart appears to have violated workers' right to distributive justice.

2. Describe one example of how Wal-Mart appears to have violated workers' right to procedural justice.

3. Choose one of Wal-Mart's actions mentioned in the case. In your opinion, who is hurt most by this action? Who benefits most? Use the answer to those two questions to determine whether the action is ethical or not. Explain your reasons.

References: "Sam Walton's 3 Basic Beliefs," Wal-Mart website, www.walmartstores.com on June 11, 2005; "Wal-Mart Union," Wal-Mart Facts website, www.walmartfacts.com on June 11, 2005; "Wal-Mart's War on Workers," video case; "Betty Dukes et. al. v. Wal-Mart Stores Inc.—Plaintiffs' Reply in Support of Class Certification," Cohen, Milstein, Hausfield & Toll website, www.cmht.com on June 11, 2005; Jonathan D. Glazer, "Attention Wal-Mart Plaintiffs: Hurdles Ahead," *New York Times*, June 27, 2004, p. BU5; Joe Hansen, "Hold Wal-Mart Accountable," UFCW website, www.ufcw.org on June 11, 2005; Joe Hansen, "More Villain than Victim," *USA Today*, April 17, 2005, www.usatoday.com on June 11, 2005.

TEST PREPPER

You have read the chapter and studied the key terms. Think you're ready to ace the exam? Take this sample test to gauge your comprehension of chapter material and check your answers at the back of the book. Want more test questions? Take the ACE quizzes found on the student website: http://college.hmco.com/business/students/ (select Griffin/Moorhead, Organizational Behavior, 8e from the Management menu).

T F 1. No one can truly be a leader without the ability to influence others.

T F 2. Simply having the potential to control others may be enough to influence them.

T F 3. A person with coercive power has the ability to physically or psychologically punish another person.

T F 4. Subtly making others aware of your education, experience, and accomplishments is a good way to use legitimate power.

T F 5. According to the model presented in this chapter, political behaviors are ethical if they respect the rights of others and adhere to the canons of justice.

T F 6. Managers should do their best to eliminate all political activity in their organizations.

T F 7. An employee who experiences interpersonal justice is likely to reciprocate by treating others with disrespect.

8. People engage in impression management for all of the following reasons, except
   a. to further their own careers.
   b. to improve the image of their company.
   c. to receive rewards and promotions.
   d. to acquire more power.
   e. to boost their own self-esteem.

9. Lawrence is a manager over fifteen employees in his organization. At a minimum, Lawrence has which base of power?
   a. Managerial
   b. Expert
   c. Legitimate
   d. Coercive
   e. Referent

10. Formal leaders have at least some _____ power, whereas informal leaders have at least some _____ power.
    a. referent; managerial
    b. legitimate; expert
    c. expert; legitimate
    d. personal; position
    e. position; personal

11. Managers who effectively use their power are most likely to engender which response from their employees?
    a. Compliance
    b. Coordination
    c. Compromise
    d. Commitment
    e. Continuity

12. To prevent accidental violations of a rule, a manager who wants to use coercive power should first
    a. make reasonable and feasible requests.
    b. fully inform subordinates about the rules and the penalties for violating them.
    c. be polite and confident.
    d. make subordinates aware of the manager's education, expertise, and accomplishments.
    e. be responsive to subordinates' problems and concerns.

13. What advice would you give managers with regard to handling political behaviors within an organization?
    a. Eliminate all political behavior.
    b. Allow political behavior at the top of the organization, but not at the bottom.
    c. Allow political behavior at the bottom of the organization, but not at the top.
    d. Minimize the potential dysfunctional consequences of abusive political behavior.
    e. Let the political "market" of the organization govern itself.

14. Why do nonprogrammed decisions often lead to political behaviors?
    a. They involve ambiguous circumstances.
    b. They involve limited resources.
    c. They involve information technology.
    d. They create zero-sum situations.
    e. They involve too many people.

15. Nicolas is upset about his salary. He knows the way the salary is calculated for him and his coworkers is fair, but he still doesn't believe he receives a fair wage. Which of the following forms of justice most concerns Nicolas?
    a. Distributive justice
    b. Procedural justice
    c. Interpersonal justice
    d. Operational justice
    e. Financial justice

Conflict and Negotiation in Organizations

After studying this chapter, you should be able to:

- ▶ **Define and discuss the nature of conflict in organizations.**

- ▶ **Identify and describe the common forms and causes of conflict.**

- ▶ **Discuss the most frequent reactions to conflict in organizations.**

- ▶ **Describe how conflict can be managed.**

- ▶ **Define negotiation in organizations and discuss its underlying processes.**

The (Functional) Family Business

Many large American businesses began as family-run ventures, including Sears, Exxon, and Anheuser-Busch. Even today, Wal-Mart is 40 percent controlled by members of the Walton family and Ford Motors is headed by William Clay Ford Jr., a great-grandson of founder Henry Ford. Family businesses account for 80 percent of all American firms and employ 62 percent of American workers.

Clearly, then, the health of family businesses is important to the nation's economy. However, with many baby boomers ready to retire, almost 40 percent of small businesses will change hands by 2008. And keeping a family business functional can be challenging, especially when it's time to pass control.

Consultant Paul Karofsky sums it up: "There's no greater thrill than sharing success with people you love. But there's no greater hell on earth than working with a dysfunctional family when things aren't going well." The joys of working for a family-run business include less bureaucracy, greater flexibility, and more access to top executives. The downside, however, can be intense, full of personal squabbles and perceptions of favoritism.

Families can be loving and nurturing, but they can also be the foundation for lifelong resentments. "Emotions run high, and the professional and the personal can often become indistinguishable," says consultant Jane Zalman. Mick Arnold, president of family-owned Arnold's Factory Supplies, struggled with other family members for years before his relatives resigned. Family members are still not speaking to each other. Other employees in family firms describe tense holidays and arguments over the breakfast table.

Even when family relationships are amicable, the differences between family and business values can cause problems. "Family relationships are supposed to be about unconditional love, valuing others for who they are," Karofsky explains. "In business, it's about competency, where people are valued for what they do and how well they do it." Strong family ties can make outsiders feel excluded and slighted. Patrick Murphy, an outsider who is president of a family-run business, acknowledges the tension, saying, "Blood is thicker than water, don't kid yourself. If push comes to shove, where do you think the allegiances are going to lie?"

Family businesses, where family members all have a self-interest in employment and income, can often use superordinate goals to resolve conflict. Increased structure and rules can help too. Intervention from third parties who lack personal involvement is also very helpful. Most families benefit from new ideas,

from reasonable challenges to their long-standing assumptions, and from the change in behavior patterns.

Finally, the family that screams together stays together. "I've found that it's actually OK—and sometimes even healthy—for family members to struggle with these issues, so long as they're ultimately reconciled," says Karofsky. Professor Joe Astrachan goes further: "Family researchers have found a linear relationship—the more you scream in your family, the healthier your family is. Those families tend to stay together longer than those that shun hostile communication." The future of family business may depend on the ability to conduct an on-going and productive argument.

For more about family business, see this chapter's boxed insert on page 397, *The Family Business and . . . Change.*

References: Jill Hamburg Coplan, "Outside Help," *Business Week Small Biz*, Summer 2004, pp. 54–58 (quotation); Paul Karofsky, "Equal Vs. Fair in Family Business," *Business Week*, January 26, 2005, www.businessweek.com on June 11, 2005; David Koeppel, "Those Family Ties Can Bind, But They Can Also Strangle," *New York Times*, February 13, 2005, pp. W1, 3; Rod Kurtz, "When Business Is In the Blood," *Business Week*, January 25, 2005, www.businessweek.com on June 11, 2005.

When people work together in organizational settings myriad consequences can result. For instance, people may leave work each day feeling happy and energized for having done a great job; they can be frustrated and unhappy because of some problem they encountered; and they can feel stressed because of the pressures being imposed upon them. Another possible outcome that occurs with regularity is conflict, the subject of this chapter. We begin with a discussion of the nature of conflict. We then examine its most common forms and the things that cause it in the first place. We then discuss reactions to conflict and how it can be managed. We conclude with a discussion of a related organizational process, negotiation.

The Nature of Conflict in Organizations

Conflict is a common occurrence in organizations. While there are numerous definitions of **conflict**, we will define it as a process resulting in the perceptions of two parties that they are working in opposition to each other in ways that result in feelings of discomfort and/or animosity. There are several elements of this definition that warrant additional comment.

First, note that conflict is a process, not a singular event. It evolves over time and draws upon previous events. While it may emerge as a result of a specific event, more than likely it has been brewing for some time. Further, the parties have to actually perceive conflict to exist in order for it to be real. If an observer witnesses what appears to be an argument between two other individuals but those people do not perceive their dialog to be conflictual, then conflict does not really exist. Finally, discomfort or animosity must occur in order for the conflict to be real. For example, a group of friends who play each other in a friendly game of softball may be competing for victory but are not in conflict.

We should also note that the parties involved in conflict may be individuals, groups, and/or organizations. Hence, conflict may involve one person in opposition to another, one group in opposition to another, or one organization in opposition to another. Conflict may also exist across levels, such as when an individual is in conflict with a group. Conflict may also result from the anticipation of future problems. For example, a person may behave antagonistically toward another person whom he or she expects to pose obstacles to goal achievement.[1]

Conflict is a process resulting in the perceptions of two parties that they are working in opposition to each other in ways that result in feelings of discomfort and/or animosity.

Conflict results from disagreement among parties (people and/or organizations). Dylan Lauren and her business partner, Jeff Rubin, have a unique way to resolve their conflicts. They each take a piece of gum, take three steps, and then blow a bubble. Whoever holds their bubble the longest wins and gets to decide how to do things. Ms. Lauren, for example, won the contest to determine the name of the candy store they opened on Manhattan's Upper East Side. The name? What else but Dylan's Candy Bar?

FIGURE 15.1

The Nature of Organizational Conflict

Either too much to too little conflict can be dysfunctional for an organization. In either case, performance may be low. However, an optimal level of conflict that sparks motivations, creativity, innovation, and initiative can result in higher levels of performance. T.J. Rodgers, CEO of Cypress Semiconductor, maintains a moderate level of conflict in his organization as a way of keeping people energized and motivated.

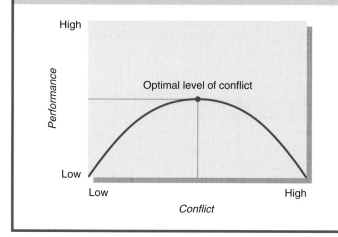

Although conflict often is considered harmful and something to avoid, it can also have some benefits. A total absence of conflict can lead to apathy and lethargy. A moderate degree of focused conflict, on the other hand, can stimulate new ideas, promote healthy competition, and energize behavior. In some organizations, especially profit-oriented ones, many managers believe that conflict is dysfunctional. On the other hand, many managers in not-for-profit organizations often view conflict as beneficial and conducive to higher-quality decision making.[2] In many cases, the impact of conflict on performance may take the form shown in Figure 15.1. Either too little or too much conflict may result in low performance, while a moderate level of conflict may lead to higher performance.

Common Forms and Causes of Conflict

Conflict may take a number of forms. In addition, it may be caused by a wide array of factors in an organization.

Common Forms of Conflict

Task conflict refers to conflict regarding the goals and content of the work.

In general, there are three basic forms of conflict that exist within an organization. There are additional forms that can relate to conflict between organizations. **Task conflict** refers to conflict regarding the goals and content of the work. For instance, suppose one manager believes that the firm should strive to maximize profits and shareholder value. This individual will feel strongly that the organization should avoid social causes and instead focus its efforts on increasing revenues and/or lowering costs to the exclusion of most other activities. Another manager in the same firm, however, may believe the business should have a pronounced social agenda and be an active participant in relevant social programs. While this manager recognizes the importance of profits, he or she also sees the importance of corporate citizenship. To the extent that their differences lead to disagreements over substantive issues, it represents task conflict.

Process conflict occurs when the parties agree on the goals and content of work, but disagree on how to achieve the goals and actually do the work.

Process conflict occurs when the parties agree on the goals and content of work, but disagree on how to achieve the goals and actually do the work. For example, suppose the two executives noted above actually both believe in the importance of a social agenda and support the concept of sharing corporate profits with society. Hence, they have no task conflict. However, one thinks the best way to do this is to simply give a portion of the firm's profits to one or more social causes. The other, however, thinks the company should be more active; for instance, she or he wants the firm to sponsor ongoing building projects through Habitat for Humanity. While they share the same goals, they see different processes being the best way to achieve those goals.

Relationship conflict occurs when the parties have interpersonal issues.

Relationship conflict occurs when the parties have interpersonal issues. For instance, suppose one person has very strict conservative religious beliefs. This person is

The Family Business and . . . **CHANGE**

Keeping It in the Family

Family businesses in America employ two-thirds of workers and contribute two-thirds of the gross domestic product. They also grow into large businesses—one-third of *Fortune* 500 companies still have family involvement. Family businesses tend to be conservative and traditional. Family name and reputation are keys to their success, making them reluctant to change. Yet family businesses are just as susceptible as larger firms to changes such as increased competition and outsourcing. How can family businesses manage change, without experiencing too much conflict?

Succession is a problem area, as families decide which members of the next generation will assume leadership of the company. The problem is so thorny that only about 30 percent of firms survive a generational change. Advance planning is essential. "Most [family-business owners] don't deal with these issues until they become a crisis," says Alfonse Mattia, a family-business accountant.

Outside advice, from consultants, accountants, or even psychologists, can help the family better manage changes. When three family-run companies merged to form Allied Beverage, the families hired consultants Bernie Tenenbaum and Dirk Drew. The consultants recommended more formalization of structure and procedures. "We wanted the owners to understand that they didn't have the right to tell people what to do just because they were owners," Tenenbaum says.

C.J. Buck, CEO of Buck Knives, believes that involving all of the family members in the business from a young age is essential. His teenagers are knowledgeable because they help out at the manufacturing plant. The family discusses the impact of business trends every night. "They all have something to say," Buck says. "It's good for them to discuss the business." Bob Paisner, a family-business owner, adds, "There is always conflict, but if you ignore it, it gets bigger."

For family-owned companies, maintaining family harmony in spite of the inevitable changes may be just as important as the bottom line.

> *"There is always conflict, but if you ignore it, it gets bigger."*
> BOB PAISNER, CEO, SCRUBADUB
> AUTO WASH CENTERS

References: Erin Chambers, "A Clan on the Cutting Edge," *Business Week*, January 25, 2005, www.businessweek.com on June 11, 2005; Jill Hamburg Coplan, "Outside Help," *Business Week Small Biz*, Summer 2004, pp. 54–58; Brian Hindo, "What Successful Successions Need," *Business Week*, January 25, 2005, www.businessweek.com on June 11, 2005 (quotation); Rod Kurtz, "When Business Is in the Blood," *Business Week*, January 25, 2005, www.businessweek.com on June 11, 2005; Amy Tsao, "Families, United to Grow," *Business Week*, January 25, 2005, www.businessweek.com on June 11, 2005.

offended by the use of vulgar language, believes strongly in the importance of regular church attendance, and has no qualms about voicing his or her beliefs to others. A coworker, however, may frequently use off-color words and joke about the need to sleep late on weekends to recover from late nights in bars. While conflict between these two individuals is not certain, there is a reasonable likelihood that they will at least occasionally let the other know that they value different things. As detailed more fully in *The Family Business and . . . Change* box, relationship conflict can be especially relevant for a family-owned business.

At a somewhat different level, **legal conflict** may arise when there are differences in perceptions between organizations. For instance, if one firm sees a competitor as engaging in predatory pricing practices or a supplier as failing to live up to the terms of a contract, it may bring legal action against the other firm. Given that legal conflict has tightly prescribed procedures and processes in place for resolution, much of our discussion will focus on task, process, and relationship conflict.

Legal conflict may arise when there are differences in perceptions between organizations.

Causes of Conflict

Interpersonal Conflict   Conflict between two or more individuals is almost certain to occur in any organization, given the great variety in perceptions, goals, attitudes, and so forth among its members. William Gates, founder and CEO of Microsoft, and Kazuhiko Nishi, a former business associate from Japan, ended a long-term business relationship because of interpersonal conflict. Nishi accused Gates of becoming too political, while Gates charged that Nishi became too unpredictable and erratic in his behavior.[3]

A frequent source of interpersonal conflict in organizations is what many people call a personality clash—when two people distrust each other's motives, dislike one another, or for some other reason simply can't get along.[4] Conflict also may arise between people who have different beliefs or perceptions about some aspect of their work or their organization. For example, one manager may want the organization to require that all employees use Microsoft Office software to promote standardization. Another manager may believe a variety of software packages should be allowed in order to recognize individuality. Similarly, a male manager may disagree with his female colleague over whether the organization is guilty of discriminating against women in promotion decisions. Defense secretary Donald Rumsfeld frequently has conflicts with others because of his abrasive and confrontational style.[5]

Conflict also can result from excess competitiveness among individuals. Two people vying for the same job, for example, may resort to political behavior in an effort to gain an advantage. If either competitor sees the other's behavior as inappropriate, accusations are likely to result. Even after the "winner" of the job is determined, such conflict may continue to undermine interpersonal relationships, especially if the reasons given in selecting one candidate are ambiguous or open to alternative explanation. Robert Allen, former CEO of Delta Airlines, disagreed with other key executives over how best to reduce the carrier's costs. After he began looking for a replacement for one of his rivals without the approval of the firm's board of directors, the resultant conflict and controversy left him with no choice but to leave.[6]

Intergroup Conflict   Conflict between two or more organizational groups is also quite common. For example, the members of a firm's marketing group may disagree with the production group over product quality and delivery schedules. Two sales groups may disagree over how to meet sales goals, and two groups of managers may have different ideas about how best to allocate organizational resources.

At a J.C. Penney's department store, conflict arose between stockroom employees and sales associates. The sales associates claimed that the stockroom employees were slow in delivering merchandise to the sales floor so that it could be priced and shelved. The stockroom employees, in turn, claimed that the sales associates did not give them enough lead time to get the merchandise delivered or acknowledge that the stockroom employees had additional duties besides carrying merchandise to the sales floor.

Just like people, different departments often have different goals. Further, these goals may often be incompatible. A marketing goal of maximizing sales, achieved partially by offering many products in a wide variety of sizes, shapes, colors, and models, probably conflicts with a production goal of minimizing costs, achieved partially by long production runs of a few items. Reebok recently confronted this very situation. One group of managers wanted to introduce a new sportswear line as quickly as possible, while other managers wanted to expand more deliberately and cautiously. Because the two groups were not able to reconcile their differences effectively, conflict between the two factions led to quality problems and delivery delays that plagued the firm for months.

Competition for scarce resources can also lead to intergroup conflict. Most organizations—especially universities, hospitals, government agencies, and businesses in depressed industries—have limited resources. In one New England town, for example, the public works department and the library battled over funds from a federal construction grant. The Buick, Pontiac, and Chevrolet divisions of General Motors have frequently fought over the rights to manufacture various new products developed by the company.

Conflict Between Organization and Environment Conflict that arises between one organization and another is called interorganizational conflict. A moderate amount of interorganizational conflict resulting from business competition is, of course, expected, but sometimes conflict becomes more extreme. For example, the owners of Jordache Enterprises Inc. and Guess? Inc. battled in court for years over ownership of the Guess label, allegations of design theft, and several other issues.[7] Similarly, General Motors and Volkswagen went to court to resolve a bitter conflict that spanned more than four years. It all started when a key GM executive, Jose Ignacio Lopez de Arriortua, left for a position at Volkswagen. GM claimed that he took with him key secrets that could benefit its German competitor. After the messy departure, dozens of charges and countercharges were made by the two firms, and only a court settlement was able to put the conflict to an end.[8] The *Xerox and . . . Technology* box provides still other examples.

Conflict can also arise between an organization and other elements of its environment. For example, an organization may conflict with a consumer group over claims it makes about its products. McDonald's faced this problem a few years ago when it published nutritional information about its products that omitted details about fat content. A manufacturer might conflict with a governmental agency such as OSHA. For example, the firm's management may believe it is in compliance with OSHA regulations, while officials from the agency feel that the firm is not in compliance. Or a firm might conflict with a supplier over the quality of raw materials. The firm may think the supplier is providing inferior materials, while the supplier thinks the materials are adequate. Finally, individual managers may obviously have disagreements with groups of workers. For example, a manager may think her workers are doing poor-quality work and that they are unmotivated. The workers, on the other hand, may believe they are doing a good job and that the manager is doing a poor job of leading them.

Task Interdependence Task interdependence can also result in conflict across any of the levels noted previously. The greater the interdependence between departments, the greater the likelihood that conflict will occur. There are three major forms of interdependence: pooled, sequential, and reciprocal.[9]

Pooled interdependence represents the lowest level of interdependence and results in the least amount of conflict. Units with pooled interdependence operate with little interaction—the output of the units is pooled at the organizational level. The Gap clothing stores operate with pooled interdependence. Each store is considered a "department" by the parent corporation. Each has its own operating budget, staff, and so forth. The profits or losses from each store are "added together" at the organizational level. The stores are interdependent to the extent that the final success or failure of one store affects the others, but they do not generally interact on a day-to-day basis.

In **sequential interdependence**, the output of one unit becomes the input for another in a sequential fashion. This creates a moderate level of interdependence and a somewhat higher potential for conflict. At Nissan, for example, one plant assembles engines and then ships them to a final assembly site at another plant where the cars are completed. The plants are interdependent in that the final assembly plant must have the

Pooled interdependence represents the lowest level of interdependence, and hence results in the least amount of conflict.

In **sequential interdependence**, the output of one unit becomes the input for another in a sequential fashion; this creates a moderate level of interdependence and a somewhat higher potential for conflict.

Xerox and . . . TECHNOLOGY

Whose Idea Was This, Anyway?

Xerox is a company long known for innovative technology. Its first copier, for instance, was an instant success, and today many people use "xeroxing" as a synonym for "photocopying." Following its success in the copier business, Xerox diversified into computers and continued to spend substantial amounts on R&D.

In the firm's research laboratory in Palo Alto, California, Xerox built one of the world's first personal computers. The Alto, released in 1981, included many elements that are still used today, such as the mouse, icons, point-and-click, and windows. In spite of the innovations, Xerox was unable to duplicate its previous success and exited the PC industry in 1989.

However, ideas from the Alto were adopted by others, and that was the beginning of Xerox's conflicts and legal troubles with competitors. In December 1989, Xerox sued Apple, alleging copyright infringement. After months in court, the case was dismissed. Apple's lawyers successfully argued that while Apple borrowed ideas from Xerox, ideas are not protected by copyrights. The judge also noted that the case was out of date because technology had already changed so much.

Ironically, at that time, Apple was vigorously defending copyrights. Apple was suing Microsoft, IBM, and Hewlett-Packard over their use of a Macintosh-style user interface called "Windows," exactly the same charge Xerox was making about Apple. Like Xerox, Apple lost their lawsuits and the market.

Unfortunately for Xerox, the players change but the problem remains the same. Xerox has bogged down in legal disputes when it develops a concept that is then adopted by a more profitable rival. In the latest example, in 1997 Xerox sued Palm (now known as palmOne) over the use of a handwriting recognition program. Xerox's claims were denied in May 2004. As before, Palm made money from Xerox's ideas and the legal challenge came far too late.

According to the firm's website, "Xerox . . . explores the unknown, invents next-generation technology . . . and creates new business opportunities." Xerox has mastered exploration and invention; now it needs to focus on selling those new products.

This chapter's closing case, "Xerox's Unique Approach to Labor-Management Relations," tells about Xerox's success in labor negotiations.

> *"Xerox . . . explores the unknown, invents next-generation technology . . . and creates new business opportunities."*
> XEROX WEBSITE

References: "Innovation," "Online Fact Book," "The Story of Xerography," Xerox website, www.xerox.com on June 11, 2005 (quotation); Andrew Pollack, "Most of Xerox's Suit Against Apple Barred," *New York Times*, March 24, 1990, www.nytimes.com on June 11, 2005; Laura Rohde, "Xerox Loses Patent Claim Against PalmOne," *Computer Weekly*, June 21, 2005; www.computerweekly.com on June 11, 2005.

engines from engine assembly before it can perform its primary function of producing finished automobiles. But the level of interdependence is generally one-way—the engine plant is not necessarily dependent on the final assembly plant. In this example, though, if the engine assembly plant is constantly late with its deliveries, it will quickly encounter problems with managers at the final assembly plant.

Reciprocal interdependence exists when activities flow both ways between units. This form is clearly the most complex, and hence has the highest potential for conflict. Within a Marriott Hotel, for example, the reservations department, front-desk check-in, and housekeeping are all reciprocally interdependent. Reservations has to provide front-desk employees with information about how many guests to expect each day, and housekeeping needs to know which rooms require priority cleaning. If any of the three units does not do its job properly, the others will all be affected and conflict is almost inevitable.

Reciprocal interdependence exists when activities flow both ways between units; this form has the highest potential for conflict.

Reactions to Conflict

The most common reactions to conflict are avoidance, accommodation, competition, collaboration, and compromise.[10] Whenever conflict occurs between groups or organizations, it is really the people who are in conflict. In many cases, however, people are acting as representatives of the groups to which they belong. In effect, they work together, representing their group as they strive to do their part in helping the group achieve its goals. Thus, whether the conflict is between people acting as individuals or people acting as representatives of groups, the five types of interactions can be analyzed in terms of relationships among the goals of the people or the groups they represent.

Reactions to conflict can be differentiated along two dimensions: how important each party's goals are to that party and how compatible the goals are, as shown in Figure 15.2. The importance of reaching a goal may range from very high to very low. The degree of **goal compatibility** is the extent to which the goals can be achieved simultaneously. In other words, the goals are compatible if one party can meet its goals without preventing the other from meeting its goals. The goals are incompatible if one party's meeting its goals prevents the other party from meeting its goals. The goals of different groups may be very compatible, completely incompatible, or somewhere in between.

> The degree of **goal compatibility** is the extent to which the goals can be achieved simultaneously.

Avoidance

Avoidance occurs when an interaction is relatively unimportant to either party's goals, and the goals are incompatible, as in the bottom left corner of Figure 15.2. Because the parties to the conflict are not striving toward compatible goals, and the issues in question seem unimportant, the parties simply try to avoid interacting with one another. For example, one state agency may simply ignore another agency's requests for information. The requesting agency can then practice its own form of avoidance by not following up on the requests.

> **Avoidance** occurs when an interaction is relatively unimportant to either party's goals, and the goals are incompatible.

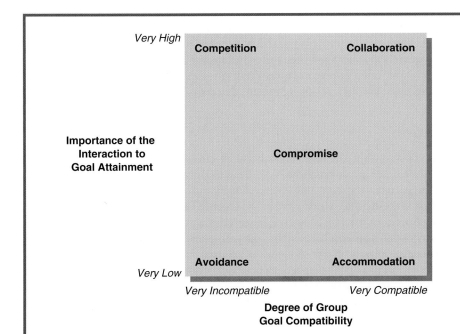

FIGURE 15.2

Five Types of Reactions to Conflict

The five types of reactions to conflict stem from the relative importance of interaction to goal attainment and the degree of goal compatibility.

Reference: Adapted from Kenneth Thomas, "Conflict and Conflict Management," in Marvin Dunnette (ed.), *Handbook of Industrial and Organizational Psychology* (Chicago: Rand McNally, 1976), pp. 889–935. Reprinted by permission.

Accommodation

Accommodation occurs when the goals are compatible, but the interactions are not considered important to overall goal attainment, as in the bottom right corner of Figure 15.2. Interactions of this type may involve discussions of how the parties can accomplish their interdependent tasks with the least expenditure of time and effort. This type of interaction tends to be very friendly. For example, during a college's course scheduling period, potential conflict may exist between the marketing and management departments. Both departments offer morning classes. Which department is allocated the 9:00 A.M. time slot and which one the 10:00 A.M. time slot is not that important to either group. Their overall goal is that the classes are scheduled so that students will be able to take courses.

Accommodation occurs when the goals are compatible, but the interactions are not considered important to overall goal attainment.

Competition

Competition occurs when the goals are incompatible, and the interactions are important to each party's meeting its goals, as in the top left corner of Figure 15.2. If all parties are striving for a goal, but only one can reach the goal, the parties will be in competition. As we noted earlier, if a competitive situation gets out of control, as when overt antagonism occurs, and there are no rules or procedures to follow, then competition can result in conflict. Thus, competition may lead to conflict. Sometimes conflict can also change to competition if the parties agree to rules to guide the interaction, and conflicting parties agree not to be hostile toward each other.

Competition occurs when the goals are incompatible, and the interactions are important to each party's meeting its goals.

In one freight warehouse and storage firm, the first, second, and third shifts each sought to win the weekly productivity prize by posting the highest productivity record. Workers on the winning shift received recognition in the company newspaper. Because the issue was important to each group, and the interests of the groups were incompatible, the result was competition.

The competition among the shifts encouraged each shift to produce more per week, which increased the company's output and eventually improved its overall welfare (and thus the welfare of each group). Both the company and the groups benefited from the competition because it fostered innovative and creative work methods, which further boosted productivity. After about three months, however, the competition got out of control. The competition among the groups led to poorer overall performance as the groups started to sabotage other shifts and inflate records. The competition became too important, open antagonism resulted, rules were ignored, and the competition changed to open conflict, resulting in actual decreases in work performance.[11]

Collaboration

Collaboration occurs when the interaction between groups is very important to goal attainment, and the goals are compatible, as in the top right corner of Figure 15.2. In the class scheduling situation mentioned earlier, conflict may arise over which courses to teach in the first semester and which ones in the second. Both departments would like to offer specific courses in the fall. However, by discussing the issue and refocusing their overall goals to match students' needs, the marketing and economics departments can collaborate on developing a proper sequence of courses. At first glance, this may seem to be simple interaction in which the parties participate jointly in activities to accomplish goals after agreeing on the goals and their importance. In many situations, however, it is no easy matter to agree on goals, their importance, and especially the means for achieving them. In a collaborative interaction, goals may differ but be compatible. Parties to a

Collaboration occurs when the interaction between groups is very important to goal attainment, and the goals are compatible.

conflict may initially have difficulty working out the ways in which all can achieve their goals. However, because the interactions are important to goal attainment, the parties are willing to continue to work together to achieve the goals. Collaborative relationships can lead to new and innovative ideas and solutions to differences among the parties.

Compromise

Compromise occurs when the interactions are moderately important to goal attainment, and the goals are neither completely compatible nor completely incompatible. In a compromise situation, parties interact with others striving to achieve goals, but they may not aggressively pursue goal attainment in either a competitive or collaborative manner because the interactions are not that important to goal attainment. On the other hand, the parties may choose to not avoid one another; however, they may also choose to not be particularly accommodating because the interactions are somewhat important. Often each party gives up something, but because the interactions are only moderately important, they do not regret what they have given up.

Compromise is frequently used to resolve conflict. Vivid examples of compromise often accompany labor disputes. Take these airline pilots, for example. They are shown here walking a picket line during a recent strike. When the strike was ultimately settled, the union achieved some of its demands, the airline achieved some of its demands, and compromises were used to settle some of the demands. In this case, for instance, the new salary structure for the pilots was higher than originally offered by the airline but lower than first demanded by the union.

> **Compromise** occurs when the interactions are moderately important to goal attainment, and the goals are neither completely compatible nor completely incompatible.

Contract negotiations between union and management are usually examples of compromise. Each side brings numerous issues of varying importance to the bargaining table. The two sides frequently give and take on the issues through rounds of offers and counteroffers. The complexity of the negotiations increases as the negotiations spread to multiple plants in different countries. Agreements between management and labor in a plant in the United States may be unacceptable to either or both parties in Canada. Weeks of negotiations ending in numerous compromises usually result in a contract agreement between the union and management.

In summary, when groups are in conflict, they may react in several different ways. If the goals of the parties are very compatible, the parties may engage in mutually supportive interactions—that is, collaboration or accommodation. If the goals are very incompatible, each may attempt to foster its own success at the expense of the other, engaging in competition or avoidance.

Managing Conflict

Managers must know when to stimulate conflict and when to resolve it if they are to avoid its potentially disruptive effects.[12] As we noted earlier, too little conflict and too much conflict are each dysfunctional in their own ways. Hence, if there is too little conflict, managers many need to stimulate a moderate degree of conflict. If conflict is excessive, however, it may need to be reduced. Figure 15.3 introduces some of the basic techniques for stimulating and resolving conflict.

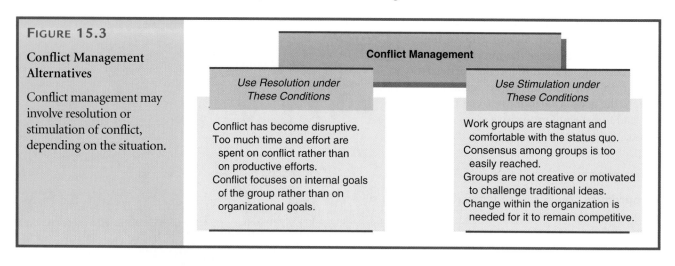

FIGURE 15.3

Conflict Management Alternatives

Conflict management may involve resolution or stimulation of conflict, depending on the situation.

Conflict Management

Use Resolution under These Conditions

Conflict has become disruptive. Too much time and effort are spent on conflict rather than on productive efforts.
Conflict focuses on internal goals of the group rather than on organizational goals.

Use Stimulation under These Conditions

Work groups are stagnant and comfortable with the status quo.
Consensus among groups is too easily reached.
Groups are not creative or motivated to challenge traditional ideas.
Change within the organization is needed for it to remain competitive.

Stimulating Conflict

Conflict stimulation is the creation and constructive use of conflict by a manager.

A complete absence of conflict may indicate that the organization is stagnant and that employees are content with the status quo. It may also suggest that work groups are not motivated to challenge traditional and well-accepted ideas. **Conflict stimulation** is the creation and constructive use of conflict by a manager. Its purpose is to bring about situations in which differences of opinion are exposed for examination by all.

For example, if competing organizations are making significant changes in products, markets, or technologies, it may be time for a manager to stimulate innovation and creativity by challenging the status quo. Conflict may give employees the motivation and opportunity to reveal differences of opinion that they previously kept to themselves. When all parties to the conflict are interested enough in an issue to challenge other groups, they often expose their hidden doubts or opinions. These, in turn, allow the parties to get to the heart of the matter and often to develop unique solutions to the problem. Indeed, the interactions may lead the groups to recognize that a problem in fact does exist. Conflict, then, can be a catalyst for creativity and change in an organization.

Several methods can be used to stimulate conflict under controlled conditions. These include altering the physical location of groups to stimulate more interactions, forcing more resource sharing, and implementing other changes in relationships among groups. In addition, training programs can be used to increase employee awareness of potential problems in group decision making and group interactions. Adopting the role of "devil's advocate" in discussion sessions is another way to stimulate conflict among groups. In this role, a manager challenges the prevailing consensus to ensure that all alternatives have been critically appraised and analyzed. Although this role is often unpopular, employing it is a good way to stimulate constructive conflict.

Conflict Resolution

Conflict resolution is a managed effort to reduce or eliminate harmful conflict.

When a potentially harmful conflict situation exists, however, a manager needs to engage in **conflict resolution**. Conflict needs to be resolved when it causes major disruptions in the organization and absorbs time and effort that could be used more productively. Conflict should also be resolved when its focus is on the group's internal goals rather than on organizational goals.

When attempting to resolve conflict, managers should first attempt to determine the source of the conflict. If the source of destructive conflict is a particular person or two, it might be appropriate to alter the membership of one or both groups. If the conflict is due to differences in goals, perceptions of the difficulty of goal attainment, or the importance of the goals to the conflicting parties, then the manager can attempt to move the conflicting parties into one of the five types of reactions to conflict, depending on the nature of the conflicting parties.

To foster collaboration, it might be appropriate to try to help people see that their goals are really not as different as they seem to be. The manager can help groups view their goals as part of a **superordinate goal** to which the goals of both conflicting parties can contribute. A superordinate goal is a goal of the overall organization and is more important to the well-being of the organization and its members than the more specific goals of the conflicting parties. If the goals are not really that important and are very incompatible, the manager may need to develop ways to help the conflicting parties avoid each other. Similarly, accommodation, competition, or compromise might be appropriate for the conflicting parties.

> A **superordinate goal** is a goal of the overall organization and is more important to the well-being of the organization and its members than the more specific goals of the conflicting parties.

Using Structure to Manage Conflict

Beyond the methods noted above, managers can also rely heavily on elements of organization structure to manage conflict. Among the more common methods are the hierarchy, rules and procedures, liaison roles, and task forces.

The Managerial Hierarchy Organizations that use the hierarchy to manage conflict place one manager in charge of people, groups, or departments in conflict. In Wal-Mart distribution centers, major activities include receiving and unloading bulk shipments from railroad cars and loading other shipments onto trucks for distribution to retail outlets. The two groups (receiving and shipping) are interdependent and may experience conflict in that they share the loading docks and some equipment. To ensure coordination and minimize conflict, one manager is in charge of the whole operation.

Rules and Procedures Routine conflict management can be handled via rules and standard procedures. In the Wal-Mart distribution center, an outgoing truck shipment has priority over an incoming rail shipment. Thus when trucks are to be loaded, the shipping unit is given access to all of the center's auxiliary forklifts. This priority is specifically stated in a rule. But, as useful as rules and procedures often are in routine situations, they are not particularly effective when coordination problems and conflict are complex or unusual.

Liaison Roles We introduced the liaison role of management in Chapter 1. As a device for managing conflict, a manager in a liaison role coordinates activities acting as a common point of contact. This individual may not have any formal authority over the groups but instead simply facilitates the flow of information between parties. Two engineering groups working on component systems for a large project might interact through a liaison. The liaison maintains familiarity with each group as well as with the overall project. She can answer questions and otherwise serve to integrate the activities of all the groups. Since the groups do not directly interact with one another, there is less chance of conflict.

Task Forces A task force may be created when the need for conflict management is acute. When interdependence is complex and several groups and/or individuals are involved, a single liaison person may not be sufficient. Instead, a task force might be assembled by drawing one representative from each group. The conflict management function is thus spread across several individuals, each of whom has special information about one of the groups involved. When the project is completed, task force members return to their original positions. For example, a college overhauling its degree requirements might establish a task force made up of representatives from each department affected by the change. Each person retains her or his regular departmental affiliation and duties but also serves on the special task force. After the new requirements are agreed on, the task force is dissolved.

Using Interpersonal Techniques to Manage Conflict

There are also several techniques that focus on interpersonal processes that can be used to manage conflict. These often fall under the heading of organization development, discussed in Chapter 19. Hence, we describe only a few examples here.

Team-building activities are intended to enhance the effectiveness and satisfaction of individuals who work in groups or teams and to promote overall group effectiveness; consequently there should be less conflict among members of the team.

Team Building
Team-building activities are intended to enhance the effectiveness and satisfaction of individuals who work in groups or teams and to promote overall group effectiveness; consequently there should be less conflict among members of the team. Given the widespread use of teams today, these activities have taken on increased importance. Caterpillar used team building as one method for changing the working relationships between workers and supervisors from confrontational to cooperative. An interesting new approach to team building involves having executive teams participate in group-cooking classes to teach them the importance of interdependence and coordination.[13]

In **survey feedback**, each employee responds to a questionnaire intended to measure perceptions and attitudes (for example, satisfaction and supervisory style).

Survey Feedback
In **survey feedback**, each employee responds to a questionnaire intended to measure perceptions and attitudes (for example, satisfaction and supervisory style). Everyone involved, including the supervisor, receives the results of the survey. The aim of this approach is usually to change the behavior of supervisors by showing them how their subordinates viewed them. After the feedback has been provided, workshops may be conducted to evaluate results and suggest constructive changes.

Team building is a common method used by organizations to help overcome conflict and promote collaboration among employees. Outward Bound was a pioneer in developing unique and challenging outdoor experiences for teams. The idea is that by spending time together in demanding situations and having to rely on each other to accomplish their goals, team members will develop improved working relationships. This group of corporate executives is in the midst of an eight-day kayaking trip through the Florida Everglades.

Third-Party Peacemaking   A somewhat more extreme form of interpersonal conflict management is **third-party peacemaking**, which is most often used when substantial conflict exists within the organization. Third-party peacemaking can be appropriate on the individual, group, or organization level. A third party, usually a trained external facilitator, uses a variety of mediation or negotiation techniques to resolve problems or conflicts between individuals or groups.

Third-party peacemaking, primarily used to address extreme conflict, involves bringing in an outsider to facilitate conflict resolution.

Negotiated Conflict Management

Finally, conflict solutions are sometimes negotiated in advance. For instance, a labor agreement often spells out in detail how union members must report a grievance, how management must respond, and how the dispute will be resolved. Conflict is thus avoided by pre-establishing exactly how it will be addressed. The following discussion of negotiation also has other implications for conflict management.

Negotiation in Organizations

Negotiation is the process in which two or more parties (people or groups) reach agreement on an issue even though they have different preferences regarding that issue. In its simplest form the parties involved may be two individuals who are trying to decide who will pay for lunch. A little more complexity is involved when two people, such as an employee and manager, sit down to decide on personal performance goals for the next year against which the employee's performance will be measured. Even more complex are the negotiations that take place between labor unions and the management of a company or between two companies as they negotiate the terms of a joint venture. The key issues in such negotiations are that at least two parties are involved, their preferences are different, and they need to reach agreement.

Negotiation is the process in which two or more parties (people or groups) reach agreement on an issue even though they have different preferences regarding that issue.

Approaches to Negotiation

Interest in negotiation has grown steadily in recent years.[14] Four primary approaches to negotiation have dominated this study: individual differences, situational characteristics, game theory, and cognitive approaches. Each of these is briefly described in the following sections.

Individual Differences   Early psychological approaches concentrated on the personality traits of the negotiators.[15] Traits investigated have included demographic characteristics and personality variables. Demographic characteristics have included age, gender, and race, among others. Personality variables have included risk taking, locus of control, tolerance for ambiguity, self-esteem, authoritarianism, and Machiavellianism. The assumption of this type of research was that the key to successful negotiation was selecting the right person to do the negotiating, one who had the appropriate demographic characteristics or personality. This assumption seemed to make sense because negotiation is such a personal and interactive process. However, the research rarely showed the positive results expected because situational variables negated the effects of the individual differences.[16]

Situational Characteristics   Situational characteristics are the context within which negotiation takes place. They include such things as the types of communication between negotiators, the potential outcomes of the negotiation, the relative power of the parties (both positional and personal), the time frame available for negotiation, the number of people representing each side, and the presence of other parties. Some of this research has contributed to our understanding of the negotiation process. However, the shortcomings of the situational approach are similar to those of the individual characteristics approach. Many situational characteristics are external to the negotiators and beyond their control. Often the negotiators cannot change their relative power positions or the setting within which the negotiation occurs. So, although we have learned a lot from research on the situational issues, we still need to learn much more about the process.

> Game theory was developed by economists using mathematical models to predict the outcome of negotiation situations.

Game Theory

Game theory was developed by economists using mathematical models to predict the outcome of negotiation situations (as illustrated in the Academy Award®–winning movie *A Beautiful Mind*). It requires that every alternative and outcome be analyzed with probabilities and numerical outcomes reflecting the preferences for each outcome. In addition, the order in which different parties can make choices and every possible move are predicted, along with associated preferences for outcomes. The outcomes of this approach are exactly what negotiators want: a predictive model of how negotiation should be conducted. One major drawback is that it requires the ability to describe all possible options and outcomes for every possible move in every situation before the negotiation starts. This is often very tedious, if possible at all. Another problem is that this theory assumes that negotiators are rational at all times. Other research in negotiation has shown that negotiators often do not act rationally. Therefore, this approach, although elegant in its prescriptions, is usually unworkable in a real negotiation situation.

Cognitive Approaches

The fourth approach is the cognitive approach, which recognizes that negotiators often depart from perfect rationality during negotiation; it tries to predict how and when negotiators will make these departures. Howard Raiffa's decision analytic approach focuses on providing advice to negotiators actively involved in negotiation.[17] Bazerman and Neale have added to Raiffa's work by specifying eight ways in which negotiators systematically deviate from rationality.[18] The types of deviations they describe include escalation of commitment to a previously selected course of action, overreliance on readily available information, assuming that the negotiations can produce fixed-sum outcomes, and anchoring negotiation in irrelevant information. These cognitive approaches have advanced the study of negotiation a long way beyond the early individual and situational approaches. Negotiators can use them to attempt to predict in advance how the negotiation might take place.

"A good negotiator can stand back and gain perspective."

www.cartoonstock.com

Negotiators may get so personally involved in a bargaining process that their objectivity suffers. Many experts caution against this mistake, and some offer advice on how to remain objective. Of course, it is also possible for a person to become so far removed from the negotiation process that they loose touch with what is actually happening.

Win-Win Negotiation

In addition to the approaches to negotiation previously described, a group of approaches proposed by consultants and advisors is meant to give negotiators a specific model to use in carrying out difficult negotiations. One of the best of these is the "Win-Win Negotiator" developed by Ross Reck and his associates.[19] The Win-Win approach does not treat negotiation as a game in which there are winners and losers. Instead, it approaches negotiation as an opportunity for each side to be a winner, for each side to get what it wants out of the agreement. The focus is on both parties reaching an agreement that both are committed to fulfilling, with the possibility for more agreements in the future. In other words, both parties want to have their needs satisfied. In addition, this approach does not advocate either a "tough guy" or a "nice guy" approach to negotiation, both of which are popular in the literature. It assumes that both parties work together to find ways to satisfy both parties at the same time.

The Win-Win approach is a four-step approach illustrated in the **PRAM model** shown in Figure 15.4. The PRAM four-step approach proposes that proper planning, building relationships, getting agreements, and maintaining the relationships are the key steps to successful negotiation.

Planning requires that each negotiator set his or her own goals, anticipate the goals of the other, determine areas of probable agreement, and develop strategies for reconciling areas of probable disagreement.

Developing Win-Win *relationships* requires that negotiators plan activities that enable positive personal relationships to develop, cultivate a sense of mutual trust, and allow relationships to develop fully before discussing business in earnest. The development of trust between the parties is probably the single most important key to success in negotiation.

Forming Win-Win *agreements* requires that each party confirm the other party's goals, verify areas of agreement, propose and consider positive solutions to reconcile areas of disagreement, and jointly resolve any remaining differences. The key in reaching agreement is to realize that both parties share many of the goals. The number of areas of disagreement is usually small.

Finally, Win-Win *maintenance* entails providing meaningful feedback based on performance, each of the parties holding up an end of the agreement, keeping in contact, and reaffirming trust between the parties. The assumption is that both parties want to keep the relationship going so that in the future mutually beneficial transactions can occur. Both parties must uphold their ends of the agreement and do what they said they would do. Finally, keeping in touch is as easy as making a telephone call or meeting for lunch.

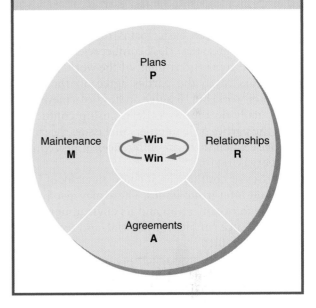

FIGURE 15.4

The PRAM Model of Negotiation

The PRAM model shows the four steps in setting up negotiation so that both parties win.

Reference: Reprinted from Brian G. Long, Ph.D., and Ross R. Reck, Ph.D., *The Win-Win Negotiator: How to Negotiate Favorable Agreements That Last.* Copyright © 1985, 1987 by Brian G. Long and Ross R. Reck. Reprinted with permission of Ross R. Reck, Ph.D.

The **PRAM model** is a four-step approach to negotiation that proposes that proper planning, building relationships, getting agreements, and maintaining the relationships are the key steps to successful negotiation.

Chapter Review

Synopsis

Conflict is a process resulting in the perceptions of two parties that they are working in opposition to each other in ways that result in feelings of discomfort and/or animosity. Although conflict often is considered harmful, and thus something to avoid, it can also have some benefits.

There are three basic forms of conflict that exist within an organization. Task conflict refers to conflict regarding the goals and content of the work. Process conflict occurs when the parties agree on the goals and content of work, but disagree on how to achieve the goals and actually do the work. Relationship conflict occurs when the parties have interpersonal issues. Legal conflict may arise when there are differences in perceptions between organizations.

Causes of conflict can include an array of interpersonal and intergroup issues. There may also be conflict between an organization and its environment. Task interdependence (pooled, sequential, and reciprocal) can also cause conflict.

The most common reactions to conflict are avoidance, accommodation, competition, collaboration, and compromise. Reactions to conflict can be differentiated along two dimensions: how important each party's goals are to that party and how compatible the goals are.

Managers must know when to stimulate conflict and when to resolve it if they are to avoid its potentially disruptive effects. There are a variety of methods that can be used to either stimulate or resolve conflict. Organization structure and various interpersonal methods may also be useful in managing conflict. Conflict resolution may also be negotiated in advance.

Negotiation is the process in which two or more parties (people or groups) reach agreement on an issue even though they have different preferences regarding that issue. Four primary approaches to negotiation focus on individual differences, situational characteristics, game theory, and cognitive approaches. The win-win approach does not treat negotiation as a game in which there are winners and losers. Instead, it approaches negotiation as an opportunity for both sides to be winners, to get what they want out of the agreement.

Discussion Questions

1. Recall instances in which you have experienced each of the three primary forms of conflict.

2. In general, is one form of conflict likely to be more costly to an organization than the others? Why or why not?

3. Are certain forms of conflict more likely than others to be associated with each level of interdependence? In what way?

4. Have you ever been a party to conflict that had positive benefits? What were the details?

5. How comfortable are you personally in dealing with conflict?

6. What is the primary risk of trying to stimulate moderate levels of conflict in a situation characterized by lethargy?

7. Relate the various methods of resolving conflict to the primary forms of conflict. That is, what conflict resolution methods are most likely to be useful in dealing with task conflict?

8. Describe various ways in which conflict and negotiations may be related.

9. Recall an instance in which you negotiated something and describe it in terms of the discussion of negotiation in this chapter.

10. Why don't people engaged in all negotiation situations try to adopt a win-win mentality?

Learning Negotiation Skills

Purpose: This exercise will help you learn more about how to prepare for and participate in a negotiation.

Format: You will participate in this exercise with one of your classmates. The two of you will attempt to negotiate an understanding regarding a hypothetical assignment.

Procedure: Assume that your instructor has assigned the two of you an out-of-class project. The hypothetical project consists of the following activities:

1. You are to interview a total of five managers in your local community. Each interview should last about an hour. The purpose of the interviews is to learn more about the nature and substance of managerial work. You will ask each manager a set of predetermined questions about their jobs.

2. The results of the interviews are to be synthesized into a single discussion of what managers do. Detailed analyses of the responses to each question are to be carefully studied and integrated into a single overall description.

3. The description is to be written up in the form of a paper of approximately ten pages. In addition to its content, issues such as language, grammar, spelling, and format will all be considered when the paper is graded.

4. Finally, the content of the paper must also be organized for an in-class presentation. The presentation needs to be of professional quality, make use of PowerPoint slides and other visual aids, and be formally presented to a group of visiting executives.

5. Your instructor is indifferent as to how the assignment is completed. That is, you and your partner can divide the work up in any way that you see fit. However, you will each receive the same overall grade on the project regardless of what you each do.

Now, you and your partner should negotiate what you will each do. Be as specific as possible when deciding how to divide up the work involved in completing the project.

Follow-up Questions

1. What factors did you consider as you reached agreement on how to divide up the work?

2. How comfortable were you with the final division of labor?

3. If this were a real assignment, what concerns would you have about having a successful outcome? What steps, if any, might you use to offset those concerns?

Comfort with Conflict

The questionnaire that follows is intended to help you better understand your personal comfort level with conflict. Respond to each statement truthfully by assigning these numbers to each statement based on their corresponding answers:

Agree = 3
Unsure = 2
Disagree = 1

1. I have no trouble taking up for myself when necessary.

2. I think a little tension in a group can be a great source of stimulation and excitement.

3. When I disagree with someone else, I make sure they know where I stand.

4. I usually have strong opinions about things and make sure those opinions are known to others.

5. When someone disagrees with me, I usually try to convince them that I am right and they are wrong.

6. I stand my ground when someone tries to intimidate me.

7. I enjoy debates over controversial subjects.

8. When it becomes necessary to argue with someone, I tend to be resolute and don't let my emotions get in the way.

9. When pushed, I push back.

10. I find it refreshing when someone disagrees with me on an issue and wants to discuss it.

Interpretation: Add up your points. A score of 10–16 indicates that you uncomfortable with conflict and try to avoid it; a score of 17–23 indicates that you have a moderate degree of comfort with conflict; a score of 24–30 suggests that you are quite comfortable with conflict.

Building Managerial Skills

Exercise Overview: A manager's interpersonal skills refer to her or his ability to understand how to motivate individuals and groups. Clearly, then, interpersonal skills play a major role in determining how well a manager can interact with others in a group setting. This exercise will allow you to practice your interpersonal skills in relation to just such a setting.

Exercise Background: You have just been transferred to a new position supervising a group of five employees. The business you work for is fairly small and has few rules and regulations. Unfortunately, the lack of rules and regulations is creating a problem that you must now address.

Specifically, two of the group members are nonsmokers. They are becoming increasingly more vocal about the fact that two other members of the group smoke at work. These two workers feel that the secondary smoke in the workplace is endangering their health and want to establish a no-smoking policy like those of many large businesses today.

The two smokers, however, argue that since the firm did not have such a policy when they started working there, it would be unfair to impose such a policy now. One of them, in particular, says that he turned down an attractive job with another company because he wanted to work in a place where he could smoke.

The fifth worker is also a nonsmoker but says that she doesn't care if others smoke. Her husband smokes at home anyway, she says, so she is used to being around smokers. You suspect that if the two vocal nonsmokers are not appeased, they may leave. At the same time, you also think that the two smokers will leave if you mandate a no-smoking policy. All five workers do good work, and you do not want any of them to leave.

Exercise Task: With this information as context, do the following:

1. Explain the nature of the conflict that exists in this work group.

2. Develop a course of action for dealing with the situation.

Organizational Behavior Case for Discussion

Xerox's Unique Approach to Labor-Management Relations

As we saw earlier in the *Xerox and . . . Technology* box, Xerox has had its share of conflict with other businesses. But one area where the firm has clearly excelled is in its relationship with its employees. "Xerox represents probably the most successful example of labor-management cooperation and labor participation in management in the United States," says Thomas A. Kochan, an MIT professor. Kochan is describing a relationship between labor and management with a twenty-five-year history of cooperation and mutual goal achievement, an unprecedented achievement for an American firm. In addition, the labor-management relationship is so strong that U.S. workers have repeatedly been successful in fending off outsourcing. How does this kind of success—for both employees and employer—happen?

In 1980, Xerox added an employee involvement program to its union contract, calling for worker participation in quality, safety, and other decisions. At first, employees simply gave input; they had no authority to change company policy or union work rules. However, in 1982, the company was losing money and outsourcing was suggested as a way to reduce expenses. Employee involvement committees developed ideas that would allow the company to save more than the outsourcing promised, but the ideas required changes to Xerox and union procedures. The company and union agreed to the changes. More importantly, they both agreed to allow employees the same opportunity for any future outsourcing decisions. The partnership was born.

Over the next fifteen years, Xerox expanded on the employee involvement program, implementing an extensive teams-based organization. As each new labor contract was negotiated, cooperation grew between labor and management. The CEO often personally sat in on negotiations, to symbolically demonstrate the firm's commitment to a fair contract. Outsourcing and moving operations offshore were considered by management more than once, but each time, employees were able to justify keeping manufacturing at the Rochester, New York, headquarters facility. When funds for salary increases were unavailable, the union agreed to accept profit sharing instead.

Today, Xerox is the only unionized office equipment maker in the world. UNITE, a labor union formed by the merger of several smaller unions, represents thousands of production and distribution workers at Xerox, mostly at the firm's Rochester, New York, headquarters facility. John Richman, Xerox's manager of industrial relations, describes the company's unique labor situation. "Management was agreeing to bring in the union as a full partner in terms of its business condition," Richman states. "In a very broad sense, that says if the union is

> **❝At the floor level, the company-union relationship will always be somewhat contentious. That's just the nature of things.❞**
> JOHN RICHMAN, MANAGER OF INDUSTRIAL RELATIONS, XEROX

our partner, we need to share with the union all the concerns and problems associated with running this business."

Richman notes that input from employees and unions has been instrumental in keeping jobs within the United States. "We brought union leadership into some of the high-level discussions on new product development and new product sourcing, which is all-important in terms of where a product is going to be made . . . and if it's going to be made with union labor."

Richman is careful to note that the management-labor relationship at Xerox is far from perfect. He believes that the company benefits because both groups hold similar goals and both groups acknowledge their mutual dependence. "At the floor level, the company-union relationship will always be somewhat contentious. That's just the nature of things," Richman explains. "However, as you move up in the hierarchy of the union and the company, you quickly find that we both recognize that our long-term objectives run parallel. Our security is their security. The only true job security is a healthy business."

Xerox seems to be emerging from its recent performance slump. CEO Anne Mulcahy, who assumed control three years ago at Xerox's lowest point, has engineered a surprising turnaround. Although Mulcahy rigorously cut costs, she maintained R&D spending, leading to several new products that will be introduced throughout 2005. Based on new product estimates, the CEO expects sales to increase for the first time since 1999. Xerox met earnings expectations for the last ten quarters, raising stock price. Updated work rules, employee commitment to efficiency and quality, and other changes proposed by unionized workers have been instrumental in bringing about Xerox's success.

The company remains committed to working cooperatively with the unions. However, Xerox is under tremendous competitive and cost pressure, so that decision will need to be continually re-examined as new opportunities and challenges arise. Xerox leaders say they will give union workers the chance to be competitive globally. Now it's up to the unions to show that they can deliver. For more on Xerox see the boxed insert in this chapter titled *Xerox and . . . Technology.*

Case Questions

1. Which reaction to conflict is demonstrated by Xerox and union leaders in this case?

2. What are the situational characteristics surrounding Xerox's labor-management negotiations? In your opinion, do each of these characteristics make the negotiations easier or more difficult? Tell why.

3. Have Xerox and union leaders adopted a win-win approach to negotiation? If so, explain what each side stands to gain from the negotiation. If not, explain the current approach and tell whether a win-win approach would be more beneficial than the current one.

References: "Online Fact Book," Xerox website, www.xerox.com on June 11, 2005; "Management and Unions Team Up at Xerox," video case (quotation); "New Xerox Employees Joint UNITE," *Northwest Labor Press*, May 5, 2000, www.nwlaborpress.org on June 11, 2005; "Our History," UNITE website, www.unitehere.org on June 11, 2005; "The Best Managers of the Year: Thomas A. Kochan, 'Futurework: Rebuilding the Social Contract at Work,' U.S. Department of Labor website, May 1, 1999, www.dol.gov on June 11, 2005; Anne Mulcahy, "Xerox" *Business Week*, January 10, 2005, p. 62; David Tyler, "Xerox Workers Ratify Union Contract," *Rochester Democrat and Chronicle*, March 23, 2005, www.democratandchronicle.com on June 11, 2005.

TEST PREPPER

You have read the chapter and studied the key terms. Think you're ready to ace the exam? Take this sample test to gauge your comprehension of chapter material and check your answers at the back of the book. Want more test questions? Take the ACE quizzes found on the student website: http://college.hmco.com/business/students/ (select Griffin/Moorhead, Organizational Behavior, 8e from the Management menu).

T   F   1. Conflict usually refers to a specific event.

T   F   2. Process conflict occurs when the parties disagree on how to achieve the goals and actually do the work.

T   F   3. Competition for scarce resources is unlikely to lead to intergroup conflict.

T   F   4. If interaction is unimportant to two parties, and their goals are incompatible, the two parties are likely to avoid interacting with each other.

T   F   5. The identification of a superordinate goal may help two parties resolve their conflict.

T   F   6. In a "win-win" negotiation, both parties are careful to be "nice guys."

T   F   7. One key in reaching agreement is to realize that both parties may share many of the same goals.

8. Which of the following is not a potential benefit of conflict?
   a. Stimulates new ideas
   b. Facilitates downsizing
   c. Energizes behavior
   d. Conducive to higher-quality decisions
   e. Promotes healthy competition

9. Conflict regarding the goals and content of the work is called
   a. task conflict.
   b. process conflict.
   c. relationship conflict.
   d. labor conflict.
   e. legal conflict.

10. Which form of interdependence results in the greatest potential for conflict?
   a. Relationship interdependence
   b. Process interdependence
   c. Reciprocal interdependence
   d. Sequential interdependence
   e. Pooled interdependence

11. Greg and Gina have incompatible goals, but in order for them each to meet their individual goals, they have to interact. Which of the following is the likely reaction to this situation?

   a. Avoidance
   b. Accommodation
   c. Competition
   d. Compromise
   e. Collaboration

12. A manager who wants to stimulate conflict may use any of the following, except
   a. place the parties in closer physical proximity.
   b. reduce the need for the parties to interact.
   c. force more resource sharing.
   d. have one party adopt the role of "devil's advocate."
   e. train the parties in group decision making.

13. The purpose of survey feedback usually is to
   a. change the behavior of supervisors by showing them how their subordinates view them.
   b. stimulate conflict between work groups.
   c. eliminate the possibility of competition by showing both parties what goals they have in common.
   d. reach "win-win" agreements in labor-management negotiations.
   e. provide opportunities for employees to learn more about themselves and their personal conflict resolution styles.

14. Which approach to negotiation uses mathematical models to predict the outcomes of negotiation situations?
   a. Individual differences
   b. Situational characteristics
   c. Game theory
   d. Cognitive
   e. Operational

15. Which of the following is not part of the PRAM model of negotiation?
   a. Proper planning
   b. Building relationships
   c. Getting agreements
   d. Holding to your position
   e. Maintaining the relationships

The Success of Groups at Starbucks

The interpersonal interactions of individuals in groups contribute greatly to the success of Starbucks. Baristas and other workers at each Starbucks location make up a group, a collection of individuals who interact with and influence each other. The Starbucks group is a command group, because the individuals are brought together by their official positions and the group includes a store manager to oversee the work of the others.

Each store's group of workers can also be a team, because they work toward a common goal. Starbucks's mission statement serves as the ultimate goal for employees and the statement is prominently displayed at every location. Baristas often hear about the company's commitment to the mission statement's values, such as caring for the environment, fostering innovation, satisfying customers, treating others with dignity and respect, making a profit, and embracing diversity. Starbucks's executives communicate details about company performance and goals with employees, to help employees contribute to the firm. Employees share short-range goals for sales, quality, efficiency, and so on. Starbucks pays bonuses based on company-wide performance, further strengthening the team concept.

However, Starbucks teams do not operate autonomously, so they are not fully mature. The store managers have discretion in hiring, rewarding, and scheduling. Workers may choose tasks and manage their own work to some extent, but store managers oversee the store's operations and direct the baristas, just as the regional and corporate officers oversee and direct the work of store managers.

Starbucks teams are fairly well developed, as members have worked together for some time. Of course, with an annual turnover of 80 percent, team membership changes frequently and there is a constant need to teach new workers about the group's norms. Starbucks provides twenty-four hours of formal training that introduces each new hire to the company's values and culture. The first training also includes an introduction to coffee. Baristas learn about different coffees and methods of coffee brewing. Later training focuses on communication, leadership, and management skills. Another way that Starbucks employees learn about group norms is through direct observation and interaction with peers. Starbucks has a "promote from within" policy, so the store managers know the company's culture and can serve as role models.

Training also helps the company to enforce group norms. At Starbucks, norms include everything from how to dress to how to manage difficult customers. The norms at Starbucks promote friendliness, efficiency, and consistency, which aid the company in accomplishing its goals. However, some feel that the strong norms at Starbucks result in too much consistency and stifle creativity and individual expression. In Canada, two female baristas of Indian ancestry were fired because they wore nose studs. Facial jewelry is prohibited by Starbucks's dress code, but the women argued that the result is unfair bias. "Starbucks' dress code accepts ear piercing . . . [but] rejects other forms of body piercing," claims a leaflet circulated in support of a lawsuit filed by the women. "In prohibiting nose studs, it degrades an important part of South Asian tradition . . . This is cultural racism, an unjustified act of discrimination."

Group performance is improved by Starbucks's diversity, where over 60 percent of the workforce is made up of minorities and women. "Embracing diversity is not only the right thing to do socially or ethically, it's good for business," according to former CEO Orin Smith. "As the world becomes more and more complex, having a diverse work team helps us be more adaptive as a company. This is especially critical because we are expanding internationally. Diversity helps us make better decisions." Diversity improves decision quality by increasing the number of different values and viewpoints brought to bear in making a decision. For instance, Starbucks employees make thousands of suggestions each year, based on their unique backgrounds. Each suggestion is investigated and hundreds are adopted, leading to increased innovation and efficiency.

In addition, workforce diversity makes it easier to attract and serve diverse customers. And seeking out diverse applicants increases the applicant pool, making it easier to find personnel when the labor supply is tight. The U.S. government predicts that, by 2008, 70 percent of those entering the workforce will be women and minorities. Thus, Starbucks must recruit from a diverse population in order to find enough workers. To recruit more diverse applicants, Starbucks visits colleges with high minority enrollment, builds relationships with advocacy organizations, and places advertisements in publications with minority readers.

Starbucks explains its stance on diversity with the phrase, "Honoring our origins, enriched by our blends." The word "origins" is equated to a single-origin coffee, "with its own unique flavor, aroma, and growing conditions." Starbucks emphasizes the importance of the individual worker, who has unique experiences, values, and skills. The word "blends" is compared to blended coffees, which "are woven together, forming a tapestry of taste and texture." This phrase emphasizes the combination of several different individuals to create a group that can do more than each of its individual parts.

Group cohesiveness is an important performance factor at Starbucks. The company works to increase cohesiveness by careful recruiting procedures that identify individuals with outgoing, energetic, and pleasant personalities. Also, store managers are trained in team building, where they learn to create a supportive and upbeat atmosphere. And Starbucks's policy of internal promotions increases cohesiveness, because store employees see managers as being similar to themselves.

Effective interpersonal processes aid the organization in leadership, decision making, and conflict management. Leadership has been an important element of Starbucks's success since 1985, when Howard Schultz bought the small chain. Schultz had two visions, inspired by an experience with Italian coffee houses, which he used to transform the lackluster company into the retailing giant it is today. First, Schultz saw that Starbucks had the potential for tremendous growth. Second, he realized the appeal of socializing, which is important to the success of European coffee houses. "Great companies must have the courage to examine strategic opportunities that are transformational—as long as they are not inconsistent with the guiding principles and values of the core business," Schultz says.

Starbucks uses a rational decision-making model for many decisions, such as product pricing and store location. However, behavioral factors play a large part in the most important decisions, including the initial concept of the firm. Schultz's decision to purchase Starbucks and change its competitive strategy was based on his intuition. His management training and experiences helped him to quickly realize the company's potential. Schultz also has a high propensity for risk, as shown by his willingness to give up his executive job and invest his own money in an uncertain undertaking. In addition, he drastically changed the focus and strategy of Starbucks, to move into a more competitive industry. Schultz says, "Seek to renew yourself even when you are hitting home runs." With this statement, the Starbucks founder shows that he will not be satisfied with excellent performance. He believes that even excellent performance can be improved, if one is willing to change and take risks.

Schultz has also demonstrated very effective transactional leadership in the years since he acquired Starbucks. He has managed a great deal of growth, international expansion, the transition to a publicly traded firm, and more. Schultz has demonstrated his transactional management abilities by his successful efforts at product development, brand management, and operational efficiencies.

Founder Schultz and other top managers are clearly excellent leaders, as demonstrated by Starbucks's long-term performance. Yet leadership at Starbucks occurs at many levels, not just at the top of the giant firm. Schultz claims as one of his guiding principles, "Don't be threatened by people smarter than you." Therefore, there is an emphasis at the company on developing the team leadership skills of every leader, down to the level of store managers. Starbucks offered a leadership training program called "Servant Leaders Workshop" to over 6,000 employees in 2004. The program emphasized "trust, collaboration, people development and ethics."

Servant leadership is an emerging view of leadership, in which the leader sees him- or herself as helping followers, rather than as guiding or directing them. Servant leadership is similar to the idea of leaders as coaches, but takes the concept a step further. Leader-coaches help employees develop the skills they need to function without a lot of oversight and direction from above. Leader-servants lead out of a genuine desire to be of service to employees and the organization, helping them to develop and be more effective. Richard Smith of Creative Leaps International developed the program used at Starbucks. Smith says that his program is designed to help leaders answer the question, "Do those served grow as persons?" Smith explains that servant leadership means that the worker, as a result of what the leader does, should grow and become a better person. Smith's course emphasizes ways that managers, through increased trust and collaboration, give to workers.

Starbucks works hard to create positive personal interactions among its employees, but in a company of this size, conflicts are inevitable. Workers need predictable schedules; managers need flexibility. Workers demand freedom to speak and dress as they please; managers demand that company policies and dress codes be upheld. Until recently, worker-management conflicts were resolved at the store level. However, in early 2004, store 7356, on Madison Avenue in Manhattan, got permission from the National Labor Relations Board (NLRB) to hold a union election. Pro-union sentiment had begun to build, with workers unhappy about pay, hours, and safety. Barista Anthony Polanco says, "Starbucks pays peanuts, and they treat the workers like elephants." Most New York City workers agree that Starbucks's $7.75 hourly rate is a poverty wage for the area. Another barista, Daniel Gross, cites a work environment that causes burns and repetitive stress injuries.

Starbucks prefers that workers are not unionized. Founder Howard Schultz takes the threat of unionization personally. "If workers had faith in me and my motives, they wouldn't need a union," he says. After the call for a union election, Starbucks executives began to visit store 7536, engaging in anti-union discussions with baristas and handing out free pizza and concert tickets. By July 2004, union activists canceled the election, perhaps fearing a loss. Most of the pro-union employees moved on to other stores or other employers.

The NLRB is investigating the possibility that Starbucks engaged in unfair labor practices. A ruling is expected in summer 2005, and with a reputation for social

> **"**. . . *A diverse work team helps us be more adaptive as a company . . . Diversity helps us make better decisions.***"**
>
> ORIN SMITH, FORMER CEO, STARBUCKS

responsibility, Starbucks is vulnerable to charges of being anti-labor or anti-worker. In the meantime, the company continues its practices: training, communicating, fostering diversity, and developing leaders. So far, these have been more than sufficient in generating growth and success for Starbucks.

Sources: "Corporate Social Responsibility Report 2004," "Diversity," "Starbucks Mission Statement," Starbucks website, www.starbucks.com on June 30, 2005; "Biography: Howard Schultz, Starbucks," Great Entrepreneurs website, 2000, www.myprimetime.com on June 30, 2005 (quotation); Sharmistha Choudhury, "Brewing Racism in Canada," *The New Nation*, October 1, 2004, nation.ittefaq.com on June 30, 2005; Anya Kamenetz, "Baristas of the World, Unite!" *New York Magazine*, May 30, 2005, www.newyorkmetro.com on June 30, 2005; A.V. Krebs, "Union in NYC Wins Battle to Vote on Union at Starbucks," *The Agribusiness Examiner*, July 14, 2004, www.organic-consumers.org on February 2, 2005; Alison Overholt, "Listening to Starbucks," *Fast Company*, July 2004, pp. 50–56.

Integrative Case Questions

1. In what ways does workforce diversity help or benefit Starbucks? In what ways does diversity present challenges or potential problems? Based on your answer, do you think Starbucks should try to increase or decrease the diversity of its workforce? Explain.

2. Starbucks carefully selects team members and offers them training about the company. What else could the company do improve team effectiveness? What outcomes does Starbucks experience as a result of good teamwork at its stores?

3. Based on what you read about attempts to unionize Starbucks, what is the company's reaction to conflict? In your opinion, is this the optimal response in this situation? If so, explain why. If not, choose a different response and explain why that response might be preferable.

Foundations of Organization Structure

CHAPTER 16

After studying this chapter, you should be able to:

Chapter Outline

The Nature of Organization Structure

Structural Configuration

Structure and Operations

Responsibility and Authority

Classic Views of Structure

Intel's Intelligent Organization Structure

Intel is the world's leading microprocessor manufacturer, providing semiconductor chips that power 80 percent of personal computers worldwide. Intel is famous for its business model, which is focused on innovative technology, developed rapidly, and produced in very large volumes that lowered costs. With a research budget of $4.4 billion annually, Intel will dominate the semiconductor industry for years. In the past, Intel's corporate structure reflected the product-centered business model, with departments focused on microprocessors, networking equipment, communications equipment, and services. As journalists Gary Rivlin and John Markoff wrote, "Every new product followed a simple pattern: the engineers figured out what was possible and then told the marketing department what to sell."

Today, the firm has switched its attention from the technology to the consumers who use that technology. The change is due in part to a saturated PC industry in the United States. Intel will have to pay more attention to customer needs to keep on growing.

To aid in the transition, Paul S. Otellini became Intel's CEO in May 2005. Otellini is an M.B.A. with sales experience and an unlikely choice to lead a company headed for decades by engineers with PhDs. The changes he has made have had profound implications for

- Define organization structure and discuss its purpose.
- Describe structural configuration and summarize its four basic dimensions.
- Discuss two structural policies that affect operations.
- Explain the dual concepts of authority and responsibility.
- Describe the classic views of organization structure.

> **"[It] takes a lot of guts and courage to push an entire company from where it's most comfortable."**
>
> LOUIS J. BURNS, VICE PRESIDENT,
> DIGITAL HEALTH GROUP, INTEL

the future of the firm. "[It] takes a lot of guts and courage to push an entire company from where it's most comfortable," says Intel manager Louis J. Burns. Otellini will oversee a new organization structure, with unit names of Mobile, Business, Home, Digital Health Group, and International.

Each of the new departments will focus on a specific group of customers, their needs, and how they use their computers. The new structure will create more variety between the departments. As each unit responds to a particular set of buyers, a unique set of solutions and devices may be developed. For example, the Digital Health Group develops technology to help individuals better manage their health. Among dozens of innovative products, one system supports individuals with Alzheimer's, prompting them to eat meals and displaying detailed cooking instructions for forgetful seniors. Another system provides monitoring of the senior and a warning system to help at-home caregivers.

In the new structure, computing, communications, networking, and services staff will be merged into every new department. This reflects the current trend in high-tech industries toward products that combine computing and other technologies.

Industry observers worry that Intel's new approach may not be good for consumers. "You'll be using a PC uniquely designed and optimized for what you do," says *InfoWorld* editor Ephraim Schwartz. "PCs will become far less interchangeable . . . It may no longer be practicable to share a mobile PC between work and home." Yet in the short run, the customized solutions serve customers well. Only time will tell whether this new organization structure can help Intel align itself more closely with its customers. For more about the long-term impacts of Intel's new focus and structure, see the boxed insert, *Intel and . . . Change* on page 427.

References: "Intel Aligns Around Platforms," "Intel Corporation in Summary," Intel website, appzone.intel.com on February 8, 2005; "Intel Corporation," Hoover's, www.hoovers.com on March 6, 2005; "Intel Shuffles Key Management Roles," *TechWeb*, October 10, 2000, www.techweb.com on February 8, 2005; Gary Rivlin and John Markoff, "Can Mr. Chips Transform Intel?" *New York Times*, September 12, 2004, pp. BU1, 4 (quotation); Ephraim Schwartz, "The Age of the Industry-Specific PC," *InfoWorld*, January 28, 2005, www.infoworld.com on February 8, 2005.

Intel has made a radical departure from their former ways of doing business. This is not unusual in business these days as companies struggle to remain competitive in a rapidly changing world. This chapter introduces many of the key concepts of organization structure and sets the stage for understanding the many aspects of developing the appropriate organization design, which is discussed in Chapter 17.

The Nature of Organization Structure

In other chapters we discuss key elements of the individual and the factors that tie the individual and the organization together. In a given organization, these factors must fit together within a common framework: the organization's structure.

Organization Defined

An **organization** is a goal-directed social entity with deliberate processes and systems.[1] In other words, an organization is a collection of people working together to accomplish something. Top management determines what that "something" is and sets the direction of the organization by defining its purpose, establishing goals to meet that purpose, and formulating strategies to achieve the goals.[2] The definition of its purpose gives the organization reason to exist; in effect, it answers the question "What business are we in?"

Establishing goals converts the defined purpose into specific, measurable performance targets. **Organizational goals** are objectives that management seeks to achieve in pursuing the purpose of the firm. Goals motivate people to work together. Although each individual's goals are important to the organization, it is the organization's overall goals that are most important. Goals keep the organization on track by focusing the attention and actions of the members. They also give the organization a forward-looking orientation. They do not address past success or failure; rather, they force members to think about and plan for the future.

Finally, strategies are specific action plans that enable the organization to achieve its goals and thus its purpose. Pursuing a strategy involves developing an organization structure and the processes to do the organization's work.

> An **organization** is a goal-directed social entity with deliberate processes and systems.

> **Organizational goals** are objectives that management seeks to achieve in pursuing the firm's purpose.

Organization Structure

Organization structure is the system of task, reporting, and authority relationships within which the work of the organization is done. Thus, structure defines the form and function of the organization's activities. Structure also defines how the parts of an organization fit together, as is evident from an organization chart.

The purpose of an organization's structure is to order and coordinate the actions of employees to achieve organizational goals. The premise of organized effort is that people can accomplish more by working together than they can separately. The work must be coordinated properly, however, if the potential gains of collective effort are to be realized. Consider what might happen if the thousands of employees at Dell Computers worked without any kind of structure. Each person might try to build a computer that he or she thought would sell. No two computers would be alike, and each would take months or years to build. The costs of making the computers would be so high that no one would be able to afford them. To produce computers that are both competitive in the marketplace and profitable for the company, Dell must have a structure in which its employees and managers work together in a coordinated manner. DaimlerChrysler was faced with similar coordination problems following its merger, due to duplication of capabilities, facilities, and product lines. It had to restructure its departments and systems to create significant savings without diluting the image of either brand.[3]

The task of coordinating the activities of thousands of workers to produce cars or computers that do the work expected of them and that are guaranteed and easy to maintain may seem monumental. Yet whether the goal is to mass produce computers or to make soap, the requirements of organization structure are similar. First, the structure must identify the various tasks or processes necessary for the organization to reach

> **Organization structure** is the system of task, reporting, and authority relationships within which the organization does its work.

Africa native Florence Wambugu has developed genetically modified foods, such as bananas and sweet potatoes, to help the starving people of her homeland. However, some governments in Africa object to genetically altered food, and people are starving despite the availability of the controversial crops. Wambugu has created a new organization, A Harvest Biotech Foundation International, to serve as a pan-African voice on the issue. With the organizational goal of increasing the availability of genetically modified crops in Africa, the organization will be better able to stay on track and continue its forward momentum.

its goals. This dividing of tasks into smaller parts is often called "division of labor." Even small organizations (those with fewer than one hundred employees) use division of labor.[4] Second, the structure must combine and coordinate the divided tasks to achieve a desired level of output. The more interdependent the divided tasks, the more coordination is required.[5] Every organization structure addresses these two fundamental requirements.[6] The various ways of approaching these requirements are what make one organization structure different from another.

Organization structure can be analyzed in three ways. First, we can examine its configuration—that is, its size and shape—as depicted on an organization chart. Second, we can analyze its operational aspects or characteristics, such as separation of specialized tasks, rules and procedures, and decision making. Finally, we can examine responsibility and authority within the organization. In this chapter, we describe organization structure from all three points of view.

Structural Configuration

An **organization chart** is a diagram showing all people, positions, reporting relationships, and lines of formal communication in the organization.

The structure of an organization is most often described in terms of its organization chart. See Figure 16.1 for an example. A complete **organization chart** shows all people, positions, reporting relationships, and lines of formal communication in the

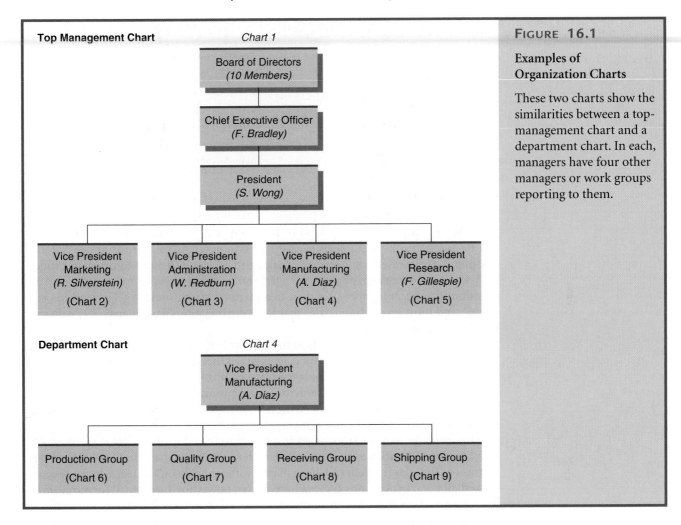

Top Management Chart — Chart 1

Board of Directors
(10 Members)

Chief Executive Officer
(F. Bradley)

President
(S. Wong)

Vice President
Marketing
(R. Silverstein)
(Chart 2)

Vice President
Administration
(W. Redburn)
(Chart 3)

Vice President
Manufacturing
(A. Diaz)
(Chart 4)

Vice President
Research
(F. Gillespie)
(Chart 5)

Department Chart — Chart 4

Vice President
Manufacturing
(A. Diaz)

Production Group
(Chart 6)

Quality Group
(Chart 7)

Receiving Group
(Chart 8)

Shipping Group
(Chart 9)

FIGURE 16.1

Examples of Organization Charts

These two charts show the similarities between a top-management chart and a department chart. In each, managers have four other managers or work groups reporting to them.

organization. (However, as we discussed in Chapter 11, communication is not limited to these formal channels.) For large organizations, several charts may be necessary to show all positions. For example, one chart may show top management, including the board of directors, the chief executive officer, the president, all vice presidents, and important headquarters staff units. Subsequent charts may show the structure of each department and staff unit. Figure 16.1 depicts two organization charts for a large firm; top management is shown in the upper portion of the figure and the manufacturing department in the lower portion. Notice that the structures of the different manufacturing groups are given in separate charts.

An organization chart depicts reporting relationships and work group memberships and shows how positions and small work groups are combined into departments, which together make up the **configuration**, or shape, of the organization. The configuration of organizations can be analyzed in terms of how the two basic requirements of structure—division of labor and coordination of the divided tasks—are fulfilled.

Division of Labor

Division of labor is the extent to which the organization's work is separated into different jobs to be done by different people. Division of labor is often referred to as

The **configuration** of an organization is its shape, which reflects the division of labor and the means of coordinating the divided tasks.

The **division of labor** is the way the organization's work is divided into different jobs to be done by different people. Division of labor is often referred to as **specialization**.

Advantages	Disadvantages
Efficient use of labor	Routine, repetitive jobs
Reduced training costs	Reduced job satisfaction
Increased standardization and uniformity of output	Decreased worker involvement and commitment
Increased expertise from repetition of tasks	Increased worker alienation
	Possible incompatibility with computerized manufacturing technologies

specialization. Division of labor is one of the seven primary characteristics of structuring described by Max Weber,[7] who is discussed later in the chapter, but the concept can be traced back to eighteenth-century economist Adam Smith. As we noted in Chapter 7, Smith used a study of pin making to promote the idea of dividing production work to increase productivity.[8] Division of labor grew more popular as large organizations became more prevalent in a manufacturing society. This trend has continued, and most research indicates that large organizations usually have more division of labor than smaller ones.[9]

Division of labor has been found to have both advantages and disadvantages (see Table 16.1). Modern managers and organization theorists are still struggling with the primary disadvantage: Division of labor often results in repetitive, boring jobs that undercut worker satisfaction, involvement, and commitment.[10] In addition, extreme division of labor may be incompatible with new, integrated computerized manufacturing technologies that require teams of highly skilled workers.[11]

However, division of labor need not result in boredom. Visualized in terms of a small organization such as a basketball team, it can be quite dynamic. A basketball team consists of five players, each of whom plays a different role on the team. In professional basketball the five positions typically are center, power forward, small forward, shooting guard, and point guard. The tasks of the players in each position are quite different, so players of different sizes and skills are on the floor at any one time. The teams that win championships, such as the Los Angeles Lakers and the Detroit Pistons, use division of labor by having players specialize in doing specified tasks, and doing them impeccably. Similarly, organizations must have specialists who are highly trained and know their specific jobs very well.

Coordinating the Divided Tasks

Three basic mechanisms are used to help coordinate the divided tasks: departmentalization, span of control, and administrative hierarchy. These mechanisms focus on grouping tasks in some meaningful manner, creating work groups of manageable size, and establishing a system of reporting relationships among supervisors and managers. When companies reorganize, they are usually changing the ways in which the division of labor is coordinated. To some people affected by reorganization, it may seem that things are still just as disorganized as they were before. But there really is a purpose for such reorganization efforts. Top management expects that the work will be better coordinated under the new system.

Departmentalization **Departmentalization** is the manner in which divided tasks are combined and allocated to work groups. It is a consequence of the division of labor. Because employees engaged in specialized activities can lose sight of overall

Departmentalization is the manner in which divided tasks are combined and allocated to work groups.

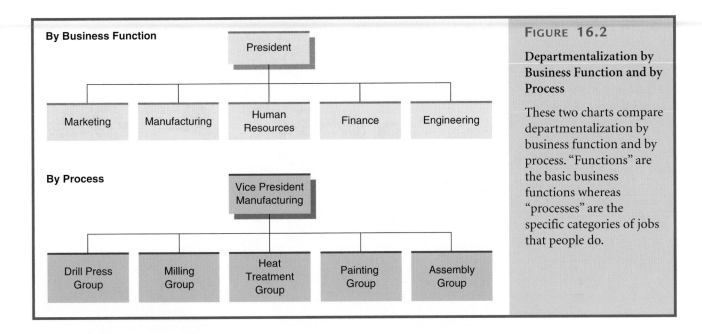

By Business Function

President

Marketing | Manufacturing | Human Resources | Finance | Engineering

By Process

Vice President Manufacturing

Drill Press Group | Milling Group | Heat Treatment Group | Painting Group | Assembly Group

FIGURE 16.2

Departmentalization by Business Function and by Process

These two charts compare departmentalization by business function and by process. "Functions" are the basic business functions whereas "processes" are the specific categories of jobs that people do.

organizational goals, their work must be coordinated to ensure that it contributes to the welfare of the organization.

There are many possible ways to group, or departmentalize, tasks. The five groupings most often used are business function, process, product or service, customer, and geography. The first two, function and process, derive from the internal operations of the organization; the others are based on external factors. Most organizations tend to use a combination of methods, and departmentalization often changes as organizations evolve.[12]

Departmentalization by business function is based on traditional business functions such as marketing, manufacturing, and human resource administration (see Figure 16.2). In this configuration employees most frequently associate with those engaged in the same function, a situation that helps in communication and cooperation. In a functional group, employees who do similar work can learn from one another by sharing ideas about opportunities and problems they encounter on the job. Unfortunately, functional groups lack an automatic mechanism for coordinating the flow of work through the organization.[13] In other words, employees in a functional structure tend to associate little with those in other parts of the organization. The result can be a narrow focus that limits the coordination of work among functional groups, as when the engineering department fails to provide marketing with product information because it is too busy testing materials to think about sales.

Departmentalization by process is similar to functional departmentalization except that the focus is much more on specific jobs grouped according to activity. Thus, as Figure 16.2 illustrates, the firm's manufacturing jobs are divided into certain well-defined manufacturing processes: drilling, milling, heat treatment, painting, and assembly. Hospitals often use process departmentalization, grouping the professional employees such as therapists according to the types of treatment they provide.

Process groupings encourage specialization and expertise among employees, who tend to concentrate on a single operation and share information with departmental colleagues. A process orientation may develop into an internal career path and managerial hierarchy within the department. For example, a specialist might become

This meeting shows Kari Barbar, vice president of sales and marketing operations for IBM's Personal Computing, chairing a meeting discussing IBM's "Think" strategy. Creating divisions, such as the Personal Computing Division, allows employees with different areas of expertise to work more closely together and focus their attention on one product or set of products, in this case personal computers.

the "lead" person for that specialty—that is, the lead welder or lead press operator. As in functional grouping, however, narrowness of focus can be a problem. Employees in a process group may become so absorbed in the requirements and execution of their operations that they disregard broader considerations such as overall product flow.[14]

Departmentalization by product or service occurs when employees who work on a particular product or service are members of the same department regardless of their business function or the process in which they are engaged. In the late 1980s, IBM reorganized its operations into five autonomous business units: personal computers, medium-size office systems, mainframes, communications equipment, and components.[15] Although the reorganization worked for a while, the company took quite a downturn in the early 1990s. Then, facing the Internet age at the beginning of the new century, IBM reorganized again by adding several new divisions: a global computer services group to provide computing services; an Internet division to develop, manufacture, and distribute products for the new Internet age; and the Personal Computing Division to develop strategies centered on devices, software, and services that make the Internet accessible anywhere, anytime. These new divisions continued IBM's departmentalization by product or service.

Intel reorganized along product lines in January 2005 by creating five new product divisions as discussed in the opening case and in the boxed insert, *Intel and . . . Change*. Their new organization chart at the executive level is shown in Figure 16.3.

Departmentalization according to product or service obviously enhances interaction and communication among employees who produce the same product or service and may reduce coordination problems. In this type of configuration, there may be less process specialization but more specialization in the peculiarities of the specific product or service. Intel expected that the new alignment would allow all employees, from designers to manufacturing workers to marketing experts, to become specialists in a particular product line. The disadvantage is that employees may become so interested

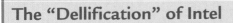

Intel and . . .   **CHANGE**

The "Dellification" of Intel

Intel's reorganization gives more attention to customers and makes it resemble Dell Computers, arguably the most customer-focused firm on the planet. Technology editor Ephraim Schwartz makes the connection when he says, "The dot-com boom saw the promise of build-to-order PCs, perfected by Dell. [With Intel's reorganization] we may be seeing the beginning of a design-components-to-order era."

Dell tries to encourage imitation, particularly in its supplier firms, but with scant success. Writer James Surowiecki says, "In theory, any of Dell's competitors could do what Dell does . . . None does, though, in large part because all of them are stuck with out-of-date business models and business structures." Founder Michael Dell says, "These things just don't happen as fast as a lot of people predict. We've seen [potential imitators] come time and time again, and you could see them struggling with the change."

Innovation expert Michael Schrage writes that "[Dell has had] unprecedented success in matching product offerings to customer demand . . . Michael Dell is too smart to think he's smart enough to predict the future . . . Dell is content to ask consumers what they want and then sell it to them." Dell's organization structure supports this sharp departure from a traditional model, where consumers are taught to want what the company can provide.

Surowiecki claims that large groups of ordinary individuals are better at innovation and problem solving than a few experts. Surowiecki applies his model to politics, popular culture, and business. Dell has turned Surowiecki's insight into bankable profits. If Surowiecki is correct, and if Dell's evident success continues, Intel may be just one of hundreds of companies that say and truly mean, "The customers are always right."

> *"Dell's competitors . . . are stuck with out-of-date business models and business structures."*
>
> JAMES SUROWIECKI, WRITER

References: Darrell Dunn, "Dell's Manifest Destiny," *Tech Builder,* February 7, 2005, www.techbuilder.org on March 6, 2005; Ephraim Schwartz, "The Age of the Industry-Specific PC," *InfoWorld,* January 28, 2005, www.infoworld.com on February 8, 2005; Michael Schrage, "The Dell Curve," *Wired,* July 2002, www.wired.com on March 6, 2005; James Surowiecki, "The New Economy Was a Myth, Right?" *Wired,* July 2002, www.wired.com on March 6, 2005.

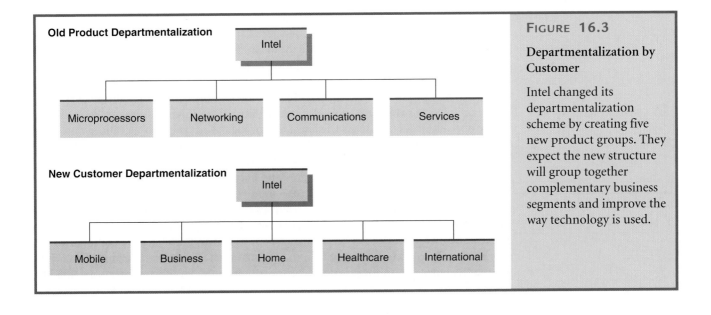

FIGURE 16.3

Departmentalization by Customer

Intel changed its departmentalization scheme by creating five new product groups. They expect the new structure will group together complementary business segments and improve the way technology is used.

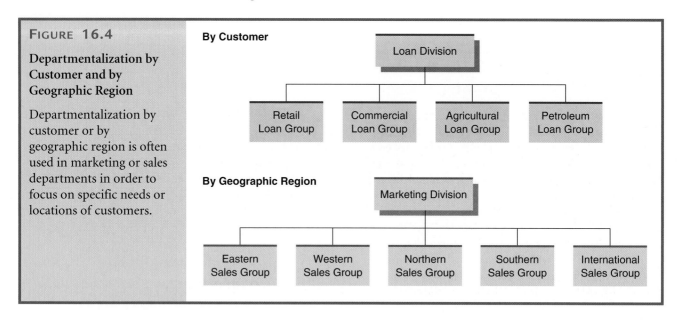

FIGURE 16.4

Departmentalization by Customer and by Geographic Region

Departmentalization by customer or by geographic region is often used in marketing or sales departments in order to focus on specific needs or locations of customers.

in their particular product or service that they miss technological improvements or innovations developed in other departments.

Departmentalization by customer is often called "departmentalization by market." Many lending institutions in Texas, for example, have separate departments for retail, commercial, agriculture, and petroleum loans similar to those shown in Figure 16.4. When significant groups of customers differ substantially from one another, organizing along customer lines may be the most effective way to provide the best product or service possible. This is why hospital nurses often are grouped by the type of illness they handle; the various maladies demand different treatment and specialized knowledge.[16] Deutsche Bank has recently changed its organization structure from a regional structure to one based on client groups in order to expand its international presence and to appeal to more international investors.[17] Dell Computers is one of the leaders in creating a structure focused on customers, as described in the *Intel and . . . Change* box.

With customer departmentalization there is usually less process specialization because employees must remain flexible to do whatever is necessary to enhance the relationship with customers. This configuration offers the best coordination of the workflow to the customer; however, it may isolate employees from others in their special areas of expertise. For example, if each of a company's three metallurgical specialists is assigned to a different market-based group, these individuals are unlikely to have many opportunities to discuss the latest technological advances in metallurgy.

Departmentalization by geography means that groups are organized according to a region of the country or world. Sales or marketing groups often are arranged by geographic region. As Figure 16.4 illustrates, the marketing effort of a large multinational corporation can be divided according to major geographical divisions. Using a geographically based configuration may result in significant cost savings and better market coverage. On the other hand, it may isolate work groups from activities in the organization's home office or in the technological community because the focus of the work group is solely on affairs within the region. Such a regional focus may foster loyalty to the work group that exceeds commitment to the larger organization. In addi-

Nissan and . . . GLOBALIZATION

Nissan's Chinese Venture

As part of sweeping changes and a major reorganization effort, Nissan Motors is increasing its investment in a joint venture with its Chinese partner, Dongfeng Automobile Company. Nissan's first investment in China came in 2000, when the automaker began its partnership with Dongfeng to produce just one sedan model. In 2003, the joint venture was at capacity with a volume of 39,000. Yet Nissan cannot afford to ignore a market that is predicted to be the third-largest purchaser of automobiles by 2012, with annual sales of two million vehicles. Imports from Japan just will not cover demand.

Dongfeng gains valuable expertise and access to resources through its partnership, while Nissan takes advantage of lower production costs and Dongfeng's knowledge of the local market. On the downside, Nissan must consider the impact on their brand if quality slips, as well as the risk of competitors gaining access to confidential information. This fear is especially acute in its relationship with Dongfeng, which also has a joint venture with Honda, one of Nissan's rivals.

Another concern is perhaps even more important, because so many are affected. What happens to global competitors if China is able to produce high-quality goods much more cheaply? One American manufacturer, seeing low-cost components similar to those made by his firm, says, "I can only assume this is 'the China price' . . . It is about half the price." Ohio State University professor and author Oded Shenkar warns firms, "If you still make any-

thing labor intensive, get out now rather than bleed to death . . . You need an entirely new business model to compete."

Nissan is cooperating in China, for now. At the same time, the company *is* adopting an entirely new business model. To read more, see the chapter closing case, "Nissan's New Organization Structure."

> *"You need an entirely new business model to compete [against Chinese firms]."*
>
> ODED SHENKAR, OHIO STATE UNIVERSITY
> PROFESSOR AND AUTHOR

References: "Dongfeng Automobile Co. Ltd.," China Cars website, www.chinacars.com on March 7, 2005; "Nissan's Revival Plan Bets on New Models in China," Xinhua News Agency, August 21, 2002, www.china.org.cn on March 7, 2005; Brian Bremner, "Nissan's Boss," *Business Week*, October 4, 2004, www.businessweek.com on March 7, 2005; Pete Engardio and Dexter Roberts, "'The China Price,'" *Business Week*, December 6, 2004, www.businessweek.com on March 7, 2005; Yuri Kageyama, "Nissan Beefing Up China Plants with New Company," *The Detroit News*, June 12, 2003, www.detnews.com on March 7, 2005; Ian Rowley, "So Much for Hollowing Out," *Business Week*, October 11, 2004, www.businessweek.com on March 7, 2005.

tion, work-related communication and coordination among groups may be somewhat inefficient.

Many large organizations use a mixed departmentalization scheme. Such organizations may have separate operating divisions based on products, but within each division, departments may be based on business function, process, customers, or geographic region (see Figure 16.5). Which methods work best depends on the organization's activities, communication needs, and coordination requirements. Another type of mixed structure often occurs in joint ventures, which are becoming increasingly popular.

Span of Control   The second dimension of organizational configuration, **span of control**, is the number of people reporting to a manager; it defines the size of the organization's work groups. Span of control is also called **span of management**. A manager who has a small span of control can maintain close control over workers and stay in contact with daily operations. If the span of control is large, close control is not

> The **span of control** is the number of people who report to a manager. Span of control is often called **span of management**.

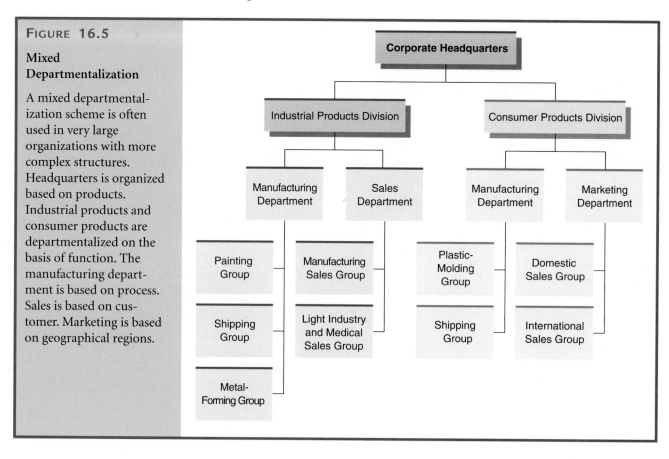

FIGURE 16.5

Mixed Departmentalization

A mixed departmentalization scheme is often used in very large organizations with more complex structures. Headquarters is organized based on products. Industrial products and consumer products are departmentalized on the basis of function. The manufacturing department is based on process. Sales is based on customer. Marketing is based on geographical regions.

possible. Figure 16.6 shows examples of small and large spans of control. Supervisors in the upper portion of the figure have a span of control of sixteen, whereas in the lower portion, supervisors have a span of control of eight.

A number of formulas and rules have been offered for determining the optimal span of control in an organization,[18] but research on the topic has not conclusively identified a foolproof method.[19] Henry Mintzberg concluded that the optimal unit size, or span of control, depends on five conditions:

1. The coordination requirements within the unit, including factors such as the degree of job specialization
2. The similarity of the tasks in the unit
3. The type of information available or needed by unit members
4. Differences in the members' need for autonomy
5. The extent to which members need direct access to the supervisor[20]

For example, a span of control of sixteen (as shown in Figure 16.6) might be appropriate for a supervisor in a typical manufacturing plant in which experienced workers do repetitive production tasks. On the other hand, a span of control of eight or fewer (as shown in Figure 16.6) might be appropriate in a job shop or custom-manufacturing facility in which workers do many different things and the tasks and problems that arise are new and unusual.[21]

Administrative Hierarchy The **administrative hierarchy** is the system of reporting relationships in the organization, from the first level up through the president or CEO. It results from the need for supervisors and managers to coordinate the activities of employees. The size of the administrative hierarchy is inversely related to the span of control: Organizations with a small span of control have many managers in the hierarchy; those with a large span of control have a smaller administrative hierarchy. Companies often rearrange their administrative hierarchies to achieve more efficient operations. Gateway 2005 rearranged its management and moved the company's headquarters from South Dakota to San Diego, California, in order to develop an organization that will enable it to provide many different computer-related products and services.[22]

Using Figure 16.6 again, we can examine the effects of small and large spans of control on the number of hierarchical levels. The smaller span of control for the supervisors in the lower portion of the figure requires that there be four supervisors rather than two. Correspondingly, another management layer is needed to keep the department head's span of control at two. Thus, when the span of control is small, the workers are under tighter supervision, and there are more administrative levels. When the span of control is large, as in the upper portion of the figure, production workers are not closely supervised, and there are fewer administrative levels. Because it measures the number of management personnel, or administrators, in the organization, the administrative hierarchy is sometimes called the "administrative component," "administrative intensity," or "administrative ratio."

The size of the administrative hierarchy also relates to the overall size of the organization. As an organization's size increases, so does its complexity and the requirements for coordination, necessitating proportionately more people to manage the business. However, this conclusion defines the administrative component as including the entire administrative hierarchy—that is, all of the support staff groups, such as personnel and financial services, legal staff, and others. Defined in this way, the administrative component in a large company may seem huge compared with the number of production workers. On the other hand, research that separates the support staff and clerical functions from the management hierarchy has found that the ratio of managers to total employees actually decreases with increases in the organization's size. Other, more recent research has shown that the size of the

FIGURE 16.6

Span of Control and Levels in the Administrative Hierarchy

These charts show how span of control and the number of levels in the administrative hierarchy are inversely related. The thirty-two first-level employees are in two groups of sixteen in the top chart and in four groups of eight in the bottom chart. Either may be appropriate, depending on the work situation.

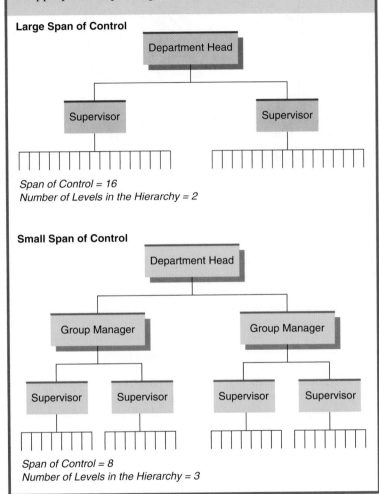

The **administrative hierarchy** is the system of reporting relationships in the organization, from the lowest to the highest managerial levels.

"JB wears many hats. He just can't delegate."

www.cartoonstock.com

In this cartoon, JB must have trouble delegating some of his tasks to others since he "wears so many hats." In effect, the failure to delegate has resulted in JB doing everything himself and making all the decisions. JB probably needs to delegate to some of his employees the right to make decisions so he does not have to make all of them himself.

administrative hierarchy and the overall size of the organization are not related in a straightforward manner, especially during periods of growth and decline.[23]

The popular movement of downsizing has been part of a reaction to the complexity that comes with increasing organization size. Much of the literature on organizational downsizing has proposed that it results in lower overhead costs, less bureaucracy, faster decision making, smoother communications, and increases in productivity.[24]

These expectations are due to the effort to reduce the administrative hierarchy by cutting out layers of middle managers. Unfortunately, when downsizing is done indiscriminately—without regard for the jobs that people actually do, the coordination needs of the organization, and the additional training that may be necessary for the survivors—it results in poorer communication, reduced productivity, and lower employee morale.[25]

Structure and Operations

Some important aspects of organization structure do not appear on the organization chart and thus are quite different from the configurational aspects discussed in the previous section. In this section, we examine the structural policies that affect operations and prescribe or restrict how employees behave in their organizational activities.[26] The two primary aspects of these policies are centralization of decision making and formalization of rules and procedures.

Centralization

> **Centralization** is a structural policy in which decision-making authority is concentrated at the top of the organizational hierarchy.

The first structural policy that affects operations is **centralization**, wherein decision-making authority is concentrated at the top of the organizational hierarchy. At the opposite end of the continuum is decentralization, in which decisions are made throughout the hierarchy.[27] Increasingly, centralization is being discussed in terms of participation in decision making.[28] In decentralized organizations, lower-level employees participate in making decisions. The changes that Jack Smith made in 1993 and 1996 at General Motors were intended to decentralize decision making throughout the company. Smith dismantled the old divisional structure, created a single unit called North American Operations, and abolished a tangle of management committees that slowed down decision making. Managers are now encouraged to make decisions on new designs and pricing that used to take weeks to circulate through the committee structure on their way to the top.[29]

Decision making in organizations is more complex than the simple centralized-decentralized classification indicates. In Chapter 8, we discussed organizational decision making in more depth. One of the major distinctions we made there was that some decisions are relatively routine and require only the application of a decision rule. These decisions are programmed decisions whereas those that are not routine are nonprogrammed. The decision rules for programmed decisions are formalized for the organization. This difference between programmed and nonprogrammed decisions tends to cloud the distinction between centralization and decentralization. For even if decision making is decentralized, the decisions themselves may be programmed and tightly circumscribed.

If there is little employee participation in decision making, then decision making is centralized, regardless of the nature of the decisions being made. At the other extreme, if individuals or groups participate extensively in making nonprogrammed decisions, the structure can be described as truly decentralized. If individuals or groups participate extensively in decision making but mainly in programmed decisions, the structure is called "formalized decentralization." Formalized decentralization is a common way to provide decision-making involvement for employees at many different levels in the organization while maintaining control and predictability.

Participative management has been described as a total management system in which people are involved in the daily decision making and management of the organization. As part of an organization's culture, participative management can contribute significantly to the long-term success of an organization.[30] It has been described as effective and, in fact, morally necessary in organizations. Thus, for many people, participation in decision making has become more than a simple aspect of organization structure. Caution is required, however, because if middle managers are to make effective decisions, as participative management requires, they must have sufficient information.[31] One of the highly touted benefits of the "Information Age" was that all employees throughout the organization would have more information and would therefore be able to participate more in decisions affecting their work, thus creating more decentralized organizations. However, some have suggested that all of this new information in organizations has had the opposite effect by enabling top managers to have more information about the organization's operations and to keep the decisions to themselves, thus creating more centralized organizations.[32]

Formalization

Formalization is the degree to which rules and procedures shape employees' jobs and activities. The purpose of formalization is to predict and control how employees behave on the job.[33] Rules and procedures can be both explicit and implicit. Explicit rules are set down in job descriptions, policy and procedures manuals, or office memos. (In one large company that continually issues directives attempting to limit employee activities, workers refer to them as "Gestapo" memos because they require employees to follow harsh rules.) Implicit rules may develop as employees become accustomed to doing things in a certain way over a period of time.[34] Though unwritten, these established ways of getting things done become standard operating procedures and have the same effect on employee behavior as written rules.

We can assess formalization in organizations by looking at the proportion of jobs that are governed by rules and procedures and the extent to which those rules permit variation. More formalized organizations have a higher proportion of rule-bound jobs and less tolerance for rule violations.[35] Increasing formalization may affect the design of jobs throughout the organization,[36] as well as employee motivation[37] and work group interactions.[38] The specific effects of formalization on employees are still unclear, however.[39]

Organizations tend to add more rules and procedures as the need for control of operations increases. Some organizations have become so formalized that they have rules for how to make new rules! One large state university created such rules in the form of a three-page document entitled "Procedures for Rule Adoption" that was added to the four-inch-thick *Policy and Procedures Manual*. The new policy first defines terms such as "university," "board," and "rule" and lists ten exceptions that describe when this policy on rule adoptions does not apply. It then presents a nine-step process for adopting a new rule within the university.

> **Formalization** is the degree to which rules and procedures shape the jobs and activities of employees.

Dummy workers holding traffic signs are common near large construction sites and oil and gas fields, such as this one in Prudhoe Bay, Alaska. These dummies do not actually enforce rules and procedures such as speeding and wearing safety equipment, but serve as friendly reminders to employees to follow the rules when on the site.

Other organizations are trying to become less formalized by reducing the number of rules and procedures employees must follow. In this effort, Chevron cut the number of its rules and procedures from over four hundred to eighteen. Highly detailed procedures for hiring were eliminated in favor of letting managers make hiring decisions based on common sense.[40]

Another approach to organizational formalization attempts to describe how, when, and why good managers should bend or break a rule.[41] Although rules exist in some form in almost every organization, how strictly they are enforced varies significantly from one organization to another and even within a single organization. Some managers argue that "a rule is a rule" and that all rules must be enforced to control employee behaviors and prevent chaos in the organization. Other managers act as if "all rules are made to be broken" and see rules as stumbling blocks on the way to effective action. Neither point of view is better for the organization; rather, a more balanced approach is recommended.

The test of a good manager in a formalized organization may be how well he or she uses appropriate judgment in making exceptions to rules. A balanced approach to making exceptions to rules should do two things. First, it should recognize that individuals are unique and that the organization can benefit from making exceptions that capitalize on exceptional capabilities. For example, suppose an engineering design department with a rule mandating equal access to tools and equipment acquires a limited amount of specialized equipment such as personal computers. The department manager decides to make an exception to the equal-access rule by assigning the computers to the designers the manager believes will use them the most and with the best results instead of making them available for use by all. Second, a balanced approach should recognize the commonalities among employees. Managers should make exceptions to rules only when there is a true and meaningful difference between individuals rather than base exceptions on features such as race, sex, appearance, or social factors.

Responsibility and Authority

Responsibility and authority are related to both configurational and operational aspects of organization structure. For example, the organization chart shows who reports to whom at all levels in the organization. From the operational perspective, the degree of centralization defines the locus of decision-making authority in the organization. However, often there is some confusion about what responsibility and authority really mean for managers and how the two terms relate to each other.

Responsibility is an obligation to do something with the expectation of achieving some act or output.

Responsibility

Responsibility is an obligation to do something with the expectation that some act or output will result. For example, a manager may expect an employee to write and present a proposal for a new program by a certain date; thus, the employee is responsible for preparing the proposal. Responsibility ultimately derives from the ownership of the organization. The owners hire or appoint a group, often a board of directors, to be responsible for managing the organization, making the decisions, and reaching the goals set by the owners. A downward chain of responsibility is then established. The board hires a chief executive officer (CEO) or president to be responsible for running the organization. The CEO or president hires more people and holds them responsible for accomplishing designated tasks that enable her or him to produce the results expected by the board and the owners. Jack Welch became famous for the way he ran GE for twenty years. Over the years he hired many managers and assigned responsibility for running various parts of the business. However, in the end, Jack Welch was responsible for all of the activities of the organization.

The chain extends throughout the organization because each manager has an obligation to fulfill: to appropriately employ organizational resources (people, money, and equipment) to meet the owners' expectations. Although managers can assign responsibility to others and expect them to achieve results, each manager is still held responsible for the outputs of those to whom he or she assigns the tasks.

A manager responsible for a work group assigns tasks to members of the group. Each group member is then responsible for doing his or her task, yet the manager still remains responsible for each task and for the work of the group as a whole. This means that managers can take on the responsibility of others but cannot shed their own responsibility onto those below them in the hierarchy.

Authority

Authority is power that has been legitimized within a specific social context.[42] (Power is discussed in Chapter 14.) Only when power is part of an official organizational role does it become authority. Authority includes the legitimate right to use resources to accomplish expected outcomes. As we discussed in the previous section, the authority to make decisions may be restricted to the top levels of the organization or dispersed throughout the organization.

Like responsibility, authority originates in the ownership of the organization. The owners establish a group of directors who are responsible for managing the organization's affairs. The directors, in turn, authorize people in the organization to make decisions and to use organizational resources. Thus, they delegate authority, or power in a social context, to others.

Authority is linked to responsibility because a manager responsible for accomplishing certain results must have the authority to use resources to achieve those results.[43] The relationship between responsibility and authority must be one of parity; that is, the authority over resources must be sufficient to enable the manager to meet the output expectations of others.

But authority and responsibility differ in significant ways. Responsibility cannot be delegated down to others (as discussed in the previous section), but authority can. One complaint often heard from employees is that they have too much responsibility but not enough authority to get the job done. This indicates a lack of parity between responsibility and authority. Managers usually are quite willing to hold individuals responsible for specific tasks but are reluctant to delegate enough authority to do the job. In effect, managers try to rid themselves of responsibility for results (which they cannot do), yet they rarely like to give away their cherished authority over resources.

Delegation is the transfer to others of authority to make decisions and use organizational resources. Delegation of authority to lower-level managers to make decisions is

> **Authority** is power that has been legitimized within a particular social context.

> **Delegation** is the transfer to others of authority to make decisions and use organizational resources.

common in organizations today. The important thing is to give lower-level managers authority to carry out the decisions they make. Managers typically have difficulty in delegating successfully. In the Self-Assessment Exercise at the end of this chapter, you will have a chance to practice delegation.

An Alternative View of Authority

So far we have described authority as a "top-down" function in organizations; that is, authority originates at the top and is delegated downward as the managers at the top consider appropriate. In author Chester Barnard's alternative perspective, authority is seen as originating in the individual, who can choose whether or not to follow a directive from above. The choice of whether to comply with a directive is based on the degree to which the individual understands it, feels able to carry it out, and believes it to be in the best interests of the organization and consistent with personal values.[44] This perspective has been called the **acceptance theory of authority** because it means that the manager's authority depends on the subordinate's acceptance of the manager's right to give the directive and to expect compliance.

> The **acceptance theory of authority** says that the authority of a manager depends on the subordinate's acceptance of the manager's right to give directives and to expect compliance with them.

For example, assume that you are a marketing analyst, and your company has a painting crew in the maintenance department. For some reason, your manager has told you to repaint your own office over the weekend. You probably would question your manager's authority to make you do this work. In fact, you would probably refuse to do it. If you received a similar request to work over the weekend to finish a report, you would be more likely to accept it and carry it out. Thus, by either accepting or rejecting the directives of a supervisor, workers can limit supervisory authority.[45] In most organizational situations, employees accept a manager's right to expect compliance on normal, reasonable directives because of the manager's legitimate position in the organizational hierarchy or in the social context of the organization. They may choose to disobey a directive and must accept the consequences if they do not accept the manager's right.

Classic Views of Structure

The earliest views of organization structure combined the elements of organization configuration and operation into recommendations on how organizations should be structured. These views have often been called "classical organization theory" and include Max Weber's concept of the ideal bureaucracy, the classic organizing principles of Henri Fayol, and the human organization view of Rensis Likert. Although all three are universal approaches, their concerns and structural prescriptions differ significantly.

Ideal Bureaucracy

> Weber's **ideal bureaucracy** is characterized by a hierarchy of authority and a system of rules and procedures designed to create an optimally effective system for large organizations.

In the early 1900s, Max Weber, a German sociologist, proposed a "bureaucratic" form of structure that he believed would work for all organizations. Weber's **ideal bureaucracy** was an organizational system characterized by a hierarchy of authority and a system of rules and procedures that, if followed, would create a maximally effective system for large organizations. Weber, writing at a time when organizations were inherently inefficient, claimed that the bureaucratic form of administration is superior to other forms of management with respect to stability, control, and predictability of outcomes.[46]

Elements	Comments
1. **Rules and Procedures**	A consistent set of abstract rules and procedures should exist to ensure uniform performance.
2. **Distinct Division of Labor**	Each position should be filled by an expert.
3. **Hierarchy of Authority**	The chain of command should be clearly established.
4. **Technical Competence**	Employment and advancement should be based on merit.
5. **Segregation of Ownership**	Professional managers rather than owners should run the organization.
6. **Rights and Properties of the Position**	These should be associated with the organization, not with the person who holds the office.
7. **Documentation**	A record of actions should be kept regarding administrative decisions, rules, and procedures.

TABLE 16.2

Elements of Weber's Ideal Bureaucracy

Weber's ideal bureaucracy had seven essential characteristics: rules and procedures, division of labor, a hierarchy of authority, technical competence, separation of ownership, rights and property differentiation, and documentation. As you can see, these characteristics utilize several of the building blocks discussed in this chapter. Weber intended these characteristics to ensure order and predictability in relationships among people and jobs in the bureaucracy. But it is easy to see how the same features can lead to sluggishness, inefficiency, and red tape. The administrative system can easily break down if any of the characteristics are carried to an extreme or are violated. For example, if endless arrays of rules and procedures bog down employees who must find the precise rule to follow every time they do something, responses to routine client or customer requests may slow to a crawl. Moreover, subsequent writers have said that Weber's view of authority is too rigid and have suggested that the bureaucratic organization may impede creativity and innovation and result in a lack of compassion for the individual in the organization.[47] In other words, the impersonality that is supposed to foster objectivity in a bureaucracy may result in serious difficulties for both employees and the organization. However, some organizations retain some characteristics of a bureaucratic structure while remaining innovative and productive.

Paul Adler has recently countered the currently popular movements of "bureaucracy busting" by noting that large-scale, complex organizations still need some of the basic characteristics that Weber described—hierarchical structure, formalized procedures, and staff expertise—in order to avoid chaos and ensure efficiency, conformance quality, and timeliness. Adler further proposes a second type of bureaucracy that essentially serves an enabling function in organizations.[48] The need for bureaucracy is not past. Bureaucracy, or at least some of its elements, is still critical for designing effective organizations.

The Classic Principles of Organizing

Also at the beginning of the twentieth century, Henri Fayol, a French engineer and chief executive officer of a mining company, presented a second classic view of the organization structure. Drawing on his experience as a manager, Fayol was the first to classify the essential elements of management—now usually called **management functions**—as planning, organizing, command, coordination, and control.[49] In addition, he presented

The **management functions** set forth by Henri Fayol include planning, organizing, command, coordination, and control.

TABLE 16.3

Fayol's Classic Principles of Organizing

Principle	Fayol's Comments
1. Division of work	Individuals and managers work on the same part or task.
2. Authority and responsibility	Authority—right to give orders; power to exact obedience; goes with responsibility for reward and punishment.
3. Discipline	Obedience, application, energy, behavior. Agreement between firm and individual.
4. Unity of command	Employee receives orders from one superior.
5. Unity of direction	One head and one plan for activities with the same objective.
6. Subordination of individual interest to general interest	Objectives of the organization come before objectives of the individual.
7. Remuneration of personnel	Pay should be fair to the organization and the individual; discussed various forms.
8. Centralization	Proportion of discretion held by the manager compared to that allowed to subordinates.
9. Scalar chain	Line of authority from lowest to top.
10. Order	A place for everyone and everyone in his or her place.
11. Equity	Combination of kindness and justice; equality of treatment.
12. Stability of tenure of personnel	Stability of managerial personnel; time to get used to work.
13. Initiative	Power of thinking out and executing a plan.
14. Esprit de corps	Harmony and union among personnel is strength.

Reference: From *General and Industrial Management,* by Henri Fayol. Copyright © Lake Publishing 1984, Belmont, CA 94002. Used with permission.

fourteen principles of organizing that he considered an indispensable code for managers (see Table 16.3).

Fayol's principles have proved extraordinarily influential; they have served as the basis for the development of generally accepted means of organizing. For example, Fayol's "unity of command" principle means that employees should receive directions from only one person, and "unity of direction" means that tasks with the same objective should have a common supervisor. Combining these two principles with division of labor, authority, and responsibility results in a system of tasks and reporting and authority relationships that is the very essence of organizing. Fayol's principles thus provide the framework for the organization chart and the coordination of work.

The classic principles have been criticized on several counts. First, they ignore factors such as individual motivation, leadership, and informal groups—the human element in organizations. This line of criticism asserts that the classic principles result in a mechanical organization into which people must fit, regardless of their interests, abilities, or motivations. The principles have also been criticized for their lack of operational specificity in that Fayol described the principles as universal truths but did not specify the means of applying many of them. Finally, Fayol's principles have been discounted because they were not supported by scientific evidence; Fayol presented them as universal principles, backed by no evidence other than his own experience.[50]

Human Organization

In the 1960s Rensis Likert developed an approach to organization structure he called **human organization**.[51]Because Likert, like others, had criticized Fayol's classic principles for overlooking human factors, it is not surprising that his approach centered on the principles of supportive relationships, employee participation, and overlapping work groups.

The term "supportive relationships" suggests that in all organizational activities, individuals should be treated in such a way that they experience feelings of support, self-worth, and importance. By "employee participation," Likert meant that the work group needs to be involved in decisions that affect it, thereby enhancing the employee's sense of supportiveness and self-worth. The principle of "overlapping work groups" means that work groups are linked, with managers serving as the "linking pins." Each manager (except the highest ranking) is a member of two groups: a work group that he or she supervises and a management group composed of the manager's peers and their supervisor. Coordination and communication grow stronger when the managers perform the linking function by sharing problems, decisions, and information both upward and downward in the groups to which they belong. The human organization concept rests on the assumption that people work best in highly cohesive groups oriented toward organizational goals. Management's function is to make sure the work groups are linked for effective coordination and communication.

Likert described four systems of organizing, which he called management systems, whose characteristics are summarized in Table 16.4. System 1, the exploitive authoritative system, can be characterized as the classic bureaucracy. System 4, the participative group, is the organization design Likert favored. System 2, the benevolent authoritative system, and system 3, the consultative system, are less extreme than either system 1 or system 4.

Likert described all four systems in terms of eight organizational variables: leadership processes, motivational forces, communication processes, interaction-influence processes, decision-making processes, goal-setting processes, control processes, and performance goals and training. Likert believed that work groups should be able to overlap horizontally as well as vertically where necessary to accomplish tasks. This feature is directly contrary to the classic principle that advocates unity of command. In addition, rather than the hierarchical chain of command, Likert favored the linking-pin concept of overlapping work groups for making decisions and resolving conflicts.

Research support for Likert's human organization emanates primarily from Likert and his associates' work at the Institute for Social Research at the University of Michigan. Although their research has upheld the basic propositions of the approach, it is not entirely convincing. One review of the evidence suggested that although research has shown characteristics of system 4 to be associated with positive worker attitudes and, in some cases, increased productivity, it is not clear that the characteristics of the human organization "caused" the positive results.[52] It may have been that positive attitudes and high productivity allowed the organization structure to be participative and provided the atmosphere for the development of supportive relationships. Likert's design has also been criticized for focusing almost exclusively on individuals and groups and not dealing extensively with structural issues. Overall, the most compelling support for this approach is at the individual and work-group levels. In some ways, Likert's system 4 is much like the team-based organization popular today.

Rensis Likert's **human organization** approach is based on supportive relationships, participation, and overlapping work groups.

TABLE 16.4

Characteristics of Likert's
Four Management
Systems

Characteristic	System 1: Exploitive Authoritative	System 2: Benevolent Authoritative	System 3: Consultative	System 4: Participative Group
Leadership				
• Trust in subordinates	None	None	Substantial	Complete
• Subordinates' ideas	Seldom used	Sometimes used	Usually used	Always used
Motivational Forces				
• Motives tapped	Security, status	Economic, ego	Substantial	Complete
• Level of satisfaction	Overall dissatisfaction	Some moderate satisfaction	Moderate satisfaction	High satisfaction
Communication				
• Amount	Very little	Little	Moderate	Much
• Direction	Downward	Mostly downward	Down, up	Down, up, lateral
Interaction-Influence				
• Amount	None	None	Substantial	Complete
• Cooperative teamwork	None	Virtually none	Moderate	Substantial
Decision Making				
• Locus	Top	Policy decided at top	Broad policy decided at top	All levels
• Subordinates involved	Not at all	Sometimes consulted	Usually consulted	Fully involved
Goal Setting				
• Manner	Orders	Orders with comments	Set after discussion	Group participation
• Acceptance	Covertly resisted	Frequently resisted	Sometimes resisted	Fully accepted
Control Processes				
• Level	Top	None	Some below top	All levels
• Information	Incomplete, inaccurate	Often incomplete, inaccurate	Moderately complete, accurate	Complete, accurate
Performance				
• Goals and Training	Mediocre	Fair to good	Good	Excellent

Reference: Adapted from Rensis Likert, *New Patterns of Management* (New York: McGraw-Hill, 1961), pp. 223–233; and Rensis Likert, *The Human Organization* (New York: McGraw-Hill, 1967), pp. 197, 198, 201, 203, 210, and 211.

Thus, the classic views of organization embody the key elements of organization structure. Each view, however, combined these key elements in different ways and with other management elements. These three classic views are typical of how the early writers attempted to prescribe a universal approach to organization structure that would be best in all situations. In the next chapter we describe other views of organization structure that may be effective, depending on the organizational situation.

Synopsis

The structure of an organization is the system of task, reporting, and authority relationships within which the organization does its work. The purpose of organization structure is to order and coordinate the actions of employees to achieve organizational goals. Every organization structure addresses two fundamental issues: dividing available labor according to the tasks to be performed and combining and coordinating divided tasks to ensure that tasks are accomplished.

An organization chart shows reporting relationships, work group memberships, departments, and formal lines of communication. In a broader sense, an organization chart shows the configuration, or shape, of the organization. Configuration has four dimensions: division of labor, departmentalization, span of control, and administrative hierarchy. Division of labor is the separation of work into different jobs to be done by different people. Departmentalization is the manner in which the divided tasks are combined and allocated to work groups for coordination. Tasks can be combined into departments on the basis of business function, process, product, customer, and geographic region. Span of control is the number of people reporting to a manager; it also defines the size of work groups and is inversely related to the number of hierarchical levels in the organization. The administrative hierarchy is the system of reporting relationships in the organization.

Structural policies prescribe how employees should behave in their organizational activities. Such policies include formalization of rules and procedures and centralization of decision making. Formalization is the degree to which rules and procedures shape employees' jobs and activities. The purpose of formalization is to predict and control how employees behave on the job. Explicit rules are set down in job descriptions, policy and procedures manuals, and office memos. Implicit rules develop over time as employees become accustomed to doing things in certain ways.

Centralization concentrates decision-making authority at the top of the organizational hierarchy; under decentralization, decisions are made throughout the hierarchy.

Responsibility is an obligation to do something with the expectation of achieving some output. Authority is power that has been legitimized within a specific social context. Authority includes the legitimate right to use resources to accomplish expected outcomes. The relationship between responsibility and authority needs to be one of parity; that is, employees must have enough authority over resources to meet the expectations of others.

Weber's ideal bureaucracy, Fayol's classic principles of organizing, and Likert's human organization cover many of the key features of organization structure. Weber's bureaucratic form of administration was intended to ensure stability, control, and predictable outcomes. Rules and procedures, division of labor, a hierarchy of authority, technical competence, separation of ownership, rights and property differentiation, and documentation characterize the ideal bureaucracy.

Fayol's classic principles included departmentalization, unity of command, and unity of direction; they came to be generally accepted as a means of organizing. Taken together, the fourteen principles provided the basis for the modern organization chart and for coordinating work.

Likert's human organization was based on the principles of supportive relationships, employee participation, and overlapping work groups. Likert described the human organization in terms of eight variables based on the assumption that people work best in highly supportive and cohesive work groups oriented toward organization goals.

Discussion Questions

1. Define "organization structure" and explain its role in the process of managing the organization.

2. What is the purpose of organization structure? What would an organization be like without a structure?

3. In what ways are aspects of the organization structure analogous to the structural parts of the human body?

4. How is labor divided in your college or university? In what other ways could your college or university be departmentalized?

5. What types of organizations could benefit from a small span of control? What types might benefit from a large span of control?

6. Discuss how increasing formalization might affect the role conflict and role ambiguity of employees.

7. How might the impact of formalization differ for research scientists, machine operators, and bank tellers?

8. How might centralization or decentralization affect the job characteristics specified in job design?

9. When a group makes a decision, how is responsibility for the decision apportioned among the members?

10. Why do employees typically want more authority and less responsibility?

11. Consider the job you now hold or one that you held in the past. Did your boss have the authority to direct your work? Why did he or she have this authority?

12. Describe at least four features of organization structure that were important parts of the classic view of organizing.

Experiencing Organizational Behavior

Understanding Organization Structure

Purpose: This exercise will help you understand the configurational and operational aspects of organization structure.

Format: You will interview at least five employees in different parts of either the college or university you attend or a small- to medium-sized organization and analyze its structure. (You may want to coordinate this exercise with the exercise in Chapter 17.)

Procedure: If you use a local organization, your first task is to find one with fifty to five hundred employees. The organization should have more than two hierarchical levels, but it should not be too complex to understand in a short period of study. You may want to check with your professor before contacting the company. Your initial contact should be with the highest-ranking manager, if possible. Be sure that top management is aware of your project and gives its approval.

If you use your local college or university, you could talk to professors, secretaries, and other administrative staff in the admissions office, student services department, athletic department, library, or many other areas. Be sure to represent a variety of jobs and levels in your interviews.

Using the material in this chapter, interview employees to obtain the following information on the structure of the organization.

1. The type of departmentalization (business function, process, product, customer, geographic region)

2. The typical span of control at each level of the organization

3. The number of levels in the hierarchy

4. The administrative ratio (ratio of managers to total employees and ratio of managers to production employees)

5. The degree of formalization (to what extent are rules and procedures written down in job descriptions, policy and procedures manuals, and memos?)

6. The degree of decentralization (to what extent are employees at all levels involved in making decisions?)

Interview three to five employees of the organization at different levels and in different departments. One should hold a top-level position. Be sure to ask the questions in a way that is clear to the respondents; they may not be familiar with the terminology used in this chapter.

Students should produce a report with a paragraph on each configurational and operational aspect of structure listed in this exercise as well as an organization chart of the company, a discussion of differences in responses from the employees interviewed, and any unusual structural features (for example, a situation in which employees report to more than one person or to no one). You may want to send a copy of your report to the company's top management.

Follow-up Questions

1. Which aspects of structure were the hardest to obtain information about? Why?

2. If there were differences in the responses of the employees you interviewed, how do you account for them?

Making Delegation Work

Tasks and decisions must be delegated to others if what remains of middle management is to survive. With downsizing, those who are left must do more with less time and fewer resources. In addition, the essence of total quality management is allowing others—teams and individuals—to make decisions about their work. On the other hand, many managers and supervisors complain that they do not know how to delegate effectively. The following eleven points should improve your delegation.

If you hold any type of managerial assignment or job at work or in a student club or association, you could delegate some job or task to another person. Try the following simple steps.

1. Choose a specific task and time frame. Know exactly what task is to be delegated and by when.

2. Specify in writing exactly why you are delegating this task.

3. Put down in writing exactly what you expect to be done and how it will be measured.

4. Be sure that the person or team is competent to do the task, or at least knows how to acquire the competence if they do not have it initially.

5. Be certain that those who must do the task really want to take on more responsibility.

6. Measure or oversee the work without being conspicuous and bothersome to those doing the task.

7. Predict how much it will cost to correct mistakes that might be made.

8. Make sure that YOUR boss knows that you are delegating this task and approves.

9. Be sure that you will be able to provide the appropriate rewards to the person or team who takes on this additional responsibility if they succeed.

10. Be ready with another task to delegate when the person or team succeeds with this one.

11. Be sure to delegate both responsibility for the task and the authority to utilize the appropriate resources to get the job done.

References: Selwyn W. Becker, "TQM Does Work: Ten Reasons Why Misguided Attempts Fail," *Management Review,* May 1993, pp. 30–33; Janet Houser Carter, "Minimizing the Risks from Delegation," *Supervisory Management,* February 1993, pp. 1–2; John Lawrie, "Turning Around Attitudes About Delegation," *Supervisory Management,* December 1990, pp. 1–2.

Exercise Overview: Managers typically inherit an existing organization structure when they are promoted or hired into a position as manager. Often, however, after working with the existing structure for a while, they feel the need to rearrange the structure to increase the productivity or performance of the organization. This exercise provides you with the opportunity to restructure an existing organization.

Exercise Background: Recall the analysis you did in the "Experiencing Organizational Behavior" exercise on page 442 in which you analyzed the structure of an existing organization. In that exercise you described the con-figurational and operational aspects of the structure of a local organization or department at your college or university.

Exercise Task: Develop a different organization structure for that organization. You may utilize any or all of the factors described in this chapter. For example, you could alter the span of control, the administrative hierarchy, and the method of departmentalization as well as the formalization and centralization of the organization. Remember, the key to structure is to develop a way to coordinate the divided tasks. You should draw a new organization chart and develop a rationale for your new design.

Conclude by addressing the following questions:

1. How difficult was it to come up with a different way of structuring the organization?

2. What would it take to convince the current head of that organization to go along with your suggested changes?

Nissan's New Organization Structure

Nissan was a traditional Japanese firm, providing lifetime employment to its workers and deeply involved in the country's *keiretsu* system, in which Japanese corporations use long-standing contractual arrangements to create a network of interrelated firms. Traditional firms and their customers and employees enjoyed a very stable and predictable future. Yet Nissan's environment was changing. The automobile industry was consolidating, competition was becoming more global, the Japanese economy was stagnating, and technology and consumer tastes were changing. The traditional approach just wasn't working in the new, more uncertain competitive landscape.

Nissan needed to adapt. When Carlos Ghosn became the first non-Japanese to head Nissan, and indeed, the first non-Japanese CEO of any major Japanese manufacturer, it was clear that the organization was ready for change. Ghosn focused on cost cutting, outsourcing some functions, reducing the number of partners, and severing some alliances. For the first time in company history, personnel were let go and facilities were closed. The CEO also worked to increase individual responsibility, rather than allowing workers to rely on group responsibility, as is common in Japanese management. "If you disagree with the plan," Ghosn told his managers, "you've got to leave the company." Ghosn admits that he was very hard on his staff, asking them to take actions that some found distasteful, but he also gave them tremendous power to make changes. He says, "You can't be demanding of someone who isn't empowered, it isn't fair."

Ghosn changed the corporate structure too. Nissan has grown closer to partner Renault and by May 2005, Ghosn will likely be CEO of the combined firm. The alliance creates the fourth-largest automaker in the world, with annual sales topping 5.7 million vehicles, giving the company greater competitive power. To coordinate and control the giant firm, Ghosn insisted that worldwide divisions work together. "[P]eople are still Japanese or French or American, but by working together, it will come together much better than if everybody was working on their own," claims Ghosn.

The result is a shared information system, supply chain management system, transportation system, and so on. Auto components are more standardized, easing production costs. In 2003, the companies saved an estimated $115 million through sharing logistics functions. The two companies exchange personnel through nineteen cross-company teams that include thousands of workers in every function of the company. "Don't expect to see us coming back to the old practices," asserts Ghosn, who has plans for even more standardization, sharing, and cost cutting. In the future, Nissan and Renault are likely to make and sell autos under their own and their partner's brand name, blurring the line between the two companies. Research and development is another area that could be improved and made more efficient by sharing resources across the two companies. The company has already opened about 150 common sales hubs, to carry both Renault and Nissan product lines, and 250 more common hubs are scheduled to start operation in 2005.

Ghosn, who has Lebanese ancestry and lived as a child in Brazil, Lebanon, and France, is perhaps ideally suited to lead Nissan through this period of extraordinary change. At first he faced such formidable resistance to his management style that he traveled with bodyguards for protection. Today, he is "adulated" at Nissan, appears as the hero of a popular *manga* comic book, and travels with a bodyguard for protection from overly friendly fans. Ghosn sees the benefits of diversity for himself and for the organization: "People have always had problems about what is different from them . . . We have a tendency to reject what is different. At the same time, we need what is different . . . If someone is different, I'm going to learn a lot . . . Whenever you understand how much difficulty is behind the situation, then you appreciate people and what they do, independently of who they are." Nissan and Renault should certainly appreciate how Ghosn's remarkable transformation has turned this once staid company into an industry leader with a new, powerful organizational structure and design.

> **" You can't be demanding of someone who isn't empowered, it isn't fair. "**
> *Carlos Ghosn, CEO, Nissan Motors*

responsibility? Is that the same way you might respond in a similar situation? Explain.

3. Consider Fayol's classical principles of organizing, found in Table 16.2 of your text. Describe how Nissan's transformation has affected the utilization of the fourteen principles at the firm.

Case Questions

1. What has Ghosn done in order to change Nissan's level of centralization? What are the likely advantages and disadvantages of Ghosn's approach to centralization?

2. In your opinion, how will Nissan workers respond to Ghosn's demand that they assume more individual

References: "Extending Their Global Partnership," "Nissan Creates New Supply Chain Management Division," "Renault-Nissan Alliance, March 2005," "The Renault-Nissan Alliance Ranks Among the Top Four Global Automakers," Nissan and Renault websites, www.nissan-global.com on March 7, 2005; "The Gaijin Who Saved Nissan: A Review of *Shift* by Carlos Ghosn," *Business Week*, January 17, 2005, www.businessweek.com on March 7, 2005; Liz Alderman, "Ghosn Shifts to All-Wheel Drive," *International Herald Tribune*, January 8–9, 2005, pp. 11, 13; Brian Bremner, "A Spin with Carlos Ghosn," *Business Week*, October 4, 2004, www.businessweek.com on March 7, 2005 (quotation).

TEST PREPPER

You have read the chapter and studied the key terms. Think you're ready to ace the exam? Take this sample test to gauge your comprehension of chapter material and check your answers at the back of the book. Want more test questions? Take the ACE quizzes found on the student website: http://college.hmco.com/business/students/ (select Griffin/Moorhead, Organizational Behavior, 8e from the Management menu).

T   F   1. An organization is a group of jobs tied together with money.

T   F   2. The system of authority relationships are part of an organization's structure.

T   F   3. A primary disadvantage of division of labor is low worker satisfaction.

T   F   4. Nearly all large organizations pick one form of departmentalization for all levels of the company.

T   F   5. Formalized decentralization is a common way to allow participation in decision making while maintaining control and predictability.

T   F   6. Authority can be delegated down to others, but responsibility cannot.

T   F   7. Fayol's classic principles of organizing were criticized because they ignore the human element in organization.

8. The purpose of an organization's structure is to
   a. avoid formal task and reporting relationships.
   b. order and coordinate the actions of employees to achieve organizational goals.
   c. focus on customer needs, not on products or geographic locations.
   d. eliminate differences in authority and responsibility.
   e. make the organization more attractive to customers.

9. Which of the following is not a common basis for departmentalization?
   a. Business function
   b. Profit levels
   c. Process
   d. Product
   e. Geography

10. With customer departmentalization there is usually less process specialization because
   a. specialists prefer to develop products rather than work with people.
   b. process specialization results in a span of control that is too large.
   c. employees must remain flexible to do whatever is necessary for customers.

   d. market coverage is better with lower process specialization.
   e. process specialization results in lower productivity and higher costs, regardless of the form of departmentalization.

11. Robert wants to work at a company that allows lower-level employees to participate in making decisions. Robert should look for a company
   a. that is departmentalized by geography.
   b. with a narrow span of control.
   c. that refuses to downsize.
   d. that is decentralized.
   e. that is departmentalized by product.

12. You can tell whether an organization is very formalized by
   a. counting the number of levels in its hierarchy.
   b. determining the last time the company downsized.
   c. looking at how many rules it has.
   d. observing whether the departmentalization is based on customers or products.
   e. verifying that responsibility is delegated.

13. The classic management theorist Rensis Likert described several systems of organizing. Which system did Likert favor?
   a. The classic bureaucracy
   b. The participative group
   c. The benevolent authoritative system
   d. The consultative system
   e. The dual-structure system

14. Rensis Likert, a renown management theorist, believed work groups should be able to overlap horizontally as well as vertically where necessary to accomplish tasks. This feature is directly contrary to which classical principle of organizing?
   a. Supportive relationships
   b. Linking pins
   c. Employee participation
   d. Unity of command
   e. Customer departmentalization

Organization Design

CHAPTER 17

After studying this chapter, you should be able to:

▶ **Describe the basic premise of contingency approaches to organization design.**

▶ **Discuss how strategy and the structural imperatives combine to affect organization design.**

▶ **Summarize five types of organization designs.**

▶ **Explain several contemporary approaches to organization design.**

A Marriage Made in Heaven

In 1998, European firm Daimler-Benz, maker of Mercedes automobiles, merged with Chrysler, which was struggling to hold onto its position as the third-largest automaker in the United States. The merger was described as "a marriage made in heaven," because it would allow both firms to better meet their strategic goals. Daimler would increase its market share in America, especially with middle-class buyers. Chrysler would benefit from the cash, technical expertise, and reputation of Mercedes. The new firm would be "a merger of equals," according to Daimler CEO Juergen Schrempp, and that was reflected in the new firm's name, Daimler-Chrysler. Although the merger showed great promise initially, it took years to see a positive impact on the combined firm's bottom line. The largest hurdle was the difficulty in creating a coherent, focused, and consistent structure and strategy across the two firms.

When Schrempp first headed Daimler-Benz in 1995, "what followed was a shake-up that was unprecedented in the culture of German management," according to business historian David Lewis. Compared to traditional American firms, traditional German companies show a greater emphasis on operational efficiency and product quality, less attention to marketing and finance, closer working relationships between labor and management, more decision making by consensus, and a focus on long-term, not short-term, results.

Schrempp, however, has often been accused of managing like an American, with one union leader calling him "a callous capitalist." His

> **"[CEO Juergen Schrempp's] plan to turn DaimlerChrysler into a global carmaker did not work out."**
>
> ANONYMOUS STOCK ANALYST

predecessor at Daimler-Benz, Edzard Reuter, did not specifically name Schrempp but complained that the company was now being run by "ice-cold calculators . . . untroubled by emotions." This harsh language was in response to Schrempp's cost-cutting approach at Daimler, when over 60,000 workers were laid off and entire factories and divisions eliminated. Schrempp said that he was trying to save the company and he was merely looking out for the company's owners: "I have to overstress the justifiable interests of the shareholders because they were not taken into account before."

Schrempp seemed the ideal leader, therefore, to craft a new organization that would combine the best of German and American business practices. Yet expected efficiencies have not materialized, as many Daimler and Chrysler products and processes could not be standardized. Schrempp mandated that Chrysler change to a more Daimler-like structure and management style, causing loss of morale and personnel. When American managers left and German management practices were implemented across the company, the anticipated benefits of Chrysler's expertise were not realized.

In addition, DaimlerChrysler has acquired a significant portion of Japanese automaker Mitsubishi, trying to duplicate its American strategy in Asia. Investors and Schrempp's own management board have rebelled, cutting off further funds for Mitsubishi. Lack of confidence in the company's future caused the stock price to fall from over $100 per share after the merger to just $27 in March 2004. *Business Week* named Schrempp "The Worst Manager of the Year" in 2004.

Schrempp concedes that progress has been slow but insists that the strategy was sound and that anticipated benefits will materialize over time. Experts and shareholders disagree and are impatient for results. When the board recently extended Schrempp's employment contract through 2008, one analyst said, "It would have been a good time to replace Schrempp—his plan to turn DaimlerChrysler into a global car maker did not work out." Shareholders are fighting back. "The decade with Schrempp . . . is a lost decade," says shareholder Jurgen Grasslin, in his shareholder motion to dismiss Schrempp. "He has missed by a long way the goals he set himself . . .[He] will go down as the biggest destroyer of jobs, shareholder value, and market capitalization in the history of Daimler-Benz."

Schrempp, always controversial at home and abroad, is facing one of his toughest challenges yet, as he tries to create a unified and effective company from diverse elements. For more about the controversy surrounding the DaimlerChrysler merger, see the boxed insert titled *DaimlerChrysler and . . . Ethics* on page 460.

References: "Annual Meeting 2005: Counter-Motions," Daimler-Chrysler website, www.daimlerchrysler.com on March 11, 2005; "Culture of German Management," Executive Planet, www.executiveplanet.com on March 9, 2005; Jim Burt, "DCX Extends Schrempp's Deal," *The Car Connection*, February 23, 2004, www.thecarconnection.com on March 9, 2005; Danny Hakim, "You Say 'Takeover.' I Say 'Merger of Equals.'" *New York Times*, December 21, 2003, pp. BU 1, 10; David Lewis, "Jurgen Schrempp: Rambo in Pinstripes or Global Pioneer?" *Financial Times*, March 2003, www.ftmastering.com on March 9, 2005; Jeffrey K. Liker, "What Was Daimler Thinking?" *Across the Board*, January/February 2005, pp. 12–13; Mark Thompson, "Daimler-Chrysler Sticks with CEO, Renews Board," *Forbes*, February 18, 2004, www.forbes.com on March 9, 2005 (quotation); David Welch, "A Shaky Automotive *Menage a Trois*," *Business Week*, May 10, 2004, www.businessweek.com on March 9, 2005.

DaimlerChrysler is not alone in its struggle to find the best organizational design in order to survive in an ever-changing environment. Many companies are constantly reorganizing to try to increase their performance, productivity, and response times—or just to survive. The primary issue is how to determine which organizational form is right for a given organization. In this chapter we describe several approaches to organization design.

Contingency Approaches to Organization Design

Organization designs vary from rigid bureaucracies to flexible matrix systems. Most theories of organization design take either a universal or a contingency approach. A **universal approach** is one whose prescriptions or propositions are designed to work in any situation. Thus, a universal design prescribes the "one best way" to structure the jobs, authority, and reporting relationships of the organization, regardless of factors such as the organization's external environment, the industry, and the type of work to be done. The classical approaches discussed in Chapter 16 are all universal approaches: Weber's ideal bureaucracy, Fayol's classic principles of organizing, and Likert's human organization. A **contingency approach**, on the other hand, suggests that organizational efficiency and effectiveness can be achieved in several ways. In a contingency design, specific conditions such as the environment, technology, and the organization's workforce determine the structure. Figure 17.1 shows the distinction between the universal

In the **universal approach** to organization design, prescriptions or propositions are designed to work in any circumstances.

Under the **contingency approach** to organization design, the desired outcomes for the organization can be achieved in several ways.

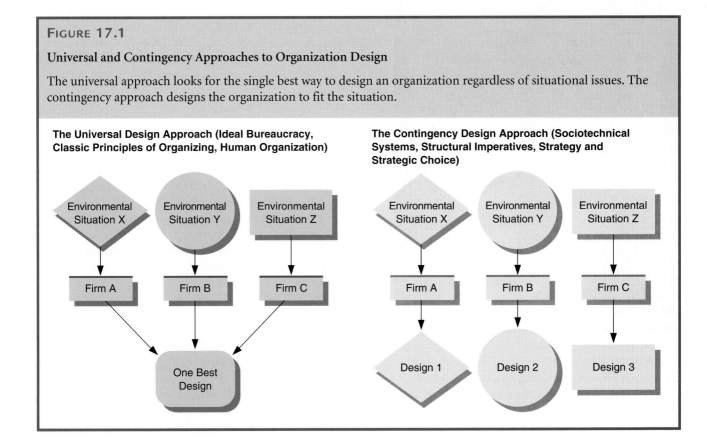

FIGURE 17.1

Universal and Contingency Approaches to Organization Design

The universal approach looks for the single best way to design an organization regardless of situational issues. The contingency approach designs the organization to fit the situation.

and contingency approaches. This distinction is similar to the one between universal and contingency approaches to motivation (Chapter 4), job design (Chapter 5), and leadership (Chapters 12 and 13). Although no one particular form of organization is generally accepted, the contingency approach most closely represents current thinking.

Weber, Fayol, and Likert (see Chapter 16) each proposed an organization design that is independent of the nature of the organization and its environment. Although each of their approaches contributed to our understanding of the organizing process and the practice of management, none has proved to be universally applicable. In this chapter we turn to several contingency designs, which attempt to specify the conditions, or contingency factors, under which they are likely to be most effective. The contingency factors include such things as the strategy of the organization, its technology, the environment, the organization's size, and the social system within which the organization operates.

The contingency approach has been criticized as being unrealistic because managers are expected to observe a change in one of the contingency factors and to make a rational structural alteration. On the other hand, Lex Donaldson has argued that it is reasonable to expect organizations to respond to lower organizational performance, which may result from a lack of response to some significant change in one or several contingency factors.[1]

> **Strategy** is the plans and actions necessary to achieve organizational goals.

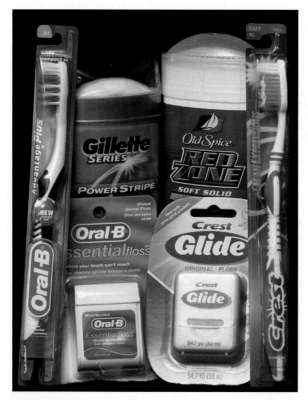

This picture shows just a few of the multiple overlapping products from Procter & Gamble and Gillette following the acquisition of Gillette by Procter & Gamble. The strategy related to personal care products will probably require that Procter & Gamble sell, spin off, license, or combine in some manner some of these overlapping products. The result will be a very different organization design for the new Procter & Gamble.

Strategy, Structural Imperatives, and Strategic Choice

The decision about how to design the organization structure is based on numerous factors. In this section, we present several views of the determinants of organization structure and integrate them into a single approach. We begin with the strategic view.

Strategy

A **strategy** is the plans and actions necessary to achieve organizational goals.[2] Every organization tries to develop a strategy that will enable it to meet its goals. Kellogg, for example, has attempted to be the leader in the ready-to-eat cereal industry by pursuing a strategy that combines product differentiation and market segmentation. Over the years, Kellogg has successfully introduced new cereals made from different grains in different shapes, sizes, colors, and flavors in its effort to provide any type of cereal the consumer might want.[3] McDonalds has been one of the leaders in the fast-food industry but has struggled lately to find the right strategy in a changing environment.[4]

After studying the history of seventy companies, Alfred Chandler drew certain conclusions about the relationship between an organization's structure and its business strategy.[5] Chandler observed that a growth strategy to expand into a new product line is usually matched with some type of decentralization, a decentralized structure being necessary to deal with the problems of the new product line.

Chandler's "structure follows strategy" concept seems to appeal to common sense. Management must decide what the organization is to do and what its goals are before deciding how to design the organization structure, which is how the organization will meet those goals. This perspective assumes a purposeful approach to designing the structure of the organization.

Structural Imperatives

The structural-imperatives approach to organization design probably has been the most discussed and researched contingency perspective of the last thirty years. This perspective was not formulated by a single theorist or researcher, and it has not evolved from a systematic and cohesive research effort. Rather, it gradually emerged from a vast number of studies that sought to address the question "What are the compelling factors that determine how the organization must be structured to be effective?" As Figure 17.2 shows, the three factors that have been identified as **structural imperatives** are size, technology, and environment.

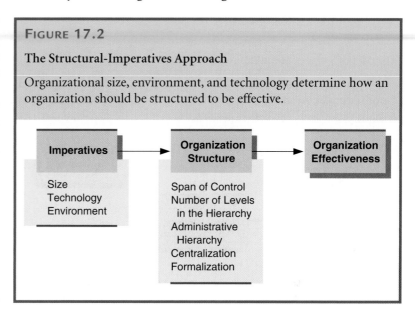

FIGURE 17.2

The Structural-Imperatives Approach

Organizational size, environment, and technology determine how an organization should be structured to be effective.

Structural imperatives—size, technology, and environment—are the three primary determinants of organization structure.

Size   The size of an organization can be gauged in many ways. Usually it is measured in terms of total number of employees, value of the organization's assets, total sales in the previous year (or number of clients served), or physical capacity. The method of measurement is very important, although the different measures usually are correlated.[6]

Generally, larger organizations have a more complex structure than smaller ones. Peter Blau and his associates concluded that large size is associated with greater specialization of labor, a larger span of control, more hierarchical levels, and greater formalization.[7] These multiple effects are shown in Figure 17.3. Increasing size leads to more specialization of labor within a work unit, which increases the amount of differentiation among work units and the number of levels in the hierarchy, resulting in a need for more intergroup formalization. With greater specialization within the unit, there is less need for coordination within groups; thus, the span of control can be larger. Larger spans of control mean fewer first-line managers, but the need for more intergroup coordination may require more second- and third-line managers and staff personnel to coordinate them. Large organizations may therefore be more efficient because of their large spans of control and reduced administrative overhead; however, the greater differentiation among units makes the system more complex. Studies by researchers associated with the University of Aston in Birmingham, England, and others have shown similar results.[8]

Economies of scale are another advantage of large organizations. In a large operation, fixed costs—for example, plant and equipment—can be spread over more units of output, thereby reducing the cost per unit. In addition, some administrative activities such as purchasing, clerical work, and marketing can be accomplished for a large number of units at the same cost as for a small number. Their cost can then be spread over the larger number of units, again reducing unit cost.

> **FIGURE 17.3**
>
> **Impact of Large Size on Organization Structure**
>
> As organizations grow larger, their structures usually change in predictable ways. Larger organizations tend to have more complex structures, larger spans of control, and more rules and procedures.

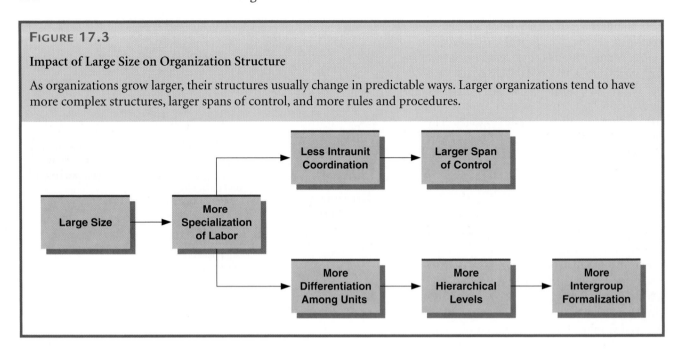

Companies such as AT&T Technologies, General Electric's Aircraft Engines products group, and S. C. Johnson & Son have gone against the conventional wisdom that larger is always better in manufacturing plants. They cite as their main reasons the smaller investment required for smaller plants, the reduced need to produce a variety of products, and the desire to decrease organizational complexity (that is, reduce the number of hierarchical levels and shorten lines of communication). In a number of instances, smaller plants have resulted in increased team spirit, improved productivity, and higher profits.[9] Other studies have found that the relationship between size and structural complexity is less clear than the Blau results indicate. These studies suggest that size must be examined in relation to the technology of the organization.[10]

Traditionally, as organizations have grown, several layers of advisory staff have been added to help coordinate the complexities inherent in any large organization. In contrast, a current trend is to cut staff throughout the organization. Known as **organizational downsizing**, this popular trend is aimed primarily at reducing the size of corporate staff and middle management to reduce costs. The results of downsizing have been mixed, with some observers noting that indiscriminate across-the-board cuts may leave the organization weak in certain key areas. Companies such as NYNEX, Eastman Kodak, Digital Equipment Corporation, and RJR Nabisco have made cutbacks with disastrous results. NYNEX Corporation, the telephone company, had to hire back hundreds of employees who had taken an early retirement program to try to build back its reputation for customer service. In addition, the New York Public Service Commission ordered NYNEX to rebate $50 million to 5 million customers because it had fallen behind in responding to problems due to its staff reductions. Eastman Kodak is paying more for contract workers who are doing the work that laid-off workers used to do. In addition, Kodak is rehiring some of those laid-off workers at increased salaries and incurring the costs of recruiting and rehiring. And Digital Equipment Corporation does not even exist anymore.

In sales, cutting costs can be disastrous. Digital Equipment Company eliminated hundreds of sales and marketing staff members because it reported losing $3 million

Organizational downsizing is a popular trend aimed at reducing the size of corporate staff and middle management to reduce costs.

per day! Customers then reported never seeing a DEC representative for months and subsequently began to use other computer equipment suppliers such as IBM and Hewlett-Packard. In fact, some of the laid-off salespeople were hired by the competitors and immediately pulled former DEC customers with them. Following a merger, RJR Nabisco decided to merge sales forces for its foods group, which handles Grey Poupon Mustard and Milkbone dog biscuits, with the Planters Life Savers Company, which makes gums, candies, and nuts. Problems arose when the lack of compatibility in product types and in outlets began to surface. Sales representatives had trouble covering the much broader array of products and selling to twice as many outlets. As a result, customers were not called on promptly, and sales suffered significantly. Initially, profit margins did improve, but the next year operating earnings fell to 25 percent of their former levels.[11]

However, positive results often include quicker decision making because fewer layers of management must approve every decision. One review of research on organizational downsizing found that it had both psychological and sociological impacts. This study suggested that in a downsizing environment, size affects organization design in very complex ways.[12]

"The dip in sales seems to coincide with the decision to eliminate the sales staff."

That becomes the common problem with downsizing: Some things just do not get done and performance of the unit can suffer. In addition, productivity of all employees can drop as they fear that they may be the next to be let go.

Technology **Organizational technology** consists of the mechanical and intellectual processes that transform raw materials into products and services for customers. For example, the primary technology employed by major oil companies transforms crude oil (input) into gasoline, motor oil, heating oil, and other petroleum-based products (outputs). Prudential Insurance uses actuarial tables and information-processing technologies to produce its insurance services. Of course, most organizations use multiple technologies. Oil companies use research and information-processing technologies in their laboratories, where new petroleum products and processes are generated.

Although there is general agreement that technology is important, the means by which this technology has been evaluated and measured have varied widely. Five approaches to examining the technology of the organization are shown in Table 17.1. For convenience, we have classified these approaches according to the names of their proponents.

In an early study of the relationship between technology and organization structure, Joan Woodward categorized manufacturing technologies by their complexity: unit or small-batch, large-batch or mass production, and continuous process.[13] Tom Burns and George Stalker proposed that the rate of change in technology determines the best method of structuring the organization.[14] Charles Perrow developed a technological continuum, with routine technologies at one end and nonroutine technologies at the other, and claimed that all organizations could be classified on his routine-to-nonroutine continuum.[15] Thompson claimed that all organizations could be classified into one of three technological categories: long-linked, mediating, and intensive.[16] Finally, a group of English researchers at the University of Aston developed three categories of technology based on the type of workflow involved: operations, material, and knowledge.[17] These perspectives on technology are somewhat

Organizational technology refers to the mechanical and intellectual processes that transform inputs into outputs.

TABLE 17.1

Summary of Approaches to Technology

Approach	Classification of Technology	Example
Woodward (1958 and 1965) (cit. no. 14)	Unit or small-batch	Customized parts made one at a time
	Large-batch or mass production	Automobile assembly line
	Continuous process	Chemical plant, petroleum refinery
Burns and Stalker (1961) (cit. no. 15)	Rate of technological change	Slow: large manufacturing; rapid: computer industry
Perrow (1967) (cit. no. 16)	Routine	Standardized products (Procter & Gamble, General Foods)
	Nonroutine	New technology products or processes (computers, telecommunications)
Thompson (1967) (cit. no. 17)	Long-linked	Assembly line
	Mediating	Bank
	Intensive	General hospital
Aston studies: Hickson, Pugh, and Pheysey (1969) (cit. no. 18)	Workflow integration; operations, materials, and knowledge technologies	Technology differs in various parts of the organization

similar in that all (except the Aston typology) address the adaptability of the technological system to change. Large-batch or mass production, routine, and long-linked technologies are not very adaptable to change. At the opposite end of the continuum, continuous-process, nonroutine, and intensive technologies are readily adaptable to change.

One major contribution of the study of organizational technology is the recognition that organizations have more than one important "technology" that enables them to accomplish their tasks. Instead of examining technology in isolation, the Aston group recognized that size and technology are related in determining organization structure.[18] They found that in smaller organizations, technology had more direct effects on the structure. In large organizations, however, they, like Blau, found that structure depended less on the operations technology and more on size considerations such as the number of employees. In large organizations, each department or division may have a different technology that determines how that department or division should be structured. In short, in small organizations the structure depended primarily on the technology, whereas in large organizations the need to coordinate complicated activities was the most important factor. Thus, both organizational size and technology are important considerations in organization design.

Global technology variations come in two forms: variations in available technology and variations in attitudes toward technology. The technology available affects how organizations can do business. Many underdeveloped countries, for example, lack electric power sources, telephones, and trucking equipment, not to mention computers and robots. A manager working in such a country must be prepared to deal with many frustrations. Some Brazilian officials convinced a U.S. company to build a high-tech plant in their country. Midway through construction, however, the government of Brazil decided it would not allow the company to import some accurate measuring instruments that it needed to produce its products. The new plant was abandoned before it opened.[19]

Build-A-Bear and . . . **TECHNOLOGY**

The High-Tech Approach to High Touch

When you walk into a Build-A-Bear Workshop (BBW) location, you immediately notice the personal touch and numerous opportunities for interaction and activity. Children select animals, then stuff and dress them. Kids place the stuffing in the clear blower tubes as a game. Staff members groom the bears and sew them up with a needle and thread. It all seems very low technology and high touch. Build-A-Bear CEO Maxine Clark says, "[The store is] the balance to high technology." Yet BBW has found a way to combine high touch with high tech.

One use of high technology is the Name Me computer, which provides games that let children customize their bear's "birth certificate." While the children think they are playing, they are in fact helping to create their own product. Another high-tech application is the insertion of sound chips into the bear during stuffing. Customers can choose from pre-recorded messages or can create their own custom sounds. Best of all, a barcode is also inserted into the bear before final stitching, allowing the toy to be reunited with its owner if it is ever lost.

The company's website has won design awards for its ease in navigation and for the imaginative children's games it provides. The website even allows customers to create a custom birthday party experience, with personalized favors and products.

Build-A-Bear has been very smart about mixing high and low tech and using technology to increase customer appeal. Chris Bryne, editor of a toy industry magazine, states, "Kids live in a technological world now, so technology alone does not impress them . . . It has to be a play experience they really love." Or as Amazon.com CEO Jeffrey P. Bezos, an advocate for online retailing, says, "The physical world is still the best medium ever invented."

> *"The physical world is still the best medium ever invented."*
>
> JEFFREY P. BEZOS, CEO, AMAZON.COM

References: "Awards, Press, Print," "Fact Sheet," "Welcome to Build-A-Bear Workshops!" Build-A-Bear website, www.buildabear.com on March 13, 2005; "Build-A-Bear Creates Value Through Organization Design," video case; Janet Ginsburg, "Xtreme Retailing," *Business Week*, December 20, 1999, www.businessweek.com on March 12, 2005 (quotation).

Attitudes toward technology also vary across cultures. Surprisingly, Japan only began to support basic research in the 1980s. For many years, the Japanese government encouraged its companies to take basic research findings discovered elsewhere (often in the United States) and figure out how to apply them to consumer products (applied research). In the mid-1980s, however, the government changed its stance and started to encourage basic research as well.[20] Most Western nations have a generally favorable attitude toward technology whereas until the 1990s, China and other Asian countries (with the exception of Japan) did not.

Despite all of the emphasis on technology's role as a primary determinant of structure, there is some support for viewing it from the perspective that the strategy and structure of the organization determine what types of technology are appropriate. For example, Wal-Mart and Dell Computers are careful to use only new information technology in ways that support their strategy and structure. Wal-Mart's information systems keep track of its inventory from receipt to shelf placement to purchase, and Dell uses technology to optimize its manufacturing processes. Because both companies started with low-tech processes and then adopted new technologies over time, the technology clearly was a result of each firm's structure and strategy, and not the other way around.[21] The *Build-a-Bear and . . . Technology* box describes how Build-a-Bear is using technology to bring the customer directly into the manufacturing process.

In a complex and dynamic environment such as the toy industry, the development of new products and re-design of existing products are very risky propositions. In addition to the influence of movies and television programs, even Barbie has a new image and has dumped poor Ken. Mattel hopes the newly redesigned "Cali Barbie" may be interested enough in Australian boogie boarder Blaine to spur sales of both dolls. Mattel's organization structure must be able to react quickly to changes in children's preferences for toys.

The **organizational environment** is everything outside an organization and includes all elements—people, other organizations, economic factors, objects, and events—that lie outside the boundaries of the organization.

The **general environment** includes the broad set of dimensions and factors within which the organization operates, including political-legal, sociocultural, technological, economic, and international factors.

Environment   The organizational environment includes all of the elements—people, other organizations, economic factors, objects, and events—that lie outside the boundaries of the organization. The environment is composed of two layers: the general environment and the task environment. The **general environment** includes all of a broad set of dimensions and factors within which the organization operates, including political-legal, social, cultural, technological, economic, and international factors. The **task environment** includes specific organizations, groups, and individuals who influence the organization. People in the task environment include customers, donors, regulators, inspectors, and shareholders. Among the organizations in the task environment are competitors, legislatures, and regulatory agencies. Economic factors in the task environment might include interest rates, international trade factors, and the unemployment rate in a particular area. Objects in the task environment include such things as buildings, vehicles, and trees. Events that may affect organizations include weather, elections, or war.

It is necessary to determine the boundaries of the organization to understand where the environment begins. These boundaries may be somewhat elusive, or at least changeable, and thus difficult to define. Many companies are spinning off some business units but then continuing to do business with them as suppliers. Therefore, one day a manager may be a member of an organization and the next day be a part of the environment of that organization. But for the most part, we can say that certain people, groups, or buildings are either in the organization or in the environment. For example, a college student shopping for a personal computer is part of the environment of HP, Dell, IBM, and other computer manufacturers. However, if the student works for one of these computer manufacturers, he or she is not part of that company's environment but is within the boundaries of the organization.

This definition of organizational environment emphasizes the expanse of the environment within which the organization operates. It may give managers the false impression that the environment is outside their control and interest. But because the environment completely encloses the organization, managers must be constantly concerned about it. Most managers these days are aware that the environment is changing rapidly. The difficulty for most is to determine how those changes affect the company.

The manager, then, faces an enormous, only vaguely specified environment that somehow affects the organization. Managing the organization within such an environment may seem like an overwhelming task. The alternatives for the manager are to (1) ignore the environment because of its complexity and focus on managing the internal operations of the company, (2) exert maximum energy in gathering information on every part of the environment and in trying to react to every environmental factor, and (3) pay attention to specific aspects of the task environment, responding only to those that most clearly affect the organization.

To ignore environmental factors entirely and focus on internal operations leaves the company in danger of missing major environmental shifts such as changes in customer preferences, technological breakthroughs, and new regulations. To expend large amounts of energy, time, and money exploring every facet of the environment may take more out of the organization than the effort may return.

The third alternative—to carefully analyze segments of the environment that most affect the organization and to respond accordingly—is the most prudent course. The issue, then, is to determine which parts of the environment should receive the manager's attention. In the remainder of this section, we examine two perspectives on the organizational environment: the analysis of environmental components and environmental uncertainty.

Forces in the environment have different effects on different companies. Hospital Corporation of America, for example, is very much influenced by government regulations and medical and scientific developments. Quite different environmental forces, on the other hand, affect McDonald's—consumer demand, disposable income, the cost of meat and bread, and gasoline prices. Thus, the task environment, the specific set of environmental forces that influence the operations of an organization, varies among organizations.

The environmental characteristic that brings together all of these different environmental influences and appears to have the most effect on the structure of the organization is uncertainty. **Environmental uncertainty** exists when managers do not have sufficient information about environmental factors, and they have difficulty predicting their impact on the organization.[22] Uncertainty has been described as resulting from complexity and dynamism in the environment. **Environmental complexity** is the number of environmental components that impinge on organizational decision making. **Environmental dynamism** is the degree to which these components change.[23] With these two dimensions, we can determine the degree of environmental uncertainty, as illustrated in Figure 17.4.

In cell 1, a low-uncertainty environment, there are few important components, and they change infrequently. A company in the cardboard container industry might have a highly certain environment when demand is steady, manufacturing processes are stable, and government regulations have remained largely unchanged.

In contrast, in cell 4, many important components are involved in decision making, and they change often. Thus, cell 4 represents a high-uncertainty environment. The banking environment is now highly uncertain. With deregulation and the advent of interstate operations, banks today must compete with insurance companies, brokerage firms, real estate firms, and even department stores. The toy industry also is in a highly uncertain environment. As they develop new toys, toy companies must stay in tune with movies, television shows, and cartoons, as well as with public sentiment. Between 1983 and 1988, Saturday morning cartoons were little more than animated stories about children's toys. Recently, however, due to the disappointing sales of many toys presented in cartoons designed to promote them, most toy companies have left the toy-based cartoon business. Many toys that are now sold are based on movies.[24]

Environmental characteristics and uncertainty have been important factors in explaining organization structure, strategy, and performance. For example, the characteristics of the environment affect how managers perceive the environment, which in turn affects how they adapt the structure of the organization to meet environmental demands.[25] The environment has also been shown to affect the degree to which a firm's strategy enhances its performance.[26] That is, a certain strategy will enhance organizational performance to the extent that it is appropriate for the environment in which the organization operates. Finally, the environment is directly related to organizational performance.[27] The environment and the organization's response to it are crucial to success.

An organization attempts to continue as a viable entity in a dynamic environment. The environment completely encloses the organization, and managers must be constantly concerned about it. The organization as a whole, as well as departments and divisions within it, is created to deal with different challenges, problems, and uncertainties. James Thompson suggested that organizations design a structure to protect the dominant technology of the organization, smooth out any problems, and keep down coordination

The task environment includes specific organizations, groups, and individuals who influence the organization.

Environmental uncertainty exists when managers have little information about environmental events and their impact on the organization.

Environmental complexity is the number of environmental components that impinge on organizational decision making.

Environmental dynamism is the degree to which environmental components that impinge on organizational decision making change.

FIGURE **17.4**

Classification of Environmental Uncertainty

This four-cell matrix describes all four levels of environmental dynamism and complexity and shows how they combine to create low or high environmental uncertainty.

Reference: Reprinted from "Characteristics of Organizational Environments and Perceived Environmental Uncertainty," by Robert B. Duncan, published in *Administrative Science Quarterly,* Sept. 1972, vol. 17, no. 3, p. 320, by permission of *Administrative Science Quarterly.* © Johnson Graduate School of Management, Cornell University.

Rate of Environmental Change

Static

Cell 1:
Low Perceived Uncertainty

1. Small number of factors and components in the environment.
2. Factors and components are somewhat similar to one another.
3. Factors and components remain basically the same.

Example: cardboard container industry

Cell 2:
Moderately Low Perceived Uncertainty

1. Large number of factors and components in the environment.
2. Factors and components are not similar to one another.
3. Factors and components remain basically the same.

Example: state universities

Dynamic

Cell 3:
Moderately High Perceived Uncertainty

1. Small number of factors and components in the environment.
2. Factors and components are somewhat similar to one another.
3. Factors and components of the environment continually change.

Example: fashion industry

Cell 4:
High Perceived Uncertainty

1. Large number of factors and components in the environment.
2. Factors and components are not similar to one another.
3. Factors and components of environment continually change.

Example: banking industry

Simple   *Complex*

Environmental Complexity

---

costs.[28] Thus, organization structures are designed to coordinate relevant technologies and protect them from outside disturbances. Structural components such as inventory, warehousing, and shipping help buffer the technology used to transform inputs into outputs. For instance, demand for products usually is cyclical or seasonal and is subject to many disturbances, but the warehouse inventory helps the manufacturing system function as if the environment accepted output at a steady rate, maximizing technological efficiency and helping the organization respond to fluctuating demands of the market.

Organizations with international operations must contend with additional levels of complexity and dynamism, both within and across cultures. Many cultures have relatively stable environments. For example, the economies of Sweden and the United States are fairly stable. Although competitive forces within each country's economic system vary, each economy remains strong. In contrast, the environments of other countries are much more dynamic. For example, France's policies on socialism versus private enterprise tend to change dramatically with each election. At present, far-reaching changes in the economic and management philosophies of most European countries make their environments far more dynamic than that of the United States.

Environments also vary widely in terms of their complexity. The Japanese culture, which is fairly stable, is also quite complex. Japanese managers are subject to an array of cultural norms and values that are far more encompassing and resistant to change than those U.S. managers face. India, too, has an extremely complex environment, which continues to be influenced by its old caste system. Although the business potential is great in China, the many environmental uncertainties faced by foreign firms who want to do business there make it a difficult proposition. Infrastructure problems, language differences, governmental regulations, inconsistent suppliers, customs issues, and irregular copyright protection make it difficult at best.[29]

Strategic Choice

The previous two sections described how structure is affected by the strategy of the organization and by the structural imperatives of size, technology, and environment. These approaches may seem to contradict each other since both approaches attempt to specify the determinants of structure. This apparent clash has been resolved by refining the strategy concept to include the role of the top management decision maker in determining the organization's structure.[30] In effect, this view inserts the manager as the decision maker who evaluates the imperatives and the organization strategy and then designs the organization structure.

The importance of the role of top management can be understood by comparing Figure 17.5 with Figure 17.2. Figure 17.5 shows structural imperatives as contextual factors within which the organization must operate and that affect the purposes and goals of the organization. The manager's choices for organization structure are affected by the organization's strategy (purposes and goals), the imperatives (contextual factors), and the manager's personal value system and experience.[31] Organizational effectiveness depends on the fit among the size, the technology, the environment, the strategies, and the structure. The Thermos Company noted new environmental conditions, reinvented its approach, and came up with an innovative new product, an electric cooking grill.[32] When Citicorp and Travelers Group merged in 1998, they installed both former CEOs as co-CEOs to run the merged company. This dual CEO arrangement dramatically affected the ways in which the new company was structured and run for several years.[33]

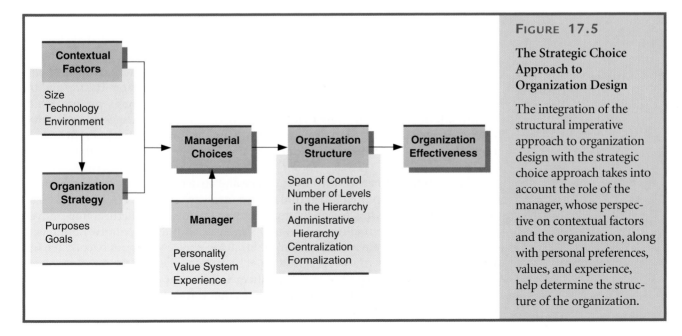

FIGURE 17.5

The Strategic Choice Approach to Organization Design

The integration of the structural imperative approach to organization design with the strategic choice approach takes into account the role of the manager, whose perspective on contextual factors and the organization, along with personal preferences, values, and experience, help determine the structure of the organization.

DaimlerChrysler and . . .

A Marriage . . . or an Abduction?

When Daimler-Benz merged with Chrysler, Daimler CEO Juergen Schrempp promised "a merger of equals." In the new organization, both Daimler and Chrysler were supposed to retain their structures and identities. On the strength of that promise, the Americans supported the merger. Yet today, Chrysler is not a true partner, but is just one of the subordinate divisions of DaimlerChrysler. So it now seems that Schrempp never meant to form an equal partnership, but instead deceived everyone, including his own managers and stockholders.

Schrempp's supporters claim he was forced to reduce Chrysler's role because of inefficiencies and poor leadership. Yet Schrempp himself has contradicted that opinion. In an interview with the *Financial Times* in 2000, Schrempp said, "The structure we have now [with Chrysler as a subordinate division] was always the structure I wanted . . . We had to go a roundabout way but it had to be done for psychological reasons. If I had gone and said Chrysler would be a division, everybody on their side would have said, 'There is no way we'll do a deal.'" After the interview, the American head of the Chrysler division was replaced by a German, leaving the eleven-person management board with just one American.

American investor Kirk Kerkorian, a large shareholder, is suing the firm for $9 billion. He claims much of his holding's value is destroyed and that if Schrempp had called the deal an acquisition, Daimler would have paid much more for his Chrysler shares. DaimlerChrysler has already settled another shareholder suit for $300 million.

Whether reducing Chrysler from a partner to a division was deliberate or not, the action has caused suffering for shareholders, customers, employees, and suppliers. "It became obvious that this was an out-and-out-takeover," writes manufacturing expert Jeffrey K. Liker. "Out the door went all of these fine [Chrysler] leaders . . . out the door went what they were trying to build."

> ### "It became obvious that this was an out-and-out-takeover."
> JEFFREY K. LIKER, MANUFACTURING EXPERT

References: "Kerkorian Sues Daimler," *CNN Money*, November 28, 2000, cnnmoney.com on March 10, 2005; Stephen Graham, "DaimlerChrysler to Trim Management," *Detroit Free Press*, February 1, 2003, www.freep.com on March 10, 2005; Danny Hakim, "You Say 'Takeover.' I Say 'Merger of Equals.'" *New York Times*, December 21, 2003, pp. BU 1, 10; Jeffrey K. Liker, "What Was Daimler Thinking?" *Across the Board*, January/February 2005, pp. 12–13.

Another perspective on the link between strategy and structure is that the relationship may be reciprocal; that is, the structure may be set up to implement the strategy, but the structure may then affect the process of decision making, influencing such matters as the centralization or decentralization of decision making and the formalization of rules and procedures.[34] Thus, strategy determines structure, which in turn affects strategic decision making. A more complex view, suggested by Herman Boschken, is that strategy is a determinant of structure and long-term performance, but only when the subunits doing the planning have the ability to do the planning well.[35]

The relationship between strategic choice and structure is actually more complicated than the concept that "structure follows strategy" conveys. However, this relationship has received less research attention than the idea of structural imperatives. And, of course, some might view strategy simply as another imperative, along with size, technology, and environment. But the strategic-choice view goes beyond the imperative perspective because it is a product of both the analyses of the imperatives and the organization's strategy. Daimler CEO Juergen Schrempp shows how the top manager has significant impact on how the organization is structured.

Organizational Designs

The previous section described several factors that determine how organizations are structured. In this section we present several different organizational designs that have been created to adapt organizations to the many contingency factors they face. We discuss mechanistic and organic structures, the sociotechnical system perspective, Mintzberg's designs, matrix designs, and virtual organizations.

Mechanistic and Organic Designs

As we discussed in the previous section, most theorists believe that organizations need to be able to adapt to changes in the technology. For example, if the rate of change in technology is slow, the most effective design is bureaucratic or, to use Burns and Stalker's term, "mechanistic." As summarized in Table 17.2, a **mechanistic structure** is primarily hierarchical in nature, interactions and communications are mostly vertical, instructions come from the boss, knowledge is concentrated at the top, and continued membership requires loyalty and obedience.

But if the technology is changing rapidly, the organization needs a structure that allows more flexibility and faster decision making so that it can react quickly to change. This design is called "organic." An **organic structure** resembles a network—interactions and communications are more lateral, knowledge resides wherever it is most useful to the organization, and membership requires a commitment to the tasks of the organization. An organic organization is generally expected to be faster at reacting to changes in the environment.

Sociotechnical Systems Designs

The foundation of the sociotechnical systems approach to organizing is systems theory, discussed in Chapter 1. There we defined a **system** as an interrelated set of elements that function as a whole. A system may have numerous subsystems, each of which, like the overall system, includes inputs, transformation processes, outputs, and feedback. An **open system** is one that interacts with its environment. A complex system is made up of numerous subsystems in which the outputs of some are the inputs to others. The **sociotechnical systems approach** views the organization as an open system structured to integrate the two important subsystems: the technical (task) subsystem and the social subsystem.

The **technical (task) subsystem** is the means by which inputs are transformed into outputs. The transformation process may take many forms. In a steel foundry, it would entail the way steel is formed, cut, drilled, chemically treated, and painted. In an insurance

A **mechanistic structure** is primarily hierarchical; interactions and communications typically are vertical, instructions come from the boss, knowledge is concentrated at the top, and loyalty and obedience are required to sustain membership.

An **organic structure** is set up like a network; interactions and communications are horizontal, knowledge resides wherever it is most useful to the organization, and membership requires a commitment to the organization's tasks.

A **system** is an interrelated set of elements that function as a whole.

An **open system** is a system that interacts with its environment.

The **sociotechnical systems approach** to organization design views the organization as an open system structured to integrate the technical and social subsystems into a single management system.

A **technical (task) subsystem** is the means by which inputs are transformed into outputs.

Characteristic	Mechanistic	Organic
Structure	Hierarchical	Network based on interests
Interactions, Communication	Primarily vertical	Lateral throughout
Work Directions, Instructions	From supervisor	Through advice, information
Knowledge, Information	Concentrated at top	Throughout
Membership, Relationship with Organization	Requires loyalty, obedience	Commitment to task, progress, expansion

TABLE 17.2

Mechanistic and Organic Organization Designs

company or financial institution, it would be the way information is processed. Often, significant scientific and engineering expertise is applied to these transformation processes to get the highest productivity at the lowest cost. For example, Fireplace Manufacturers of Santa Ana, California, a manufacturer of prefabricated metal fireplaces, implemented "just in time" (JIT) manufacturing and inventory systems to improve the productivity of its plant.[36] Under this system, component parts arrive "just in time" to be used in the manufacturing process, reducing the costs of storing them in a warehouse until they are needed. In effect, JIT redesigns the transformation process, from the introduction of raw materials to the shipping of the finished product. In three years, Fireplace Manufacturers' inventory costs dropped from $1.1 million to $750,000 while sales doubled during the same period. The transformation process usually is regarded as technologically and economically driven; that is, whatever process is most productive and costs the least is generally the most desirable.

> A **social subsystem** includes the interpersonal relationships that develop among people in organizations.

The **social subsystem** includes the interpersonal relationships that develop among people in organizations. Employees learn one another's work habits, strengths, weaknesses, and preferences while developing a sense of mutual trust. The social relationships may be manifested in personal friendships and interest groups. Communication, about both work and employees' common interests, may be enhanced by friendship or hampered by antagonistic relationships. The Hawthorne studies, conducted between 1927 and 1932 at Western Electric's Hawthorne plant near Chicago, were the first serious studies of the social subsystems in organizations.[37]

The sociotechnical systems approach was developed by members of the Tavistock Institute of England as an outgrowth of a study of coal mining. The study concerned new mining techniques that were introduced to increase productivity but failed because they entailed splitting up well-established work groups.[38] The Tavistock researchers concluded that the social subsystem had been sacrificed to the technical subsystem. Thus, improvements in the technical subsystem were not realized because of problems in the social subsystem.

> **Autonomous work groups** are used to integrate an organization's technical and social subsystems for the benefit of the larger system.

The Tavistock group proposed that an organization's technical and social subsystems could be integrated through autonomous work groups. The aim of **autonomous work groups** is to make technical and social subsystems work together for the benefit of the larger system. These groups are developed using concepts of task design, particularly job enrichment, and ideas about group interaction, supervision, and other characteristics of organization design. To structure the task, authority, and reporting relationships around work groups, organizations should delegate to the groups themselves decisions regarding job assignments, training, inspection, rewards, and punishments. Management is responsible for coordinating the groups according to the demands of the work and task environment. Autonomous work groups often evolve into self-managing teams, as was discussed in Chapter 10.

Organizations in turbulent environments tend to rely less on hierarchy and more on the coordination of work among autonomous work groups. Sociotechnical systems theory asserts that the role of management is twofold: to monitor the environmental factors that impinge on the internal operations of the organization and to coordinate the social and technical subsystems. Although the sociotechnical systems approach has not been thoroughly tested, it has been tried with some success in the General Foods plant in Topeka, Kansas; the Saab-Scania project in Sweden; and the Volvo plant in Kalmar, Sweden.[39] The development of the sociotechnical systems approach is significant in its departure from the universal approaches to organization design and in its emphasis on jointly harnessing the technical and human subsystems. The popular movements in management today include many of the principles of the sociotechnical systems design approach. The development of cross-functional teams to generate and design new products and services is a good example (see Chapter 10).

Mintzberg's Designs

In this section we describe five specific organization designs proposed by Henry Mintzberg. The universe of possible designs is large, but fortunately we can divide designs into a few basic forms. Mintzberg proposed that the purpose of organizational design was to coordinate activities, and he suggested a range of coordinating mechanisms that are found in operating organizations.[40] In Mintzberg's view, organization structure reflects how tasks are divided and then coordinated. He described five major ways in which tasks are coordinated: by mutual adjustment, by direct supervision, and by standardization of worker (or input) skills, work processes, or outputs (see Figure 17.6). These five methods can exist side by side within an organization.

Coordination by mutual adjustment (1 in Figure 17.6) simply means that workers use informal communication to coordinate with one another, whereas *coordination by direct supervision* (2 in Figure 17.6) means that a manager or supervisor coordinates the actions of workers. As noted, *standardization* may be used as a coordination mechanism in three different ways: (1) We can standardize the *input skills* (3 in Figure 17.6)—that is, the worker skills that are inputs to the work process; (2) we can standardize the *work processes* themselves (4 in Figure 17.6)—that is, the methods workers use to transform inputs into outputs; and (3) we can standardize the *outputs* (5 in Figure 17.6)—that is, the products or services or the performance levels expected of workers. Standardization usually is developed by staff analysts and enforced by management such that skills, processes, and output meet predetermined standards.

Mintzberg further suggested that the five coordinating mechanisms roughly correspond to stages of organizational development and complexity. In the very small organization, individuals working together communicate informally, achieving coordination by mutual adjustment. As more people join the organization, coordination needs

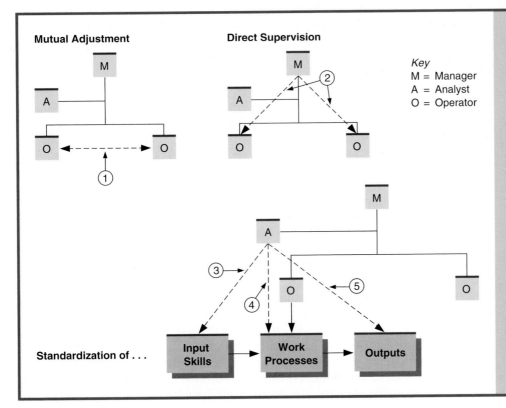

FIGURE 17.6

Mintzberg's Five Coordinating Mechanisms

Mintzberg described five methods of coordinating the actions of organizational participants. The dashed lines in each diagram show the five different means of coordination: (1) mutual adjustment, (2) direct supervision, and standardization of (3) input skills, (4) work processes, and (5) outputs.

Reference: Henry Mintzberg, *The Structuring of Organizations: A Synthesis of the Research.* © 1979, p. 4. Reprinted by permission of Prentice Hall, Inc., Englewood Cliffs, NJ.

become more complex, and direct supervision is added. For example, two or three people working in a small fast-food business can coordinate the work simply by talking to each other about the incoming orders for hamburgers, fries, and drinks. However, direct supervision becomes necessary in a larger restaurant with more complex cooking and warming equipment and several shifts of workers.

In large organizations, standardization is added to mutual adjustment and direct supervision to coordinate the work. The type of standardization depends on the nature of the work situation—that is, the organization's technology and environment. Standardization of work processes may achieve the necessary coordination when the organization's tasks are fairly routine. Thus, the larger fast-food outlet may standardize the making of hamburger patties: The meat is weighed, put into a hamburger press, and compressed into a patty. McDonald's is well known for this type of standardized process.

In other complex situations, standardization of the output may allow employees to do the work in any appropriate manner as long as the output meets specifications. Thus, the cook may not care how the hamburger is pressed, only being concerned that the right amount of meat is used and that the patty is the correct diameter and thickness. In other words, the worker may use any process as long as the output is a standard burger.

A third possibility is to coordinate work by standardizing worker skills. This approach is most often adopted in situations in which processes and outputs are difficult to standardize. In a hospital, for example, each patient must be treated as a special situation; the hospital process and output therefore cannot be standardized. Similar diagnostic and treatment procedures may be used with more than one patient, but the hospital relies on the skills of the physicians and nurses, which are standardized through their professional training, to coordinate the work. Organizations may have to depend on workers' mutual adjustment to coordinate their own actions in the most complex work situations or when the most important elements of coordination are the workers' professional training and communication skills. In effect, mutual adjustment can be an appropriate coordinating mechanism in both the simplest and the most complex situations. Analysis of the success of McDonald's shows that some part of its success is due to the degree of standardization.

Mintzberg pointed out that the five methods of coordination could be combined with the basic components of structure to develop five structural forms: the simple structure, the machine bureaucracy, the professional bureaucracy, the divisionalized form, and the adhocracy. Mintzberg called these structures pure or ideal types of designs.

Simple Structure   The simple structure characterizes relatively small, usually young organizations in a simple, dynamic environment. The organization has little specialization and formalization, and its overall structure is organic. Power and decision making are concentrated in the chief executive, often also the owner-manager, and the flow of authority is from the top down. The primary coordinating mechanism is direct supervision. The organization must adapt quickly to survive because of its dynamic and often hostile environment. Most small businesses—a car dealership, a locally owned retail clothing store, or a candy manufacturer with only regional distribution—have a simple structure.

Machine Bureaucracy   The machine bureaucracy is typical of large, well-established companies in simple, stable environments. Work is highly specialized and formalized, and decision making is usually concentrated at the top. Standardization of work processes is the primary coordinating mechanism. This highly bureaucratic

The **simple structure**, typical of relatively small or new organizations, has little specialization or formalization; power and decision making are concentrated in the chief executive.

In **machine bureaucracy**, which typifies large, well-established organizations, work is highly specialized and formalized, and decision making is usually concentrated at the top.

structure does not have to adapt quickly to changes because the environment is both simple and stable. Examples include large mass-production firms such as Container Corporation of America, some automobile companies, and providers of services to mass markets, such as insurance companies.

Professional Bureaucracy

Professional Bureaucracy Usually found in a complex and stable environment, the **professional bureaucracy** relies on standardization of skills as the primary means of coordination. There is much horizontal specialization by professional areas of expertise but little formalization. Decision making is decentralized and takes place where the expertise is. The only means of coordination available to the organization is standardization of skills—those of the professionally trained employees.

Although it lacks centralization, the professional bureaucracy stabilizes and controls its tasks with rules and procedures developed in the relevant profession. Hospitals, universities, and consulting firms are examples.

A **professional bureaucracy** is characterized by horizontal specialization by professional areas of expertise, little formalization, and decentralized decision making.

Divisionalized Form

Divisionalized Form The **divisionalized form** is characteristic of old, very large firms operating in a relatively simple, stable environment with several diverse markets. It resembles the machine bureaucracy except that it is divided according to the various markets it serves. There is some horizontal and vertical specialization between the divisions (each defined by a market) and headquarters. Decision making is clearly split between headquarters and the divisions, and the primary means of coordination is standardization of outputs. The mechanism of control required by headquarters encourages the development of machine bureaucracies in the divisions.

The classic example of the divisionalized form is General Motors, which, in a reorganization in the 1920s, adopted a design that created divisions for each major car model.[41] Although the divisions have been reorganized and the cars changed several

The **divisionalized form**, typical of old, very large organizations, is divided according to the different markets served; horizontal and vertical specialization exists between divisions and headquarters, decision making is divided between headquarters and divisions, and outputs are standardized.

This dog is wearing the latest in specialty doggie wear, Doggles, created by Roni and Ken DiLullo for their pet MidKnight. Not just providing protection from the sun, these anti-UVA doggie goggles can protect dogs' eyes from external materials following surgery or from harmful debris when searching building explosions or natural disasters. This small million-dollar company has a very simple structure composed of the DiLullos, who primarily do marketing and distribution of the Doggles, while the product is manufactured in Asia.

times, the concept of the divisionalized organization is still very evident at GM.[42] General Electric uses a two-tiered divisionalized structure, dividing its numerous businesses into strategic business units, which are then further divided into sectors.[43]

Adhocracy   The **adhocracy** is typically found in young organizations engaged in highly technical fields in which the environment is complex and dynamic. Decision making is spread throughout the organization, and power is in the hands of experts. There is horizontal and vertical specialization but little formalization, resulting in a very organic structure. Coordination is by mutual adjustment through frequent personal communication and liaison. Specialists are not grouped together in functional units but are instead deployed into specialized market-oriented project teams.

In an **adhocracy**, typically found in young organizations in highly technical fields, decision making is spread throughout the organization, power resides with the experts, horizontal and vertical specialization exists, and there is little formalization.

The typical adhocracy is usually established to foster innovation, something to which the other four types of structures are not particularly well suited. Numerous U.S. organizations—Johnson & Johnson, Procter & Gamble, Monsanto, and 3M, for example—are known for their innovation and constant stream of new products.[44] These organizations are either structured totally as adhocracies or have large divisions set up as adhocracies. Johnson & Johnson established a new-products division over thirty years ago to encourage continued innovation, creativity, and risk taking. The division continues to succeed; Johnson & Johnson in the United States has introduced more than two hundred new products in the past several years. The majority of the start-up "dot-com" companies were most likely structured as adhocracies.

Mintzberg believed that fit among parts is the most important consideration in designing an organization. Not only must there be a fit among the structure, the structural imperatives (technology, size, and environment), and organizational strategy, but the components of structure (rules and procedures, decision making, specialization) must also fit together and be appropriate for the situation. Mintzberg suggested that an organization could not function effectively when these characteristics are not put together properly.[45]

Matrix Organization Design

One other organizational form deserves attention here: the matrix organization design. Matrix design is consistent with the contingency approach because it is useful only in certain situations. One of the earliest implementations of the matrix design was at TRW Systems Group in 1959.[46] Following TRW's lead, other firms in aerospace and high-technology fields created similar matrix structures.

The matrix design combines two different designs to gain the benefits of each; typically combined are a product or project departmentalization scheme and a functional structure.

The **matrix design** attempts to combine two different designs to gain the benefits of each. The most common matrix form superimposes product or project departmentalization on a functional structure (see Figure 17.7). Each department and project has a manager; each employee, however, is a member of both a functional department and a project team. The dual role means that the employee has two supervisors, the department manager and the project leader.

A matrix structure is appropriate when three conditions exist:

1. There is external pressure for a dual focus, meaning that factors in the environment require the organization to focus its efforts equally on responding to multiple external factors and on internal operations.
2. There is pressure for a high information-processing capacity.
3. There is pressure for shared resources.[47]

In the aerospace industry in the early 1960s, all these conditions were present. Private companies had a dual focus: their customers, primarily the federal government,

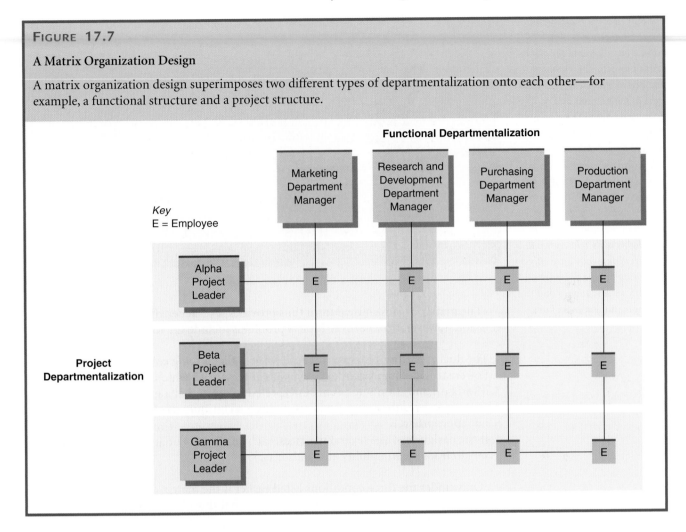

FIGURE **17.7**

A Matrix Organization Design

A matrix organization design superimposes two different types of departmentalization onto each other—for example, a functional structure and a project structure.

and the complex engineering and technical fields in which they were engaged. Moreover, the environments of these companies were changing very rapidly. Technological sophistication and competition were increasing, resulting in growing environmental uncertainty and an added need for information processing. The final condition stemmed from the pressure on the companies to excel in a very competitive environment despite limited resources. The companies concluded that it was inefficient to assign their highly professional—and highly compensated—scientific and engineering personnel to just one project at a time.

Built into the matrix structure is the capacity for flexible and coordinated responses to internal and external pressures. Members can be reassigned from one project to another as demands for their skills change. They may work for a month on one project, be assigned to the functional home department for two weeks, and then be reassigned to another project for the next six months. The matrix form improves project coordination by assigning project responsibility to a single leader rather than dividing it among several functional department heads. Furthermore, it improves communication because employees can talk about the project with members of both the project team and the functional unit to which they belong. In this way, solutions to project problems may emerge from either group. Many different types of organizations have used the matrix form of organization, notably large-project manufacturing firms, banks, and hospitals.[48]

The Star Alliance is an alliance of sixteen different commercial airlines based around the globe. While the airlines remain separate and independent, they cooperate in reservations and ticketing and code share many flights. The result is they bring business to each other and provide global service to their clients. A single flight might have passengers with tickets from two or three different cooperating airlines in the alliance. This allows flights to fly relatively full, yet each airline may have only a third or half of the passengers. The airlines save money and passengers can get lower fares.

The matrix organizational form thus provides several benefits for the organization. It is not, however, trouble-free. Typical problems include the following:

1. The dual reporting system may cause role conflict among employees.
2. Power struggles may occur over who has authority on which issues.
3. Matrix organization often is misinterpreted to mean that a group must make all decisions; as a result, group decision-making techniques may be used when they are not appropriate.
4. If the design involves several matrices, each laid on top of another, there may be no way to trace accountability and authority.[49]

Only under the three conditions listed earlier is the matrix design likely to work. In any case, it is a complex organizational system that must be carefully coordinated and managed to be effective.

Virtual Organizations

Some companies do one or two things very well, such as sell to government clients, but struggle with most others, such as manufacturing products with very tight precision. Other companies might be great at close-tolerance manufacturing but lousy at reaching out to certain types of clients. What is needed is some way for those two organizations to get together to utilize each other's strengths, yet still retain their independence. They can, and many are doing so in what are called "virtual organizations."

A **virtual organization** is a temporary alliance between two or more organizations that band together to accomplish a specific venture. Each partner contributes to the partnership what it does best. The opportunity is usually something that needs a quick response to maximize the market opportunity. A slow response will probably result in losses. Therefore, a virtual organization allows different organizations to bring their best capabilities together without worrying about learning how to do something that they have never done before. Thus, the reaction time is faster, mistakes are fewer, and profits are quicker. Sharing of information among partners is usually facilitated by electronic technology such as computers, faxes, and electronic mail systems, thereby avoiding the expenses of renting new office space for the venture or costly travel time between companies.

A **virtual organization** is a temporary alliance between two or more organizations that band together to undertake a specific venture.

There are no restrictions on how large or small organizations or projects need to be to take advantage of this type of alliance. In fact, some very small organizations are working together quite well. In Phoenix, Arizona, a public relations firm, a graphic design firm, and a management consulting firm are working together on projects that have multiple requirements beyond those offered by any single firm. Rather than turn down the business or try to hire additional staff to do the extra work, the three firms work together to better serve client needs. The clients like the arrangement because they get high-quality work and do not have to shop around for someone to do little pieces of work. The networking companies feel that the result is better creativity, more teamwork, more efficient use of resources, and better service for their clients.

More typically, however, large companies create virtual organizations. Corning is involved in nineteen partnerships on many different types of projects, and it is pleased with most of its ventures and plans to do more. Intel worked with two Japanese organizations to manufacture flash memory chips for computers. One of the Japanese companies was not able to complete its part of the project, leaving Intel with a major product-delivery problem. Intel's chairman at the time, Andrew Grove, was not too happy about that venture and may not participate in others.[50]

The virtual organization is not just another management fad. It has become one way to deal with the rapid changes brought about by evolving technology and global competition. Management scholars have mixed opinions on the effectiveness of such arrangements. Although it may seem odd, this approach can produce substantial benefits in some situations.

Contemporary Organization Design

The current proliferation of design theories and alternative forms of organization gives practicing managers a dizzying array of choices. The task of the manager or organization designer is to examine the firm and its situation and to design a form of organization that meets its needs. A partial list of contemporary alternatives includes such approaches as downsizing, rightsizing, reengineering the organization, team-based organizations, and the virtual organization. These approaches often make use of total quality management, employee empowerment, employee involvement and participation, reduction in force, process innovation, and networks of alliances. Practicing managers must deal with the new terminology, the temptation to treat such new approaches as fads, and their own organizational situation before making major organization design shifts. In this section we describe two currently popular approaches—reengineering and rethinking the organization—as well as global organization structure and design issues. We conclude with a summary of the dominant themes in contemporary organization design.

Reengineering the Organization

Reengineering is the radical redesign of organizational processes to achieve major gains in cost, time, and provision of services. It forces the organization to start from scratch to redesign itself around its most important, or core, processes rather than beginning with its current form and making incremental changes. It assumes that if a company had no existing structure, departments, jobs, rules, or established ways of doing things, reengineering would design the organization as it should be for future success. The process starts with determining what the customers actually want from the organization and then developing a strategy to provide it. Once the strategy is in place, strong leadership from top management creates teams of people to design an organiza-

Reengineering is the radical redesign of organizational processes to achieve major gains in cost, time, and provision of services.

tional system to achieve the strategy.[51] The aim of reengineering is to fundamentally change the way everybody in the organization conceives his or her role. Rather than view their role as a position in a hierarchy, reengineering creates a horizontal flow of teams that focus on core processes that deliver the product or service. Throughout a decade of reengineering, the forces of change have been intensified by information technology—the Internet—that has accelerated all of these processes. This has led to what some have called "X-engineering," which takes these same reengineering processes across organizational boundaries, searching for new efficiencies from suppliers to distributors.[52]

Rethinking the Organization

Rethinking the organization means looking at organization design in totally different ways, perhaps even abandoning the classic view of the organization as a pyramid.

Also currently popular is the concept of rethinking the organization. **Rethinking** the organization is also a process for restructuring that throws out traditional assumptions that organizations should be structured with boxes and horizontal and vertical lines. Robert Tomasko makes some suggestions for new organizational forms for the future.[53] He suggests that the traditional pyramid shape of organizations may be inappropriate for current business practices. Traditional structures, he contends, may have too many levels of management arranged in a hierarchy to be efficient and to respond to dynamic changes in the environment.

Rethinking organizations might entail thinking of the organization structure as a dome rather than a pyramid, the dome being top management, which acts as an umbrella, covering and protecting those underneath but also leaving them alone to do their work. Internal units underneath the dome would have the flexibility to interact with each other and with environmental forces. Companies such as Microsoft Corporation and Royal Dutch Petroleum have some of the characteristics of this dome approach to organization design. American Express Financial Advisors restructured from a vertical organization into a horizontal organization as a result of its rethinking everything about the ways it needed to meet customers' needs.[54]

Global Organization Structure and Design Issues

Managers working in an international environment must consider not only similarities and differences among firms in different cultures but also the structural features of multinational organizations.

Between-Culture Issues   "Between-culture issues" are variations in the structure and design of companies operating in different cultures. As might be expected, such companies have both differences and similarities. For example, one study compared the structures of fifty-five U.S. and fifty-one Japanese manufacturing plants. Results suggested that the Japanese plants had less specialization, more "formal" centralization (but less "real" centralization), and taller hierarchies than their U.S. counterparts. The Japanese structures were also less affected by their technology than the U.S. plants.[55]

Many cultures still take a traditional view of organization structure not unlike the approaches used in this country during the days of classical organization theory. For example, Tom Peters, a leading U.S. management consultant and coauthor of *In Search of Excellence*, spent some time lecturing to managers in China. They were not interested in his ideas about decentralization and worker participation, however. Instead, the most frequently asked question concerned how a manager determined the optimal span of control.[56]

In contrast, many European companies are increasingly patterning themselves after successful U.S. firms, a move stemming in part from corporate raiders in Europe emulating their U.S. counterparts and partly from the managerial workforce becoming better educated. Together, these two factors have caused many European firms to become less centralized and to adopt divisional structures by moving from functional to product departmentalization.[57]

Multinational Organization More and more firms have entered the international arena and have found it necessary to adapt their designs to better cope with different cultures.[58] For example, after a company has achieved a moderate level of international activity, it often establishes an international division, usually at the same organizational level as other major functional divisions. Levi-Strauss uses this organization design. One division, Levi-Strauss International, is responsible for the company's business activities in Europe, Canada, Latin America, and Asia.

For an organization that has become more deeply involved in international activities, a logical form of organization design is the international matrix. This type of matrix arrays product managers across the top. Project teams headed by foreign-market managers cut across the product departments. A company with three basic product lines, for example, might establish three product departments (of course, it would include domestic advertising, finance, and operations departments as well). Foreign-market managers can be designated for, say, Canada, Japan, Europe, Latin America, and Australia. Each foreign-market manager is then responsible for all three of the company's products in his or her market.[59]

Finally, at the most advanced level of multinational activity, a firm might become an international conglomerate. Nestlé and Unilever N.V. fit this type. Each has an international headquarters (Nestlé in Vevey, Switzerland, and Unilever in Rotterdam, the Netherlands) that coordinates the activities of businesses scattered around the globe. Nestlé has factories in fifty countries and markets its products in virtually every country in the world. Over 96 percent of its business is done outside of Switzerland, and only about 7,000 of its 160,000 employees reside in its home country.

Dominant Themes of Contemporary Designs

The four dominant themes of current design strategies are (1) the effects of technological and environmental change, (2) the importance of people, (3) the necessity of staying in touch with the customer, and (4) the global organization. Technology and the environment are changing so fast and in so many unpredictable ways that no organization structure will be appropriate for long. The changes in electronic information processing, transmission, and retrieval alone are so vast that employee relationships, information distribution, and task coordination need to be reviewed almost daily.[60] The emphasis on productivity through people that was energized by Thomas Peters and Robert Waterman Jr. in the 1980s continues in almost every aspect of contemporary organization design.[61] In addition, Peters and Nancy Austin further emphasized the importance of staying in touch with customers at the initial stage in organization design.[62] Superimposed over these four dominant themes are the rapid changes in technology, competition, and globalization. Organizations must be adaptive to new circumstances in order to survive.[63]

These popular contemporary approaches and the four dominant factors argue for a contingency design perspective. Unfortunately, there is no "one best way." Managers must consider the impact of multiple factors—sociotechnical systems, strategy, the structural imperatives, changing information technology, people, global considerations, and a concern for end users—on their particular organization and design the organization structure accordingly.

Chapter Review

Synopsis

Universal approaches to organization design attempt to specify the one best way to structure organizations for effectiveness. Contingency approaches, on the other hand, propose that the best way to design organization structure depends on a variety of factors. Important contingency approaches to organization design center on the organizational strategy, the determinants of structure, and strategic choice.

Initially, strategy was seen as the determinant of structure: The structure of the organization was designed to implement its purpose, goals, and strategies. Taking managerial choice into account in determining organization structure is a modification of this view. The manager designs the structure to accomplish organizational goals, guided by an analysis of the contextual factors, the strategies of the organization, and personal preferences.

The structural imperatives are size, technology, and environment. In general, large organizations have more complex structures and usually more than one technology. The structures of small organizations, on the other hand, may be dominated by one core operations technology. The structure of the organization is also established to fit with the environmental demands and buffer the core operating technology from environmental changes and uncertainties.

Organization designs can take many forms. A mechanistic structure relies on the administrative hierarchy for communication and directing activities. An organic design is structured like a network; communications and interactions are horizontal and diagonal across groups and teams throughout the organization.

In the sociotechnical systems view, the organization is an open system structured to integrate two important subsystems: the technical (task) subsystem and the social subsystem. According to this approach, organizations should structure the task, authority, and reporting relationships around the work group, delegating to the group decisions on job assignments, training, inspection, rewards, and punishments. The task of management is to monitor the environment and coordinate the structures, rules, and procedures.

Mintzberg's ideal types of organization design were derived from a framework of coordinating mechanisms. The five types are simple structure, machine bureaucracy, professional bureaucracy, divisionalized form, and adhocracy. Most organizations have some characteristics of each type, but one is likely to predominate. Mintzberg believed that the most important consideration in designing an organization is the fit among parts of the organization.

The matrix design combines two types of structure (usually functional and project departmentalization) to gain the benefits of each. It usually results in a multiple command and authority system. Benefits of the matrix form include increased flexibility, cooperation, and communication and better use of skilled personnel. Typical problems are associated with the dual reporting system and the complex management system needed to coordinate work.

Virtual organizations are temporary alliances between several organizations that agree to work together on a specific venture. Reaction time to business opportunities can be very fast with these types of alliances. In effect, organizations create a network of other organizations to enable them to respond to changes in the environment.

Contemporary organization design is contingency oriented. Currently popular design strategies are reengineering the organization and rethinking the organization. Four factors influencing design decisions are the changing technological environment, concern for people as valued resources, the need to keep in touch with customers, and global impacts on organizations.

Discussion Questions

1. What are the differences between universal approaches and contingency approaches to organization design?

2. Define "organizational environment" and "organizational technology." In what ways do these concepts overlap?

3. Identify and describe some of the environmental and technological factors that affect your college or university. Give specific examples of how they affect you as a student.

4. How does organization design usually differ for large and small organizations?

5. What might be the advantages and disadvantages of structuring the faculty members at your college or university as an autonomous work group?

6. What do you think are the purposes, goals, and strategies of your college or university? How are they reflected in its structure?

7. Which of Mintzberg's pure forms is best illustrated by a major national political party (Democratic or Republican)? A religious organization? A football team? The U.S. Olympic Committee?

8. In a matrix organization, would you rather be a project leader, a functional department head, or a highly trained technical specialist? Why?

9. Discuss what you think the important design considerations will be for organization designers in the year 2020.

10. How would your college or university be different if you rethought or reengineered the way in which it is designed?

Studying a Real Organization

Purpose: This exercise will help you understand the factors that determine the design of organizations.

Format: You will interview at least five employees in different parts of the college or university that you attend or employees of a small- to medium-sized organization and analyze the reasons for its design. (You may want to coordinate this exercise with the "Experiencing Organizational Behavior" exercise in Chapter 16.)

Procedure: If you use a local organization, your first task is to find one with between fifty and five hundred employees. (It should not be part of your college or university.) If you did the exercise for Chapter 16, you can use the same company for this exercise. The organization should have more than two hierarchical levels, but it should not be too complex to understand with a short period of study. You may want to check with your professor before contacting the company. Your initial contact should be with the highest-ranking manager you can reach. Make sure that top management is aware of your project and gives its approval.

If you use your local college or university, you could talk to professors, secretaries, and other administrative staff in the admissions office, student services department, athletic department, library, and many others. Be sure to include employees from a variety of jobs and levels in your interviews.

Using the material in this chapter, you will interview employees to obtain the following information on the structure of the organization:

1. What is the organization in business to do? What are its goals and its strategies for achieving them?

2. How large is the company? What is the total number of employees? How many work full-time? How many work part-time?

3. What are the most important components of the organization's environment?

4. Is the number of important environmental components large or small?

5. How quickly or slowly do these components change?

6. Would you characterize the organization's environment as certain, uncertain, or somewhere in between? If in between, describe approximately how certain or uncertain.

7. What is the organization's dominant technology; that is, how does it transform inputs into outputs?

8. How rigid is the company in its application of rules and procedures? Is it flexible enough to respond to environmental changes?

9. How involved are employees in the daily decision making related to their jobs?

10. What methods are used to ensure control over the actions of employees?

Interview at least five employees of the college or company at different levels and in different departments.

One should hold a top-level position. Be sure to ask the questions in a way the employees will understand; they may not be familiar with some of the terminology used in this chapter.

The result of the exercise should be a report describing the technology, environment, and structure of the company. You should discuss the extent to which the structure is appropriate for the organization's strategy, size, technology, and environment. If it does not seem appropriate, you should explain the reasons. If you also used this company for the exercise in Chapter 16, you can comment further on the organization chart and its appropriateness for the company. You may want to send a copy of your report to the cooperating company.

Follow-up Questions

1. Which aspects of strategy, size, environment, and technology were the most difficult to obtain information about? Why?

2. If there were differences in the responses of the employees you interviewed, how do you account for them?

3. If you were the president of the organization you analyzed, would you structure it in the same way? Why or why not? If not, how would you structure it differently?

4. How did your answers to questions 2 and 3 differ from those in the exercise in Chapter 16?

Self-Assessment Exercise

Diagnosing Organization Structure

Introduction: You are probably involved with many different organizations—the place you work, a social or service club, a church, the college or university you attend. This assessment will help you diagnose the structure of one of those organizations. You could use this assessment on the organization that you analyzed in the preceding "Experiencing Organizational Behavior" exercise.

Instructions: First, pick one of the organizations you belong to or know a lot about. Then read each of the following statements and determine the degree to which you agree or disagree with that statement about your organization by using the following scale.

5	4	3	2	1
Strongly Agree	Agree	Don't know	Disagree	Strongly Disagree

Then place the number of the response that best represents your organization in the space before each statement.

_____ 1. If people believe that they have the right approach to carrying out their job, they can usually go ahead without checking with their superior.

_____ 2. People in this organization don't always have to wait for orders from their superiors on important matters.

_____ 3. People in this organization share ideas with their superior.

_____ 4. Different individuals play important roles in making decisions.

_____ 5. People in this organization are likely to express their feelings openly on important matters.

_____ 6. People in this organization are encouraged to speak their minds on important matters, even if it means disagreeing with their superior.

_____ 7. Talking to other people about the problems someone might have in making decisions is an important part of the decision-making process.

_____ 8. Developing employees' talents and abilities is a major concern of this organization.

_____ 9. People are encouraged to make suggestions before decisions are made.

_____10. In this organization, most people can have their point of view heard.

_____ 11. Superiors often seek advice from subordinates before making decisions.

_____ 12. Subordinates play an active role in running this organization.

_____ 13. For many decisions, the rules and regulations are developed as we go along.

_____ 14. It is not always necessary to go through channels in dealing with important matters.

_____ 15. Employees do not consistently follow the same rules and regulations.

_____ 16. There are few rules and regulations for handling any kind of problem that may arise in making most decisions.

_____ 17. People from different departments are often put together in task forces to solve important problems.

_____ 18. For special problems, we usually set up a temporary task force until we meet our objectives.

_____ 19. Jobs in this organization are not clearly defined.

_____ 20. In this organization, adapting to changes in the environment is important.

_____ = Total Score

When you have finished, add up the numbers to get a total score. Your instructor can help you interpret your scores by referring to the _Instructor's Resource Manual._

Reference: From Ricky W. Griffin, _Management,_ 5/e, which is adapted from Robert T. Keller, _Type of Management System._ Griffin copyright © 1996 by Houghton Mifflin Company. Keller copyright © 1988. Used by permission of Houghton Mifflin Company and Robert T. Keller.

Building Managerial Skills

Exercise Overview: When organizations utilize a matrix organizational structure (see Figure 17.7), every employee and manager in the system has dual reporting relationships, a situation that puts additional pressure on the managerial skills of everybody in the system. This exercise provides you with an opportunity to analyze some of the managerial requirements for success in a matrix organizational structure.

Exercise Background: The matrix organizational structure was initially established to overcome the inadequacies of traditional structures when the environment and technology of certain organizations required additional information-processing capabilities. It has been hailed as a great innovation in certain situations, but it has also caused some problems when utilized in other organizations.

Exercise Task: Working alone, look again at the managerial roles and critical managerial skills described in Chapter 2. See if you can describe how each of these managerial roles and skills is affected when an organization uses a matrix structure. Go through each role and each skill, first listing each one along with a simple one-sentence description. Then, reread the section on matrix organizations in this chapter and write a description of the roles and skills required of managers in a matrix structure.

Exchange papers with a classmate or share papers in a small group. Make notes about how others saw the roles and skills differently than you did. Discuss the differences and similarities that you find.

Conclude by addressing the following questions:

1. To what extent does the matrix organization structure put additional pressure on managers?

2. What should organizations using a matrix structure do to help their managers be prepared for those additional pressures?

3. Would you like to work in a matrix organizational structure? Why or why not?

Organizational Behavior
Case For Discussion

The Right Structure for Build-A-Bear Workshop

In 1995, Maxine Clark resigned from the presidency of Payless ShoeSource. She left the chain of 4,500 stores to start up a new kind of retail firm, Build-A-Bear Workshop. "My ability to connect with people wasn't being tapped," Clark says. "I wanted to . . . make retailing fun again." She has certainly succeeded. Today, Build-A-Bear Workshop (BBW) operates 170 stores in the U.S. and Canada, is franchising in Japan and Korea, and opens thirty new stores each year.

BBW is based on a unique retailing concept. Clark claims, "We don't think of ourselves as a toy company. We sell an experience." Kids of all ages choose a pre-sewn animal body, have it stuffed, and complete it with sounds, grooming, clothes, and accessories. The entire store is designed to create maximum opportunities for interaction between customers and staff. Store visitors are given lavish personal attention. Children enjoy the atmosphere of wacky, kid-friendly fun, and customers also appreciate the opportunity to customize the product.

Build-A-Bear is at the forefront of a trend toward customization, interaction, and entertainment in retailing. For example, popular "skater" shoe company Vans has added a skate park to a Los Angeles store. Gibson Guitar allows clients to watch their custom instruments being built. Bass Pro Shops has trout ponds and aquariums at some locations. Lands' End online clothing retailer allows customers to order pants and shirts tailored to their exact body measurements. "Build-A-Bear is a new type of toy store where there's interactivity. Kids love differentiation. They like to have something that's their own," says Jim Silver, toy industry expert.

In the retailing industry, personal service and customization are necessary to counteract "the Wal-Mart" problem, according to Clark. Wal-Mart's low prices have allowed the firm to dominate retailing for more than a decade, yet many customers are now yearning for a different type of retail experience and are willing to pay more to get it. "We're so opposite from [Wal-Mart]," says Clark. "We're not about price."

Build-A-Bear Workshop is a mid-sized retail chain and is rapidly growing, both in the United States and abroad. Therefore, the organization structure needs to be flexible, to accommodate change. At the same time, the organization needs to emphasize standardization, to gain the efficiencies that can come with larger size.

BBW uses small-batch technology—virtually every product is one of a kind. This too, has an effect on organization structure, causing the firm to adopt a flexible structure with a need for close coordination between units and individuals. Finally, BBW faces a fairly high level of environmental uncertainty, with constantly changing customer tastes being the most dynamic element. Many "hot" toy concepts, for example, have suffered dramatic drops in sales after the fad cools off. High uncertainty also mandates an organization structure that has lots of flexibility and need for coordination.

It comes as no surprise, then, that Build-A-Bear Workshop uses an organization structure that is relatively organic. Sales associates, due to their constant interaction with the customers, are a valuable source of information and expertise for the firm. Relationships are relatively informal and information sharing occurs laterally as well as vertically. Everyone in the firm is encouraged and expected to be creative, to suggest improvements, to independently resolve problems within their units, and to participate in making important decisions. In addition, the work environment is fun and relaxed.

Build-A-Bear Workshop uses a simple structure, which is appropriate for a young, small, and growing company, headed by a powerful and effective owner-manager. Again, the simple structure maximizes flexibility, open communication, informality, interaction with customers, and creativity.

Build-A-Bear is continuing to creatively expand the business, licensing BBW-brand clothing, books, and home décor. The firm is also experimenting with non-traditional locations, for example, at the Philadelphia Phillies' baseball park, where customers purchase Major League Baseball merchandise for their bears. Some experts fear that BBW, like any specialty retailer, may be a passing fad or limited in growth beyond their specialty niche. Clark, however, has an answer. "Stuffed animals . . . are one of the most difficult to merchandise . . . They usually get thrown on the shelves," she says. "But I think each shopper is looking for something that appeals to them personally and connects with them, and Build-A-Bear is about connection."

Case Questions

> **❝** *We don't think of ourselves as a toy company. We sell an experience.* **❞**
> *MAXINE CLARK, CEO AND FOUNDER,*
> *BUILD-A-BEAR WORKSHOP*

1. Which type of standardization (work processes, output, or worker skills, as described by Mintzberg) should Build-A-Bear Workshop use, and why?

2. There are a number of possible factors that influence the choice of an organization structure. Consider BBW's situation. Do the various factors lead BBW to choose compatible strategies, or do the various influences lead the firm in several different directions as they choose a structure? What effect does this level of agreement or disagreement have on the firm?

3. In your opinion, what will BBW's structure look like after more growth, say, in five to ten years? What factors will lead to the changes you expect?

References: David Barry, "Exit Strategies," *Fast Company*, April 2000, www.fastcompany.com on March 12, 2005; Janet Ginsburg, "Xtreme Retailing," *Business Week*, December 20, 1999, www.businessweek.com on March 12, 2005; Olga Kharif, "Of Mice, Men, and Baby Bears," *Business Week*, December 17, 2004, www.businessweek.com on March 12, 2005; Lawrence Meyers, "Build-A-Bear Gets Stuffed," *Motley Fool*, March 8, 2005, biz.yahoo.com on March 12, 2005; Angela Moore, "Build-A-Bear Builds on the Basics," *Reuters*, March 5, 2005, news.yahoo.com on March 12, 2005 (quotation); Ian Ritter, "Build-A-Bear's Maxine Clark," *Globe Street Retailing*, March 7, 2005, www.globest.com on March 12, 2005; Amey Stone, "In Toytown, a New Set of Rules," *Business Week*, December 20, 2004, www.businessweek.com on March 12, 2005.

TEST PREPPER

You have read the chapter and studied the key terms. Think you're ready to ace the exam? Take this sample test to gauge your comprehension of chapter material and check your answers at the back of the book. Want more test questions? Take the ACE quizzes found on the student website: http://college.hmco.com/business/students/ (select Griffin/Moorhead, Organizational Behavior, 8e from the Management menu).

T F 1. A universal approach considers all the different ways a manager might approach a particular situation.

T F 2. Organizational downsizing usually reduces the size of corporate staff and middle management.

T F 3. Uncertainty in the environment results from the complexity of the environment and the degree to which environmental components change.

T F 4. The technical subsystem in a university is the means by which new freshmen students are turned into graduating seniors.

T F 5. Professional bureaucracies are usually found in simple but rapidly changing environments.

T F 6. The virtual organization appears to be another management fad—its popularity will likely wane in the coming years.

T F 7. Nestlé is an example of a firm that has successfully maintained exclusively domestic operations—in this case, in Switzerland.

8. The contingency factors that affect organizational design include all of the following except
   a. the environment.
   b. the organization's technology.
   c. the organization's structure.
   d. the social system within which the organization operates.
   e. the organization's size.

9. Amanda works in a larger firm than Bruce. Based on what you know about organizational size, which of the following is true?
   a. Bruce's firm will be larger than Amanda's.
   b. Bruce's firm will be more specialized than Amanda's.
   c. Amanda's firm will be less formalized than Bruce's.
   d. Span of control will be larger in Amanda's firm.
   e. Differentiation will be greater in Bruce's firm.

10. In large organizations the need to coordinate complicated activities is the most important factor in determining the firm's structure. In small organizations, the most important factor is
    a. strategy.
    b. technology.
    c. culture.
    d. environment.
    e. size.

11. Structural components such as inventory, warehousing, and shipping help buffer an organization's technology from
    a. the effects of organizational size.
    b. environmental disturbances.
    c. the effects of organizational strategy.
    d. interpersonal conflicts among managers.
    e. interpersonal conflict between managers and subordinates.

12. Thomas is a manager in a very small organization. Which of the following mechanisms would Thomas most likely use to coordinate employees efforts?
    a. Standardized input skills
    b. Standardized work processes
    c. Mutual adjustment
    d. Direct supervision
    e. Contingency design

13. The best design that is best suited to foster innovation is the
    a. simple structure.
    b. professional bureaucracy.
    c. divisionalized form.
    d. machine bureaucracy.
    e. adhocracy.

14. For years, Steven's company has lagged behind the competition. Steven has decided to adopt the reengineering approach and completely redesign organizational processes. His first step should be to
    a. start a parallel subsidiary company that offers the same product, but employs completely different workers.
    b. adopt a matrix design and eliminate traditional lines of hierarchy.
    c. eliminate excess staff and as many layers of middle management as possible.
    d. determine what customers actually want from the organization and then provide a strategy to provide it.
    e. "x-engineer" the old processes into new, innovative processes that motivate employees.

Organization Culture

CHAPTER 18

After studying this chapter, you should be able to:

Chapter Outline

The Nature of Organization Culture

Creating the Organization Culture

Approaches to Describing Organization Culture

Emerging Issues in Organization Culture

Managing Organization Culture

Shell Updates Its Nineteenth-Century Culture, Again

▶ **Define organization culture, explain how it affects employee behavior, and understand its historical roots.**

▶ **Describe how to create organization culture.**

▶ **Describe two different approaches to culture in organizations.**

▶ **Identify emerging issues in organization culture.**

▶ **Discuss the important elements of managing the organizational culture.**

Shell Oil, founded in 1892, merged with Royal Dutch Oil in 1907. The English and Dutch company maintained a dual organization structure, with duplicate headquarters, boards, and shareholders. Royal Dutch/Shell also maintained its conservative nineteenth-century organization culture. Senior executives, known as "peetvaders" (grandfathers), made the important decisions. The system created a traditional culture that avoided risk. Shell's culture was described as "reclusive and proud," "secretive and arrogant."

In the 1990s, managers began to update Shell's culture for a greater emphasis on efficiency. While other energy companies went through mergers to increase growth and cut costs, then CEO Sir Mark Moody-Stuart insisted Shell succeed alone. Managers were no longer chosen by the peetvaders but applied for job openings. "The practical consequence was that the most talented people no longer went to the places where we needed them the most," says one executive. Jeroen van der Veer, Shell's current CEO, adds, "Shell wound up with gifted amateurs in key jobs."

To shake up smug managers, outside consultants suggested new rituals. One was called the "fishbowl." The fishbowl was designed to overcome resistance to change and build consensus. Anyone who

> **"When everyone starts leaning on the same side of the canoe, sooner or later it's going to capsize."**
>
> *AN OIL COMPANY EXECUTIVE*

spoke out against a group decision had to sit alone in the middle of a circle. The fishbowl reduced resistance to change, but it encouraged groupthink.

For a time, the "new" culture seemed to work. Sir Philip Watts became CEO in 2001 and took credit for rising oil reserves and profits. However, by early 2004, it was clear that the changes were not improvements. Innovative techniques caused the firm to overstate oil reserves, an accounting asset. In January 2004, Shell reduced its oil reserve valuation by $130 billion, shocking investors.

Lack of oversight by directors allowed the problem to go unnoticed. "The care and feeding of the board members had become something of an art," one former senior manager at Shell says. "We really didn't care too much about them, and we fed them very little." Vincent Cable, Shell's former chief economist, agrees, "[The board] seemed to have a largely decorative function."

Investigators discovered that top managers were aware of the problems and had covered them up for years, ignoring whistleblowers. Managers were pressured to overstate reserves, because compensation was tied to reserves. This pressure, combined with the groupthink mentality that now prevailed, led to the cover-up. "When everyone starts leaning on the same side of the canoe, sooner or later it's going to capsize," comments an executive from a rival firm.

Shell directors decided to reveal the problems and address them with radical change. One insider says, "We could either trample over ourselves or wait for others to do it to us." Today, Shell is under the leadership of van der Veer, who promises to "enforce a culture of compliance." His first major step is consolidating the dual structure of Shell to increase accountability.

Shell will make other changes. Its new pay plan will tie performance-based pay to share price, rather than to accounting measures. Yet Shell will find it difficult to change its long-standing culture. Some top managers still reject outside ideas and values. "Shell will have no new gurus," announced van der Veer in November 2004. "We will do it ourselves." For more about Shell's culture, see the boxed insert titled *Royal Dutch Shell and . . . Globalization* on page 487.

References: "Making a Sustainable Contribution," "Shell Proposes Revised Remuneration Policies for Executive Directors," "Shell Hosts Strategy Review," Royal Dutch Shell website, www.shell.com on April 26, 2005; Rob Arnott, "Royal Dutch Shell: Putting at Risk Reputation as a Resource," *Oxford Energy Report*, www.oxfordenergy.org on April 26, 2005; Chip Cummins and Almar Latour, "How Shell's Move to Revamp Culture Ended in Scandal," *Wall Street Journal*, November 2, 2004, pp. A1, A14; Chris Redman, "Shell Rebuilds Itself," *Corporate Board Member*, March/April 2005, www.boardmember.com on April 26, 2005 (quotation).

The Nature of Organization Culture

In the early 1980s, organization culture became a central concern in the study of organizational behavior. Hundreds of researchers began to work in this area. Numerous books were published, important academic journals dedicated entire issues to the discussion of culture, and, almost overnight, organizational behavior textbooks that omitted culture as a topic of study became obsolete.

Interest in organization culture was not limited to academic researchers. Businesses expressed a far more intense interest in culture than in other aspects of organizational behavior. *Business Week, Fortune,* and other business periodicals published articles that touted culture as the key to an organization's success and suggested that managers who could manage through their organization's culture almost certainly would rise to the top.[1]

Although the enthusiasm of the early 1980s has waned somewhat, the study of organization culture remains important. The assumption is that organizations with a strong culture perform at higher levels than those without a strong culture.[2] For example, studies have shown that organizations with strong cultures that are strategically appropriate and that have norms that permit the organization to change actually do perform well.[3] Other studies have shown that different functional units may require different types of cultures.[4] The research on the impact of culture on organizational performance is mixed, however, depending on how the research is done and what variables are measured.

Many researchers have begun to weave the important aspects of organization culture into their research on more traditional topics. Now there are fewer headline stories in the popular business press about culture and culture management, but organization culture can have powerful effects on organizational performance, as the opening case about Shell Oil illustrates. The enormous amount of research on culture completed in the last twenty years has fundamentally altered the way both academics and managers look at organizations. Some of the concepts developed in the analysis of organization culture have become basic parts of the business vocabulary, and the analysis of organization culture is one of the most important specialties in the field of organizational behavior.

What Is Organization Culture?

A surprising aspect of the recent rise in interest in organization culture is that the concept, unlike virtually every other concept in the field, has no single widely accepted definition. Indeed, it often appears that authors feel compelled to develop their own definitions, which range from very broad to highly specific. For example, T. E. Deal and A. A. Kennedy define a firm's culture as "the way we do things around here."[5] This very broad definition presumably could include the way a firm manufactures its products, pays its bills, treats its employees, and performs any other organizational operation. More specific definitions include those of E. H. Schein ("the pattern of basic assumptions that a given group has invented, discovered, or developed in learning to cope with its problems of external adaptation and internal integration"[6]) and Tom Peters and Robert Waterman ("a dominant and coherent set of shared values conveyed by such symbolic means as stories, myths, legends, slogans, anecdotes, and fairy tales"[7]). Table 18.1 lists these and other important definitions of organization culture.

Despite the apparent diversity of these definitions, a few common attributes emerge. First, all the definitions refer to some set of values held by individuals in a firm. These values define what is good or acceptable behavior and what is bad or unacceptable behavior. In some organizations, for example, it is unacceptable to blame customers when problems arise. Here the value "the customer is always right" tells managers what actions are acceptable (not blaming the customer) and what actions are not acceptable (blaming the customer). In other organizations, the dominant values might support blaming customers for problems, penalizing employees who make mistakes, or treating employees as the firm's most valuable assets. In each case, values help members of an organization understand how they should act.

TABLE 18.1

Definitions of Organization Culture

Definition	Source
"A belief system shared by an organization's members"	J. C. Spender, "Myths, Recipes and Knowledge-Bases in Organizational Analysis" (Unpublished manuscript, Graduate School of Management, University of California at Los Angeles, 1983), p. 2.
"Strong, widely shared core values"	C. O'Reilly, "Corporations, Cults, and Organizational Culture: Lessons from Silicon Valley Firms" (Paper presented at the Annual Meeting of the Academy of Management, Dallas, Texas, 1983), p. 1.
"The way we do things around here"	T. E. Deal and A. A. Kennedy, *Corporate Cultures: The Rites and Rituals of Corporate Life* (Reading, MA: Addison-Wesley, 1982), p. 4.
"The collective programming of the mind"	G. Hofstede, *Culture's Consequences: International Differences in Work-Related Values* (Beverly Hills, CA: Sage, 1980), p. 25.
"Collective understandings"	J. Van Maanen and S. R. Barley, "Cultural Organization: Fragments of a Theory" (Paper presented at the Annual Meeting of the Academy of Management, Dallas, Texas, 1983), p. 7.
"A set of shared, enduring beliefs communicated through a variety of symbolic media, creating meaning in people's work lives"	J. M. Kouzes, D. F. Caldwell, and B. Z. Posner, "Organizational Culture: How It Is Created, Maintained, and Changed" (Presentation at OD Network National Conference, Los Angeles, October 9, 1983).
"A set of symbols, ceremonies, and myths that communicates the underlying values and beliefs of that organization to its employees"	W. G. Ouchi, *Theory Z: How American Business Can Meet the Japanese Challenge* (Reading, MA: Addison-Wesley, 1981), p. 41.
"A dominant and coherent set of shared values conveyed by such symbolic means as stories, myths, legends, slogans, anecdotes, and fairy tales"	T. J. Peters and R. H. Waterman Jr., *In Search of Excellence: Lessons from America's Best-Run Companies* (New York: Harper & Row, 1982), p. 103.
"The pattern of basic assumptions that a given group has invented, discovered, or developed in learning to cope with its problems of external adaptation and internal integration"	E. H. Schein, "The Role of the Founder in Creating Organizational Culture," *Organizational Dynamics,* Summer 1985, p. 14.

A second attribute common to many of the definitions in Table 18.1 is that the values that make up an organization's culture are often taken for granted; that is, they are basic assumptions made by the firm's employees rather than prescriptions written in a book or made explicit in a training program. It may be as difficult for an organization to articulate these basic assumptions as it is for people to express their personal beliefs and values. Several authors have argued that organization culture is a powerful influence on individuals in firms precisely because it is not explicit but instead becomes an implicit part of employees' values and beliefs.[8]

Southwest Airlines chairman Herb Kelleher is shown here greeting employees at the celebration of the opening of service to the Philadelphia International Airport. Kelleher is responsible for starting the airline and creating the culture that fuels its success. The unique culture produces loyal and motivated employees, leading to outstanding performance. Although Kelleher has stepped down from the daily running of the company, the culture lives on through the values, stories, and rituals that have developed through the years.

Some organizations have been able to articulate the key values in their cultures. Some have even written down these values and made them part of formal training procedures. E*Trade Group, Inc., the online stock and mutual fund trading company, uses unique ways of creating the company culture. Chief Executive Officer Christos M. Cotsakos is building a culture that is edgy, a bit bizarre, and sometimes brilliant; he sums it up in five words as "a lust for being different." He tells new recruits that the company has to be on the offensive and predatory, like infantrymen in a war. He once asked his newly hired vice president of international business development to stand on a chair and reveal something about himself to forty strangers in the company.[9]

Even when firms can articulate and describe the basic values that make up their cultures, however, the values most strongly affect actions when people in the organization take them for granted. An organization's culture is not likely to influence behavior powerfully when employees must constantly refer to a handbook to remember what the culture is. When the culture becomes part of them—when they can ignore what is written in the book because they already have embraced the values it describes—the culture can have an important impact on their actions.

The final attribute shared by many of the definitions in Table 18.1 is an emphasis on the symbolic means through which the values in an organization's culture are communicated. Although, as we noted, companies sometimes could directly describe these values, their meaning is perhaps best communicated to employees through the use of stories, examples, and even what some authors call "myths" or "fairy tales." Stories typically reflect the important implications of values in a firm's culture. Often they develop a life of their own. As they are told and retold, shaped and reshaped, their relationship to what actually occurred becomes less important than the powerful impact the stories have on the way that people behave every day. Nike uses a group of technical representatives called "Ekins" ("Nike" spelled backwards) who run a nine-day training session for large retailers, telling them stories about Nike's history and traditions, such as the stories about CEO Phil Knight selling shoes from the trunk of his car and co-founder Bill Bowerman using the family's waffle iron to create the first waffle-soled running shoe.[10]

Some organization stories have become famous. At E*Trade, CEO Cotsakos has done many things that have become famous around the company because he does not follow the rules for the typical investment company. To make people move faster, he organized a day of racing in Formula One cars at speeds of around 150 miles per hour. To create a looser atmosphere around the office, he has employees carry around rubber chickens or wear propeller beanies. To bond the employees together, he organized gourmet-cooking classes.[11] The stories of these incidents and others are told to new employees and are spread throughout the company, thus affecting the behavior of many more people than those who actually took part in each event.

> **Organization culture** is the set of values that helps the organization's employees understand which actions are considered acceptable and which are unacceptable.

We can use the three common attributes of definitions of culture just discussed to develop a definition with which most authors probably could agree: **Organization culture** is the set of shared values, often taken for granted, that help people in an organization understand which actions are considered acceptable and which are considered unacceptable. Often these values are communicated through stories and other symbolic means.

Historical Foundations

Although research on organization culture exploded onto the scene in the early 1980s, the antecedents of this research can be traced to the origins of social science. Understanding the contributions of other social science disciplines is particularly important in the case of organization culture because many of the dilemmas and debates that continue in this area reflect differences in historical research traditions.

Anthropological Contributions   Anthropology is the study of human cultures.[12] Of all the social science disciplines, anthropology is most closely related to the study of culture and cultural phenomena. Anthropologists seek to understand how the values and beliefs that make up a society's culture affect the structure and functioning of that society. Many anthropologists believe that to understand the relationship between culture and society, it is necessary to look at a culture from the viewpoint of the people who practice it—from the "native's point of view."[13] To reach this level of understanding, anthropologists immerse themselves in the values, symbols, and stories that people in a society use to bring order and meaning to their lives. Anthropologists usually produce book-length descriptions of the values, attitudes, and beliefs that underlie the behaviors of people in one or two cultures.[14]

Whether the culture is that of a large, modern corporation or a primitive tribe in New Guinea or the Philippines, the questions asked are the same: How do people in this culture know what kinds of behavior are acceptable and what kinds are unacceptable? How is this knowledge understood? How is this knowledge communicated to new members? Through intense efforts to produce accurate descriptions, the values and beliefs that underlie actions in an organization become clear. However, these values can be fully understood only in the context of the organization in which they developed. In other words, a description of the values and beliefs of one organization is not transferable to those of other organizations; each culture is unique.

Sociological Contributions   Sociology is the study of people in social systems such as organizations and societies. Sociologists have long been interested in the causes and consequences of culture. In studying culture, sociologists have most often focused on informal social structure. Émile Durkheim, an important early sociologist, argued that the study of myth and ritual is an essential complement to the study of structure and rational behavior in societies.[15] By studying rituals, Durkheim argued, we can understand the most basic values and beliefs of a group of people.

Many sociological methods and theories have been used in the analysis of organization cultures. Sociologists use systematic interviews, questionnaires, and other quantitative research methods rather than the intensive study and analysis of anthropologists. Practitioners using the sociological approach generally produce a fairly simple typology of cultural attributes and then show how the cultures of a relatively large number of firms can be analyzed with this typology.[16] The major pieces of research on organization culture that later spawned widespread business interest—including Ouchi's *Theory Z,* Deal and Kennedy's *Corporate Cultures,* and Peters and Waterman's *In Search of Excellence*[17]—used sociological methods. Later in this chapter, we review some of this work in more detail.

Social Psychology Contributions   Social psychology is a branch of psychology that includes the study of groups and the influence of social factors on individuals. Although most research on organization culture has used anthropological or sociological methods and approaches, some has borrowed heavily from social psychology. Social psychological theory, with its emphasis on the creation and manipulation of symbols, lends itself naturally to the analysis of organization culture.

For example, research in social psychology suggests that people tend to use stories or information about a single event more than they use multiple observations to make judgments.[18] Thus, if your neighbor had trouble with a certain brand of automobile, you will probably conclude that the brand is bad even though the car company can generate reams of statistical data to prove that the situation with your neighbor's car was a rarity.

The impact of stories on decision making suggests an important reason that organization culture has such a powerful influence on the people in an organization. Unlike other organizational phenomena, culture is best communicated through stories and examples, and these become the basis that individuals in the organization use to make judgments. If a story says that blaming customers is a bad thing to do, then blaming customers is a bad thing to do. This value is communicated much more effectively through the cultural story than through some statistical analysis of customer satisfaction.[19]

Economics Contributions   The influence of economics on the study of organization culture is substantial enough to warrant attention, although it has been less significant than the influence of anthropology and sociology. Economic analysis treats organization culture as one of a variety of tools that managers can use to create some economic advantage to the organization.

The economics approach attempts to link the cultural attributes of firms with their performance rather than simply describing the cultures of companies as the sociological and anthropological perspectives do. In *Theory Z,* for example, Ouchi does not just say that Type Z companies differ from other kinds of companies—he asserts that Type Z firms outperform other firms.[20] When Peters and Waterman say they are in search of excellence, they define "excellence," in part, as consistently high financial performance.[21] These authors are using cultural explanations of financial success.

Researchers disagree about the extent to which culture affects organization performance. Several authors have investigated the conditions under which organization culture is linked with superior financial performance.[22] This research suggests that under some relatively narrow conditions, a link between culture and performance may exist. However, the fact that a firm has a culture does not mean it will perform well; indeed, a variety of cultural traits can actually hurt performance, as we discussed for Shell Oil.

For example, a firm could have a culture that includes values like "customers are too ignorant to be of much help," "employees cannot be trusted," "innovation is not important," and "quality is too expensive." The firm would have a strong culture, but the culture might impair its performance. Wal-Mart, known for its retailing expertise and its culture of respect for individuals, is also becoming known as a company whose culture does not lead to success for women.[23] The relationship between culture and performance depends, to some extent at least, on the values expressed in the organization's culture.

Culture Versus Climate

During the past twenty years, since the concept of organization culture has become popular, managers have often asked about the similarities and differences between organization culture and organization climate. Some people, managers and researchers alike, have argued that they are really the same thing, although their research bases are different, as we explain next.

The two concepts are similar in that both are concerned with the overall work atmosphere of an organization. In addition, they both deal with the social context in organizations, and both are assumed to affect the behaviors of people who work in organizations.[24]

The two concepts differ in several significant ways, however. Much of the study of climate was based in psychology, whereas the study of organization culture was based in anthropology and sociology. **Organization climate** usually refers to current situations in an organization and the linkages among work groups, employees, and work performance. Climate, therefore, is usually more easily manipulated by management to directly affect the behavior of employees. Organization culture, on the other hand, usually refers to the historical context within which a situation occurs and the impact of this context on the behaviors of employees. Organization culture is generally considered much more difficult to alter in short-run situations because it has been defined over the course of years of history and tradition.

The two concepts also differ in their emphases. Organization culture is often described as the means through which people in the organization learn and communicate what is acceptable and unacceptable in an organization—its values and norms.[25] Most descriptions of organization climate do not deal with values and norms. Therefore, descriptions of organization climate are concerned with the current atmosphere in an organization, whereas organization culture is based on the history and traditions of the organization and emphasizes values and norms about employee behavior.

> **Organization climate** usually refers to current situations in an organization and the linkages among work groups, employees, and work performance.

Creating the Organization Culture

To the entrepreneur who starts a business, creating the culture of the company may seem secondary to the basic processes of creating a product or service and selling it to customers or clients. However, as the company grows and becomes successful, it usually develops a culture that distinguishes it from other companies and that is one of the reasons for its success. In other words, a company succeeds as a result of what the company does, its strategy, and how it does it, its culture. The culture is linked to the strategic values, whether one is starting up a new company or trying to change the culture of an existing company.[26] The process of creating an organization culture is really a process of linking its strategic values with its cultural values, much as the structure of the organization is linked to its strategy, as we described in Chapter 17. The process is shown in Table 18.2.

Royal Dutch Shell and . . . GLOBALIZATION

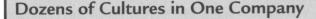

Dozens of Cultures in One Company

Royal Dutch Shell is experiencing problems in updating its organization culture. To complicate matters further, the English and Dutch company is conducting business in dozens of countries with different national cultures. For example, in India, Royal Dutch Shell faces many business opportunities but also many cultural challenges.

While English and Dutch societies have well-developed financial markets and consistent governmental policies, the situation in India is still evolving and more changeable. For instance, Shell is a supplier in a project to build a giant dam in Kashmir, near the disputed border between India and Pakistan. Project managers must include negotiators from India, Pakistan, two provinces, and many government agencies including those regulating water, safety, the environment, farming, employment, and foreign direct investment. In addition, several prominent families control many of the largest businesses in the region. The family cultures of these businesses must also be considered.

Another factor complicating Shell's dealings in India are the different values and expectations underlying Indian, English, and Dutch national cultures. Indians value personal relationships and have a relaxed attitude about time. English and Dutch cultures, on the other hand, place a high value on impersonal business relationships, promptness, and speed. English, Dutch, and Indian managers judge new ideas on their merits. Yet, "compared to other cultures, relationships and feelings play a larger role in decisions in India . . . Thus, [the source's] credibility and trustworthiness are critical," according to Madhukar Shukla, a management professor in India.

As Royal Dutch Shell works to update its organization culture, it must create an organization culture that has a strong identity, yet remains flexible enough to adapt to other national cultures. Whether the firm can sustain the enormous effort needed to change a deep-seated culture remains to be seen.

> **"Compared to other cultures, relationships and feelings play a larger role in decisions in India."**
>
> MADHUKAR SHUKLA, PROFESSOR, XLRI UNIVERSITY, INDIA

References: "Shell: Superior Brand Name with 100 Years History," *The Nation* (Lahore, Pakistan), April 5, 2005, nation.com.pk on April 28, 2005; Ahmad Fraz Khan, "Mangla Raising Project Delayed," *Dawn*, April 12, 2005, www.dawn.com on April 29, 2005; Madhukar Shukla, "Indian Business Culture," Executive Planet website, www.executiveplanet.com on April 29, 2005 (quotation); Jacob Vossestein, "Dutch Business Culture," Executive Planet website, www.executiveplanet.com on April 29, 2005.

Creating Organization Culture
Step 1—Formulate Strategic Values
Step 2—Develop Cultural Values
Step 3—Create Vision
Step 4—Initiate Implementation Strategies
Step 5—Reinforce Cultural Behaviors

TABLE 18.2

Creating Organization Culture

Establish Values

The first two steps in the process involve establishing values. First, management must determine the strategic values of the organization. **Strategic values** are the basic beliefs about an organization's environment that shape its strategy. They are developed following an environmental scanning process and strategic analysis that evaluate economic,

Strategic values are the basic beliefs about an organization's environment that shape its strategy.

demographic, public policy, technological, and social trends to identify needs in the marketplace that the organization can meet. Strategic values, in effect, link the organization with its environment. Dell Computer believed that customers would buy computers from a catalogue if the price was right, rather than go to computer stores as the conventional wisdom dictated they would. A $6.8 billion business resulted.[27] The second set of required values is the cultural values of the organization. **Cultural values** are the values employees need to have and to act on for the organization to carry out its strategic values. They should be grounded in the organization's beliefs about how and why the organization can succeed. Organizations that attempt to develop cultural values that are not linked to their strategic values may end up with an empty set of values that have little relationship to their business. In other words, employees need to value work behaviors that are consistent with and support the organization's strategic values: low-cost production, customer service, or technological innovation. Herb Kelleher, former CEO and current chairman of the board of Southwest Airlines, believed that the culture, the "espirit de corps," was the most valuable asset of the company.[28]

> **Cultural values** are the values that employees need to have and act on for the organization to act on the strategic values.

Create Vision

After developing its strategic and cultural values, the organization must establish a vision of its direction. This "vision" is a picture of what the organization will be like at some point in the future. It portrays how the strategic and cultural values will combine to create the future. For example, an insurance company might establish a vision of "protecting the lifestyles of 2 million families by the year 2010." In effect, it synthesizes both the strategic and cultural values as it communicates a performance target to employees. The conventional wisdom has been that the vision statement is written first, but experience suggests that the strategic and cultural values must be established first for the vision to be meaningful.

Initiate Implementation Strategies

The next step, initiating implementation strategies, builds on the values and initiates the action to accomplish the vision. The strategies cover many factors, from developing the organization design to recruiting and training employees who share the values and will carry them out. Consider a bank that has the traditional orientation of handling customer loans, deposits, and savings. If the bank changes, placing more emphasis on customer service, it may have to recruit a different type of employee, one who is capable of building relationships. The bank will also have to commit to serious, long-term training of its current employees to teach them the new service-oriented culture. The strategic and cultural values are the stimuli for the implementation practices.

Reinforce Cultural Behaviors

The final step is to reinforce the behaviors of employees as they act out the cultural values and implement the organization's strategies. Reinforcement can take many forms. First, the formal reward system in the organization must reward desired behaviors in ways that employees value. Second, stories must be told throughout the organization about employees who engaged in behaviors that epitomize the cultural values. Third, the organization must engage in ceremonies and rituals that emphasize employees doing the things that are critical to carrying out the organization's vision. In effect, the organization must "make a big deal out of employees doing the right things." For example, if parties are held only for retirement or to give out longevity and service pins, the employees get the message that retirement and length of service are the only things that matter. On the other hand, holding a ceremony for a group of employees who provided exceptional customer service reinforces desirable employee behaviors. Reinforcement practices are the final link between the strategic and cultural values and the creation of the organization culture.

Approaches to Describing Organization Culture

The models discussed in this section provide valuable insights into the dimensions along which organization cultures vary. No single framework for describing the values in organization cultures has emerged; however, several frameworks have been suggested. Although these frameworks were developed in the 1980s, their ideas about organization culture are still influential today. Some of the "excellent" companies that they described are not as highly lauded now, but the concepts are still in use in companies all over the world. Managers should evaluate the various parts of the frameworks described and use the parts that fit the strategic and cultural values of their own organizations.

The Ouchi Framework

One of the first researchers to focus explicitly on analyzing the cultures of a limited group of firms was William G. Ouchi. Ouchi analyzed the organization cultures of three groups of firms, which he characterized as (1) typical U.S. firms, (2) typical Japanese firms, and (3) **Type Z** U.S. firms.[29]

Through his analysis, Ouchi developed a list of seven points on which these three types of firms can be compared. He argued that the cultures of typical Japanese firms and Type Z U.S. firms are very different from those of typical U.S. firms, and that these differences explain the success of many Japanese firms and Type Z U.S. firms and the difficulties faced by typical U.S. firms. The seven points of comparison developed by Ouchi are presented in Table 18.3.

Commitment to Employees According to Ouchi, typical Japanese and Type Z U.S. firms share the cultural value of trying to keep employees. Thus, both types of firms lay off employees only as a last resort. In Japan, the value of "keeping employees on" often takes the form of lifetime employment, although some Japanese companies, reacting to the economic troubles of the past few years, are challenging this value. A person who begins working at some Japanese firms usually has a virtual guarantee that he or she

The **Type Z firm** is committed to retaining employees; evaluates workers' performance based on both qualitative and quantitative information; emphasizes broad career paths; exercises control through informal, implicit mechanisms; requires that decision making occur in groups and be based on full information sharing and consensus; expects individuals to take responsibility for decisions; and emphasizes concern for people.

Cultural Value	Expression in Japanese Companies	Expression in Type Z U.S. Companies	Expression in Typical U.S. Companies
Commitment to Employees	Lifetime employment	Long-term employment	Short-term employment
Evaluation	Slow and qualitative	Slow and qualitative	Fast and quantitative
Careers	Very broad	Moderately broad	Narrow
Control	Implicit and informal	Implicit and informal	Explicit and formal
Decision Making	Group and consensus	Group and consensus	Individual
Responsibility	Group	Individual	Individual
Concern for People	Holistic	Holistic	Narrow

TABLE 18.3

The Ouchi Framework

will never be fired. In Type Z U.S. companies, this cultural value is manifested in a commitment to what Ouchi called "long-term employment." Under the Japanese system of lifetime employment, employees usually cannot be fired. Under the U.S. system, workers and managers can be fired, but only if they are not performing acceptably.

Ouchi suggested that typical U.S. firms do not have the same cultural commitment to employees that Japanese firms and Type Z U.S. firms do. In reality, U.S. workers and managers often spend their entire careers in a relatively small number of companies. Still, there is a cultural expectation that if there is a serious downturn in a firm's fortunes, change of ownership, or a merger, workers and managers will be let go. For example, when Wells Fargo Bank bought First Interstate Bank in Arizona, it expected to lay off about 400 employees in Arizona and 5,000 in the corporation as a whole. However, eight months after the purchase, Wells Fargo had eliminated over 1,000 employees in Arizona alone and laid off a total of 10,800 workers. Wells Fargo has a reputation as a vicious cutter following a takeover and seems to be living up to it.[30]

Evaluation   Ouchi observed that in Japanese and Type Z U.S. companies, appropriate evaluation of workers and managers is thought to take a very long time—up to ten years—and requires the use of qualitative as well as quantitative information about performance. For this reason, promotion in these firms is relatively slow, and promotion decisions are made only after interviews with many people who have had contact with the person being evaluated. In typical U.S. firms, on the other hand, the cultural value suggests that evaluation can and should be done rapidly and should emphasize quantitative measures of performance. This value tends to encourage short-term thinking among workers and managers.

Careers   Ouchi next observed that the careers most valued in Japanese and Type Z U.S. firms span multiple functions. In Japan, this value has led to very broad career paths, which may lead to employees' gaining experience in six or seven distinct business functions. The career paths in Type Z U.S. firms are somewhat narrower.

However, the career path valued in typical U.S. firms is considerably narrower. Ouchi's research indicated that most U.S. managers perform only one or two different business functions in their careers. This narrow career path reflects, according to Ouchi, the value of specialization that is part of so many U.S. firms.

Control   All organizations must exert some level of control to achieve coordinated action. Thus, it is not surprising that firms in the United States and Japan have developed cultural values related to organizational control and how to manage it. Most Japanese and Type Z U.S. firms assume that control is exercised through informal, implicit mechanisms. One of the most powerful of these mechanisms is the organization's culture. In contrast, typical U.S. firms expect guidance to come through explicit directions in the form of job descriptions, delineation of authority, and various rules and procedures, rather than from informal and implicit cultural values.

From a functional perspective, organization culture could be viewed as primarily a means of social control based on shared norms and values.[31] Control comes from knowing that someone who matters is paying close attention to what we do and will tell us if our actions are appropriate or not. In organizations, control can come from formal sources, such as the organization structure or your supervisor, or from social sources, such as the organization's culture. In Ouchi's view, control is based in formal organizational mechanisms in typical U.S. firms, whereas control is more social in nature and derived from the organization culture's shared norms and values in Japanese and Type Z U.S. firms.

Decision Making   Japanese and Type Z U.S. firms have a strong cultural expectation that decision making occurs in groups and is based on principles of full information sharing and consensus. In most typical U.S. firms, individual decision making is considered appropriate.

Responsibility   Closely linked to the issue of group versus individual decision making are ideas about responsibility. Here, however, the parallels between Japanese firms and Type Z U.S. firms break down. Ouchi showed that in Japan, strong cultural norms support collective responsibility; that is, the group as a whole, rather than a single person, is held responsible for decisions made by the group. In both Type Z U.S. firms and typical U.S. firms, individuals expect to take responsibility for decisions.

Linking individual responsibility with individual decision making, as typical U.S. firms do, is logically consistent. Similarly, group decision making and group responsibility, the situation in Japanese firms, seem to go together. But how do Type Z U.S. firms combine the cultural values of group decision making and individual responsibility?

Ouchi suggested that the answer to this question depends on a cultural view we have already discussed: slow, qualitative evaluation. The first time a manager uses a group to make a decision, it is not possible to tell whether the outcomes associated with that decision resulted from the manager's influence or from the quality of the group. However, if a manager works with many groups over time, and if these groups consistently do well for the organization, it is likely that the manager is skilled at getting the most out of the groups. This manager can be held responsible for the outcomes of group decision-making processes. Similarly, managers who consistently fail to work effectively with the groups assigned to them can be held responsible for the lack of results from the group decision-making process.

Concern for People   The last cultural value examined by Ouchi deals with a concern for people. Not surprisingly, in Japanese firms and Type Z firms, the cultural value that dominates is a holistic concern for workers and managers. Holistic concern extends beyond concern for a person simply as a worker or manager to concern about that person's home life, hobbies, personal beliefs, hopes, fears, and aspirations. In typical U.S. firms, the concern for people is a narrow one that focuses on the workplace. A culture that emphasizes a strong concern for people, rather than one that emphasizes a work or task orientation, can decrease worker turnover.[32]

Theory Z and Performance   Ouchi argued that the cultures of Japanese and Type Z firms help them outperform typical U.S. firms. Toyota imported the management style and culture that succeeded in Japan into its manufacturing facilities in North America. Toyota's success has often been attributed to the ability of Japanese and Type Z firms to systematically invest in their employees and operations over long periods, resulting in steady and significant improvements in long-term performance.

The Peters and Waterman Approach

Tom Peters and Robert Waterman, in their bestseller *In Search of Excellence,* focused even more explicitly than Ouchi on the relationship between organization culture and performance. Peters and Waterman chose a sample of highly successful U.S. firms and sought to describe the management practices that led to their success.[33] Their analysis rapidly turned to the cultural values that led to successful management practices. These "excellent" values are listed in Table 18.4.

TABLE 18.4	**Attributes of an Excellent Firm**
The Peters and Waterman Framework	

1. Bias for action	5. Hands-on management
2. Stay close to the customer	6. Stick to the knitting
3. Autonomy and entrepreneurship	7. Simple form, lean staff
4. Productivity through people	8. Simultaneously loose and tight organization

Bias for Action   According to Peters and Waterman, successful firms have a bias for action. Managers in these firms are expected to make decisions even if all the facts are not in. Peters and Waterman argued that for many important decisions, all the facts will never be in.

Delaying decision making in these situations is the same as never making a decision. Meanwhile, other firms probably will have captured whatever business initiative existed. On average, according to these authors, organizations with cultural values that include a bias for action outperform firms without such values.

Stay Close to the Customer   Peters and Waterman believe that firms whose organization cultures value customers over everything else outperform firms without this value. The customer is a source of information about current products, a source of ideas about future products, and the ultimate source of a firm's current and future financial performance. Focusing on the customer, meeting the customer's needs, and pampering the customer when necessary all lead to superior performance. After losing money for years, Scandinavian Airlines focused its culture on customer service and finally started making money in 1989, when many other airlines were experiencing financial difficulties.[34]

Autonomy and Entrepreneurship   Peters and Waterman maintained that successful firms fight the lack of innovation and the bureaucracy usually associated with large size. They do this by breaking the company into smaller, more manageable pieces and then encouraging independent, innovative activities within smaller business segments. Stories often exist in these organizations about the junior engineer who takes a risk and influences major product decisions, or of the junior manager, dissatisfied with the slow pace of a product's development, who implements a new and highly successful marketing plan.

Productivity Through People   Like Ouchi, Peters and Waterman believe successful firms recognize that their most important assets are their people—both workers and managers—and that the organization's purpose is to let its people flourish. It is a basic value of the organization culture—a belief that treating people with respect and dignity is not only appropriate but essential to success.

Hands-on Management   Peters and Waterman noted that the firms they studied insisted that senior managers stay in touch with the firms' essential business. It is an expectation, reflecting a deeply embedded cultural norm, that managers should manage not from behind the closed doors of their offices but by "wandering around" the plant, the design facility, the research and development department, and so on.

Stick to the Knitting   Another cultural value characteristic of excellent firms is their reluctance to engage in business outside their areas of expertise. These firms reject the concept of diversification, the practice of buying and operating businesses in unrelated industries. This notion is currently referred to as relying on the company's "core competencies," or what the company does best.

Simple Form, Lean Staff According to Peters and Waterman, successful firms tend to have few administrative layers and relatively small corporate staff groups. In excellently managed companies, importance is measured not only by the number of people who report to a manager but also by the manager's impact on the organization's performance. The cultural values in these firms tell managers that their staffs' performance rather than their size is important.

Simultaneously Loose and Tight Organization The final attribute of organization culture identified by Peters and Waterman appears contradictory. How can a firm be simultaneously loosely and tightly organized? The resolution of this apparent paradox is found in the firms' values. The firms are tightly organized because all their members understand and believe in the firms' values. This common cultural bond is a strong glue that holds the firms together. At the same time, however, the firms are loosely organized because they tend to have less administrative overhead, fewer staff members, and fewer rules and regulations. The result is increased innovation and risk taking and faster response times.

The loose structure is possible only because of the common values held by people in the firm. When employees must make decisions, they can evaluate their options in terms of the organization's underlying values—whether the options are consistent with a bias for action, service to the customer, and so on. By referring to commonly held values, employees can make their own decisions about what actions to take. In this sense, the tight structure of common cultural values makes possible the loose structure of fewer administrative controls.

This shows children aged 5 and older participating in activities at one of IBM's sixty-seven worldwide childcare centers. IBM is attempting to meet the needs of an increasingly diverse workforce by providing childcare for employees with families. Employees can remain employed and on a career track without worrying about the quality of childcare for their little ones, while still being close enough to be involved in some of the children's activities in the center. This is just one way that companies are showing concern for their employees and developing a people-oriented culture.

Emerging Issues in Organization Culture

As the implementation of organization culture continues, it inevitably changes and develops new perspectives. Many new ideas about productive environments build on earlier views such as those of Ouchi, Peters and Waterman, and others. Typical of these approaches are the total quality management movement, worker participation, procedural justice, and team-based management, which were discussed in earlier chapters. Three other movements are briefly discussed in this section: innovation, empowerment, and appropriate cultures.

Innovation

Innovation is the process of creating and doing new things that are introduced into the marketplace as products, processes, or services. Innovation involves every aspect of

> **Innovation** is the process of creating and doing new things that are introduced into the marketplace as products, processes, or services.

the organization, from research through development, manufacturing, and marketing. One of the organization's biggest challenges is to bring innovative technology to the needs of the marketplace in the most cost-effective manner possible.[35] Note that innovation does not only involve the technology to create new products. True organizational innovation is pervasive throughout the organization. According to *Fortune* magazine, the most admired organizations are those that are the most innovative.[36] Those companies are innovative in every way—staffing, strategy, research, and business processes.

Many risks are associated with being an innovative company. The most basic is the risk that decisions about new technology or innovation will backfire. As research proceeds, and engineers and scientists continue to develop new ideas or solutions to problems, there is always the possibility that innovations will fail to perform as expected. For this reason, organizations commit considerable resources to testing innovations.[37] A second risk is the possibility that a competitor will make decisions enabling it to get an innovation to the market first. The marketplace has become a breeding ground for continuous innovation. Motorola, for example, is striving to build a company in which customer needs shape new-product development without crippling the firm's technological leadership in its basic products.

Types of Innovation   Innovation can be either radical, systems, or incremental. A **radical innovation** is a major breakthrough that changes or creates whole industries. Examples include xerography (which was invented by Chester Carlson in 1935 and became the hallmark of Xerox Corporation), steam engines, and the internal combustion engine (which paved the way for today's automobile industry). **Systems innovation** creates a new functionality by assembling parts in new ways. For example, the gasoline engine began as a radical innovation and became a systems innovation when it was combined with bicycle and carriage technology to create automobiles. **Incremental innovation** continues the technical improvement and extends the applications of radical and systems innovations. There are many more incremental innovations than there are radical and systems innovations. In fact, several incremental innovations are often necessary to make radical and systems innovations work properly. Incremental innovations force organizations to continuously improve their products and keep abreast or ahead of the competition.

New Ventures   New ventures based on innovations require entrepreneurship and good management to work. The profile of the entrepreneur typically includes a need for achievement, a desire to assume responsibility, a willingness to take risks, and a focus on concrete results. Entrepreneurship can occur inside or outside large organizations. Outside entrepreneurship requires all of the complex aspects of the innovation process. Inside entrepreneurship occurs within a system that usually discourages chaotic activity.

Large organizations typically do not accept entrepreneurial types of activities. Thus, for a large organization to be innovative and develop new ventures, it must actively encourage entrepreneurial activity within the organization. This form of activity, often called **intrapreneurship**, usually is most effective when it is a part of everyday life in the organization and occurs throughout the organization rather than in the research and development department alone.

Corporate Research   The most common means of developing innovation in the traditional organization is through corporate research, or research and development. Corporate research is usually set up to support existing businesses, provide incremental innovations in the organization's businesses, and explore potential new technology

---

Radical innovation is a major breakthrough that changes or creates whole industries.

Systems innovation creates a new functionality by assembling parts in new ways.

Incremental innovation continues the technical improvement and extends the applications of radical and systems innovations.

Intrapreneurship is entrepreneurial activity that takes place within the context of a large corporation.

bases. It often takes place in a laboratory, either on the site of the main corporate facility or some distance away from normal operations.

Corporate researchers are responsible for keeping the company's products and processes technologically advanced. Product life cycles vary a great deal, depending on how fast products become obsolete and whether substitutes for the product are developed. Obviously, if a product becomes obsolete or some other product can be substituted for it, the profits from its sales will decrease. The job of corporate research is to prevent this from happening by keeping the company's products current.

The corporate culture can be instrumental in fostering an environment in which creativity and innovation occur. Sony and Hewlett-Packard are examples of two companies that are trying to change their organization cultures to be more innovative. Hewlett-Packard had quite a struggle merging with Compaq, especially in combining the two cultures; in fact, there was so much trouble that it may have cost CEO Carley Fiorino her job.[38]

Ed Sabol and his son, Steve, developed NFL Films into a $50 million business by doing what they love: watching and filming professional football. Based on Ed's passions for football and videotaping his son's football games, the company has become an innovator in the industry. Its first foray into filming the professional game focused on showing the beauty and passion of the game. Since then, in the face of mountains of competition, it still innovates in the use of color, camera positioning, the use of music, and narration. As a result the company has 89 Emmy awards. Always the creative one, Steve has been president since 1987. They used to give a $1,000 award to the most spectacular failure in order to stimulate ingenuity, innovation, and risk taking. Each cameraperson is his or her own director by selecting location and shots, all of which encourages creativity.

Empowerment

One of the most popular buzzwords in management today is "empowerment." Almost every new approach to quality, meeting the competition, getting more out of employees, productivity enhancement, and corporate turnarounds, deals with employee empowerment. As we discussed in Chapter 5, **empowerment** is the process of enabling workers to set their own goals, make decisions, and solve problems within their spheres of responsibility and authority. Fads are often dismissed as meaningless and without substance because they are misused and overused, and the concept of empowerment, too, can be taken too lightly.

Empowerment is the process of enabling workers to set their own work goals, make decisions, and solve problems within their sphere of responsibility and authority.

Empowerment is simple and complex at the same time. It is simple in that it tells managers to quit bossing people around so much and to let them do their jobs. It is complex in that managers and employees typically are not trained to do that. A significant amount of time, training, and practice may be needed to truly empower employees. In Chapter 5, we discussed some techniques for utilizing empowerment and conditions in which empowerment can be effective in organizations.

Empowerment can be much more than a motivational technique, however. In some organizations it is the cornerstone of organizational culture. At E*Trade, CEO Cotsakos believes that people should be empowered and then encouraged to take responsibility and solve their own problems. When the chief information officer and the chief financial officer got into what seemed to be an irresolvable spat, they turned to Cotsakos for resolution. He insisted that they work it out between them for the good of the company. He sent them each a bouquet of roses bearing the message "We're a team. Let's work it out." and made each think that the other had sent the flowers. The two executives resolved their problems and developed a better understanding of each other's role in the company.[39]

Empowerment can be viewed as liberating employees, but sometimes "empowerment" entails little more than delegating a task to an employee and then watching over the employee too closely. Employees may feel that this type of participation is superficial and that they are not really making meaningful decisions. The concept of liberating employees suggests that they should be free to do what they think is best without fear that the boss is standing by to veto or change the work they do.[40]

Appropriate Cultures

Much of the literature on organization culture has focused on describing the concept of organization culture, linking culture to performance, and then creating an organizational culture. For example, the Peters and Waterman framework described eight attributes that successful firms all had, the implication being that those same attributes would be desirable in all organizations. But one need only examine a few successful organizations, such as Southwest Airlines, General Electric, and Microsoft, with vastly different cultures to legitimately question the appropriateness of one culture for all organizations. Rob Goffee and Gareth Jones have questioned the idea that there is one best organization culture and propose that there are only "appropriate cultures."[41] After all, flying airplanes and moving people from one place to another at the lowest possible cost is vastly different from writing new software for personal computers. Goffee and Jones suggest that the nature of the value chain and the dynamism of the environment are two factors that may determine what type of culture is appropriate for a particular organization. The determining factors may prove to be quite elusive, however, as nobody has been able to successfully copy Southwest Airlines, although many have tried. Much more research is needed on the prospect of a contingency theory of organization culture.

Managing Organization Culture

The work of Ouchi, Peters and Waterman, and many others demonstrates two important facts. First, organization cultures differ among firms; second, these different organization cultures can affect a firm's performance. Based on these observations, managers have become more concerned about how to best manage the cultures of their organizations. The three elements of managing organization culture are (1) taking advantage of the existing culture, (2) teaching the organization culture, and (3) changing the organization culture.

Taking Advantage of the Existing Culture

Most managers are not in a position to create an organization culture; rather, they work in organizations that already have cultural values. For these managers, the central issue in managing culture is how best to use the cultural system that already exists. It may be easier and faster to alter employee behaviors within the existing culture than it is to change the history, traditions, and values that already exist.[42]

To take advantage of an existing cultural system, managers must first be fully aware of the culture's values and what behaviors or actions those values support. Becoming fully aware of an organization's values usually is not easy, however; it involves more than reading a pamphlet about what the company believes in. Managers must develop a deep understanding of how organizational values operate in the firm—an understanding that usually comes only through experience.

This understanding, once achieved, can be used to evaluate the performances of others in the firm. Articulating organizational values can be useful in managing others' behaviors. For example, suppose a subordinate in a firm with a strong cultural value of "sticking to its knitting" develops a business strategy that involves moving into a new industry. Rather than attempting to argue that this business strategy is economically flawed or conceptually weak, the manager who understands the corporate culture can point to the company's organizational value: "In this firm, we believe in sticking to our knitting."

Senior managers who understand their organization's culture can communicate that understanding to lower-level individuals. Over time, as these lower-level managers begin to understand and accept the firm's culture, they will require less direct supervision. Their understanding of corporate values will guide their decision making.

Teaching the Organization Culture: Socialization

Socialization is the process through which individuals become social beings.[43] As studied by psychologists, it is the process through which children learn to become adults in a society—how they learn what is acceptable and polite behavior and what is not, how they learn to communicate, how they learn to interact with others, and so on. In complex societies, the socialization process takes many years.

Organizational socialization is the process through which employees learn about their firm's culture and pass their knowledge and understanding on to others. Employees are socialized into organizations, just as people are socialized into societies; that is, they come to know over time what is acceptable in the organization and what is not, how to communicate their feelings, and how to interact with others. They learn both through observation and through efforts by managers to communicate this information to them. Research into the process of socialization indicates that for many employees, socialization programs do not necessarily change their values, but instead they make employees more aware of the differences between personal and organization values and help them develop ways to cope with the differences.[44]

A variety of organizational mechanisms can affect the socialization of workers in organizations. Probably the most important are the examples that new employees see in the behavior of experienced people. Through observing examples, new employees develop a repertoire of stories they can use to guide their actions. When a decision needs to be made, new employees can ask, "What would my boss do in this situation?" This is not to suggest that formal training, corporate pamphlets, and corporate statements about organization culture are unimportant in the socialization process. However, these factors tend to support the socialization process based on people's close observations of the actions of others.

In some organizations, the culture described in pamphlets and presented in formal training sessions conflicts with the values of the organization as they are expressed in the actions of its people. For example, a firm may say that employees are its most important asset but treat employees badly. In this setting, new employees quickly learn that the rhetoric of the pamphlets and formal training sessions has little to do with the real organization culture. Employees who are socialized into this system usually come to accept the actual cultural values rather than those formally espoused.

Socialization is the process through which individuals become social beings.

Organizational socialization is the process through which employees learn about the firm's culture and pass their knowledge and understanding on to others.

Fortunately, while most organizations have a distinct corporate culture with specific organizational values, not all employees would classify their office "families" as "dysfunctional." A strong organizational culture can enhance performance and create loyal employees. However, not all organizations have cultures that value and promote high performance, and in these cases attempting to change the organization's culture, while often difficult, can be rewarding in terms of productivity and performance.

"At my office we're not just coworkers, we're like a family. A very dysfunctional family."

© 1996 Randy Glasbergen.
www.glasbergen.com

Whole Foods Market and . . .   **CHANGE**

Putting the "Super" Back into "Supermarket"

In 2003, an animal-rights activist lectured Whole Foods CEO John Mackey about the unpleasant lives of farmed ducks. When Mackey investigated and found that farm-raised ducks never swam, he invited the activist to join him in pressuring the duck-raising industry. Today, Grimaud Farms, a Whole Foods supplier, is building a duck swimming area.

Whole Foods has grown from one store in 1978 to become the largest retailer of natural foods in the United States; with over 160 stores, it exerts considerable buying power. As Whole Foods becomes more successful, more suppliers provide natural foods. Dole, a traditional fruit producer, now supplies organic bananas and pineapples, half of which go to conventional stores. Organic Valley sells 16 percent of its organic milk to Whole Foods, but their biggest account is Publix, a traditional grocery store, and 60 percent of their sales are made to mainstream grocery sellers.

Supermarkets are under attack from discounters and profitability is suffering. Some stores compete by decreasing customer service and price, but this tactic has not improved performance. Industry analyst Dan Bagan says, "If a store starts to look, feel, and act like Wal-Mart, it *is* a Wal-Mart. That's when it's in trouble."

Whole Foods is having a tremendous influence on the mass-market grocery chains, challenging them to introduce more organic and natural foods. "If you look back 100 years from now," says editor Doug Greene, "history will show that Whole Foods will be in the top-five companies that changed the world." Mackey himself puts it a little differently. "Business is the most transformative agency in the world," he says. "[Businesses] can make money *and* do good."

The chapter's closing case, titled "The Fast-Breaking Culture of Whole Foods Market," tells more about culture and performance at Whole Foods.

"If a store starts to look, feel, and act like Wal-Mart, it is a Wal-Mart. That's when it's in trouble."

DAN BAGAN, INDUSTRY ANALYST, SUPERMARKET NEWS

References: Parija Bhatnagar, "Supermarkets Strike Back," *CNN/Money*, April 29, 2005, www.cnnmoney.com on April 30, 2005 (quotation); Charles Fischman, "The Anarchist's Cookbook," *Fast Company*, July 2004, pp. 70–78; Evan Smith, "John Mackey," *Texas Monthly*, March 2005, pp. 122–132; Amy Tsao, "Whole Foods' Natural High," *Business Week*, July 17, 2003, www.businessweek.com on April 30, 2005.

Changing the Organization Culture

Much of our discussion to this point has assumed that an organization's culture enhances its performance. When this is the case, learning what an organization's cultural values are and using those values to help socialize new workers and managers is very important, for such actions help the organization succeed. However, as Ouchi's and Peters and Waterman's research indicates, not all firms have cultural values that are consistent with high performance. Ouchi found that Japanese firms and Type Z U.S. firms have performance-enhancing values. Peters and Waterman identified performance-enhancing values associated with successful companies. By implication, some firms not included in Peters and Waterman's study must have had performance-reducing values. What should a manager who works in a company with performance-reducing values do?

The answer to this question is, of course, that top managers in such firms should try to change their organization's culture. However, this is a difficult thing to do.[45] Organization culture resists change for all the reasons that it is a powerful influence on behavior—it embodies the firm's basic values, it is often taken for granted, and it is typically most effectively communicated through stories or other symbols. When managers attempt to change organization culture, they are attempting to change people's basic assumptions about what is and is not appropriate behavior in the organization. Changing from a traditional organization to a team-based organization (discussed in Chapter 10) is one example of an organization culture change. Another is Boeing's decision in 1999 to change from a family culture to a performance culture.[46]

Despite these difficulties, some organizations have changed their cultures from performance-reducing to performance-enhancing.[47] This change process is described in more detail in Chapter 19. The earlier section on creating organization culture describes the importance of linking the strategic values and the cultural values in creating a new organization culture. We briefly discuss other important elements of the cultural change process in the following sections.

Managing Symbols

Research suggests that organization culture is understood and communicated through the use of stories and other symbolic media. If this is correct, managers interested in changing cultures should attempt to substitute stories and myths that support new cultural values for those that support old ones. They can do so by creating situations that give rise to new stories.

Suppose an organization traditionally has held the value "employee opinions are not important." When management meets in this company, the ideas and opinions of lower-level people—when discussed at all—are normally rejected as foolish and irrelevant. The stories that support this cultural value tell about managers who tried to make a constructive point only to have that point lost in personal attacks from superiors.

An upper-level manager interested in creating a new story, one that shows lower-level managers that their ideas are valuable, might ask a subordinate to prepare to lead a discussion in a meeting and follow through by asking the subordinate to take the lead when the topic arises. The subordinate's success in the meeting will become a new story, one that may displace some of the many stories suggesting that the opinions of lower-level managers do not matter.

The Difficulty of Change

Changing a firm's culture is a long and difficult process. A primary problem is that upper-level managers, no matter how dedicated they are to implementing some new cultural value, may sometimes inadvertently revert to old patterns of behavior. This happens, for example, when a manager dedicated to implementing the value that lower-level employees' ideas are important vehemently attacks a subordinate's ideas.

This mistake generates a story that supports old values and beliefs. After such an incident, lower-level managers may believe that the boss seems to want employee input and ideas, but nothing could be further from the truth. No matter what the boss says or how consistent his/her behavior is, some credibility has been lost, and cultural change has been made more difficult.

The Stability of Change   The process of changing a firm's culture starts with a need for change and moves through a transition period in which efforts are made to adopt new values and beliefs. In the long run, a firm that successfully changes its culture will find that the new values and beliefs are just as stable and influential as the old ones. Value systems tend to be self-reinforcing. Once they are in place, changing them requires an enormous effort. Thus, if a firm can change its culture from performance-reducing to performance-enhancing, the new values are likely to remain in place for a long time.

Synopsis

Organization culture has become one of the most discussed subjects in the field of organization behavior. It burst on the scene in the 1980s with books by Ouchi, Peters and Waterman, and others. Interest has not been restricted to academics, however. Practicing managers are also interested in organization culture, especially as it relates to performance.

There is little agreement about how to define organization culture. A comparison of several important definitions suggests that most have three things in common: They define culture in terms of the values that individuals in organizations use to prescribe appropriate behavior, they assume that these values are usually taken for granted, and they emphasize the stories and other symbolic means through which the values are typically communicated.

Current research on organization culture reflects various research traditions. The most important contributions have come from anthropology and sociology. Anthropologists have tended to focus on the organization cultures of one or two firms and have used detailed descriptions to help outsiders understand organization culture from the "natives' point of view." Sociologists typically have used survey methods to study the organization cultures of larger numbers of firms. Two other influences on current work in organization culture are social psychology, which emphasizes the manipulation of symbols in organizations, and economics. The economics approach sees culture both as a tool used to manage and as a determinant of performance.

Creating organization culture is a four-step process. It starts with formulating strategic and cultural values for the organization. Next, a vision for the organization is created, followed by the institution of implementation strategies. The final step is reinforcing the cultural behaviors of employees.

Although no single framework for describing organization culture has emerged, several have been suggested. The most popular efforts in this area have been Ouchi's comparison of U.S. and Japanese firms and Peters and Waterman's description of successful firms in the United States. Ouchi and Peters and Waterman suggested several important dimensions along which organization values vary, including treatment of employees, definitions of appropriate means for decision making, and assignment of responsibility for the results of decision making.

Emerging issues in the area of organization culture include innovation, employee empowerment, and appropriate cultures. Innovation is the process of creating and doing new things that are introduced into the marketplace as products, processes, or services. The organization culture can either help or hinder innovation. Employee empowerment, in addition to being similar to employee participation as a motivation technique, is now viewed by some as a type of organization culture. Empowerment occurs when employees make decisions, set their own work goals, and solve problems in their own area of responsibility. Finally, experts are beginning to suggest that there are cultures that are appropriate for particular organizations rather than there being any one best type of culture. Managing the organization culture requires attention to three factors. First, managers can take advantage of cultural values that already exist and use their knowledge to help subordinates understand them. Second, employees need to be properly socialized, or trained, in the cultural values of the organization, either through formal training or by experiencing and observing the actions of higher-level managers. Third, managers can change the culture of the organization through managing the symbols, addressing the extreme difficulties of such a change, and relying on the durability of the new organization culture once the change has been implemented.

Discussion Questions

1. A sociologist or anthropologist might suggest that the culture in U.S. firms simply reflects the dominant culture of the society as a whole. Therefore, to change the organization culture of a company, one must first deal with the inherent values and beliefs of the society. How would you respond to this claim?

2. Psychology has been defined as the study of individual behavior. Organizational psychology is the study of individual behavior in organizations. Many of the theories described in the early chapters of this book are based in organizational psychology. Why was this field not identified as a contributor to the study of organization culture along with

anthropology, sociology, social psychology, and economics?

3. Describe the culture of an organization with which you are familiar. It might be one in which you currently work, one in which you have worked, or one in which a friend or family member works. What values, beliefs, stories, and symbols are significant to employees of the organization?

4. Discuss the similarities and differences between the organization culture approaches of Ouchi and Peters and Waterman.

5. Describe how organizations use symbols and stories to communicate values and beliefs. Give some examples of how symbols and stories have been used in organizations with which you are familiar.

6. What is the role of leadership (discussed in Chapters 12 and 13) in developing, maintaining, and changing organization culture?

7. Review the characteristics of organization structure described in earlier chapters and compare them with the elements of culture described by Ouchi and Peters and Waterman. Describe the similarities and differences, and explain how some characteristics of one may be related to characteristics of the other.

8. Discuss the role of organization rewards in developing, maintaining, and changing the organization culture.

9. Describe how the culture of an organization can affect innovation.

Experiencing Organizational Behavior

Culture of the Classroom

Purpose: This exercise will help you appreciate the fascination as well as the difficulty of examining culture in organizations.

Format: The class will divide into groups of four to six. Each group will analyze the organization culture of a college class. Students in most classes that use this book will have taken many courses at the college they attend and therefore should have several classes in common.

Procedure: The class is divided into groups of four to six on the basis of classes the students have had in common.

1. Each group should first decide which class it will analyze. Each person in the group must have attended the class.

2. Each group should list the cultural factors to be discussed. Items to be covered should include

   a. Stories about the professor
   b. Stories about the exams
   c. Stories about the grading
   d. Stories about other students
   e. The use of symbols that indicate the students' values

   f. The use of symbols that indicate the instructor's values
   g. Other characteristics of the class as suggested by the frameworks of Ouchi and Peters and Waterman.

3. Students should carefully analyze the stories and symbols to discover their underlying meanings. They should seek stories from other members of the group to ensure that all aspects of the class culture are covered. Students should take notes as these items are discussed.

4. After twenty to thirty minutes of work in groups, the instructor will reconvene the entire class and ask each group to share its analysis with the rest of the class.

Follow-up Questions

1. What was the most difficult part of this exercise? Did other groups experience the same difficulty?

2. How did your group overcome this difficulty? How did other groups overcome it?

3. Do you believe your group's analysis accurately describes the culture of the class you selected? Could

other students who analyzed the culture of the same class come up with a very different result? How could that happen?

4. If the instructor wanted to try to change the culture in the class you analyzed, what steps would you recommend that he or she take?

An Empowering Culture: What It Is and What It Is Not

What does it mean to empower people? Below is a brief definition, along with three behaviors that masquerade as empowerment, often with devastating results. See how well you can distinguish among them by choosing the one that best describes the supervisory behavior. Answers appear in *the Instructor's Resource Manual*. The quiz and answers were prepared by Donna Deeprose of Deeprose Consulting in New York.

Empower: To enable an employee to set work goals, make decisions, and solve problems

Exploit: To take advantage of an employee to meet an unspoken goal of one's own

Abandon: To delegate but provide no support

Delude: To give the appearance of empowering but to withhold the freedom the employee needs to be successful

1. A supervisor gives an employee authority to handle a project. When the employee complains about difficulties, the supervisor responds, "Don't worry, I'll handle it from now on."

   Behavior: _____

2. Same situation as (1), except that when the employee comes to the supervisor for help, the supervisor's response is "This is your project. You take care of it."

   Behavior: _____

3. Same as (1) and (2), except that the supervisor discusses the problem with the employee and guides the employee into determining an appropriate next move.

   Behavior: _____

4. An employee has asked for additional responsibilities. The supervisor delegates to the employee total responsibility for a time-consuming report. The supervisor leaves at 5 P.M. each day while the employee works late to complete the report.

   Behavior: _____

5. A supervisor keeps up with the company's changing mission, objectives, and plans, and keeps employees informed of how well all these changes influence the work unit.

   Behavior: _____

Reference: Reprinted from "Understanding the E-Word," *Supervisory Management,* November 1993, pp. 7–8. American Management Association International. Reprinted by permission of American Management Association International, New York, NY. All rights reserved.

Exercise Overview: Typically, managers are promoted or selected to fill jobs in an organization with a given organization culture. As they begin to work, they must recognize the culture and either learn how to work within it or figure out how to change it. If the culture is a performance-reducing one, managers must figure out how to change the culture to a performance-enhancing one. This exercise will give you a chance to develop your own ideas about changing organization culture.

Exercise Background: Assume that you have just been appointed to head the legislative affairs committee of your local student government. As someone with a double major in business management and government, you are eager to take on this assignment and really make a difference. This committee has existed at your university for several years, but it has done little because the members use the committee as a social group and regularly throw great parties. In all the years of its existence, the committee has done nothing to impact the local state legislature in relation to the issues important to university students, such as tuition. Since you know that the issue of university tuition will come before the state legislature during the current legislative session, and you know that many students could not afford a substantial raise in tuition, you are determined to use this committee to ensure that any tuition increase is as small as possible. However, you are worried that the party culture of the existing committee may make it difficult for you to use it to work for your issues. You also know that you cannot "fire" any of the volunteers on the committee and can add only two people to the committee.

Exercise Task: Using this information as context, do the following:

1. Design a strategy for utilizing the existing culture of the committee to help you impact the legislature regarding tuition.

2. Assuming that the existing culture is a performance-reducing culture, design a strategy for changing it to a performance-enhancing culture.

Organizational Behavior Case for Discussion

The Fast-Breaking Culture of Whole Foods Market

Most large supermarkets are standardized with a warehouse environment, offer minimal customer service, and use centralized, bureaucratic decision making. According to John Mackey, CEO of Whole Foods Market, these stores "have command and control models . . . They're cookie cutters. They have a formula that works . . . It's the mass-market football model of executing the game plan—don't fumble the ball, don't make any mistakes." In 2005, Kroger's, the nation's largest supermarket chain with 3,750 stores, lost $100 million.

Yet one company, Whole Foods Market, stands out from the rest. In 2004, the 160-store chain earned $137 million. It has a unique organization culture, described by Mackey as "a fast-breaking basketball team. We're driving down the court, but we don't exactly know how the play is going to evolve." Can the differences in performance be attributed to differences in organization culture?

In 1978, Mackey, then a student at the University of Texas, started a tiny natural foods store called SaferWay. As the store grew and changed its name to Whole Foods, Mackey studied Japanese management techniques. The result was an organization culture that is democratic, participative, egalitarian, innovative, team-based, and transparent.

Democratic—Almost all decisions are made by consensus or after intense consultation with a wide variety of employees. Over sixty employees helped write the company's "Declaration of Interdependence." Among the values expressed in the declaration are a commitment to high-quality natural and organic food, customer service guidelines, and support for "team member excellence and happiness."

Participative—Whole Foods believes that decisions should be made closest to the place they'll be carried out and should directly involve the people affected. Store employees design the store, pick the products that will sell locally, and establish prices. Mackey prefers to stay out of local choices, and claims his favorite decisions are "decisions that are *not* my decision."

Egalitarian—Executive pay is limited to no more than 14 times the average salary of a front-line worker. Compare this to the $3.7 million earned by David Dillon, CEO of Kroger's. Dillon's pay is 122 times the average Kroger's employee's salary. Every employee qualifies for stock options and 94 percent is awarded to non-executive staff.

Innovative—At Whole Foods, employees are encouraged to experiment. "The team leader at every store can spend up to $100,000 a year without asking for permission," says Mackey. "We want them to try different things,

> **"We're driving down the court, but we don't exactly know how the play is going to evolve."**
> JOHN MACKEY, CEO, WHOLE FOODS MARKET

and the things that are successful we'll study and copy and improve on."

Team-based—After a four-week trial period, a two-thirds vote by team members is needed to permanently hire a new employee. Team members are careful in their hires because pay is linked to the performance of small teams at every location.

Transparent—The company releases far more financial data than most companies and most of it is aimed at employees. Every employee has easy access to pay data for every Whole Foods employee, by name.

Other cultural elements have added to the success of Whole Foods. Mackey is a conscientious cost-cutter, flying economy class on commercial airlines and asking visiting managers to stay at his home in Austin. Supplier relationships are crucial when the organic nature of the products must be verified. Whole Foods works with suppliers on issues as diverse as support for family farms and development of USDA standards for organic foods.

Social responsibility is taken seriously here. Whole Foods donates 5 percent of after-tax profits to charity. It also pays employees for up to twenty hours of community service each year and allows each employee to donate $50 of company money to a charity of their choice. Whole Foods created the Animal Compassion Foundation to support meat producers in improving the quality of life for farm animals.

Grocery sales have grown by 2.5 percent annually in the United States over the last five years. Whole Foods had an annual growth of about 19 percent over that same time. Chris Hitt, former president of Whole Foods, claims the growth is due to happy customers, and happy customers are a result of the unique culture. "Customers experience the food and the space, but what they really experience is the work culture. The true hidden secret of the company is the work culture. That's what delivers the stores to the customers."

Case Questions

1. What are the basic assumptions and values that make up the organization culture of Whole Foods Market?

2. Using the Ouchi framework, analyze the organization culture at Whole Foods. Is the company a typical Japanese company, a typical U.S. company, or a Type Z American company? Explain.

3. What would it take for a traditional supermarket such as Safeway or Kroger's to change its organization culture to become more like Whole Foods? In your opinion, would such an effort be likely to be successful? Why or why not?

References: "Declaration of Interdependence," Whole Foods Market website, www.wholefoodsmarket.com on May 1, 2005; "David B. Dillon," *Forbes*, www.forbes.com on April 29, 2005; "The Kroger Co.," *Hoover's*, www.hoovers.com on April 29, 2005; Charles Fischman, "The Anarchist's Cookbook," *Fast Company*, July 2004, pp. 70–78; Evan Smith, "John Mackey," *Texas Monthly*, March 2005, pp. 122–132 (quotation); Amy Tsao, "Whole Foods' Natural High," *Business Week*, July 17, 2003, www.businessweek.com on April 30, 2005.

TEST PREPPER

You have read the chapter and studied the key terms. Think you're ready to ace the exam? Take this sample test to gauge your comprehension of chapter material and check your answers at the back of the book. Want more test questions? Take the ACE quizzes found on the student website: http://college.hmco.com/business/students/ (select Griffin/Moorhead, Organizational Behavior, 8e from the Management menu).

T F 1. The research on the impact of culture has come to the firm conclusion that strong cultures enhance performance.

T F 2. Culture is often communicated through stories.

T F 3. The terms organizational culture and organizational climate mean essentially the same thing, and are, for all purposes, interchangeable.

T F 4. According to William Ouchi, a Type Z firm is a typical Japanese firm that tries to develop an American firm culture.

T F 5. Managers with a bias for action make decisions even if all the facts are not in.

T F 6. Entrepreneurial activity within an organization is called intrapreneurship.

T F 7. Organizations that use formal socialization programs to teach employees their culture are usually successful at changing employees' values.

8. A variety of definitions of culture exist. All of the following are common attributes that emerge among these definitions, except
   a. culture refers to some set of values held by individuals.
   b. the values that make up an organization's culture are often taken for granted.
   c. cultural elements create positive situations in the organization.
   d. an organization's culture is communicated through symbolic means.
   e. All of the above are common attributes among the definitions of culture.

9. Paul is interested in studying organizational culture. Which of the following areas would likely be the least helpful to Paul in his research?
   a. Sociology
   b. Engineering
   c. Anthropology
   d. Social psychology
   e. Economics

10. Lauren is an entrepreneur and is about to open a new business. She wants to start things off correctly by creating a healthy organizational culture. Which of the following would you recommend be Lauren's first step?

a. Become a Type Z organization.
b. Tell as many stories as possible.
c. Let the culture rapidly develop a "taken for granted" nature.
d. Determine the strategic values of the organization.
e. Reinforce cultural behaviors.

11. According to the research performed by William Ouchi, Type Z U.S. and typical Japanese firms share certain cultural values that may explain their success. Which of the following is not one of these values?
   a. Trying to keep employees
   b. Rapid employee evaluation and promotion
   c. Control through informal, implicit mechanisms
   d. Group decision making
   e. Holistic concern for workers and managers

12. One suggestion in Peters and Waterman's *In Search of Excellence* is to "stick to the knitting." This means
   a. staying close to the customer.
   b. achieving productivity through people.
   c. reluctance to engage in business outside their areas of expertise.
   d. managers should manage by "wandering around" the organization.
   e. breaking the company into smaller pieces and then re-attaching each piece in sequence.

13. Peters and Waterman identified simultaneously loose and tight organization as a valuable cultural characteristic. How is it possible to be simultaneously loosely and tightly organized?
   a. All members understand the firm's values, but there are formal fewer rules and regulations.
   b. Prices are strictly based on market values, but prices are allowed to fluctuate with the market.
   c. Managers have formal authority, but they allow a wide degree of participation by subordinates.
   d. Employees have specific assignments, but they are allowed to schedule their work as they please.
   e. The organization has few administrative layers, and each layer is staffed with only the necessary number of employees.

Organization Change and Development

CHAPTER 19

After studying this chapter, you should be able to:

Chapter Outline

Forces for Change

Processes for Planned Organization Change

Organization Development

Resistance to Change

Managing Successful Organization Change and Development

▶ **Summarize the dominant forces for change in organizations.**

▶ **Describe the process of planned organization change.**

▶ **Discuss several approaches to organization development.**

▶ **Explain resistance to change.**

▶ **Identify the keys to managing successful organization change and development.**

Shutting Down Rocky Flats

Built in 1952, Rocky Flats produced nuclear weapons at an 11-square-mile site located just 16 miles from Denver and 8 miles from Boulder. The work was done in secrecy and high security. Rocky Flats experienced several accidents and fires, including one in 1969 that released radioactive plutonium into the air. Production was suspended in 1989 and when Trident warhead production ceased in 1992, the site was closed. Yet the remaining radiation required ongoing maintenance and security, costing the government $1.5 million daily. Meanwhile, suburban growth brought people closer to the site.

The site had to be cleaned up. Initially, the cost of the cleanup was estimated at $36 billion and would last until 2062. The site's plutonium and the 8,000 other chemicals that are there make cleanup expensive. Workers must wear fully enclosed suits connected to oxygen and undergo extensive decontamination. Concrete buildings and huge steel machines must be cut into pieces for transportation. Thousands of tons of soil and an estimated 7,000 semi-truck loads of radioactive material must be removed.

Kaiser-Hill, the cleanup contractor, hired laid-off plant workers, because they already knew the site and understood the dangers. But how could these workers be motivated? "How in the world do you get people to work as fast as they can to put themselves out of work?" asks professor Kim Cameron. He provides four answers: incentives, meaning, symbolic leadership, and culture change.

Rocky Flats offered annual cash bonuses, but first they developed quantifiable performance measures to measure each tiny step forward. The company could earn up to $100 million in bonuses. Each employee may receive between $200,000 and $400,000 if goals are met. To give meaning to the shutdown, managers shifted workers' focus away from the demolition and toward the ultimate goal—creation of a wildlife refuge. Workers envisioned themselves as environmentalists, not polluters.

Symbols were important too. On the first week, the guardhouse was demolished, visibly destroying the old culture of secrecy and replacing it with openness. Creation of a new culture has been challenging. Many of the workers have decades of employment at Rocky Flats, so old ways are slow to change. Kaiser-Hill increased innovation by creating broader job descriptions and giving autonomous teams greater decision-making power.

The results have been impressive. The work will finish in 2006 at a cost of less than $7 billion. Kaiser-Hill used some of its profits to create a full-time, free job relocation program for employees who will soon be out of work. It's a win-win situation. "It's the right thing to do, but it also plays into our business model," says Len Martinez, Kaiser-Hill chief financial officer. "If you have people worried about what they're going to do and how their families will be affected, they won't be focused on being safe and doing the job." See the boxed insert titled *The U.S. Army and . . . Change* on page 517 for more information about motivation at Rocky Flats and other organizations.

References: "Rocky Flats Environmental Technology Site," U.S. Department of Energy website, web.em.doe.gov on May 2, 2005; "Rocky Flats Public Exposure Studies," Colorado Department of Public Health and Environment website, www.cdphe.state.co.us on May 3, 2005; "Toward a 2006 Deadline," *Nuclear Engineering International*, February 2000, www.findarticles.com on May 2, 2005; Jena McGregor, "Rocky Mountain High," *Fast Company*, July 2004, pp. 58–64 (quotation).

Forces for Change

An organization is subject to pressures for change from far too many sources that can be discussed here. Moreover, it is difficult to predict what types of pressures for change will be most significant in the next decade because the complexity of events and the rapidity of change are increasing. However, it is possible—and important—to discuss the broad categories of pressures that probably will have major effects on organizations. The four areas in which the pressures for change appear most powerful involve people, technology, information processing and communication, and competition. Table 19.1 gives examples of each of these categories.

Category	Examples	Type of Pressure for Change
People	Generation X, Y, Z Twixters Global Labor Supplies Senior citizens Workforce diversity	Demands for different training, benefits, workplace arrangements, and compensation systems
Technology	Manufacturing in space Internet Global design teams	More education and training for workers at all levels, more new products, products move faster to market
Information Processing and Communication	Computer, satellite communications Global Sourcing Videoconferencing	Faster reaction times, immediate responses to questions, new products, different office arrangements, telecommuting
Competition	Global markets International trade agreements Emerging nations	Global competition, more competing products with more features and options, lower costs, higher quality

TABLE 19.1

Pressures for Organization Change

People

Approximately 56 million people were born between 1945 and 1960. These baby boomers differ significantly from previous generations with respect to education, expectations, and value systems.[1] As this group has aged, the median age of the U.S. population has gradually increased, passing 32 for the first time in 1988[2] and further increasing to 35.6 in 1999.[3] The special characteristics of baby boomers show up in distinct purchasing patterns that affect product and service innovation, technological change, and marketing and promotional activities.[4] Employment practices, compensation systems, promotion and managerial succession systems, and the entire concept of human resource management are also affected.

Other population-related pressures for change involve the generations that sandwich the baby boomers: the increasing numbers of senior citizens and those born after 1960. The parents of the baby boomers are living longer, healthier lives than previous generations, and today they expect to live the "good life" that they missed when they were raising their children. The impact of the large number of senior citizens is already evident in part-time employment practices, in the marketing of everything from hamburgers to packaged tours of Asia, and in service areas such as healthcare, recreation, and financial services. The post-1960 generation of workers who entered the job market in the 1980s were different from the baby boomers. Sociologists and psychologists have identified a new group, from age eighteen to the late twenties, that seems to be experiencing a distinct and separate life stage in between adolescence and adulthood in which young people may jump from job to job and relationship to relationship, often living at home with few responsibilities and experimenting with life. This in-between age group, often called "twixters" or "emerging adults," is putting off marriage, childbearing, home purchases, and most adult responsibilities.[5] These changes in demographics extend to the composition of the workforce, family lifestyles, and purchasing patterns worldwide.

The increasing diversity of the workforce in coming years will mean significant changes for organizations. This increasing diversity was discussed in some detail in Chapter 2. In addition, employees are facing a different work environment in the twenty-first century. The most descriptive word for this new work environment is "change." Employees must be prepared for constant change. Change is occurring in organizations' cultures, structures, work relationships, and customer relationships, as well as in the actual jobs that people do. People will have to be completely adaptable to new situations while maintaining productivity under the existing system.[6]

Technology

Not only is technology changing, but the rate of technological change is also increasing. In 1970, for example, all engineering students owned slide rules and used them in almost every class. By 1976, slide rules had given way to portable electronic calculators. In the mid-1980s, some universities began issuing microcomputers to entering students or assumed that those students already owned them. In 1993, the Scholastic Aptitude Test (SAT), which many college-bound students take to get into college, allowed calculators to be used during the test! Today students cannot make it through the university without owning or at least having ready access to a personal computer. The dormitory rooms at many universities are wired for direct computer access for email and class assignments and for connection to the Internet. Many buildings at many universities are set up for wireless access for faculty, students, staff, and campus guests. Technological development is increasing so rapidly in almost every field that it is quite difficult to predict which products will dominate ten years from now. DuPont is an example of a company that is making major changes due to new technological developments. Although its business had been based on petrochemicals since the end of the nineteenth century, as new technology has developed in the life sciences, DuPont has changed its basic business strategy, reorganized its eighty-one business units into three, and invested heavily in agrichemicals and the life sciences. Realizing that a biotechnology-based business changes much more rapidly than a petrochemical-based business, Chairman Chad Holliday has had to make cultural changes as well as structural ones in order to make the strategy work.[7]

Interestingly, organization change is self-perpetuating. With the advances in information technology, organizations generate more information, and it circulates more quickly. Consequently, employees can respond more quickly to problems, so the organization can respond more quickly to demands from other organizations, customers, and competitors.[8] Toyota is a leader in developing and using new technologies in its plants, as described in the *Toyota and . . . Technology* box.

New technology will affect organizations in ways we cannot yet predict. Artificial intelligence—computers and software programs that think and learn in much the same way as humans do—is already assisting in geological exploration.[9] Several companies are developing systems to manufacture chemicals and exotic electronic components in space. The Internet and the World Wide Web are changing the way companies and individuals communicate, market, buy, and distribute faster than organizations can respond. Thus, as organizations react more quickly to change, change occurs more rapidly, which in turn necessitates more rapid responses.

Information Processing and Communication

Advances in information processing and communication have paralleled each other. A new generation of computers, which will mark another major increase in processing power, is being designed. Satellite systems for data transmission are already in use. Today people can carry telephones in their pockets that double as their portable computers, pocket-size televisions, music players, and pagers, all in one device.

Toyota and . . . **TECHNOLOGY**

The Robot-Worker Interface at Toyota

Toyota is pushing the technology envelope with the development of a *kokino robotto*, "advanced robot," that can perform several complex tasks simultaneously. Personal assistant robots are designed to carry heavy packages and help the elderly and the ill out of bed. Another robot is an exoskeleton, shaped like a chair on legs. A disabled person rides the robot, opening doors with its arms and climbing stairs, tasks impossible for traditional wheelchairs.

The robots will also be used in factory production. While traditional robots perform large-scale operations in welding, painting, and gross assembly, the *kokino robotto* are super robots capable of performing a task as delicate as tightening a screw. Toyota's super robots can manage final assembly and trim operations.

The machines are quick and consistent. Unlike humans, robots never tire, get hurt, or retire, reducing Toyota's short- and long-term expenses. "The two-armed [super robot] is as labor efficient as a human, if not more efficient," says industry observer Burritt Sabin. A Toyota official states, "[With robots], we aim to reduce production costs to the levels in China."

Robots replace factory workers, in short supply in Japan, and keep costs low, in a high-wage country. The company plans to add 1,000 super robots to its 3,000 to 4,000 standard robots. "Even this super robot will not result in the total replacement of man by machine; rather,

it will reinforce the strengths of the production line," says Sabin.

Competitors are awed by Toyota's high-tech equipment. However, Toyota managers claim their success is founded on training, responsibility, shared values, and respect. Consultant Dennis Pawley sees the performance gap between American and Japanese automakers. Referring to the Detroit Big Three, he says, "They don't understand that they don't understand."

See "Toyota Reinvented," this chapter's closing case, to learn more about changes at Toyota.

> *"[With robots], we aim to reduce production costs to the levels in China."*
>
> *A TOYOTA MANAGER*

References: "Toyota to Employ Robots," News24.com website, January 6, 2005, www.news24.com on May 4, 2005; "Toyota's Global New Body Line," Toyota Motor Manufacturing website, www.toyotageorgetown.com on May 4, 2005; Burritt Sabin, "Robots for Babies—Toyota at the Leading Edge," Japan.com website, www.japan.com on May 5, 2005; Christine Tierney, "Big Three Play Catch-Up to Toyota Plant Prowess," *The Detroit News,* February 22, 2004, www.detnews.com on May 4, 2005.

In the future, people may not need offices as they work with computers and communicate through new data transmission devices. Work stations, both in and outside of offices, will be more electronic than paper and pencil. For years, the capability has existed to generate, manipulate, store, and transmit more data than managers could use, but the benefits were not fully realized. Now the time has come to utilize all of that information-processing potential, and companies are making the most of it. Typically, companies received orders by mail in the 1970s, by toll-free telephone numbers in the 1980s, by fax machine in the late 1980s and early 1990s, and by electronic data exchange in the mid-1990s. Orders used to take a week; now they are placed instantaneously, and companies must be able to respond immediately, all because of changes in information processing and communication.[10] Suppliers and end users in some industries now have the parts systems integrated so closely that orders for new parts shipments sometimes are not even ordered: They just show up at the receiving dock when they are needed. Systems integrators such as Context Integration are providing new knowledge management

Cell phone giants such as Nokia, Motorola, and Ericsson have had a stranglehold on the worldwide cellular phone market. All three have major operations in China, manufacturing and selling in Asia as well as the rest of the world. That world is changing fast, however. The new competition may soon be from Chinese companies. More than 30 Chinese companies are now manufacturing cellular phones and working with software providers Microsoft and Qualcomm Inc. to develop much lower-priced handsets. Nokia and the others had better watch out!

systems to help companies outthink their competition.[11]

Competition

Although competition is not a new force for change, competition today has some significant new twists. First, most markets are global because of decreasing transportation and communication costs and the increasing export orientation of business. The adoption of trade agreements such as the North American Free Trade Agreement (NAFTA) and the presence of the World Trade Organization (WTO) have changed the way business operates. In the future, competition from industrialized countries such as Japan and Germany will take a back seat to competition from the booming industries of developing nations, such as China and India. The Internet is creating new competitors overnight and in ways that could not have been imagined five years ago. Companies in developing nations may soon offer different, newer, cheaper, or higher-quality products while enjoying the benefits of low labor costs, abundant supplies of raw materials, expertise in certain areas of production, and financial protection from their governments that may not be available to firms in older industrialized states. Nokia, a Finnish company, is locked in a battle with Motorola and Ericsson for the worldwide cellular phone market. In order to meet the global competitive challenges, Nokia changed its approach to marketing by holding global strategy sessions and training managers to think globally yet act locally by developing a good understanding of local cultures. The firm had to adjust to the fact that mass marketing differs widely among the United States, Europe, and Asia.[12] Organizations that are not ready for these new sources of competition may not last long in the new century. Korean manufacturers, such as LG Electronics and Samsung Electronics, have joined the fray, making competition in the cellular phone industry extremely fierce.[13]

Processes for Planned Organization Change

External forces may impose change on an organization. Ideally, however, the organization will not only respond to change but will also anticipate it, prepare for it through planning, and incorporate it in the organization strategy. Organization change can be viewed from a static point of view, such as that of Lewin (see next section), or from a dynamic perspective.

Lewin's Process Model

Planned organization change requires a systematic process of movement from one condition to another. Kurt Lewin suggested that efforts to bring about planned change in organizations should approach change as a multistage process.[14] His model of planned change is made up of three steps—unfreezing, change, and refreezing—as shown in Figure 19.1.

Unfreezing is the process by which people become aware of the need for change. If people are satisfied with current practices and procedures, they may have little or no interest in making changes. The key factor in unfreezing is making employees understand the importance of a change and how their jobs will be affected by it. The employees who will be most affected by the change must be made aware of why it is needed, which in effect makes them dissatisfied enough with current operations to be motivated to change. Creating in employees the awareness of the need for change is the responsibility of the leadership of the organization.[15]

> **Unfreezing** is the process by which people become aware of the need for change.

Change itself is the movement from the old way of doing things to a new way. Change may entail installing new equipment, restructuring the organization, implementing a new performance appraisal system—anything that alters existing relationships or activities.

Refreezing makes new behaviors relatively permanent and resistant to further change. Examples of refreezing techniques include repeating newly learned skills in a training session and role playing to teach how the new skill can be used in a real-life work situation. Refreezing is necessary because without it, the old ways of doing things might soon reassert themselves while the new ways are forgotten. For example, many employees who attend special training sessions apply themselves diligently and resolve

> **Refreezing** is the process of making new behaviors relatively permanent and resistant to further change.

FIGURE 19.1

Lewin's Process of Organization Change

In Lewin's three-step model, change is a systematic process of transition from an old way of doing things to a new way. Inclusion of an "unfreezing" stage indicates the importance of preparing for the change. The refreezing stage reflects the importance of following up on the change to make it permanent.

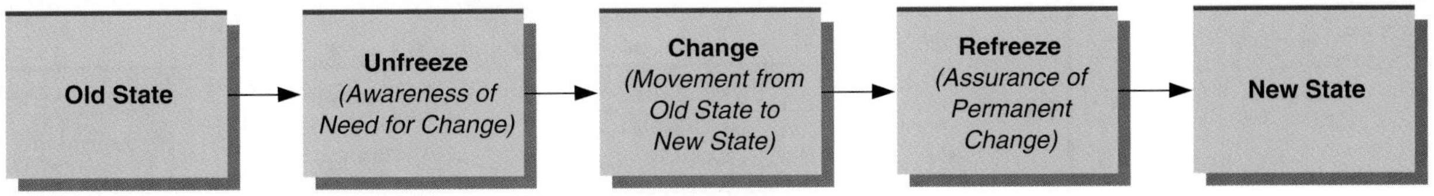

| Old State | → | **Unfreeze** (Awareness of Need for Change) | → | **Change** (Movement from Old State to New State) | → | **Refreeze** (Assurance of Permanent Change) | → | New State |

to change things in their organizations. But when they return to the workplace, they find it easier to conform to the old ways than to make waves. There usually are few, if any, rewards for trying to change the organizational status quo. In fact, the personal sanctions against doing so may be difficult to tolerate. Learning theory and reinforcement theory (see Chapter 4) can play important roles in the refreezing phase.

The Continuous Change Process Model

Perhaps because Lewin's model is very simple and straightforward, virtually all models of organization change use his approach. However, it does not deal with several important issues. A more complex, and more helpful, approach is illustrated in Figure 19.2. This approach treats planned change from the perspective of top management and indicates that change is continuous. Although we discuss each step as if it were separate and distinct from the others, it is important to note that as change becomes continuous in organizations, different steps are probably occurring simultaneously throughout the organization. The model incorporates Lewin's concept into the implementation phase.

In this approach, top management perceives that certain forces or trends call for change, and the issue is subjected to the organization's usual problem-solving and decision-making processes (see Chapter 8). Usually, top management defines its goals in terms of what the organization or certain processes or outputs will be like after the change. Alternatives for change are generated and evaluated, and an acceptable one is selected.

Early in the process, the organization may seek the assistance of a **change agent**—a person who will be responsible for managing the change effort. The change agent may also help management recognize and define the problem or the need for the change and may be involved in generating and evaluating potential plans of action. The change agent

A **change agent** is a person responsible for managing a change effort.

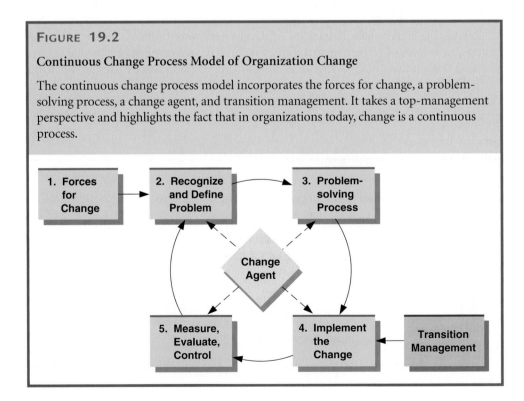

FIGURE 19.2

Continuous Change Process Model of Organization Change

The continuous change process model incorporates the forces for change, a problem-solving process, a change agent, and transition management. It takes a top-management perspective and highlights the fact that in organizations today, change is a continuous process.

may be a member of the organization, an outsider such as a consultant, or even someone from headquarters whom employees view as an outsider. An internal change agent is likely to know the organization's people, tasks, and political situations, which may be helpful in interpreting data and understanding the system; but an insider may also be too close to the situation to view it objectively. (In addition, a regular employee would have to be removed from his or her regular duties to concentrate on the transition.) An outsider, then, is often received better by all parties because of his or her assumed impartiality. Under the direction and management of the change agent, the organization implements the change through Lewin's unfreeze, change, and refreeze process. The final step is measurement, evaluation, and control. The change agent and the top management group assess the degree to which the change is having the desired effect; that is, they measure progress toward the goals of the change and make appropriate changes if necessary. The more closely the change agent is involved in the change process, the less distinct the steps become. The change agent becomes a "collaborator" or "helper" to the organization as she or he is immersed in defining and solving the problem with members of the organization. When this happens, the change agent may be working with many individuals, groups, and departments within the organization on different phases of the change process. When the change process is moving along from one stage to another, it may not be readily observable because of the total involvement of the change agent in every phase of the project. Throughout the process, however, the change agent brings in new ideas and viewpoints that help members look at old problems in new ways. Change often arises from the conflict that results when the change agent challenges the organization's assumptions and generally accepted patterns of operation.

This is Michael Eisner at the time he became CEO and savior of Disney in 1984 when the company was in the midst of a troubled period. That year the company had a flagging film division that produced few hits. Eisner became the change agent who spurred growth by engaging in what previously would have been considered some very un-Disney like activities. In effect, he was an internal change agent. Two decades later, in 2004, the board ousted Eisner. Evidently, Eisner, once an agent for change, became the one who needed to be changed.

Through the measurement, evaluation, and control phase, top management determines the effectiveness of the change process by evaluating various indicators of organizational productivity and effectiveness or employee morale. It is hoped that the organization will be better after the change than before. However, the uncertainties and rapid change in all sectors of the environment make constant organization change a certainty for most organizations.

Transition management is the process of systematically planning, organizing, and implementing change, from the disassembly of the current state to the realization of a fully functional future state within an organization.[16] No matter how much we plan and how well we implement the change, because we are dealing with people there will always be unanticipated and unpredictable things happen along the way.[17] One key role of transition management is to deal with these unintended consequences. Once change begins, the organization is in neither the old state nor the new state, yet business must go on. Transition management also ensures that business continues while the change is occurring; therefore, it must begin before the change occurs. The members of the regular management team must take on the role of transition managers and coordinate organizational activities with the change agent. An interim management structure or interim positions may be created to ensure continuity and control

Transition management is the process of systematically planning, organizing, and implementing change.

of the business during the transition. Communication about the changes to all involved, from employees to customers and suppliers, plays a key role in transition management.[18]

Organization Development

On one level, organization development is simply the way organizations change and evolve. Organization change can involve personnel, technology, competition, and other areas. Employee learning and formal training, transfers, promotions, terminations, and retirements are all examples of personnel-related changes. Thus, in the broadest sense, organization development means organization change.[19] However, the term as used here means something more specific. Over the past thirty years, organization development has emerged as a distinct field of study and practice. Experts now substantially agree as to what constitutes organization development in general, although arguments about details continue.[20] Our definition of organization development is an attempt to describe a very complex process in a simple manner. It is also an attempt to capture the best points of several definitions offered by writers in the field.

Organization Development Defined

Organization development is the process of planned change and improvement of the organization through application of knowledge of the behavioral sciences.

Organization development (OD) is the process of planned change and improvement of organizations through the application of knowledge of the behavioral sciences. Three points in this definition make it simple to remember and use. First, organization development involves attempts to plan organization changes, which excludes spontaneous, haphazard initiatives. Second, the specific intention of organization development is to improve organizations. This point excludes changes that merely imitate those of another organization, are forced on the organization by external pressures, or are undertaken merely for the sake of changing. Third, the planned improvement must be based on knowledge of the behavioral sciences such as organizational behavior, psychology, sociology, cultural anthropology, and related fields of study rather than on financial or technological considerations. Under our definition, the replacement of manual personnel records with a computerized system would not be considered an instance of organization development. Although such a change has behavioral effects, it is a technology-driven reform rather than a behavioral one. Likewise, alterations in record keeping necessary to support new government-mandated reporting requirements are not a part of organization development because the change is obligatory and the result of an external force. The three most basic types of techniques for implementing organization development are systemwide, task and technological, and group and individual.

At one time in the 1960s and 1970s organization development was treated as a field of study and practiced by specially trained OD professionals. However, as organization change became the order of the day in progressive organizations around the world, it became clear that all organizational leaders needed to become leaders and teachers of change throughout their organizations if their organizations were going to survive. Excellent examples of organizations that have embraced OD are the U.S. Army, General Electric, and Royal Dutch Shell.[21] *The U.S. Army and . . . Change* box describes how a complete organization structure and culture change.

Systemwide Organization Development

Structural change is a systemwide organization development involving a major restructuring of the organization or instituting programs such as quality of work life.

The most comprehensive type of organization change involves a major reorientation or reorganization—usually referred to as a **structural change** or a systemwide

The U.S. Army and . . . CHANGE

Motivating Workers out of a Job

Kaiser-Hill is changing the organization culture in order to motivate employees at Rocky Flats. Many other organizations face a similar task—motivating workers at a time of intense organization change.

The fall of the Berlin Wall, in 1989, caused U.S. Army leaders to realize that "the Army . . . had been perfected for a world that suddenly no longer existed," claim Colonel Michael V. Harper and General Gordon R. Sullivan. "[T]he challenge was to displace a sense of satisfaction . . . and imbed a passion for growth. The challenge was to keep the Army ready to fight while we were demobilizing 600,000 people. The Army was good—very good—at gradual change, but it was poorly prepared to handle the avalanche of change thrust upon it . . ."

In this chapter's opening case, professor Kim Cameron recommends that organizations change their cultural values and symbols to increase motivation. In 1995, the Army did that, with an organization redesign and cultural shift called Force XXI, which improved flexibility. Glen R. Hawkins and James Jay Carafano, of the Army's Center for Military History, write, "The great challenge for designers is to build organizations that meet [today's] strategic requirements, but are sufficiently flexible to adapt to changes."

It seems that a permanent change in the fundamental purpose, direction, and strategy of an organization must be accompanied by a change in its culture, if it is to succeed. In *The Wisdom of the Sands,* author Antoine de Saint-Exupery writes, "If you want to build a ship, don't drum up the men to gather wood, divide the work, and give orders. Instead, teach them to yearn for the vast and endless sea." Saint-Exupery understands that workers don't need to be told what to do. To motivate them, a manager has only to inspire them with a vision of change.

> *"The challenge was to keep the Army ready to fight while we were demobilizing 600,000 people."*
>
> COLONEL MICHAEL V. HARPER AND GENERAL GORDON R. SULLIVAN, AUTHORS OF HOPE IS NOT A METHOD.

References: Glen R. Hawkins and James Jay Carafano, "Prelude to Army XXI," United States Army Center of Military History website, 1997, www.fas.org on May 4, 2005; Jena McGregor, "Rocky Mountain High," *Fast Company*, July 2004, pp. 58–64; "Toward a 2006 Deadline," *Nuclear Engineering International*, February 2000, www.findarticles.com on May 2, 2005; Gordon R. Sullivan and Michael V. Harper, *Hope Is Not a Method* (New York: Random House, 1996) (quotation).

rearrangement of task division and authority and reporting relationships. A structural change affects performance appraisal and rewards, decision making, and communication and information-processing systems. As we discussed in Chapter 17, reengineering and rethinking the organizations are two contemporary approaches to systemwide structural change. Reengineering can be a difficult process, but it has great potential for organizational improvement. It requires that managers challenge long-held assumptions about everything they do and set outrageous goals and expect that they will be met. An organization may change the way it divides tasks into jobs, combines jobs into departments and divisions, and arranges authority and reporting relationships among positions. It may move from functional departmentalization to a system based on products or geography, for example, or from a conventional linear design to a matrix or a team-based design. Other changes may include dividing large groups into smaller ones or merging small groups into larger ones. In addition, the degree to which rules and procedures are written down and enforced, as well as the locus of decision-making authority, may be altered. Supervisors may become "coaches" or "facilitators" in a team-based organization. The organization will have transformed both the configurational and the operational aspects of its structure if all of these changes are made.

No systemwide structural change is simple.[22] A company president cannot just issue a memo notifying company personnel that on a certain date they will report to a different supervisor and be responsible for new tasks and expect everything to change overnight. Employees have months, years, and sometimes decades of experience in dealing with people and tasks in certain ways. When these patterns are disrupted, employees need time to learn the new tasks and to settle into the new relationships. Moreover, they may resist the change for a number of reasons; we discuss resistance to change later in this chapter. Therefore, organizations must manage the change process.

Ford Motor Company is pretty typical of organizations that have had to make major organization-wide and worldwide changes. Over the years, Ford had developed several regional fiefdoms, such as Ford of Europe, Ford United States, and Ford Australia, which all operated relatively independently. When Jacques Nasser was named CEO, he set out to tear down those regionally based organizations and to create a truly globally integrated car manufacturer. As his plan was unfolding, however, Ford continued to lose market share, so on October 30, 2001, Nasser was replaced as CEO by Ford family member William Clay Ford Jr., who is continuing to develop the global integration of the design, development, and manufacture of Ford automobiles.[23] Only time will tell if the new plan will work.

Another systemwide change is the introduction of quality-of-work-life programs. J. Lloyd Suttle defined **quality of work life** as the "degree to which members of a work organization are able to satisfy important personal needs through their experiences in the organization."[24] Quality-of-work-life programs focus strongly on providing a work environment conducive to satisfying individual needs. The emphasis on improving life at work developed during the 1970s, a period of increasing inflation and deepening recession. The development was rather surprising because an expanding economy and substantially increased resources are the conditions that usually induce top management to begin people-oriented programs. However, top management viewed improving life at work as a means of improving productivity.

Any movement with broad and ambiguous goals tends to spawn diverse programs, each claiming to be based on the movement's goals, and the quality-of-work-life movement is no exception. These programs vary substantially, although most espouse a goal of "humanizing the workplace." Richard Walton divided them into the eight categories shown in Figure 19.3.[25] Obviously, many types of programs can be accommodated by the categories, from changing the pay system to establishing an employee bill of rights that guarantees workers the rights to privacy, free speech, due process, and fair and equitable treatment.

> **Quality of work life** is the extent to which workers can satisfy important personal needs through their experiences in the organization.

FIGURE 19.3

Walton's Categorization of Quality-of-Work-Life Programs

Quality-of-work-life programs can be categorized into eight types. The expected benefits of these programs are increased employee morale, productivity, and organizational effectiveness.

Reference: Adapted from Richard E. Walton, "Quality of Work Life: What Is It?" *Sloan Management Review,* Fall 1973, pp. 11–21, by permission of the publisher. Copyright © 1973 by the Sloan Management Review Association. All rights reserved.

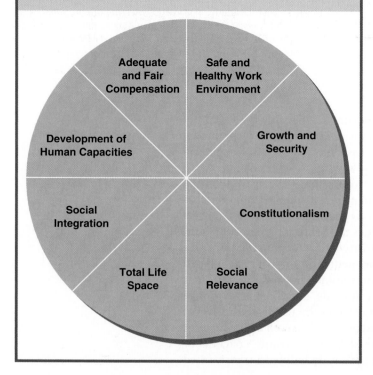

Adequate and Fair Compensation

Safe and Healthy Work Environment

Growth and Security

Development of Human Capacities

Social Integration

Constitutionalism

Total Life Space

Social Relevance

Total quality management, which was discussed in several earlier chapters, can also be viewed as a systemwide organization development program. In fact, some might consider total quality management as a broad program that includes structural change as well as quality of work life. It differs from quality of work life in that it emphasizes satisfying customer needs by making quality-oriented changes rather than focusing on satisfying employee needs at work. Often, however, the employee programs are very similar to it.

The benefits gained from quality-of-work-life programs differ substantially, but generally they are of three types. A more positive attitude toward the work and the organization, or increased job satisfaction, is perhaps the most direct benefit.[26] Another is increased productivity, although it is often difficult to measure and separate the effects of the quality-of-work-life program from the effects of other organizational factors. A third benefit is increased effectiveness of the organization as measured by its profitability, goal accomplishment, shareholder wealth, or resource exchange. The third gain follows directly from the first two: If employees have more positive attitudes about the organization and their productivity increases, everything else being equal, the organization should be more effective.

Task and Technological Change

Another way to bring about systemwide organization development is through changes in the tasks involved in doing the work, the technology, or both. The direct alteration of jobs usually is called "task redesign." Changing how inputs are transformed into outputs is called "technological change" and also usually results in task changes. Strictly speaking, changing the technology is typically not part of organization development whereas task redesign usually is.

The structural changes discussed in the preceding section are explicitly systemwide in scope. Those we examine in this section are more narrowly focused and may not seem to have the same far-reaching consequences. It is important to remember, however, that their impact is felt throughout the organization. The discussion of task design in Chapter 5 focused on job definition and motivation and gave little attention to implementing changes in jobs. Here we discuss task redesign as a mode of organization change.

Several approaches to introducing job changes in organizations have been proposed. One is by a coauthor of this book, Ricky W. Griffin. Griffin's approach is an integrative framework of nine steps that reflect the complexities of the interfaces between individual jobs and the total organization.[27] The process, shown in Table 19.2, includes the steps usually associated with change such as recognizing the need for a change, selecting the appropriate intervention, and evaluating the change. But Griffin's approach inserts four additional steps into the standard sequence: diagnosis of the overall work system and context, including examination of the jobs, workforce, technology, organization design, leadership, and group dynamics; evaluating the costs and benefits of the change; formulating a redesign strategy; and implementing supplemental changes.

Diagnosis includes analysis of the total work environment within which the jobs exist. It is important to evaluate the organization structure, especially the work rules and decision-making authority within a department, when job changes are being considered.[28] For example, if jobs are to be redesigned to give employees more freedom in choosing work methods or scheduling work activities, diagnosis of the present system must determine whether the rules will allow that to happen. Diagnosis must also include evaluation of the work group and teams and intragroup dynamics (discussed in Chapters 9 and 10). Furthermore, it must determine whether workers have or can easily obtain the new skills to perform the redesigned task.

TABLE 19.2
 	
Integrated Framework for Implementation of Task Redesign in Organizations
	Step 1: Recognition of a need for a change
	Step 2: Selection of task redesign as a potential intervention
	Step 3: Diagnosis of the work system and context
	     a. Diagnosis of existing jobs
	     b. Diagnosis of existing workforce
	     c. Diagnosis of technology
	     d. Diagnosis of organization design
	     e. Diagnosis of leader behavior
	     f. Diagnosis of group and social processes
	Step 4: Cost-benefit analysis of proposed changes
	Step 5: Go/no-go decision
	Step 6: Formulation of the strategy for redesign
	Step 7: Implementation of the task changes
	Step 8: Implementation of any supplemental changes
	Step 9: Evaluation of the task redesign effort
	
	Reference: Ricky W. Griffin, *Task Design: An Integrative Framework* (Glenview, IL: Scott, Foresman, 1982), p. 208. Used by permission.

It is extremely important to recognize the full range of potential costs and benefits associated with a job redesign effort. Some are direct and quantifiable; others are indirect and not quantifiable. Redesign may involve unexpected costs or benefits; although these cannot be predicted with certainty, they can be weighed as possibilities. Factors such as short-term role ambiguity, role conflict, and role overload can be major stumbling blocks to a job redesign effort.

Implementing a redesign scheme takes careful planning, and developing a strategy for the intervention is the final planning step. Strategy formulation is a four-part process. First, the organization must decide who will design the changes. Depending on the circumstances, the planning team may consist of only upper-level management or may include line workers and supervisors. Next, the team undertakes the actual design of the changes based on job design theory and the needs, goals, and circumstances of the organization. Third, the team decides the timing of the implementation, which may require a formal transition period during which equipment is purchased and installed, job training takes place, new physical layouts are arranged, and the bugs in the new system are worked out. Fourth, strategy planners must consider whether the job changes require adjustments and supplemental changes in other organizational components such as reporting relationships and the compensation system.

Group and Individual Change

Groups and individuals can be involved in organization change in a vast number of ways. Retraining a single employee can be considered an organization change if the training affects the way the employee does his or her job. Familiarizing managers with the leadership grid or the Vroom decision tree (Chapter 12) is an attempt at change. In the first case, the goal is to balance management concerns for production and people; in the second, the goal is to increase the participation of rank-and-file employees in the organization's decision making. In this section, we present an overview of four popular types of people-oriented change techniques: training, management development programs, team building, and survey feedback.

Training   Training generally is designed to improve employees' job skills. Employees may be trained to run certain machines, taught new mathematical skills, or acquainted

David Hunt, assistant director of the Language Training Center, teaches Spanish during a class for workers at Delta Faucet in Indianapolis. This is an example of training to increase employees' skills to help them better interact with Hispanic coworkers and customers. An increasing number of companies are offering Spanish-language and cultural awareness training to their English-speaking employees. Some do it to tap into a new customer base, others to enrich the lives of employees who increasingly interact with their Hispanic neighbors.

with personal growth and development methods. Stress management programs are becoming popular for helping employees, particularly executives, understand organizational stress and develop ways to cope with it.[29] Training may also be used in conjunction with other, more comprehensive organization changes. For instance, if an organization is implementing a management-by-objectives program, training in establishing goals and reviewing goal-oriented performance is probably needed. One important type of training that is becoming increasingly more common is training people to work in other countries. Companies such as Motorola give extensive training programs to employees at all levels before they start an international assignment. Training includes intensive language courses, cultural courses, and courses for the family.

Among the many training methods, the most common are lecture, discussion, a lecture-discussion combination, experiential methods, case studies, and films or videotapes. Training can take place in a standard classroom, either on company property or in a hotel, at a resort, or at a conference center. On-the-job training provides a different type of experience in which the trainee learns from an experienced worker. Most training programs use a combination of methods determined by the topic, the trainees, the trainer, and the organization.

A major problem of training programs is transferring employee learning to the workplace. Often an employee learns a new skill or a manager learns a new management technique, but upon returning to the normal work situation, he or she finds it easier to go back to the old way of doing things. As we discussed earlier, the process of refreezing is a vital part of the change process, and some way must be found to make the accomplishments of the training program permanent.

Management Development Programs Management development programs, like employee training programs, attempt to foster certain skills, abilities, and perspectives. Often, when a highly qualified technical person is promoted to manager of a work group, he or she needs training in how to manage or deal with people. In such cases, management development programs can be important to organizations, both for the new manager and for his or her subordinates.

Typically, management development programs use the lecture-discussion method to some extent but rely most heavily on participative methods such as case studies and role playing. Participative and experiential methods allow the manager to experience the problems of being a manager as well as the feelings of frustration, doubt, and success that are part of the job. The subject matter of this type of training program is problematic, however, in that management skills, including communication, problem diagnosis, problem solving, and performance appraisal, are not as easy to identify or to transfer from a classroom to the workplace as the skills required to run a machine. In addition, rapid changes in the external environment can make certain managerial skills obsolete in a very short time. As a result, some companies are approaching the development of their management team as an ongoing, careerlong process and require their managers to attend refresher courses periodically.

Jack Welch was so committed to making cultural changes within GE that he created the now famous Crotonville training facility to develop an army of change leaders. GE put more than 10,000 managers a year through a three-step workshop series called the Change Acceleration Program (CAP). Leadership was redefined as a teaching activity in which leaders taught their direct reports how to change the way they did their jobs. In order to make the systemwide changes Welch thought were needed, he turned to individual OD.[30]

As corporate America invests hundreds of millions of dollars in management development, certain guiding principles are evolving: (1) Management development is a multifaceted, complex, and long-term process to which there is no quick or simple approach; (2) organizations should carefully and systematically identify their unique developmental needs and evaluate their programs accordingly; (3) management development objectives must be compatible with organizational objectives; and (4) the utility and value of management development remain more an article of faith than a proven fact.[31]

Team Building   When interaction among group members is critical to group success and effectiveness, team development, or team building, may be useful. Team building emphasizes members' working together in a spirit of cooperation and generally has one or more of the following goals:

1. To set team goals and priorities
2. To analyze or allocate the way work is performed
3. To examine how a group is working—that is, to examine processes such as norms, decision making, and communications
4. To examine relationships among the people doing the work[32]

Total quality management efforts usually focus on teams, and the principles of team building must be applied to make them work. Team participation is especially important in the data-gathering and evaluation phases of team development. In data gathering, the members share information on the functioning of the group. The opinions of the group thus form the foundation of the development process. In the evaluation phase, members are the source of information about the effectiveness of the development effort.[33]

Like total quality management and many other management techniques, team building should not be thought of as a one-time experience, perhaps something undertaken on a retreat from the workplace; rather, it is a continuing process. It may take weeks, months, or years for a group to learn to pull together and function as a team. Team development can be a way to train the group to solve its own problems in the future. Research on the effectiveness of team building as an organization development tool so far is mixed and inconclusive. For more details on developing teams in organizations, please refer to Chapter 10.

In this photo, managers of Motorola, Inc., in Chicago are working on their presentation skills with members of the famous improvisational troupe, Second City Communications. This type of training combines improvisational techniques with traditional corporate training methods to help these managers communicate more effectively. Working with this troupe is fun and provides some unique tips not found in many traditional management development programs.

Survey Feedback Survey feedback techniques can form the basis for a change process. In this process, data are gathered, analyzed, summarized, and returned to those who generated them to identify, discuss, and solve problems. A survey feedback process is often set in motion either by the organization's top management or by a consultant to management. By providing information about employees' beliefs and attitudes, a survey can help management diagnose and solve an organization's problems. A consultant or change agent usually coordinates the process and is responsible for data gathering, analysis, and summary. The three-stage process is shown in Figure 19.4.[34]

The use of survey feedback techniques in an organization development process differs from their use in traditional attitude surveys. In an organization development process, data are (1) returned to employee groups at all levels in the organization and (2) used by all employees working together in their normal work groups to identify and solve problems. In traditional attitude surveys, top management reviews the data and may or may not initiate a new program to solve problems the survey has identified.

In the data-gathering stage, the change agent interviews selected personnel from appropriate levels to determine the key issues to be examined. Information from these interviews is used to develop a survey questionnaire, which is distributed to a large sample of employees. The questionnaire may be a standardized instrument, an instrument developed specifically for the organization, or a combination of the two. The questionnaire data are analyzed and aggregated by group or department to ensure that respondents remain anonymous.[35] Then the change agent prepares a summary of the results for the group feedback sessions. From this point on, the consultant is involved in the process as a resource person and expert.

The feedback meetings generally involve only two or three levels of management. Meetings are usually held serially, first with a meeting of the top management group, which is then followed by meetings of employees throughout the organization. The group manager rather than the change agent typically leads sessions to transfer "ownership" of the data from the change agent to the work group. The feedback consists

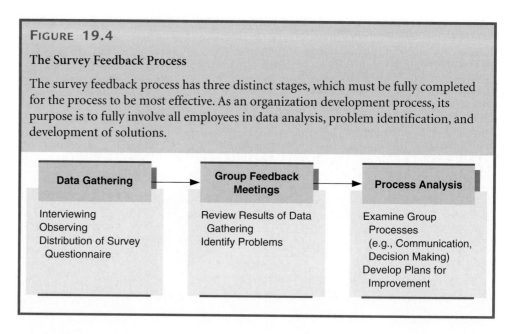

FIGURE 19.4

The Survey Feedback Process

The survey feedback process has three distinct stages, which must be fully completed for the process to be most effective. As an organization development process, its purpose is to fully involve all employees in data analysis, problem identification, and development of solutions.

Data Gathering	Group Feedback Meetings	Process Analysis
Interviewing Observing Distribution of Survey Questionnaire	Review Results of Data Gathering Identify Problems	Examine Group Processes (e.g., Communication, Decision Making) Develop Plans for Improvement

primarily of profiles of the group's attitudes toward the organization, the work, the leadership, and other topics on the questionnaire. During the feedback sessions, participants discuss reasons for the scores and the problems that the data reveal.

In the process analysis stage, the group examines the process of making decisions, communicating, and accomplishing work, usually with the help of the consultant. Unfortunately, groups often overlook this stage as they become absorbed in the survey data and the problems revealed during the feedback sessions. Occasionally, group managers simply fail to hold feedback and process analysis sessions. Change agents should ensure that managers hold these sessions and that they are rewarded for doing so. The process analysis stage is important because its purpose is to develop action plans to make improvements. Several sessions may be required to discuss the process issues fully and to settle on a strategy for improvements. Groups often find it useful to document the plans as they are discussed and to appoint a member to follow up on implementation. Generally, the follow-up assesses whether communication and communication processes have actually been improved. A follow-up survey can be administered several months to a year later to assess how much these processes have changed since they were first reported.

The survey feedback method is probably one of the most widely used organization change and development interventions. If any of its stages are compromised or omitted, however, the technique becomes less useful. A primary responsibility of the consultant or change agent, then, is to ensure that the method is fully and faithfully carried through.

Resistance to Change

Change is inevitable; so is resistance to change. Paradoxically, organizations both promote and resist change. As an agent for change, the organization asks prospective customers or clients to change their current purchasing habits by switching to the company's product or service, asks current customers to change by increasing their purchases, and asks suppliers to reduce the costs of raw materials. The organization resists change in that its structure and control systems protect the daily tasks of producing a

TABLE 19.3

Organizational and
Individual Sources of
Resistance

Organizational Sources	Examples
Overdetermination	Employment system, job descriptions, evaluation and reward system, organization culture
Narrow Focus of Change	Structure changed with no concern given to other issues, e.g., jobs, people
Group Inertia	Group norms
Threatened Expertise	People move out of area of expertise
Threatened Power	Decentralized decision making
Resource Allocation	Increased use of part-time help

Individual Sources	Examples
Habit	Altered tasks
Security	Altered tasks or reporting relationships
Economic Factors	Changed pay and benefits
Fear of the Unknown	New job, new boss
Lack of Awareness	Isolated groups not heeding notices
Social Factors	Group norms

product or service from uncertainties in the environment. The organization must have some elements of permanence to avoid mirroring the instability of the environment, yet it must also react to external shifts with internal change to maintain currency and relevance in the marketplace.

A commonly held view is that all resistance to change needs to be overcome, but that is not always the case. Resistance to change can be used for the benefit of the organization and need not be eliminated entirely. By revealing a legitimate concern that a proposed change may harm the organization or that other alternatives might be better, resistance may alert the organization to reexamine the change.[36] For example, an organization may be considering acquiring a company in a completely different industry. Resistance to such a proposal may cause the organization to examine the advantages and disadvantages of the move more carefully. Without resistance, the decision might be made before the pros and cons have been sufficiently explored.

Resistance may come from the organization, the individual, or both. Determining the ultimate source is often difficult, however, because organizations are composed of individuals. Table 19.3 summarizes various types of organizational and individual sources of resistance.

Organizational Sources of Resistance

Daniel Katz and Robert Kahn have identified six major organizational sources of resistance: overdetermination, narrow focus of change, group inertia, threatened expertise, threatened power, and changes in resource allocation.[37] Of course, not every organization or every change situation displays all six sources.

Overdetermination   Organizations have several systems designed to maintain stability. For example, consider how organizations control employees' performance. Job candidates must have certain specific skills so that they can do the job the organization needs them to do. New employees are given a job description, and the supervisor trains, coaches, and counsels the employee in job tasks. The new employee usually serves some type of probationary period that culminates in a performance review; thereafter, the employee's performance is regularly evaluated. Finally, rewards, punishment, and

Overdetermination, or structural inertia, occurs because numerous organizational systems are in place to ensure that employees and systems behave as expected to maintain stability.

discipline are administered, depending on the level of performance. Such a system is said to be characterized by **overdetermination**, or **structural inertia**,[38] in that one could probably have the same effect on employee performance with fewer procedures and safeguards. In other words, the structure of the organization produces resistance to change because it was designed to maintain stability. Another important source of overdetermination is the culture of the organization. As discussed in Chapter 18, the culture of an organization can have powerful and long-lasting effects on the behavior of its employees.

Narrow Focus of Change   Many efforts to create change in organizations adopt too narrow a focus. Any effort to force change in the tasks of individuals or groups must take into account the interdependencies among organizational elements such as people, structure, tasks, and the information system. For example, some attempts at redesigning jobs fail because the organization structure within which the jobs must function is inappropriate for the redesigned jobs.[39]

Group Inertia   When an employee attempts to change his or her work behavior, the group may resist by refusing to change other behaviors that are necessary complements to the individual's changed behavior. In other words, group norms may act as a brake on individual attempts at behavior change.

Threatened Expertise   A change in the organization may threaten the specialized expertise that individuals and groups have developed over the years. A job redesign or a structural change may transfer responsibility for a specialized task from the current expert to someone else, threatening the specialist's expertise and building his or her resistance to the change.

Threatened Power   Any redistribution of decision-making authority, such as with reengineering or team-based management, may threaten an individual's power relationships with others. If an organization is decentralizing its decision making, managers who wielded their decision-making powers in return for special favors from others may resist the change because they do not want to lose their power base.

Resource Allocation   Groups that are satisfied with current resource allocation methods may resist any change they believe will threaten future allocations. Resources in this context can mean anything from monetary rewards and equipment to additional seasonal help to more computer time.

These six sources explain most types of organization-based resistance to change. All are based on people and social relationships. Many of these sources of resistance can be traced to groups or individuals who are afraid of losing something—resources, power, or comfort in a routine.

Individual Sources of Resistance

Individual sources of resistance to change are rooted in basic human characteristics such as needs and perceptions. Researchers have identified six reasons for individual resistance to change: habit, security, economic factors, fear of the unknown, lack of awareness, and social factors (see Table 19.3).[40]

Habit   It is easier to do a job the same way every day if the steps in the job are repeated over and over. Learning an entirely new set of steps makes the job more difficult. For the same amount of return (pay), most people prefer to do easier rather than harder work.

This little guy brags to his coworkers that he is not worried about the reorganization when he really is worried about it. In any organization change, most people worry about how the changes will affect their job and their future. Most people learn how to survive in the job and the work environment and fear the unknowns that changes might bring.

Security   Some employees like the comfort and security of doing things the same old way. They gain a feeling of constancy and safety from knowing that some things stay the same despite all the change going on around them. People who believe their security is threatened by a change are likely to resist the change.

Economic Factors   Change may threaten employees' steady paychecks. Workers may fear that change will make their jobs obsolete or reduce their opportunities for future pay increases.

Fear of the Unknown   Some people fear anything unfamiliar. Changes in reporting relationships and job duties create anxiety for such employees. Employees become familiar with their bosses and their jobs and develop relationships with others within the organization, such as contact people for various situations. These relationships and contacts help facilitate their work. Any disruption of familiar patterns may create fear because it can cause delays and foster the belief that nothing is getting accomplished. The cartoon shows how people sometimes appear brave, but when alone, they worry about what the changes might bring.

Lack of Awareness   Because of perceptual limitations such as lack of attention or selective attention, a person may not recognize a change in a rule or procedure and thus may not alter his or her behavior. People may pay attention only to things that support their point of view. As an example, employees in an isolated regional sales office may not notice—or may ignore—directives from headquarters regarding a change in reporting procedures for expense accounts. They may therefore continue the current practice as long as possible.

Social Factors   People may resist change for fear of what others will think. As we mentioned before, the group can be a powerful motivator of behavior. Employees may believe change will hurt their image, result in ostracism from the group, or simply make them "different." For example, an employee who agrees to conform to work rules established by management may be ridiculed by others who openly disobey the rules.

Managing Successful Organization Change and Development

In conclusion, we offer seven keys to managing change in organizations. They relate directly to the problems identified earlier and to our view of the organization as a comprehensive social system. Each can influence the elements of the social system and may help the organization avoid some of the major problems in managing the change. Table 19.4 lists the points and their potential impacts.

Consider International Issues

One factor to consider is how international environments dictate organization change. As we have already noted, the environment is a significant factor in bringing about organization change. Given the additional environmental complexities multinational organizations face, it follows that organization change may be even more critical to them than it is to purely domestic organizations.

A second point to remember is that acceptance of change varies widely around the globe. Change is a normal and accepted part of organization life in some cultures. In other cultures, change causes many more problems. Managers should remember that techniques for managing change that have worked routinely back home may not work at all and may even trigger negative responses if used indiscriminately in other cultures.[41]

Take a Holistic View

Managers must take a holistic view of the organization and the change project. A limited view can endanger the change effort because the subsystems of the organization are interdependent. A holistic view encompasses the culture and dominant coalition as well as the people, tasks, structure, and information subsystems.

Start Small

Peter Senge claims that every truly successful, systemwide change in large organizations starts small.[42] He recommends that change start with one team, usually an executive

TABLE 19.4	Key	Impact
Keys to Managing Successful Organization Change and Development	**Consider international issues.**	Keeps in touch with the latest global developments and how change is handled in different cultures
	Take a holistic view of the organization.	Helps anticipate the effects of change on the social system and culture
	Start small.	Works out details and shows the benefits of the change to those who might resist
	Secure top management support.	Gets dominant coalition on the side of change: safeguards structural change, heads off problems of power and control
	Encourage participation by those affected by the change.	Minimizes transition problems of control, resistance, and task redefinition
	Foster open communication.	Minimizes transition problems of resistance and information and control systems
	Reward those who contribute to change.	Minimizes transition problems of resistance and control systems

team. One team can evaluate the change, make appropriate adjustments along the way, and most importantly, show that the new system works and gets desired results. If the change makes sense, it begins to spread to other teams, groups, and divisions throughout the system. Senge described how at Shell and Ford, significant changes started small, with one or two parallel teams, and then spread as others recognized the benefits of the change. When others see the benefits, they automatically drop their inherent resistance and join in. They can voluntarily join and be committed to the success of the change effort.

Secure Top Management Support

The support of top management is essential to the success of any change effort. As the organization's probable dominant coalition, it is a powerful element of the social system, and its support is necessary to deal with control and power problems. For example, a manager who plans a change in the ways in which tasks are assigned and responsibility is delegated in his or her department must notify top management and gain its support. Complications may arise if disgruntled employees complain to high-level managers who have not been notified of the change or do not support it. The employees' complaints may jeopardize the manager's plan—and perhaps her or his job.

Encourage Participation

Problems related to resistance, control, and power can be overcome by broad participation in planning the change. Allowing people a voice in designing the change may give them a sense of power and control over their own destinies, which may help to win their support during implementation.

Foster Open Communication

Open communication is an important factor in managing resistance to change and overcoming information and control problems during transitions. Employees typically recognize the uncertainties and ambiguities that arise during a transition and seek information on the change and their place in the new system. In the absence of information, the gap may be filled with inappropriate or false information, which may endanger the change process. Rumors tend to spread through the grapevine faster than accurate information can be disseminated through official channels. A manager should always be sensitive to the effects of uncertainty on employees, especially during a period of change; any news, even bad news, seems better than no news.

Reward Contributors

Although this last point is simple, it can easily be neglected. Employees who contribute to the change in any way need to be rewarded. Too often, the only people acknowledged after a change effort are those who tried to stop it. Those who quickly grasp new work assignments, work harder to cover what otherwise might not get done during the transition, or help others adjust to changes deserve special credit—perhaps a mention in a news release or the internal company newspaper, special consideration in a performance appraisal, a merit raise, or a promotion. From a behavioral perspective, individuals need to benefit in some way if they are to willingly help change something that eliminates the old, comfortable way of doing the job.

In the current dynamic environment, managers must anticipate the need for change and satisfy it with more responsive and competitive organization systems. These seven keys to managing organization change may also serve as general guidelines for managing organizational behavior because organizations must change or face elimination.

Chapter Review

Synopsis

Change may be forced on an organization, or an organization may change in response to the environment or an internal need. Forces for change are interdependent and influence organizations in many ways. Currently, the areas in which the pressures for change seem most powerful involve people, technology, information processing and communication, competition, and social trends.

Planned organization change involves anticipating change and preparing for it. Lewin described organization change in terms of unfreezing, the change itself, and refreezing. In the continuous change process model, top management recognizes forces encouraging change, engages in a problem-solving process to design the change, and implements and evaluates the change.

Organization development is the process of planned change and improvement of organizations through the application of knowledge of the behavioral sciences. It is based on a systematic change process and focuses on managing the culture of the organization. The most comprehensive change involves altering the structure of the organization through reorganization of departments, reporting relationships, or authority systems.

Quality-of-work-life programs focus on providing a work environment in which employees can satisfy individual needs. Task and technological changes alter the way the organization accomplishes its primary tasks. Along with the steps usually associated with change, task redesign entails diagnosis, cost-benefit analysis, formulation of a redesign strategy, and implementation of supplemental changes.

Frequently used group and individual approaches to organization change are training and management development programs, team building, and survey feedback techniques. Training programs are usually designed to improve employees' job skills, to help employees adapt to other organization changes (such as a management-by-objectives program), or to develop employees' awareness and understanding of problems such as workplace safety or stress. Management development programs attempt to foster in current or future managers the skills, abilities, and perspectives important to good management. Team-building programs are designed to help a work team or group develop into a mature, functioning team by helping it define its goals or priorities, analyze its tasks and the way they are performed, and examine relationships among the people doing the work. As used in the organization development process, survey feedback techniques involve gathering data, analyzing and summarizing them, and returning them to employees and groups for discussion and to identify and solve problems.

Resistance to change may arise from several individual and organizational sources. Resistance may indicate a legitimate concern that the change is not good for the organization and may warrant a reexamination of plans.

To manage change in organizations, international issues must be considered, and managers should take a holistic view of the organization and start small. Top management support is needed, and those most affected by the change must participate. Open communication is important, and those who contribute to the change effort should be rewarded.

Discussion Questions

1. Is most organization change forced on the organization by external factors or fostered from within? Explain.

2. What broad category of pressures for organization change other than the four discussed in the chapter can you think of? Briefly describe it.

3. Which sources of resistance to change present the most problems for an internal change agent? For an external change agent?

4. Which stage of the Lewin model of change do you think is most often overlooked? Why?

5. What are the advantages and disadvantages of having an internal change agent rather than an external change agent?

6. How does organization development differ from organization change?

7. How and why would organization development differ if the elements of the social system were not interdependent?

8. Do quality-of-work-life programs rely more on individual or organizational aspects of organizational behavior? Why?

9. Describe how the job of your professor could be redesigned. Include a discussion of other subsystems that would need to be changed as a result.

10. Which of the seven keys for successfully managing an organizational change effort seem to be the most difficult to manage? Why?

Experiencing Organizational Behavior

Planning a Change at the University

Purpose: This exercise will help you understand the complexities of change in organizations.

Format: Your task is to plan the implementation of a major change in an organization.

Procedure:

Part 1

The class will divide into five groups of approximately equal size. Your instructor will assign each group one of the following changes:

1. A change from the semester system to the quarter system (or the opposite, depending on the school's current system)

2. A requirement that all work—homework, examinations, term papers, problem sets—be done on computers and submitted via computers

3. A requirement that all students live on campus

4. A requirement that all students have reading, writing, and speaking fluency in at least three languages, including English and Japanese, to graduate

5. A requirement that all students room with someone in the same major

First, decide what individuals and groups must be involved in the change process. Then decide how the change will be implemented using Lewin's process of organization change (Figure 19.1) as a framework. Consider how to deal with resistance to change, using Tables 19.3 and 19.4 as guides. Decide whether a change agent (internal or external) should be used. Develop a realistic timetable for full implementation of the change. Is transition management appropriate?

Part 2

Using the same groups as in Part 1, your next task is to describe the techniques you would use to implement the change described in Part 1. You may use structural changes, task and technology methods, group and individual programs, or any combination of these. You may need to go to the library to gather more information on some techniques.

You should also discuss how you will utilize the seven keys to successful change management discussed at the end of the chapter.

Your instructor may make this exercise an in-class project, but it is also a good semester-ending project for groups to work on outside class. Either way, the exercise is most beneficial when the groups report their implementation programs to the entire class. Each group should report on which change techniques are to be used, why they were selected, how they will be implemented, and how problems will be avoided.

Follow-up Questions

Part 1

1. How similar were the implementation steps for each change?

2. Were the plans for managing resistance to change realistic?

3. Do you think any of the changes could be successfully implemented at your school? Why or why not?

Part 2

1. Did various groups use the same technique in different ways or to accomplish different goals?

2. If you did outside research on organization development techniques for your project, did you find any techniques that seemed more applicable than those in this chapter? If so, describe one of them.

Self-Assessment Exercise

Support for Change

Introduction: The following questions are designed to help people understand the level of support or opposition to change within an organization. Scores on this scale should be used for classroom discussion only.

Instructions: Think of an organization for which you have worked in the past or an organization to which you currently belong and consider the situation when a change was imposed at some point in the recent past. Then circle the number that best represents your feeling about each statement or question.

1. Values and Vision

   (*Do people throughout the organization share values or vision?*)

1	2	3	4	5	6	7
Low						High

2. History of Change

   (*Does the organization have a good track record in handling change?*)

1	2	3	4	5	6	7
Low						High

3. Cooperation and Trust

   (*Do they seem high throughout the organization?*)

1	2	3	4	5	6	7
Low						High

4. Culture

   (*Is it one that supports risk taking and change?*)

1	2	3	4	5	6	7
Low						High

5. Resilience

   (*Can people handle more?*)

1	2	3	4	5	6	7
Low						High

6. Rewards

   (*Will this change be seen as beneficial?*)

1	2	3	4	5	6	7
Low						High

7. Respect and Face

   (*Will people be able to maintain dignity and self-respect?*)

1	2	3	4	5	6	7
Low						High

8. Status Quo

   (*Will this change be seen as mild?*)

1	2	3	4	5	6	7
Low						High

A Guide to Scoring and explanation is available in the *Instructor's Resource Manual.*

Reference: From Rick Maurer, *Beyond the Wall of Resistance,* 1996 (Austin, TX: Bard Press), pp. 104–105. Used by permission of Bard Press.

Building Managerial Skills

Exercise Overview: Many organizations utilize surveys to assess the needs and concerns of their employees. On the basis of the results of such surveys, many organizations make significant organizational changes. This exercise will help you understand more about organizational surveys.

Exercise Background: Your organization has a new CEO who has been brought in to make changes. Her first priority is to survey all employees to find out what employees think about the company, what they want from the company, and what their needs and concerns are.

Exercise Task: You have been assigned to find several organizational surveys that could be used by your company. Search the Internet for resources that might assist you in finding several different surveys and other related resources. Describe the kinds of information you were able to locate and explain its likely value to you.

Finally, respond to the following questions:

1. What additional information would you need, besides what was available on the Internet, to actually use one of the surveys that you found?

2. How would the type of survey you use be different if you were a large multinational company as opposed to a small manufacturing company with employees at only one location?

Organizational Behavior Case for Discussion

Toyota Reinvented

In 2003, Toyota Motors was catching up with the Big Three U.S. automakers—GM, Ford, and Chrysler. It was a risky strategy to overtake the industry's largest competitors, but one that would pay off with a gradual increase in sales and profits. What did Toyota do next? The company immediately set out to reinvent itself.

One of the first changes was the introduction of a host of new designs. Although an earlier version of the hybrid-fuel Prius came to the American market in 2000, an improved design was unveiled in 2004. Ford licensed Toyota's hybrid technology because, "Toyota is ahead of the game. Ford is playing catch up," claim writers James Mackintosh and Michiyo Nakamoto. Toyota capitalized on the popularity of the hybrid Prius by introducing the world's first hybrid luxury sport-utility vehicle, the RX 400h. Toyota engineers in Europe designed the compact Yaris for sale there. The Yaris is now being imported to Japan for sale to buyers who prefer a European look. Sales of the Scion, designed for hip younger buyers, are double Toyota's initial prediction.

Toyota has a reputation as one of the world's leading cost-cutters, beginning with the company's invention of the *kaizen* (continuous improvement) and *kanban* (just-in-time inventory) systems. Even so, managers have begun to search even more diligently for ways to reduce expenses. Katsuaki Watanabe, executive vice president, targeted 180 key parts and asked for a 30 percent price reduction. No part was too small, or too large. Designers cut the number of parts in a door grip from thirty-four to five, reducing purchasing costs by 40 percent and installation time by 75 percent. From 2000 to 2005, Toyota cut costs by $10 billion, without any layoffs or plant closings, and it plans to cut another $2 billion this year.

Toyota is making a number of low-tech changes to bring cost savings and improve speed and quality. One simple change requires designers, engineers, suppliers, and workers to meet face to face as they hash out the details of a new product design. An over-reliance on teleconferencing and email was inefficient. It took Toyota just nineteen months to develop the new Solara, compared to the industry average of three years. However, the auto giant has not forgotten the high technology for which it is famous. The process technology has been improved with the change to a global production line that allows Toyota to build multiple models on the same production line at the same time. A robotic system assists workers in identifying defects, flashing lights when a mistake is spotted. Toyota's research and development budget has been steadily rising. In 2004, Toyota spent $15 billion on R&D, compared to $7 billion at GM and $7.4 at Ford.

Toyota is not content to make changes only in design, processes, and technology. The firm is also updating its organization structure and replacing many of its top managers. It is further integrating some of its other divisions, such as the business unit that is the biggest seller of single-family homes in Japan. Alliances with Peugeot and even GM are being revitalized and clarified. Katsuaki Watanabe, known for his aggressive cost-cutting and quality control measures, will succeed CEO Fujio Cho when he retires in June 2005. That choice is "part of a wide reshuffle designed to bring new blood to the ranks of upper management," according to business writer Chester Dawson. Watanabe's promotion signals Toyota's continuing commitment to change.

To support these many changes, Toyota leaders are updating the organization's culture. Toyota has often been accused of being too conservative in design, too focused on the Japanese market, and too timid and slow in adopting revolutionary innovations. Maryann Keller, an auto industry consultant, offers faint praise for Toyota, saying, "They find a hole and they plug it. They methodically study problems and they solve them." But that is about to change. Watanabe says, "I feel that being successful may make us arrogant and want to stay in a comfort zone. That is the threat." The CEO-to-be plans on pushing for more reform, more openness, more alliances, more speed, and more risk taking. CEO Fujio Cho adds, "This is a company that does not fear failure."

Toyota is racking up win after win. The Prius was named North American Car of the Year for 2004. That year also showed Toyota producing more than 30 percent of the new cars sold in America, a record high, and becoming the world's second-largest car maker, after GM. In April 2005, Toyota had its best-ever sales month with 210,000 vehicles sold, a 21.3 percent increase. Meanwhile, sales at General Motors fell 5.2 percent in the last quarter of 2004. According to writers David Welch and Dan Beucke, "Toyota Motor Corp., Nissan Motor Corp., and other more nimble competitors ate GM's lunch." Growth has not come at the expense of profits—operating profit margins at Toyota were an impressive 9.4 percent in December 2004. The company also has $30 billion in liquid assets, to fuel further R&D and growth. Reinvention, at

> **❝ This is a company that does not fear failure. ❞**
> *FUJIO CHO, CEO, TOYOTA*

Toyota, looks like a winning strategy.

Case Questions

1. What are the forces acting for change in the auto industry?

2. What areas of Toyota are undergoing organization change? Give an example of a change taking place in each area.

3. In your opinion, are Toyota workers likely to resist the changes? Why or why not? How might Toyota help workers overcome their resistance to change?

References: "Scoring the World's Carmakers," Standard and Poor's Ratings News, www2.standardandpoors.com on May 4, 2005; "Toyota, Nissan Lift U.S. Auto Sales—SUV Sales Slide," *Agence France Presse*, dailynews.yahoo.com on May 4, 2005; Jeff Bennett, "New Direction for Lexus," *Detroit Free Press*, January 7, 2004, www.freep.com on May 4, 2005; Brian Bremmer and Chester Dawson, "Can Anything Top Toyota?" *Business Week*, November 17, 2003, pp. 114–122 (quotation); Chester Dawson, "The New Boss Driving Toyota," *Business Week*, February 10, 2005, www.business-week.com on May 4, 2005; Gail Edmondson, "Revved Up For Battle," *Business Week*, January 10, 2005, www.businessweek.com on May 4, 2005; James Mackintosh and Michiyo Nakamoto, "Japanese Carmakers Reach Milestone: 30 Percent of U.S. Auto Sales," *The Financial Times*, January 6, 2005, www.newstarget.com on May 4, 2005; Jathon Sapsford, "Toyota Revs Up Operations to Rival GM as No. 1," *The Wall Street Journal*, November 2, 2004, pp. A1, A12; David Welch and Dan Beucke, "Why GM's Plan Won't Work," *Business Week*, May 9, 2005, pp. 85–93.

TEST PREPPER

ACE self-test

You have read the chapter and studied the key terms. Think you're ready to ace the exam? Take this sample test to gauge your comprehension of chapter material and check your answers at the back of the book. Want more test questions? Take the ACE quizzes found on the student website: http://college.hmco.com/business/students/ (select Griffin/Moorhead, Organizational Behavior, 8e from the Management menu).

T   F   1. Baby boomers differ from previous generations in terms of their education; however, they hold similar value systems.

T   F   2. Advances in information processing and communication have actually slowed business operations because of the extra time needed to enter data.

T   F   3. A change agent may come from inside or outside the organization.

T   F   4. Quality-of-work-life programs are used by medical research firms to extend the average career length of working adults.

T   F   5. A major problem of training programs is transferring employee learning to the workplace.

T   F   6. Managers should learn that all resistance to change needs to be overcome.

T   F   7. Truly successful, systemwide changes in large organizations start off small.

8. Which of the following is not one of the major categories of pressures that influence organizations to change?
   a. Competition
   b. Information processing and communication
   c. Legislation
   d. Technology
   e. People

9. Most markets are now global because of
   a. limits on competition.
   b. emergent organizational change.
   c. planned organizational change.
   d. decreasing transportation and communication costs.
   e. smaller domestic markets.

10. Brian has been assigned the role of transition manager as part of a change effort in his company. Brian's role will likely involve which of the following?
   a. Act as a liaison between the organization and its competitors during the change.
   b. Bridge the gap between potential and actual performance.
   c. Change the organization back to the way it was initially.
   d. Deal with unintended consequences of the change.
   e. Eliminate resistance to the change.

11. Quality-of-work-life programs generally result in which of the following benefits?
   a. Limited resistance to change
   b. Increased job satisfaction
   c. A shorter "refreezing" stage
   d. Fewer unintended consequences of change
   e. Innovative technological change

12. Daniel wants to analyze the way work is performed, examine relationships among the people doing the work, and examine how the work groups he supervises are working. Daniel ought to consider which of the following change techniques?
   a. Training
   b. Management development programs
   c. Team building
   d. Survey feedback
   e. Total quality management

13. Structural inertia means
   a. the culture of the organization has initiated a change effort.
   b. the technology of the organization has become obsolete but is still in use.
   c. the strategy of the organization is to resist change for as long as possible, but not indefinitely.
   d. the people in the organization have adopted a positive attitude toward organizational change efforts.
   e. the structure of the organization produces resistance because it was designed to maintain stability.

14. Open communication during a change effort is important because
   a. in the absence of accurate information, the gap may be filled with rumors and false information.
   b. open communication can replace the need for top management support.
   c. it allows an organization to begin its change effort on a small scale.
   d. a holistic view requires communication among lower-level employees.
   e. employees are used to open communication during periods of stability.

Structure and Success at Starbucks

Founder Howard Schultz purchased Starbucks Coffee Company in 1985 and transformed the little company into one of the most powerful retailing operations in the world. Along with individual and interpersonal forces, organizational factors play a significant role in Starbucks's success.

For the last twenty years, the firm's organizational structure has remained the same. At the lowest level, stores are organized into regions. Regional managers report to one of two executive vice presidents, one for the United States and one for international locations. Top managers oversee support functions such as purchasing, marketing, legal, human resources, and information resources. Other groups at the highest level of the company oversee corporate social responsibility and organization culture. Starbucks also has high-level executives in charge of innovation. They focus on emerging businesses and the company's new entertainment ventures.

To attain economies of scale and to ensure consistent quality, most decisions, such as purchasing coffee, developing drinks, store design, and so on, are centralized. Company policies are centrally determined to ensure fairness. However, some decisions are decentralized. Store managers hire and evaluate baristas, and local managers are responsible for ensuring that operational goals are met. Starbucks uses the distinction between centralized and decentralized issues to allow decisions to be made at the most appropriate level—the level where the decision makers are most involved in gathering information and implementing the decision.

The organization design that Starbucks has evolved relies on differentiation strategy; Starbucks presents itself as a distinctive and superior company. The organization design supports the company's differentiation strategy by offering unique and desirable features to customers. These include selling high-quality products, providing excellent customer service, and creating an upscale, entertaining environment. Another important part of Starbucks's strategy is growth. Again, the organization design is simple and consists of multiple small, one-store units. This structure makes it easy to add stores, accommodating growth.

The relative youth of the firm is another important factor affecting organization structure. Starbucks began its current strategic direction just eighteen years ago. Therefore, the organization structure is fairly simple. Although the company has grown tremendously, it does not have many layers of management for a firm of its size. Middle managers and support staff are fewer than in older, more established firms. However, as Starbucks grows and ages, a more complex organization structure will be required. Already the firm is moving away from a simple structure, as defined by Mintzberg, toward a machine bureaucracy. A machine bureaucracy relies more on administrative coordination and standardization of work. At Starbucks, a machine bureaucracy structure is demonstrated when important decisions are made centrally and workers are trained to ensure product consistency.

Finally, the environment has a significant impact on organization structure. The quick-serve food industry, including technology, the economy, and competitors, is changing slowly. Since Starbucks itself is responsible for much of the change that has occurred in coffee houses in recent years (formulating new drinks, selling CDs), this makes the changes very easy for Starbucks to predict. An environment that is low in uncertainty allows Starbucks to concentrate attention internally. This leads to rapid growth, high efficiency, and innovation.

Along with an effective and evolving organization design, Starbucks has a unique organization culture. Schultz and other leaders at Starbucks understand the importance of organization culture in creating a successful firm. "It's extremely valuable to have people proud to work for Starbucks and we make decisions that are consistent with what our employees expect of us," Schultz says.

The culture began with the values held by founder Howard Schultz. He states again and again two important purposes for Starbucks: "to build a company with a soul" and "to pursue the perfect cup of coffee." Company executives, led by then CEO Schultz, wrote the first official statement about the organization culture in 1990. The vision statement that resulted said, "Put people first and profits last." The mission statement elaborated further, laying out principles such as respect, diversity, and excellence. Many U.S. corporations uphold similar values, but Starbucks places a uniquely strong emphasis on ethics and social responsibility, as well as innovation.

The company has a number of policies that demonstrate its ethical treatment of workers. For example, every employee is referred to as a "partner." Workers, even many part-timers, receive generous benefits. The company is committed to a total pay package that provides a decent standard of living for its workers.

Starbucks is more transparent than most organizations. It shares financial and other information with workers, and it also actively solicits input and feedback from workers. It publishes several newsletters and has education programs for workers. A business conduct help line is available for anonymous help with questions about ethics and business conduct. Starbucks conducts a Mission Review program that encourages workers to submit reports and questions about the company's performance on the values stated in the firm's mission. In 2004, workers contacted the company 3,500 times, resulting in many changes in operations and policies.

Starbucks is also active in philanthropic giving. Store managers can donate funds and merchandise for local projects. The company supports causes related to education, youth, and poverty, such as Head Start, a preschool education organization. Starbucks also spends millions of dollars supporting healthcare, sanitation, and literacy in coffee-producing countries. Starbucks gains positive publicity from its charitable programs, which is especially useful in courting young, affluent customers. Barista Daniel Gross says, "Starbucks is selling an image more than coffee."

Observing Starbucks's growth and development over the last eighteen years, the most striking aspect of the firm is its commitment to innovation. No part of the firm is too important or too insignificant to escape change. Starbucks was the first firm to popularize Italian-style specialty coffee beverages in the United States. There are 167 million Americans who drink coffee, about the same number as ten years ago. However, Americans spend $31 per capita on coffee, a sharp increase over the last decade. The increase is due to increased consumption of more expensive specialty drinks. Starbucks constantly develops new products, including iced coffees, teas, hot chocolate, coffee ice creams, and even seasonal flavors, such as pumpkin spice coffee at Halloween. New food offerings include sandwiches and salads. Lunch food sales are expected to contribute $30,000 in profits per store.

Starbucks has expanded its product offerings beyond food and drink. The firm offers CDs, publishes a children's holiday book, and sells the board game Cranium. One in every ten Americans holds a Starbucks prepaid card. The company offers a branded Visa card and most locations offer wireless Internet service. That creates what Schultz refers to as "the Third Place," a space for socializing that is somewhere between home and work. The usual Starbucks visit is just five minutes long, but Internet users stay forty-five minutes on average, creating more sales opportunities. Also, Internet customers visit after peak morning hours, generating revenue during otherwise "light" periods. "If we'd only thought of ourselves as a coffee company, we wouldn't have done this," says Anne Saunders, marketing senior vice president.

Operations provides another area for innovation. One-third of new stores now offer drive-through lanes for speedier service. The company has switched to faster, automated espresso machines. New store designs increase the selling space, provide more effective displays, and optimize inventory and food preparation areas. The company acquired several smaller coffee companies to increase brand depth. Alternate distribution channels include whole-bean, bottled coffee, and ice cream sales through traditional supermarkets, as well as deals with food wholesaler Sysco. Starbucks's brewed coffee is available in Borders bookstores and Safeway supermarkets.

Starbucks is expanding its demographic base to attract more young, urban, and diverse customers. The firm is trying to move beyond its narrow niche market of white, educated, wealthy consumers. Peter Kafka of *Forbes* writes, "Starbucks may be the only consumer company in the U.S. that boasts that its customer base is becoming less affluent." The company has begun to build stores in small towns and inner cities, allowing them to reach a broader market.

The company continually reinvents itself. "Whenever you reach a plateau, it's time to rethink," Schultz says. "If you're number one. . . maybe it's time to reconsider . . . Create a broader definition of the industry, and develop a new plan to conquer it." Starbucks has certainly heeded that advice. First it switched from coffee bean retailer to coffee house. Then it became the "Third Place" for socializing and working. Its next concept, called Hear Music, is the company's third major transformation in less than twenty years.

With Hear Music customers can purchase CDs or create their own. Hear Music's marketing plan helped *Genius Loves Company*, an album of Ray Charles duets, win a Grammy. The CD sold over 1 million copies in just three months and earned Album of the Year for 2004. In southern California, Miami, and Austin, stores provide tablet PCs for customers to select and legally burn music CDs from the company's library of more than 150,000 songs. The buyer chooses the music ($8.99 for the first seven songs, $.99 for each additional song) and can create label and cover art. "In the time it takes you to order a latte, you could have any CD burned on demand for you," says vice president Don MacKinnon. The service is likely to appeal to older buyers who are not technology savvy and who feel ignored by traditional music stores and radio stations. "This is training wheels for digital," MacKinnon says. These customers are willing to pay for ease and convenience.

Innovation is ongoing at Starbucks. "Schultz is doing something quite unusual in business. He's already looking ahead, doing the arithmetic and saying, 'Well, our current model is not forever.' There are probably a few more years of growth left in coffee shops, and he's asking, 'How do we manage that inevitable slowdown a couple of years from now?'" says consultant Adrian Slywotzky. Starbucks plans to continue growing. It will add over 1,000 new U.S. locations and 500 international locations in 2005. Yet while the company is growing and changing, Starbucks's leaders are working to help the company retain its culture, image, and small-store appeal. "The hardest thing is to stay small while you get big, to figure out how to stay intimate with your customers and your people, even as your reach gets bigger," says Schultz.

> ❝ *The hardest thing is to stay small while you get big.* ❞
>
> HOWARD SCHULTZ, FOUNDER, STARBUCKS

References: "Corporate Social Responsibility Report 2004," "Mission Statement," "Ray Charles Nominated for 10 Grammy Awards," "Starbucks Recaps 2002–2004 Successes," "Starbucks Lays Out Global Growth Strategy," "Starbucks' Strong Innovation Pipeline," Starbucks website, www.starbucks.com on February 2, 2005; "U.S. Coffee Consumption Shows Impressive Growth," *Food and Drink Weekly*, February 16, 2004, www.foodanddrink.com on June 30, 2005; Robert D. Hof, "Building an Idea Factory," *Business Week*, October 11, 2004, www.businessweek.com on January 31, 2005; Stanley Holmes, "Maybe They'll Call It Starbooks," *Business Week*, October 25, 2004, www.businessweek.com on January 31, 2005; Stanley Holmes, "Starbucks Tunes In to Digital Music," *Business Week*, March 16, 2004, www.businessweek.com on January 31, 2005; Peter Kafka, "Bean Counter," *Forbes*, February 28, 2005, www.forbes.com on June 30, 2005; Anya Kamenetz, "Baristas of the World, Unite!" *New York Metro*, www.newyorkmetro.com on June 30, 2005; Alison Overholt, "Listening to Starbucks," *Fast Company*, July 2004, pp. 50–56 (quotation); Christopher Palmeri, "March of the Toys—Out of the Toy Section," *Business Week*, November 29, 2004, www.businessweek.com on January 31, 2005; Amy Tsao, "Starbucks: A Bit Overheated?" *Business Week*, April 5, 2004, www.businessweek.com on January 31, 2005; Amy Tsao, "Starbucks' Plan to Brew Growth," *Business Week*, April 5, 2004, www.businessweek.com on January 31, 2005.

Integrative Case Questions

1. What changes in organization structure do you anticipate the firm will make as it grows and ages? What benefits will these structure changes bring? What are some potential problems that these structure changes will bring?

2. Use the Ouchi framework to describe the organization culture at Starbucks. Is the company most like a Japanese firm, a Type Z U.S. company, or a typical U.S. company?

3. What types of resistance to change is Starbucks likely to encounter? What can the company do to overcome resistance to change?

Research Methods in Organizational Behavior

We have referred to theories and research findings as a basis for our discussion throughout this book. In this appendix, we further examine how theories and research findings about organizational behavior are developed. First, we highlight the role of theory and research. We then identify the purposes of research and describe the steps in the research process, types of research designs, and methods of gathering data. We conclude with a brief discussion of some related issues.

The Role of Theory and Research

Some managers—and many students—fail to see the need for research. They seem confused by what appears to be an endless litany of theories and by sets of contradictory research findings. They often ask, "Why bother?"

Indeed, few absolute truths have emerged from studies of organizational behavior. Management in general and organizational behavior in particular, however, are in many ways fields of study still in their infancy. Thus, it stands to reason that researchers in these fields have few theories that always work. In addition, their research cannot always be generalized to settings other than those in which the research was originally conducted.

Still, theory and research play valuable roles.[1] Theories help investigators organize what they do know. They provide a framework that managers can use to diagnose problems and implement changes. They also serve as road signs that help managers solve many problems involving people. Research also plays an important role. Each study conducted and published adds a little more to the storehouse of knowledge available to practicing managers. Questions are posed and answers developed. Over time, researchers can become increasingly confident of findings as they are applied across different settings.[2]

Purposes of Research

As much as possible, researchers try to approach problems and questions of organizational behavior scientifically. **Scientific research** is the systematic

> **Scientific research** is the systematic investigation of hypothesized propositions about the relationships among natural phenomena.

539

Basic research is concerned with discovering new knowledge rather than solving specific problems.

Applied research is conducted to solve particular problems or answer specific questions.

investigation of hypothesized propositions about the relationships among natural phenomena. The aims of science are to describe, explain, and predict phenomena.[3] Research can be classified as basic or applied. **Basic research** is concerned with discovering new knowledge rather than solving particular problems. The knowledge made available through basic research may not have much direct application to organizations, at least when it is first discovered.[4] Research scientists and university professors are the people who most often conduct basic research in organizational behavior.

Applied research, on the other hand, is conducted to solve particular problems or answer specific questions. The findings of applied research are, by definition, immediately applicable to managers. Consultants, university professors, and managers themselves conduct much of the applied research performed in organizations.

The Scientific Research Process

To result in valid findings, research should be conducted according to the scientific process shown in Figure AA.1. The starting point is a question or problem.[5] For example, a manager wants to design a new reward system to enhance employee motivation but is unsure about what types of rewards to offer or how to tie them to performance. This manager's questions therefore are "What kinds of rewards will motivate my employees?" and "How should those rewards be tied to performance?"

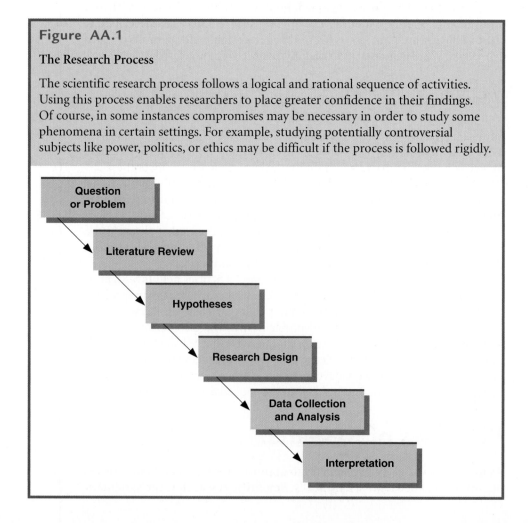

Figure AA.1

The Research Process

The scientific research process follows a logical and rational sequence of activities. Using this process enables researchers to place greater confidence in their findings. Of course, in some instances compromises may be necessary in order to study some phenomena in certain settings. For example, studying potentially controversial subjects like power, politics, or ethics may be difficult if the process is followed rigidly.

Question or Problem → Literature Review → Hypotheses → Research Design → Data Collection and Analysis → Interpretation

The next step is to review existing literature to determine what is already known about the phenomenon. Something has probably been written about most problems or questions today's managers face. Thus, the goal of the literature review is to avoid "reinventing the wheel" by finding out what others have already learned. Basic research generally is available in journals such as the *Academy of Management Journal, Academy of Management Review, Administrative Science Quarterly, Journal of Applied Psychology, Organizational Behavior and Human Decision Processes, Journal of Management,* and *Organization Science.* Applied research findings are more likely to be found in such sources as the *Harvard Business Review, Academy of Management Executive, Organizational Dynamics, HRMagazine,* and *Personnel Psychology.*

Based on the original question and the review of the literature, researchers formulate hypotheses—predictions of what they expect to find. The hypothesis is an important guide for the researcher's design of the study because it provides a very clear and precise statement of what the researcher wants to test. That means that the study can be specifically designed to test the hypothesis.

The research design is the plan for doing the research. (We discuss the more common research designs later.) As part of the research design, the researcher must determine how variables will be measured. Thus, if satisfaction is one factor being considered, the researcher must decide how to measure it.

After data have been collected, they must be analyzed. (We also discuss common methods for gathering data later.) Depending on the study design and hypotheses, data analysis may be relatively simple and straightforward or may require elaborate statistical procedures. Methods for analyzing data are beyond the scope of this discussion.

Finally, the results of the study are interpreted; that is, the researcher figures out what they mean. They may provide support for the hypothesis, fail to support the hypothesis, or suggest a relationship other than that proposed in the hypothesis. An important part of the interpretation process is recognizing the limitations imposed on the findings by weaknesses in the research design.

Many researchers go a step further and try to publish their findings. Several potential sources for publication are the journals mentioned in the discussion of literature review. Publication is important because it helps educate other researchers and managers and also provides additional information for future literature reviews.[6]

Types of Research Designs

A **research design** is the set of procedures used to test the predicted relationships among natural phenomena. The design addresses such issues as how the relevant variables are to be defined, measured, and related to one another. Managers and researchers can draw on a variety of research designs, each with its own strengths and weaknesses. Four general types of research designs often are used in the study of organizational behavior (see Table AA.1); each type has several variations.[7]

> A **research design** is the set of procedures used to test the predicted relationships among natural phenomena.

Type	Dominant Characteristic
Case Study	Useful for thorough explanation of unknown phenomena
Field Study	Provides easily quantifiable data
Laboratory Experiment	Allows researcher high control of variables
Field Experiment	Takes place in realistic setting

TABLE AA.1

Types of Research Designs

Case Study

A **case study** is an in-depth analysis of a single setting. This design frequently is used when little is known about the phenomena being studied and the researcher wants to look at relevant concepts intensively and thoroughly. A variety of methods are used to gather information, including interviews, questionnaires, and personal observation.[8]

The case study research design offers several advantages. First, it allows the researcher to probe one situation in detail, yielding a wealth of descriptive and explanatory information. The case study also facilitates the discovery of unexpected relationships. Because the researcher observes virtually everything that happens in a given situation, she or he may learn about issues beyond those originally chosen for the study.

The case study design also has several disadvantages. The data it provides cannot be readily generalized to other situations because the information is so closely tied to the situation studied. In addition, case study information may be biased by the researcher's closeness to the situation. Case study research also tends to be very time-consuming.

Nevertheless, the case study can be an effective and useful research design as long as the researcher understands its limitations and takes them into account when formulating conclusions.

Field Survey

A **field survey** usually relies on a questionnaire distributed to a sample of people chosen from a larger population.

If a manager is conducting the study, the sample often is drawn from a group or department within her or his organization. If a researcher is conducting the study, the sample typically is negotiated with a host organization interested in the questions being addressed. The questionnaire generally is mailed or delivered by hand to participants at home or at work and may be returned by mail or picked up by the researcher. The respondents answer the questions and return the questionnaire as directed. The researcher analyzes the responses and tries to make inferences about the larger population from the representative sample.[9] Field surveys can focus on a variety of topics relevant to organizational behavior, including employees' attitudes toward other people (such as leaders and coworkers), attitudes toward their jobs (such as satisfaction with the job and commitment to the organization), and perceptions of organizational characteristics (such as the challenge inherent in the job and the degree of decentralization in the organization).[10]

Field surveys provide information about a much larger segment of the population than do case studies. They also provide an abundance of data in easily quantifiable form, which facilitates statistical analysis and the compilation of normative data for comparative purposes.

Field surveys also have several disadvantages. First, survey information may reveal only superficial feelings and reactions to situations rather than deeply held feelings, attitudes, or emotions. Second, the design and development of field surveys require a great deal of expertise and can be very time-consuming. Furthermore, relationships among variables tend to be accentuated in responses to questionnaires because of what is called common method variance. This means that people may tend to answer all the questions in the same way, creating a misleading impression. A final, very important point is that field surveys give the researcher little or no control. The researcher may lack control over who completes the questionnaire, when it is filled out, the mental or physical state of the respondent, and many other important conditions. Thus, the typical field survey has many inherent sources of potential error.[11]

Nonetheless, surveys can be a very useful means of gathering large quantities of data and assessing general patterns of relationships among variables.

Laboratory Experiment

The **laboratory experiment** gives the researcher the most control. By creating an artificial setting similar to a real work situation, the researcher can control almost every possible factor in that setting. He or she can then manipulate the variables in the study and examine their effects on other variables.[12]

As an example of how laboratory experiments work, consider the relationship between how goals are developed for subordinates and the subordinates' subsequent level of satisfaction. To explore this relationship, the researcher structures a situation in which some subjects (usually students but occasionally people hired or recruited from the community) are assigned goals while others determine their own goals. Both groups then work on a hypothetical task relevant to the goals, and afterward all subjects fill out a questionnaire designed to measure satisfaction. Differences in satisfaction between the two groups could be attributed to the method used for goal setting.

Laboratory experiments prevent some of the problems of other types of research. Advantages include a high degree of control over variables and precise measurement of variables. A major disadvantage is the lack of realism; rarely does the laboratory setting exactly duplicate the real-life situation. A related problem is the difficulty in generalizing the findings to organizational settings. Finally, some organizational situations, such as plant closings or employee firings, cannot be realistically simulated in a laboratory.

A **laboratory experiment** involves creating an artificial setting similar to a real work situation to allow control over almost every possible factor in that setting.

Field Experiment

A **field experiment** is similar to a laboratory experiment except that it is conducted in a real organization. In a field experiment, the researcher attempts to control certain variables and to manipulate others to assess the effects of the manipulated variables on outcome variables. For example, a manager interested in the effects of flexible working hours on absenteeism and turnover might design a field experiment in which one plant adopts a flexible work schedule program and another plant, as similar as possible to the first, serves as a control site. Attendance and turnover are monitored at both plants. If attendance increases and turnover decreases in the experimental plant and there are no changes at the control site, the manager probably will conclude that the flexible work schedule program was successful.

The field experiment has certain advantages over the laboratory experiment. The organizational setting provides greater realism, making generalization to other organizational situations more valid. Disadvantages include the lack of control over other events that might occur in the organizational setting (such as additional changes the firm introduces), contamination of the results if the various groups discover their respective roles in the experiment and behave differently because of that knowledge, greater expense, and the risk that the experimental manipulations will contribute to problems within the company.

A **field experiment** is similar to a laboratory experiment but is conducted in a real organization.

Methods of Gathering Data

The method of gathering data is a critical concern of the research design. Data-gathering methods may be grouped into four categories: questionnaires, interviews, observation, and nonreactive measures.[13]

Questionnaires

A *questionnaire* is a collection of written questions about the respondents' attitudes, opinions, perceptions, demographic characteristics, or some combination of these factors. Usually the respondent fills out the questionnaire and returns it to the researcher. To facilitate scoring, the researcher typically uses questions with a variety of answers, each of which has an associated score. Some questionnaires have a few open-ended questions that allow respondents to elaborate on their answers. Designing a questionnaire that will provide the information the researcher desires is a very complex task and one that has received considerable attention. Some researchers have recently begun using computer networks to distribute questionnaires and collect responses. Indeed, web-based survey methodologies are quickly supplanting paper-and-pencil surveys.

Interviews

An *interview* resembles a questionnaire, but the questions are presented to the respondent orally by an interviewer. The respondent usually is allowed to answer questions spontaneously rather than being asked to choose among alternatives defined by the researcher. Interviews generally take much more time to administer than questionnaires, and they are more difficult to score. The benefit of interviews is the opportunity for the respondent to speak at length on a topic, thereby providing a richness and depth of information not normally yielded by questionnaires.

Observation

Observation, in its simplest form, is watching events and recording what is observed. Researchers use several types of observation. In structured observation, the observer is trained to look for and record certain activities or types of events. In participant observation, the trained observer actually participates in the organizational events as a member of the work team and records impressions and observations in a diary or daily log. In hidden observation, the trained observer is not visible to the subjects. A hidden camera or a specially designed observation room may be used.

Nonreactive Measures

When a situation is changed because of data gathering, we say the activity has caused a reaction in the situation. *Nonreactive measures,* also called "unobtrusive measures," have been developed for gathering data without disturbing the situation being studied. When questionnaires, interviews, and obtrusive observations may cause problems in the research situation, the use of nonreactive measures may be an appropriate substitute. Nonreactive measures include examination of physical traces, use of archives, and simple observation. At some universities, for example, sidewalks are not laid down around a new building until it has been in use for some time. Rather than ask students and faculty about their traffic patterns or try to anticipate them, the designers observe the building in use, see where the grass is most heavily worn, and put sidewalks there.

Related Issues in Research

Three other issues are of particular interest to researchers: causality, reliability and validity, and ethical concerns.[14]

Causality

Scientific research attempts to describe, explain, and predict phenomena. In many cases, the purpose of the research is to reveal causality; that is, researchers attempt to describe, explain, and predict the cause of a certain event. In everyday life, people commonly observe a series of events and infer causality about the relationship among them. For example, you might observe that a good friend is skipping one of her classes regularly. You also know that she is failing that class. You might infer that she is failing the class because of her poor attendance. But the causal relationship may be just the reverse: Your friend may have had a good attendance record until her poor performance on the first test destroyed her motivation and led her to stop attending class. Given the complexities associated with human behavior in organizational settings, the issues of causality, causal inference, and causal relations are of considerable interest to managers and researchers alike.

In the behavioral sciences, causality is difficult to determine because of the interrelationships among variables in a social system. Causality cannot always be empirically proven, but it may be possible to infer causality in certain circumstances. In general, two conditions must be met for causality to be attributed to an observed relationship among variables. The first is temporal order: If x causes y, then x must occur before y. Many studies, especially field surveys, describe the degree of association among variables with highly sophisticated mathematical techniques, but inferring a causal relationship is difficult because the variables are measured at the same point in time. On the basis of such evidence, we cannot say whether one variable or event caused the other, whether they were both caused by another variable, or whether they are totally independent of each other.

The second condition is the elimination of spuriousness. If we want to infer that x caused y, we must eliminate all other possible causes of y. Often a seemingly causal relationship between two variables is due to their joint association with a third variable, z. To be able to say the relationship between x and y is causal, we must rule out z as a possible cause of y. In the behavioral sciences, so many variables may influence one another that tracing causal relationships is like walking in an endless maze. Yet despite the difficulties of the task, we must continue trying to describe, explain, and predict social phenomena in organizational settings if we are to advance our understanding of organizational behavior.[15]

Reliability and Validity

The **reliability** of a measure is the extent to which it is consistent over time. Suppose that a researcher measures a group's job satisfaction today with a questionnaire and then measures the same thing in two months. Assuming that nothing has changed, individual responses should be very similar. If they are, the measure can be assessed as having a high level of reliability. Likewise, if question 2 and question 10 ask about the same thing, responses to these questions should be consistent. If measures lack reliability, little confidence can be placed in the results they provide.

Validity describes the extent to which research measures what it was intended to measure. Suppose that a researcher is interested in employees' satisfaction with their jobs. To determine this, he asks them a series of questions about their pay, supervisors, and working conditions. He then averages their answers and uses the average to represent job satisfaction. We might argue that this is not a valid measure. Pay, supervision, and working conditions, for example, may be unrelated to the job itself. Thus, the researcher has obtained data that do not mean what he thinks they mean—they are not valid. The researcher, then, must use measures that are valid as well as reliable.[16]

The **reliability of a measure** is the extent to which it is consistent over time.

Validity is the extent to which a measure actually reflects what it was intended to measure.

Ethical Concerns

Last, but certainly not least, the researcher must contend with ethical concerns. Two concerns are particularly important.[17] First, the researcher must provide adequate protection for participants in the study and not violate their privacy without their permission. For example, suppose that a researcher is studying the behavior of a group of operating employees. A good way to increase people's willingness to participate is to promise that their identities will not be revealed. Having made such a guarantee, the researcher is obligated to keep it.

Likewise, participation should be voluntary. All prospective subjects should have the right to not participate or to withdraw their participation after the study has begun. The researchers should explain all procedures in advance to participants and should not subject them to any experimental conditions that could harm them either physically or psychologically. Many government agencies, universities, and professional associations have developed guidelines for researchers to use to guarantee protection of human subjects.

The other issue involves how the researcher reports the results. In particular, it is important that research procedures and methods be reported faithfully and candidly. This enables readers to assess for themselves the validity of the results reported. It also allows others to do a better job of replicating (repeating) the study, perhaps with a different sample, to learn more about how its findings generalize.

The Historical Development of Organizational Behavior

T his appendix traces the historical development of the field of organizational behavior.

The Roots of Organizational Behavior

Many disciplines, such as physics and chemistry, are literally thousands of years old. Management has also been around in one form or another for centuries. For example, the writings of Aristotle and Plato abound with references to and examples of management concepts and practices. But because serious interest in the study of management did not emerge until around the turn of the twentieth century, the study of organizational behavior is only a few decades old.[1]

One reason for the relatively late development of management as a scientific field is that few large business organizations existed until the nineteenth century.[2] Although management is just as important to a small organization as to a large one, large firms were needed to provide both a stimulus and a laboratory for management research. A second reason is that many of the first people who took an interest in studying organizations were economists who initially assumed that management practices at the organizational level are by nature efficient and effective; therefore, they concentrated on higher levels of analysis such as national economic policy and industrial structures.

Interestingly, many contemporary managers today have come to appreciate the value of history. For example, managers glean insights from Homer's *Iliad*, Machiavelli's *The Prince*, Sun Tsu's *The Art of War*, Musashi's *The Book of Five Rings*, and Chaucer's *The Canterbury Tales*. And some organizations, such as Polaroid and Wells Fargo, even have corporate historians. Others, such as Shell Oil and Coca-Cola, openly proclaim their heritage as part of their employee orientation programs and often stress their rich histories as part of their advertising and public relations activities.[3]

The Scientific Management Era

The **scientific management** approach focused on the efficiency of individual workers and assumed that employees were motivated by money.

One of the first approaches to the study of management, popularized during the early 1900s, was **scientific management**. Scientific management was developed primarily in the United States. It focused primarily on the efficiency of individual workers. Several individuals helped develop and promote scientific management, including Frank and Lillian Gilbreth (whose lives were portrayed in a book and a subsequent movie, *Cheaper by the Dozen*—not the recent Steve Martin version!), Henry Gantt, and Harrington Emerson. But Frederick W. Taylor is most closely identified with this approach.[4] Early in his life, Taylor developed an interest in efficiency and productivity. While working as a foreman at Midvale Steel Company in Philadelphia from 1878 to 1890, he became aware of employees working at a pace much slower than their capabilities, a phenomenon he called soldiering. Because most managers had never systematically studied jobs in the plant—and, in fact, had little idea how to gauge worker productivity—they were completely unaware of this practice.

To counteract the effects of soldiering, Taylor developed several innovative techniques. For example, he scientifically studied all the jobs in the Midvale plant and developed a standardized method for performing each one. He also installed a piece-rate pay system in which each worker was paid for the amount of work that individual completed during the workday rather than for the time spent on the job. (Taylor believed that money was the only important motivational factor in the workplace.) These innovations boosted productivity markedly and are the foundation of scientific management.

After leaving Midvale, Taylor spent several years working as a management consultant for industrial firms. At Bethlehem Steel Company, he developed several efficient techniques for loading and unloading rail cars. At Simonds Rolling Machine Company, he redesigned jobs, introduced rest breaks to combat fatigue, and implemented a piece-rate pay system. In every case, Taylor claimed his ideas and methods greatly improved worker output. His book *Principles of Scientific Management*, published in 1911, was greeted with enthusiasm by practicing managers and quickly became a standard reference.

Scientific management quickly became a mainstay of business practice. Among other things, it facilitated job specialization and mass production, profoundly influencing the U.S. business system.[5] It also demonstrated to managers the importance of enhancing performance and productivity and confirmed their influence on these matters. For example, firms such as UPS and McDonald's still use some of the basic concepts introduced during the scientific management era today in their efforts to become ever more efficient.

Taylor had his critics, however. Labor opposed scientific management because its explicit goal was to get more output from workers. Congress investigated Taylor's methods and ideas because some argued that his incentive system would dehumanize the workplace and reduce workers to little more than drones. Later theorists recognized that Taylor's views of employee motivation were inadequate and narrow. And recently there have been allegations that Taylor falsified some of his research findings and paid someone to do his writing for him. Nevertheless, scientific management represents a key milestone in the development of management thought.[6]

Classical Organization Theory

Classical organization theory was concerned with the effective structuring of organizations.

During the same era, another perspective on management theory and practice was also emerging. Generally referred to as **classical organization theory**, this perspective was concerned with structuring organizations effectively. Whereas scientific

Elements	Comments	
1. **Rules and Procedures**	A consistent set of abstract rules and procedures should exist to ensure uniform performance.	**TABLE AB.1**
2. **Distinct Division of Labor**	Each position should be filled by an expert.	**Elements of Weber's Ideal Bureaucracy**
3. **Hierarchy of Authority**	The chain of command should be clearly established.	
4. **Technical Competence**	Employment and advancement should be based on merit.	
5. **Segregation of Ownership**	Professional managers rather than owners should run the organization.	
6. **Rights and Properties of the Position**	These should be associated with the organization, not with the person who holds the office.	
7. **Documentation**	A record of actions should be kept regarding administrative decisions, rules, and procedures.	

management studied how individual workers could be made more efficient, classical organization theory focused on how a large number of workers and managers could be organized most effectively into an overall structure. Interestingly, whereas scientific management was generally an American phenomenon, classical organization theory has a much more international heritage.

Henri Fayol (a French executive and engineer), Lyndall Urwick (a British executive), and Max Weber (a German sociologist) were major contributors to classical organization theory. Weber, the most prominent of the three, proposed a "bureaucratic" form of structure that he believed would work for all organizations.[7] Although today the term "bureaucracy" conjures up images of paperwork, red tape, and inflexibility, in Weber's model bureaucracy embraced logic, rationality, and efficiency. Weber assumed that the bureaucratic structure would always be the most efficient approach. (Such a blanket prescription represents what is now called a universal approach.) Table AB.1 summarizes the elements of Weber's ideal bureaucracy.

In contrast to Weber's views, contemporary organization theorists recognize that different organization structures may be appropriate in different situations. However, like scientific management, this perspective played a key role in the development of management thought, and Weber's ideas and the concepts associated with his bureaucratic structure are still interesting and relevant today.

The Emergence of Organizational Behavior

Rationality, efficiency, and standardization were the central themes of both scientific management and classical organization theory. The roles of individuals and groups in organizations were either ignored altogether or given only minimal attention. A few early writers and managers, however, recognized the importance of individual and social processes in organizations.[8]

Precursors of Organizational Behavior

In the early nineteenth century, Robert Owen, a British industrialist, attempted to better the condition of industrial workers. He improved working conditions, raised minimum ages for hiring children, introduced meals for employees, and shortened working hours. In the early twentieth century, the noted German psychologist Hugo Munsterberg argued that the field of psychology could provide important insights into areas such as motivation and the hiring of new employees. Another writer in the early 1900s, Mary Parker Follett, believed that management should become more democratic in its dealings with employees. An expert in vocational guidance, Follett argued that organizations should strive harder to accommodate their employees' human needs.[9]

Like Follett's perspective, the views of Owen and Munsterberg were not widely shared by practicing managers. Not until the 1930s did management's perception of the relationship between the individual and the workplace change significantly. At that time, a series of now classic research studies led to the emergence of organizational behavior as a field of study.

The Hawthorne Studies

The **Hawthorne studies** were conducted between 1927 and 1932 at Western Electric's Hawthorne plant near Chicago. (General Electric initially sponsored the research but withdrew its support after the first study was finished.) Several researchers were involved, the best known being William Dickson, chief of Hawthorne's Employee Relations Research Department, who initiated the research, and Elton Mayo and Fritz Roethlisberger, Harvard faculty members and consultants, who were called in after some of the more interesting findings began to surface.[10]

The first major experiment at Hawthorne investigated the effects of different levels of lighting on productivity. The researchers systematically manipulated the lighting of the area in which a group of women worked. The group's productivity was measured and compared with that of another group (the control group), whose lighting was left unchanged. As lighting was increased for the experimental group, productivity went up—but, surprisingly, so did the productivity of the control group. Even when lighting was subsequently reduced, the productivity of both groups continued to increase. Not until the lighting had become almost as dim as moonlight did productivity start to decline. This led the researchers to conclude that lighting had no relationship to productivity—and it was at this point that General Electric withdrew its sponsorship of the project!

In another major experiment, a piecework incentive system was established for a nine-man group that assembled terminal banks for telephone exchanges. Scientific management would have predicted that each man would work as hard as he could to maximize his personal income. But the Hawthorne researchers instead found that the group as a whole established an acceptable level of output for its members. Individuals who failed to meet this level were dubbed "chiselers," and those who exceeded it by too much were branded "rate busters." A worker who wanted to be accepted by the group could not produce at too high or too low a level. Thus, as a worker approached the accepted level each day, he slowed down to avoid overproducing.

After a follow-up interview program with several thousand workers, the Hawthorne researchers concluded that the human element in the workplace was considerably more important than previously believed. The lighting experiment, for example, suggested that productivity might increase simply because workers were singled out for special treatment and thus perhaps felt more valued. In the incentive system experiment, being accepted as a part of the group evidently meant more to the workers than earning extra money. Several other studies supported the overall conclusion that individual and social processes are too important to ignore.

Like the work of Taylor, unfortunately, the Hawthorne studies recently have been called into question. Critics cite deficiencies in research methods and alternative

The Hawthorne studies were conducted between 1927 and 1932 and led to some of the first discoveries of the importance of human behavior in organizations.

explanations of the findings. Again, however, these studies played a major role in the advancement of the field and are still among its most frequently cited works.[11]

The Human Relations Movement

The Hawthorne studies created quite a stir among managers, providing the foundation for an entirely new approach to management known as the human relations movement. The basic premises underlying the **human relations movement** were that people respond primarily to their social environment, that motivation depends more on social needs than on economic needs, and that satisfied employees work harder than unsatisfied employees. This perspective represented a fundamental shift away from the philosophy and values of scientific management and classical organization theory.

The works of Douglas McGregor and Abraham Maslow perhaps best exemplified the values of the human relations approach to management.[12] McGregor is best known for his classic book, *The Human Side of Enterprise*, in which he identified two opposing perspectives that he believed to typify managerial views of employees. Some managers, McGregor said, subscribed to what he labeled Theory X, whose characteristics are summarized in Table AB.2. **Theory X** takes a pessimistic view of human nature and employee behavior. In many ways, it is consistent with the premises of scientific management. A much more optimistic and positive view of employees is found in Theory Y, also summarized in Table AB.2. **Theory Y**, which is generally representative of the human relations perspective, was the approach McGregor himself advocated.

In 1943, Abraham Maslow published a pioneering theory of employee motivation that became well known and widely accepted among managers. Maslow's theory, which we describe in detail in Chapter 4, assumes that motivation arises from a hierarchical series of needs. As the needs at each level are satisfied, the individual progresses to the next-higher level.

> The **human relations movement** was based on the assumptions that employee satisfaction played a key role in performance.

> **Theory X** reflects a management approach that takes a negative and pessimistic view of workers.

> **Theory Y** reflects a management approach that takes a positive and optimistic view of workers.

Theory X Assumptions	Theory Y Assumptions
1. People do not like work and try to avoid it.	1. People do not naturally dislike work; work is a natural part of their lives.
2. People do not like work, so managers have to control, direct, coerce, and threaten employees to get them to work toward organizational goals.	2. People are internally motivated to reach objectives to which they are committed.
3. People prefer to be directed, to avoid responsibility, to want security; they have little ambition.	3. People are committed to goals to the degree that they receive personal rewards when they reach their objectives.
	4. People will seek and accept responsibility under favorable conditions.
	5. People have the capacity to be innovative in solving organizational problems.
	6. People are bright, but under most organizational conditions, their potentials are underutilized.

TABLE AB.2

Theory X and Theory Y

Reference: Douglas McGregor, *The Human Side of Enterprise* (New York: McGraw-Hill, 1960), pp. 33–34, 47–48.

The Hawthorne studies and the human relations movement played major roles in developing the foundations for the field of organizational behavior. Some of the early theorists' basic premises and assumptions were incorrect, however. For example, most human relationists believed that employee attitudes such as job satisfaction are the major causes of employee behaviors such as job performance. As we explain in Chapter 5, however, this usually is not the case at all. Also, many of the human relationists' views were unnecessarily limited and situation specific. Thus, there was still plenty of room for refinement and development in the emerging field of human behavior in organizations.

Toward Organizational Behavior: The Value of People

Organizational behavior began to emerge as a mature field of study in the late 1950s and early 1960s.[13] That period saw the field's evolution from the simple assumptions and behavioral models of the human relationists to the concepts and methodologies of a true scientific discipline. Since that time, organizational behavior as a scientific field of inquiry has made considerable strides, although there have been occasional steps backward as well. Overall, however, managers increasingly recognize the value of human resources and strive to better understand people and their role in complex organizations and competitive business situations.[14]

Endnotes

Chapter 1

1. For a classic discussion of the meaning of organizational behavior, see Larry Cummings, "Toward Organizational Behavior," *Academy of Management Review*, January 1978, pp. 90–98. For recent updates, see the annual series *Research in Organizational Behavior* (Greenwich, CT: JAI Press) and *Trends in Organizational Behavior* (New York: John Wiley & Sons). See also Nigel Nicholson, Pino Audia, and Madan Pillutla, eds., *Organizational Behavior*, vol. XI of *The Blackwell Encyclopedia of Management* (London: Blackwell Publishing, 2005).

2. Henry Mintzberg, "Rounding Out the Manager's Job," *Sloan Management Review*, Fall 1994, pp. 11–26; see also "All in a Day's Work," *Harvard Business Review*, December 2001, pp. 55–60.

3. "In Praise of Middle Managers," *Harvard Business Review*, September 2001, pp. 72–81.

4. Mauro F. Guillen, "The Age of Eclecticism: Current Organizational Trends and the Evolution of Managerial Models," *Sloan Management Review*, Fall 1994, pp. 75–86.

5. Henry Mintzberg, "The Manager's Job: Folklore and Fact," *Harvard Business Review*, July–August 1975, pp. 49–61.

6. Robert L. Katz, "The Skills of an Effective Administrator," *Harvard Business Review*, September–October 1987, pp. 90–102.

7. "SBC Chief Says Deal Preserves an 'Icon,'" *USA Today*, February 1, 2005, pp. 1B, 2B.

8. "Most Important Qualities for a CEO," *USA Today*, March 11, 2002, p. A1.

9. Max Bazerman, "Conducting Influential Research: The Need for Prescriptive Implications," *Academy of Management Review*, January 2005, pp. 25–31.

10. Joseph W. McGuire, "Retreat to the Academy," *Business Horizons*, July–August 1982, pp. 31–37; Kenneth Thomas and Walter G. Tymon, "Necessary Properties of Relevant Research: Lessons from Recent Criticisms of the Organizational Sciences," *Academy of Management Review*, July 1982, pp. 345–353. See also Jeffrey Pfeffer, "The Theory-Practice Gap: Myth or Reality?" *Academy of Management Executive*, February 1987, pp. 31–32.

11. Fremont Kast and James Rosenzweig, "General Systems Theory: Applications for Organization and Management," *Academy of Management Journal*, December 1972, pp. 447–465.

12. See Fremont Kast and James Rozenzweig, eds., *Contingency Views of Organization and Management* (Chicago: SRA, 1973), for a classic overview and introduction.

13. James Terborg, "Interactional Psychology and Research on Human Behavior in Organizations," *Academy of Management Review*, October 1981, pp. 569–576; Benjamin Schneider, "Interactional Psychology and Organizational Behavior," in *Research in Organizational Behavior*, eds. Larry Cummings and Barry Staw (Greenwich, CT: JAI Press, 1983), V, pp. 1–32; Daniel B. Turban and Thomas L. Keon, "Organizational Attractiveness: An Interactionist Perspective," *Journal of Applied Psychology*, vol. 78, no. 2, 1993, pp. 184–193.

Chapter 2

1. M. J. Gent, "Theory X in Antiquity, or the Bureaucratization of the Roman Army," *Business Horizons*, January–February 1984, pp. 53–54.

2. Ricky Griffin and Michael Pustay, *International Business*, 4th ed. (Upper Saddle River, NJ: Prentice-Hall, 2005).

3. Brian O'Reilly, "Your New Global Workforce," *Fortune*, December 14, 1992, pp. 58–66.

4. Simcha Ronen and Oded Shenkar, "Clustering Countries on Attitudinal Dimension: A Review and Synthesis," *Academy of Management Review*, July 1985, pp. 435–454.

5. Nancy J. Adler, Robert Doktor, and Gordon Redding, "From the Atlantic to the Pacific Century," *Journal of Management*, Summer 1986, pp. 295–318.

6. Brian O'Reilly, "Japan's Uneasy U.S. Managers," *Fortune*, April 25, 1988, pp. 245–264.

7. "Learning to Accept Cultural Diversity," *Wall Street Journal*, September 12, 1990, pp. B1, B9.

8. Tamotsu Yamaguchi, "The Challenge of Internationalization," *Academy of Management Executive*, February 1988, pp. 33–36.

9. Geert Hofstede, *Culture's Consequences: International Differences in Work-Related Values* (Beverly Hills, CA: Sage Publications, 1980).

10. André Laurent, "The Cultural Diversity of Western Conceptions of Management," *International Studies of Management and Organization*, Spring–Summer 1983, pp. 75–96.

11. See Brian O'Reilly, "Your New Global Workforce," *Fortune*, December 14, 1992, pp. 58–66; Richard I. Kirkland Jr., "Europe's New Managers," *Fortune*, September 29, 1986, pp. 56–60.

12. Michael L. Wheeler, "Diversity: Making the Business Case," *Business Week*, December 9, 1996; special advertising section.

13. For example, see Joshua Sacco and Neal Schmitt, "A Dynamic Multilevel Model of Demographic Diversity and Misfit Effects," *Journal of Applied Psychology*, 2005, vol. 90, no. 2, pp. 203–232.

14. Elaine Carter, Elaine Kepner, Malcolm Shaw, and William Brooks Woodson, "The Effective Management of Diversity," *S. A. M. Advanced Management Journal*, Autumn 1982, pp. 49–53.

15. Marilyn Loden and Judy B. Rosener, *Workforce America! Managing Employee Diversity as a Vital Resource* (Homewood, IL: Business One Irwin, 1991), pp. 58–62.

16. Ibid., p. 60.

17. Ibid., pp. 68–70.

18. Loden and Rosener, *Workforce America!* p. 19.

19. Howard N. Fullerton Jr. and Mitra Toossi, "Labor Force Projections to 2010: Steady Growth and Changing Composition," *Monthly Labor Review*, November 2001, pp. 21–38.

20. Ibid., p. 22.

21. Michael Crawford, "The New Office Etiquette," *Canadian Business*, May 1993, pp. 22–31.

22. Harish C. Jain and Anil Verma, "Managing Workforce Diversity for Competitiveness: The Canadian Experience," *International Journal of Manpower*, April–May 1996, pp. 14–30.

23. "Plenty of Muck, Not Much Money," *Economist,* May 8, 1999, p. 52.

24. Barry Louis Rubin, "Europeans Value Diversity," *HRMagazine,* January 1991, pp. 38–41, 78.

25. Ron Corben, "Thailand Faces a Shrinking Work Force," *Journal of Commerce and Commercial,* December 26, 1996, p. 5a.

26. Martha Irvine, "EEOC Sues Illinois Company Over 'English-Only' Policy," *Legal Intelligence,* September 2, 1999, p. 4.

27. Wheeler, "Diversity: Making the Business Case."

28. Lennie Copeland, "Making the Most of Cultural Differences at the Workplace," *Personnel,* June 1988, pp. 52–60.

29. See Anil Khurana, "Managing Complex Production Processes," *Sloan Management Review,* Winter 1999, pp. 85–98.

30. "How to Fix Corporate Governance," *Business Week,* May 6, 2002, pp. 68–78.

31. Max Boisot, *Knowledge Assets* (Oxford: Oxford University Press, 1998).

32. M. L. Tushman and C. A. O'Reilly, *Winning Through Innovation* (Cambridge, MA: Harvard Business School Press, 1996).

33. M. A. Von Glinow, *The New Professionals* (Cambridge, MA: Ballinger, 1988).

34. T. W. Lee and S. D. Maurer, "The Retention of Knowledge Workers with the Unfolding Model of Voluntary Turnover," *Human Resource Management Review,* 1997, vol. 7, pp. 247–276.

35. G. T. Milkovich, "Compensation Systems in High-Technology Companies," in *High Technology Management,* eds. A. Klingartner and C. Anderson (Lexington, MA: Lexington Books, 1987).

Chapter 3

1. Denise M. Rousseau and Judi McLean Parks, "The Contracts of Individuals and Organizations," in *Research in Organizational Behavior,* vol. 15, eds. Larry L. Cummings and Barry M. Staw (Greenwich, CT: JAI Press, 1993), pp. 1–43. See also Guillermo Dabos and Denise Rousseau, "Mutuality and Reciprocity in the Psychological Contracts of Employees and Employers," *Journal of Applied Psychology,* 2004, vol. 89, no. 1, pp. 52–72.

2. Denise M. Rousseau, "Changing the Deal While Keeping the People," *Academy of Management Executive,* February 1996, pp. 50–58; see also Violet Ho, "Social Influence on Evaluations of Psychological Contract Fulfillment," *Academy of Management Review,* January 2005, pp. 113–128.

3. Richard A. Guzzo, Katherine A. Noonan, and Efrat Elron, "Expatriate Managers and the Psychological Contract," *Journal of Applied Psychology,* vol. 79, no. 4, pp. 617–626.

4. Amy L. Kristof, "Person-Organization Fit: An Integrative Review of Its Conceptualizations, Measurement, and Implications," *Personnel Psychology,* Spring 1996, pp. 1–49.

5. See Daniel Goleman, *Emotional Intelligence: Why It Can Matter More Than IQ* (New York: Bantam Books, 1995).

6. Daniel Goleman, "Leadership That Gets Results," *Harvard Business Review,* March–April 2000, pp. 78–90.

7. J. B. Rotter, "Generalized Expectancies for Internal vs. External Control of Reinforcement," *Psychological Monographs,* 1966, vol. 80, pp. 1–28; Bert De Brabander and Christopher Boone, "Sex Differences in Perceived Locus of Control," *Journal of Social Psychology,* 1990, vol. 130, pp. 271–276.

8. T. W. Adorno, E. Frenkel-Brunswick, D. J. Levinson, and R. N. Sanford, *The Authoritarian Personality* (New York: Harper & Row, 1950).

9. "The Rise and Fall of Dennis Kozlowski," *Business Week,* December 23, 2002, pp. 64–77.

10. Leon Festinger, *A Theory of Cognitive Dissonance* (Palo Alto, CA: Stanford University Press, 1957).

11. Patricia C. Smith, L. M. Kendall, and Charles Hulin, *The Measurement of Satisfaction in Work and Behavior* (Chicago: Rand-McNally, 1969).

12. Linda Grant, "Happy Workers, High Returns," *Fortune,* January 12, 1998, p. 81.

13. See Timothy Judge, Carl Thoresen, Joyce Bono, and Gregory Patton, "The Job-Satisfaction-Job Performance Relationship: A Qualitative and Quantitative Review," *Psychological Bulletin,* 2001, vol. 127, no. 3, pp. 376–407.

14. James R. Lincoln, "Employee Work Attitudes and Management Practice in the U.S. and Japan: Evidence from a Large Comparative Study," *California Management Review,* Fall 1989, pp. 89–106.

15. See Michael Riketta, "Attitudinal Organizational Commitment and Job Performance: A Meta-Analysis," *Journal of Organizational Behavior,* 2002, vol. 23, no. 3, pp. 257–266.

16. Lincoln, "Employee Work Attitudes and Management Practice."

17. Leslie E. Palich, Peter W. Hom, and Roger W. Griffeth, "Managing in the International Context: Testing Cultural Generality of Sources of Commitment to Multinational Enterprises," *Journal of Management,* 1995, vol. 21, no. 4, pp. 671–690.

18. For an example of research in this area, see Jennifer M. George and Gareth R. Jones, "The Experience of Mood and Turnover Intentions: Interactive Effects of Value Attainment, Job Satisfaction, and Positive Mood," *Journal of Applied Psychology,* 1996, vol. 81, no. 3, pp. 318–325. For a recent review, see Arthur P. Brief and Howard M. Weiss, "Organizational Behavior: Affect in the Workplace," in *Annual Review of Psychology,* vol. 53 (Annual Reviews: Palo Alto, CA, 2002), pp. 279–307.

19. "One Man's Accident Is Shedding New Light on Human Perception," *Wall Street Journal,* September 30, 1993, pp. A1, A13.

20. William H. Starbuck and John M. Mezias, "Opening Pandora's Box: Studying the Accuracy of Managers' Perceptions," *Journal of Organizational Behavior,* 1996, vol. 17, pp. 99–117.

21. Mark J. Martinko and William L. Gardner, "The Leader/Member Attribution Process," *Academy of Management Review,* April 1987, pp. 235–249; Jeffrey D. Ford, "The Effects of Causal Attributions on Decision Makers' Responses to Performance Downturns," *Academy of Management Review,* October 1985, pp. 770–786.

22. "Chick-fil-A Cuts Job Turnover Rates," *Houston Chronicle,* January 9, 2002, p. B3.

23. See Anne O'Leary-Kelly, Ricky W. Griffin, and David J. Glew, "Organization-Motivated Aggression: A Research Framework," *Academy of Management Review,* January 1996, pp. 225–253.

24. See Dennis W. Organ, "Personality and Organizational Citizenship Behavior," *Journal of Management,* 1994, vol. 20, no. 2, pp. 465–478. For more recent information, see Jeffrey LePine,

Amir Erez, and Diane Johnson, "The Nature and Dimensionality of Organizational Citizenship Behavior: A Critical Review and Meta-Analysis," *Journal of Applied Psychology,* 2002, vol. 87, no. 1, pp. 52–65, and Mark Bolino and William Turnley, "Going the Extra Mile: Cultivating and Managing Employee Citizenship Behavior," *Academy of Management Executive,* 2003, vol. 17, no. 3, pp. 60–70.

Chapter 4

1. See Craig Pinder, *Work Motivation in Organizational Behavior* (Upper Saddle River, NJ: Prentice Hall, 1998).
2. Richard M. Steers, Gregory A. Bigley, and Lyman W. Porter, *Motivation and Leadership at Work,* 6th ed. (New York: McGraw-Hill, 1996). See also Ruth Kanfer, "Motivational Theory and Industrial and Organizational Psychology," in *Handbook of Industrial and Organizational Psychology,* 2nd ed., eds. M. D. Dunnette and L. M. Hough (Palo Alto, CA: Consulting Psychologists Press), vol. 1, pp. 75–170; and M. L. Ambrose, "Old Friends, New Faces: Motivation Research in the 1990s," *Journal of Management,* 1999, vol. 25, no. 2, pp. 110–131.
3. Roland E. Kidwell Jr. and Nathan Bennett, "Employee Propensity to Withhold Effort: A Conceptual Model to Intersect Three Avenues of Research," *Academy of Management Review,* July 1993, pp. 429–456.
4. Jeffrey Pfeiffer, *The Human Equation* (Boston: Harvard Business School Press, 1998).
5. E. L. Deci and R. M. Ryan, "The 'What' and 'Why' of Goal Pursuits: Human Needs and the Self-Determination of Behavior," *Psychological Inquiry,* 2000, vol. 11, no. 4, pp. 227–269.
6. Frederick W. Taylor, *Principles of Scientific Management* (New York: Harper, 1911).
7. Elton Mayo, *The Social Problems of an Industrial Civilization* (Boston: Harvard University Press, 1945); Fritz J. Rothlisberger and W. J. Dickson, *Management and the Worker* (Boston: Harvard University Press, 1939).
8. Gerald R. Salancik and Jeffrey Pfeiffer, "An Examination of Need-Satisfaction Models of Job Attitudes," *Administrative Science Quarterly,* September 1977, pp. 427–456.
9. Abraham H. Maslow, "A Theory of Human Motivation," *Psychological Review,* 1943, vol. 50, pp. 370–396; Abraham H. Maslow, *Motivation and Personality* (New York: Harper & Row, 1954). Maslow's most famous work includes Abraham Maslow, Deborah C. Stephens, and Gary Heil, *Maslow on Management* (New York: John Wiley and Sons, 1998); and Abraham Maslow and Richard Lowry, *Toward a Psychology of Being* (New York: John Wiley and Sons, 1999).
10. See "Professionals Sick of Old Routine Find Healthy Rewards in Nursing," *USA Today,* August 16, 2004, pp. 1B, 2B.
11. See Nancy Adler, *International Dimensions of Organizational Behavior,* 3rd ed. (Boston: PWS-Kent), 1997.
12. Mahmond A. Wahba and Lawrence G. Bridwell, "Maslow Reconsidered: A Review of Research on the Need Hierarchy Theory," *Organizational Behavior and Human Performance,* April 1976, pp. 212–240.
13. Clayton P. Alderfer, *Existence, Relatedness, and Growth* (New York: Free Press, 1972).
14. Ibid.
15. Frederick Herzberg, Bernard Mausner, and Barbara Synderman, *The Motivation to Work* (New York: John Wiley and Sons, 1959); Frederick Herzberg, "One More Time: How Do You Motivate Employees?" *Harvard Business Review,* January–February 1968, pp. 53–62.
16. Herzberg, Mausner, and Synderman, *The Motivation to Work.*
17. Ibid.
18. Ibid.
19. Ricky W. Griffin, *Task Design: An Integrative Approach* (Glenview, IL: Scott, Foresman, 1982).
20. Pinder, *Work Motivation in Organizational Behavior.*
21. Frederick Herzberg, *Work and the Nature of Man* (Cleveland, OH: World, 1966); Valerie M. Bookman, "The Herzberg Controversy," *Personnel Psychology,* Summer 1971, pp. 155–189; Benedict Grigaliunas and Frederick Herzberg, "Relevance in the Test of Motivation-Hygiene Theory," *Journal of Applied Psychology,* February 1971, pp. 73–79.
22. Marvin Dunnette, John Campbell, and Milton Hakel, "Factors Contributing to Job Satisfaction and Job Dissatisfaction in Six Occupational Groups," *Organizational Behavior and Human Performance,* May 1967, pp. 143–174; Charles L. Hulin and Patricia Smith, "An Empirical Investigation of Two Implications of the Two-Factor Theory of Job Satisfaction," *Journal of Applied Psychology,* October 1967, pp. 396–402.
23. Adler, *International Dimensions of Organizational Behavior.*
24. David McClelland, *The Achieving Society* (Princeton, NJ: Nostrand, 1961). See also David C. McClelland, *Human Motivation* (Cambridge, UK: Cambridge University Press, 1988).
25. Michael J. Stahl, "Achievement, Power, and Managerial Motivation: Selecting Managerial Talent with the Job Choice Exercise," *Personnel Psychology,* Winter 1983, pp. 775–790.
26. Stanley Schachter, *The Psychology of Affiliation* (Palo Alto, CA: Stanford University Press, 1959).
27. As reported in "Best Friends Good for Business," *USA Today,* December 1, 2004, pp. 1B, 2B.
28. David McClelland and David H. Burnham, "Power Is the Great Motivator," *Harvard Business Review,* March–April 1976, pp. 100–110.
29. Pinder, *Work Motivation in Organizational Behavior;* McClelland and Burnham, "Power Is the Great Motivator."
30. J. Stacy Adams, "Toward an Understanding of Inequity," *Journal of Abnormal and Social Psychology,* November 1963, pp. 422–436. See also Richard T. Mowday, "Equity Theory Predictions of Behavior in Organizations," in *Motivation and Work Behavior,* 4th ed., eds. Richard M. Steers and Lyman W. Porter (New York: McGraw-Hill, 1987), pp. 89–110.
31. Priti Pradham Shah, "Who Are Employees' Social Referents? Using a Network Perspective to Determine Referent Others," *Academy of Management Journal,* 1998, vol. 41, no. 3, pp. 249–268.
32. J. Stacy Adams, "Inequity in Social Exchange," in *Advances in Experimental Social Psychology,* vol. 2, ed. L. Berkowitz (New York: Academic Press, 1965), pp. 267–299.
33. Pinder, *Work Motivation in Organizational Behavior.*
34. See Kerry Sauler and Arthur Bedeian, "Equity Sensitivity: Construction of a Measure and Examination of Its Psychometric Properties," *Journal of Management,* 2000, vol. 26,

no. 5, pp. 885–910; Mark Bing and Susan Burroughs, "The Predictive and Interactive Effects of Equity Sensitivity in Teamwork-Oriented Organizations," *Journal of Organizational Behavior,* 2001, vol. 22, pp. 271–290.

35. Victor Vroom, *Work and Motivation* (New York: John Wiley and Sons, 1964).

36. Lyman W. Porter and Edward E. Lawler, *Managerial Attitudes and Performance* (Homewood, IL: Dorsey Press, 1968).

37. See Terence R. Mitchell, "Expectancy Models of Job Satisfaction, Occupational Preference, and Effort: A Theoretical, Methodological, and Empirical Appraisal," *Psychological Bulletin,* 1974, vol. 81, pp. 1096–1112; and John P. Campbell and Robert D. Pritchard, "Motivation Theory in Industrial and Organizational Psychology," in *Handbook of Industrial and Organizational Psychology,* ed. Marvin D. Dunnette (Chicago: Rand McNally, 1976), pp. 63–130, for reviews.

38. Pinder, *Work Motivation and Organizational Behavior.*

39. Ibid.

40. Campbell and Pritchard, "Motivation Theory in Industrial and Organizational Psychology."

41. Adler, *International Dimensions of Organizational Behavior.*

42. David A. Nadler and Edward E. Lawler, "Motivation: A Diagnostic Approach," in *Perspectives on Behavior in Organizations,* 2nd ed., eds. J. Richard Hackman, Edward E. Lawler, and Lyman W. Porter (New York: McGraw-Hill, 1983), pp. 67–78. See also Anne Fisher, "Turning Clock-Watchers into Stars," *Fortune,* March 22, 2004, p. 60.

43. Ivan P. Pavlov, *Conditional Reflexes* (New York: Oxford University Press, 1927).

44. Albert Bandura, "Social Cognitive Theory: An Agentic Perspective," *Annual Review of Psychology,* 2001, vol. 52, pp. 1–26.

45. B. F. Skinner, *Science and Human Behavior* (New York: Macmillan, 1953), and *Beyond Freedom and Dignity* (New York: Knopf, 1972).

46. Fred Luthans and Robert Kreitner, *Organizational Behavior Modification and Beyond* (Glenview, IL: Scott, Foresman, 1985).

47. "Workers: Risks and Rewards," *Time,* April 15, 1991, pp. 42–43.

48. See Richard Arvey and John M. Ivancevich, "Punishment in Organizations: A Review, Propositions, and Research Suggestions," *Academy of Management Review,* April 1980, pp. 123–132, for a review of the literature on punishment.

49. Fred Luthans and Robert Kreitner, *Organizational Behavior Modification* (Glenview, IL: Scott, Foresman, 1975); Luthans and Kreitner, *Organizational Behavior Modification and Beyond.*

50. Alexander D. Stajkovic, "A Meta-Analysis of the Effects of Organizational Behavior Modification on Task Performance, 1975–95," *Academy of Management Journal,* 1997, vol. 40, no. 5, pp. 1122–1149.

51. "At Emery Air Freight: Positive Reinforcement Boosts Performance," *Organizational Dynamics,* Winter 1973, pp. 41–50; W. Clay Hamner and Ellen P. Hamner, "Organizational Behavior Modification on the Bottom Line," *Organizational Dynamics,* Spring 1976, pp. 3–21.

52. Hamner and Hamner, "Organizational Behavior Modification on the Bottom Line."

53. Edwin Locke, "The Myths of Behavior Mod in Organizations," *Academy of Management Review,* 1977, vol. 2, pp. 543–553.

Chapter 5

1. Ricky W. Griffin and Gary C. McMahan, "Motivation Through Job Design," in *Organizational Behavior: State of the Science,* ed. Jerald Greenberg (New York: Lawrence Erlbaum and Associates, 1994), pp. 23–44.

2. Frederick W. Taylor, *The Principles of Scientific Management* (New York: Harper & Row, 1911).

3. C. R. Walker and R. Guest, *The Man on the Assembly Line* (Cambridge, MA: Harvard University Press, 1952).

4. Jia Lin Xie and Gary Johns, "Job Scope and Stress: Can Job Scope Be Too High?" *Academy of Management Journal,* 1995, vol. 38, no. 5, pp. 1288–1309.

5. Ricky W. Griffin, *Task Design: An Integrative Approach* (Glenview, IL: Scott, Foresman, 1982).

6. "These Six Growth Jobs Are Dull, Dead-End, Sometimes Dangerous," *Wall Street Journal,* December 1, 1994, pp. A1, A8, A9.

7. H. Conant and M. Kilbridge, "An Interdisciplinary Analysis of Job Enlargement: Technology, Cost, Behavioral Implications," *Industrial and Labor Relations Review,* 1965, vol. 18, no. 7, pp. 377–395.

8. Frederick Herzberg, "One More Time: How Do You Motivate Employees?" *Harvard Business Review,* January–February 1968, pp. 53–62; Frederick Herzberg, "The Wise Old Turk," *Harvard Business Review,* September–October 1974, pp. 70–80.

9. R. N. Ford, "Job Enrichment Lessons from AT&T," *Harvard Business Review,* January–February 1973, pp. 96–106.

10. E. D. Weed, "Job Enrichment 'Cleans Up' at Texas Instruments," in *New Perspectives in Job Enrichment,* ed. J. R. Maher (New York: Van Nostrand, 1971).

11. Griffin, *Task Design;* Griffin and McMahan, "Motivation Through Job Design."

12. J. Richard Hackman and Greg Oldham, "Motivation Through the Design of Work: Test of a Theory," *Organizational Behavior and Human Performance,* 1976, vol. 16, pp. 250–279. See also Michael A. Campion and Paul W. Thayer, "Job Design: Approaches, Outcomes, and Trade-Offs," *Organizational Dynamics,* Winter 1987, pp. 66–78.

13. J. Richard Hackman, "Work Design," in *Improving Life at Work: Behavioral Science Approaches to Organizational Change,* eds. J. Richard Hackman and J. L. Suttle (Santa Monica, CA: Goodyear, 1977).

14. Griffin, *Task Design.*

15. Griffin, *Task Design.* See also Karlene H. Roberts and William Glick, "The Job Characteristics Approach to Task Design: A Critical Review," *Journal of Applied Psychology,* 1981, vol. 66, pp. 193–217; and Ricky W. Griffin, "Toward an Integrated Theory of Task Design," in *Research in Organizational Behavior,* eds. Larry L. Cummings and Barry M. Staw (Greenwich, CT: JAI Press, 1987), vol. 9, pp. 79–120.

16. Ricky W. Griffin, M. Ann Welsh, and Gregory Moorhead, "Perceived Task Characteristics and Employee Performance: A Literature Review," *Academy of Management Review,* October 1981, pp. 655–664.

17. For a discussion of these issues, see Timothy Butler and James Waldroop, "Job Sculpting," *Harvard Business Review,* September–October 1999, pp. 144–152.

18. David J. Glew, Anne M. O'Leary-Kelly, Ricky W. Griffin, and David D. Van Fleet, "Participation in Organizations: A Preview of the Issues and Proposed Framework for Future Analysis," *Journal of Management,* 1995, vol. 21, no. 3, pp. 395–421; for a recent update, see Russ Forrester, "Empowerment: Rejuvenating a Potent Idea," *Academy of Management Executive,* 2002, vol. 14, no. 1, pp. 67–78.

19. John A. Wagner III, "Participation's Effects of Performance and Satisfaction: A Reconsideration of Research Evidence," *Academy of Management Review,* 1994, vol. 19, no. 2, pp. 312–330.

20. "9 to 5 Isn't Working Anymore," *Business Week,* September 20, 1999, pp. 94–98.

21. A. R. Cohen and H. Gadon, *Alternative Work Schedules: Integrating Individual and Organizational Needs* (Reading, MA: Addison-Wesley, 1978).

22. See Barbara Rau and MaryAnne Hyland, "Role Conflict and Flexible Work Arrangements: The Effects on Applicant Attraction," *Personnel Psychology,* 2002, vol. 55, no. 1, pp. 111–136.

23. "Working 9-to-5 No Longer," *USA Today,* December 6, 2004, pp. 1B, 2B.

24. For a recent analysis, see Sumita Raghuram, Raghu Garud, Batia Wiesenfeld, and Vipin Gupta, "Factors Contributing to Virtual Work Adjustment," *Journal of Management,* 2001, vol. 27, pp. 383–405.

Chapter 6

1. Jon R. Katzenbach and Jason A. Santamaria, "Firing Up the Front Line," *Harvard Business Review,* May–June 1999, pp. 107–117.

2. A. Bandura, *Social Learning Theory* (Englewood Cliffs, NJ: Prentice-Hall, 1977).

3. See Edwin A. Locke, "Toward a Theory of Task Performance and Incentives," *Organizational Behavior and Human Performance,* 1968, vol. 3, pp. 157–189.

4. Gary P. Latham and Gary Yukl, "A Review of Research on the Application of Goal Setting in Organizations," *Academy of Management Journal,* 1975, vol. 18, pp. 824–845.

5. Gary P. Latham and J. J. Baldes, "The Practical Significance of Locke's Theory of Goal Setting," *Journal of Applied Psychology,* 1975, vol. 60, pp. 187–191.

6. Gary P. Latham, "The Importance of Understanding and Changing Employee Outcome Expectancies for Gaining Commitment to an Organizational Goal," *Personnel Psychology,* 2001, vol. 54, pp. 707–720.

7. See Anthea Zacharatos, Julian Barling, and Roderick Iverson, "High-Performance Work Systems and Occupational Safety," *Journal of Applied Psychology,* 2005, vol. 90, no. 1, pp. 77–94.

8. H. John Bernardin and Richard W. Beatty, *Performance Appraisal: Assessing Human Behavior at Work* (Boston: Kent, 1984).

9. See Bruce Pfau and Ira Kay, "Does 360-Degree Feedback Negatively Affect Company Performance?" *HR Magazine,* June 2002, pp. 54–59.

10. Joan Brett and Leanne Atwater, "360° Feedback: Accuracy, Reactions, and Perceptions of Usefulness," *Journal of Applied Psychology,* 2001, vol. 86, no. 5, pp. 930–942; Terry Beehr, Lana Ivanitskaya, Curtiss Hansen, Dmitry Erefeev, and David Gudanowski, "Evaluation of 360-Degree Feedback Ratings: Relationships with Each Other and with Performance and Selection Predictors," *Journal of Organizational Behavior,* 2001, vol. 22, pp. 775–788.

11. Vanessa Urch Druskat and Steven B. Wolff, "Effects and Timing of Developmental Peer Appraisals in Self-Managing Work Groups," *Journal of Applied Psychology,* 1999, vol. 84, no. 1, pp. 58–74.

12. See Edward E. Lawler, *Pay and Organization Development* (Reading, MA: Addison-Wesley, 1981).

13. Brian Boyd and Alain Salamin, "Strategic Reward Systems: A Contingency Model of Pay System Design," *Strategic Management Journal,* 2001, vol. 22, pp. 777–792.

14. Alfred Rappaport, "New Thinking on How to Link Executive Pay with Performance," *Harvard Business Review,* March–April 1999, pp. 91–99.

15. Steve Bates, "Piecing Together Executive Compensation," *HR Magazine,* May 2002, pp. 60–69.

16. "Rich Benefit Plan Gives GM Competitors Cost Edge," *Wall Street Journal,* March 21, 1996, pp. B1, B4.

17. "Painless Perks," *Forbes,* September 6, 1999, p. 138. See also "Does Rank Have Too Much Privilege?" *Wall Street Journal,* February 26, 2002, pp. B1, B4.

18. Charlotte Garvey, "Meaningful Tokens of Appreciation," *HR Magazine,* August 2004, pp. 101–106.

19. John R. Deckop, Robert Mangel, and Carol C. Cirka, "Getting More Than You Pay For: Organizational Citizenship Behavior and Pay-for-Performance Plans," *Academy of Management Journal,* 1999, vol. 42, no. 4, pp. 420–428.

20. Charlotte Garvey, "Steering Teams with the Right Pay," *HR Magazine,* May 2002, pp. 70–80.

21. Andrea Poe, "Selection Savvy," *HR Magazine,* April 2002, pp. 77–80.

22. Ricky W. Griffin and Michael W. Pustay, *International Business—A Managerial Perspective,* 4th ed. (Upper Saddle River, NJ: Prentice Hall, 2005).

Chapter 7

1. See Richard S. DeFrank and John M. Ivancevich, "Stress on the Job: An Executive Update," *Academy of Management Executive,* 1998, vol. 12, no. 3, pp. 55–65.

2. See James C. Quick and Jonathan D. Quick, *Organizational Stress and Preventive Management* (New York: McGraw-Hill, 1984), for a review.

3. "Job Stress Beginning to Take Toll on Some Airline Workers," *USA Today,* November 30, 2004, pp. 1B, 2B.

4. Hans Selye, *The Stress of Life* (New York: McGraw-Hill, 1976).

5. For example, see Steve M. Jex and Paul D. Bliese, "Efficacy Beliefs as a Moderator of the Impact of Work-Related Stressors: A Multilevel Study," *Journal of Applied Psychology,* 1999, vol. 84, no. 3, pp. 349–361.

6. Meyer Friedman and Ray H. Rosenman, *Type A Behavior and Your Heart* (New York: Knopf, 1974).

7. "Prognosis for the 'Type A' Personality Improves in a New Heart Disease Study," *Wall Street Journal,* January 14, 1988, p. 27.

8. Susan C. Kobasa, "Stressful Life Events, Personality, and Health: An Inquiry Into Hardiness," *Journal of Personality and Social Psychology,* January 1979, pp. 1–11; Susan C. Kobasa, S. R. Maddi, and S. Kahn, "Hardiness and Health: A Prospective Study," *Journal of Personality and Social Psychology,* January 1982, pp. 168–177.

9. Findings reported by Carol Kleiman, *Chicago Times,* March 31, 1988, p. B1.

10. Todd D. Jick and Linda F. Mitz, "Sex Differences in Work Stress," *Academy of Management Review,* October 1985, pp. 408–420; Debra L. Nelson and James C. Quick, "Professional Women: Are Distress and Disease Inevitable?" *Academy of Management Review,* April 1985, pp. 206–218.

11. "Complex Characters Handle Stress Better," *Psychology Today,* October 1987, p. 26.

12. Robert L. Kahn, D. M. Wolfe, R. P. Quinn, J. D. Snoek, and R. A. Rosenthal, *Organizational Stress: Studies in Role Conflict and Role Ambiguity* (New York: Wiley, 1964).

13. David R. Frew and Nealia S. Bruning, "Perceived Organizational Characteristics and Personality Measures as Predictors of Stress/Strain in the Work Place," *Academy of Management Journal,* December 1987, pp. 633–646.

14. Thomas H. Holmes and Richard H. Rahe, "The Social Readjustment Rating Scale," *Journal of Psychosomatic Research,* 1967, vol. 11, pp. 213–218.

15. Evelyn J. Bromet, Mary A. Dew, David K. Parkinson, and Herbert C. Schulberg, "Predictive Effects of Occupational and Marital Stress on the Mental Health of a Male Workforce," *Journal of Organizational Behavior,* 1988, vol. 9, pp. 1–13.

16. "I Can't Sleep," *Business Week,* January 26, 2004, pp. 66–74.

17. Edward Hallowell, "Why Smart People Underperform," *Harvard Business Review,* January 2005, pp. 54–62.

18. "Employers on Guard for Violence," *Wall Street Journal,* April 5, 1995, p. 3A; Joel H. Neuman and Robert A. Baron, "Workplace Violence and Workplace Aggression: Evidence Concerning Specific Forms, Potential Causes, and Preferred Targets," *Journal of Management,* 1998, vol. 24, no. 3, pp. 391–419.

19. Raymond T. Lee and Blake E. Ashforth, "A Meta-Analytic Examination of the Correlates of the Three Dimensions of Job Burnout," *Journal of Applied Psychology,* 1996, vol. 81, no. 2, pp. 123–133.

20. For a recent update, see Iain Densten, "Re-thinking Burnout," *Journal of Organizational Behavior,* 2001, vol. 22, pp. 833–847.

21. John M. Kelly, "Get a Grip on Stress," *HR Magazine,* February 1997, pp. 51–57.

22. John W. Lounsbury and Linda L. Hoopes, "A Vacation from Work: Changes in Work and Nonwork Outcomes," *Journal of Applied Psychology,* 1986, vol. 71, pp. 392–401.

23. "Overloaded Staffers Are Starting to Take More Time Off Work," *Wall Street Journal,* September 23, 1998, p. B1.

24. "Eight Ways to Help You Reduce the Stress in Your Life," *Business Week Careers,* November 1986, p. 78. See also Holly

Weeks, "Taking the Stress out of Stressful Conversations," *Harvard Business Review,* July–August 2001, pp. 112–116.

25. Richard A. Wolfe, David O. Ulrich, and Donald F. Parker, "Employee Health Management Programs: Review, Critique, and Research Agenda," *Journal of Management,* Winter 1987, pp. 603–615.

26. "Workplace Hazard Gets Attention," *USA Today,* May 5, 1998, pp. 1B, 2B.

27. "Work and Family," *Business Week,* September 15, 1997, pp. 96–99.

28. Samuel Aryee, E. S. Srinivas, and Hwee Hoon Tan, "Rhythms of Life: Antecedents and Outcomes of Work-Family Balances in Employed Parents," *Journal of Applied Psychology,* 2005, vol. 90, no. 1, pp. 132–146.

Chapter 8

1. Herbert Simon, *The New Science of Management Decision* (New York: Harper & Row, 1960), p. 1.

2. Nandini Rajagopalan, Abdul M. A. Rasheed, and Deepak K. Datta, "Strategic Decision Processes: Critical Review and Future Directions," *Journal of Management,* Summer 1993, vol. 19, no. 2, pp. 349–384.

3. See George P. Huber, *Managerial Decision Making* (Glenview, IL: Scott, Foresman, 1980), pp. 90–115, for a discussion of decision making under conditions of certainty, risk, and uncertainty.

4. See David Garvin and Michael Roberto, "What You Don't Know About Making Decisions," *Harvard Business Review,* September 2001, pp. 108–115.

5. "'90s Style Brainstorming," *Forbes ASAP,* October 25, 1993, pp. 44–61.

6. Henry Mintzberg, Duru Raisinghani, and Andre Thoret, "The Structure of 'Unstructured' Decision Processes," *Administrative Science Quarterly,* June 1976, pp. 246–275; Milan Zeleny, "Descriptive Decision Making and Its Application," *Applications of Management Science,* 1981, vol. 1, pp. 327–388.

7. See E. Frank Harrison, *The Managerial Decision-Making Process,* 5th ed. (Boston: Houghton Mifflin, 1999), pp. 55–60, for more on choice processes.

8. Ari Ginsberg and N. Ventrakaman, "Contingency Perspectives of Organizational Strategy: A Critical Review of the Empirical Research," *Academy of Management Review,* July 1985, pp. 412–434; Donald C. Hambrick and David Lei, "Toward an Empirical Prioritization of Contingency Variables for Business Strategy," *Academy of Management Journal,* December 1985, pp. 763–788.

9. Leon Festinger, *A Theory of Cognitive Dissonance* (Palo Alto, CA: Stanford University Press, 1957).

10. Patricia Sellers, "The Dumbest Marketing Ploys," *Fortune,* October 5, 1992, pp. 88–94.

11. See Harrison, *The Managerial Decision-Making Process,* pp. 74–100, for more on the rational approach to decision making.

12. Craig D. Parks and Rebecca Cowlin, "Group Discussion as Affected by Number of Alternatives and by a Time Limit," *Organizational Behavior and Human Decision Processes,* 1995, vol. 62, no. 3, pp. 267–275.

13. See James G. March and Herbert A. Simon, *Organizations* (New York: Wiley, 1958), for more on the concept of bounded rationality.

14. Herbert A. Simon, *Administrative Behavior: A Study of Decision Making Processes in Administrative Organizations,* 3rd ed. (New York: Free Press, 1976).

15. Richard M. Cyert and James G. March, *A Behavioral Theory of the Firm* (Englewood Cliffs, NJ: Prentice Hall, 1963), p. 113; Simon, *Administrative Behavior.*

16. Kathleen M. Eisenhardt, "Making Fast Strategic Decisions in High-Velocity Environments," *Academy of Management Journal,* September 1989, pp. 543–576.

17. Irving L. Janis and Leon Mann, *Decision Making: A Psychological Analysis of Conflict, Choice, and Commitment* (New York: Free Press, 1977).

18. "Stage Set for Conflict at Disney Meeting," *USA Today,* February 22, 2005, p. B1.

19. Kimberly D. Elsbach and Greg Elofson, "How the Packaging of Decision Explanations Affects Perceptions of Trustworthiness," *Academy of Management Journal,* 2000, vol. 43, pp. 80–89.

20. Charles P. Wallace, "Adidas—Back in the Game," *Fortune,* August 18, 1997, pp. 176–182.

21. Barry M. Staw and Jerry Ross, "Good Money After Bad," *Psychology Today,* February 1988, pp. 30–33; D. Ramona Bobocel and John Meyer, "Escalating Commitment to a Failing Course of Action: Separating the Roles of Choice and Justification," *Journal of Applied Psychology,* 1994, vol. 79, pp. 360–363.

22. Mark Keil and Ramiro Montealegre, "Cutting Your Losses: Extricating Your Organization When a Big Project Goes Awry," *Sloan Management Review,* Spring 2000, pp. 55–64.

23. Gerry McNamara and Philip Bromiley, "Risk and Return in Organizational Decision Making," *Academy of Management Journal,* 1999, vol. 42, pp. 330–339.

24. See Brian O'Reilly, "What It Takes to Start a Startup," *Fortune,* June 7, 1999, pp. 135–140, for an example.

25. See Richard W. Woodman, John E. Sawyer, and Ricky W. Griffin, "Toward a Theory of Organizational Creativity," *Academy of Management Review,* April 1993, pp. 293–321.

26. John Simons, "The $10 Billion Pill," *Fortune,* January 20, 2003, pp. 58–68.

27. Christina E. Shalley, Lucy L. Gilson, and Terry C. Blum, "Matching Creativity Requirements and the Work Environment: Effects on Satisfaction and Intentions to Leave," *Academy of Management Journal,* 2000, vol. 43, no. 2, pp. 215–223; see also Filiz Tabak, "Employee Creative Performance: What Makes it Happen?" *The Academy of Management Executive,* 1997, vol. 11, no. 1, pp. 119–122.

Chapter 9

1. See John J. Gabarro, "The Development of Working Relationships," in *Handbook of Organizational Behavior,* ed. Jay W. Lorsch (Englewood Cliffs, NJ: Prentice-Hall, 1987), pp. 172–189; see also "Team Efforts, Technology, Add New Reasons to Meet," *USA Today,* December 8, 1997, pp. 1A, 2A.

2. Marvin E. Shaw, *Group Dynamics: The Psychology of Small Group Behavior,* 3rd ed. (New York: McGraw-Hill, 1991), p. 11.

3. Francis J. Yammarino and Alan J. Dubinsky, "Salesperson Performance and Managerially Controllable Factors: An Investigation of Individual and Work Group Effects," *Journal of Management,* 1990, vol. 16, pp. 97–106.

4. Rob Cross and Laurence Prusak, "The People Who Make Organizations Go—Or Stop," *Harvard Business Review,* June 2002, pp. 104–114.

5. William L. Sparks, Dominic J. Monetta, and L. M. Simmons Jr., "Affinity Groups: Developing Complex Adaptive Organizations," working paper, The PAM Institute, Washington, DC, 1999.

6. Shawn Tully, "The Vatican's Finances," *Fortune,* December 21, 1997, pp. 29–40.

7. Bernard M. Bass and Edward C. Ryterband, *Organizational Psychology,* 2nd ed. (Boston: Allyn & Bacon, 1979), pp. 252–254. See also Scott Lester, Bruce Meglino, and M. Audrey Korsgaard, "The Antecedents and Consequences of Group Potency: A Longitudinal Investigation of Newly Formed Work Groups," *Academy of Management Journal,* 2002, vol. 45, no. 2, pp. 352–369.

8. Susan Long, "Early Integration in Groups: A Group to Join and a Group to Create," *Human Relations,* April 1994, pp. 311–332.

9. For example, see Mary Waller, Jeffrey Conte, Cristina Gibson, and Mason Carpenter, "The Effect of Individual Perceptions of Deadlines on Team Performance," *Academy of Management Review,* 2001, vol. 26, no. 4, pp. 596–600.

10. Steven L. Obert, "Developmental Patterns of Organizational Task Groups: A Preliminary Study," *Human Relations,* January 1993, pp. 37–52.

11. Bass and Ryterband, *Organizational Psychology,* pp. 252–254.

12. Bernard M. Bass, "The Leaderless Group Discussion," *Psychological Bulletin,* September 1954, pp. 465–492.

13. Jill Lieber, "Time to Heal the Wounds," *Sports Illustrated,* November 2, 1997, pp. 96–91.

14. Connie J. G. Gersick, "Marking Time: Predictable Transitions in Task Groups," *Academy of Management Journal,* 1999, vol. 32, pp. 274–309.

15. James H. Davis, *Group Performance* (Reading, MA: Addison-Wesley, 1964), pp. 92–96.

16. Shaw, *Group Dynamics,* pp. 89–92.

17. Charles A. O'Reilly III, David F. Caldwell, and William P. Barnett, "Work Group Demography, Social Integration, and Turnover," *Administrative Science Quarterly,* March 1999, vol. 34, pp. 21–37.

18. See Sheila Simsarian Webber and Lisa Donahue, "Impact of Highly and Less Job-Related Diversity on Work Group Cohesion and Performance: A Meta-Analysis," *Journal of Management,* 2001, vol. 27, pp. 141–162.

19. Nancy Adler, *International Dimensions of Organizational Behavior,* 4th ed. (Cincinnati: Thomson Learning, 2002), chapter 5.

20. Shaw, *Group Dynamics,* pp. 173–177.

21. See Jennifer Chatman and Francis Flynn, "The Influence of Demographic Heterogeneity on the Emergence and Consequences of Cooperative Norms in Work Teams," *Academy of Management Journal,* 2001, vol. 44, no. 5, pp. 956–974.

22. Daniel C. Feldman, "The Development and Enforcement of Group Norms," *Academy of Management Review*, January 1994, pp. 47–53.

23. William E. Piper, Myriam Marrache, Renee Lacroix, Astrid M. Richardson, and Barry D. Jones, "Cohesion as a Basic Bond in Groups," *Human Relations*, February 1993, pp. 93–109.

24. Daniel Beal, Robin Cohen, Michael Burke, and Christy McLendon, "Cohesion and Performance in Groups: A Meta-Analytic Clarification of Construct Relations," *Journal of Applied Psychology*, 2003, vol. 88, no. 6, pp. 989–1004.

25. Robert T. Keller, "Predictors of the Performance of Project Groups in R & D Organizations," *Academy of Management Journal*, December 1996, pp. 715–726.

26. Irving L. Janis, *Groupthink*, 2nd ed. (Boston: Houghton Mifflin, 1992), p. 9.

27. Blake E. Ashforth and Fred Mael, "Social Identity Theory and the Organization," *Academy of Management Review*, January 1999, pp. 20–39.

28. Reed E. Nelson, "The Strength of Strong Ties: Social Networks and Intergroup Conflict in Organizations," *Academy of Management Journal*, June 1999, pp. 377–401, reprinted by permission.

29. M. A. Wallach, N. Kogan, and D. J. Bem, "Group Influence on Individual Risk Taking," *Journal of Abnormal and Social Psychology*, August 1962, pp. 75–86; James A. F. Stoner, "Risky and Cautious Shifts in Group Decisions: The Influence of Widely Held Values," *Journal of Experimental Social Psychology*, October 1968, pp. 442–459.

30. Dorwin Cartwright, "Risk Taking by Individuals and Groups: An Assessment of Research Employing Choice Dilemmas," *Journal of Personality and Social Psychology*, December 1971, pp. 361–378.

31. S. Moscovici and M. Zavalloni, "The Group as a Polarizer of Attitudes," *Journal of Personality and Social Psychology*, June 1969, pp. 125–135.

32. Janis, *Groupthink*.

33. Gregory Moorhead, Christopher P. Neck, and Mindy West, "The Tendency Toward Defective Decision Making Within Self-Managing Teams: Relevance of Groupthink for the 21st Century," *Organizational Behavior and Human Decision Processes*, February–March 1998, pp. 327–351.

34. Gregory Moorhead, Richard Ference, and Chris P. Neck, "Group Decision Fiascoes Continue: Space Shuttle Challenger and a Revised Groupthink Framework," *Human Relations*, 1991, vol. 44, pp. 539–550.

35. See Robert Cross and Susan Brodt, "How Assumptions of Consensus Undermine Decision Making," *Sloan Management Review*, Winter 2001, pp. 86–95.

36. Irving L. Janis, *Victims of Groupthink* (Boston: Houghton Mifflin, 1972), pp. 197–198.

37. Janis, *Groupthink*.

38. Janis, *Groupthink*, pp. 193–197; Gregory Moorhead, "Groupthink: Hypothesis in Need of Testing," *Group & Organization Studies*, December 1982, pp. 429–444.

39. Gregory Moorhead and John R. Montanari, "Empirical Analysis of the Groupthink Phenomenon," *Human Relations*, May 1986, pp. 399–410; John R. Montanari and Gregory Moorhead, "Development of the Groupthink Assessment Inventory," *Educational and Psychological Measurement*, Spring 1989, pp. 209–219.

40. Frederick W. Taylor, *The Principles of Scientific Management* (New York: Harper & Row, 1911).

41. Chris Argyris, *Personality and Organization* (New York: Harper & Row, 1957); Rensis Likert, *New Patterns of Management* (New York: McGraw-Hill, 1961).

42. Lester Coch and John R. P. French, "Overcoming Resistance to Change," *Human Relations*, 1948, vol. 1, pp. 512–532; N. C. Morse and E. Reimer, "The Experimental Change of a Major Organizational Variable," *Journal of Abnormal and Social Psychology*, January 1956, pp. 120–129.

43. Victor Vroom, "Leadership and the Decision-Making Process," *Organizational Dynamics* (Spring 2000).

44. For a recent example, see Carsten K. W. De Dreu and Michael West, "Minority Dissent and Team Innovation: The Importance of Participation in Decision Making," *Journal of Applied Psychology*, 2001, vol. 86, no. 6, pp. 1191–1201.

Chapter 10

1. Eric L. Trist and K. W. Bamforth, "Some Social and Psychological Consequences of the Longwall Method of Goal-Getting," *Human Relations*, February 1951, pp. 3–38; Jack D. Orsburn, Linda Moran, and Ed Musselwhite, with John Zenger, *Self-Directed Work Teams: The New American Challenge* (Homewood, IL: Business One Irwin, 1990).

2. See Jon R. Katzenbach and Douglas K. Smith, *The Wisdom of Teams: Creating the High-Performance Organization* (Boston: Harvard Business School Press, 1993), p. 45.

3. See Ruth Wageman, "How Leaders Foster Self-Managing Team Effectiveness: Design Choices Versus Hands-on Coaching," *Organization Science*, 2001, vol. 12, no. 5, pp. 559–577.

4. See Michelle Marks, John Mathieu, and Stephen Zaccaro, "A Temporally Based Framework and Taxonomy of Team Processes," *Academy of Management Review*, 2001, vol. 26, no. 3, pp. 356–376.

5. Michele Williams, "In Whom We Trust: Group Membership as an Affective Context for Trust Development," *Academy of Management Review*, 2001, vol. 26, no. 3, pp. 377–396.

6. Katzenbach and Smith, *The Wisdom of Teams*, p. 3.

7. See Michelle Marks, Mark Sabella, C. Shawn Burke, and Stephen Zaccaro, "The Impact of Cross-Training on Team Effectiveness," *Journal of Applied Psychology*, 2002, vol. 87, no. 1, pp. 3–13.

8. Orsburn, Moran, Musselwhite, and Zenger, *Self-Directed Work Teams*, p. 15.

9. Charles C. Manz and Henry P. Sims Jr., *Business Without Bosses* (New York: Wiley, 1993), pp. 10–11.

10. See Deborah Ancona, Henrik Bresman, and Katrin Kaeufer, "The Competitive Advantage of X-Teams," *Sloan Management Review*, Spring 2002, pp. 33–42.

11. Katzenbach and Smith, *The Wisdom of Teams*, pp. 184–189.

12. Manz and Sims, *Business Without Bosses*, pp. 74–76.

13. Jason Colquitt, Raymond Noe, and Christine Jackson, "Justice in Teams: Antecedents and Consequences of Procedural Justice Climate," *Personnel Psychology*, 2002, vol. 55, pp. 83–95.

14. Nigel Nicholson, Pino Audia, and Madan Pillutla, eds., *Encyclopedic Dictionary of Organizational Behavior*, 2nd ed. (Cambridge, MA: Blackwell, 2005), pp. 337–338.

15. Brian Dumaine, "The Trouble with Teams," *Fortune*, September 5, 1994.

16. Ibid.

17. Ibid.

18. Ibid.

19. Ellen Hart, "Top Teams," *Management Review*, February 1996, pp. 43–47.

20. Dan Dimancescu and Kemp Dwenger, "Smoothing the Product Development Path," *Management Review*, January 1996, pp. 36–41.

21. Ibid.

22. Manz and Sims, *Business Without Bosses*, pp. 27–28.

23. Ibid., pp. 29–31.

24. Ibid., p. 130.

25. Ibid., p. 200.

26. Ibid., p. 200

Chapter 11

1. Otis W. Baskin and Craig E. Aronoff, *Interpersonal Communication in Organizations* (Santa Monica, CA: Goodyear, 1980), p. 2.

2. "How Merrill Lynch Moves Its Stock Deals All Around the World," *Wall Street Journal*, November 9, 1987, pp. 1, 8.

3. Jeanne D. Maes, Teresa G. Weldy, and Marjorie L. Icenogle, "A Managerial Perspective: Oral Communication Competency Is Most Important for Business Students in the Workplace," *Journal of Business Communication*, January 1997, pp. 67–80.

4. Melinda Knight, "Writing and Other Communication Standards in Undergraduate Business Education: A Study of Current Program Requirements, Practices, and Trends," *Business Communication Quarterly*, March 1999, p. 10.

5. Robert Nurden, "Graduates Must Master the Lost Art of Communication," *The European*, March 20, 1997, p. 24.

6. Silvan S. Tompkins and Robert McCarter, "What and Where Are the Primary Affects? Some Evidence for a Theory," *Perceptual and Motor Skills*, February 1964, pp. 119–158.

7. See Everett M. Rogers and Rekha Agarwala-Rogers, *Communication in Organizations* (New York: Free Press, 1976), for a brief review of the background and development of the source-message-channel-receiver model of communication.

8. Charles A. O'Reilly III, "Variations in Decision Makers' Use of Information Sources: The Impact of Quality and Accessibility of Information," *Academy of Management Journal*, December 1982, pp. 756–771.

9. See Jerry C. Wofford, Edwin A. Gerloff, and Robert C. Cummins, *Organizational Communication* (New York: McGraw-Hill, 1977), for a discussion of channel noise.

10. Donald R. Hollis, "The Shape of Things to Come: The Role of IT," *Management Review*, June 1996, p. 62.

11. Kym France, "Computer Commuting Benefits Companies," *Arizona Republic*, August 16, 1993, pp. E1, E4.

12. Paul S. Goodman and Eric D. Darr, "Exchanging Best Practices Through Computer-Aided Systems," *Academy of Management Executive*, May 1996, pp. 7–18.

13. Jenny C. McCune, "The Intranet: Beyond E-Mail," *Management Review*, November 1996, pp. 23–27.

14. See Daniel Katz and Robert L. Kahn, *The Social Psychology of Organizations*, 2nd ed. (New York: John Wiley and Sons, 1978), for more about the role of organizational communication networks.

15. For good discussions of small-group communication networks and research on this subject, see Wofford, Gerloff, and Cummins, *Organizational Communication*; and Marvin E. Shaw, *Group Dynamics: The Psychology of Small Group Behavior*, 3rd ed. (New York: McGraw-Hill, 1981), pp. 150–161.

16. See R. Wayne Pace, *Organizational Communication: Foundations for Human Resource Development* (Englewood Cliffs, NJ: Prentice Hall, 1983), for further discussion of the development of communication networks.

17. David Krackhardt and Lyman W. Porter, "The Snowball Effect: Turnover Embedded in Communication Networks," *Journal of Applied Psychology*, February 1986, pp. 50–55.

18. "Has Coke Been Playing Accounting Games?" *Business Week*, May 13, 2002, pp. 98–99.

19. See "E-mail's Limits Create Confusion, Hurt Feelings," *USA Today*, February 5, 2002, pp. 1B, 2B.

20. "Talk of Chapter 11 Bruises Kmart Stock," *USA Today*, January 3, 2002, p. 1B.

21. Thomas J. Peters and Robert H. Waterman Jr., *In Search of Excellence: Lessons from America's Best-Run Companies* (New York: Harper & Row, 1982), p. 121.

22. Shari Caudron, "Monsanto Responds to Diversity," *Personnel Journal*, November 1990, pp. 72–78; "Trading Places at Monsanto," *Training and Development Journal*, April 1993, pp. 45–49.

Chapter 12

1. Ralph M. Stogdill, *Handbook of Leadership* (New York: Free Press, 1974). See also Bernard Bass, *Bass and Stogdill's Handbook of Leadership*, 3rd ed. (Riverside, NJ: Free Press, 1990); and "In Search of Leadership," *Business Week*, November 15, 1999, pp. 172–176.

2. See Gary Yukl and David D. Van Fleet, "Theory and Research on Leadership in Organizations," in *Handbook of Industrial and Organizational Psychology*, vol. 3, eds. M. D. Dunnette and L. M. Hough (Palo Alto, CA: Consulting Psychologists Press, 1992), pp. 148–197.

3. Arthur G. Jago, "Leadership: Perspectives in Theory and Research," *Management Science*, March 1982, pp. 315–336.

4. Melvin Sorcher and James Brant, "Are You Picking the Right Leaders?" *Harvard Business Review*, February 2002, pp. 78–85.

5. See John P. Kotter, "What Leaders Really Do," *Harvard Business Review*, May–June 1990, pp. 103–111. See also Abraham Zaleznik, "Managers and Leaders: Are They Different?" *Harvard Business Review*, March–April 1992, pp. 126–135; and John Kotter, "What Leaders Really Do," *Harvard Business Review*, December 2001, pp. 85–94.

6. Ronald Heifetz and Marty Linsky, "A Survival Guide for Leaders," *Harvard Business Review*, June 2002, pp. 65–74.

7. Frederick Reichheld, "Lead for Loyalty," *Harvard Business Review,* July–August 2001, pp. 76–83.

8. David D. Van Fleet and Gary A. Yukl, "A Century of Leadership Research," in *Papers Dedicated to the Development of Modern Management,* eds. D. A. Wren and J. A. Pearce II (Chicago: The Academy of Management, 1986), pp. 12–23.

9. Shelly A. Kirkpatrick and Edwin A. Locke, "Leadership: Do Traits Matter?" *Academy of Management Executive,* May 1991, pp. 48–60; see also Robert J. Sternberg, "Managerial Intelligence: Why IQ Isn't Enough," *Journal of Management,* 1997, vol. 23, no. 3, pp. 475–493.

10. Philip M. Podsakoff, Scott B. MacKenzie, Mike Ahearne, and William H. Bommer, "Searching for a Needle in a Haystack: Trying to Identify the Illusive Moderators of Leadership Behaviors," *Journal of Management,* 1995, vol. 21, no. 3, pp. 422–470.

11. Rensis Likert, *New Patterns of Management* (New York: McGraw-Hill, 1961).

12. Edwin Fleishman, E. F. Harris, and H. E. Burtt, *Leadership and Supervision in Industry* (Columbus, OH: Bureau of Educational Research, Ohio State University, 1955).

13. See Edwin A. Fleishman, "Twenty Years of Consideration and Structure," in *Current Developments in the Study of Leadership,* eds. Edward A. Fleishman and James G. Hunt (Carbondale, IL: Southern Illinois University Press, 1973), pp. 1–40.

14. Fleishman, Harris, and Burtt, *Leadership and Supervision in Industry.*

15. For a recent update, see Timothy Judge, Ronald Piccolo, and Remus Ilies, "The Forgotten Ones? The Validity of Consideration and Initiating Structure in Leadership Research," *Journal of Applied Psychology,* 2004, vol. 89, no. 1, pp. 36–51.

16. Robert R. Blake and Jane S. Mouton, *The Managerial Grid* (Houston: Gulf Publishing, 1964); Robert R. Blake and Jane S. Mouton, *The Versatile Manager: A Grid Profile* (Homewood, IL: Dow Jones-Irwin, 1981).

17. Robert Tannenbaum and Warren H. Schmidt, "How to Choose a Leadership Pattern," *Harvard Business Review,* March–April 1958, pp. 95–101.

18. Fred E. Fiedler, *A Theory of Leadership Effectiveness* (New York: McGraw-Hill, 1967). Reprinted by permission of the author.

19. See Fred E. Fiedler, "Engineering the Job to Fit the Manager," *Harvard Business Review,* September–October 1965, pp. 115–122.

20. See Fred E. Fiedler, Martin M. Chemers, and Linda Mahar, *Improving Leadership Effectiveness: The Leader Match Concept* (New York: John Wiley and Sons, 1976).

21. Chester A. Schriesheim, Bennett J. Tepper, and Linda A. Tetrault, "Least Preferred Co-Worker Score, Situational Control, and Leadership Effectiveness: A Meta-Analysis of Contingency Model Performance Predictions," *Journal of Applied Psychology,* 1994, vol. 79, no. 4, pp. 561–573.

22. See Martin G. Evans, "The Effects of Supervisory Behavior on the Path-Goal Relationship," *Organizational Behavior and Human Performance,* May 1970, pp. 277–298; Robert J. House, "A Path-Goal Theory of Leadership Effectiveness," *Administrative Science Quarterly,* September 1971, pp. 321–339; Robert J. House and Terence R. Mitchell, "Path-Goal Theory of Leadership," *Journal of Contemporary Business,* Autumn 1974, pp. 81–98.

23. See Victor H. Vroom and Philip H. Yetton, *Leadership and Decision Making* (Pittsburgh: University of Pittsburgh Press, 1973); Victor H. Vroom and Arthur G. Jago, *The New Leadership* (Englewood Cliffs, NJ: Prentice-Hall, 1988).

24 Victor Vroom, "Leadership and the Decision-Making Process," *Organizational Dynamics,* Spring 2000.

25. Vroom and Jago, *The New Leadership.*

26. See Madeline E. Heilman, Harvey A. Hornstein, Jack H. Cage, and Judith K. Herschlag, "Reaction to Prescribed Leader Behavior as a Function of Role Perspective: The Case of the Vroom-Yetton Model," *Journal of Applied Psychology,* February 1984, pp. 50–60; R. H. George Field, "A Test of the Vroom-Yetton Normative Model of Leadership," *Journal of Applied Psychology,* February 1982, pp. 523–532.

Chapter 13

1. George Graen and J. F. Cashman, "A Role-Making Model of Leadership in Formal Organizations: A Developmental Approach," in *Leadership Frontiers,* eds. J. G. Hunt and L. L. Larson (Kent, OH: Kent State University Press, 1975), pp. 143–165; Fred Dansereau, George Graen, and W. J. Haga, "A Vertical Dyad Linkage Approach to Leadership Within Formal Organizations: A Longitudinal Investigation of the Role-Making Process," *Organizational Behavior and Human Performance,* 1975, vol. 15, pp. 46–78.

2. See Charlotte R. Gerstner and David V. Day, "Meta-Analytic Review of Leader-Member Exchange Theory: Correlates and Construct Issues," *Journal of Applied Psychology,* 1997, vol. 82, no. 6, pp. 827–844; John Maslyn and Mary Uhl-Bien, "Leader-Member Exchange and Its Dimensions: Effects of Self-Effort and Others' Effort on Relationship Quality," *Journal of Applied Psychology,* 2001, vol. 86, no. 4, pp. 697–708.

3. Paul Hersey and Kenneth H. Blanchard, *Management of Organizational Behavior: Utilizing Human Resources,* 3rd ed. (Englewood Cliffs, NJ: Prentice Hall, 1977).

4. See Fred Fiedler and Joe Garcia, *New Approaches to Effective Leadership: Cognitive Resources and Organizational Performance* (New York: Wiley, 1987).

5. Vicki Goodwin, J. C. Wofford, and J. Lee Whittington, "A Theoretical and Empirical Extension to the Transformational Leadership Construct," *Journal of Organizational Behavior,* 2001, vol. 22, pp. 759–774.

6. See James MacGregor Burns, *Leadership* (New York: Harper & Row, 1978), and Karl W. Kuhnert and Philip Lewis, "Transactional and Transformational Leadership: A Constructive/Developmental Analysis," *Academy of Management Review,* October 1987, pp. 648–657. See also Nick Turner, Julian Barling, Olga Epitropaki, Vicky Butcher, and Caroline Milner, "Transformational Leadership and Moral Reasoning," *Journal of Applied Psychology,* vol. 87, no. 3, pp. 304–311.

7. Francis J. Yammarino and Alan J. Dubinsky, "Transformational Leadership Theory: Using Levels of Analysis to Determine Boundary Conditions," *Personnel Psychology*, 1994, vol. 47, pp. 787–800.

8. Juan-Carlos Pastor, James Meindl, and Margarita Mayo, "A Network Effects Model of Charisma Attributions," *Academy of Management Journal*, 2002, vol. 45, no. 2, pp. 410–420.

9. See Robert J. House, "A 1976 Theory of Charismatic Leadership," in *Leadership: The Cutting Edge*, eds. J. G. Hunt and L. L. Larson (Carbondale, IL: Southern Illinois University Press, 1977), pp. 189–207. See also Jay A. Conger and Rabindra N. Kanungo, "Toward a Behavioral Theory of Charismatic Leadership in Organizational Settings," *Academy of Management Review*, October 1987, pp. 637–647.

10. "Play Hard, Fly Right," *Time, Bonus Section: Inside Business*, June 2002, pp. Y15–Y22.

11. David A. Nadler and Michael L. Tushman, "Beyond the Charismatic Leader: Leadership and Organizational Change," *California Management Review*, Winter 1990, pp. 77–97.

12. David A. Waldman and Francis J. Yammarino, "CEO Charismatic Leadership: Levels-of-Management and Levels-of-Analysis Effects," *Academy of Management Review*, 1999, vol. 24, no. 2, pp. 266–285.

13. Jane Howell and Boas Shamir, "The Role of Followers in the Charismatic Leadership Process: Relationships and Their Consequences," *Academy of Management Review*, January 2005, pp. 96–112.

14. See Steven Kerr and John M. Jermier, "Substitutes for Leadership: Their Meaning and Measurement," *Organizational Behavior and Human Performance*, 1978, vol. 22, pp. 375–403. See also Charles C. Manz and Henry P. Sims Jr., "Leading Workers to Lead Themselves: The External Leadership of Self-Managing Work Teams," *Administrative Science Quarterly*, March 1987, pp. 106–129.

15. Jon P. Howell, David E. Bowen, Peter W. Dorfman, Steven Kerr, and Philip Podsakoff, "Substitutes for Leadership: Effective Alternatives to Ineffective Leadership," *Organizational Dynamics*, Summer 1990, pp. 20–38. See also Philip M. Podsakoff, Scott B. Mackenzie, and William H. Bommer, "Transformational Leader Behaviors and Substitutes for Leadership as Determinants of Employee Satisfaction, Commitment, Trust, and Organizational Citizenship Behaviors," *Journal of Management*, 1996, vol. 22, no. 2, pp. 259–298.

16. J. Richard Hackman and Ruth Wageman, "A Theory of Team Coaching," *Academy of Management Review*, April 2005, pp. 269–287.

17. Russell L. Kent and Sherry E. Moss, "Effects of Sex and Gender Role of Leader Emergence," *Academy of Management Journal*, 1994, vol. 37, no. 5, pp. 1335–1346.

18. A. H. Eagly, M. G. Makhijani, and R. G. Klonsky, "Gender and the Evaluation of Leaders: A Meta-Analysis," *Psychological Bulletin*, 1992, vol. 111, pp. 3–22.

19. "The Best (& Worst) Managers of the Year," *Business Week*, January 10, 2005, p. 55.

20. See Kurt Dirks and Donald Ferrin, "Trust in Leadership," *Journal of Applied Psychology*, 2002, vol. 87, no. 4, pp. 611–628.

Chapter 14

1. Robert W. Allen and Lyman W. Porter, eds., *Organizational Influence Processes* (Glenview, IL: Scott, Foresman, 1983).

2. Alan L. Frohman, "The Power of Personal Initiative," *Organizational Dynamics*, Winter 1997, pp. 39–48; see also James H. Dulebohn and Gerald R. Ferris, "The Role of Influence Tactics in Perceptions of Performance Evaluations' Fairness," *Academy of Management Journal*, 1999, vol. 42, no. 3, pp. 288–303.

3. For reviews of the meaning of power, see Henry Mintzberg, *Power In and Around Organizations* (Englewood Cliffs, NJ: Prentice-Hall, 1983); Jeffrey Pfeffer, *Power in Organizations* (Marshfield, MA: Pitman Publishing, 1981); John Kenneth Galbraith, *The Anatomy of Power* (Boston: Houghton Mifflin, 1983); Gary A. Yukl, *Leadership in Organizations*, 3rd ed. (Englewood Cliffs, NJ: Prentice-Hall, 1994).

4. John R. P. French and Bertram Raven, "The Bases of Social Power," in *Studies in Social Power*, ed. Darwin Cartwright (Ann Arbor: University of Michigan Press, 1959), pp. 150–167. See also Philip M. Podsakoff and Chester A. Schriesheim, "Field Studies of French and Raven's Bases of Power: Critique, Reanalysis, and Suggestions for Future Research," *Psychological Bulletin*, 1985, vol. 97, pp. 387–411.

5. Yukl, *Leadership in Organizations*, Chapter 10.

6. See Darren Treadway, Wayne Hochwarter, Charles Kacmar, and Gerald Ferris, "Political Will, Political Skill, and Political Behavior," *Journal of Organizational Behavior*, 2005, vol. 26, pp. 229–245.

7. Victor Murray and Jeffrey Gandz, "Games Executives Play: Politics at Work," *Business Horizons*, December 1980, pp. 11–23. See also Jeffrey Gandz and Victor Murray, "The Experience of Workplace Politics," *Academy of Management Journal*, June 1980, pp. 237–251.

8. Gerald F. Cavanaugh, Dennis J. Moberg, and Manuel Valasquez, "The Ethics of Organizational Politics," *Academy of Management Review*, July 1981, pp. 363–374.

9. Pfeffer, *Power in Organizations*; Mintzberg, *Power In and Around Organizations*.

10. The techniques are based on Pfeffer, *Power in Organizations*; Mintzberg, *Power In and Around Organizations*; and Galbraith, *Anatomy of Power*.

11. "How the 2 Top Officials of Grace Wound Up in a Very Dirty War," *Wall Street Journal*, May 18, 1995, pp. Al, A8.

12. See Jerald Greenberg and Jason Colquitt, *Handbook of Organizational Justice* (Mahwah, NJ: Lawrence Erlbaum Associates, 2004), for a comprehensive discussion and review of the literature on justice in organization.

Chapter 15

1. See Stephen P. Robbins, *Managing Organizational Conflict* (Englewood Cliffs, NJ: Prentice Hall, 1974), for a classic review.

2. Charles R. Schwenk, "Conflict in Organizational Decision Making: An Exploratory Study of Its Effects in For-Profit and Not-for-Profit Organizations," *Management Science*, April 1990, pp. 436–448.

3. "How 2 Computer Nuts Transformed Industry Before Messy Breakup," *Wall Street Journal*, August 27, 1996, pp. A1, A10.

4. Bruce Barry and Greg L. Stewart, "Composition, Process, and Performance in Self-Managed Groups: The Role of Personality," *Journal of Applied Psychology*, 1997, vol. 82, no. 1, pp. 62–78.

5. "Rumsfeld's Abrasive Style Sparks Conflict With Military Command," *USA Today*, December 10, 2002, pp. 1A, 2A.

6. "Delta CEO Resigns After Clashes With Board," *USA Today*, May 13, 1997, p. B1.

7. "A 'Blood War' in the Jeans Trade," *Business Week*, November 13, 1999, pp. 74–81.

8. Peter Elkind, "Blood Feud," *Fortune*, April 14, 1997, pp. 90–102.

9. James Thompson, *Organizations in Action* (New York: McGraw-Hill, 1967). For another discussion, see Bart Victor and Richard S. Blackburn, "Interdependence: An Alternative Conceptualization," *Academy of Management Review*, July 1987, pp. 486–498.

10. Kenneth Thomas, "Conflict and Conflict Management," in *Handbook of Industrial and Organizational Psychology*, ed. Marvin Dunnette (Chicago: Rand McNally, 1976), pp. 889–935.

11. Alfie Kohn, "How to Succeed Without Even Vying," *Psychology Today*, September 1986, pp. 22–28.

12. See Carsten K.W. De Dreu and Annelies E. M. Van Vianen, "Managing Relationship Conflict and the Effectiveness of Organizational Teams," *Journal of Organizational Behavior*, 2001, vol. 22, pp. 309–328.

13. "Memo To the Team: This Needs Salt!" *Wall Street Journal*, April 4, 2000, pp. B1, B14.

14. See Kimberly Wade-Benzoni, Andrew Hoffman, Leigh Thompson, Don Moore, James Gillespie, and Max Bazerman, "Barriers to Resolution in Ideologically Based Negotiations: The Role of Values and Institutions," *Academy of Management Review*, 2002, vol. 27, no. 1, pp. 41–57.

15. J. Z. Rubin and B. R. Brown, *The Social Psychology of Bargaining and Negotiation* (New York: Academic Press, 1975).

16. R. J. Lewicki and J. A. Litterer, *Negotiation* (Homewood, IL: Irwin, 1985).

17. Howard Raiffa, *The Art and Science of Negotiation* (Cambridge, MA: Belknap, 1982).

18. K. H. Bazerman and M. A. Neale, *Negotiating Rationally* (New York: Free Press, 1992).

19. Ross R. Reck and Brian G. Long, *The Win-Win Negotiator* (Escondido, CA: Blanchard Training and Development, 1985).

Chapter 16

1. See Richard L. Daft, *Organization Theory and Design*, 8th ed. (Mason, OH: South-Western, 2004), p.11, for further discussion of the definition of *organization*.

2. John R. Montanari, Cyril P. Morgan, and Jeffrey S. Bracker, *Strategic Management* (Hinsdale, IL: Dryden Press, 1990), pp. 1–2.

3. Alex Taylor III, "Schrempp Shifts Gears," *Fortune*, March 18, 2002. www.fortune.com on June 6, 2002; Christine Tierney and Joann Muller, "DaimlerChrysler's Foggy Forecast," *Business Week*, February 14, 2002. www.businessweek.com on June 6, 2002; "DaimlerChrysler Chief Seeks Greater Brand Integration," as reported in the *Financial Times*, reprinted in *Wall Street Journal Online*, May 21, 2002. online.wsj.com on June 6, 2002.

4. A. Bryman, A. D. Beardworth, E. T. Keil, and J. Ford, "Organizational Size and Specialization," *Organization Studies*, September 1983, pp. 271–278.

5. Joseph L. C. Cheng, "Interdependence and Coordination in Organizations: A Role System Analysis," *Academy of Management Journal*, March 1983, pp. 156–162.

6. Henry Mintzberg, *The Structuring of Organizations* (Englewood Cliffs, NJ: Prentice Hall, 1979), for further discussion of the basic elements of structure.

7. Max Weber, *The Theory of Social and Economic Organization*, trans. A. M. Henderson and Talcott Parsons (New York: Free Press, 1947).

8. Adam Smith, *An Inquiry into the Nature and Causes of the Wealth of Nations* (London: Dent, 1910).

9. Nancy M. Carter and Thomas L. Keon, "The Rise and Fall of the Division of Labour, the Past 25 Years," *Organization Studies*, 1986, pp. 54–57.

10. Glenn R. Carroll, "The Specialist Strategy," *California Management Review*, Spring 1984, pp. 126–137.

11. "Management Discovers the Human Side of Automation," *Business Week*, September 29, 1986, pp. 70–75.

12. See Robert H. Miles, *Macro Organizational Behavior* (Santa Monica, CA: Goodyear, 1980), pp. 28–34, for a discussion of departmentalization schemes.

13. Mintzberg, *The Structuring of Organizations*, p. 125.

14. Miles, *Macro Organizational Behavior*, pp. 122–133.

15. "Big Blue Wants to Loosen Its Collar," *Fortune*, February 29, 1988, p. 8; "Inside IBM: Internet Business Machines," *Business Week*, December 13, 1999, pp. EB20–28.

16. Peggy Leatt and Rodney Schneck, "Criteria for Grouping Nursing Subunits in Hospitals," *Academy of Management Review*, March 1984, pp. 150–165.

17. "Fact Sheets," "Organizational Structure," Deutsche Bank website. group.deutsche-bank.de on June 7, 2002; Marcus Walker, "Lean New Guard at Deutsche Bank Sets Global Agenda—But Cultural Rifts Prevent More-Aggressive Cost Cuts—The Traditionalists Haven't Gone Quietly," *Wall Street Journal*, February 14, 2002. www.wsj.com on April 4, 2002; Stephen Graham, "Deutsche Bank Says 2001 Profit Plummeted, Proceeds with Management Shake-Up," *National Business Stream*, January 31, 2002; "Deutsche Bank Names Next CEO, Continuity Seen," *National Business Stream*, September 21, 2000.

18. Lyndall F. Urwick, "The Manager's Span of Control," *Harvard Business Review*, May–June 1956, pp. 39–47.

19. Dan R. Dalton, William D. Tudor, Michael J. Spendolini, Gordon J. Fielding, and Lyman W. Porter, "Organization Structure and Performance: A Critical Review," *Academy of Management Review*, January 1980, pp. 49–64.

20. Mintzberg, *The Structuring of Organizations*, pp. 133–147.

21. See David Van Fleet, "Span of Management Research and Issues," *Academy of Management Journal*, September 1983, pp. 546–552, for an example of research on span of control.

22. "New Home. New CEO. Gateway Is Moo and Improved," *Fortune,* December 20, 1999, pp. 44–46; "Weitzen to Become Gateway's New CEO; Waitt Still Chairman," *Wall Street Journal,* December 9, 1999, p. B16; William J. Holstein and Susan Gregory Thomas, "Gateway Gets Citified," *U.S. News & World Report,* May 3, 1999, p. 42; Elizabeth Corcoran, "Gateway 2005," *Forbes,* March 8, 1999, p. 52.

23. John R. Montanari and Philip J. Adelman, "The Administrative Component of Organizations and the Rachet Effect: A Critique of Cross-Sectional Studies," *Journal of Management Studies,* March 1987, pp. 113–123.

24. D. A. Heenan, "The Downside of Downsizing," *Journal of Business Strategy,* November–December 1989, pp. 18–23.

25. Wayne F. Cascio, "Downsizing: What Do We Know? What Have We Learned?" *Academy of Management Executive,* February 1993, pp. 95–104.

26. Dalton et al., "Organization Structure and Performance."

27. See John Child, *Organization: A Guide to Problems and Practice,* 2nd ed. (New York: Harper & Row, 1984), pp. 145–153, for a detailed discussion of centralization.

28. Richard H. Hall, *Organization: Structure and Process,* 3rd ed. (Englewood Cliffs, NJ: Prentice Hall, 1982), pp. 87–96.

29. "Can Jack Smith Fix GM?" *Business Week,* November 1, 1993, pp. 126–131; John McElroy, "GM's Brand Management Might Work," *Automotive Industries,* September 1996, p. 132.

30. Daniel R. Denison, "Bringing Corporate Culture to the Bottom Line," *Organizational Dynamics,* Autumn 1984, pp. 4–22.

31. Leonard W. Johnson and Alan L. Frohman, "Identifying and Closing the Gap in the Middle of Organizations," *Academy of Management Executive,* May 1989, pp. 107–114.

32. Michael Schrage, "I Know What You Mean, and I Can't Do Anything About It," *Fortune,* April 2, 2001, p. 186.

33. Mintzberg, *The Structuring of Organizations,* pp. 83–84.

34. Arthur P. Brief and H. Kirk Downey, "Cognitive and Organizational Structures: A Conceptual Analysis of Implicit Organizing Theories," *Human Relations,* December 1983, pp. 1065–1090.

35. Jerald Hage, "An Axiomatic Theory of Organizations," *Administrative Science Quarterly,* December 1965, pp. 289–320.

36. Gregory Moorhead, "Organizational Analysis: An Integration of the Macro and Micro Approaches," *Journal of Management Studies,* April 1981, pp. 191–218.

37. J. Daniel Sherman and Howard L. Smith, "The Influence of Organizational Structure on Intrinsic Versus Extrinsic Motivation," *Academy of Management Journal,* December 1984, pp. 877–885.

38. John A. Pearce II and Fred R. David, "A Social Network Approach to Organizational Design-Performance," *Academy of Management Review,* July 1983, pp. 436–444.

39. Eileen Farihurst, "Organizational Rules and the Accomplishment of Nursing Work on Geriatric Wards," *Journal of Management Studies,* July 1983, pp. 315–332.

40. "Chevron Corp. Has Big Challenge Coping with Worker Cutbacks," *Wall Street Journal,* November 4, 1986, pp. 1, 25.

41. Neil F. Brady, "Rules for Making Exceptions to Rules," *Academy of Management Review,* July 1987, pp. 436–444.

42. See Jeffrey Pfeiffer, *Power in Organizations* (Boston: Pittman, 1981), pp. 4–6, for a discussion of the relationship between power and authority.

43. John B. Miner, *Theories of Organizational Structure and Process* (Hinsdale, IL: Dryden Press, 1982), p. 360.

44. Chester Barnard, *The Functions of the Executive* (Cambridge, MA: Harvard University Press, 1938), pp. 161–184.

45. Pfeiffer, *Power in Organizations,* pp. 366–367.

46. Weber, *The Theory of Social and Economic Organization.*

47. For more discussion of these alternative views, see Miner, *Theories of Organizational Structure and Process,* p. 386.

48. Paul S. Adler, "Building Better Bureaucracies," *Academy of Management Executive,* November 1999, pp. 36–46.

49. This summary of the classic principles of organizing is based on Henri Fayol, *General and Industrial Management,* trans. Constance Storrs (London: Pittman, 1949); Miner, *Theories of Organizational Structure and Process,* pp. 358–381; and the discussions in Arthur G. Bedeian, *Organizations: Theory and Analysis,* 2nd ed. (Chicago: Dryden, 1984), pp. 58–59.

50. Miner, *Theories of Organizational Structure and Process,* pp. 358–381.

51. See Rensis Likert, *New Patterns of Management* (New York: McGraw-Hill, 1961), and Rensis Likert, *The Human Organization: Its Management and Value* (New York: McGraw-Hill, 1967), for a complete discussion of the human organization.

52. Miner, *Theories of Organizational Structure and Process,* pp. 17–53.

Chapter 17

1. Lex Donaldson, "Strategy and Structural Adjustment to Regain Fit and Performance: In Defense of Contingency Theory," *Journal of Management Studies,* January 1987, pp. 1–24.

2. John R. Montanari, Cyril P. Morgan, and Jeffrey Bracker, *Strategic Management* (Hinsdale, IL: Dryden Press, 1990), p. 114.

3. See Arthur A. Thompson Jr. and A. J. Strickland III, *Strategic Management,* 3rd ed. (Plano, TX: Business Publications, 1984), pp. 19–27.

4. David Stires, "Fallen Arches," *Fortune,* April 26, 1999, pp. 146–152.

5. Alfred D. Chandler, *Strategy and Structure: Chapters in the History of the American Industrial Enterprise* (Cambridge, MA: MIT Press, 1962).

6. John R. Kimberly, "Organizational Size and the Structuralist Perspective: A Review, Critique, and Proposal," *Administrative Science Quarterly,* December 1976, pp. 571–597.

7. Peter M. Blau and Richard A. Schoenherr, *The Structure of Organizations* (New York: Basic Books, 1971).

8. The results of these studies are thoroughly summarized in Richard H. Hall, *Organizations: Structure and Process,* 3rd ed. (Englewood Cliffs, NJ: Prentice Hall, 1982), pp. 89–94. For another study in this area, see John H. Cullen and Kenneth S. Anderson, "Blau's Theory of Structural Differentiation Revisited: A Theory of Structural Change or Scale?" *Academy of Management Journal,* June 1986, pp. 203–229.

9. "Small Is Beautiful Now in Manufacturing," *Business Week,* October 22, 1984, pp. 152–156.

10. Richard H. Hall, J. Eugene Haas, and Norman Johnson, "Organizational Size, Complexity, and Formalization," *American Sociological Review,* December 1967, pp. 903–912.

11. Catherine Arnst, "Downsizing out One Door and in Another," *Business Week,* January 22, 1996, p. 41; Peter Elstrom, "Dial A for Aggravation," *Business Week,* March 11, 1996, p. 34; Alex Markels and Matt Murray, "Call It Dumbsizing: Why Some Companies Regret Cost-Cutting," *Wall Street Journal,* May 14, 1996, pp. A1, A5.

12. Robert I. Sutton and Thomas D'Anno, "Decreasing Organizational Size: Untangling the Effects of Money and People," *Academy of Management Review,* May 1989, pp. 194–212.

13. Joan Woodward, *Management and Technology: Problems of Progress in Industry,* no. 3 (London: Her Majesty's Stationery Office, 1958); Joan Woodward, *Industrial Organizations: Theory and Practice* (London: Oxford University Press, 1965).

14. Tom Burns and George M. Stalker, *The Management of Innovation* (London: Tavistock, 1961).

15. Charles B. Perrow, "A Framework for the Comparative Analysis of Organizations," *American Sociological Review,* April 1967, pp. 194–208.

16. James D. Thompson, *Organizations in Action* (New York: McGraw-Hill, 1967).

17. David J. Hickson, Derek S. Pugh, and Diana C. Pheysey, "Operations Technology and Organization Structure: An Empirical Reappraisal," *Administrative Science Quarterly,* September 1969, pp. 378–397.

18. Ibid.

19. Andrew Kupfer, "How to Be a Global Manager," *Fortune,* March 14, 1988, pp. 52–58.

20. "Going Crazy in Japan—In a Break from Tradition, Tokyo Begins Funding a Program for Basic Research," *Wall Street Journal,* November 10, 1986, p. D20.

21. "About Wal-Mart," "Wal-Mart Stores, Inc., at a Glance," Wal-Mart website. www.walmartstores.com on June 12, 2002; "Dell at a Glance," "Dell Worldwide," Dell website. www.dell.com on June 12, 2002; Brian Dumaine, "What Michael Dell Knows That You Don't," *Fortune,* June 3, 2002. www.fortune.com on June 12, 2002; Andy Serwer, "Dell Does Domination," *Fortune,* January 21, 2002, pp. 71–75; Eryn Brown, "America's Most Admired Companies," *Fortune,* March 1, 1999, pp. 68–73 (quotation p. 70).

22. Richard L. Daft, *Organization Theory and Design,* 8th ed. (South-Western a division of Thomson Learning.2004), p. 141.

23. Robert B. Duncan, "Characteristics of Organizational Environments and Perceived Uncertainty," *Administrative Science Quarterly,* September 1972, pp. 313–327.

24. "Toy Makers Lose Interest in Tie-Ins with Cartoons," *Wall Street Journal,* April 28, 1988, p. 29.

25. Masoud Yasai-Ardekani, "Structural Adaptations to Environments," *Academy of Management Review,* January 1986, pp. 9–21.

26. John E. Prescott, "Environments as Moderators of the Relationship Between Strategy and Performance," *Academy of Management Journal,* June 1986, pp. 329–346.

27. Timothy M. Stearns, Alan N. Hoffman, and Jan B. Heide, "Performance of Commercial Television Stations as an Outcome of Interorganizational Linkages and Environmental Conditions," *Academy of Management Journal,* March 1987, pp. 71–90.

28. Thompson, *Organizations in Action,* pp. 51–82.

29. Lori Ioannou, "American Invasion," *Fortune,* May 13, 2002. www.fortune.com on June 12, 2002; Jesse Wong, "How to Start a Business Without a Road Map," *Fortune,* April 1, 2002. www.fortune.com on June 12, 2002; Camilla Ojansivu, "Strategy for a Stronger Market Economy: Corporate Restructuring the PRC," *Business Beijing,* November, 2001, pp. 38–39.

30. For more information on managerial choice, see John Child, "Organizational Structure, Environment, and Performance: The Role of Strategic Choice," *Sociology,* January 1972, pp. 1–22; John R. Montanari, "Managerial Discretion: An Expanded Model of Organizational Choice," *Academy of Management Review,* April 1978, pp. 231–241.

31. H. Randolph Bobbitt and Jeffrey D. Ford, "Decision Maker Choice as a Determinant of Organizational Structure," *Academy of Management Review,* January 1980, pp. 13–23.

32. "Thermos Fires Up Grill Lines," *Weekly Home Furnishings Newspaper,* August 24, 1992, p. 54; Brian Dumaine, "Payoff from the New Management," *Fortune,* December 13, 1993, pp. 102–110.

33. "Three's Company," *Economist,* October 30, 1999, p. 80; "Citigroup: So Much for 50–50," *Business Week,* August 16, 1999, p. 80; Carol J. Loomis, "Citigroup: Scenes from a Merger," *Fortune,* January 11, 1999, pp. 76–88.

34. James W. Frederickson, "The Strategic Decision Process and Organization Structure," *Academy of Management Review,* April 1986, pp. 280–297.

35. Herman L. Boschken, "Strategy and Structure: Reconceiving the Relationship," *Journal of Management,* March 1990, pp. 135–150.

36. "Small Manufacturers Shifting to 'Just-In-Time' Techniques," *Wall Street Journal,* December 21, 1987, p. 25.

37. Elton Mayo, *The Human Problems of an Industrial Civilization* (New York: Macmillan, 1933); F. J. Roethlisberger and W. J. Dickson, *Management and the Worker* (Cambridge, MA: Harvard University Press, 1939).

38. Eric L. Trist and K. W. Bamforth, "Some Social and Psychological Consequences of the Longwall Method of Coal-Getting," *Human Relations,* February 1951, pp. 3–38.

39. Richard E. Walton, "How to Counter Alienation in the Plant," *Harvard Business Review,* November–December 1972, pp. 70–81; Pehr G. Gyllenhammar, "How Volvo Adapts Work to People," *Harvard Business Review,* July–August 1977, pp. 102–113; Richard E. Walton, "Work Innovations at Topeka: After Six Years," *Journal of Applied Behavioral Science,* July–August–September 1977, pp. 422–433.

40. Henry Mintzberg, *The Structuring of Organizations: A Synthesis of the Research* (Englewood Cliffs, NJ: Prentice Hall, 1979).

41. See Harold C. Livesay, *American Made: Men Who Shaped the American Economy* (Boston: Little, Brown, 1979), pp. 215–239, for a discussion of Alfred Sloan and the development of the divisionalized structure at General Motors.

42. Anne B. Fisher, "GM Is Tougher Than You Think," *Fortune,* November 10, 1986, pp. 56–64.

43. Thompson and Strickland, *Strategic Management,* p. 212.

44. Kenneth Labich, "The Innovators," *Fortune,* June 6, 1988, pp. 51–64.

45. Henry Mintzberg, "Organization Design: Fashion or Fit," *Harvard Business Review,* January–February 1981, pp. 103–116.

46. Harvey F. Kolodny, "Managing in a Matrix," *Business Horizons,* March–April 1981, pp. 17–24.

47. Stanley M. Davis and Paul R. Lawrence, *Matrix* (Reading, MA: Addison-Wesley, 1977), pp. 11–36.

48. Lawton R. Burns, "Matrix Management in Hospitals: Testing Theories of Matrix Structure and Development," *Administrative Science Quarterly,* September 1989, pp. 355–358.

49. Ibid., pp. 129–154.

50. "The Virtual Corporation," *Business Week,* February 8, 1993, pp. 98–102; William H. Carlile, "Virtual Corporation a Real Deal," *Arizona Republic,* August 2, 1993, pp. E1, E4.

51. Thomas A. Stewart, "Reengineering: The Hot New Managing Tool," *Fortune,* August 23, 1993, pp. 41–48.

52. James A. Champy, "From Reengineering to X-Engineering," in *Organization 21C: Someday All Organizations Will Lead This Way,* ed. Subir Chowdury (Upper Saddle River, NJ: Financial Times Prentice Hall, 2003), pp. 93–95.

53. Robert Tomasko, *Rethinking the Corporation* (New York: AMA-COM, 1993).

54. Rahul Jacob, "The Struggle to Create an Organization for the 21st Century," *Fortune,* April 3, 1995, pp. 90–99; Gene G. Marcial, "Don't Leave Your Broker Without It?" *Business Week,* February 5, 1996, p. 138; Jeffrey M. Laderman, "Loading Up on No-Loads," *Business Week,* May 27, 1996, p. 138.

55. James R. Lincoln, Mitsuyo Hanada, and Kerry McBride, "Organizational Structures in Japanese and U.S. Manufacturing," *Administrative Science Quarterly,* September 1986, pp. 338–364.

56. "The Inscrutable West," *Newsweek,* April 18, 1988, p. 52.

57. Richard I. Kirkland Jr., "Europe's New Managers," *Fortune,* September 29, 1980, pp. 56–60; Shawn Tully, "Europe's Takeover Kings," *Fortune,* July 20, 1987, pp. 95–98.

58. Henry W. Lane and Joseph J. DiStefano, *International Management Behavior* (Ontario: Nelson, 1988).

59. William H. Davison and Philippe Haspeslagh, "Shaping a Global Product Organization," *Harvard Business Review,* July–August 1982, pp. 125–132.

60. John Child, *Organizations: A Guide to Problems and Practice* (New York: Harper & Row, 1984), p. 246.

61. Thomas J. Peters and Robert H. Waterman Jr., *In Search of Excellence: Lessons from America's Best-Run Companies* (New York: Harper & Row, 1982), pp. 235–278.

62. Thomas J. Peters and Nancy K. Austin, "A Passion for Excellence," *Fortune,* May 13, 1985, pp. 20–32.

63. Michael Beer, "Building Organizational Fitness" in *Organization 21C: Someday All Organizations Will Lead This Way,* ed. Subir Chowdury (Upper Saddle River, NJ: Financial Times Prentice Hall, 2003), pp. 311–312.

Chapter 18

1. See "Corporate Culture: The Hard-to-Change Values That Spell Success or Failure," *Business Week,* October 27, 1980, pp. 148–160; Charles G. Burck, "Working Smarter," *Fortune,* June 15, 1981, pp. 68–73.

2. Charles A. O'Reilly and Jennifer A. Chatman, "Culture as Social Control: Corporations, Cults, and Commitment," in *Research in Organizational Behavior,* eds. Barry M. Staw and L. L. Cummings, vol. 18, pp. 157–200 (Stamford, CT: JAI Press, 1996).

3. J. P. Kotter and J. L. Heskett, *Corporate Culture and Performance* (New York: Free Press, 1992).

4. Michael Tushman and Charles A. O'Reilly, *Staying on Top: Managing Strategic Innovation and Change for Long-Term Success* (Boston: Harvard Business School Press, 1996).

5. T. E. Deal and A. A. Kennedy, *Corporate Cultures: The Rites and Rituals of Corporate Life* (Reading, MA: Addison-Wesley, 1982), p. 4.

6. E. H. Schein, "The Role of the Founder in Creating Organizational Culture," *Organizational Dynamics,* Summer 1983, p. 14.

7. Thomas J. Peters and Robert H. Waterman Jr., *In Search of Excellence: Lessons from America's Best-Run Companies* (New York: Harper & Row, 1982), p. 103.

8. See M. Polanyi, *Personal Knowledge* (Chicago: University of Chicago Press, 1958); E. Goffman, *The Presentation of Self in Everyday Life* (New York: Doubleday, 1959); and P. L. Berger and T. Luckman, *The Social Construction of Reality* (Garden City, NY: Anchor Books, 1967).

9. Louise Lee, "Tricks of E*Trade," *Business Week E.Biz,* February 7, 2000, pp. EB18–EB31.

10. Eric Ransdell, "The Nike Story? Just Tell It!" *Fast Company,* January– February 2000, pp. 44–46 (quotation on p. 46); Claude Solnik, "Co-Founder of Nike Dies Christmas Eve," *Footwear News,* January 3, 2000, p. 2; Rosemary Feitelberg, "Bowerman's Legacy Runs On," *WWD,* December 30, 1999, p. 8.

11. Lee, "Tricks of E*Trade."

12. A. L. Kroeber and C. Kluckhohn, "Culture: A Critical Review of Concepts and Definitions," in *Papers of the Peabody Museum of American Archaeology and Ethnology,* vol. 47, no. 1 (Cambridge, MA: Harvard University Press, 1952).

13. C. Geertz, *The Interpretation of Cultures* (New York: Basic Books, 1973).

14. See, for example, B. Clark, *The Distinctive College* (Chicago: Adline, 1970).

15. E. Durkheim, *The Elementary Forms of Religious Life,* trans. J. Swain (New York: Collier, 1961), p. 220.

16. See William G. Ouchi, *Theory Z: How American Business Can Meet the Japanese Challenge* (Reading, MA: Addison-Wesley, 1981); and Peters and Waterman, *In Search of Excellence.*

17. See Ouchi, *Theory Z;* Deal and Kennedy, *Corporate Cultures;* and Peters and Waterman, *In Search of Excellence.*

18. E. Borgida and R. E. Nisbett, "The Differential Impact of Abstract vs. Concrete Information on Decisions," *Journal of Applied Social Psychology,* July–September 1977, pp. 258–271.

19. J. Martin and M. Power, "Truth or Corporate Propaganda: The Value of a Good War Story," in Pondy et al., pp. 93–108.

20. W. G. Ouchi, "Markets, Bureaucracies, and Clans," *Administrative Science Quarterly,* March 1980, pp. 129–141; A. Wilkins and W. G. Ouchi, "Efficient Cultures: Exploring the Relationship Between Culture and Organizational Performance," *Administrative Science Quarterly,* September 1983, pp. 468–481.

21. Peters and Waterman, *In Search of Excellence.*

22. J. B. Barney, "Organizational Culture: Can It Be a Source of Sustained Competitive Advantage?" *Academy of Management Review,* July 1986, pp. 656–665.

23. Michelle Conlin, "Is Wal-Mart Hostile to Women?" *Business Week,* July 16, 2001. www.businessweek.com on June 21, 2002.

24. Daniel R. Denison, "What Is the Difference Between Organizational Culture and Organizational Climate? A Native's Point of View on a Decade of Paradigm Wars," *Academy of Management Review,* July 1996, pp. 619–654.

25. O'Reilly and Chatman, "Culture as Social Control."

26. Richard L. Osborne, "Strategic Values: The Corporate Performance Engine," *Business Horizons,* September–October 1996, pp. 41–47.

27. See Osborne, "Strategic Values: The Corporate Performance Engine"; and Gary McWilliams, "Dell's Profit Rises Slightly, As Expected," *Wall Street Journal,* February 11, 2000, p. A3.

28. "The Jack and Herb Show," *Fortune,* January 11, 1999, p. 166.

29. Ouchi, *Theory Z.*

30. Catherine Reagor, "Wells Fargo Riding Roughshod in State, Some Say," *Arizona Republic,* September 8, 1996, pp. D1, D4; Catherine Reagor, "Wells Fargo to Cut 3,000 Additional Jobs," *Arizona Republic,* December 20, 1996, pp. E1, E2.

31. O'Reilly and Chatman, "Culture as Social Control."

32. John E. Sheridan, "Organizational Culture and Employee Retention," *Academy of Management Journal,* December 1992, pp. 1036–1056; Lisa A. Mainiero, "Is Your Corporate Culture Costing You?" *Academy of Management Executive,* November 1993, pp. 84–85.

33. Peters and Waterman, *In Search of Excellence.*

34. Kenneth Labich, "An Airline That Soars on Service," *Fortune,* December 31, 1990, pp. 94–96.

35. Watts S. Humphrey, *Managing for Innovation: Leading Technical People* (Englewood Cliffs, NJ: Prentice Hall, 1987).

36. Brian O'Reilly, "Secrets of the Most Admired Corporations: New Ideas and New Products," *Fortune,* March 3, 1997, pp. 60–64.

37. Laurie K. Lewis and David R. Seibold, "Innovation Modification During Intraorganizational Adoption," *Academy of Management Review,* April 1993, vol. 10, no. 2, pp. 322–354.

38. Bill Saporito, Chris Taylor, Laura A. Locke, Daren Fonda, and Jyoti Thottam, "Why Carly's Out," *Time,* February 21, 2005, p. 34. http://infotrac-college.thomsonlearning.com/itw/infomark/956/467/88159836w3/purl=rcl_..2/20/05 on February 20, 2005.

39. Lee, "Tricks of E*Trade."

40. Oren Harari, "Stop Empowering Your People," *Management Review,* November 1993, pp. 26–29.

41. Rob Goffee and Gareth Jones, "Organizational Culture," in *Organization 21C: Someday All Organizations Will Lead This Way,* ed. Subir Chowdhury (Upper Saddle River, NJ: Financial Times Prentice Hall, 2003), pp. 273–290.

42. See Warren Wilhelm, "Changing Corporate Culture—Or Corporate Behavior? How to Change Your Company," *Academy of Management Executive,* November 1992, pp. 72–77.

43. "Socialization" has also been defined as "the process by which culture is transmitted from one generation to the next." See J. W. M. Whiting, "Socialization: Anthropological Aspects," in *International Encyclopedia of the Social Sciences,* vol. 14, ed. D. Sils (New York: Free Press, 1968), p. 545.

44. J. E. Hebden, "Adopting an Organization's Culture: The Socialization of Graduate Trainees," *Organizational Dynamics,* Summer 1986, pp. 54–72.

45. J. B. Barney, "Organizational Culture: Can It Be a Source of Sustained Competitive Advantage?" *Academy of Management Review,* July 1986, pp. 656–665.

46. Bellamy Pailthorp, "Safe Landing for Boeing," *U.S. News & World Report,* September 13, 1999, p. 43; Janet Rae-Dupree, "Can Boeing Get Lean Enough?" *Business Week,* August 30, 1999, p. 182; Aaron Bernstein, "Boeing's Unions Are Worried About Job Security—The CEO's," *Business Week,* July 5, 1999, p. 30; Kenneth Labich, "Boeing Finally Hatches a Plan," *Fortune,* March 1, 1999, pp. 101–106.

47. James R. Norman, "A New Teledyne," *Forbes,* September 27, 1993, pp. 44–45.

Chapter 19

1. "Baby Boomers Push for Power," *Business Week,* July 2, 1984, pp. 52–56.

2. "Americans' Median Age Passes 32," *Arizona Republic,* April 6, 1988, pp. A1, A5.

3. "Population Estimates Program," Population Division, U.S. Census Bureau, Washington, DC.

4. Geoffrey Colvin, "What the Baby Boomers Will Buy Next," *Fortune,* October 15, 1984, pp. 28–34.

5. Lev Grossman, "Grow Up? Not So Fast," *Time,* January 24, 2005, p. 42.

6. John Huey, "Managing in the Midst of Chaos," *Fortune,* April 5, 1993, pp. 38–48.

7. "DuPont Adopts New Direction in China," Xinhua News Agency, September 7, 1999, p. 1008250h0104; Alex Taylor III, "Why DuPont Is Trading Oil for Corn," *Fortune,* April 26, 1999, pp. 154–160; Jay Palmer, "New DuPont: For Rapid Growth, an Old-Line Company Looks to Drugs, Biotechnology," *Barron's,* May 11, 1998, p. 31.

8. Peter Nulty, "How Personal Computers Change Managers' Lives," *Fortune,* September 3, 1984, pp. 38–48.

9. "Artificial Language Is Here," *Business Week,* July 9, 1984, pp. 54–62.

10. Thomas A. Stewart, "Welcome to the Revolution," *Fortune,* December 13, 1993, pp. 66–80.

11. "Intellectual Assets Network (IAN)," "Our Approach," Context Integration website. www.context.com on June 19, 2002; Suzanne Koudsi, "Actually, It Is Like Brain Surgery," *Fortune,* March 20, 2000, pp. 233–234; Chuck Salter, "Ideas.com," *Fast Company,* September 1999, p. 292.

12. "Nokia's Restructured," *Television Digest,* September 4, 1995, p. 15; Rahul Jacob, "Nokia Fumbles, but Don't Count It Out," *Fortune,* February 19, 1996, pp. 86–88; Gail Edmondson, "At Nokia, A Comeback—and Then Some," *Business Week,* December 2, 1996, p. 106.

13. *The Economic Times,* February 16, 2005. http://infotrac-college.thomsonlearning.com/itw/infomark/236/789/

62103544w5/purl=rc1_WAD_0_CJ128751249&dyn=4!xrn_10_0_CJ128751249?sw_aep=olr_wad on February 29, 2005.

14. Kurt Lewin, *Field Theory in Social Science* (New York: Harper & Row, 1951).

15. W. Warner Burke, "Leading Organizational Change," in *Organization 21C: Someday All Organizations Will Lead This Way,* ed. Subir Chowdhury (Upper Saddle River, NJ: Financial Times Prentice Hall, 2003), pp. 291–310.

16. Linda S. Ackerman, "Transition Management: An In-Depth Look at Managing Complex Change," *Organizational Dynamics,* Summer 1982, pp. 46–66; David A. Nadler, "Managing Transitions to Uncertain Future States," *Organizational Dynamics,* Summer 1982, pp. 37–45.

17. Burke, "Leading Organizational Change."

18. Noel M. Tichy and David O. Ulrich, "The Leadership Challenge—A Call for the Transformational Leader," *Sloan Management Review,* Fall 1984, pp. 59–68.

19. W. Warner Burke, *Organization Development: Principles and Practices* (Boston: Little, Brown, 1982).

20. Michael Beer, *Organization Change and Development* (Santa Monica, CA: Goodyear, 1980); Burke, *Organization Development.*

21. Noel M. Tichy and Christopher DeRose, "The Death and Rebirth of Organizational Development," in *Organization 21C: Someday All Organizations Will Lead This Way,* ed. Subir Chowdhury (Upper Saddle River, NJ: Financial Times Prentice Hall, 2003), pp.155–177.

22. Danny Miller and Peter H. Friesen, "Structural Change and Performance: Quantum Versus Piecemeal-Incremental Approaches," *Academy of Management Journal,* December 1982, pp. 867–892.

23. "Ford Enters New Era of E-Communication: New Web Sites Connect Dealers, Consumer, Suppliers," *PR Newswire,* January 24, 2000, p. 7433; Suzy Wetlaufer, "Driving Change," *Harvard Business Review,* March–April 1999, pp. 77–85; "Ford's Passing Fancy," *Business Week,* March 15, 1999, p. 42.

24. J. Lloyd Suttle, "Improving Life at Work—Problems and Prospects," in *Improving Life at Work: Behavioral Science Approaches to Organizational Change,* eds. J. Richard Hackman and J. Lloyd Suttle (Santa Monica, CA: Goodyear, 1977), p. 4.

25. Richard E. Walton, "Quality of Work Life: What Is It?" *Sloan Management Review,* Fall 1983, pp. 11–21.

26. Daniel A. Ondrack and Martin G. Evans, "Job Enrichment and Job Satisfaction in Greenfield and Redesign QWL Sites," *Group & Organization Studies,* March 1987, pp. 5–22.

27. Ricky W. Griffin, *Task Design: An Integrative Framework* (Glenview, IL: Scott, Foresman, 1982).

28. Gregory Moorhead, "Organizational Analysis: An Integration of the Macro and Micro Approaches," *Journal of Management Studies,* April 1981, pp. 191–218.

29. James C. Quick and Jonathan D. Quick, *Organizational Stress and Preventive Management* (New York: McGraw-Hill, 1984).

30. Tichy and DeRose, "The Death and Rebirth of Organizational Development."

31. Kenneth N. Wexley and Timothy T. Baldwin, "Management Development," *1986 Yearly Review of Management of the Journal of Management,* in the *Journal of Management,* Summer 1986, pp. 277–294.

32. Richard Beckhard, "Optimizing Team-Building Efforts," *Journal of Contemporary Business,* Summer 1972, pp. 23–27, 30–32.

33. Bernard M. Bass, "Issues Involved in Relations Between Methodological Rigor and Reported Outcomes in Evaluations of Organizational Development," *Journal of Applied Psychology,* February 1983, pp. 197–201; William M. Vicars and Darrel D. Hartke, "Evaluating OD Evaluations: A Status Report," *Group & Organization Studies,* June 1984, pp. 177–188.

34. Beer, *Organization Change and Development.*

35. Jerome L. Franklin, "Improving the Effectiveness of Survey Feedback," *Personnel,* May–June 1978, pp. 11–17.

36. Paul R. Lawrence, "How to Deal with Resistance to Change," *Harvard Business Review,* May–June 1954, reprinted in *Organizational Change and Development,* eds. Gene W. Dalton, Paul R. Lawrence, and Larry E. Greiner (Homewood, IL: Irwin, 1970), pp. 181–197.

37. Daniel Katz and Robert L. Kahn, *The Social Psychology of Organizations,* 2nd ed. (New York: John Wiley and Sons, 1978), pp. 36–68.

38. See Michael T. Hannah and John Freeman, "Structural Inertia and Organizational Change," *American Sociological Review,* April 1984, pp. 149–164, for an in-depth discussion of structural inertia.

39. Moorhead, "Organizational Analysis: An Integration of the Macro and Micro Approaches."

40. G. Zaltman and R. Duncan, *Strategies for Planned Change* (New York: John Wiley and Sons, 1977); David A. Nadler, "Concepts for the Management of Organizational Change," *Perspectives on Behavior in Organizations,* 2nd ed., eds. J. Richard Hackman, Edward E. Lawler III, and Lyman W. Porter (New York: McGraw-Hill, 1983), pp. 551–561.

41. Alfred M. Jaeger, "Organization Development and National Culture: Where's the Fit?" *Academy of Management Review,* January 1986, pp. 178–190.

42. Alan M. Webber, "Learning for a Change," *Fast Company,* May 1999, pp. 178–188.

Appendix A

1. Jeffrey Pfeffer, "The Theory-Practice Gap: Myth or Reality?" *Academy of Management Executive,* February 1987, pp. 31–33.

2. Eugene Stone, *Research Methods in Organizational Behavior* (Santa Monica, CA: Goodyear, 1978).

3. Fred N. Kerlinger and Howard B. Lee, *Foundations of Behavioral Research,* 4th ed. (New York: Harcourt College Publishers, 1999).

4. Richard L. Daft, Ricky W. Griffin, and Valerie Yates, "Retrospective Accounts of Research Factors Associated with Significant and Not-So-Significant Research Outcomes," *Academy of Management Journal,* December 1987, pp. 763–785.

5. Richard L. Daft, "Learning the Craft of Organizational Research," *Academy of Management Review,* October 1983, pp. 539–546.

6. Larry L. Cummings and Peter Frost, *Publishing in Organizational Sciences* (Homewood, IL: Irwin, 1985). See also Ellen

R. Girden, *Evaluating Research Articles From Start to Finish* (Thousand Oaks, CA: Sage, 1996).

7. D. T. Campbell and J. C. Stanley, *Experimental and Quasi-Experimental Designs for Research* (Boston: Houghton Mifflin, 1966).

8. R. Yin and K. Heald, "Using the Case Study Method to Analyze Policy Studies," *Administrative Science Quarterly,* June 1975, pp. 371–381.

9. Kerlinger and Lee, *Foundations of Behavioral Research.*

10. Ramon J. Aldag and Timothy M. Stearns, "Issues in Research Methodology," *Journal of Management,* June 1988, pp. 253–276.

11. See C. A. Schriesheim et al., "Improving Construct Measurement in Management," *Journal of Management,* Summer 1993, pp. 385–418.

12. Cynthia D. Fisher, "Laboratory Experiments," in *Method and Analysis in Organizational Research,* eds. Thomas S. Bateman and Gerald R. Ferris (Reston, VA: Reston, 1984); Edwin Locke, ed., *Generalizing from Laboratory to Field Settings* (Lexington, MA: Lexington Books, 1986).

13. Stone, *Research Methods in Organizational Behavior.*

14. Phillip M. Podsakoff and Dan R. Dalton, "Research Methodology in Organizational Studies," *Journal of Management,* Summer 1987, pp. 419–441.

15. Stone, *Research Methods in Organizational Behavior.*

16. Kerlinger and Lee, *Foundations of Behavioral Research.*

17. Mary Ann Von Glinow, "Ethical Issues in Organizational Behavior," *Academy of Management Newsletter,* March 1985, pp. 1–3.

Appendix B

1. Daniel A. Wren, *The Evolution of Management Thought,* 4th ed. (New York: Wiley, 1994), Chapters 1 and 2. See also Stephen J. Carroll and Dennis A. Gillen, "Are the Classical Management Functions Useful in Describing Managerial Work?" *Academy of Management Review,* January 1987, pp. 38–51; and Daniel A. Wren, "Management History: Issues and Ideas for Teaching and Research," *Journal of Management,* Summer 1987, pp. 339–350.

2. "Builders & Titans of the 20th Century," *Time,* December 7, 1998, pp. 70–217.

3. Alfred Kieser, "Why Organization Theory Needs Historical Analyses—And How This Should be Performed," *Organization Science,* November 1994, pp. 608–617.

4. Frederick W. Taylor, *Principles of Scientific Management* (New York: Harper, 1911).

5. See "The Line Starts Here," *Wall Street Journal,* January 11, 1999, pp. R25–R28.

6. For critical analyses, see Charles D. Wrege and Amedeo G. Perroni, "Taylor's Pig-Tale: A Historical Analysis of Frederick W. Taylor's Pig-Iron Experiment," *Academy of Management Journal,* March 1974, pp. 6–27; and Charles D. Wrege and Ann Marie Stoka, "Cooke Creates a Classic: The Story Behind Taylor's Principles of Scientific Management," *Academy of Management Review,* October 1978, pp. 736–749. For a more favorable review, see Edwin A. Locke, "The Ideas of Frederick W. Taylor: An Evaluation," *Academy of Management Review,* January 1982, pp. 14–24. See Oliver E. Allen, "'This Great Mental Revolution,'" *Audacity,* Summer 1996, pp. 52–61, for another discussion of the practical value of Taylor's work.

7. Max Weber, *Theory of Social and Economic Organization,* trans. A. M. Henderson and T. Parsons (London: Oxford University Press, 1921).

8. Raymond A. Katzell and James T. Austin, "From Then to Now: The Development of Industrial-Organizational Psychology in the United States," *Journal of Applied Psychology,* 1992, vol. 77, no. 6, pp. 803–835.

9. Hugo Munsterberg, *Psychology and Industrial Efficiency* (Boston: Houghton Mifflin, 1913); and Wren, *Evolution of Management Thought.* See also Frank J. Landy, "Hugo Munsterberg: Victim or Visionary?" *Journal of Applied Psychology,* 1992, vol. 77, no. 6, pp. 787–802: and Frank J. Landy, "Early Influences on the Development of Industrial and Organizational Psychology," *Journal of Applied Psychology,* 1997, vol. 82, no. 4, pp. 467–477.

10. Elton Mayo, *The Human Problems of Industrial Civilization* (New York: Macmillan, 1933); Fritz J. Roethlisberger and William J. Dickson, *Management and the Worker* (Cambridge, MA: Harvard University Press, 1939).

11. Alex Carey, "The Hawthorne Studies: A Radical Criticism," *American Sociological Review,* June 1967, pp. 403–416; Lyle Yorks and David A. Whitsett, "Hawthorne, Topeka, and the Issue of Science versus Advocacy in Organizational Behavior," *Academy of Management Review,* January 1985, pp. 21–30.

12. Douglas McGregor, *The Human Side of Enterprise* (New York: McGraw-Hill, 1960); Abraham Maslow, "A Theory of Human Motivation," *Psychological Review,* July 1943, pp. 370–396. See also Paul R. Lawrence, "Historical Development of Organizational Behavior," in *Handbook of Organizational Behavior,* ed. Jay W. Lorsch (Englewood Cliffs, NJ: Prentice-Hall, 1987), pp. 1–9.

13. See "Conversation with Lyman W. Porter," *Organizational Dynamics,* Winter 1990, pp. 69–79.

14. Jeffrey Pfeffer and John F. Veiga, "Putting People First for Organizational Success," *Academy of Management Executive,* 1999, vol. 13, no. 2, pp. 37–48.

Test Prepper Answers

Chapter 1

1. F	6. T	11. e
2. F	7. T	12. d
3. T	8. d	13. c
4. F	9. b	14. d
5. F	10. c	

Chapter 2

1. F	6. T	11. a
2. F	7. T	12. c
3. T	8. d	13. b
4. T	9. b	
5. T	10. e	

Chapter 3

1. F	6. T	11. d
2. T	7. F	12. d
3. F	8. c	13. b
4. T	9. e	14. a
5. T	10. b	15. c

Chapter 4

1. F	6. T	11. d
2. F	7. T	12. b
3. T	8. d	13. b
4. T	9. a	14. e
5. F	10. a	15. c

Chapter 5

1. F	6. T	11. a
2. F	7. F	12. b
3. T	8. c	13. e
4. F	9. d	14. a
5. F	10. b	

Chapter 6

1. T	6. T	11. b
2. F	7. b	12. a
3. T	8. d	13. d
4. T	9. c	
5. T	10. e	

Chapter 7

1. T	6. F	11. d
2. F	7. T	12. a
3. T	8. d	13. c
4. T	9. b	14. e
5. F	10. e	15. e

Chapter 8

1. F	6. T	11. b
2. T	7. F	12. d
3. F	8. b	13. a
4. T	9. c	14. e
5. T	10. d	

Chapter 9

1. T	6. T	11. d
2. F	7. T	12. a
3. F	8. d	13. c
4. F	9. b	14. b
5. T	10. d	15. a

Chapter 10

1. F	6. T	11. e
2. T	7. T	12. d
3. T	8. b	13. c
4. T	9. c	14. b
5. F	10. a	15. a

Chapter 11

1. T	6. F	11. e
2. T	7. T	12. b
3. F	8. b	13. a
4. T	9. e	14. d
5. F	10. d	15. c

Chapter 12

1. F	6. T	11. e
2. F	7. T	12. c
3. F	8. a	13. b
4. F	9. e	14. d
5. T	10. b	

Chapter 13

1. F	6. F	11. c
2. T	7. d	12. e
3. T	8. a	13. a
4. F	9. d	14. e
5. T	10. d	

Chapter 14

1. T	6. F	11. d
2. T	7. F	12. b
3. T	8. b	13. d
4. F	9. c	14. a
5. T	10. e	15. a

Chapter 15

1. F	6. F	11. c
2. T	7. T	12. b
3. F	8. b	13. a
4. T	9. a	14. c
5. T	10. c	15. d

Chapter 16

1. F	6. F	11. d
2. T	7. T	12. c
3. T	8. b	13. b
4. F	9. b	14. d
5. T	10. c	

Chapter 17

1. F	6. F	11. b
2. T	7. F	12. c
3. T	8. c	13. e
4. T	9. d	14. d
5. F	10. b	

Chapter 18

1. F	6. T	11. b
2. T	7. F	12. c
3. F	8. c	13. a
4. F	9. b	
5. T	10. d	

Chapter 19

1. F	6. F	11. b
2. F	7. T	12. c
3. T	8. c	13. e
4. F	9. d	14. a
5. T	10. d	

Name Index

Organization Index

Subject Index

Supplements Designed to Aid Instructors and Students

For Students:

Student Web Site provides chapter synopses and objectives, ACE practice tests, links to companies highlighted in the text, Flashcards, a visual glossary, career snapshots, OB Online, Experiencing Organizational Behavior and Self-Assessment exercises from end of chapter, a resource center with links to OB related sites, and additional cases and experiential exercises.

OB in Action, Eighth Edition written by Steven B. Wolff provides additional cases and hands-on experiential exercises to help students bridge the gap between theory and practice. Working individually or with teams, students tackle problems and find solutions, using organizational theories as their foundation.

For Instructors:

Online Instructor's Resource Manual, written by Paul Keaton of the University of Wisconsin-La Crosse, includes a chapter overview, chapter learning objectives, lecture outline, text discussion questions with suggested answers, notes on the experiential exercises (Building Managerial Skills, Experiencing Organizational Behavior, Self-Assessment), Organizational Behavior case questions with suggested answers, a minilecture, and additional experiential exercise ideas. Also included are a table of contents, a transition guide, sample syllabi, suggested course outlines, and a section on learning and teaching ideologies. Printed copies are available upon request to the Faculty Service Group.

Online Test Bank, written by David Glew of the University of North Carolina, Wilmington, contains completely updated true/false, multiple-choice, matching, completion, and essay questions for each chapter. A text page reference and a learning-level indicator accompany each question. Printed copies are available upon request to the Faculty Service Group.

Online OB in Action Instructor's Resource Manual correlates with *OB in Action* exercises. It includes a topic area grid, a section with icebreaker materials, and teaching notes for all cases and exercises in the OB in Action text.

Instructor Web Site includes downloadable files for the IRM, PowerPoint slides, Video Guide, and Transparencies, as well as a resource center that includes sample syllabi, a table of contents, learning and teaching ideologies, a visual glossary, chapter overviews, mini-lectures, notes on the experiential exercises (Building Managerial Skills, Experiencing Organizational Behavior, OB Online, Self-Assessments), text discussion questions with suggested answers, *OB in Action* Instructor Notes and notes on additional cases, and Organizational Behavior case questions with suggested answers